3725

D1570529

Jews and the Left

Contemporary Religious Movements:

A Wiley-Interscience Series

Edited by IRVING I. ZARETSKY

Jews and the Left

Arthur Liebman

JOHN WILEY & SONS · New York · Chichester · Brisbane · Toronto

Library of Congress Cataloging in Publication Data

Liebman, Arthur.
  Jews and the left.

  (Contemporary religious movements)

  Bibliography: p.
  Includes indexes.
    1. Jews in the United States—Politics and
government.   2.   Socialists, Jewish—United
States.   3.   Radicalism—Jews.   4.   Radicalism—
United States.   5.   United States—Politics and
government.   I.   Title.
E184.J5L666   301.45'19'24073   78-20871
ISBN 0-471-53433-1

For my father, Sol Liebman
a member of the working class, who represented the past
and
For my children, Michael, Lisa, and Amy,
who represent the future

Series Editor's Preface

This volume presents a fine-grained and well documented analysis of Jewish participation in the political movements of the Left in America. Beginning in the 1880s with the immigrants from the Pale of Eastern Europe and bringing us to the early 1970s, the post—New Left period, this study spans up to four generations of Jewish Americans who were involved with a century's evolution of the politics of social change and social reform.

Among American Jewry, only a minority were active in formulating the ideology, building the institutions, and carrying out the activities of the Left, which includes here the labor movements, the Socialist and Communist parties, and *ad hoc* political radicalism. Yet this minority of Jews, relative to other immigrant and ethnic groups in America, provided the Left during the past century with a disproportionately large number of its leaders, activists, and supporters. Today this Jewish support is declining. The questions are posed: Why the initial support from Jews? and, What accounts for its recent decline?

At the very outset, Professor Liebman abandons previous explanations, no longer satisfactory, that argued either that Jews were somehow "inherently prone" to political radicalism, or that within Jewish religious thought the Jew could find a legitimating charter for radical political action. Instead, Liebman uses the craft of the historian and social scientist to uncover data, through archival, librarial, literary, and participant—observer field research, that demonstrate the relationship and interplay between ethnicity, class, and politics—the dialectic between individual and socioeconomic environment—in industrialized, multiethnic American society. In so doing he provides us with a bifocal lens through which we can at once focus closely on an important aspect of Jewish history in the United States, and gain a more distant view of the merger of that historical process with the larger American experience of which it is a part.

This work is relevant, therefore, not only in demonstrating and explaining the unique relationship between Jews and the Left in America, but also more generally in exploring the dynamics of political radicalism at various periods during the past century. Through comparative analyses we begin to discover the relationships of other ethnic and immigrant groups to political processes that accentuate social change rather than political reform.

This is the eighth volume to appear in the series *Contemporary Religious Movements*. It continues our exploration of the interface between religious groups and the sociopolitical process. Its publication at this time coincides with a national trend toward decline in political activism and toward an increase in religious pursuits within the frameworks of recently formed religious groups and within the quasireligious Human Potential movement. Many activists and supporters of the New Left, still committed to timely and effective social change, have moved to the religious arena and now maintain that social change can best be achieved through individualized efforts at personal transformation and renewal. For some, this transformation has been expressed through a spiritual rebirth in their natal religious traditions. For others, it has been expressed through the painful efforts to discover their ethnic roots and to affirm their personal and social identities. While it remains for the future to reveal how this personal renewal will be expressed politically, the chapters that follow should help us to focus in on the determinants of that historical pattern underlying the transition from political activism to religious meditation—"out of Babylon, by way of Bethlehem, on the way once again to the new Jerusalem."

This volume, like others in this series, was edited during several research periods supported by grants from several Foundations. I gratefully acknowledge the generous support and encouragement that I received from the Edward W. Hazen Foundation, The Lilly Endowment, Inc., The Lucius N. Littauer Foundation, and the Wenner-Gren Foundation for Anthropological Research.

IRVING I. ZARETSKY

Preface

This is a sociohistorical case study of the relationship between the Jews and the Left in the United States in the twentieth century. It is designed to illuminate the interplay between ethnicity, class, and politics in modern capitalist society.

The decision to study the association between the Jews and the Left was not initially dictated by a concern for the building of sociological theory. Rather, the motivation derived from at least two not entirely independent sources: one, personal experiences, and the other, curiosity.

In the course of my formal and informal sociological and political education I gained the impression that many Leftists or Marxists were Jews or persons of Jewish parentage. Some of the most impressive socialist thinkers and political activists of the Western world, I discovered, emerged out of a Jewish background. These included Karl Marx, Leon Trotsky, and Rosa Luxemburg.

I also found that this was not a phenomenon limited to a few European giants of the nineteenth and early twentieth centuries. As I proceeded through undergraduate and graduate school, I read or heard about Leftists in America who were also of Jewish descent. They first appeared in my consciousness as somewhat blurred, romanticized, and stereotyped figures. There was the "Lower-East-Side Garment Worker Socialist Jew" and his son, the "City College Radical." Out of this haze emerged names of prominent Jewish Leftists like Morris Hillquit, Abraham Cahan, and David Dubinsky.

Later, at Berkeley I was to meet for the first time people who had actually been radicals in the 1930s at the City College of New York and others my own age, most of whom were Jews. These encounters provided me with "objective" proof that such people really did exist and led me to realize that this relationship between Jews and the Left was a very live and, to me, very meaningful phenomenon.

Yet the reactions of those with whom I discussed this discovery were generally disturbing. Some who had grown up in a Jewish-Left milieu thought it to be a trite bit of insight. Others thought it interesting but not very relevant or politically significant, particularly since they saw blacks as more likely and more eligible recruits for Marxism.

Still others argued the negative historical relationship between socialism on the one hand and Judaism and Zionism on the other, and some insisted that alluding to the existence of ethnic and religious differences among comrades and potential comrades was damaging to "the cause." These types of ascribed differences were defined as atavistic obstacles, which educated people in general and educated radicals in particular were supposed to surmount in the interest of a greater unity.

These varied responses to my observations about Jews and the Left appeared to make a good deal of surface sense to me. After all, radicalism, and more specifically, Marxism, offered an ideology and movement for the oppressed; and by no standard did American Jews in the early 1960s appear very oppressed. Socially, owing to the then low level of anti-Semitism, and economically, they were relatively well off. I, too, believed that "irrational" distinctions based on race, ethnicity, and religion had impaired the socialist cause in the United States. So why raise an issue that in the past had proven so damaging to radicalism?

Not only did the logic and tone of these responses make me want to acquiesce in their position, but also who the responders were and the character of their life styles. The fact of being born a Jew seemed to have very little significance in their lives as I saw it in Berkeley. Associations and friendships crossed Jewish–non-Jewish lines with great ease and frequency. The only important factors that appeared to matter in terms of social interaction were personality and ideas.

I almost managed to suppress my feelings about this Jewish angle on radicalism, but two major factors prevented my doing so. One had to do with somewhat intangible personal feelings, and the other with the nature of my academic training as a sociologist.

The arguments of my radical Jewish contemporaries, while persuasive, were for me undercut by the fervor and uneasiness of the speakers communicating them. I had the distinct feeling that they were trying to convince not only me but themselves as well. Perhaps they had earlier in their lives made the same observation as I had, and did not know how to deal with it. Perhaps they also had trouble dealing with their being Jewish.

My feelings about them and their Jewishness was also reinforced by their reactions to new recruits. Non-Jews seemed to be received with much more open and positive feelings than Jews were. It was almost as if the recruiting of a Gentile was a greater achievement than the recruiting of a Jew.

The graduate education that I was then undergoing at Berkeley also gave me reason to continue to question the nature of the relationship between Jews and the Left. Sociological methodology teaches that one of the most important pieces of information a researcher can gather on a social movement is the socioeconomic composition of its membership. Such information allows the analyst to more adequately comprehend the reasons why certain tactics, strategies, and ideologies are accepted while others are rejected. Yet the movement in which I was most intimately involved expected and encouraged people to forget about the ethnic and religious components of its social base.

This was disturbing. If the modes of analysis that I was learning in the classroom were good enough to utilize when studying the Ku Klux Klan or the Zengahkuren, why then were they not applicable to my own Socialist Party? Were these movements that I was acquainted with from personal experience so drastically different from others distant from me that classic sociological analytic probes could not be effectively employed? I thought not, yet it was difficult to understand why I and other sociologists—socialists were so reluctant to subject our own movement to the questions we asked of others in our research. Why, in particular, was the question of the relationship of Jews to socialism one to be so studiously avoided by all concerned?

Another related but somewhat analytically distinct factor that drew me to this study was the desire to explain a seeming paradox—the disproportionate support of Jews for the Left in the United States, particularly in the post–World War II era.

This study then is a way of my coming to grips with these and other apparent paradoxes. At the same time, it is designed to make a contribution to the understanding of the interrelationship between ethnicity, class, and politics in a modern capitalist society.

I have attempted to approach and to deal with the data in as scholarly a fashion as possible. I have tried wherever possible to double- and triple-check facts, especially those provided by informants. I am well aware of the problems presented by selective perception, faulty memories, and the need to justify one's life, particularly crucial portions within it. I have dealt with these methodological problems in ways designed to correct for distortions.

At this point I would like to say a few words about my sources. In doing this study I relied on various types of data that included primary and secondary sources and my own impressions and experiences. The primary data were interviews, archival materials, the attitudes and opinions of key persons garnered from their autobiographies and writings, and newspapers. The sources of secondary data were principally biographies, histories, sociological studies, and surveys.

Between 1971 and 1977 I conducted approximately 35 in-depth interviews. My interviewees were former or current members of the Communist Party, the Socialist Party, the Trotskyist Socialist Workers Party, the New Left, and the Jewish New Left. Twenty-five of my respondents were Jewish, all but four were men, and ranged in age from 20 to 85.

I make no claim to randomness. I interviewed people who I believe had important information to impart. Names were gathered on the basis of my own knowledge about possible informants and leads that interviewees were kind enough to give me. I wanted essentially three things from these people—one, their knowledge and impressions about their movements and their experiences within them; two, information as to the factors that inclined them toward the Left; and three, their own feelings and attitudes about Jews, their own Jewish identities (for Jewish respondents), and the relationships between Jews and the Left. Not each was able to give me all the information in each of the three areas, but all did contribute to my storehouse of knowledge.

I typically did not cite informants by name—there were two major reasons for this: one, many of my interviewees asked to remain anonymous, radicals and former radicals familiar with modern American political history having good reason to feel anxious about being publicly identified and having attention called to their political actions and beliefs; and two, there was no pressing reason to cite most by name. The type of information that I obtained from them generally did not necessitate the revealing of their identities. For the most part I treated them as representatives of different generations of radicals with therefore no social scientific reason to be identified.

I think that if there is any methodological bias pertaining to these interviews, the most serious has to do with geography. Owing to limitations on finances, time, and energy, I restricted my interviewing to people currently located on the East Coast, primarily in New York City, and believe that this geographical concentration of respondents poses no very substantial methodological drawback.

First, New York City and the East Coast, from the 1910s to the present, was the major area of concentration for parties of the Left. My sample therefore reflects a social reality. Second, although now located in the East, many of my interviewees did not live all of their natural or movement lives in this area of the country. Third, my own primary involvement with the Socialist Party took place in California. This allowed me to introduce some sort of geographical control or check on what my interviewees reported. Fourth, the interviews, while important, were not my only source of information on my subject. In general, I believe that this study was not in any serious or significant way negatively affected by the geographical nature of my interviewee sample.

In the course of this study, I utilized various archival sources. The data from them consisted of letters, personal papers, internal memorandums, minutes of meetings, and newspapers. The archives whose resources I made use of were: the Tamiment Library of New York University, the State Historical Society of Wisconsin, the YIVO Institute for Jewish Research, the New York Public Library, the Labor-Management Documentation Center of Cornell University, the Syracuse University Library, the Duke University Library, and the Columbia University Library.

This monograph would not have been possible without the active assistance of many people. Much as I would like to be able to thank all of them, this is not possible. I would, however, like to express my gratitude to some by name. First is my wife Edna. Although ambivalent about me and my work she did her best to provide me with a supportive ambience necessary to complete this task. The next in line for thanks are my children, Michael, Lisa, and Amy. They did not always understand the necessity of my reading and typing for so many hours (and years), but they, with love and good humor, agreed to share me with my typewriter and books. Each also helped to type the the manuscript. I would also like to single out for special thanks my former mentor and friend, Seymour Martin Lipset. Marty showed me by example how superior sociological research should be conducted. I am also indebted to the assistance and cooperation that I received from the librarians and staff at the Tamiment Library, the State Historical Society of Wisconsin, the YIVO Institute for Jewish Research, the New York Public Library, the Labor Management Documentation Center of Cornell University, the Syracuse University Library, Duke University Library, Columbia University Library, and my own Library of the State of New York at Binghamton. Those in particular who went far out of their way for me include Dorothy Thomas at Tamiment, Mark Webb at YIVO, Richard Strassberg at Cornell, and Flossy Lee and Rachelle Moore at SUNY–Binghamton.

I am also indebted to those who allowed me to interview them both formally and informally. These busy men and women kindly allowed me to invade their lives. I learned much from them, and I am most grateful. One who helped me a great deal with ideas for the interviews and opened a number of important doors was Joseph Starobin, who recently passed away. I did not have the opportunity to thank him and can only belatedly do so now.

There are numerous others whose advice and assistance merit the mention of their names. Two scholarly editors carefully read every page of this manuscript and were instrumental in helping me to improve it. Irving Zaretsky, a professional sociologist and an expert in the sociology of religion, offered me numerous sociological insights and enthusiastic encouragement. I am most grateful for the scholarly assistance that he offered above and beyond the call of duty as an editor. And Morris U. Schappes, editor of *Jewish Currents*, challenged a number of my facts and many of my interpretations. I almost always agreed with him about the facts, and sometimes about the interpretations. My wife, Edna, read much of this work and helped to sharpen some of my arguments. Others who read various portions of this manuscript and gave me useful advice include (in alphabetical order) Philip G. Altbach, David Biale, Fran Clifton, Richard Dalfiume, Ronald Efon, Al Geddicks, James A. Geschwender, Mickey and Penina Glazer, Charles Leinenweber, David Makofsky, Gary T. Marx, Helen and Stuart Perry, Jack Nusan Porter, Richard Rehberg, and Cedrick Robinson. I alone am responsible for any remaining errors of fact or judgment.

There were others who helped me in the course of my study. Fran and Valerie Clifton, Ed Goldman and Susan Lowes, Earl Landau, and Sydelle Feinberg, and Sam and Leila Rosenstock allowed me to reside in their homes as a non-paying guest while I did research in libraries or interviewed informants. Patricia Doloway did most of the typing and a good deal of editing. Nettie Rathje and Nancy Hall also typed portions of the manuscript. To each individual I would like once more to say, "Thank you."

Finally, I would like to convey my appreciation to those who provided me with funds necessary to carry this project to its successful conclusion. They include Norman Cantor in his capacity as Provost of the State University of New York at Binghamton, the SUNY Research Foundation Awards Program through Fellowships and Grants in Aid, and, my wife, Edna.

Arthur Liebman

Binghamton, New York
November 1978

Contents

Jews and the Left

1 A Theoretical Overview

INTRODUCTION

The Jewish contribution to the Left in the United States during the twentieth century ranks the highest of any immigrant or ethnic group. From the early 1900s until the present, American Jewry has provided socialist organizations and movements with a disproportionate number—at times approaching or surpassing a majority—of their leaders, activists, and supporters. This was the situation in the case of the Socialist Labor party at the turn of the century and in the case of the New Left in the 1960s as well.

At the same time this support for the Left on the part of Jews was neither monolithic nor consistently high throughout. Those Jews who nurtured the Left generally constituted a minority of the American Jewish population in any given period. And although the size of this minority fluctuated during the century, the overall tendency was for it to diminish the further the Jews moved from their immigrant experience. This tendency was particularly pronounced in the post–World War II decade.

The major objective of this study is to further our understanding of this unique relationship between Jews and the Left in the United States and by so doing advance our knowledge of the interplay between ethnicity, class, and politics in modern, multiethnic, capitalist society. Specifically, I will address two questions: (1) Why the Jewish community in America relative to other ethnic communities gave such disproportionate support to the Left. (2) Why that support declined.

To respond to these issues I have used a sociohistorical approach to American Jewry. The period covered runs from the turn of the century to the 1970s. Emphasis will be given to those historical and structural factors within and associated with the Jewish community that significantly influenced its association with the Left. Throughout, comparisons and contrasts will be made between Left Jews and non-Left Jews as well as between Jews and other ethnic groups in order to isolate and highlight the most important factors that affected the relationship between American Jewry and socialism in this century.

It would be helpful at this point to clarify some key terms that will be used extensively in this work. The term *Left* is used to designate a political ideology that is in some way or to some significant extent informed by Marxism. In this sense it is used to describe the politics of individuals, groups, or movements. It is also employed to characterize collectively the various groups, organizations, parties, and movements that in any given era or decade had or claimed to have a Marxist or at least quasi-Marxist orientation. This common label in no way implies a unity of action or purpose among these collectivities, for this commonality did not prevent bitter rivalries and internecine warfare from erupting regularly.

The most important organizations that comprised the Left in the United States throughout the period under consideration are the Socialist party (SP) and the Communist party (CP), along with their associated youth groups, fraternal orders, language federations, and other organized affiliates. In addition to these, there were and are a variety of smaller political bodies that can also be considered part of the Left. Among the more important of these smaller groups dealt with here are the Socialist Labor party (SLP), the *Poale Zion*, or Labor Zionists, and the Socialist Workers party and its offshoots.

Leftists, then, are persons "associated" with these groups and organizations. They can be people who formally belong as nonmembers who give special support to them through political action such as voting or other actions such as financial contributions. Regrettably, this is a loose definition of Leftist, but it does, I believe, mirror social reality.

The terms *Jew* and *Jewish* are also fraught with the same problem. The principal criteria used here to define a person as a Jew are: (1) self-definition; (2) definition by significant others; and (3) having one or both parents who define themselves as Jewish or are defined by "significant others" (such as political elites, government officials, teachers, or peer groups) as Jewish. If one of these criterion apply, then for our purposes the individual or individuals will be considered as Jewish.

The adjective *Jewish* will be utilized to describe geographical areas, economic and occupational arenas, and social, economic, and political organizations when they contain a majority, plurality, or a significant percentage of Jewish individuals. This appellation may apply when either the ordinary residents, members, or supporters are being considered or when the activists and leadership are under consideration. Thus, for example, the International Ladies' Garment Workers' Union (ILGWU) can be treated as a "Jewish" union on the basis of both the percentage of Jews in its membership and leadership in the years prior to 1920. Afterward, particularly from the 1930s to the present, it is Jewish only on the basis of the percentage of Jews among its officers.

In this study Jews will be treated primarily as an ethnic group. Here I shall rely on Max Weber's definition: "Those human groups that entertain a subjective belief in their common descent—because of similarities of physical type or of customs or both, or because of memories of colonization and migration—in such a way that this belief is impor-

tant for the continuation of non-kinship communal relationships."[1]
Dealing with Jews as an ethnic group in the manner defined by Weber
allows the study to include a wider variation of individuals and
groups than would a purely religious definition of Jewry. Thus, the
Jewish label can be applied to those who are religious, secular, cultural, assimilated, unassimilated, or even self-denying.

THE THEORETICAL FRAMEWORK

The observation that Jews are disproportionately found on the Left
(and more so on the liberal) end of the political spectrum is not one
that is new or peculiar to this work. In Europe from the mid-nineteenth century on, social commentators have noted the existence of
this relationship. Such disparate and keen political analysts as Benjamin Disraeli in 1852, Vladimir Lenin in 1913, and Robert Michels in
1915 called attention to the fact that the Jews of Europe to a disproportionate degree were to be found among the ranks of revolutionaries
and socialists.[2] In America, a variety of political and social scientists
have already commented upon the existence of a similar type of association between the Jews and the Left that obtained from the early
1900s through the 1960s.[3]

Within the body of this work I have attempted to make some unique
contributions to the understanding of the relationship between Jews
and socialism that have not been previously dealt with by other analysts in a systematic fashion. First, the account offered here is more
historic, more far-ranging, and more detailed than any other. Second,
it systematically analyzes not only the factors that contributed to the
association between the Jews and the Left but also to those that weakened and impaired it. Third, this study provides a theoretical framework for understanding this relationship that is more extensive and of
greater validity than those of previous analysts.

This does not mean that previous theories were wrong or that the
one presented here is the correct one. The framework developed here
is, of course, indebted to the analyses of others. This theoretical
framework is in part a synthesis of the positive contributions offered
by my predecessors but, at the same time, goes beyond them.

The key to understanding the relationship between the Jews and the
Left in America lies in the class-linked socialist subculture that a portion of the Jewish community erected on these shores after the turn of
the century. This subculture as an entity in and of itself and in conjunction with other socio-political forces inside and outside of the
Jewish community was the crucial factor in the making of generations
of Jewish Leftists.

Before elaborating on this position, we will consider other prominent theses that have been advanced to explain Jewish radicalism and
shall indicate their problems and limitations as well as their
strengths. In this way, it will also become evident that it is necessary

to go beyond them in order to comprehend more fully the relationship that obtained between the Jews and the Left in America during the twentieth century.

RELIGION

Those that have sought to locate in Judaism the nexus between Jews and socialism have generally employed two interrelated approaches. One has been to stress the similarities between socialism and Judaism in broad themes and general outlines. The other has been to examine religious scriptures, texts, and commentaries for more specific elements that could be interpreted as causing, predisposing, or facilitating Jews to move toward the Left. In both cases, the assumption was that the basic source of Jewish radicalism flowed from the religion and the religious experiences of the Jewish people.

Exponents of the first approach include the contemporary historian Moses Rischin and former Russian Marxist Nicolas Berdyaev. It was Rischin who claimed that ". . . For most Jewish socialists, although unaware of it, socialism was Judaism secularized."[4] Berdyaev seized on the same theme and developed it by comparing basic elements in Marxism with those in the Jewish religion.

. . . the most important aspect of Marx's teaching concerning the proletariat's messianic vocation is the fact that he applied to the proletariat the characteristics of God's chosen people. Marx was a Jew; he had abandoned the faith of his fathers, but the messianic expectation of Israel remained in his subconsciousness, and for him the proletariat is a New Israel, God's chosen people, the liberator and builder of an earthly kingdom that is to come. His proletarian Communism is a secularized form of the ancient Jewish chiliasm. A Chosen Class takes the place of the chosen people. It was impossible to reach such an idea by means of science. It is an idea of a religious kind. Here we have the very marrow of the Communist religion. For a messianic consciousness is surely always of ancient Hebrew origin.[5]

This was also a perspective that was shared by Saint Simon, the French leader of the first socialist movement in Europe during the nineteenth century.

Others have looked to more specific aspects of Judaism to explain the Jewish propensity for liberal and Left politics. Emma Lazarus, the poet of Statue of Liberty fame, believed that a key to this phenomenon could be found in the Mosaic Code. Her position was summarized by Louis Harap, a literary critic, thusly: "The modern movement for reform and for socialism," "has its roots in the Mosaic Code . . . which formulated the principle of the rights of labor, denying the right of private property in land, asserting that . . . gleanings of the harvest belonged in *justice*, not in charity, to the poor and the stranger."[6]

This position has found its most articulate proponent in contemporary times in Lawrence Fuchs, a political scientist at Brandeis University. Fuchs contends that this type of Jewish politics was based in part on three primary and distinctively Jewish values: learning (*Torah*); charity (*zedakeh*); and life's pleasures, or nonasceticism. The deep Jewish concern and respect for learning, Fuchs indicates, prompt Jews to support intellectual candidates, who are usually on the liberal-Left of the political spectrum and on issues such as rational social planning, intellectual independence, and civil liberties. The value of *zedakeh* enjoins Jews as a religious duty to ameliorate the plight of the poor and needy. This, then, becomes a motor force in modern times for Jewish support of social welfare programs and social justice for the deprived and oppressed. Nonasceticism is the third value cluster according to Fuchs, who feels that ". . . by its emphasis on this worldliness and the enjoyment of life here and now, Jews have been made more receptive to plans for a better life, for reconstructing society . . . for socialism."

Fuchs further buttresses his position by comparing Jewish values to orthodox Christian ones and indicating their respective effects upon the politics of Jews and Christians in the United States. "While Orthodox Christianity stresses man's sinfulness, repentance, and otherworldliness, the Jews appeared to have emphasized man's potentialities, works, and life here and now. Orthodox Christian theology has tended to color American politics with a conservative cast from which Jews have been largely exempt. On the other hand, Jewish cultural and theological values have promoted a liberal and radical political style." [7]

The "Judaic" theory of socialism, whether of the broad or more narrow variety, is, however, fraught with too many inconsistencies and problems to be of any significant value in accounting for the relationship between the Jews and the Left in the United States, Europe, or even Israel. One of the most glaring of its shortcomings is the existence of Jewish conservatives, not to mention moderates or centrists. How can Judaism be credited with the generation of Jewish Leftists while at the same time bearing no responsibility for the production of Jewish rightists?

It is true that some of the world-renowned socialists were Jews or of Jewish descent. These include Karl Marx and Ferdinand Lassalle in Germany, Rosa Luxemburg in Poland, Leon Trotsky in Russia, and Morris Hillquit and Moissaye Olgin in America. But it is also true that eminent conservatives came from the same religious origins. In this category there are Benjamin Disraeli in England, Friedrich Julius Stahl and Gerson von Bleichroder (Bismarck's financial adviser) in Germany, Emile Durkheim in France, and Milton Friedman, and Irving Kristol in the United States. In Israel from 1948 to 1977, all the Prime Ministers were members of the Labor Party and considered to be on the liberal to Left end of the political spectrum. Yet in 1977 a leading Israeli conservative, Menachem Begin, became the Prime Minister.

The issue is not one restricted to individuals. The same inconsistency or perhaps consistency holds when a larger number of Jews are involved. In Europe, the United States, and Israel, the parties and candidates of the Left have not always garnered the support of the majority of the Jews. At various times, moderate and conservative parties and their candidates have proved quite successful in attracting Jews to their standards. In prerevolutionary Russia the Constitutional Democrats, a liberal centrist party, received a considerable amount of Jewish support that at times surpassed the support given to more left-wing parties. In Poland, during much of the inter-war period, the bulk of the Jewish electorate gave its support to center and right wing parties.[8] In America, until 1928, with the exception of the election of 1916, the majority or plurality of the Jewish vote for President routinely went to the Republican Party.[9] Throughout the century, in elections for municipal, state, federal-legislative, and executive offices, Jewish voters in the United States have at times given a majority or plurality of their votes to moderate and conservative candidates despite opportunities to vote for more liberal or Left alternatives. One example is the 1969 mayoralty election in New York where conservative Mario Procaccino attracted more Jewish votes than his more liberal opponent John Lindsay.[10] In Israel, after nearly 30 years of rule by a coalition dominated by a liberal to left Labor party, the government is now dominated by an economically and socially conservative coalition headed by the right wing Herut.

This inconsistency is not the only weakness of the Judaic thesis of socialism. If we consider the thesis in its broadest form, even more serious problems arise. One lies within the nature of its formulation. It is generally stated in such a way as to make empirical testing impossible. For example, in the statements of Rischin and Berdyaev cited above, both claim, independently of one another, that the Jewish influence upon socialism was transmitted to Jewish socialists through some kind of unconscious process. This approach leaves us at an impasse as far as empirical verification is concerned.

Empirical testing, however, is not the only way of assessing the validity of this thesis. Historical data and logical procedures can also be employed. In this regard, let us focus on a key element in the broadly conceived formulation—messianism. This phenomenon is a central feature in both Judaism and Marxism. Since Marx was a Jew, and since Judaism preceded Marxism, it appears logical that messianism came to Marxism via Marx the Jew. It is necessary to take issue with this logical approach on two counts, however.

One concerns Karl Marx and his Jewish background. Marx at the age of six, at the wish of his convert father, was baptized a Lutheran Christian. As a child and adolescent he received no systematic or even quasi-systematic exposure to the ideas, tenets, and values of Judaism. His immediate family did not provide this exposure, and there was not much interaction between the Christian and Jewish branches of the wider Marx family. Little in his writings as an adult indicates that he harbored any favorable notions about his Jewish ancestry. It does not then seem very plausible to conclude that Jewish messianism could have been positively implanted in Marx's subconsciousness.[11]

The second problem with this approach is the fact that there were important differences between Jewish and socialist messianism. Jewish messianism was closely tied to the conception of Jews as a chosen people. Socialists rejected, were even hostile to, this type of messianism and to what they considered to be its secular forms—Jewish nationalism and Zionism. This type of messianism in their eyes had as a major consequence the preservation of a Jewish separateness and a Jewish nationalism. Both were an anathema to socialists, especially Jewish socialists. Socialist messianism was universal in character, not particular. Jewish Leftists in most cases rejected Judaism as a religion precisely because of its particularistic elements. For Jews and non-Jews alike in the socialist movement, a major obstacle to the triumph of their messianism was the pernicious influence of religion and nationalism.[12]

This does not mean that no positive influences were carried from Judaism to socialism. Undoubtedly some were, and undoubtedly a few were transmitted through the subconsciousness of individuals. However, it does not seem very reasonable to build a major thesis on the basis of these plausibilities and the above-cited facts.

The narrower and more easily testable formulation of the Judaic thesis of socialism is also fraught with problems. Here, too, there are difficulties in empirical verification. In order to test the proposition that specific elements and values within Judaism predispose Jews to adopt a liberal to Left political perspective, let us assume this proposition to be a given. If this is so, then it should logically follow that those Jews who are most religious should be the ones who are most likely to be found on or near the left of the political spectrum. Concretely this means that Orthodox Jews in particular and observant Jews in general should be more liberal or Left than their coreligionists. Unfortunately for this hypothesis all of the available empirical evidence indicates that this is not the case. It is the non-Orthodox and least observant Jews who are most likely to be to the Left.

The Jewish man and woman of the Left have generally been "non-Jewish Jews," to use a phrase emanating from an article of the same name by Isaac Deutscher. In his consideration of famous Jewish radicals and heretics, Deutscher found that they were individuals whose greatness as radicals derived from their transcending the boundaries of Judaism. These included persons such as Marx, Trotsky, and Luxemburg.[13]

Let us now systematically present evidence to refute the hypothesis that those closest to Judaism are the Jews more likely to be to the Left.

The chief embodiment, carrier, and teacher of Jewish values has been the rabbinate, particularly the Orthodox rabbinate. If the hypothesis is valid, it is reasonable to expect this group to have a large proportion of Leftists and to be supportive of Leftist positions.

This has not been the case. It has been the rabbinate, particularly its most Orthodox members, who have been most opposed to movements and organizations of or associated with the Left. In czarist Russia, the Orthodox rabbis vehemently opposed the ideas and actions of Jewish radicals. Conversely, it was they who continually and publicly espoused support for the constituted government, in this case an anti-Semitic and oppressive government.[14] In the United States throughout this century, the Orthodox rabbinate, relative to its counterparts in the Conservative and Reform denominations, has been the least likely to espouse liberal or Left positions on political, economic, or social issues. Of the three major branches of Judaism, only the Orthodox religious and lay bodies offered public support for the Vietnam War policies of the American government in the 1960s.[15]

Nor have the Conservative and Reform rabbinates been noted for their secular progressivism. Historically, despite the instances of major deviations, their politics have generally been characterized by political quiescence and tacit accommodation to the existing order. And when Conservative and Reform rabbis have spoken out or acted on behalf of liberal or Left causes or issues, it has usually been in response to pressure from their congregations rather than as a demonstration of leadership.[16]

A similar type of overall pattern between religion and politics obtains when Jewish laymen are concerned. The relatively few social science studies bearing on this subject indicate that Orthodox and observant Jews, compared with their coreligionists, are least likely to be liberals or Leftists.[17] One of the best of these studies was done by Seymour M. Lipset and E. C. Ladd, Jr., entitled, "Jewish Academics in the United States: Their Achievements, Culture and Politics." In this study Lipset and Ladd questioned more than 5000 Jewish faculty members in American colleges and universities in 1969, a sample large enough to permit the use of multivariate analysis. The researchers found that of all professors of Jewish parentage, those who defined their present religious status as "none" were the most likely to designate themselves as "Leftists." These could be considered less famous versions of Deutscher's non-Jewish Jewish radicals. Among those who defined themselves as Jewish and attended religious services, the faculty members who went least often had the largest percentage of self-identified Leftists. Conversely, the most frequent attenders were the group with the highest proportion of self-designated "conservatives."[18] Similar results were obtained by using a smaller but more socioeconomically heterogeneous sample of Jews in a study of Jews residing on the upper West Side of Manhattan in the latter 1960s. Those who described themselves as Orthodox Jews were more likely to hold conservative positions on various social and economic issues than were the non-Orthodox Jews.[19]

The patterns of voter preferences and election results in recent New York City elections also suggest that the Orthodox and more observant are the least liberal of the city's Jews. In the Democratic primary in the Fourteenth Congressional District (CD) in 1972, the votes of the Hasidic Jews meant victory for the conservative incumbent, John Rooney, and defeat for his Jewish liberal challenger, Allard Lowenstein. Of the Assembly Districts (AD) within the Thirteenth Congressional District in Brooklyn, the Forty-eighth is the one containing the highest proportion of Orthodox Jews. In the presidential election of 1972 and the United States Senatorial primary of 1974, this Assembly District gave the highest proportion of votes to conservative and moderate candidates like Richard Nixon and Daniel Patrick Moynihan and the smallest proportion to liberals such as George McGovern, Bella Abzug, Ramsay Clark, and Paul O'Dwyer of any other AD in the Thirteenth CD.[20] Prior to the run-off mayoralty primary in 1973, a survey of Jewish voters suggested that the more observant Jews were more likely to prefer (Jewish) Abe Beame, the more conservative of the two candidates, over Herman Badillo.[21]

The editorial positions of Jewish newspapers provide further evidence of the nexus between Orthodox Judaism and political conservatism. The first Yiddish-language daily newspaper to be published in America and the world was the *Tageblatt* (1885). From its inception the *Tageblatt* reflected the viewpoints of Orthodox Judaism and political conservatism. In 1901 the *Yiddisher Morgen Journal* appeared; it followed the same religious and political orientation as the *Tageblatt*. Both of these newspapers supported Republican candidates for office. Of the Yiddish-language press, the *Tageblatt* and the *Yiddisher Morgen Journal* were probably the furthest to the right on the political spectrum.[22]

At the present time among the English-language Jewish newspapers, the one that is closest to Orthodoxy and at the same time is conservative in its politics is the *Jewish Press*. This paper usually supports the more conservative of the candidates running for political office, whether the office is that of mayor of New York City or president of the United States. It also supported the policies of Lyndon Johnson and Richard Nixon on the Vietnam War until the very end. Orthodox rabbis, Menachem Begin, and Meier Kahane (the founder of the Jewish Defense League) are regular columnists for the *Jewish Press*. For a period of time Kahane also served as associate editor of this paper.

This association between Orthodoxy and conservative politics is not a phenomenon unique to Jews in America. In pre-World War II Poland, the political representation of Orthodoxy, the *Agudat Yisrael*, the largest Jewish party in that country, aligned itself with the right wing and even anti-Semitic government of Marshal Joseph Pilsudski. In Israel, the National Religious Party, the major Orthodox party, currently is a member of the conservative Likud government of Begin.[23]

This relationship between Judaism and politics clearly does not support a Judaic thesis of socialism. In fact, there is more evidence in support of a Jewish theory of conservatism than of radicalism. Indeed, such a thesis has been postulated. One hundred and twenty-five years ago, Benjamin Disraeli espoused such a thesis. On the basis of his estimation of the influence that the dominant values of Jews and Judaism had on their political outlook, he asserted: ". . . all the tendencies of the Jewish race are conservative. Their bias is to religion, property, and natural aristocracy. . . . The native tendency of the Jewish race . . . is against the equality of man." Disraeli was sharply critical of what he believed to be the shortsighted, anti-Semitic policies of European governments, which in his view forced Jews to depart from their natural conservatism and enlist on the side of their "un-natural" allies, revolutionaries. "The people of God cooperate with atheists; the most skillful accumulators of property ally themselves with communists, and low castes of Europe! And all this because they wish to destroy that ungrateful Christendom which owes to them even its name, and whose tyranny they can no longer endure."[24]

The conservatizing values embedded in Judaism have also been noted by more contemporary observers. A noted sociologist of Jewry, Charles Liebman, has called attention to the existence of such values, values that run counter to those regarded as positive by Jewish radicals. "Jewish values," according to that author, ". . . are folk oriented rather than universalistic, ethnocentric rather than cosmopolitan, and at least one major strand in Jewish tradition expresses indifference, fear, and even hostility toward the non-Jew."[25]

There is also no consensus concerning the transferability of religious values into the secular sphere and the political direction toward which they incline their adherents. Torah or traditional Jewish learning, a value that Fuchs believes to be supportive of a liberal to Left political orientation, is one of those values in dispute. Recent studies have shown that there is a considerable divergence in style, content, and goals between traditional Jewish education and secular education. As with some Christian doctrines, Orthodox Judaism was often hostile to science and resistant to secular education.[26] From this point of view, the traditional value that was placed upon Jewish education could as well represent an obstacle as a launching pad into the secular world in general or the radical world in particular.

The conservative thesis receives further support from the Jewish values pertaining to government and the Law. There is a strong tradition within Judaism that exhorts Jews to be obedient to and respectful of secular as well as religious laws. Laws, courts of law, and the legal process backed by the power of the state are from the perspective of Judaic tradition as well as Jewish historical experience the major defenses that Jews have against the anti-Semitic passions of the masses.[27] In this sense, then, government, even one that is oppressive to Jews such as that of czarist Russia, merits Jewish support; for a strong functioning state is the last line of Jewish defense against the worse treatment that could be expected from the hands of the people. Thus, the Talmud requires ". . . that every day men should bless God for the government because without it they would devour each other alive."[28]

It seems very clear that both conservatives and radicals can find within Judaism support for their respective positions. But their ability to judiciously select themes and values from the Judaic tradition to buttress their respective political convictions is in no way evidence for the claim that Judaism facilitates or predisposes Jews toward the holding of a left-wing or right-wing political orientation. Similarly the demonstration that radicals or conservatives utilize rituals, chants, and forms similar to those found within Orthodox Judaism is also not evidence to support such hypotheses. It is evidence only of the use of religion by politicians to legitimate and marshal support for their particular brand of politics.

The order of the variables in both the radical and conservative thesis of Judaism is actually the reverse of the original postulation. It is not values and themes within Judaism that necessarily lead to a particular type of politics. Jewish politicians and ideologues of all stripes seek to find within the Jewish tradition those values and themes that will buttress their politics. Or, as Irving Howe so aptly phrased it: "With enough wrenching one could find 'ancestors' in the Jewish past for almost any position."[29]

In summary, there is little evidence to support the hypothesis that Judaism predisposes its adherents (or former adherents) toward a socialist political identification or support for socialism. It is necessary, then, to look elsewhere for the factors that have led a disproportionate number of Jews into or near the Left.

ANTI-SEMITISM AS A ROOT CAUSE

Another major thesis that seeks to explain the connection between socialism and Jews identifies anti-Semitism as one or even the primary cause of the association. The general outline of this position is the following: anti-Semitism emanating from or supported by societal authorities arbitrarily penalizes Jews in a wide variety of arenas. They suffer psychological, social, economic, and political hardships largely because of an accident of birth. Their identification as Jews by others bars them from a wide range of economic, educational, and social opportunities. Conversely, they are confined to a narrow range of occupations as well as to limited geographical areas. As Jews, their abilities, talents, and demonstrated merit can do little to improve their situation except in cases of isolated individuals. Such treatment arouses in Jews a strong sense of injustice and a burning desire to bring about a societal change that will assure their recognition as equals. It is this treatment and the feelings stemming from it that cause Jews to throw in their lot with radical parties and movements.

The anti-Semitism thesis of Jewish radicalism also has several variants that merit our attention: self-hatred and status incongruity. The argument for the self-hatred thesis is that anti-Semitism and its historical product—a parochial Jew with a denigrated status—causes Jews living in Christian societies to hate themselves as individuals or as a group. For these, membership in the socialist movement served as a way of transcending their ethnically derived stigma.

This movement, according to the proponents of the thesis, had much to offer such Jews. It provided them with a way of escaping an onerous situation that Christendom had shaped over centuries and from which Christendom had denied relief to all but a handful of Jews. Specifically: "It offered a medium of escape from an obsolete religion, from a language—Yiddish—that was no better than jargon; and from an attachment to worldly goods that was the very epitome of the bourgeois spirit." [30]

But socialism was more than a medium of escape for Jews. It also had positive things to offer its Jewish adherents. Ideally, Jews who came to the movement gained access to the scientific and modern world that existed outside of the ghetto walls. They gained acceptance (or at least thought they had) into a fellowship of equals that did not require conversion to Christianity. Also, socialism did not require denial of their ethnic origins. Socialism gave these Jews a means by which they could subvert Christianity and strike back and even overthrow unjust Christian societies that had treated them and their ancestors so contemptuously. In the bosom of the socialist movement, they were no longer despised and crippled Jews but free, equal, and modern men inspired by a secular messianic mission to create a free, equal, and modern society devoid of ethnic particularisms.

Socialism for some of the self-hating Jews, again according to this thesis, also provided them with a way of striking back or destroying their hated community of origin. However, unlike the motives and methods of the Crusaders and pogromists, this was to be done scientifically for the "best" of reasons. The triumph of socialism in addition to its other meanings meant for them and for non-Jews like Kautsky, Lenin, and Stalin the demise of the Jews as a group, as a people with a corporate identity.

The status-incongruity or status-disequilibrium variant of the anti-Semitic thesis of Jewish radicalism takes a related but analytically distinct approach from that of the self-hatred hypothesis. It also considers the pain of a Jewish status determined by anti-Semitic Christian authorities as a major social psychological impetus drawing Jews toward socialism. A difference, and an important one, between this thesis and the self-hatred or general anti-Semitic theses is that it identifies and predicts which Jews will be most likely to associate with radicalism and utilizes sociological categories in so doing.

Basically, it contends that not all categories of Jews experience the same degree of strain or pain emanating from anti-Semitism. According to the logic of this thesis, Jews most likely to suffer acute discomfort are those who rank high in achieved status—that is, status based on effort or accomplishment. They are in a position of extreme status disequilibrium because their high achieved status based on wealth, prestigious occupation, or years of secular schooling conflicts with the low ascribed status—that is, a quality inherent to the individual such as age, sex, or in this case religio-ethnicity—that society assigns to Jews. It then follows that the rich, well educated, and professionals within the Jewish community should be the ones that the status disequilibrium thesis would predict to be most inclined to the Left.

The logic underlying this expectation is, according to contemporary sociologists, applicable to any individuals who are torn between a high-achieved and low-ascribed status.

No matter how high one rises on the educational, occupational or income ladders, in many realms a person of low ethnic status will still encounter social barriers that he cannot change. Hence his only recourse—should he wish to escape his status inconsistency—will be to seek broad scale social change through political action. A similar argument cannot be applied to persons of high ascribed but low achieved status, since normally they should be able to attain relative status congruence through individual mobility without sociopolitical change.[31]

The anti-Semitic and status-incongruity theses of Jewish socialism were probably earliest and most elegantly stated by the famous European political sociologist Robert Michels in 1915. His is a position that still receives prominent academic endorsement today.

The origin of this predominant position [of the Jews in the Left] is to be found, as far at least as concerns Germany and the countries of eastern Europe, in the peculiar position which the Jews have occupied and in many respects still occupy. The legal emancipation of the Jews has not there been followed by their social and moral emancipation. In large sections of the German people a hatred of the Jews and the spirit of the Jew-baiter still prevails, and contempt for the Jews is a permanent feeling. The Jew's chances in public life are injuriously affected; he is practically excluded from the judicial profession, from a military career, and from official employment. Yet everywhere in the Jewish race there continues to prevail an ancient and justified spirit of rebellion against the wrongs from which it suffers, and this sentiment idealist in its origin, animating the members of an impassioned race, becomes in them more easily than in those of Germanic blood transformed into a revolutionary impulse towards a grandly conceived world-amelioration.

Even when they are rich, the Jews constitute, at least in eastern Europe, a category of persons who are excluded from the social advantages which the prevailing political, economic, and intellectual system ensures for the corresponding portion of the Gentile population. Society, in the narrower sense of the term, is distrustful of them and public opinion is unfavorable to them. Besides the sentiment which is naturally aroused in their minds by this injustice, they are often affected by that cosmopolitan tendency which has been highly developed in the Jews by the historical experiences of the race and these combine to push them into the arms of the working class party.[32]

The anti-Semitic thesis and its variants are not devoid of merit. Anti-Semitism has undoubtedly been a factor in the generation of Jewish Leftists. Certainly some of the social psychological processes indicated in these theories have functioned to move some Jews toward the Left. But at the same time these theses are fraught with weaknesses and problems that undermine their contributions.

A major flaw in the anti-Semitic thesis lies in its discriminatory power. If anti-Semitism is a major force in the production of Jewish Leftists, then it should logically follow that most Jews in most European countries and America should have at one time or another been radicals. This obviously has not been the case. Rarely in any country at any one time in the Western Diaspora in the nineteenth and twentieth centuries has the proportion of Leftist Jews even approached a majority among their coethnics.

In fact, there seems to be no strong correlation between the degree and extent of anti-Semitism and the proportion of Jews identifying with radical politics. In France at the time of the controversy surrounding the Dreyfus case in the late 1800s and early 1900s, the level of anti-Semitism was at least as high as in Germany and Austria if not higher. Yet during that period the proportion of Jews who were radicals appeared to be lower in France than in Germany and Austria. Robert Michels, for example, admitted that in France in those decades ". . . the role of the Jews [in the socialist movement] is less conspicuous [than in Germany, Austria, and eastern Europe]."[33] Others have also shared Michels's general estimate of the Jewish presence in the socialist movement in France during these years. The overt and militant anti-Semitism stoked by the Dreyfus affair did not inspire a significant turn to the Left on the part of the Jewish community in France. Instead, the predominant reaction was one of caution and hope that the controversy would soon die down.

In the United States in the years immediately following the end of World War I the level of anti-Semitism rose. Yet during the decade of the 1920s, Jewish membership in and electoral support of socialist parties declined.[34]

More contemporary studies of the relationship between anti-Semitism and the political ideology of Jews also fail to validate this thesis. A study of the Jewish voters in the Boston area at the time of the 1972 election revealed that the conservative Nixon did better among those who were most concerned about discrimination against Jews and less well among Jewish voters who did not have strong feelings on the matter.[35] In 1960 a report of an analysis of Jews in a northeastern city of the United States concluded that: "Jews who feel socially and psychologically subordinate because of their ethnic affiliation are least likely to be tolerant of political non-conformists and altruistic toward other deprived groups."[36] It should also be noted that the founders and early recruits of the antisocialist and antiliberal Jewish Defense League came from Jewish populations in New York City, where feelings about anti-Semitism ran high.[37]

Another related problem with the anti-Semitic thesis bears on the issue of the character of Jewish responses to anti-Semitism. First, aside from the status-inconsistency variant, which will be considered separately below, this thesis does not adequately explain why Jews who are subjected to anti-Semitism, either directly or indirectly, turn to politics as a means of striking back or alleviating their condition. History has provided us with numerous cases of Jews who under such circumstances have chosen various responses other than politics. These have included suicide, conversion, rapid assimilation, and a reaffirmation of faith. For those Jews who do turn to politics, this thesis does not explain why they and not others equally burdened by anti-Semitism chose this particular alternative.

Second, the thesis has shortcomings bearing specifically on the issue of a Leftist response to anti-Semitism. Among those Jews who do turn to politics as a means of reacting to anti-Semitism, radicalism is not the only possible alternative. Political Zionism is one logical alternative that has been exercised historically in numerous instances. The anti-Semitic thesis does not provide us with the wherewithal to explain why some Jews chose Zionism rather than socialism. In general, we lack the guidance that will allow us to predict systematically which Jews or categories of Jews will be Leftist or more Left than others among their coreligionists.

The self-hatred variant of the anti-Semitic thesis shares virtually all of the weaknesses of its parent, in addition to having drawbacks of its own. This hypothesis provides no logical basis for explaining why self-hating Jews would turn to politics in general and radical politics in particular in order to deal with their situation. Again the problem of prediction appears. It does not allow us to predict who from among the self-hating Jews will be Leftists.

The self-hatred hypothesis of Jewish radicalism is a difficult one to validate. In order to do so it would be necessary to define "self-hatred" and construct empirical indicators to measure it. Next, a random sample of Jews would have to be selected and divided into groups on the basis of the degree of their self- or group-hatred. At the same time it would be necessary to ensure that these different groupings were similar in terms of background. After this procedure was completed the politics of each category would be determined. If there was a clear, direct, and strong positive relationship between the degree of self-hatred and Left or liberal politics then that would constitute validation of the hypothesis.

Unfortunately, such a study has never been carried out. Instead, the usual procedures followed by advocates of this hypothesis virtually guarantee unreliable results. Typically, the methodological shortcomings begin with the handling of the reputed causal variable, self-hatred. Generally, there is no adequate conceptualization of the concept, nor are empirical indicators of it spelled out in any detail in advance of the investigation. Evidence of self-hatred then becomes whatever the researcher declares it to be after the fact. Usually the "evidence" consists of hostile statements about Jews or negative experiences with them that are culled from writings, speeches, and conversations of or about the subject or subjects being studied. Even the absence of any statements concerning Jews by a Jewish-born socialist is regarded as "proof" of contempt of his ethnic origins.[38] Generally we are given no independent means of determining how important this negativism about Jews was in shaping the radical politics of these individuals.

The underlying assumption about the motivation for the discovered self-hatred is usually biased in favor of psychology. Psychological factors are given prominence, and other possible causal ones are given short shrift. Scarcely any effort is made to place the "evidence" within an historical or political context in order to ascertain the existence or extent of other forces that could have contributed to the same result.

The sample typically consists of one or several radicals of Jewish birth, who tend to be selected on the basis of their prominence as radicals. Such a sample precludes in advance the ability to make any generalization about the relationship between self-hatred and socialism. We do not know how typical or atypical these individuals were of (a) self-hating Jews, (b) non-self hating Jews, (c) Jewish socialists, or (d) non-Jewish socialists.

The problem with the self-hatred thesis is not only logical and methodological in character. It also has the associated burden of accounting for nonself-hating Jewish socialists. Moses Hess and Leon Blum were proud to be Jews and exhibited far fewer instances of alleged self-hatred than Karl Marx or Ferdinand Lassalle, but the former were Leftists as were the latter.[39] The much larger problem is that of accounting for the existence of tens of thousands of Bundists and Labor Zionists who purposely retained their Jewish identity and involvement in the Jewish community at the same time that they adhered to socialism. The existence of such exceptions and the seriously flawed methodology of those who have "tested" the self-hatred hypothesis lead to the inescapable conclusion that other hypotheses and theses have to be sought to explain the relationship between the Jews and the Left.

The status-inconsistency hypothesis has distinct advantages over the anti-Semitic and self-hatred theses of Jewish radicalism. It, unlike the other two, makes distinctions among Jews on the basis of nonpolitical variables and identifies the particular category of Jews who are most likely to be to the Left. In addition, this hypothesis indicates in advance why a particular combination of factors will tend to produce a socialist response among Jews. Despite these strengths, however, the status-incongruity hypothesis shares with the anti-Semitic and self-hatred hypotheses important weaknesses and inconsistencies. It should also be noted that these drawbacks are also present when non-Jewish groups are used to test the potency of the status-inconsistency proposition.[40]

In part, the problem with respect to Jews stems from the way in which the hypothesis has been tested. Guided by the logic of the hypothesis, we should expect that Jews most subject to strain because of discrepant statuses should be the ones most likely to be Left or near to the Left in their politics. Unfortunately, no study of Jewish subjects has been done to test this hypothesis. The principal difficulty centers around the variable of status-induced pain, which has not been given its own set of empirical indicators. Instead, discrepant statuses are assumed to generate discomfort, with the greater imbalance producing the more pain. Those who stand highest in accomplishment or achieved status are assumed to suffer the most pain and are expected to be the most Left.

There is historical and comparative data that on its surface appear to support this contention. A large proportion of the major figures of nineteenth- and twentieth-century European socialist movements were persons of Jewish origin from bourgeois backgrounds. Ferdinand Lassalle, Rosa Luxemburg, Victor Adler, Otto Bauer, Leon Blum, Julius Martov, Leon Trotsky, and Karl Marx himself shared such characteristics. It should also be noted that all of them were a part of a very small minority of their general age cohort or persons in their age bracket and an even smaller part of the Jewish age cohort that attended institutions of advanced education.[41]

It would be a mistake, however, to draw conclusions or to generalize about the validity of the status-incongruity hypothesis on the basis of such evidence. We do not know how representative these major figures are of the much more numerous ordinary Jewish socialists. Leaders, by definition, are different. They form a small minority of Jewish radicals and a small minority of the socialists within their organizations. Also, one expects that in radical parties and structures within capitalist societies a substantial portion of the leadership is made up of articulate men and women familiar with ideas and the use of words—in other words individuals from bourgeois and student backgrounds.[42]

In order to adequately test this hypothesis and determine if it has any validity among the masses of Jews, as opposed to a few special individuals, other types of data are needed. We should know for the country or region under scrutiny (a) the approximate size of the various classes and strata within the Jewish community; (b) the class background of Jews in the socialist movement; and (c) similar information for other ethnic groups both higher and lower on the status scale than Jews. Only if these data are available can valid conclusions be drawn about the political effects of discrepant statuses among Jews. Unfortunately, no studies containing such information have been done. In the absence of reliable data, we are forced to rely on other types of data that have some relevance and reliability in order to submit the status-incongruity hypothesis to some kind of testing. History provides us with some relevant cases. The examples presented below are by no means random or representative, but they do suggest that this hypothesis has serious problems.

Consider, for example, the following European cases. A detailed analysis of the background of Jewish cabinet ministers in the Hungarian Soviet Republic from March to August 1919 reveals that Jews from wealthy families had little if any representation in this group. Instead, virtually all were the progeny of minor officials and provincial professionals.[43] Another similar counterexample is that provided by the General Jewish Workers Union in Russia, Poland, and Lithuania or, as it was popularly known, the Bund. Although a large proportion of the leadership of the Bund was students, many of them from bourgeois families, the vast majority of the larger rank and file were workers or petty merchants or both.[44]

In America in the twentieth century the case against the status-disequilibrium thesis is much clearer. If the wealthier Jews have been the ones to experience the most strain and if these have been the ones most likely to move to the Left, then it should follow that a large proportion of the German Jewish men of wealth in the earlier decades should have been radicals. This was not so. The well-to-do German Jews tended to vote for conservative candidates, particularly Republicans. Herbert Lehman, as we shall see, was considered a renegade by his circle for aligning himself politically with Franklin D. Roosevelt and the Democratic party.[45] At virtually no time in twentieth-century America have wealthy Jews, whether of German or Eastern European background, joined in any significant numbers the Socialist or Communist parties or voted for their candidates. The Jews who have belonged and cast ballots for these parties have been overwhelmingly from the working and lower middle classes.[46]

The weakness of the status-disequilibrium hypothesis in terms of American Jews is further demonstrated by the situation that obtained in the 1920s. In the first half of this decade, anti-Semitism, as noted earlier, grew in intensity. At the same time the numbers of Jews experiencing economic mobility, owing in large part to World War I, increased considerably. According to the status-disequilibrium hypothesis, we could have expected that the coincidence of rising levels of anti-Semitism and Jewish social mobility would have produced an increasing number of radical Jews. It did not. In fact, the number of radical Jews as measured by electoral support for or membership in the Socialist or Communist parties continually decreased throughout the 1920s.[47] This observation in particular should also alert us to the danger of considering sociological hypotheses in an historical void. It is necessary to take into account the historical context and the existence of political and social forces that contribute to the shaping of individuals' and groups' political responses. We shall return to this point later.

History also presents us with a problem in the testing of the status-inconsistency hypothesis in the post–World War II decades in the United States. The virtual demise of the leading Left parties, the Socialist and Communist parties, in this era means that Jewish membership in or electoral support for them cannot be used as a dependent variable. We are then forced to rely primarily upon data gathered from Jewish voting patterns, positions on issues, or measures of liberalism devised by social scientists. These data are not as good as support for or membership in actual socialist organizations. The limited differences between the Democratic and the Republican parties and the abstract or trivial nature of many questionnaire items do not offer individuals desirous of basic structural change a means to express it. These types of data also lump together in one grouping those who are left of center and those who stand at the far left of the political spectrum. These may be the distinctions that are important to preserve.

Bearing in mind the shortcomings of these contemporary data, what do they reveal about the relationship between Jewish politics and status inconsistency? Similar to the richer historical and comparative data, the more recent evidence gives weak and mixed support to the contention that disequilibriant statuses among Jews produces a liberal to Left propensity. Since World War II studies of party preferences and electoral results have usually found that the pattern of politics of Jews by class is similar to that of Christians, although there have been significant exceptions to this pattern, particularly in the last 10 years, as the issues of race and law and order have come to the fore. The higher the socioeconomic status of Jews the more likely they are, compared to their less favored coreligionists, to vote for and prefer the Republican party, the more conservative of the two major parties.[48]

It is interesting to note in view of this discussion that social scientists working with the status-inconsistency hypothesis and utilizing samples from different ethnic and religious groups in the United States have invariably found that the Jews are the group most likely to provide positive proof of the hypothesis. In part this finding has usually been the result of weakness in the design of these studies. Class has generally not been controlled for. Typically, the higher status Jew is compared with his peers in other ethnic or religious groups and found to be more liberal. At this point the analysis stops, and this finding is presented as the evidence. Rarely is the comparison made between higher and lower status Jews and between Jews and Christians at the same socioeconomic levels. The failure to introduce this form of control invalidates any claim that the Jewish case is the best validator of the status-discontinuity hypothesis.

There has, however, been at least one study that has controlled for class differences among Jews and non-Jews. It was found that the relationship between status incongruity and liberal to Left politics among Jews was rather weak. But when the results for Jews were compared to those for non-Jews, the relationship was found to be strongest among Jews.[49] It is also interesting to note that the ethnic group with the political pattern most similar to that of the Jews was the blacks.[50] These recent findings have prompted some methodologically sophisticated social scientists to come to two conclusions. One is that the status-inconsistency hypothesis is of quite limited potency and not worthy of much more significant attention. The second is that other avenues of inquiry should be opened.[51] The fact that the predicted relationship was relatively strongest for Jews and blacks has led to the suggestion that one of these avenues should be that of an ethnic subculture. In fact, in considering the findings that obtained among these two groups and the weakness of the supporting data in general, two sociologists who have closely examined the status-inconsistency argument have virtually abandoned it and concluded that ". . . it is the persistency of traits characteristic of ethnic subcultures that leads to these results."[52]

The argument in favor of an ethnic-subculture explanation over a status-inconsistency thesis of Jewish liberal to Left politics is supported by two other pieces of evidence. One is that Jews, compared with non-Jews at any given socioeconomic level, are more likely to be liberal to Left politically. The second is that the extent of measured political difference or distance between high and low socioeconomic status Jews is generally less than that for any non-Jewish group.[53] This unique political profile suggests that attention must be paid to the experience and condition of Jews as a group, as a subculture.

HISTORICAL TRADITION

Historical tradition has been invoked as another explanation for the nexus between the Jews and the Left. This school of thought argues that anti-Semitism and the unique situation of the Jews in Christian Europe determined both the political choices available to them and the attitudes of non-Jewish political parties toward them. The long-term political consequence has been that the Jews have been close to the Left and distant from the Right.[54] This school contends that the formal emancipation of the Jews and the increased secularization and democratization of Europe in the wake of the French Revolution did not lead to their acceptance in the main stream of social, economic, and political life. Politically, there was one sector, made up of right-wing parties, that adamantly refused to accept them as equals. These parties, according to a major proponent of the historical tradition thesis, Werner Cohn, ". . . clung to the view that the state must be Christian. Not one of these—from the bitterly anti-Semitic Monarchists in Russia through the staunchly Catholic 'Noires' in France to the amiable Tories in England—could reconcile itself to Jewish political equality. . . . adherence to the Christian religion was made a prerequisite for joining the parties of the right, *Jews had no alternative but to side with those of the left*" [emphasis mine].[55]

This Jewish move to the Left, according to this perspective, was not only a result of the rejection by the Right but also of the attraction of the Left. On a formal or impersonal level, the radical parties were attractive to Jews because they fought for Jewish interests. Typically, it was these organizations who led the fight to maintain Jewish civil rights and to ban religious considerations from the sphere of public concern. It was the socialist parties that offered Jews and non-Jews alike a vision of a future commonwealth devoid of racial and religious prejudices. There were also more informal or personal reasons that led Jews to align themselves with the Left. Generally, the socialist parties were the most willing to welcome Jews into their ranks as party members. Religious and ethnic backgrounds of recruits and members were defined by these organizations as irrelevant. It was their political beliefs that mattered, not their religious ones. But it was not only a formal egalitarian fraternity that Jews found so appealing about these parties. Once inside them, they had the opportunity to exercise their talents and move in considerable numbers to the forefront of these bodies. Usually, the most prominent Jewish politicians and political journalists in a European country were men or women of the Left.[56]

Proponents of the historical-tradition thesis contend that many of the Jews who immigrated to the United States from Europe carried with them as baggage the political memories of a comparatively friendly Left and an antagonistic Right. These memories, it is argued, were reinforced in the decades prior to World War II by such factors as the warmth and openness of the Socialist party, the Communist party's vehement opposition to anti-Semitism in the latter 1930s and early 1940s, and the New Deal's recruitment of Jews to government service as well as its reform legislation.

The "historical traditionists," however, do recognize that the preponderant weight of the American experience did not reinforce the pro-Left reminiscences of European Jews. The permanent and prevailing conditions of life in the United States were effective in dulling the European political memories of the Jews and combined to make them less Left or more American in their day-to-day politics. These conditions included the absence of a significant Christian conservative tradition, a generally more accepting political and social climate, and the opening of opportunities to Jews in a relatively wide variety of arenas. Similar to the other theses dealt with, the historical-tradition thesis has some compelling aspects to it. Of special importance is that here for the first time specific historical conditions and experiences are introduced to explain the Jewish-Left propensity. However, similar to the others, it also has important problems and inconsistencies.

One of the most important of these inconsistencies is that the historical-tradition thesis does not account for the presence of Jewish conservatives among European Jewish immigrants, especially during the period of their early years in America. As noted earlier, a large proportion of the first generation German American Jews in the late nineteenth and early twentieth centuries were moderates or conservatives. The same was true for the Eastern European Jews who arrived before 1900. Currently, the chasidim, the most recent arrivals from Europe, are probably the most politically conservative Jews in the United States.

Also, if the historical-tradition thesis were valid, it would allow us to make accurate predictions about the politics of Jews in the United States based on their length of time in the country. It would follow from the thesis that the immigrant or first generation would be consistently more to the Left on the political spectrum than the second and third generations would be. The data that bear on this question indicate that this has not been the case, despite the fact that the first-generation Americans are generally of a lower socioeconomic status than their progeny. Neither the number of years nor the number of generations spent in the United States by themselves adequately account for the differences between Left and non-Left Jews.[57]

This particular shortcoming stems in part from another that is intrinsic to this thesis as it has been formulated. Paradoxically, this weakness lies in its area of greatest strength—historical specificity. Specifically, the thesis assumes a more uniform political tradition among Jews than actually obtained in the various countries of Europe prior to their departure. It does not take into account the fact that many European Jews in the nineteenth and twentieth centuries refrained from participating in non-Jewish politics. For some, the Zionist movement—a largely non-Leftist phenomenon—probably had a greater political impact on their lives than Christian political parties. For others, their political tradition was largely informed by participation in or exposure to conservative Jewish parties associated with Orthodoxy.[58]

The thesis also does not take into account the historical fact that socialist and conservative parties in nineteenth and twentieth century Europe were not always poles apart in their attitude toward Jews and Jewish affairs. In Austria, for example, socialists were noted for their hostility toward purely Jewish interests and concerns. The Austrians were not unique in this regard. Antagonism toward Jews that at times bordered on anti-Semitism was present either at the leadership or mass base of the Russian, Polish, German, French, and English socialist movements in this same time period. Conversely, there were conservative parties that were protective of Jewish interests and allowed them to enter their ranks. Practical political concerns such as votes often made a principled position on the "Jewish question" too heavy a burden for both socialists and conservatives.[59]

In order to give the historical-tradition thesis a proper test and demonstrate whether or not it had the power to differentiate Left from non-Left Jews, it would have to go beyond its present formulation and become more specific. It would require describing the formal and informal attitude toward Jews of the major parties (and Leftist ones if they were not among these) in those countries that sent many Jews to the United States at that particular time. The next step would be to determine the politics of these Jews from each of these various countries at the time of their arrival and at one or more later periods. Unfortunately, no one has yet conducted this type of research. Therefore, in its absence, it is to be expected that the historical-tradition thesis lacks the power to differentiate Left from non-Left Jews. The failure to take into consideration the heterogeneity of the political traditions of the immigrant Jews virtually guarantees this result.

There is another flaw to this thesis, also historical in character. This flaw concerns the assumptions the thesis makes concerning the process of the transmission and continuation of the pro-Left tradition among Jews in the United States. The historical tradition argument gives virtually no weight to Jewish experiences and institutions in America that sustained a socialist proclivity among Jews in this country. To explain the linkages between the Jews and the Left in the United States, the advocates of this thesis turn their attention almost solely upon the politics and political situation of Jews in the Old World. These differential emphases constitute a serious flaw in the historical tradition thesis. Any school of thought concerned with tracing and explaining the linkages between Jews and the Left in the United States must pay serious attention to the conditions of Jews in this country and to the political structures and subcultures they built here. Many important *American* factors not only sustained and perpetuated a European-inspired Leftist heritage, but they also reinvigorated it. Thus socialist politics were as much a reality for Jews in the New World as they had been in the Old (as we shall see presently). The American contribution in no way denigrates the significance of the European impetus. These are two interrelated factors, and both are necessary for understanding the association between the Jews and the Left in the United States.

The introduction of a Jewish subculture (or perhaps more appropriately a sub-subculture) in America as a key political factor also elucidates a related drawback in the historical-tradition thesis. Without the concept and structure of this subculture, we have to rely on weak, individualistic, and ad hoc means to explain how the socialist tradition is transmitted and perpetuated over time and generations. These vehicles, rarely if ever spelled out in any detail by advocates of the historical-tradition argument, are memory and positive sentiment as transmitted by individuals and families.

Memories and sentiments are significant factors in explaining the perpetuation of a political tradition. Individuals and families are important conveyors of that tradition. All this is true, but it does not go far enough. Unless they are embedded in a supportive subculture, memories and sentiments will fade and lose their ability to influence political behavior in the present and future. They are likely to be relegated to the status of a pleasant grandfatherly tale having little to do with life on this side of the Atlantic. Similarly, individuals and families by themselves cannot be relied upon to transmit a tradition that has the capability of affecting politics in the present and future. In such situations, the continual interest of many individuals and families in perpetuating the tradition cannot be counted upon, for they have little reason to do this other than the desire to pass on a positive and continually fading memory. Also, if institutions and groups outside the home either do not reinforce this tradition or oppose it, the odds against its having any sort of contemporary "clout" are considerable.

The perpetuation and maintenance of a socialist tradition among Jews in America that is still powerful enough to influence them politically is dependent upon more than interested individuals with positive memories. The institutions and values of the prevailing capitalist culture in the United States could easily overcome and vitiate any socialist influence of importance passed on by such means. In such a circumstance, the capitalist culture acting through its cultural and political leaders could rather easily remove the potency of such a tradition by defining it as "un-American" in character and relevant only to a distant past.

The fact that a significant Left tradition as well as actual Left politics survived in the American Jewish community for decades after the cessation of mass immigration indicates that something more than memories of European politics sustained them. This something, we contend, was in large part a unique and vibrant Leftist subculture. The proponents of the historical-tradition thesis do not give sufficient attention to the spokesmen, educators, leaders, organizations, institutions, and values of this subculture as they acted in the New World to breathe fresh life into a socialist tradition largely imported from the Old World.

There is another related drawback of the historical-tradition thesis that must also concern us here. Nowhere does this thesis give significant attention to the role of economic factors in explaining (a) the Jews' original turn to the Left in nineteenth-century Europe—the period in which the "tradition" first started—and (b) their maintenance of this tradition afterward in Europe and America. It is difficult to believe that the politics of Jews in these times and places were not affected by economic considerations.

The failure to deal with economic considerations—societal, non-Jewish, and Jewish—at specific times severely limits our ability to understand Jewish political behavior. It means that we must believe that only noneconomic Jewish factors influence Jewish politics and the attitudes of political parties toward Jews and that these factors affect all classes of Jews in the same way. It also means that we are to believe that the definite economic views of the socialist parties play little if any role in attracting Jews to them. These beliefs—that the historical-tradition thesis demands of us—are not in accord with historical facts, as we shall presently see.

The Judaic, anti-Semitic, and historical-tradition theses of Jewish radicalism have positive and negative features. Unfortunately, their weaknesses override their strengths. Thus, a new thesis is needed—one that will build on the contributions of the former and at the same time develop a more potent and valid framework for the understanding of the relations between the Jews and the Left.

The radical-subculture thesis proposed here avoids the major pitfalls of the theses of Jewish radicalism discussed above. First the issue of homogeneity is addressed. Important differences between Jews do exist and these differences do matter in terms of the politics of particular Jews. Social class distinctions are among the more important variables that differentiate Jews, particularly in terms of explaining the various Jewish responses to the Left. The tendency to treat Jews as a homogeneous unit precludes in advance any theory's ability to adequately differentiate Left from non-Left Jews.

A second issue—very closely related to the first—deals with broadness or scope. This is also confronted. Left Jews in any time and place were generally a minority among their fellow Jews. A theory seeking to explain the politics of this minority cannot rely on one factor or several factors that characterize or affect virtually all Jews. This problem is compounded when Jews are treated as a homogeneous unit.

A third problem with the previous theses of Jewish radicalism is their ahistorical nature. They do not give adequate attention to specific historical contexts and the changing historical conditions of Jews. I will clearly show that Jews exist in history and their politics flow and change from the different historical positions in which they find themselves.

Another pitfall of the theses described is their tendency to be apolitical. Little attention is given to the role of political parties and organizations, Jewish and non-Jewish, in the shaping of the politics of the masses of Jews. The historical-tradition thesis is an exception in this respect but not a very major exception. The political choices of individuals do not occur in a political vacuum. As my thesis will show, individuals are affected by a variety of factors including political organizations operative in their social environments.

Finally, a fifth problem area that the radical-subculture thesis avoids is the propensity of the other theses to view Jewish politics as reflexive politics. From their perspective, the political decisions of Jews are almost solely the product of the action of other people, particularly anti-Semites. Little attention is given to the manner in which Jews initiate and innovate in the political arena nor to the political manner in which Jews receive and deal with input coming from non-Jewish sources. The failure to define Jews as political initiators and innovators distorts reality and makes it very difficult to properly understand the relationship between the Jews and the Left.

A RADICAL SUBCULTURE

At this juncture I will outline the thesis of this book. It will be broadly sketched here with the main points briefly summarized. A more detailed treatment will be found in the body of this work. My objective here is to make the reader aware of the components of the thesis around which this volume is constructed. Given this approach, references to specific sources and related work will be kept to a minimum here, but they can be found in the body of the study. The two contentions underlying this work are: (1) class-linked factors enabled and motivated largely working class Jews at the turn of the century and for some years thereafter in the Pale of Settlement and in the major ghettoes of the United States to make Left political choices and to build a radical subculture; (2) once in place this radical subculture, in conjunction with, as well as independent of, those elements responsible for its establishment, functioned to create, recreate, and sustain a vital link between the Jews and the Left.

The concept of subculture as used here refers to a system of norms, values, cultural patterns, and related structures different from and smaller than that of society. The ideal typical subculture encompasses the two sexes, a range of ages, and different sets of groups and institutional arrangements for individuals as they move through the life cycle.[60]

The Jewish Left subculture of the United States in the twentieth century—a major focus of this study—is a special type of subculture because it is at one and the same time an ethnic and political subculture. It is ethnic because its members derive primarily from one ethnic group, and norms and values of that ethnic group color and characterize the component elements of the Jewish Left subculture. It is political because Leftist values are its dominant ones, and adherence in one form or another is generally a sine qua non for membership, at least for an adult.

It would probably be more enlightening if we were to characterize this Jewish Left subculture as a form of contraculture.[61] This indicates that conflict with or antagonism toward society is a central feature of this subculture and that many of its values and cultural patterns are contradictions of those existing in the surrounding society. In these respects the Jewish Left subculture is a contraculture vis-à-vis American society and the American Jewish community. These definitions should not be applied rigidly. The Jewish Left contraculture was not an independent and hostile entity with respect to America or the Jewish community. First, it could not be independent because it was not economically self-sustaining. The vast majority of its members earned their livelihoods working for capitalists or the bourgeois state. Second, this subculture was not a thoroughly hostile one. As we shall see, its values and cultural patterns were not always contradictory to those of the Jewish and American communities. In many instances overlaps occurred. The subculture as an entity also acknowledged the legitimacy of the larger United States society through its continual participation in the electoral system.

It is important to keep in mind that the Jewish Left subculture was not homogeneous nor was it resistant to change. In reality, this subculture was an amalgam of different forces that at times were more hostile to one another than to capitalists or Orthodox Jews who shared no Leftist commitments. Also, change was usually a constant within this subculture. Internal developments and external factors continually forced the leaders and agencies of the Jewish Left subculture to modify or alter positions and values. This was particularly true as Jews became more Americanized and the chances of a socialist revolution taking place here became more remote.

At its height, in the early decades of this century, the Jewish socialist contraculture in America was a force of significance. Its values and structures were richly informed by a variety of Jewish and socialist values and traditions. Structurally, as we shall see, it was composed of a myriad of informal groups and formal organizations and institutions. These touched upon or related to almost all facets of organized social life including education, culture, amusement, and, of course, politics. In its most developed form, this Leftist subculture provided Jews within its geographical scope with the means of living their lives almost totally within its ideological and structural confines. And during this period even non-Leftists within the Jewish community were required to exercise caution in the expression of their hostility to this Jewish Leftist phenomenon.

It should also be noted that the radical subculture was only one of several subcultures that existed within the American Jewish community. Throughout its existence, the Jewish Leftist contraculture continually had to struggle with religious, bourgeois, and nationalist adversaries for the allegiance of Jews. It was only for short periods of time primarily in New York City that the Jewish Left was able to be a leading force within the Jewish community. Generally this was not the case. Usually the majority of Jews within a given geographical unit including New York resisted its allure. Adherence to this subculture could, at times, prove costly in terms of jobs, economic well-being, and family peace and stability. Many who were a part of this subculture were only occasional or token participants, limiting their involvement to selected organizations and institutions. Many Jewish Leftists were simultaneously involved in non-Left Jewish and American organizations and institutions. Those Jews who constituted the core of the Leftist subculture were always a small minority in any given Jewish community. But its minority status should not obscure the significance of this phenomenon. As I will detail, the leaders and activists of this minority subculture often proved capable of mobilizing large numbers, sometimes majorities, on behalf of particular causes or issues. Even when past its prime, the socialist subculture and its component institutions proved capable of influencing the course of events and decisions within Jewish communities. And although it was a minority subculture, when compared with radical subcultures among other ethnic groups in the same geographical areas at the same time, the Jewish one was typically the largest, the best organized, and frequently the most influential.

It is now necessary to turn our attention to those factors that led to the establishment of the radical subculture in the first place. These were the class-linked elements that initially moved certain Jews to a Left or pro-Left position and to their building a radical contraculture.

Facilitating and Predisposing Factors

The factors that facilitated and predisposed Jews in America toward a positive Left orientation are very similar to the variables that Karl Marx, Max Weber, and more contemporary social scientists employed in their analysis of the formation of class consciousness.[62] The analysis developed here and in the body of the volume is much indebted to the work of these scholars. The reason for the similarity in approach is that in both cases—the classic working-class and the Leftist Jews—the key to their class consciousness and politics stemmed from their confrontation with capitalism.

The ideal-typical pattern leading to class conflict or Leftist politics was briefly the following: Capitalism disrupted traditional relationships and subverted traditions that upheld the status quo. Developing capitalism forced artisans and small shops out of business, forcing the occupants of these positions into cities and larger and larger factories doing the same type or level of work as exploited wage laborers. The concentrated numbers of workers sharing common grievances facilitated intraclass communication. All of these conditions combined to produce a feeling of solidarity among workers and place them in a position of antagonism against their common exploiters— the bourgeoisie—the revealed source of their economic plight. The final step in this process was the formation of socialist political organizations.

Naturally, no two groups underwent this process in the same manner. Much depended upon particular historical conditions and stages of development. Ethnicity was a factor that could both strengthen or weaken the development of class consciousness or Leftist proclivity depending upon the unique conditions prevailing at a particular juncture in history.[63] The role, or roles, that Jewish ethnicity played in this regard is the subject upon which I will now focus.

The analysis of the relationship between the Jews and the Left and the factors that facilitated and encouraged this association must commence with the situation of the Jews in the czarist empire during the nineteenth century. This is because of the vital part that Russian Jewish immigrants played in building a Jewish Left subculture in the United States. The early leaders, activists, and masses that erected and supported this subculture were overwhelmingly Russian Jews. Therefore, their experiences, traditions, and associations become significant elements in understanding the nexus between the Jews and the Left in America.

The unique manner and conditions under which Jews encountered capitalism in the Russian empire during the nineteenth and early twentieth centuries shaped their reaction to socialism for decades and generations both in Russia and the United States. The Jews commenced their experience with capitalism as pariahs. This politicoeconomic system did nothing to change that status. Capitalism respected the bigotry and barriers that confronted Jews. The result was that by the turn of the century Russian Jews were largely an exploited and impoverished class as well as an oppressed people. It was primarily as a reaction to this dual status and condition that many turned toward radicalism.

The essence of capitalism's role in unintentionally radicalizing Jews lies in its proletarianization of a large segment of the Russian Jewish community. The details of this process will be presented later, but indicated below are the lines along which this development occurred. First, the traditional Jewish economic roles such as middle men, managers, and independent artisans were undermined. Capitalism was a factor either in their demise or in their transformation to a proletarianlike status. For example, in the case of artisans, although formally not wage laborers, their work was increasingly controlled by others who in effect functioned as their employers. Secondly, capitalism as it developed simply generated more wage labor positions. Thus, by the turn of the century, there were large numbers of Jews in Russia who were either proletarians, felt like proletarians, or realized that they were en route to becoming proletarians. These Jews proved more receptive to socialism than the relatively stable Jewish bourgeoisie. It was from among these Jews, too, that the bulk of Jewish supporters of socialism was drawn. This new and large class of Jewish proletarians was probably the single most important factor in understanding why the Jewish Left rose and developed in Russia and America.

Capitalist development in Russia was largely responsible for the severe deterioration in living standards that the Jews experienced in the latter part of the nineteenth century. Jews suffered economically whether they remained in their traditional occupational roles or sought existing alternatives. The fact that they were Jews severely restricted their economic opportunities. Those who were fortunate enough to find positions in the new economic order occupied many of the dirtiest, most dangerous, lowest paying, and most marginal positions that the Russian economy had to offer. Non-Jewish Russians also held these kinds of jobs, but for Jews it was worse. These negative economic changes propelled Jews toward a socialist orientation.

They were propelled along this route even faster because of the role that the government played in these developments. In absolutist czarist Russia the state was intimately and publicly involved in bringing capitalism into the country and overseeing its actual operation in the society. It was the state that also took purposeful and public action against Jews as a group to deprive them of existing livelihoods, while at the same time denying them the economic opportunities that flowed from the capitalist expansion and that might have improved their situation. The czarist regime left little doubt as to its responsibility for the miserable economic condition of the Jews in Russia. Jews might still berate individual exploiting employers, ruthless competitors, or even G-d for their plight, but it was only with great difficulty that the state could be exempted from this list of oppressors. The role of the czarist government in the economic and ethnic oppression of Jews facilitated the focusing of their hostility onto the political arena and back upon the state, the ultimate source of their misery. For many, a radical political movement that attacked both the state and capitalism was considered an effective vehicle for the expression of the anger that flowed from their treatment as workers and as Jews. The attraction was even greater when these radical movements also included as objectives the elimination of ethnic discrimination.

The "natural" workings of the capitalist system and the purposeful action of the czarist state combined to create other conditions that facilitated and motivated Jews to move in a Left direction. Together they unintentionally laid the foundation for a Jewish socialist subculture. These two forces pushed and pulled many thousands of Jews from villages and small towns into larger towns and cities and did so in a relatively short period of time. In these urban areas they were confined en masse by laws, popular ethnic hostility generated by the Church and tsarist rulers, and a desire for security to crowded, unsafe, and unsanitary quarters. The classic ingredients for the development of a working-class consciousness—large numbers, geographical concentration, similar harsh jobs, a common lowly economic fate, shared grievances, and common enemies—could be found in these Russian Jewish ghettoes. But the unique Jewish factor must also be added. These Jewish poor and workers were not only developing a working-class consciousness, they were also developing a *Jewish* working-class consciousness. At this juncture the ethnic and class factors reinforced one another and moved the Jews more quickly to a Left position.

There were two ways in which the Jewish factor developed a socialist consciousness within the Russian Jewish community. First, the anti-Semitism that pervaded the Czarist state and society made the economic and living conditions imposed by the "normal" workings of a developing capitalist order more onerous for Jews than for non-Jews. Anti-Semitism tended to increase or make bitter the grievances and enemies they in a sense already "enjoyed" as workers. Their Jewishness also contributed to their feeling of commonality as a group. Not only did they share common enemies and grievances as Jews but common background experiences as well. All of this made it easier for them to communicate with one another and to spread political ideas and arguments.

This commonality and ease of communication was also fostered and reinforced by the Jewish factor in another way: through the Jewish language and its related culture. Yiddish and Yiddish culture were something that virtually all Jews in Russia had in common. Yiddish gave Jews their own unique means of communication, and the Yiddish culture allowed them to be culturally self-reliant. Yiddish and Yiddish culture along with geographical isolation also insulated the Jews from contact with societal values that fostered political conformity.

Russian capitalism and the czarist regime further contributed to the rise of Jewish radicalism by their treatment of two important Jewish strata—traditional Jewish authorities and secular Jewish intellectuals. In the case of the former, they did this through inadvertently undermining their position in the Jewish community. These authorities— the rabbinate and the wealthy elite—backed by tradition had been the primary agencies of social control among Jews. In this capacity they were also the primary bulwarks of the political and socioeconomic status quo in the society as well as within the Jewish community. Their own social position and social control functions were buttressed by the social context in which they were located—small, stable, and self-contained communities. But it was precisely such entities that capitalist development and anti-Semitic czarist edicts affected so adversely. Both of these created conditions that led Jews to move from the towns and villages to the cities. Urban economies meant class division and antagonism among Jews and increased secularization of the Jewish population. In such settings, the rabbis and the rich had a difficult time establishing or reestablishing their authority. In their weakened state, they lacked the power to inhibit the development of a radical consciousness and movement among urbanized and proletarianized Jews.

At this point, the only element missing to launch a radical movement among the urbanized and proletarianized Jews was leadership.

Here again capitalism in tandem with czarism obliged. This strata was produced from among those Jews who were denied access to schools and colleges and those who were the skillful artisans. Both of these groups found their hopes for personal improvement or social mobility frustrated by the state and Christian competitors or employers. It was from among these frustrated and angry Jews that the radical leaders were drawn.

As all of the necessary elements fell into place at about the turn of the century, Jews did launch a radical Jewish movement as well as participate as individuals in non-Jewish radical groups. The principal organizational component of the Jewish movement was the General Jewish Workers' Union or, as it was more popularly known, the Bund. The Bund and other Jewish Left groups focused their efforts on increasing the breadth and depth of Jewish support for socialism. In the process, they developed a Jewish Left subculture replete with institutions, values, and cultural patterns.

The Jewish Left in America owed much to the work of its counterpart in Russia. It especially benefitted after 1900 from the arrival in the New World of thousands and thousands of Russian Jews who had either been involved in the Left or whose lives had been touched by it in a positive manner. It was from the Russian movement that many of the leaders and cadres of the American Jewish Left were drawn. The Jewish Left in the United States was not an emigre movement or subculture totally indebted to Russian Jewish activists and memories of experiences in Russia. The resources and conditions flowing from the American environment and American capitalism were sufficient in combination with the "assistance" provided by Russian Jews to permit the building of a Jewish Left subculture in America. The Jewish confrontation with American capitalism and American society was not as harsh as it had been in Russia, but I contend that the forms and pattern of this confrontation in the New World were not all that dissimilar from those of the Old. This will be made clearer in the body of this work.

As in Russia, the Russian and Eastern European Jewish immigrants in America possessed their own language and culture, Yiddish. This provided them with another basis of unity as well as shielding them, to a degree, from the conservatizing influences emanating from American culture. It is also important to note that the Yiddish culture in the United States after the turn of the century was a culture that Russian Jewish radicals had succeeded in "tilting" to the Left. In America, emigre intellectuals continued to push Yiddish in that direction making it for a short period of time a Left-oriented language and culture.

In America in the first several decades of this century, the conservative forces within the Jewish community—the wealthy and the rabbis—did not represent significant obstacles to the development of a Left subculture. The wealthy Russian-born Jews were too few and too lacking in prestige. The German-American elite were too different from and too hostile toward the Yiddish-speaking Eastern Europeans, socialist or non-socialist, to successfully establish their political hegemony over these Jews. The rabbis did not represent much of a force at this time either. Not many came to the New World. Those that did were not generally most learned or respected individuals. Furthermore they were generally not prepared to cope with life in the New World themselves, much less help others.

The political weakness of organized religion, the rabbinate, and the rich in the early 1900s gave socialism and the socialists a major opportunity. It gave them a crucial breathing space in which to establish and legitimize a Jewish Left subculture. This relative political void also facilitated the socialists' ascension to positions of leadership within the Jewish community. The growth of a Left and pro-Left orientation among Jews in the United States was also facilitated by a factor indigenous to this country—a relatively strong Socialist Party. Prior to 1920 this was the only prominent political party to welcome Jewish immigrants both into its ranks as equals and into its leadership positions. Its stands against anti-Semitism and for more state services to the poor attracted large numbers of Jews to its banners.

These were the factors that facilitated and motivated the growth and development of Jewish radicalism and of a Jewish Left subculture in America. Basically, the Jewish confrontation with capitalism in Russia and America and ethnic divisions and hostilities prevailing in both countries combined to produce in America for a short period of time a large, concentrated, and culturally self-sustaining Jewiah working class oriented toward socialism. It was this base that nourished a Jewish Left subculture. At the same time, it is important to keep in mind that this subculture itself continually strengthened the socialist commitment of Jews. But this Left subculture did more than interact with and become dependent upon a particular segment of the Jewish community. It was also able, for a limited period of time, to take on a life of its own and stand almost independent of the forces that had brought it into being. In this capacity, the Jewish Left subculture made its own contribution to bringing Jews closer to socialism in America.

The Decline of Jewish Radicalism

We now turn our attention to the second question of concern in this study: Why did Jewish support for the Left decline? The response to this query forces us to retrace our steps. Much of the answer to this question can be found in the very elements that contributed to the positive association between the Jews and the Left. Here again we shall sketch the thesis broadly and wait until the body of this work to paint in the detail.

Before dealing with the decline of socialism among Jews, it is important to stress the fact that, even in the heyday of Jewish socialism in Czarist Russia or in the United States, most Jews are not active or committed Leftists. Jews, as was true of other peoples in these two societies, were usually too preoccupied with family and job concerns to become active politicians of any stripe, especially of a radical variety. It took a great deal of pressure and courage for Jews to put non-political concerns and interests aside and defy social inertia, employers, civil authorities, and their own religious leaders to enter the political arena as socialists. For most Jews in America again, as was true for most non-Jews, the barriers that separated them from radicalism proved too formidable to ever overcome.

Let us now commence by noting some of the more obvious factors that worked to undermine the relationship between this ethnic group and the socialist movement. Although they are considered separately here, it is important to realize that there was considerable interaction between them and that their political impact was felt cumulatively as well as separately. First, conservative forces, even at the height of the Jewish support for the Left, continued to exist within the Jewish community in Russia and in America. This implies that even at their weakest points, the rabbinate and the bourgeoisie, backed by religious traditions, were able to exert some political influence to counter the Left. In America, especially in the decades after World War I, these elements grew stronger and became more potent politically, thus attenuating the ties between Jews and the Left.

Second, if such factors as poverty, exploitation, ethnic oppression, and large numbers living in concentrated areas contributed to the growth of a socialist consciousness among Jews, then it should logically follow that their diminution would eventually lead to a diminution of support for the Left. A people who do not suffer from poverty, exploitation, and ethnic oppression and who are dispersed throughout various locations lack the structural facilities and the motivation needed to become members or supporters of the Left. Increasingly, throughout the twentieth century in America, Jews came to resemble such a people.

Third, the Jewish Left in America over time lost its protective Yiddish culture. With the passage of generations, the influence of this culture waned while that of the larger American society waxed. This meant that Jews came increasingly into contact with bourgeois and anti-Left values and cultural patterns. Eventually such a process had to lead to decreased support for the Left among Jews.

Fourth, the seeds of the decline of the Jewish Left were sown in the occupations of a large portion of the Jewish workers. Traditional Jewish customs and anti-Semitism combined to limit Jewish economic opportunities and to push them toward marginal or low capitalization industries, most notably the garment industry. The conditions that prevailed in these industries were not such that could sustain for any great length of time a large socialist-oriented Jewish working class. For example, the actual places in which Jews worked were small and characterized by frequent contact between employer and employees. These industries also offered Jewish workers ample opportunity to become "bosses." The poor wages and working conditions of thousands of Jews sharing a common occupation in conjunction with a heightened sense of ethnic solidarity stemming from oppression were sufficient to give rise to a militant Jewish working-class consciousness. But in America, when this consciousness became increasingly reliant on only occupational factors, it foundered. The occupational conditions in these Jewish-dominated industries, by themselves, were not as capable as those of more Christian-dominated industries like mining or automobile manufacturing of sustaining a socialist-oriented working class.

Fifth, the success of the organizations that comprised the Jewish Left subculture attenuated their commitment to the Left and the Jewish population which they served. In the context of a stable capitalist environment, success for these organizations generally meant that they had directly or indirectly improved living and working conditions, with, for instance, the creation of unions. It also meant, particularly for their own activists, the provision of skills, experiences, and contacts necessary to improve their personal life situations. But by facilitating or causing such improvements, these organizations subverted some of the very factors that had been responsible (a) for the development of socialism in the Jewish community and (b) for their own development as Leftish organizations.

A similar and related process also obtained at the organizational level. The leaders' decisions to pursue reformist as opposed to revolutionary objectives locked them and their organizations into a conservatizing cycle. Effectiveness in the sense of improving the situation of Jewish constituents within the context of the capitalist system required these Leftists to cooperate with bourgeois parties and groups and to develop ties and commitments to the very system ultimately responsible for the plight of their constituents. As the years passed, such a position pushed these Left organizations and their leaders to the point where organizational survival and the maintenance of a constituency became virtually the only objectives. Leftist goals were consigned to warm reminiscences.

Finally, success undermined their radical commitment in another fashion. These organizations' increased effectiveness in defending and promoting the interests of the Jewish poor and working class caused other sectors of the Jewish community, those not engaged in direct and immediate conflict with them, to seek out these Jewish Left bodies for assistance. The appeal or contact was made on the basis of their sharing a commitment to Jews and in some cases a shared constituency. In this manner, the Left organizations were increasingly pressed to function as Jewish communal structures as opposed to Jewish working class or Left ones.

Sixth, the seeds for the evolution of Jewish Left institutions into non-Left Jewish bodies were sown at the time of their origin in Russia and in their early years in the United States. The fact that they were exclusively Jewish creations largely confined to Jewish constituents and quarters made them vulnerable to conservatizing pressures from the Jewish community. In the United States, particularly after World War I, this meant a community whose leaders and those of primary influence were increasingly drawn from the ranks of the wealthy, the rabbinate, the professionals, and the nationalists—all of which were groups whose political interests and values and definitions of Jewish concerns were typically antithetical to those of the Jewish or non-Jewish Left. As Jewish organizations, Jewish Left institutions could not afford to alienate their Jewish constituents and potential constituents who felt strongly about Jewish concerns—as defined largely by non-Leftist Jewish elites. Similarly, Jewish Left organizations could not consistently remain oblivious or hostile to non-Left movements such as Zionism that gained the emotional commitment of large numbers of Jews in every socioeconomic category. The more that Jewish Leftist leaders and their institutions responded to and cooperated with these forces and the closer that they became to the Jewish community under the sway of non-Leftists, the more Jewish and the less Left these Jewish radicals became.

This Judaizing pressure became more acute over time for two interrelated reasons. The first was that the Left's natural constituency in America—the poor and working class immigrant Yiddish-speaking Jews—were dwindling in size and significance. In such a circumstance, the only way to avoid becoming small and insignificant organizations was to compromise and become more communal in scope, which in essence meant becoming more open and vulnerable to non-Leftist interests and values.

Another reason this pressure became so acute was because the Jewish Left leaders did not choose to leave the Jewish community and throw in their lot and their organizations' with that of the American Left. To have done so would have been to run the risk of becoming minor political actors on someone else's stage. This is not a risk that individuals who were or are major figures enjoy taking. But by not taking such action, they made themselves and their organizations vulnerable to non-Leftist pressures emanating from an increasingly bourgeois Jewish community.

Finally, the explanation for the decline in the Jewish support for the Left in the United States must eventually turn to factors outside of the Jewish community. Politically in America the Jews and the Jewish Left could not stand apart from the parties and other forces that shaped American politics. The more assimilated the Jews became and the less-contained their community, the more sensitive they became to American developments and the more they resembled other Americans in their politics. Jews, like non-Jews, also turned away from the Left during years of economic growth or relative stability and during those periods when the socialist movement was subjected to popular and governmental oppression.

The attenuation of the Jews' relationship with the Left, like that of the non-Jews, also stemmed from the attitudes, actions, and policies of socialist parties. Jews were not committed to the Left in such a manner as to be impervious to what they perceived to be its faults. During periods of internal power struggles and bitter internecine warfare, Jews as well as non-Jews quit the Jewish Left and non-Jewish Left parties.

Jews in the socialist movement also responded adversely to what they believed to be violations of Jewish sensibilities or interests. Socialist parties, whether Jewish or non-Jewish, were never so completely philo-Semitic as to be completely free within their ranks from hostility to Jews or from policies that large numbers of Jews considered injurious to their ethnic interests. Similarly, few Jews inside and around Jewish or non-Jewish Left parties were so ethnically liberated or assimilated as to consider their Jewish identities and things Jewish as trivial matters. Thus, when Jewish and socialist interests clashed, the usual response was a decline in Jewish membership and support. When hostility to Jews and Jewish styles of behavior surfaced within Left parties, Jews felt pressured to leave them.

Weight must also be given to the role of the major bourgeois parties in weakening Jewish ties to the Left. These parties had always competed with the socialists for Jewish support. Increasingly after World War I their indirect and direct appeals to Jews and their actions on behalf of them bore fruit in terms of Jewish votes. Also, even those Jews sympathetic to the Left became more and more cognizant of the fact that in a stable capitalist society, a bourgeois party was better able than a socialist one to further concrete and immediate Jewish interests.

CONCLUSION

The rise and fall of Jewish radicalism is rooted in the ways in which Jews in czarist Russia and in the United States confronted capitalism. The Jewish institutions and the social and economic divisions that emerged from this confrontation were the immediate contexts in which Jews related to radicalism. The radical Jewish subculture was one such product of this confrontation. The decline of Jewish socialism in large part flows from the accommodation of Jews to a stable capitalist society. During both the rise and decline of Jewish support for the Left, Jews did not merely respond reflexively to societal forces, they made political choices. It is to these decisions and their determinants that we now turn in order to substantiate the thesis of this work.

2 The Left Parties and the Jews: The "Dependent" Variable

INTRODUCTION

This chapter will demonstrate the extent to which the Left in America was Jewish. In this context the Jewish composition of Left leaders, activists, members, voters, and supporters will be detailed. To this end political party data have been selected as the single best measure of the Jews' relationship to and involvement with the Left.

The exclusive use of political party data in this chapter in reality understates the extent of the Jews' Left affiliation. Jews and other groups related to socialism in this country not only through political parties but also through other organizational vehicles—trade unions, fraternal orders, newspapers, and cooperative enterprises. To ignore these would be to omit an important dimension of the association between Jews and the Left, but we leave the analysis of these organizational ties to subsequent chapters.

Membership figures for these Left nonparty groupings and readership statistics of radical papers, while giving a more complete assessment, would, at the same time, exaggerate the Jews' ties to the Left. Membership in a radical union, fraternal order, or cooperative does not signify that the individual subscribes to the politics of that organization or its leaders. A person might join such groups for other than political reasons. In the case of unions, those in factories with closed shops would not even have a choice.

In the case of a radical political party, it is somewhat different. Here politics can be assumed to be a primary reason for support or membership. Yet even in this case, such actions do not necessarily mean that the person or persons performing them are socialists. A vote for a Left party can indicate dissatisfaction with a major party or support for a particular policy that may have little to do with socialism. However, in the absence of more accurate data, figures on Jewish leaders, members, voters, and supporters of radical parties will be the primary indication of the extent of radicalism among Jews.

The discussion here will be limited to those factors most susceptible to quantification. This does not mean that qualitative variables are unimportant. They are. Nonquantifiable "feelings" and attitudes also have to be figured into the equation to obtain a more rounded picture. These less quantifiable variables will be considered later.

Most attention will be paid to the Socialist and Communist parties, the two largest and most influential radical organizations in the United States during the twentieth century. At different periods of time one or the other was *the* political embodiment of socialism in America. Consideration will also be given to the Socialist Labor party at the end of the nineteenth century and to the New Left during the 1960s. During these years these Left bodies defined what it meant to be radical in America. Most of the radical parties that have existed within the last 100 years will not be considered in this chapter. Generally their numbers were too great, their members too few, and their existence too short to be of importance to the central question under study here.[1] In addition, for the vast majority of these groups, adequate data are not available.

The data that are used here are far from perfect. Membership and voting statistics are not as complete as one would desire. Individual Jews and Leftist parties did not for their own particular reasons always wish to reveal who was or was not a Jew. In such situations I have had to rely on a variety of sources to obtain valid or nearly valid data on Jews in Left organizations. These include official and unofficial Jewish statistics supplied by these organizations and their leaders, government agencies that have spied upon them, and knowledgeable informants.[2]

This approach is not problem-free. No one of the above sources may actually know the total number of Left Jews in any given period. In addition, a motive can be found in each case for distorting the figures. The Leftist party may wish to deflate the importance of Jews in its midst to show how ethnically broad-based or American it is. Government agencies may also desire to deflate the figures. An accurate report could stir up anti-Semitism or leave the reporter vulnerable to charges of anti-Semitism. Similarly, individuals may have their own axes to grind. Anti-Semites might want to inflate the importance of Jews while philo-Semites for opposite reasons might wish to underplay the significance of Jews in Leftist movements. The only way out of this morass or potential morass is to judge the sources carefully and check for consistency among them.

Thus, in the pages to follow, the extent of the Jewish involvement with the Left will be demonstrated by utilizing the hardest data possible. Through the use of party data, this relationship will be reduced to its most skeletal form. The fact that such data by itself can establish the relatively high degree of Jewish participation in the Left allows us the freedom in subsequent chapters to utilize other types of materials to give a more complete and rounded analysis and assessment of the relationship between the Jews and the Left in the United States.

THE LATE 1800'S AND THE SOCIALIST LABOR PARTY

The Russian Jewish involvement with the Left in America coincided with the beginnings of their mass immigration in the 1880s. At that time the Left within the Jewish community consisted of a variety of small, short-lived, and feuding socialist and anarchist organizations. For a brief period from the late 1880s to the early 1890s, anarchism was the most popular of the competing tendencies among Russian Jews in the United States. However, the longer lasting commitment was to socialism, as embodied in the non-Jewish Socialist Labor party (SLP). The SLP was, from the 1880s through the early 1900s, the leading political organization of American socialism. It was within and through the SLP that Jews had their first major contact and involvement with a non-Jewish socialist organization in the United States.[3]

Initially, the Jewish association with the SLP was neither direct nor immediate. It was mediated by a small Jewish Left group, the Jewish Workers' Verein (or Association). This organization, founded in 1885, was the successor to various other short-lived vereins, commencing with the Propaganda Verein in 1882. Each of these associations, despite the ideological disputes that helped to destroy them, was a socialist organization—a combination of political party, trade union, political school, and debating society. In essence they were training grounds for which emerged seasoned cadres that eventually built a large, stable Jewish radical movement. The JWV was both similar to and different from the other *vereins* that preceded it. Although larger than most of the others, it was small, with a membership of perhaps 20 to 30. The JWV, as was true of its predecessors, also lacked a sizable following within the Jewish community. As with the others, much of the organization's time was spent in internal debates. Its leaders and activists, like their counterparts in other *vereins*, were largely Russian-educated intellectuals who thought of themselves as cosmopolitan socialists. They did not consider their own Jewishness or that of the workers among whom they propagandized as being of special importance.

The Jewish Workers' Verein was also different from its predecessors. Although it was Jewish in composition, it had a broader base in terms of class and nationality than the others. The JWV's membership included Jews not only from czarist Russia but from Galicia, Romania, and Hungary as well. The JWV also had a greater proportion of workers. Perhaps most important, the Jewish Workers' Verein was the first to take the formal step of affiliating with the American socialist movement, the Socialist Labor party. It took this action in July 1886.[4]

The Socialist Labor party with which the Jewish Workers' Verein became affiliated was an organization that was far from being American in composition. German-born and German-speaking immigrants constituted the vast majority of the leaders and the rank and file. Of its 2000 to 3000 members at the end of the 1880s, about 10 percent were

native Americans, according to the estimate of one of its most distinguished alumni, Morris Hillquit. The rest were largely German, with a
thin sprinkling of Scandinavians and Czechs.[5] Its leaders were very
much aware of the ethnic composition of the largest socialist party in
the United States. "Let us not conceal the truth," commented Wihelm
L. Rosenberg, the non-Jewish German Secretary of the SLP, "the Socialist Labor Party is only a German colony, an adjunct of the German-
speaking Social Democracy."[6]

The Germans who headed and peopled the SLP were men who had
had some experience or contact with the German Social Democratic
party or social democracy. In the latter nineteenth century this was
the largest and most admired socialist party in the world. Many of the
Germans who left Germany for the United States had come because of
the persecution they had suffered for being associated with that party.
In America their political experience and their links with German
social democracy propelled them into the leadership of the socialist
movement.

The major problem of the Socialist Labor party was not so much its
Germanic composition but the fact that so little effort was made by its
leadership to make it into an American party. German was the language of communication between leaders and members and was the
language in which the major party newspaper was printed. Party
meetings were conducted in German-populated areas, generally in
rooms behind German beer halls. Only one of its sections was designated as American. In essence, the SLP could well have been the Ba-
varian division of the German Social Democratic party geographically
situated in America. In actual fact much of it was physically located in
New York City. This was the city that housed the SLP's headquarters
and the party's major newspaper, the New Yorker Volkszeitung.[7] This
was the party through which the immigrant Russian and Eastern European Jews initially came to American socialism. This was the party
from which Jewish Leftists sought political education.

Two astute observers of the Socialist Labor party commented on the
Germanic nature of this organization and its leaders and its relationship to the success of socialism in America. One was Abraham
Cahan, a member of the SLP, who, by choice, was most active in an
English-speaking branch; the other was Friedrich Engels, Marx's close
collaborator. Cahan, reflecting on the SLP and his own experience
within it, observed:

The German comrades understood that by themselves they could not achieve
socialism in America. It was necessary to spread the doctrine and the party
among native Americans. They did much in this direction, but one could not
escape the impression they were doing so only half-heartedly. Actually, they
looked condescendingly on the American masses and conducted their affairs
as if the German-language socialist movement were the entire movement. . . .
Examining our party, one could easily suppose that the German immigrants
were the natives and the American natives were the foreigners.[8]

If Jewish and Yiddish were to be substituted for the term *German* in Cahan's statement, it would not be very far from describing the attitude of the men who came to the fore a few years later within the Jewish Left.

Friedrich Engels assessed the strengths and weaknesses of the Socialist Labor party in 1887. His observations shed light not only on the SLP but also on the condition and situation that would confront the Jewish Left as it emerged as a power to be reckoned with.

It is . . . to a certain extent, foreign to America, having until lately been made up almost exclusively of German immigrants, using their own language and, for the most part, little conversant with the common language of the country. But if it came from a foreign stock it came, at the same time, armed with the experience earned during long years of class struggle in Europe and with an insight into the general conditions of working class emancipation far superior to that hitherto gained by American workingmen. This is a fortunate circumstance for the American proletarians, who thus are enabled to appropriate and to take advantage of the intellectual and moral fruits of the forty year struggle of their European classmates and thus to hasten on the time of their own victory. . . . there cannot be any doubt that the ultimate platform of the American working class must and will be essentially the same as that now adopted by the whole militant working class of Europe, the same as that of the German-American Socialist Labor Party, insofar as this party is called upon to play a very important part in the movement. But in order to do so they will have to doff every remnant of foreign garb. They will have to become out-and-out Americans. They cannot expect the Americans to come to them; they, the minority and the immigrants, must go to the Americans who are the vast majority and the natives. And to do that they must, above all things, learn English.[9]

Affiliation with the Socialist Labor party was not the only action taken by Jewish Leftists to bring them closer to left wing politics in America. In 1886 the Jewish Workers' Verein, along with the SLP, decided to endorse the candidacy of Henry George, a liberal reformer, for Mayor of New York City. Despite their hesitations, owing to the fact that George was a reformer and not a socialist, these radicals campaigned for him and affiliated themselves with George's United Labor party. The George campaign of 1886 was in many ways an important experience for the nascent Jewish Left. It gave these radicals their first practical experience in conducting an election campaign in America and taught them many practical lessons about American politics. But this campaign was also significant because it helped to weaken, if not break, the ties of the immigrant radicals and their constituents with the Old World while bringing them all closer to the life of the New World. At one point in the campaign the JWV through its weekly organ, the *New Yorker Yiddishe Folkszeitung*, enjoined their fellow foreign-born Jews: "Jewish immigrants, become citizens! We remind our brothers who are already five years in this country to take out their citizenship papers to enable them to fight, in common with all other workers, for their political freedom." [10]

The campaign involved far more Jews than the relative handful who belonged to the Jewish Workers' Verein. For the first time in America, thousands of Jews, primarily workers, became actively involved in American politics. Their first entry was on behalf of a third-party candidate endorsed by socialists and defined by many of his supporters and opponents as a man of the Left. The election results, in many ways, presaged the pattern for the future. The third-party candidate favored by the Jewish voters lost, although in George's case he did quite well. The United Labor party nominee *officially* received 68,110 votes, some 8000 more than his Republican rival and 22,000 less than the Democratic winner. (It is widely contended that an honest vote count would have given the victory to George.) The proportion of Jewish votes that went to George was very high. Estimates as to the actual size of his Jewish vote vary from a low of 5000 to a high of 15,000. Either figure represents a significant percentage of the total Jewish vote, since the number of all Jewish voters in New York City as of 1880 (some six years earlier) was said to be 11,000. [11] The official New York City records for the Eighth Assemby District (A.D.) allow us to gauge the extent of the Jewish support for George, as this district was located in the heart of the Lower East Side, making it the most Jewish of all assembly districts. In the Eighth A.D. George outpolled the Democratic winner, Abraham Hewitt. The former received 2671 votes, the latter 2241. However, George did run behind Republican Theodore Roosevelt, a popular figure among Jews, by about 750 votes. [12]

In 1886 the size of the Jewish vote for George, given the context of the times, was quite remarkable. His organizational apparatus was hastily thrown together, an unwieldy coalition that had never before been tested. George and his campaigners could not rival the Democratic organization in terms of offering minor (and some major) benefits in return for votes; nor would they rival the Democrats in the field of more direct electoral chicanery. Another contextual factor was the political nature of the Jewish immigrant community at the time. The Eastern European Jews in New York City in 1886 were much less politically inclined and certainly much less socialistically oriented than their fellow Jews who would come after the turn of the century. Yet despite all of these inhibiting factors, the Jews disproportionately gave their electoral support to a left-wing candidate endorsed by socialists.

The Jewish commitment to the Left in the late nineteenth century, as assessed by membership in the SLP and electoral support for socialist candidates, was considerable in relative but not objective terms. In the election of 1892, for example, the SLP won 6000 votes in New York City with one-quarter of these coming from Jewish districts. In the 1890s the SLP vote in New York City was about 2 to 3 percent.

During the same period, in the Lower East Side's Eighth A.D., SLP candidates averaged about 10 percent.[13]

This was not a phenomenon limited to New York City. In Newark, New Jersey, in the election of 1894, the SLP received less than 2 percent of the total vote; but in Jewish and German-American wards, the percentage was much higher. There the SLP attracted from 5 to 18 percent of the voters. In New Haven and Paterson, the pattern was the same.[14]

By the end of the century, it was quite clear that working-class Jewish immigrants along with German-Americans were the electoral mainstay of American socialism. Proportionately, Jews gave more of their votes to the SLP than any other ethnic or nationality group (with the possible exception of the Germans). But Jewish SLP voters were a distinct minority of those Jews who cast ballots. It is not as easy to assess the number and importance of Jewish members of the SLP by the end of the 1890s. However, the available information suggests that their size and influence had become considerable by this time. Several Jews—Morris Hillquit, Victor Berger, and Louis Miller—were major figures within the party. The SLP's autocratic leader was Daniel De-Leon, a man of Jewish parentage, which he never publicly acknowledged.

The Jewish coloration of the party could also be gauged to some extent by the foreign-language branches of the organization. The SLP, as was true of earlier radical parties, was organized into branches or sections according to the language or nationality of the members. The first Jewish or Yiddish-speaking branch was Section 8. This was organized in 1887 in New York City and had at its founding about 25 individuals who were former members of the Jewish Workers' Union. However, not all Jews in the SLP in New York City joined Section 8. Others in the same area shortly after formed Section 17—a Russian-speaking section. As more Jews entered the SLP a similar phenomenon occurred in other areas of the country. Some Jews joined Jewish sections and others non-Jewish sections, a development that would occur later in other socialist parties. Many Jewish Leftists did not want to belong to Jewish sections of their respective parties. (This, of course, means that the researcher cannot use size only of Jewish sections to determine Jewish membership in socialist political organizations.) However, bearing this in mind, the number of Jewish branches did grow in the 1890s. In the early years of this decade, 14 Jewish sections were added to the party—a figure higher than that for any other foreign-language group except the Germans.[15]

By the end of the century, when the SLP was at its peak, it was quite clear that the Jews in the leadership and the rank and file of the organization had come to rival the Germans in terms of numbers and influence.[16] This was especially true for New York City. In approximately two decades the Russian Jews in America had become a major force within the socialist movement.

This change in the ethnic coloration of the SLP was the result of a variety of factors. Probably most important, it reflected a rise in the tide of Jewish immigration and a decline in that of the Germans. It also reflected the change in the political character of the German immigrants. In 1890 the German Social Democratic party regained its legality, and thus socialists had much less cause to flee Germany than before. The changing ethnic composition of the SLP also mirrored the increasing integration of Germans into American society, particularly German workers into American trade unions during the 1890s. Jewish immigrants, on the other hand, were still in one way or another motivated by political repression. And the Jews who flocked to American shores replaced the Germans as political outsiders. This position traditionally facilitated, if not encouraged, its occupants to move in the direction of socialism.[17]

The 1890s did not mark the end of the German-Americans' association with socialism. It continued for decades, especially in Milwaukee, a German-American population center that elected Socialists as mayors through the 1950s. The period did mark the end of their predominant role in socialist politics. Now it was the turn of the Jews and other ethnic groups from the Russian Empire to move to the fore within radical politics in America.

THE SOCIALIST PARTY OF AMERICA

The Socialist Party of America (SPA) was founded in 1901 and swiftly superseded the Socialist Labor party as the primary socialist party in the United States. From 1901 to 1919 the Left in the United States was for all intents and purposes embodied in the SPA. At its inception this new party was an amalgam of various groups. These included native Americans, unionists, clergymen, intellectuals, and progressives, as well as foreign-born Jews. (All Jews involved in radical politics from the 1880s to the 1920s were foreign-born, generally from Russia and Eastern Europe.) The Jews who entered the Socialist party in 1901 were primarily men who had earlier seceded from the Socialist Labor party. In fact, a major purpose of the first Socialist party convention in 1901 was to join these dissident SLP members together with the Social Democratic party led by Eugene V. Debs. But Jews did not constitute either a majority, a plurality, or a large minority of the membership of this new organization.[18]

The unique aspect of the Socialist Party of America and one of its strongest assets was its native American character. The Socialist party gave an American face and voice to socialism, an ideology and a movement previously associated only with foreigners. At its founding convention in Debs's home state of Indiana in July 1901, three-fourths of the delegates were native-born Americans (which automatically meant that they were not Jews, as virtually all radical Jews were born abroad at that time). Similarly, a majority of the delegates to the next five SP conventions were also native Americans, many of whom were third- and fourth-generation Americans. In 1908 a canvas of the general membership revealed that about 70 percent were born in the United States.[19] This, it should be stressed, was a year in which almost all Eastern European Jewish adults living in the United States were born abroad. In fact, it was the American character of the new party (albeit only second generation), epitomized by its midwestern, all-American leader Eugene Debs, that proved to be one of the strong attractions for the immigrant Jews.[20]

The Socialist party also drew its electoral support from Americans who lived in areas where there were relatively few foreigners. "Until 1918," observed the radical historian James Weinstein, "the greatest relative voting strength of the movement [SP] lay west of the Mississippi River in the states where mining, lumbering, and tenant farming prevailed. New York . . . placed twenty-ninth and twenty-fourth in the percentage of Socialist voters in 1912 and 1916. . . . The states with the greatest percentage of Socialist voters in the pre-war years were Oklahoma, Nevada, Montana, Washington, California, Idaho, Florida, Arizona, Wisconsin and Texas. In that order, all appeared among the top dozen states in the Presidential elections of both 1912 and 1916."[21]

If the Jews did not constitute a numerically important component of the Socialist party's members or voters, however, they did constitute a significant part of the leadership. Debs may have been the national leader and the most popular public figure in the SP, but it was not Debs and his immediate followers who dominated its internal organization. The two most important men in this regard were Morris Hillquit and Victor Berger, both immigrant Jews and dissident members of the SLP. Hillquit was also regarded as the SP's leading Marxist theoretician.[22] Other influential Jews in the early days of the Socialist party included Abraham Cahan, Leon Greenbaum, and Louis Miller. But, with the exception of Victor Berger, these Jewish leaders had few direct followers during much of the first decade of the party's existence, a deficiency that was considerably remedied by the large influx of Jews who soon began to arrive in America in the next several decades.

Despite its large native-American base, the Socialist party recognized the political potential represented by the great numbers of working class immigrants in the country. Although it was divided over the best way of tapping that potential, the party reorganized itself in 1910 in order to facilitate and encourage recruitment of these immigrants. This new organizational device was the foreign-language federation. According to the amended party constitution, any foreign-language group with at least 500 members could affiliate with the SP.[23] Once instituted, various immigrant nationalities began to utilize the federation mechanism in order to affiliate with the SP. The Finns were the first group. By 1915 there were a total of 14 federations, including the Jewish Socialist Federation, which came into existence in 1912. In that year, when the party was at or near its zenith in terms of its appeal to the American-born, 13 percent of its membership (or 16,000 of its 118,000 members) was located in foreign-language federations. In 1918 the percentage within the federations had increased to about 30 percent, and by the end of 1919 it had risen to 53 percent, representing 57,000 out of a total of 108,504 Socialists. These figures for the members of the federations actually understate the total number of foreign-born within the party, as not all in this category chose to join the Socialist party through this organizational affiliation.[24]

The increasing influence of the foreign-born within American socialism could also be observed through the rapid rise of the foreign-language socialist press. Between 1912 and 1916 the number of foreign-language dailies increased from eight to 13. Conversely, the figure for their English-language counterparts declined from five to two in the same period. A similar pattern also obtained when circulation figures for the English- and foreign-language press are compared.[25] The ballot box also reflected the importance of the immigrant to the Socialist party. After 1912 the importance of the Socialist vote began to be felt in areas where the foreign-born were concentrated. Increasingly, the two largest sources of Socialist votes were among the German-Americans in Wisconsin and the Eastern European Jews in New York City. Reflective of this is the fact that the only two Socialists ever sent to the House of Representatives were Victor Berger from Wisconsin and Meyer London from New York.

Various reasons can be offerred to explain the ethnic shift in the ranks of Socialist Party members. The ascendancy of the foreign-born occurred during a period of internal strife revolving around the political direction of the Socialist party. Many of the most reformist members who departed were American born Christians. In these same years the farmer base of the SP, which was largely native American in composition, was undercut by increased economic security and relative prosperity flowing from government reform legislation and higher commodity prices. Also, during World War I, Socialist Party units in the south and west, areas of American and non-Jewish concentrations, were subjected to legal, political, and physical attacks by local state and federal agencies as well as by vigilante groups. Socialist locals and chapters in which there were large numbers of Jews were generally not as viciously dealt with by the authorities and the mobs. The location of these Jewish socialists in the midst of a disproportionately anti-war ethnic community was another factor that gave them support vis-a-vis pro-war anti-socialist crusaders. In any event, as the native Americans left or were forced out of the Socialist Party, they were replaced by large number of immigrants, an increasing proportion of whom were Jews.[26]

After 1912 Jewish influence and importance within the Socialist

party and socialist politics rose as the party took on a more ethnic coloration. This can be demonstrated in a variety of areas: electoral politics, party membership, internal organization, organized support, and
party finances. By 1920 it was quite clear that the Jews and their organizations constituted the major underpinning of the Socialist Party of
America.

Voting

As the 1910s progressed it became increasingly evident that the Jewish voters, particularly those concentrated in New York City, were
becoming the party's single largest repository of electoral support. In
numbers alone the Socialist vote among Jews was probably unrivaled
among nationality groups in the country by the end of the decade. In
terms of proportion, the Jewish balloting on behalf of socialism was
perhaps exceeded only by that of the German-Americans and the
Finnish-Americans. By the end of the decade, there was no doubt that
the Jews constituted and would probably continue to constitute the
Socialist party's electoral bulwark.

This development can best be seen by viewing various election
results, primarily those in New York City, since this was the most important Jewish population center in the United States and the principal Jewish voting area as well. Prior to 1914 New York's Jews had
not been able to elect a Socialist to the House of Representatives. In
1912 Meyer London, the Socialist party's nominee from the East
Side's Congressional District, obtained 31 percent (or 3646 votes) of
the ballots cast in a four-sided race. In the next election from the same
Twelfth Congressional District two years later, London's vote increased to nearly 6000, or almost 50 percent, in a three-man race. This
was more than sufficient for victory, and Meyer London took his seat
in the House of Representatives as the only Socialist until joined in
1916 by Victor Berger, a fellow Socialist and immigrant Jew from
Milwaukee. (Berger had been the first Socialist to sit in the House,
having been elected in 1910.)[27]

Meyer London was not the only beneficiary of the rising tide of Jewish socialist ballots. Jewish Assembly Districts in New York (such as
New York County's Second, Fourth, Sixth, and Eighth; and Bronx
County's Third and Fourth), which had given Socialist candidates 10
to 15 percent of their votes prior to 1914, began giving them from one-
third to one-half in the remaining years of the decade. In the 1917
elections, a high point in Jewish electoral socialism, Jewish votes
were largely responsible for the victories of 10 Socialist state assemblymen, seven Socialist aldermen, and one Socialist municipal
judge. Only the well-organized Germans in Wisconsin could match
this electoral triumph. In the same election, the Socialist mayoralty
nominee, Morris Hillquit, won 145,332 votes, the most cast for a Socialist candidate in the United States other than the party's presiden-

tial standard bearers. Hillquit received 22 percent of all ballots cast in New York City, which was insufficient, even in the four-man race, to bring him victory. However, the Jewish districts gave him about half of all their votes. In the East Side's Fourth, Sixth, and Eighth Assembly Districts, Hillquit received 11,911 votes out of 22,299 counted.[28]

Another way of assessing the growing importance of the Jewish votes within the Socialist party is through an examination of the balloting for president, with a focus on New York State. This admittedly is a crude indicator as many New Yorkers who voted for Socialist presidential nominees were not Jewish. However, this particular and important shortcoming need not totally invalidate the use of this indicator. Although many New York Socialist voters may not have been Jewish, the Jewish proportion of the Socialist presidential vote in this state was the largest for any state in the union. There are several grounds for this assertion. First, most Socialist votes in New York State after 1912 were cast in New York City, which was responsible for between 66 to 70 percent of the state's Socialist ballots in 1920 and 1932. Second, Jews of all groups in New York City were, disproportionately, most likely to vote Socialist.[29] As Nathan Fine, an historian of Left parties in the United States, observed: "The Socialist Party never made any real headway in any section of New York City not dominated by Jewish Americans."[30] Therefore it seems permissible to utilize the New York State presidential vote as a suggestive indicator of the extent of Jewish support.

In 1912 approximately 63,000 votes in New York State went to the Socialist candidate, Eugene V. Debs. This represented 4 percent of all ballots cast in the state. In terms of percentages, this was below the national level of 6 percent and below that of 29 other states. In Oklahoma and Nevada, 16 percent of the voters voted Socialist. Even numerically this vote was not very substantial. In 1912 New York, the state with the largest number of the nation's voters, gave fewer ballots to Debs than California, Illinois, Ohio, and Pennsylvania. By 1920 the situation had changed dramatically. Debs was once again the party's standard bearer. This time he received 203,201 votes in New York State, about two-thirds of which came from New York City. This was the largest total number for any state. The New York City vote alone— 130,827—surpassed that of any state vote. The total vote in New York State came within 60,000 ballots of exceeding the combined vote of the four states that had outpolled it in 1912. In the 1920 presidential balloting New York provided the party with 22 percent of its total vote, compared with 7 percent in 1912.[31]

The 1920 election placed New York and its Jewish voters in the forefront of the party's electoral supporters, a position they were to maintain in subsequent elections. In the 1928 presidential election approximately 40 percent of the SP's votes came from New York, about one-quarter from New York City alone. In 1932 the vote dropped to 22 percent, but the New York vote was still larger than that of any other state. In the 1936 presidential balloting almost half of all Norman Thomas's votes were cast in New York. Even in 1940, when Jewish support for the Socialist party was at its nadir (for reasons we shall presently discuss), New York supplied 19 percent of the party's 99,557 votes.[32]

The election results, particularly prior to 1920, do not give an adequate indication of the degree of popular support for Socialism among American Jewry. From the early 1900s through 1920, Socialist electoral campaigns in predominantly Jewish working class districts galvanized these communities. Irving Howe tells us that, "Apart from strikes, the most exciting activity open to the Jewish Socialist was the recurrent election campaigns. . . . On the East Side a lively street meeting meant an evening's free entertainment and casual enlightenment: it was an important part of neighborhood life."[33]

Toward the end of the election campaign in 1916, the Socialists held 50 rallies per evening on the Lower East Side and 15 per night in Brownsville and Harlem—all districts with heavy Jewish concentrations.[34] During these years orators and bands would attract to these rallies crowds of thousands whose numbers were far more than sufficient to assure victory to the Socialist candidates. Harry Rogoff, an astute observer of these scenes, described the impressive campaigns and the unimpressive election day results: "During campaign weeks the East Side districts rocked with Socialist agitation. The Socialist candidates were hailed as Messiahs. Their open-air meetings were monster demonstrations. . . . The marvels of the Socialist strength would grow until the day of election. Then during the 12 hours between the opening of the polls and their closing, the strength would melt away."[35] "When election day came around," Charles Edward Russell wryly noted, "we had the cheering and the old parties had the votes."[36]

The discrepancy between the cheering and the voting was primarily the result of two major factors. One was the chicanery of Tammany Hall. Tammany did not bother to challenge the campaign efforts of the Socialists. Their election efforts were more quiet and personal, consisting of bribes, favors, threats, multiple voting, plus a unique way of counting ballots. However, Tammany was aware of Jewish sensibilities. Jews received free milk, while others received free beer.[37]

The second major reason for the difference between the size of the Socialists' campaign turnout and their electoral results centered around who could and who would register to vote. Prior to World War I only male citizens who were 21 or older were eligible. This excluded noncitizens, females, and those less than 21 years old from both registering and voting. Yet among the Jews, people from these categories were strong supporters of the Socialist party.[38]

Jews as a whole had relatively few registered voters in their midst. In 1912 the proportion of registered voters on the East Side was the lowest in New York City.[39] The Census of 1910 revealed that in the predominantly Jewish Second, Fourth, and Eighth Assembly Districts less than 20 percent of the foreign-born males over 21 were naturalized.[40] Nor had the situation improved appreciably by 1920. Census data indicated that 60 percent of the largely Jewish Russian-born residents in the country were still not naturalized. One study revealed that in the case of Jews, the average interval between the date of immigration and the filing of the final petition for naturalization was about 10 years.[41]

The Socialists were probably more adversely affected than the major parties by the relative failure of Jews to become citizens and registered voters. Supporters of the SP were more likely to be recent arrivals than were those of the SP's political rivals. About two-thirds of the SP's new recruits in the several years prior to World War I were noncitizens.[42] Also, it appears that among those Jews who were quickest to become citizens and to register to vote there was a disproportionate number of Democratic voters. This was no accident. These were the peddlers and businessmen who needed licenses and favors to establish and maintain their businesses. It was Tammany Hall, not the Socialist party, that was most able to supply both. These petty favors and the ability to get things done, inside or outside of the law, secured for Tammany a good many votes in Jewish and non-Jewish districts.[43] Perhaps it was more than the relative ability to do favors that distinguished Tammany Democrats from Socialists in these matters. Socialists felt more tightly constrained by bourgeois laws than did the minions of Tammany Hall. One informant told of the plight of a poor Jewish mother who was seeking help for her son, who had fallen afoul of the law. When she approached her Socialist alderman for assistance, he inquired as to the lad's innocence or guilt with the clear implication that if guilty there was nothing he could do. When she went to her Tammany district leader he inquired as to how many registered voters she had in her family.

Despite these drawbacks, Socialist candidates did manage to get elected in Jewish districts. By 1917 it seemed that the Socialist party, owing primarily to Jewish popular support, might emerge as the second most powerful party in the city. These election results do not only reflect popular Jewish sentiment, they also indicate the existence of a Socialist organization. In New York City the heart of the party's electoral machine was formed by the Jewish trade unions, the Workmen's Circle and the *Jewish Daily Forward*. It was this Jewish labor movement that supplied the bulk of the manpower and funds needed to turn out the sizable Jewish Socialist vote.

Members

Numerically, Jews were not only important as Socialist voters but also as Socialist party members. Their quantitative weight inside the party can be ascertained in several ways. First and most directly, there was

the Jewish Socialist Federation (JSF). Until 1919 the JSF, which affiliated with the Socialist party in 1913, was the third largest foreign-
language federation in the party. Between 1913 and 1918 its membership was exceeded only by that of the Finnish and German Socialist Federations. At or near its height around 1916, the JSF was estimated as having a membership of 5000 to 8000.[44] The JSF was more
important than its numbers alone might indicate, largely because of
its close ties with the garment unions and because of its reputation as
". . . the most Americanized of the language federations."[45]

It would be a mistake to equate the membership of the Jewish Socialist Federation with the number of Jews in the Socialist party. Not
all Jews within the SP were to be found within the JSF. Indeed there
were many more Socialist Jews outside of the JSF than there were in
it. This was also true for the German Americans with respect to the
German Socialist Federation. "It was the less-assimilated," according
to sociologist Nathan Glazer, "more newly arrived immigrants who
participated in the party by way of the foreign language federations.
Many immigrants who had arrived young, the children of immigrants,
and the more assimilated immigrants were not members of foreign
language federations."[46] Benjamin Gitlow, an SP member, estimated
that in 1918 half of those in the English-speaking groups were persons
who had been born abroad.[47] Party influentials such as Morris Hillquit, Abraham Cahan, Victor Berger, and Meyer London preferred to
participate in the English-speaking branch of the party, since this was
the organizational heart of the SP. The foreign-language federations,
including the JSF, were quasi-independent organizations located on
the party's periphery.

There were other foreign-born Jews in the SP who chose, for various
reasons, to affiliate with neither the JSF nor with the English-speaking
branch. Instead, they elected to become members in other foreign-
language federations, particularly the Russian Federation, which after
the Bolshevik Revolution in 1917 became one of the fastest growing
foreign-language bodies in the SP. Leon Trotsky, for example, while
in the United States, was an active member of the Russian Socialist
Federation. About the time this federation split from the SP in 1919,
many of its leaders, including Nicholas Hourwich, Gregory Weinstein,
and Lazar Becker, were individuals of Jewish origin.[48]

The numerical weight of Jews in the Socialist party can also be determined in another manner—calculations based on the membership
of the New York State division of the party. Of course, not all who
belonged to the SP in New York State were Jews, just as not all Socialist voters in New York were Jews. Conversely, not all Socialist party
members outside of New York were of Christian origin. However, it
can be safely assumed that the bulk of Jewish Socialists resided in
New York City. Historical evidence does reveal that after 1908 they
constituted the largest and strongest single element within New York

State Socialism.[49] In turn, Socialists within New York State, at least as of 1914, constituted the largest single element within the national party. In that year they numbered approximately 11,000, a figure that meant that close to 11 percent of the nation's Socialists resided in New York State. In 1936 New York continued to house the largest number of registered Socialists of any state in the union, 3153. This meant that in 1936 slightly more than one out of four Socialists in the United States resided in New York. Given the fact that the Jews represented a large proportion of the largest state party, it is obvious that they comprised a major numerical segment of the national Socialist party.[50]

The same sort of configuration also held true for the youth affiliate of the Socialist party, the Young People's Socialist League (YPSL). It was organized in 1907 and was officially affiliated with the SP in 1913. From its inception it contained a large proportion of residents from the New York City metropolitan area, again the area of greatest Jewish concentration. New York YPSL was the first YPSL local to be officially recognized. In the 1920s from one-quarter to one-third of the members of YPSL were New Yorkers. In 1931 they constituted one-third of the national organization. From then to the post–World War II decade, New York YPSL continued to be the largest unit of the organization in the country. Other YPSL circles, as these units were referred to in the SP, were to be found in Jewish areas in Boston, Milwaukee, Chicago, and Rochester.

The Jewish composition of YPSL cannot be precisely determined by official statistics since the organization did not provide this type of data. However, there are other indications in addition to geographical location that point to the predominance of Jews within YPSL. The growing proportion of college students on its rolls, particularly in New York City, also suggests a large Jewish presence. In 1931, about half of the YPSLrs in New York City were college students, with another quarter being high school students. In fact, as early as 1914 a YPSL publication warned that the increasing tendency of "Jewish comrades" to attend college would dilute the working class composition of the organization.[51]

Other indications that the Jewish element was a major one in YPSL comes from the testimony of scholars who have studied it and from others familiar with the organization. One scholar on the basis of her research into YPSL concluded:

Ethnically the YPSL was heavily Jewish. When League circles first grew up in New York, certain ones were labelled Jewish and Yiddish was the language spoken at meetings. In Boston, Milwaukee, and other urban areas of New York and New Jersey, as well as Los Angeles there were also Jewish circles. . . . Even those League circles that were not labelled "Jewish" circles had a predominantly Jewish membership. This can be discerned by reading the available membership lists.[52]

Jews in Other Capacities

The importance of Jews in and to the Socialist party went beyond the level of formal membership. They played significant roles at other levels and in other contexts as well. The Jewish needle trade unions, particularly the International Ladies' Garment Workers' Union, emerged shortly prior to World War I as one of the most important sources of organized labor support for Socialism. Their most prominent rival in this regard in the prewar period was the heavily German Brewery Workers' Union centered in Wisconsin. In New York City, the SP's organizational strength was largely based upon, if not coterminous with, the Jewish garment workers and their unions as well as among Jewish painters, bakers, jewelers and their unions.

After World War I the importance of the Jewish garment unions to the Socialist party became even more pronounced. In fact, until 1936 when they defected to Franklin Roosevelt, these unions constituted the strongest labor organizations associated with socialism. After their shift in loyalty to FDR, one of the few remaining unions that publicly supported the Socialist party was the largely Jewish American Federation of Teachers.[53]

Financially the SP became increasingly dependent on Jewish Socialists and their organizations beginning in the period just before World War I. This financial dependence was pronounced in the 1920s and 1930s. The principal source of funds that kept the Party solvent and allowed it to mount major electoral campaigns emanated from the coffers of the *Jewish Daily Forward,* the garment unions, and the Workmen's Circle. Subsidies from these Jewish organizations also proved significant in the maintenance of party institutions and projects such as the Rand School, the party's educational center; New York *Call,* the English-language socialist newspaper; radio station WEVD (Eugene Victor Debs) in New York City; the periodical *New Leader;* and Camp Tamiment. Significantly, when a split occurred in the Socialist party in 1936 that section of the party most closely associated with the *Jewish Daily Forward* wound up in control of these institutions (except for the *Call* which had previously folded), even though it did not control the national headquarters.[54]

Numerous Jews were also prominent in the leadership of the Socialist party. Morris Hillquit and Victor Berger, as we have already noted, were probably the men in the first two decades of the SP's life that had the most control over its inner structure. Both men continued to play leading roles after World War I. Hillquit, in addition to being the party's leading Marxist theorist, was also National Chairman from 1929 to his death in 1933, having succeeded to that position upon the death of Victor Berger. Other official and unofficial influentials and policy makers of Jewish background included Louis Waldman, B. Charney Vladeck, Julius Gerber, and Abraham Cahan.

The leading positions of these and other Jews in the Socialist party were not primarily a function of their political acumen and devotion to the party. Although these qualities were no doubt present and did help them in attaining these positions, other, less personal, factors were more important. Most significant was the fact that (with the exception of the German and Wisconsin-based Berger) they represented and symbolized one of the party's strongest constituencies—New York Jewry. The support of this constituency, particularly the organized segments within it, was sufficient to secure a position of importance within the national party. While being of Jewish background usually helped garner this support, non-Jews also benefited by it. Norman Thomas, the long-time leader and presidential standard-bearer, was catapulted into the upper echelons of the Socialist party because of this backing.[55] Algernon Lee was another case in point. Although he was not Jewish, Lee had his political base among New York Jewry. He successfully ran for New York City alderman from a Jewish district in 1917 and throughout his political life was intimately associated with New York Jewish Socialism. It was about him that B. Charney Vladeck, a leading Jewish Socialist, wrote: ". . . you could almost forget . . . that he is not a Jew . . . [he was] our good Jew."[56]

An organized power base within the Jewish constituency was also extremely useful as a ladder into the upper ranks of American socialism. Leaders of the powerful needle trades unions, like David Dubinsky, were assured roles as leading party influentials because of their union posts. Abraham Cahan, by virtue of his control of the *Jewish Daily Forward*, became a long-time power within the SP. Norman Thomas testified, albeit not very positively, to this fact in a private letter to B. Charney Vladeck on August 3, 1934: "I believe that Cahan exercises a highly autocratic and hurtful degree of power in the Socialist and Jewish labor movement, not merely because of the *Foward's* circulation but because of his power over the money bags."[57]

THE COMMUNISTS

The Socialist party was not the only major Left party in the United States in the twentieth century to attract support among American Jews. It had a prominent rival in this regard—the Communist party (CP). As with the SP, Jewish individuals and organizations provided the Communist party with a disproportionate amount of its political backing and internal leadership.

The Communist movement emerged on the American political scene as a result of a purge of the left-wing of the Socialist party by the right-wing leaders of the party in 1919. A split, which had been brewing for several years, came to a head in May 1919, when the party's National Executive Committee met and began to suspend and expel the left wingers. Before the purge was over the Socialist party's leadership had expelled or suspended approximately two-thirds of the organization's members. In January 1919 the SP was 109,589 strong;

six months later there were only 39,750 remaining members. The 70,000 former Socialists were the reservoir from which the Communist movement derived its members and leaders.

The Communist movement that was born in the wake of this split was predominantly a foreign-born movement. Ninety percent of the membership of the two Communist parties, the Communist party and the Communist Labor party, that emerged in 1919 was derived from the seven foreign-language federations forced out of the Socialist party earlier in the year. These were the Russian, Lettish, Lithuanian, Ukrainian, Hungarian, South Slavic, and Polish. The composition of the original Communist party, about which there is fairly accurate information, testified to the weight of these Eastern European groups. In 1919 more than three-fourths of the membership were Eastern European immigrants, with the Russians alone accounting for one-fourth of the total. Only 7 percent was listed as English-speaking, and there were immigrants even among these.[58]

The proportion of the foreign-born in this party rose even higher six months after its birth. The major cause was the governmental raids against the Communist movement that took place in the latter part of 1919 and early 1920. The most notable and most important was the national campaign launched by Attorney General A. Mitchell Palmer with the assistance of J. Edgar Hoover, the head of the Justice Department's alien radical division. After these attacks the Communist party lost 1200 of its original 1900 English-speaking members, who now constituted five percent of the membership.

The raids were responsible not only for the increase in the proportion of immigrants, but also for reducing the size of the Communist movement and for driving it underground. Before the raids occurred the Communist party and the Communist Labor party were estimated to have a combined membership of 25,000 to 40,000 people. After the raids this figure was reduced to about 10,000.[59] To protect against future raids of this kind, the Communist parties became an underground movement. The recent immigrants and the unassimilated in their ethnic enclaves seemed more capable of coping with this illegal life than did the American-born and the more assimilated.

By the end of 1921 the Communist parties had united in the form of the Communist Party of America. At approximately the same time the CP, still an underground organization, created the Workers' party to serve as its legal arm or "periscope" and to compete in elections. Shortly afterward the Communist party surfaced and merged with the Workers' party. (In 1925 the name was changed to the Workers' (Communist) party and in 1929 to the Communist Party of the USA.)[60]

The ethnic or national configuration of the Communist movement did not change after the formation of a legal party. In 1922 the Workers' party numbered about 12,000 (approximately the same size as the SP), but only 10 percent of its members belonged to English-speaking branches. Despite directives from the Communist Internationale and exhortations from Lenin to reach the American-born, the proportion of foreign-born continued to remain very high. In 1925 they accounted for at least 90 percent of the membership and in 1930, 70 percent. It was not until 1936 that the Communist party had a majority of American-born members.[61]

The Jews and Communism

The Jews' association with the Communist movement is apparent at several levels. Let us begin by examining the Jewish membership. It is generally agreed that throughout most of its history the American Communist party contained a disproportionate number of Jews. That is, the proportion of Jews in the Communist party was higher than its proportion in the general society. Or, stated another way, the proportion of Jews in the CP, throughout much of its history, was greater than that for any other ethnic group in the country. Indeed, for a good part of the Communist party's existence, Jews constituted the single largest ethnic or nationality group within it.[62] At no point, however, did more than a very small percentage of the total Jewish population of the United States belong to the Communist party. Coincidentally, these assertions can also be made with respect to such diverse Communist parties as those in Britain and Hungary between the wars, and the Tunisian CP before independence.[63]

As with the Socialist party, it is difficult to state with any degree of precision the total number of Jews in the CP at any given period. The two organizations in the best position to provide such information, the Communist party and the United States government, have been very reluctant to comment publicly on this issue. "From the party's point of view, to discuss straightforwardly the question of the Jewish membership would have been to raise doubts as to the party's success in reaching and representing the American working class; from the point of view of the government agencies, there would have been enormous political repercussions in discussing such a question."[64] Nevertheless, there is sufficient data, largely of an indirect, partial, and circumstantial nature, to support the claim that the Jews were present to a disproportionate degree within the ranks of the Communist party.

Let us commence our investigation of the Jewish participation in the Communist Party by scrutinizing one important source that supplied it with a large proportion of its earliest members. A large majority of the earliest Communists were left-wing socialists who had either quit or been expelled from the Socialist Party. The major stronghold of these militants was New York City, the most important concentration point for all Jewish socialists. It is no surprise then to find that many of these left-wingers were Jews. At least six of the eight men who formed the executive committee of the Left-Wing Section, Socialist Party, Local Greater New York (the first and most important organized nucleus of the SP left-wing) in 1919 were of Jewish origin.[65] One very knowledgeable source, a former Communist who was active in the Party for a great number of years, Melech Epstein, estimated that the large majority of left-wing Socialists in New York who voluntarily or involuntarily departed from the Socialist Party at the time of its split were Jews.[66]

Second, the Communist Party, similar to the Socialist Party at least until 1925, also had foreign-language federations. In 1922 the Jewish Federation totaled 975 members and was the third largest language federation in the CP, behind the Finnish Federation (5846) and the South Slavic Federation (1077). By 1925 its membership had increased to 1447, making it the second largest federation in the Party. The Finnish Federation was still first with 6410. However, as with Socialist Jews, not all Communist Jews preferred membership in the Jewish Federation. Many were to be found in the Russian and Hungarian Federations and in the English-speaking section. Again, similar to the Jews in the Socialist party, Jews in the Communist party were either recently arrived, relatively unassimilated, non-English-speaking workers, or relatively acculturated immigrants who knew and preferred to speak English.[67]

Still a third way of approaching the issue of Jewish membership in the CP is to examine the geographical distribution of the Communist party membership in the 1920s. Most, but by no means all, of the Jewish Communists during the 1920s lived in New York City. Between 1922 and 1925 from 22 to 26 percent of the nation's Communists were located in New York City.[68] The same type of geographical distribution also held true for the Young Workers League (which later became the Young Communist League), the youth affiliate of the CP. In the 1920s from 20 to 33 percent of its membership came from New York City. Young Jews (many from CCNY), together with Finns, provided the bulk of the membership, according to Herbert Zam, who was the head of this group for several years in the 1920s.[69]

One of the most informed estimates of the percentage of Jews within the Communist party in the 1920s comes from Theodore Draper, the man who has made the most intensive investigation of the Communist party during its early years. According to Draper, "In the 1920's perhaps as much as 15 percent of the party membership was Jewish." He goes on to point out, ". . . but only a minute percentage of the 4,000,000 Jews in the United States were Communists."[70] It would also be correct to state that only a minute percentage of the nation's population in this decade were Communists. After unification of the movement in 1921, the Communist party's high point in terms of average membership for a single year was 17,363 in 1924, a number that had declined by 1929 to slightly less than 10,000 members. (These figures are underestimates since "turnover" of members in these years was very high. At the same time, even if the turnover factor is considered, it was not substantial enough to invalidate the basic point of the very small size of the Communist Party.)[71] Of this small number, Jews were the largest single ethnic group within the party by the end of the decade.

In the following decades, particularly in the period of the Communist party's greatest strength, the mid-1930s through the late 1940s, the Jewish proportion among the membership was even higher than it had been in the 1920s. Again, it is difficult to arrive at precise figures; but Nathan Glazer, the sociologist who has to date most closely studied this subject, claims that from the 1930s through the early 1950s ". . . a large proportion of . . . [the CP's] membership were of Jewish origin."[72] In an interview with the author, a former leading Communist of Jewish origin stated his belief that the Jewish membership of the party constituted about 50 percent of the total. Melech Epstein, another former Communist and a man very interested in the relationship between the Jews and the party, also arrived at a similar figure—approximately 40 to 50 percent of the membership in the latter 1930s was Jewish.[73]

A consideration of the party's strength in New York City provides further support for the proposition that Jews were a most significant element within the CP. From the 1930s through the 1950s about half of the party's strength was concentrated in New York State, primarily New York City. In the mid-1940s, New York County (later Manhattan) accounted for about one-fifth of the national membership and Brooklyn for approximately one-seventh. Interpretation of party membership statistics leads to the conclusion that more than 50 percent of the former county's members during this period were Jews. In 1945 party spokesman John Williamson complained that the membership in Brooklyn was concentrated in Brownsville, Williamsburg, Coney Island, and Bensonhurst, which he correctly assessed to be "primarily Jewish American communities."[74] New York City, while the most important concentration point for Jewish Communists, was not the only one of significance. There were other locales in which Jews were numerically important to the Communist organization. In Boston, for example, in the mid-1930s, CP organizer George Charney observed that the ethnic base of the CP there was largely Jewish.[75] The same phenomenon also obtained in the Los Angeles branch in the late 1920s and early 1930s. A CP writer, commenting disapprovingly on the party's lack of success among non-Jews, stated: ". . . practically 90 percent of the membership [in Los Angeles] is Jewish."[76]

Despite the relatively large number of Jews within the Communist party ranks and the frequent complaints by party leaders and spokesmen of the failure of the party to expand much beyond a Jewish base, these very same leaders and spokesmen also realized how few Jews there were among its ranks, particularly when compared with the total number of Jews in the country. In 1939, for example, party leader, James Ford, complained: "The sad commentary is that of the

4,500,00 Jews, the Communist party, which has a total of about 100,000 [an exaggeration] has as one of its weaknesses the failure to recruit sufficiently among the Jewish masses."[77]

Jews were also a large minority, and at certain times a majority, of the Communist party's activists, cadres, and leaders. In the early 1920s, 25 to 35 percent of the Central Executive Committee of the Workers' party and the Workers' (Communist) party were of Jewish origin, as were two of the most powerful men in the life of the organization in the 1920s, Jay Lovestone and Benjamin Gitlow. During this period each held the position of General Secretary of the party. Gitlow also served as editor-in-chief of the *Daily Worker* and was the party's candidate for Vice-President in 1924 and 1928. Alexander Bittelman, another individual of Jewish origin, was one of the Communist party's influential power brokers throughout most of the 1920s and 1930s and was reputed to be the organization's leading Marxist theoretician. Jews were particularly preponderant among the leadership of the party's youth affiliation, the Young Workers' League and the Young Communist League before World War II and the Labor Youth League after the war. Jewish heads of these various affiliates included Herbert Zam, Gil Greene, Max Weiss, and Leon Wofsey.

The Jewish leadership role in the party was very visible in those decades. In 1934 Abraham Cahan was moved to observe that Jews led all the Communist demonstrations at Union Square and that they provided most of the Communist leadership at the colleges.[78] A former party intimate, editor of the *Morning Freiheit* and close observer of the role of the Jews in the CP, Melech Epstein, provided the broadest assessment of their position in the leadership of the party:

In the twenties the top leadership was primarily Jewish: Jay Lovestone, Ben Gitlow, William Weinstone, Bertram D. Wolfe and Israel Amter. . . . In the thirties the top leadership was mixed. However the second level was largely Jewish, although some of them paraded under non-Jewish names. The party organizers in California, Los Angeles, Chicago, Pittsburgh and Minnesota were Jewish during the 1930's. (I mean the top leaders, the secretaries). In New York City most of the local organizers were Jewish too. . . . Of the more than 1,100 members in 'closed' branches—people occupying sensitive positions—in 1938 in New York City, the majority were Jews.[79]

This preponderance of Jews in the leadership and among the activists of the CP continued into the post–World War II era. This was particularly true among those who managed and edited the *Daily Worker*. In the latter 1940s and 1950s the editor-in-chief was John Gates, the managing editor was Alan Max, the foreign editor was Joseph Starobin and afterwards Joseph Clark, and the labor editor was George Morris, all Jews.[80] Almost half of the Communist leaders whom the United States government chose to indict and try for violation of the Smith Act in 1949 and later were Jewish. A Department of Justice study in 1947 reported on the ethnic origins of approximately 5000 long-term and office-holding Communists. It found that 56 percent of them were either born in Russia or in countries adjacent to it, had one or both parents born in that area, or were married to a person with similar characteristics.[81] Most of those with this background were Jewish.[82]

The large percentage of Jews who constituted the core of the Communist party accentuated the Jewish tone of the organization. The considerable turnover in membership among the rank and file, which bedeviled the CP from its inception, meant that the long-term and office-holding Communists became more important than numbers and official titles alone might indicate. Between 1919 and 1929, for example, ". . . about 100,000 people entered, . . . of whom only about 10,000 stayed long enough to represent a basic membership."[83] In the early to mid-1940s, the CP lost nearly 50,000 members and gained an almost equal amount.[84] Given the fact that Jews were so large a proportion of the party's "permanent" membership and leadership, their role was even more important than their total numbers would indicate.

The location of the CP headquarters, key organizational apparatus, and authoritative English-language publications also highlighted the Jewish prominence within the party. On January 24, 1927, the party moved all of these from Chicago to New York City.[85] Thus, virtually everything of organizational importance within this highly centralized body after this date was to be found in the most Jewish city in the country and the urban area containing the most Jewish Communists and most Jewish Communist groups. Even if the Jewish proportion in the national party had been minuscule, the move to New York City would have given this minuscule element far more prominence than its numerical size alone.

It was not only as individuals that Jews were important to and within the Communist party. Jewish organizations relative to those of other nationality groups within the party (or closely associated with it) were also quite significant. In terms of party press, the Yiddish-language daily, the *Morning Freiheit* (founded in April 1922, some two years before the *Daily Worker*), was probably the largest Communist foreign-language periodical in the country. At various points in its existence, such as the 1920s and the 1950s, its circulation surpassed that of the *Daily Worker*, the party's principal and most authoritative newspaper. At its peak in 1930 the *Freiheit* claimed a paid readership of almost 65,000.[86]

The *Freiheit*'s significance to the party transcended that of a newspaper. It was also an important source of funds. Money from the paper was not only given to specifically Jewish Communist or Left endeavors, such as the "coops" a cooperative housing project in the Bronx, but to general party causes as well. *Freiheit* funds helped to subsidize the *Daily Worker* as well as pay the salaries of full-time functionaries engaged in work outside of the Jewish sector. This fiduciary role was not unique to the *Freiheit;* other foreign-language organs and bodies were also dunned for contributions. Given its relative size, the *Freiheit's* monetary donations were, in all probability, the most substantial of any emanating from the foreign sectors of the party. As mentioned previously, the *Freiheit* stood at the core of and played a strategic role in the formation, development, and maintenance of a Jewish Communist subculture. Again, this was not a role unique to the *Freiheit.* However, the Jewish Communist subculture that the *Freiheit* guided and nurtured was generally larger and more important to the party. Thus, by implication if not directly, whatever praise or credit the Jewish sector received from the party, the *Freiheit* also received. This contributed to its relative stature, vis-a-vis the other foreign-language organs.[87]

In the arena of organized labor, Jewish unions or Jewish unionists, concentrated in the needle trades unions, constituted one of the Communist party's strongest sources of support. Throughout the 1920s the predominantly Jewish needle trade unionists provided the Communist party with one of its most important entrees into organized labor. By the middle to late 1920s, the clothing workers were the largest single group of workers in the party. In 1928, 15 percent of the membership was made up of workers in the garment trades, while miners, second in number of members, accounted for 12 percent. This Jewish role became so pronounced that in the late 1920s: "The Comintern insisted that the working class base of the Communist Party must be radically changed from a preponderance of Jewish needle trade workers to non-Jewish workers employed in basic and mass production industries."[88]

Despite this admonition from the Comintern, Jewish needle trade workers in the early 1930s continued to constitute a plurality of those workers organized by the Communists. Of all the unions within the Communist-sponsored Trade Union Unity League (TUUL), the largest was the Needle Trades Workers Industrial Union (NTWIU). Its membership varied from 6000 to 25,000, depending on whether one accepts the claims of Communists eager to inflate the figures or anti-Communists desirous of deflating them. In any event, both anti-Communist and Communist sources agree on the relative position of the Needle Trades Workers Industrial Union within the TUUL. It should also be noted that even if the Communist claims are accepted, the NTWIU's membership was much smaller than that of the non-Communist needle trades unions.[89]

The relative position of the Jewish unions among unions within the Communist party orbit changed during the mid- to latter 1930s. Communists in this period finally managed to gain greater influence over organized labor than ever before. They became influential in unions in the transport, mining, electrical, maritime, metal, meatpacking, and longshore and warehouse sectors. These were unions containing few persons of Jewish origin in the rank and file and were generally larger than the predominantly Jewish unions that the Communists controlled or guided.

Despite the party's incursions into non-Jewish economic arenas, Jewish workers continued to remain a numerically important component of the CP's actual membership. As of 1942 garment workers in the party numbered approximately 1900 and were second in size (in terms of manual worker group in the party) to the building trades employees, who totaled about 2100.[90] Where were the steel, auto, and rubber workers among whom the Communists were making so many gains? They were not in the party in large numbers because the Communist party in the mid- to latter 1930s was not making a major effort to recruit them en masse. Party policy evidently was to focus upon the leadership of the unions in these heavy industries. The party seemed more interested in building unions and influencing their direction than in actually capturing them as a Communist organization. Therefore, in cases such as the Transport Workers Union, in which the Communists were reputed to have had so great a role, few members of that union were actually party members, and the party dealt mainly with a handful of top leaders.[91]

There were unions in which Communists represented a relatively high proportion of the membership. These tended to be the smaller unions and, with the notable exception of the National Maritime Union, labor organizations located in the white-collar section. These "red" white-collar unions encompassed teachers, social workers, office workers, retail clerks, and government employees. Among the Communist members of these unions, Jews were either a disproportionate minority or a majority. In the 1930s and 1940s, in fact, the two unions reputed to have the largest proportion of Communists or Communist sympathizers—the Social Service Employees Union (affiliated with the United Office and Professional Workers of America) and the New York City District 65 of the Retail, Wholesale, and Department Store Union, which in 1948 became an independent union, the Distributive Workers Union—were based largely or totally in New York City and had a mainly Jewish membership.[92]

In the latter 1940s and early 1950s, the Communist party's base of support in the union, as well as other sectors, was significantly reduced as a result of government oppression and self-defeating party tactics. Of the few unions that remained in the camp or orbit of the Communist party in this period, those with a large Jewish membership represented a significant proportion. In this period the International Fur and Leather Workers' Union (IFLWU), a "Jewish" needle trades union, was one of the last of the party's bright spots on the union scene. The ILFWU, for example, was one of a handful of unions in the country to support the candidacy of Henry Wallace. Also, its leader, Ben Gold, an admitted Communist, was almost alone among union officers in the United States to refuse to sign the non-Communist affidavit required by the Taft-Hartley Law and to continue to have the backing of a large majority of his union members for his stand. Of the 11 unions expelled from the CIO in 1949 and 1950 on grounds of Communist domination, the ILFWU, with some 100,000 members, was the second largest. (The United Electrical, Radio, and Machine Workers (UE) was the biggest.)[93]

Finally, the disproportionate support provided to the Communist party by unions with a relatively high proportion of Jewish members or leaders can be roughly discerned by considering the composition of these 11 purged unions. Three of these 11 (the International Fur and Leather Workers Union, the United Public Workers, and the United Office and Professional Workers of America) contained a considerable number and proportion of Jews in their ranks and among their leaders. The combined total of the membership of these three unions was approximately 256,000, and they represented from 28 to 38 percent of all those expelled (depending on which of the various estimates for the grand total are used).[94] Thus, as of 1950, among the small number of unions and the relatively few unionists who were in some way associated with the Communist party, Jewish unions, as in decades earlier, continued to constitute a disproportionate and significant segment.

Electoral Politics

The disproportionate Jewish support for the Communist party can also be seen at the level of electoral politics. The Jewish vote was usually a significant portion of whatever votes the Communists were able to amass. The extent of the Jewish balloting for the Communist party candidates can best be determined by considering the voting returns from areas of Jewish concentration, particularly New York. In the national elections of 1924 and 1928, the Communists ran their own candidates for the offices of president and vice-president. On each occasion William Z. Foster was the nominee for president and Benjamin Gitlow the nominee for vice-president. In neither election did the Communist candidates obtain as many as 50,000 votes. This was owing in part to the fact that in 1924 they could only get on the ballot in 14 states and in 1928, 32. But in each of these national elections, New York State was the single largest supplier of Communist votes. In 1924 and again in 1928, about one-quarter of the national ballots cast for the Communist candidates came from New York.[95]

This tendency for a disproportionate number of Jewish voters to cast their ballots for Communist candidates can also be observed in Boston. In 1936 the Communist presidential candidate, Earl Browder, received 42 percent of all the votes cast for him in Boston from the three municipal wards containing the largest number of Jews. (In none of these wards, however, did the Communist vote reach as high as 2 percent.) In other elections in the 1930s and 1940s, particularly those for minor offices, the percentage of the Communist vote in the heavily Jewish wards was generally at least twice as high as the vote from other wards.[96] But it was in New York City and not Boston or elsewhere that the Communists did their best on election day. However, much of this relative success in New York City came via candidates they supported who ran on the platform of the American Labor party (ALP). Although organized in 1936 by anti-Communist former Socialists, the ALP soon became the Communist party's major electoral vehicle in New York, even though many, if not most, who ran on its line or voted for its candidates were not themselves Communists. The vast bulk of the ALP vote came from New York City, primarily its Jewish voters.[97] In fact the Communist party in 1949 openly acknowledged that Jews were an important electoral base of the ALP.[98]

The period from 1941 to 1948 in New York City was probably the best the Communists ever enjoyed in terms of relative electoral success. In 1941 a Communist, Peter V. Cacchione, running on the Communist line was elected from Brooklyn to a seat on the New York City Council. This was the first time that a Communist had been elected to a public office in the United States. He was reelected in 1943 and 1945. In these years he was joined in the City Council by his Communist colleague, Benjamin J. Davis of Harlem. (Their victories were in large part due to a system of proportional representation that was later abolished primarily because of Cacchione's and Davis's triumphs.) Councilman Davis credited the votes of blacks and Jews with being the most important element in these electoral successes.[99]

In subsequent elections Communist-backed candidates did rather well in election districts containing a large proportion of Jewish voters. In the campaigns for state comptroller and state attorney general in 1946, Communist or ALP candidates were most successful in areas of the city containing large numbers of Jewish voters such as the Lower East Side, the Upper West Side, Coney Island, and East New York. Then, in a 1946 by-election in the East Side's Nineteenth Congressional District, a district that still housed a high percentage of Jewish voters, the Communist-supported ALP candidate, Johannes Steel (a political unknown), came within 4000 votes of upsetting the New Deal Democratic incumbant, Arthur Klein. In another by-election some two years later, this time in the heavily Jewish Twenty-fourth Congressional District in the Bronx, another Communist-backed candidate, Leo Isaacson, won.[100]

In the 1948 presidential election CP-supported candidates received more Jewish support than at any time since World War I. In this campaign the party organized and worked for Henry Wallace, Roosevelt's former vice-president and a man whom many considered to be FDR's legitimate political heir. Wallace, running as the standard-bearer of the newly formed Progressive party, emphasized a program of peace and civil rights and (as we shall see shortly) appealed to Jews on Jewish issues. The Jewish voters were much more favorably disposed toward this left-wing Democrat than the electorate-at-large. They gave him 10 to 15 percent of their votes, compared with 2 percent given to him by the non-Jewish national electorate. It is estimated that about one-third of the Wallace votes came from Jews.

The Progressive party's standard-bearer did best in areas with large Jewish populations. More than half of Wallace's national total of 1,157,172 votes came from New York State with its many Jewish voters. Another 190,000 came from California, the bulk presumably from the state's largest city, Los Angeles, with a residence of 323,000 Jews at the time. (New York and California were also the largest state units in the Communist party in the late 1940s.) In certain Jewish Assembly Districts in New York City the Wallace vote was more than 20 percent; in one case, the heavily Jewish Bronx Seventh A.D., it reached nearly 30 percent. The former vice-president also did well in Jewish districts in Boston and Atlanta. Even among nonvoting college students, Jewish students were most likely to be Wallace supporters.[101]

The 1948 elections were just about the last hurrah as far as significant Communist involvement in mass electoral politics was concerned. As the pall of anti-Communism descended upon America, the CP was increasingly denied access to the ballot in its own name. Even when successful or when it supported candidates of other parties sympathetic or aligned with it, such as the Progressive party or the American Labor party, the votes they obtained were negligible. For example, the ALP in the New York gubernatorial election of 1954 could not obtain the 50,000 votes necessary to stay on the ballot. Even among the handful who still voted for such candidates, Jewish voters were a disproportionate element.[102]

It is clear from the evidence that Jewish voters constituted a major proportion of whatever electoral support the Communist party was able to win, either directly or indirectly, throughout most of its history. It should be noted that these specific voters constituted only a small percentage of all Jewish voters. The vast bulk of Jewish votes, as with non-Jewish votes, went to the nominees of the Republican and Democrat parties, even in New York State. By the time the Communists became seriously and significantly involved in electoral politics, the Jewish electorate was firmly in the camp of the Democratic Party. In the 1940 and 1944 elections, for example, more than nine out of 10 Jewish votes went to FDR. In the 1948 election the Jewish vote for Harry Truman was five times greater than the vote for Wallace. In this election more Jewish votes probably were cast for the Republican, Dewey, than for the Progressive, Wallace.[103]

THE NEW LEFT

In the late 1950s and 1960s the most prominent movement on or near the left end of the political spectrum in the United States was the New Left. It was not socialist in the same way that the Socialist and Communist parties could be described as socialist. However, even though it was more eclectic in its ideology and programs than these parties, the New Left was similar to them in various important respects. The movement's ideals and goals were informed by Marxism as well as by liberalism, anarchism, radical pacifism, and existentialism. Also, similar to the SP and CP, the New Left located much of the source of America's problems in the capitalist system. Again, like the others, it did espouse a socialist vision for this country, although its version was far more humanistic and utopian. And like the Left parties, a significant proportion of the leaders and participants in the New Left were Jewish.[104]

The procedures for examining the degree and extent of the Jewish involvement in the New Left will be different from those previously used in the other cases. Electoral data cannot be employed as the New Left did not run candidates for political office. Membership statistics are of limited use as much of this movement was made up of "membership" organizations. The Students for a Democratic Society (SDS) was most notable in this regard. In general the New Left was comprised of undergraduate or graduate students or people of college-age who identified themselves as leftists or participated in demonstrations such as those pertaining to civil rights, civil liberties, and the Vietnam War.

Let us begin our examination of the Jewish role in the New Left by considering the Jewish involvement with the Students for a Democratic Society (SDS)—the structural core of the movement. In the early to mid-1960s, during which time membership in SDS rose from 250 to more than 30,000, the percentage of Jews within it was considerable, ranging from 30 to 50 percent. Later in the 1960s as the SDS approached a size of 100,000, the percentage of Jews declined, although their raw numbers remained significant. (In the same period the number of Jews among American college students averaged about 325,000 a year.) At the end of the decade, the SDS had not only increased in numbers but had also broadened its ethnic and class base.[105]

Jews were, however, almost always a significant proportion of the leaders and activists within SDS. At the 1966 SDS convention 46 percent of the delegates who identified themselves as having a particular religious background were Jewish. (This probably underestimates their percentage as Jews more so than non-Jews seem prone to answer "none" to such questions.) Later in the decade one-third of the SDS Weathermen arrested by the police were Jewish. Throughout the 1960s the top national officers were heavily Jewish. These included the "founder" Al Haber, as well as Richard Flacks, Steve Max, Bob Ross, Mike Spiegel, Mike Klonsky, and Mark Rudd.[106]

An examination of the New Left beyond the SDS reveals a similarly high concentration of Jews. This can be seen in important civil rights activities. In the summer of 1961 Jews made up two-thirds of the white Freedom Riders that traveled into the South to desegregate interstate transportation. Three years later Jews comprised from one-third to one-half of the Mississippi Summer volunteers. Two of the white youths martyred during this experience, Michael Schwerner and Andrew Goodman, were Jews. Several social scientists, in examining the Jewish role in the New Left, claim that, almost until the end of the 1960s, ". . . students of Jewish background constituted anywhere from 50 to 70 percent of the New Left." [107]

The change of the focus of activities of the New Left to the northern campuses in the mid-1960s did not lead to a diminution of the role of Jews. The Free Speech Movement (FSM) at Berkeley in 1964 set the pattern for Jewish involvement in New Left actions on campuses. A majority of the FSM's leadership (Steering Committee) was Jewish. During the sit-in at the university administration building—at the height of the FSM—a Chanukah service was held and the Hatikvah, a Jewish anthem, was sung. And it was Jewish students within the student body at Berkeley who gave the FSM its strongest base of support.[108]

This disproportionate participation of Jewish students could also be seen at other universities after 1964. At the University of Chicago in 1965, Jews constituted 45 percent of the participants demonstrating against that school's cooperation with the Selective Service System.[109] At Columbia University in 1968 one-third of those who participated in the massive demonstrations were Jews.[110] Finally, in May 1970, in the wake of the Cambodian invasion and the killings of 4 students at Kent State, (3 of whom were Jewish), 90 percent of Jewish students attending schools at which there were demonstrations claim to have participated. Indeed, in a major study of student activism conducted by the American Council of Education during the 1966–1967 school year, a Jewish background was the single most important predictor of participation in anti-war or anti-(college) administration protests.[111] It is quite clear then, that a very large proportion of campus activists during the 1960s were Jews. Overall, in the course of the decade, it has been estimated that from one-third to one-half of the most committed activists at the most volatile schools were Jews.[112]

There are also other indicators of the extent of Jewish identification with the New Left in the 1960s. Surveys regularly showed that of all religious groups Jews were the most likely to be found on the left end of the political spectrum. In the May 1970 Harris survey of a national sample of students, for example, 23 percent of the Jewish students designated themselves as "Far Left," compared with 4 percent for Catholic and 2 percent for Protestant students.[113] Also, at the 1970 riot-conspiracy trial of the "Chicago 7" (stemming from the demonstrations at the 1968 Democratic Convention), at least three of the seven defendants were Jewish—Jerry Rubin, Abby Hoffman, and Lee Weiner—as was the primary defense attorney, William Kunstler.

These data on leadership, membership, participation, and identification make it quite clear that Jews were a most significant part of the New Left. In this respect the New Left was quite similar to the Old Left and to the leftist student movement of the 1930s. In fact, one of the important reasons for this pattern in the New Left was that many Jewish New Lefters were the children of Jewish Old Lefters, a large percentage of whom had been the college activists of their day (see Chapter 6).

CONCLUSION

The review of the evidence from the birth of the Socialist Labor party at the end of the nineteenth century to the more contemporary New Left leaves no doubt as to degree of Jewish involvement in and with the major socialist parties and movements in the United States. Although a majority of the Jews in America were never leftists in any given decade, a *disproportionate* number relative to their size did participate in and support the Left. In fact, since the beginning of the mass arrival of Russian and Eastern European Jews in the 1880s, they and their progeny have been the mainstay of the Left in America. The remainder of this volume is devoted to an analysis of the roots of this nexis and its consequences.

3 In the Beginning: Czarist Russia

INTRODUCTION

This chapter details the forces that produced a Jewish Left in Russia in the late nineteenth and early twentieth centuries. It demonstrates that the interplay among Russian capitalism, official and unofficial anti-Semitism, and the character and structure of the Russian Jewish community during this period shaped the direction and flow of Jewish politics in Russia and later in America.

We will see that this interplay led to the emergence of a large and concentrated urban Jewish proletariat as well as a sizable cadre of Jewish secular intellectuals—two of the most important building blocks of what was to become the Jewish Left. This chapter will concern itself not only with the growth and development of Jewish radicalism in Russia but also with its fragility and vulnerability. Not all of the factors that helped to produce a Jewish Left were positive; several had negative dimensions that over time in Russia and especially later in America proved to be highly constrictive of and corrosive to this Left. The most significant of these factors are the Jewish occupational structure and the multifaceted issue of Jewish identity and nationality. With respect to the development and maintenance of a Jewish Left, these factors were positive or negative not so much because of their intrinsic qualities, but because of the character of the social, economic, and political environment in which they were embedded at different periods of capitalist development and the manner in which these peculiarly Jewish issues were politically dealt with by Jews and non-Jews.

Much attention will be given here and in other chapters to "the Jewish question" or the manner in which Jews would be defined and treated by the Left, and the relationship between Jewish nationality and socialism. These were matters of political concern to both Jews and non-Jews on the Left. The ways in which the Jews approached and dealt with these issues here in the United States significantly affected the forms and content of the association between Jews and the Left in this country. It was in Russia, however, that Jews first learned to frame the questions bearing upon Jewish nationality and political radicalism.

This chapter deals exclusively with the Jews of czarist Russia. These Jews and their progeny constituted the principal political actors in the twentieth-century American Jewish community. In the 1880s Russian Jewish immigrants began to arrive in the United States in such massive numbers that within several decades they had virtually become the American Jewish community. They brought with them from the Old Country political memories, experiences, and attitudes. This political "baggage," as we shall see, made a difference in the way they adapted to political life in the New World. It was the Russian Jews with their rich experience in politics that set the tone for the immigrant Jewsih community and provided it with the bulk of its political leadership in its encounter with America.

IMMIGRATION AND POLITICS

The Russian Jews were no strangers to politics. Politics had been the key determinant of their original entrance into Russia and was almost as decisive in their departure from it. Until 1772 only a handful of Jews lived in Russia because the government made them unwelcome. But by 1800 about 800,000 Jews were living in the empire of the czars. It was not they who had moved, however; it was the Russians. The czarist state in three successive partitions of Poland, in 1772, 1793, and 1795, had acquired as part of its booty Jews in the hundreds of thousands from Poland, Lithuania, and White Russia.

Once inside the Russian Empire, the Jews were forced to live in areas designated by the government. Through a maze of laws, edicts, and decrees, almost all of Russian Jewry was confined to the area known as the Pale of Settlement. This consisted of 10 Polish and 15 adjoining Russian provinces. In square miles, the Pale constituted about five percent of the empire; in terms of natural resources and the fertility of the soil, it was one of its poorer areas.[1] It should also be pointed out that the Pale was not an exclusively Jewish area. At the turn of the century Jews in the Polish section constituted 14 percent of the population, in the Russian section, 11 percent. This meant that Jews represented only 12 percent of all inhabitants of the Pale.[2]

Economic life for Jews in Russia throughout the nineteenth century was generally harsh. Large proportions of this community subsisted at a poverty level. In this arena of life, the hand of the state was quite visible. Despite more than a fourfold increase in the Jewish population in Russia from 1800 to 1880, Jews were still almost totally contained within the Pale. They were limited not only in terms of space but in terms of employment opportunities as well. The government directly and indirectly placed numerous occupations, professions, and careers out of the reach of Jews. Even when the government was not an immediate factor, the economic situation of the Jews remained inferior. The hostility and competition of non-Jews plus the nature of capitalist development in Russia supplemented the economic constraints imposed by the government. The result was a relatively large population occupying a limited amount of generally unproductive land with few employment opportunities open to it; in short, the Jewish community was nearly pauperized.[3]

In spite of these conditions, however, the Jews did not leave Russia in any sizable number prior to the 1880s. One rough estimate places the number of Jewish emigrants from Russia for any given year between 1820 and 1870 at about 151.[4] After 1880 the situation changed dramatically. It was no longer a movement of individuals but one of masses. From April 1881 to June 1882, some 225,000 Jews left Russia. This one-year figure rivaled that of the absolute total number of Jewish emigrants during the period from 1800 to 1880.[5] This mass emigration marked the beginning of a tidal wave that did not finally recede until after World War I.

Why did these Russian Jews leave when they did? The decision to uproot one's life and family and undertake a long and arduous journey to begin life anew under strange and difficult circumstances is not made for one reason or incident. But when such large numbers do this in so short a time, there can be little doubt that their decision has been inspired by some major event or calamity. In the case of the Russian Jews, it was the pogroms, which began in April 1881 and lasted until 1884, and the context in which they occurred that led to this massive exodus.[6]

These pogroms were without precedent in modern European history. Hundreds of Jews were raped or killed. Over twenty thousand were made homeless. More than 80 million dollars worth of Jewish property was destroyed. Most of this occurred in the first wave of the pogroms. There is some debate among scholars as to whether the government instigated these attacks, but there was little doubt in the minds of Jews as to the state's attitude toward those who attacked and those who received the blows. Authorities generally stood aside until mobs had done their worst and threatened to get out of hand, which generally meant endangering non-Jewish lives and property.[7]

The violence was soon followed by official or "paper" pogroms. Here there was no doubt as to authorship. They emanated from the highest circles of government. Police expelled thousands of Jews overnight from their "illegal" residences in cities, citing old ordinances that rarely if ever had hitherto been enforced. In 1882 the state implemented the May Laws. These laws, issued under the signature of the czar himself, were designed to wreak economic havoc on the Jews. Under their provisions, Jews were not allowed to live in villages, even in the Pale. Those who did live in the proscribed areas were ordered to leave. Jewish mortgages on landed estates were suspended, and Jews were denied the right of attorney in the managing of estates. The May Laws also made it illegal for Jews to conduct business on Sundays and Christian holidays, the very times that allowed many the opportunity to gain the few extra roubles necessary to sustain themselves above the margin of subsistence.[8]

These official and unofficial attacks on Jews followed a period in which the Jewish community had had reason to hope for better conditions. During the reign of Alexander II from 1856 to 1881, the government had adopted a more liberal policy toward the Jews. One of Alexander II's first acts was to abolish the practice of Jewish child conscription. The doors of secondary schools and universities were opened to Jews, although not widely, of course. Also, secular schools were relieved of the mandate to convert Jews. Jewish university graduates were allowed into medical and legal professions as well as government service. The privilege of residence outside the Pale was granted to university graduates, wealthy merchants, skilled artisans, and military veterans. Although only a small fraction of the Jewish population benefitted directly from this liberalization, there was a growing feeling that soon increasing numbers of Jews would be able to take advantage of it. There was also the hope that the regime would become even more liberal and enlightened.[9]

Any grounds for optimism were smashed shortly after the assassination of Alexander II in 1881. The ensuing pogroms and the new harsh policies of the government were convincing evidence that the future of the Jews in Russia held out no hope. Emigration was seized as one of the very few options open to Jews. As if to underscore this, Count Ignatev, the Minister of Interior, publicly invited the Jews to leave even though emigration for anybody was technically illegal under Russian law.[10] The new czar's advisor, Constantine Pobedonostsev, offered his own solution to the Jewish problem in Russia. "One-third will die out, one-third will leave the country, and one-third will be completely dissolved in the surrounding population."[11]

The ensuing anti-Semitic policies and edicts demonstrated that these men were in no way engaged in idle chatter. After promulgating the May Laws of 1882, the state instituted a rigid quota system for Jews in secondary schools and universities. This action eliminated for many the hope of social mobility, since a degree, especially for a Jew, was a necessary condition for entrance into a profession or middle-class career. It also functioned as a permit to leave the Pale and enter the larger Russian society, thus widening one's cultural and economic opportunities. In 1891 there was a mass expulsion of hitherto privileged Jews from Moscow. A year later the government again underscored its desire to see the Jews leave Russia by officially lifting the ban on emigration for only one category of the population—Jews.[12]

It was quite evident that the Jews had received the message, although most were unable or unwilling to act upon it. Emigration was but one choice. Many, after a pogrom or harsh government action, would turn to prayer and their religion for solace. Others on similar occasions converted to Christianity.[13]

The relationship between officially inspired or condoned pogroms, whether "paper" or violent, on the one hand and flight on the other hand was a clear and consistent one. The immigration figures of Russian Jews entering the United States from the 1880s on are sensitive indicators of this. (America was the immediate destination of about 80 percent of those Jews who left Russia between 1880 and World War I.) [14] Each punitive action against Jews immediately led to higher numbers emigrating. Conversely, when there was some respite from these attacks, the figure declined. [15] It was as if the Jews believed that their persecution had ended after each instance of persecution.

It is also interesting to note that economics was not a major independent causal factor of emigration. Although the 1890s was a period of increasing economic hardship for Russian Jews, after the expulsion from Moscow, there were few notable cases of official or inspired attacks on Jews. Thus after 1892 the number of Russian Jews immigrating to the United States, their principal destination, receded and remained fairly stable throughout the 1890s.

Shortly after the turn of the century, however, the cycle dramatically reemerged. This time the numbers were greater because emigration to the United States had become a well-established phenomenon, and because the crises affecting the Russian Jews had become more extensive and intensive than others. In 1903 the worst pogrom in modern Jewish history up to that time occurred in Kishinev. Forty-five Jews were killed; 86 were severely injured; and 1500 Jewish homes and stores were looted or destroyed. [16] This pogrom, condoned, if not inspired, by the authorities, was responsible for a flood of immigrants. In 1904, 77,544 Russian Jews were admitted to the United States, more than had been admitted in any previous single year. This record was immediately broken, however, and new ones were set in the next several years.

This period of rising official anti-Semitism in Russia was conditioned and exacerbated by the Russo-Japanese War of 1904–1905 and the abortive revolution of 1905. Jews were most directly affected by the government-endorsed pogroms that commenced after October 1905 in which 800 were killed and more than 7000 injured. They were also driven to despair by the political strife in the economic arena, which led to numerous strikes and lock-outs during these same years. Flight seemed the only viable solution. And in these turbulent years from 1904 to 1908, about half a million Jews from Russia arrived in the United States. This type of pattern continued, although interrupted by World War I, until 1925, when America officially closed its gates to mass immigration. [17]

It should also be noted that this relationship was not confined to Russia. In Rumania and to a lesser extent in the Polish-dominated Austro-Hungarian province of Galicia, the two other major sources of immigrants to the United States during the same years, hostile governmental action at all levels resulted in high rates of Jewish emigration. Both Rumania and to a lesser degree Austria-Hungary were similar to czarist Russia in the political and socioeconomic environment that affected and shaped Jewish political attitudes. In all three, the ruler was an autocrat, and power was tightly concentrated in the hands of high clergy, large landowners, nobility, and prominent officials. Also, there was an intimate association between an official religion and the state; those with different religions were penalized. Such was the common climate in which the Russian, Rumanian, and Galician Jews lived.[18]

The stimulation provided by political oppression and economic hardship produced, once a secure outlet was established, a virtual flood of Jewish emigration from this region. Thus, by 1914, after about 33 years of flight, almost half of all Russian and Eastern European Jews no longer resided in the lands of their birth. But the absolute size of the Jewish population in these areas did not decline appreciably due to natural increase of the Jewish population. Another consequence of this emigration was that the United States, the eventual destination of about 90 percent of them, emerged after World War I as the leading center of world Jewry, the home of approximately 30 percent of all the Jews on earth.[19]

The significance of ethnically inspired governmental oppression in the emigration of Jews can also be gauged by comparing Russian Jewish rates of arrival in the United States with those of other emigres from the czarist empire. (The United States figures are used because they are the best available.) Between 1899 and 1914 the Jewish rate of emigration far exceeded that of any other ethnic group—about 13 per 1000 Russian Jews. The comparable statistic for emigrants from the major Russian stocks (Russians, Ukranians, and White Russians) was less than one per thousand. Between these two ethnic groups came the other oppressed nationalities—Finns, Poles, and Lithuanians. Their rate of emigration to the United States in these years averaged about five per thousand. In fact, 85 percent of the non-Jewish Russians arriving in America from the czarist empire in this period were minority nationalities. Therefore, it is clear that the government's policy of ethnic discrimination toward groups in addition to Jews played a significant role in the pattern of emigration.[20]

The further importance of politics as a factor in the emigration of Russian Jews can also be observed in another type of emigration statistic. This is the figure for emigration from the United States. Jewish rates of departure from America, unlike those of their immigrant contemporaries from other lands, tended not to vary with economic conditions here. Recent arrivals of other nationalities were generally much more likely to leave the United States when economic opportunities in their adopted homeland constricted.[21]

The same conclusion can be drawn by comparing rates of departure solely among Jews from different countries of origin. The economic situation of Jews in Galicia was as bad and probably worse than that of their confreres in Russia over the same period of time. Politically, however, the lot of the Galician Jews was somewhat better than that of the Russian Jews. Their national administration was not as unrelentingly anti-Semitic as that of the czar. What do the departure figures reveal? In the period from 1908 to 1912, for every 100 Galician Jews admitted to the United States, 14 departed. The comparable figure for the Russian Jews was seven.

Finally, the departure rates of Jews leaving the United States compared with those of non-Jews for the same period suggest the prominence of political over economic factors in the Jewish case. From 1908 to 1912 for every 100 immigrants admitted to this country 32 left. For some specific nationalities the figure was higher than that for the average rising to more than 50 in the case of Southern Italians and Magyars. For the Jews the figure was eight, the lowest for any national group except the Irish, whose immigration was in its latter stages by that time and thus not truly comparable.[22] The picture is the same if we look at figures for a longer period, 1908 to 1925. During these years, the Jewish ratio drops to five while that of the Magyars, Italians, and Rumanians is about 60.[23] Thus, the Jews had come to America to stay, irrespective of economic cycles. For them, there was no homeland to which they could return.

Politics, therefore, has to be regarded as a root cause of the presence of so many Russian Jews in the United States. But it would be misleading and a gross exaggeration as well to isolate politics from other spheres of life or to ignore nonpolitical factors affecting the decision to emigrate. Immigration to America was facilitated for Jews by these nonpolititical considerations. The demand for labor in the United States and the sharp reduction of transatlantic fares were among these. The presence of relatives in America, their encouraging letters, and the money they sent also stirred Jews to emigrate from Russia.

These nonpolitical factors were not unique to Russian Jews. They were also facilitating factors for non-Jewish Poles, Italians, Magyars, and Russians. The Jews, however, disproportionately availed themselves of these opportunities and were more receptive to the openings for immigration to America than were other nationalities. For the Jews of the czarist empire the almost relentless hostility of an autocratic, nationalist, and quasi-theocratic state toward the Jews could not help but color all areas of existence. Russians of the Jewish faith suffered penalties and humiliation because state authorities decided that they should be treated differently from Russians of the Christian faith. The generally low economic standard of living of the masses of Russian Jewry was inextricably tied to state policy. The situation of the Jews in Russia appeared quantitatively and qualitatively worse than that of any other ethnic minority in the czarist empire.

There is no guarantee, of course, that had the Russian government chosen to adopt a policy of benign neglect toward its Jews their economic situation would have been substantially different from the generally low material level of the masses of Russians. But the state did not benignly neglect its Jews in matters of economics. Through numerous edicts, laws, taxes, and bureaucratic caprices, the Jewish community was enmeshed in an economically constrictive web that all but ensured that it would be a society of paupers and near paupers. Paradoxically, the government's perniciousness could perhaps be seen most clearly during and shortly after the brief periods when its restraints on Jews were most relaxed. The ability of even a relatively few Jews substantially to improve their lives during these intervals could not but highlight the "normal" periods before and after when the barriers were in place. In order for the Jews to have survived in such an environment, it was necessary for them to become highly sensitized to political trends and developments and politics in general.

In the face of the many government inspired hardships that befell the Jewish people, it was not surprising that growing numbers of Jews turned increasingly to political philosophies and movements hostile to autocracy. Nor did the political consciousness forged in the Pale over a number of years disappear when Russian Jews left their country for the United States. Indeed, as we shall see, this Russian inspired oppositional political frame of reference was perhaps the most important legacy that many Jews brought with them to the New World.

State policies toward Jews in the czarist empire were not the only factors shaping the receptivity of Russian Jews in America to Left politics. Other forces, interwoven with state actions, made their own independent contributions to Jewish political development. Some of these structures and forces were not historically specific to Russia. As we shall see below, some were transplanted or replicated in America, reinforcing their original political impact.

URBANIZATION

One of these factors was urbanization. By the time of the mass immigration of Jews to the United States, Jews in Russia were that nation's most urban ethnic group. This was not by any means a "natural" occurrence. Czarist policy throughout the nineteenth century was directed toward removing Jews from rural regions and villages. In addition, there were two distinguishing characteristics to Jewish urbanism. One was its concentration and the other the rapidity with which the whole process occurred for the Jews.

The Jews were an urban people by the end of the nineteenth century. They were urban within a very limited and specific area—the Pale of Settlement. Throughout this region, they constituted 38 percent of the urban population but only 12 percent of the total inhabitants. They were a majority of the city population in nine out of 15 provinces that formed the Pale. Also, Jews were often in or near the majority in some of the larger cities of the Pale. In Pinsk, they were 74 percent of the population; in Brest-Litovsk, 65 percent; in Bialystok, 52 percent; and in Vilna, 41 percent. Even in Warsaw and Odessa they accounted for one-third of the total. The same was true of the approximately 5 percent who had managed to escape the confines of the Pale. The great majority of them were to be found in the major cities such as Moscow and St. Petersburg.[24]

This urbanization took place quickly and was largely the product of the combined influences of czarist policy, economic developments, and Jewish birth rates. After 1861 the legal emancipation of the serfs (which helped to transform them into economic competitors with Jews) and the growth of capitalism in Russia reduced economic opportunities for Jews in the countryside, forcing large numbers into the cities. After 1882 the joint pressure of both government and economic forces on Jews in the rural regions and smaller towns and villages became even more intense. At the same time the Jewish birth rate was rising rapidly. Between 1820 and 1880 the Jewish population of Russia, of whom 95 percent were residents of the Pale, rose from 1,600,000 to 4,000,000. This was an increase of 150 percent, compared with an 87 percent rate of growth for the non-Jewish Russian population. In the cities of the Pale, all of these developments helped to produce doubling, tripling, and in some cases quadrupling of the Jewish population within a 50-year period.[25]

These cities in the late nineteenth and early twentieth centuries proved to be fertile territory for the development of Jewish labor and radical movements in particular and for the spread of secular ideas in general. These urban entities were more socially and economically complex than the towns and villages. In the former, class divisions were real and meaningful. In this new environment it was more difficult for the traditional agencies of social control to be as effective as in the smaller, stabler, and homogenous communities. Numbers, new experiences, contact with different types of Jews and non-Jews cut the ground from under the rabbinate and the authority of the wealthy. Their traditional mechanism of social control such as shame and ostracism lost their impact in the large cities.

The same conditions that weakened the old authorities strengthened their challengers. Social and economic diversity plus contact with varying types of Jews and non-Jews and their ideas facilitated Jewish receptivity to secularism and radicalism. As Isaac Deutscher expressed it in identifying the structural sources of Jewish intellectual and political revolutionaries: ". . . they dealt on the borderlines of various civilizations, religions, and national cultures. . . . Their minds matured where the most diverse cultural influences crossed and fertilized each other. They lived on the margins or in the nooks and crannies of their respective nations. . . ."[26] If there was any city in Eastern Europe that could be considered the model of what Deutscher had in mind, it was Vilna in the latter nineteenth and early twentieth centuries. In this Lithuanian-Polish-Jewish city of the czarist Empire the Bund was born, and Zionism and the secular Jewish enlightenment found their stronghold. In Vilna and cities like it in the Pale thousands of Jews, who would later emigrate to the United

States, had their contact and association with radicals and labor movements.[27]

ECONOMIC CHANGE AND DECLINE

The movement to the urban areas coincided with important changes in the economic life of the Jewish community. The last several decades of the nineteenth century witnessed a fairly steady deterioration in the standard of living of the Jewish masses. By the 1880s there was mass poverty. During this time almost one in five Jewish families applied for communal charity in order to observe the Passover holiday.[28] A Russian newspaper described life in the Jewish section of Vilna in the following manner:

. . . . They live in miserable hovels, dirty and badly ventilated. Filth is everywhere. . . . In the same dwelling may be found four, five, or even six families. . . . To add to the misery, neither beds, nor chairs, nor tables are to be seen in the wretched hovels, but everyone has to lie on the damp and infected ground. Meat is an unknown luxury, even on the Sabbath. Today bread and water, tomorrow water and bread, and so on day after day.[29]

Whereas the specific causes of this economic deterioration need not concern us here, the way in which it affected specific socioeconomic and occupational strata among Russian Jewry is highly relevant. By the latter decades of the nineteenth century, czarist policies, in conjunction with the peculiarities of capitalist development within Russia, had succeeded in virtually destroying the economic underpinnings of the Jewish middle class and stable artisanry. The plethora of laws, edicts, and administrative decisions, especially the May Laws of 1882, either severely constricted the access of Jewish goods and services to village and rural markets or simply made it impossible for Jews legally to ply middle-class occupations in the countryside. Confronted by such barriers and bereft of choice, many thousands of Jewish leaseholders, estate managers, merchants, innkeepers, and restauranteurs poured into the cities of the Pale and descended into the ranks of petty traders, artisans, and laborers, thereby worsening the economic lot of that strata as well. In 1891 many of the previously privileged professionals and merchants in Moscow, St. Petersburg, and Kiev suffered similar fates upon their expulsion from these cities.

The expansion of capitalism in Russia during this same period proved injurious to almost all strata of Jews. With a few notable exceptions, Jewish businessmen generally could neither accumulate sufficient capital nor obtain sufficient credit to compete adequately with their Russian and foreign counterparts. The building of factories and the introduction of modern machinery proved for the most part to be injurious to the interests of this strata of Jews. This was not only true for the Jewish bourgeoisie. Jewish artisans and workers in older and more poorly equipped factories suffered as much, if not more, as the products of their labor ceased to be competitive in the marketplace. Fewer sales and lower prices for goods were translated into layoffs and diminished wages and income.

Competition was not primarily limited to that of non-Jewish capitalists and factory owners. It also came from the non-Jewish entrepreneurs, artisans, and workers. After the liberation of the serfs in 1861, many peasants began to develop their own handicraft industries and sell their own products, both agricultural and handicrafts. In so doing, they dealt Jewish economic interests a two-fold blow. On the one hand, this new economic activity eliminated the need for the Jewish middlemen. On the other hand, it meant that Jewish artisans had to compete against them as well as the factories. The Jewish artisans proved to be at a competitive disadvantage with both the artisan-peasant and the modern factory.[30]

Factory owners and employees further contributed to the hardship of Jews in still another fashion. Factories located in the cities of the Pale were regarded as places in which hard-pressed Jews might seek employment. Although some did, and the numbers grew until about 20 percent, or 50,000, of the factory workers in the Pale were Jews, many other Jews were unable to find employment in factories. This stemmed from a variety of factors. First, the majority of employers were non-Jews and preferred not to hire Jews. Second, many of those Jews who owned factories also shared this preference for non-Jewish factory hands. Some felt that they would be unable to maintain proper and distant relationships with their coreligionist employees, thus limiting their ability to treat them as they would non-Jewish workers. For others, including non-Jewish employers, the labor troubles that Jews caused compared with non-Jews made them a more costly risk. Third, Gentile workers, many of them former peasants, were reluctant to work alongside Jews. Fourth, Jews were generally averse to entering factories. For many, values acquired during their occupations as traders and artisans prevented them from seeking the regimented employment of the factories. For others, religious scruples meant that they could not work on Saturday (the Jewish Sabbath), a normal work day for Gentiles and mechanized factories. A fifth reason was that Jews, after the various edicts of the 1880s, could not work in factories situated in areas forbidden to Jews as residences.

The factories in which Jews did work were generally qualitatively different in several ways from those employing non-Jews. At the turn of the century, almost 90 percent of all those engaged in factory labor in Russia worked in enterprises that had 50 or more workers. For Jewish factory workers, the figures could easily be reversed. The overwhelming majority of Jews who worked in factories labored in enterprises where the work force was below 30. In many places, the work force consisted of 10 or fewer individuals. Thus factories where Jews were employed tended to be smaller.

Also, these factories differed from others in their reliance on labor power. Machinery in establishments where Jews were employed tended to be minimal and fairly primitive. Even in those industries where the factories were large, such as the cigarette industry, labor power was relied on quite heavily. They were more like handworkshops than factories.[31]

For the most part, then, Jews throughout the late nineteenth and early twentieth centuries were not to be found in the large, modern factories. Instead they were concentrated in small workshops where the conditions were both primitive and hazardous. In such places of employment, they labored hard and long, without the benefit of industrial laws whose ostensible purpose was to protect the health and welfare of factory workers. Government-appointed factory inspectors rarely appeared in the small and dirty Jewish workshops. And in their absence such laws as those limiting the hours of factory work to 11½ hours a day had no real meaning.

The industries in which the Jews worked were highly seasonal and competitive in nature. The clothing industry is the single best example of this. The annual wages, particularly in the industries with the short work year, were barely minimal for the subsistence of their families. This forced many Jewish wives and children into the factories in order to survive.[32]

In summary, the growth of capitalism in Russia, particularly with respect to factories, did not improve the economic and occupational conditions of Jews. Instead, it made a bad economic situation worse as far as this group was concerned.

JEWISH ARTISANS

Jewish artisans or skilled workers were a numerically significant economic group in the Pale. The Jews were the craftsmen of this region. By the latter 1890s from two-thirds to three-quarters of all artisans there were Jewish. In fields such as tailoring and shoemaking, there were almost no Christians to be found. By the turn of the century, there were approximately 500,000 Jewish artisans in the Pale. This category comprised about 44 percent of the Jewish labor force. Among all Jews officially designated as workers—which included day laborers, factory operatives, and artisans—more than three-quarters were artisans or craftsmen.[33]

The lines between craftsmen and other occupational categories should not be regarded as immutable ones. There was considerable overlapping of categories and shading of one into another. At times it was difficult to differentiate the artisan from the factory worker. In addition, many craftsmen also sold the products of their labor, thus placing themselves in the position of petty traders as well as artisans. More than one-third of the Jewish labor force was officially listed as engaging in commerce. Together, these two categories, which again often overlapped, accounted for about 70 percent of the Jewish labor force. The significance of this figure can be better grasped when contrasted to the comparable percentage for the combined category among the non-Jewish employed population. In this latter group it was about 14 percent, consisting of 4 percent in trade and 10 percent in manufacture. On the other hand, almost three-quarters of this population was engaged in agriculture, compared with 4 percent for the Jews.[34]

These Jewish craftsmen were concentrated in several major occupational areas. The largest was in the preparation of clothing. More than 25 percent of Jewish artisans was tailors. This, in part, stemmed from the requirement of religious law, sha'atnez, which forbade Jews to wear clothing that mixed wool and linen together. To conform to this, it became necessary to have Jews make and repair clothes for other Jews. The next largest group was shoemakers, 14 percent, followed by carpenters, with 6 percent. Next bakers with 5 percent and butchers with 4 percent. Again, with shoes and foods, the necessity to conform to religious law, especially in terms of ritual preparation and the avoidance of goods emanating from proscribed animals, generated a demand for Jewish artisans in these areas.[35]

The 1880s marked a turning point in the economic fortunes of Jewish artisans. Until then their real wages and standard of living had been increasing. However, from 1880 on their standard of living rapidly declined. This was owing to the aforementioned competition with goods from factories and peasant handicraft shops. This situation was greatly exacerbated by the large numbers of Jews entering the ranks of the artisanry. Jews forced from the countryside, villages, and towns were pouring into the delimited areas of the Pale and becoming or trying to become artisans. Too many artisans crowded too close together plus too many goods being produced for a limited market were the ingredients for a formula that proved to be an economic disaster.[36]

The economic plight of the artisans, however, is only one aspect of our concern. Their composition, organization, and adaptation to that hardship were also significant factors in influencing their politics. The artisan's workshop was small. Generally, it averaged about two to three persons. The artisan was usually the master or employer, who labored alongside his workers, a journeyman, and an apprentice. In many shops there was only the master craftsman, aided by members of his family. The prototypical artisan workplace was the tailor shop. The employees in such shops were not generally receptive to the ideology of class consciousness. The journeyman's desire was not to improve his condition as an employee, but to better his situation by becoming an employer in his own right. Many, indeed, did become employers only to return to the ranks, sometimes in less than a year.[37]

This journey back and forth from employee to employer was facilitated by the nature of the industry. The crafts industry was heavily labor intensive; and machinery, especially in the small shops, was not very costly in absolute or relative terms. This meant that capital was not a major factor in setting up a small business. If a worker had the training and the labor power, which often meant one's family, plus a small sum of money, he could readily transform himself into an employer. Many did follow this path only to tumble back down. The weight of the competition plus the seasonal boom-and-bust nature of the crafts consumer-oriented industries proved too heavy to maintain at the elevated status of employer.[38] Ber Borochov, labor Zionist and astute contemporary sociological observer, claimed that these types of conditions plus the anti-Semitic policies limiting options for Jews sent proportionately more of this people's petty bourgeoisie into the ranks of the proletariat and unemployed than was true for any other nationality.[39]

These objective conditions of the Jewish artisan industry produced ideological and subjective correlates. They tended to produce an identity of interest between worker, especially journeyman, and employer. This common interest was reflected in their mutual membership in the craft guild. The journeyman, who worked only or largely with the master and in many cases lived with him as well, lacked a cohort to function as a social counterweight to the values and norms of his employer. This meant that he lived and worked in the same value and normative sphere as the employer. In short, these conditions obstructed the development of a working-class consciousness.[40]

The values of the Jewish social structure also impelled worker-artisans and even employer-artisans to bend their energies on behalf of social mobility. Artisan was not a highly regarded status in the Jewish community. The learned man and then the wealthy one stood at the apex of the social hierarchy. This was not, however, a social pyramid peculiar to Jews.[41] The Jews did differ from other people, however, in terms of differential emphasis and occupational vehicles for the attainment of upward mobility. Owning a small business often did lead to success. There were frequent examples of this in the Jewish community in the latter nineteenth century. The Jews in Russia fortunate enough to live outside of the Pale were generally more successful in business than their confreres inside the Pale.[42] Also, in the Pale, stories of success, however temporary, abounded. Again, this in large part stemmed from the nature of the Jewish industry—the small shop. Thus, the traditional Jewish social-status hierarchy combined with the objective nature of Jewish industry led to the installation of the success ethic in the Jewish proletariat. As Ber Borochov observed:

This desire to achieve "success" is a deeply ingrained characteristic of the Jewish laboring masses. Tailors, shoemakers, and cigarmakers eagerly await the opportunity to rid themselves of their tools, and to climb into the higher strata of insurance, dentistry, medicine, law, or into an independent business. This continuous exodus of thousands from the ranks of Jewish labor, and the necessary influx of thousands to replace them, furnishes the explanation for the instability of the Jewish laboring masses.[43]

These conditions did not only affect the attitude and ideology of the Jewish workers and employers. As we shall soon see, they also affected the attitude and ideology of the Jewish radicals and socialists with respect to the Jewish masses. From the 1870s through the 1880s, Jewish radicals tended to look with scorn at the Jewish masses. They dismissed them as a proper field for political work, in large part because they lumped worker and employer together into the despised category of petty bourgeoisie. The radicals' neglect of the Jewish masses, therefore, contributed also to the weakness of the development of class consciousness among them.

It is ironic that some of the very reasons for which the radicals abhored the artisan-workers were, in conjunction with other factors, stimulants to or facilitators of labor and political militancy. The Jewish artisan, and particularly those among them from the ranks of the bourgeoisie, came out of a tradition and social environment that required them to have greater need of money than their non-Jewish counterparts. It cost money to observe Jewish religious rituals. The Christians came out of a background where the standard of living was lower than that of the Jews. This agrarian background produced a worker of greater physical strength and afforded him an economic "cushion" in the countryside during periods of economic downturns. The Jewish worker had no such advantages. He could not return to a farm or village in the countryside to find food, shelter, and security until the hard times passed. The Jewish artisans were more dependent on their job in the shop and factory than were the Christians and wanted or needed more economic returns from that position than non-Jews. Consequently, the Jewish worker more than the non-Jew would be more likely to do battle with his employer over wages and working conditions.[44]

The heterogeneity of the Jewish workers was also a double-edged factor. On the one hand, it inhibited the development of a sense of consciousness of kind and contributed to the petty bourgeois aura of the Jewish artisans. On the other hand, the *forced* presence in the ranks of workers of many who had either been in a higher class or strata or who had been very desirous of moving up into that category produced a volatile quality within the Jewish artisanry. Those whose mobility had been blocked or had regressed could clearly discern the external cause of their plight. It was the state and the anti-Semitism of officials and employers that socially punished and deprived them. As a result, they shared a mutual foe with the socialists, although for different reasons. To the extent that the downwardly mobile and those who had strong aspirations to rise were trapped and felt aggrieved, they tended to be ready allies in the economic and political struggles of the socialists.

Not all, of course, took this route to express their resentment. Some seized upon the opportunity to emigrate, and others turned their anger back toward themselves in the form of Jewish self-hatred. It is difficult, if not impossible, to estimate the proportion in each category. Aside from the absence of hard data such as surveys, the categories were not mutually exclusive. However, it is possible to deduce from the available evidence the fact that there did exist, among the ranks of the Jewish workers, persons from middle-class backgrounds and aspirants for higher status who were quite active and militant.

This situation can be contrasted with the reaction of the downwardly mobile in other contexts. Where the external causes of downward or blocked mobility are not clear or are ideologically "camouflaged," such as in societies that claim to be open, the skidder is forced to place much of the blame for his plight on his own shoulders. Self-blame is generally dealt with quite differently from the way it is handled when the enemy is perceived as being outside of oneself. In the former case, one is more likely to turn to alcohol, drugs, randomized violence, or apathy than to labor or political militancy.

The changes in the economic substructure of the Jewish crafts industries were additional factors facilitating the growth of militancy among the Jewish artisan-workers. One such change produced the economic restructuring of the master or self-employed artisan. Owing to forces beyond his control, it became increasingly difficult for the artisan to define himself as an independent craftsman or a man who was his own boss. The most important factor was that the small craftsman in the latter decades of the nineteenth century was no longer producing solely for the open market. In ever-growing numbers craftsmen became dependent on a wholesaler or store owner for the sale of their goods. These middlemen progressively dictated to the "independent" artisans the quantity and type of goods that an artisan should produce. Thus, objectively at least, the status of the independent craftsman was by the turn of the century closer to the level of an employee.[45]

As the status of the employer-craftsman deteriorated, that of the journeyman also worsened. Workdays lasting 16 to 18 hours were common. In fact, in the 1890s a campaign was launched to establish a 12-hour work day. Long work days were accompanied by long periods of unemployment, as much work was seasonal in nature. For many, the meager wages earned during the short work period were not sufficient to relieve the continual poverty of their families. Also, unlike their Christian competitors, they did not have a village family to fall back on when unemployed. By the turn of the century, their position was nearly desperate.[46]

Size in terms of number of employees in a shop was another ambivalent variable. Although the smallness of the Jewish workplace inhibited class consciousness, at the same time this same size-factor placed employers of such shops in a more vulnerable position than those with a much larger number of employees. The employer of a larger shop had more resources to defend or use as a counterattack against labor or political militants. The loss of services of two, three, or five employees caused greater economic damage to the owner of a small shop than to the owner of a large shop. This is compounded in artisan industries by the fact that workers cannot be replaced as easily as in the case of industries involving relatively unskilled labor. It is interesting to note that later, in the period from 1900 to 1904, Jewish workers in small shops went on strike more often than those in larger places of employment and at the same time were more likely to win their demands.[47]

In the 1880s and 1890s, however, shop sizes did change in response to economic forces. Increasingly, craftsmen found employment in larger shops. There the distinctions between employer and employee were greater than in the small shops. Also, employees in the larger workplaces were more likely than those in the smaller ones to define themselves as hired laborers as opposed to future employers.[48] This, then, sharpened the class divisions in the Jewish community.

The Jewish working class that emerged in Russia by the turn of the century was rife with these apparent contradictions. Factors that should have inhibited the development of militancy appeared to be contributing to it.[49]

In order to understand this phenomenon, as well as the politics of the Jewish workers, it is necessary to make the distinction between militancy and radicalism. By militancy we mean aggressive behavior *unassociated* with any specific ideology. Radicalism, on the other hand, is an ideology whose focus is upon socialist or anarchist ideas and beliefs. Jewish workers who were active in protest activities tended to be more militant than radical. The economic and social conditions of the Jewish worker and the Jewish artisan-oriented industry around the turn of the century were conducive to the rise of worker militancy. Radicals and socialists played upon and encouraged this while not fully aware during the heady periods of labor strife and turmoil that striking workers joining unions and defying Czarist authorities did not equal recruits for socialism.

Often the Jewish socialists in Russia and later in America would confuse form with substance. Often they would mistake an overlap or temporary convergence of interests and objectives between themselves and the Jewish workers as an indication of the latter's move toward a permanent commitment to socialism. Relatively few Jewish laborers, however, completed the journey from militancy to socialism. The peculiar nature of Jewish occupations and industry as well as the unique traditions and experiences of the Jewish people combined in the cauldron that was the Czarist empire to produce a special kind of working class. But, despite these impediments, the commitment and fervor of the Jewish laboring masses did prove sufficient in both Russia and America for the emergence from their ranks of numerous socialists.

From the perspective of the 1890s, such distinctions between militancy and radicalism seemed of little consequence. Jewish workers, more than their non-Jewish counterparts, were not passive observers of their fate. They did things to change their life circumstances. Whereas for some this action was limited to emigration, for other Jews it involved a more militant course. They launched hunger demonstrations, conducted sabotage, and spontaneously erupted in numerous strikes. Trade unions and other forms of worker organization also began to emerge. By the late 1890s a powerful and increasingly organized force developed to which the label of a Jewish labor movement could be affixed.

THE EDUCATED SUBVERSIVES

A key element in the formation of a Jewish labor movement, a term that encompasses radical and trade union organizations, lay outside the ranks of the workers. This was the radical students and intelligentsia of Jewish origin. It was this element that developed a fairly coherent ideology. It was this element that articulated the demands of the Jewish workers. And, it was this element that hammered out the organizational structure.

These architects and leaders of the Jewish labor movement were drawn from the ranks of young Jews who had been exposed to secular ideas and education. Recall that the ascension of Alexander II to the throne in 1856 marked a period of relaxation of governmental hostility toward the Jews. Youthful Jews desirous of a secular education were among the prime beneficiaries of this "liberal" period. In the gymnasium or secondary schools of the Pale, Jews rose as a percentage of the student body from virtually zero in 1833 to 7.5 percent in 1865. By 1872 this figure had doubled to 15 percent. Jewish enrollments at the universities also displayed a similar pattern. Between 1865 and 1886 the percentage of Jews among students increased from 3 to 14 percent, or in absolute numbers there were 129 Jewish students in 1865 and 1857 some two decades later. These figures also do not take into account those students in government-supported seminaries, most notably the Governmental Rabbinical Seminary in Vilna, who also became familiar with contemporary secular intellectual trends.[50] Thus, from the 1860s through the 1880s, a Jewish desire for education, coupled with opportunity provided by the government, resulted in the production of a sizable reservoir of Jewish young men and women familiar with ideas and thinkers at variance with traditional Eastern European Judaism. This pool was produced at a time of intellectual ferment in Russia. Positivism, utilitarianism, evolutionism, humanism, and nationalism were some of the intellectual forces that attracted and seduced the minds of the students, Jew and non-Jew alike. This was especially true for students in Vilna, a city of Jews, Poles, Lithuanians, Germans, and Russians and a constant hothouse for various intellectual currents.

Many of the Jewish students were transformed into *maskilim* or enlighteners, disciples of the *Haskalah* or enlightenment that had originated in the German Jewish community. A major aim of the *Haskalah* was to secularize and modernize Jewry. For the *maskilim*, as well as converts to other intellectual faiths, the secularization and the modernization of Jewry was a necessary step in the solution of the Jewish problem. The *Haskalah* texts advocated the abandonment of obscure customs, dress, and "jargon," or Yiddish, that served to isolate Jews from their Christian peers. They urged that secular studies be incorporated into the education of Jewish students. The *Haskalah* in its examination of Judaism selected and gave positive emphasis to the rational, optimistic, and universal qualities of faith. These were also the same qualities that were emphasized in the intellectual movements outside of the *Haskalah*.[51]

All of this appealed to these young Russian Jewish students, particularly those who did not want to break abruptly from their community. It should also be pointed out that this was a period in which the Russian rabbinate was becoming more traditionalist. In response to the *Haskalah* and other social and economic forces that disturbed and disrupted the traditional and cohesive Jewish community, the rabbis drew the lines of religious conformity ever tighter.[52] The slightest deviations from custom were interpreted almost as acts of heresy. "Cutting one's earlocks, wearing a coat shorter than traditional style, reading 'modern' books—these," according to historian Lucy S. Dawidowicz, "were the most pernicious sins of all."[53] The rabbis' action, of course, led to an even greater polarity between themselves and Jewish religion, over whose definition they had a monopoly, and Jewish students and young persons touched by the new and different ideas.

The ideas of the *Haskalah* as well as the conceptions inherent in the writings of Russian and Western thinkers dovetailed to produce a consensus about the social nature of the Jews in Russia. The Jews, as seen through the prism of these intellectual currents, were social parasites. They did not produce anything. They did not work the land. Instead, they existed by living by the productive work of others. Money, not creativity, was their motivating force. The popular poets and novelists that appealed to the radical young Jewish and non-Jewish students, such as Gogol, Pushkin, and Turgenev, reinforced this view.[54] One Jewish student radical of the 1870s expressed the feelings of his generation: "I am myself a Jew but I have seen few Jewish workers. Russian Jews are only interested in petty earnings and they are ready to sell everything including their own honor. It is not worth wasting effort on them."[55]

These intellectual forces did not only attenuate or break the ties between Judaism and the Jewish students, they also paved the way for these students to become radicals. Once their wall of faith had been penetrated by the writings of philosophers, literateurs, and scientists, they searched for membership in other worlds of meaning. After their own particularistic tradition and religion had been subverted, they were not very likely to adopt those of the quasi-theocratic czarist state. Instead they turned to and became absorbed by the works of radicals and socialists like Bakunin and Plekhanov who offered them more rational, universal, and egalitarian worlds.

Their own despised minority status was also obviously a factor in their propensity to look leftward. As educated Jews they were acutely aware of the disabilities of being Jewish, even under a "liberal" regime. Although some sought to escape through conversion and many more through assimilation, Russian society as then constituted was not willing to collude in their escapism. A Jew was a Jew. And the discrimination and prejudice of the czarist officialdom and others who controlled access to desired careers and professions further heightened their antagonism toward the powers of Russian society.[56]

All of these intellectual and social forces combined to make these Jewish students of the last decades of the nineteenth century seekers of movements that would offer them a new world of equality and acceptance. In the 1870s many thought that they had found their solution in populism. This was a movement that looked to the Russian peasant and his communal institutions as the summation of the basic virtues of Russian society. This would be the mold that would shape a new, positive, and egalitarian Russian society.

A RETURN TO THE JEWS

The peasant, or rather the romantic image of the peasant, offered the Jewish student a model for hope and emulation. The peasant was a basic producer. He was the truest expression of the Russian soul. His institutions were positive and egalitarian. In short, the peasant embodied all that the Jew was not.

Jewish students, along with thousands of their Russian peers, eagerly embraced populism. However, a problem quickly arose. In 1873–1874 and again in 1876–1877, thousands of Russian students went to the countryside to live and work with the Russian peasants. The Jewish students, however, experienced great difficulty. Their language, customs, and mannerisms prevented them from getting close to the peasants. The real peasant differed from the idealized peasant in various ways, especially in his tendency to be anti-Semitic.

This induced some of these Jewish students to seek similar solutions closer to their own people. These urbane intellectuals began to dream and plan for agricultural communal colonies of Jews. They would demonstrate that Jews could, like the Russian peasants, be motivated by self-sacrifice and engage in physical labor. The *Haskalah* as well as the Bible provided them with Jewish intellectual inspiration and support for their endeavors.[57]

The outbreak of the pogroms on April 15, 1881, caused the educated and assimilationist young Jews, particularly the radicals among them to reconsider their positions concerning their identities. Although there had been a pogrom in Odessa in 1871, those that occurred in 1881 and after were more shocking and horrifying. The shock and the horror of the pogroms were compounded for the Jewish students, intellectuals, and radicals by the reaction of their educated Christian mentors, peers, and comrades. Except for isolated instances, no support for the Jews was expressed by the Russian press, intelligentsia, liberals, or radicals. These were the strata and groups that had inducted the Jewish students into the realm of Western enlightenment and socialism. The pogroms, this lack of support, and the actual physical blows some of them received forced them into an agonizing reappraisal of their identity as Jews.[58]

The Jewish radicals associated with the populist and socialist causes were particularly disheartened. Their Christian comrades-in-arms, with but few exceptions, refused to condemn the pogroms. The overwhelming response of the revolutionary movement to the attacks on Jews was to interpret them as objectively positive phenomena. From this perspective the pogroms represented the beginning of a political awakening of the peasant masses. The non-Jewish revolutionaries believed the pogroms to be almost a necessary prelude to the revolution that would soon follow. To denounce the pogromists and evince any public sympathy for the Jews in this context was to risk compromising one's position as a radical.[59] One Russian socialist coldly summarized his comrades' analysis of the pogroms thusly:

. . . sixty percent of the Jewish people are engaged in commerce. This is the background against which the peasant hunts down the Jew . . . To be sure, from a humanitarian standpoint, it is a piece of social barbarism . . . Take, however, this event in the context of social dynamics. Why does he beat? Because this is, in the meantime, his political ballot. He has no other way of venting his wrath against his exploitation by the government. It is indeed a pity that the peasant beat the Jew—the most innocent of his exploiters. But he beats, and this is the beginning of his struggle for liberation. When . . . his fists have grown strong and hard, he will strike those who are above the Jews.[60]

The leading populist group, *Narodnaya Volya* or People's Will, an organization whose founders included Jews, seized by the logic of this analysis went even further. In its newspaper the groups publicly defended and justified the peasants' attacks on Jews. In one pamphlet issued by an irresponsible faction of this organization, the Executive Committee of the People's Will in the Ukraine, the peasants were urged to continue their assaults on Jews. Three years later in 1884 leaders of the People's Will publicly acknowledged that their organization had erred, both morally and politically, in welcoming and encouraging the pogroms. But, this change of heart years afterward, had no impact upon the way radical and educated Jews felt at the time about their Christian peers' objective and subjective support of the pogromists.[61]

The pogroms and the lack of sympathy and understanding that educated and revolutionary Russians showed to the plight of the Jews, coming as they did after several decades of a seemingly growing enlightenment within Russia, drove Jewish radicals and intelligentsia back into the fold of the Jewish community. This was to prove a crucial historic event that was to have reverberations for decades and influence the course of Jewish radicalism in Russia and America. In the early 1880s radical Jews in Russia came to the conclusion that in the eyes of socialist and nonsocialist Russians, Jews, regardless of occupational, religious, or political differences, were one people, and that membership in this peoplehood was their major defining characteristic. Impelled by this realization, Jewish radicals for the first time since their process of secularization had begun returning to their previously neglected people. The most notable example of this was the organized entrance in February 1882 by the Jewish students and intelligentsia into synagogues, institutions that until then they had regarded with contempt. They did this to demonstrate their solidarity with their coreligionists, who were praying and fasting for relief from the pogroms. "We are Jews like you. We regret that we have hitherto considered ourselves as Russians. Events of the last years have shown us how sadly mistaken we have been. Yes, we are Jews."[62]

Despite the disillusionment with the non-Jewish radicals, the impact of the populists, including the People's Will, was far from negative with respect to the development of a left movement within Russian Jewry. I concur with the assessment of the historian, Nora Levin, in her contention that:

"Virtually every shade of Jewish radicalism later on, and every subsequent radical movement in Russia were affected by populism . . . The movement failed; it did not create a new order in Russia, but it was an indispensable consciousness-raising and politically maturing experience for a generation of idealistic youth who left a legacy of ideas and personal commitment to revolutionary action that made subsequent changes possible.[63]

In addition, the increasingly worsening situation of the Jews in the 1880s trivialized the ethnic obtuseness of the populists as a factor motivating Jews to break with the Left. The continuance of the pogroms in these years and the heightened legal oppression of the Jewish community reinforced the underlying forces that had originally prompted many young Jews to move toward the Left. The major consequence of their disillusioning experience with the populists was that after 1882 their milieu and social base became primarily Jewish.

One of the Jewish groups formed in the aftermath of the pogroms that carried the radical ideas of the populists into the Russian Jewish community was *Am Olam* or Eternal People. It was originally founded in 1881 by two *maskilim* but soon became inundated by Russified Jewish students and intellectuals. This organization reflected a variety of influences. Similar to the populists, they looked toward the establishment of socialist or communal agricultural settlements as the most positive means of constructing a socialist society. They also felt it necessary that the Jewish people be redeemed by a return to the land in the context of communal farms. The pogroms and the reaction of Russian society convinced them that there was no future for them in Russia. Instead, similar to some other Russian populists groups of a decade or so earlier, they decided to remove themselves and their dreams to America.

This group captured the emotional allegiance of large numbers of students, although only 350 members were to make the journey to the United States. It also attracted the attention and affection of many Jews and socialists outside of Russia.[64] One of the leaders of the *Am Olam* described the reception that these pioneers received and the way in which they symbolically embodied Jewish and socialist aspirations:

The news that a party of students was going to America to establish communistic colonies ran ahead of us. Throughout the way . . . committees of socialist minded students were organized to assist us. . . . In Krakow, we were presented with a copy of *Das Kapital*, by Karl Marx. In Lemberg, orthodox Jews gave us a Torah and a large banner with the inscription *Degel Machne Yisroel* (Banner of the Army of Israel) . . . /upon arrival in/New York. We formed lines, took out the Torah, unfurled the banner and, with Russian revolutionary songs on our lips, marched to Castle Garden.[65]

The few hundred were not very successful in their endeavors to establish communistic agrarian colonies in America. They did, however, become very important, way out of proportion to their numbers, in helping the socialist movement among Jews in the United States. Their ranks supplied the fledgling Jewish socialist movement in America with cadres, organizers, and editors.[66] One close observer, writing in 1908, claimed that: "From 1882 on the work of organizing the Jews in a Jewish labor movement was carried on almost exclusively by young students who had come over in groups of the eternal people."[67] This was also the assessment of the leading Jewish socialist newspaper in the United States, the *Jewish Daily Forward*. Of the contributions made by the members of the *Am Olam* to the cause of Jewish socialism in America, this paper stated: "they were the fathers of all that was good and wholesome that we have accomplished here."[68]

The *Am Olam* represented one type of response to the pogroms and reaction of the Russians. Other Jewish students and radicals, similarly influenced by the ideology of populism, also organized to establish agricultural communal settlements. Their target destination, however, was Palestine and not America. The most prominent group was called *Bilu*. As in the case of *Am Olam*, *Bilu* and other Palestinophile groups also attracted emotional and popular support from the Jewish populace. It should be noted that both with *Bilu* and *Am Olam*, there was a great disparity between the size of its supporters and well-wishers and the actual number of members and yet still the figure of pioneers that finally did go abroad to the agricultural settlements.[69]

Both *Am Olam* and *Bilu* had symbolic importance beyond their relatively small numbers. They embodied within them the strains and contradictions of two forces that from that point on were to compete with one another for the political loyalty of the Jewish community, socialism and Zionism. It was to be a long struggle, as both movements not only influenced one another but often coexisted within individuals and organizations as well as within the Jewish community. However, despite, or perhaps because of this, the organizational embodiments of each of these ideologies became from the 1880s through the Bolshevik Revolution ardent and bitter political foes.

Those socialists who did not emigrate, turn to Zionism, or leave politics sought paths to socialism that went beyond the populists. Although populism remained an influential force, Marxism, beginning in the 1880s, made increasing inroads among Jewish students and intellectuals. Many of the future leaders of the Jewish socialist movement came under the influence of George Plekhanov, the father of Russian Marxism. He was the first in the early and mid-1880s to apply Marxism to the conditions of Russian society.[70]

Marxism was to prove a more compatible variant of socialism for these Jewish radicals than populism. Its emphasis on cities and workers as opposed to rural areas and peasants struck a responsive chord in young men whose roots had been cut off from the soil and who had been born and bred in cities. It also did not attribute near mystical qualities to sectors of the Russian population or their particular institutions.

It was a cosmopolitan ideology not bound by national or particularistic forms and themes. Equality would flow from class membership, which was devoid of a national or ethnic context. At the same time this ideology did not require the renunciation of a Jewish heritage. In fact, many of the elements within it, such as its universalistic ethos, messianic vision, and utopian goal, were quite compatible with key elements in the Jewish tradition. Marxism, in addition to being a faith, also laid claim to being a science. Its creators and apostles considered it to be a science of the dynamics of human society. This sat well with the educated radicals. Many of them had originally found their way to the Left via an early commitment to humanistic ideals and the principles of the natural sciences.

Young educated Jewish men were attracted to Marxism because they saw in it the seeds of a society that they could embrace and by which in turn they would be wholeheartedly accepted as equals. The rootless cosmopolitans who stood outside of traditional Russian and Jewish society increasingly commited themselves to Marxism as a faith, science, and home. These young Marxists, armed with this egalitarian and cosmopolitan faith, were determined to build a movement. In practical terms, this meant finding a mass base outside of their own narrow strata. It was at this point that political ideology clashed with practical political considerations. They found, similar to their populist predecessors, that they could not effectively propagandize and politicize non-Jews. The only workers that were accessible to them were Jews. This ran contrary to their expectations and desires. They did not want to organize a Jewish socialist organization or a Jewish labor movement. Despite the pogroms and the reactions of Russian radicals, these Jewish students and intellectuals still remained ardent cosmopolitans, which in practical terms meant Russophile intellectuals. From this perspective, Jewish life and culture were still regarded as narrow and inferior.

As Marxists, they were also troubled by the material with which they had to politicize. Marxism singled out the working class as the force that would carry the socialist revolution to triumph. In the latter 1880s and early 1890s, there appeared to be little similarity between the ideal typical proletariat of Marxist literature and the Jewish workers. Only a small percentage of Jewish workers were factory workers; and even they were not found in the large modern factories. Jewish workers were not located in the basic industries but in consumer-oriented industries. These Jewish Marxists observed the Jewish workers through glasses still colored by their Russian and populist education. What they saw was not a working class but a crude amalgam of artisans and petty traders. This was hardly the material from which a force for revolution would be forged. A leading Jewish Marxist commented on this problem: "We looked upon artisans almost as exploiters. Because the majority of the Jewish toilers were artisans and had to occupy themselves with small trade, we were ready to classify them as business people. To conduct any propaganda among them and yet in jargon [Yiddish] appeared to us, if not harmful, at least a waste of time and energy."[71] But there was no choice. This "inferior" working class was the only one to which they had entry.[72]

TO THE "EDUCATED" MASSES: THE ARTISANS

The major medium through which the educated Jewish radicals worked with their Jewish material proved to be one that was very congenial to their prejudices and own backgrounds. This was the study circle, a predominant institution of the 1880s and early 1890s. The circle was established largely because of Plekhanov's insistence that the Marxist movement in Russia needed to create an intelligentsia well versed in the science of Marxism.[73] In this context, the educated Jewish radicals could avoid dealing with the Jewish masses. Instead, individual Jewish workers could be selected and appropriately educated under the rationale of preparing them for cadre and leadership positions in the worker revolutionary movement that would soon arise.

The first step on this road was education of these mostly self-selected worker recruits. The leading item on the circle curriculum was not socialism, it was Russian. As Russophile intellectuals, the leaders of the circles felt it necessary first to teach Russian, then to expose their students to Russian literature and science, and finally to introduce them to socialism. The ideal typical graduate from such an education would, among other things, be an assimilated intellectual or, in other words, a mirror image of the leaders and teachers of the circles.

This may not have been the intended objective, but it was in accordance with the outlook of the educated radicals. The dominant outlook remained assimilationist. From this perspective it was easy to rationalize that the separatism and uniqueness of the Jewish masses were the factors that isolated them from their Russian peers. If the masses could be Russified, there would be no Jewish problem. This would, of course, make the tasks and lives of the educated Jewish radicals, desirous of escaping from their own onerous ethnic burden, that much more positive. One educated radical-circle leader summed up the conscious dominant feeling of his peers: "We wanted the Jewish masses to assimilate as quickly as possible; everything that smelled of Jewishness called forth among many of us a feeling of contempt, if not more. . . . We all deeply believed that as soon as Jews began to speak Russian, they would just as we had, become 'people in general.' "[74]

The circles proved to be severely flawed instruments for hastening the cause of the socialist revolution. Given the premises that guided them, as well as the workers who came to them, their failure as revolution facilitators was almost unavoidable. The worker-students proved to be ardent pupils, who greatly admired their radical teachers, treating them in some cases as would befit a rabbi. Many, indeed, were so influenced by their socialist mentors that they aspired to become like them, not socialists but intellectuals. It was not their attitude toward education that was the problem but their motive for wanting the education. These workers, again largely self-selected, were using the secular education obtained in the circles for advancing their own social mobility and not the cause of socialism.

Another related problem was the occupational composition of the workers who joined the circles. There were virtually no factory workers among their ranks. Almost all were artisans. And, of the artisans who did come, most were of the aristocracy of the crafts such as printers, engravers, jewelers, binders, and watchmakers. In general, these were the crafts with the highest pay, skills, and prestige. The radical leaders found it quite difficult to convey to them the message of socialism, partcularly class differences and conflict. These products of the small workshops just could not visualize their employers as class exploiters. Instead these workers viewed their bosses positively as hardworking and honest men. In contrast, they would complain about the poor work habits and attitudes of their fellow workers. They could not draw upon their real life experiences to reinforce and make concrete concepts like class conflict and class solidarity that their Marxist mentors were preaching to them. The world of modern industry and factories was for them, in the words of one Marxist leader, "some fairy tale kingdom." [75]

By 1894 the Jewish Marxist intellectuals had reassessed their position and made the decision to abandon the circles in order to agitate and organize the masses. This change of direction was not only informed by their own experiences in the circles but also, once again, by Plekhanov. In 1892 he changed his thinking and persuasively argued that socialists had to work directly with the masses. "A sect can be satisfied with propaganda in the narrow sense of the word. A political party—never. . . . A propagandist gives many ideas to one or a few people, but an agitator gives only *one* or a *few* ideas, but to *masses* of people. . . . Yet, history is made by the masses." [76]

In accord with this change in policy, other alterations became necessary. In order for Jewish students and intellectuals to agitate among the Jewish masses and share their work experiences, the workers had to be approached on their own terms. This meant that the intellectuals had to abandon the teaching of Russian and subjects distant from the lives of the people with whom they worked and politicized. Now it was Yiddish and concrete action in the forms of strikes and demonstrations that would link the fates of the Marxists and the Jewish workers.

The major opposition to this new direction came, not unexpectedly, from the worker-students. They correctly realized that this new policy would injure their opportunity for social mobility. The abandonment of the circles meant that the educational ladder to better jobs and higher living standards would be smashed to pieces without anything to replace it. These worker-students turned the original arguments and attitudes of their mentors back upon them insisting that workers needed education more than agitation. They were particularly incensed when Russian was replaced with Yiddish. The feelings of the worker-students were so strong that in the mid-1890s in many circles the intellectuals were left almost isolated. Here was a great irony. The intellectuals wanted to go to the masses, but the "masses" whom they had taught wanted to go the other way, toward the world of the intellectuals and the middle class, the life their mentors wanted to abandon. [77]

The new policy, in conjunction with other events, led to and helped to stimulate significant consequences, short and long range, intended and unintended. One of the first was the formation of an organized Jewish labor movement. Prior to the agitation policy's adoption, Jewish workers had engaged in sporadic strikes and demonstrations and had thrown up either limited or short-lived organizations. After the socialist intellectuals went among them, however, the situation changed. The socialists brought with them intense dedication, new ideas, and organizational experience. These proved to be crucial in forging a more stable and organized labor movement.

The decision to agitate among Jewish workers was, perforce, a decision to agitate among the artisans. It proved to be a correct judgment. Artisans, more so than factory workers and casual laborers, responded to the socialists. They were among the earliest to conduct strikes, to organize, and to produce leaders and cadres for the Jewish labor movement. The radical students and intellectuals in overcoming their socialist inhibitions had found what they believed to be a vanguard force for socialism. Artisans might not resemble the classic proletariat of Marxist philosophy, but in their political behavior they more closely resembled this ideal type than did other workers at the time.

The success of the socialists in their work with the artisans was in large part a matter of timing and special circumstances. As we shall see, several decades later under a different set of circumstances in America the original misgivings of socialists proved not to be groundless. Some socialists in Russia, even during the period when the artisans were highly responsive, realized that this could not be an enduring phenomenon, nor could it play an integral role in the eventual triumph of socialism. This judgment did not flow from abstract ideological reasoning alone. It was grounded in a socioeconomic analysis of the structure and economics of the Jewish artisan industries of late nineteenth- and early twentieth-century Russia. Artisan industries were typically characterized by a plethora of small shops operating very close to the profit margin. In such a situation, particularly if the economic situation were to improve, ambitious workers would constantly be enticed with the prospect of starting their own businesses. Obversely, given the actual poor economic conditions, socialist victories in the form of increased wages, decreased hours, and militant unions would eventually lead to the economic destruction of the small employers. In that eventuality, the previous victories would be for nought. From this perspective, the success of socialism still came to rest on factory workers. Any long-term optimism with respect to artisans depended upon their being transformed into factory workers.[78]

The debate over the appropriate role of artisans in the socialist movement was not peculiar to the Jewish socialists of the Pale. Socialists in other parts of Europe (before and after them) were similarly troubled by this issue. Engels and even their own Russian contemporary Lenin had indeed adopted a very hostile position concerning the artisans. These socialist thinkers believed that the artisans or "aristocracy of labor," as they labeled them, were basically conservative in their political orientation. Their involvement in the nineteenth- and early twentieth-century labor and socialist movements, these Marxist intellectuals held, flowed from a reaction to their own threatened status or a desire to protect their special privileges. The labor and political organizations that were led or created by artisans in the nineteenth- and early twentieth-centuries were characterized by many Marxists as narrow and exclusive bodies lacking a proper socialist vision. Their main objective was depicted as the improvement or protection of the immediate interests of the artisans. In striving for such an objective, Marxists contended, these aristocrats of labor would move toward an accommodation with capitalism at the expense of their less favored brethren. From this perspective, the artisans were not the vanguard of socialism but the petty bourgeois betrayers of the working class.[79] Despite the polemics, however, these socialists, like their counterparts in the Pale, were confronted with the fact that labor and socialist movements (in many places, interchangeable phenomena) throughout Europe and America in the nineteenth and early twentieth centuries were led and cadred by skilled craftsmen. The nonskilled were not as radical as the skilled (if we use participation in the labor and socialist movements as the primary indicators of radicalism). The less-skilled workers were more likely than their skilled counterparts to be apathetic or conservative.[80]

At the time when large numbers of artisans in the Pale were striking, organizing, and moving toward socialism, few of the Jewish radical intellectuals let such pessimistic analyses hinder them in cooperating with and organizing these skilled workers. Neither did these socialists seriously examine the special conditions that had contributed to their apparent success among the artisans. These Jewish socialists, generally unbeknownst to themselves, had struck at a propitious historic moment. A combination of economic forces generated by developing capitalism, occupational traditions, and the fact of being Jewish in czarist Russia richly fertilized the soil in which the socialists sowed.

Jewish artisans in the Pale, similar to non-Jewish artisans elsewhere, did not fare well in their confrontation with capitalism. In the new economic order, particularly after the 1880s, the pay and standard of living of the Jewish artisans declined. This decline, coming as it did after a period of economic improvement, was deeply felt. The new circumstances pushed the artisans closer to the position of proletarians while at the same time reducing them to or nearly to the level of paupers. It was not economic adversity alone that they suffered. Jewish artisans, in their meeting with industrial capitalism, were also injured by the blows to their independence, self-esteem, and skill that accompanied their economic decline. In this predicament, the call of the socialists to hit back at the system responsible for their plight could not but fall on sympathetic ears. At the same time these Jews in their capacity as artisans possessed traditions and qualities unique to them, as compared with factory workers or day laborers, that further facilitated their receptivity to socialism. The central focus of these traditions and qualities was the fact of a shared and learned skill. It was around this that they built their craft guilds and mutual aid organizations. It was around this that they developed a positive attitude toward education. This shared and learned skill gave them respect and dignity and made them different from other workers.

The socialists' appeals and rhetoric fell upon ears made receptive by a common occupational position and by fate. When the socialists identified socialism with education and self-improvement, the Jewish artisans, as well as their non-Jewish counterparts elsewhere, could take note of the similarity between this movement and their occupational heritage. When socialists called upon them to organize and collectively resist their employers and the state, the artisans could identify these with their own traditions of organization and solidarity. In short, the skilled craftsmen were in a better position initially to accept and legitimate socialism than the nonskilled. The artisans' work experiences and occupational histories facilitated their receptivity to socialism.

One must not overlook practical and mundane factors that also facilitated the artisans' move toward unionism and socialism. They had, by definition, a skill. The possession of this meant that they had leverage, albeit weakened during times of artisan surpluses, with their employers. This learned skill meant that they could not be easily replaced. Thus, they had greater leeway than other workers to agitate and participate in union and socialist activities.

Again, the Jewish factor cannot be separated from the occupational in the radicalization of Jewish artisans. The fact that they were Jewish made their confrontation with emerging capitalism harsher than it was for their non-Jewish counterparts. Being Jewish reduced their options and thus their capacity to resist and protect themselves from the negative impact of capitalism. Christian antagonism and government hostility historically combined to produce a situation in which approximately two-thirds of all Jewish artisans at the turn of the century could be found in just three occupational categories—clothing and wearing apparel, leather goods, and food products. These occupations, even in so-called good times, were not noted for their economic stability.[81] Furthermore, Jewish residential restrictions, particularly after the 1880s when they became more intense, meant that Jewish artisans, unlike Christian ones, were not physically free to pursue job opportunities. Jobs in cities outside of the Pale or in nonurban areas inside of it were generally beyond the reach of Jewish artisans. Thus, Jewishness can be presumed to have contributed to their economic grievances and, also, to their receptivity to socialism.

There was another markedly Jewish condition that accommodated this development in the late 1800s and early 1900s: the presence in the ranks of Jewish artisans of many young men and women from middle-class backgrounds. They were there because they were Jewish. Few were there by choice. The opportunities for Jews to enter into middle-class positions had always been limited in Russia, but in the 1880s they became even more constricted. Capitalist development, as discussed earlier, had undercut traditional Jewish middle-class occupational roles. Interwoven with this were the anti-Semitic policies of the government, which helped to shape the Jews' economic misfortune. Frustrated aspirants to university education and professional careers, many from middle-class and educated families, were forced down into the ranks of artisans. They were thus present in sizable numbers when the Jewish socialists made their decision to agitate among the artisans. They aided the socialist cause in at least two ways. One, due to their previous or aspired statuses, they reduced the social distance between their fellow workers and the radical intellectuals. Two, the labor movement was seized upon by them as a vehicle through which to channel their anger and talents. Many soon after in Russia and later America were to emerge as leaders and cadres in this cause.[82]

The specific historic factors underlying the relative success of the socialists among the artisans were not amenable to control by socialists. They were also factors that history would not again replicate in America. Without special cognizance paid to these forces, the lessons to be drawn and the experiences to be transferred would, of necessity, be flawed. This, as we shall see, was one of the problems that would confront Russian Jews in America in their attempt to build a labor movement.

THE UNIQUELY JEWISH MOVEMENT

Another historic consequence flowed from the decision of the socialists to agitate among the Jewish masses. This, as mentioned above, was the construction of a uniquely Jewish labor movement. Again, this was certainly not the desire of these Jewish cosmopolitan radicals at that time. Through the 1880s the formation of a Russian socialist movement, not a Jewish socialist movement, was their major life's goal. The few among them that thought in terms of a Jewish movement were isolated and had little impact.

Jewish socialists, despite their best intentions, major efforts, and the fact that they were the standard-bearers of a universalistic creed were unable to break through the social barriers that divided and separated the nationalities in the czarist empire. The social divisions among them were too strong. These barriers were even stronger when it came to Jews, who were widely seen as the perennial aliens whose main motivation in life was to separate Christians from their money. The Jewish populists of the 1870s who had gone out among the Russian peasantry were among the first to be rudely awakened to the impact of anti-Semitism and national differences on a face-to-face basis. The Jewish socialists of the 1880s fared little better when they tried to reach the non-Jewish workers. It should be noted at this juncture that anti-Semitism among the non-Jewish workers was not only an historic carry-over. The church and the government, particularly after the 1880s, were rather consistent reinforcers of that virus. Employers, both Jewish and Christian, also found it a convenient device for dividing workers and thus reducing labor costs. However, regardless of the underlying reasons, non-Jewish workers in the latter decades of the nineteenth century were not prepared to associate intimately with Jews or work next to them, much less be organized by them into groups in which Jews held leadership positions. To these workers it did not make much difference whether the Jew in question was a religious or nonobservant Jew, a socialist or a nonsocialist. The major issue was not politics or degree of religiosity but the fact that the individual was a Jew.[83]

Class divisions were also a factor that impeded association and communication between the Jewish radicals and the Christian workers. The Jewish socialists were, for the most part, highly educated young men from middle-class backgrounds, whereas the workers had little education and were generally from worker or peasant families. They lacked a common basis for discourse, despite the good intentions of the young radicals. Class together with religioethnic differences formed a rather formidable barrier separating the two groups.

The difficulty of establishing a relationship was not entirely the fault of the Christian worker. The Jewish students and intellectuals also felt a sense of estrangement in their interaction with non-Jewish workers. Even Jewish intellectuals could not totally liberate themselves from the anti-Christian sentiments prevalent in the Jewish community. And, despite their socialist convictions, the unfamiliar and alien customs and values of the Christian workers often proved too significant an obstacle in the development of a necessary relationship. The experience of one Jewish socialist succinctly highlights and summarizes the problem:

Very often someone would send along a bottle of *monopolke* (whiskey). They would pour it into tea glasses and drink it down like a glass of water. I had to drink along with them, otherwise I would not have been a "good brother." I hoped that by becoming their "good brother" I would be able to make them class conscious. In the end neither of us achieved anything. They could not make me a drunkard, and I could not make them class conscious.[84]

There was also another aspect to the issue of national divisions and rivalries that pushed the Jewish socialists further into a Jewish orientation. The intellectual Jewish radicals located primarily in the Pale spoke and carried out their political work prior to the turn of the century in the Russian language. The non-Jewish inhabitants of the Pale, however, were not Great Russians for the most part. Many were Poles, Ukranians, and Lithuanians. These groups, especially the Poles, were quite concerned about maintaining their cultural identity and resisting the cultural domination by the Great Russians. In this context, the Jewish socialists' use of Russian was seen as abetting the czarist policy of Russifying the border areas of the empire. The Polish socialists who had organized themselves into the Polish Socialist Party called upon the Jewish socialists to cease speaking and writing in Russian and to use Polish instead.

The Jewish socialists, particularly the important group in Vilna, a largely Polish city, were in a dilemma. They did not view their immersion in Russian culture as a demonstration of hostility to the Poles and the cause of Polish independence. Russian was simply perceived as a language of greater cultural importance and as a way of reaching into the wider world. In this respect, Jewish socialists resembled educated Jews throughout the Pale and Eastern Europe. This group tended, irrespective of the ethnicity of the particular population in whose midst they were located, to speak the language of the dominant imperial power—which at the time was either German or Russian. But in an era of rising nationalism, particularly Polish nationalism, there was no explanation that the Poles would accept for Jews speaking and teaching Russian on Polish territory.

Then there was the other side of the problem. In some cases, when Jews did join national socialist movements, they were attacked by the Great Russians. The liberals and socialists from this nationality contended that such action constituted a weakening of a unified socialist movement. They argued the necessity of maintaining unity. For them, it was only natural and proper that a unified movement be one in which the Russian language and culture were dominant. There was no easy solution for the Jewish socialists. Language and culture could no longer be defined as politically neutral. The use of Russian or Polish evoked hostility from either side. Yiddish, then, seemed an expedient in extracating themselves from this cultural political cross fire.

This cultural struggle and the rise of nationalism in the Russian and Austro-Hungarian empires sensitized the Jewish socialists to their own position. The fact that socialist parties also followed the contours of the national divisions made them even more alert to their own base. Despite their cosmopolitan identities and allegiances, the examples of national socialist parties struggling with one another and marking out their own political and territorial preserves made the Jewish socialists ever more jealous and protective of their own national constituency.[85]

The decision to go to the masses in 1893 and 1894 rapidly accelerated the process leading to the formation of a Jewish labor movement. The outlines of this process were, to be sure, already embedded in the virtually ethnically homogeneous circles. But various aspects of the circle did impede its evolution. Assimilation was not a stated formal objective of the circle movement, although it was an unintended, almost necessary, outcome of a successfully functioning circle. The Jewish students and intellectuals were the dominant element in the organization with respect to leadership and to the setting of the hierarchy of values. Even the physical location, apart from the shop or the immediate work area, contributed to this tone. Thus, in forging a socialist workers' elite, the intended goal, Russian was the language of communication, although the workers generally had a poor command of it. They read Russian literature and scientific materials that were, of course, printed in Russian. The Yiddish-speaking worker members did not contest this. Indeed, they wanted to emulate their mentors and become educated cosmopolitans. Few, if any, questioned that this socialization process would lead to the transformation of the Yiddish-speaking worker into a Russian-speaking individual immersed in Russian culture.

Paradoxically, it was this individual by-product of the circle movement that in large part provided the leverage for the policy change to mass agitation. Whether owing to the motives of those who joined or to the socialization experience itself, many workers who had benefitted from their education within the circle were reluctant to commit themselves to spending more years back in their shops and factories, even as messengers of socialism. These fledgling intellectuals and cosmopolitans were more interested in furthering their own individual causes. In their pursuit of a socialist transformation of society, the radical intellectuals and students had caused the social transformation of individuals for whom socialism was not a top priority.

The socialist students and intellectuals who remained faithful to the radical movement were, unbeknownst to themselves, about to undergo their own personal transformation. Their decision to go to the Jewish masses set into motion a chain of events that led to their becoming increasingly Jewish in their interests and orientations. These unintended consequences flowing from this change in policy made not only themselves as individuals more Jewish, but their movement as well.

What did going to the masses mean? First, it meant that the intellectuals approached the workers on the workers' turf. This meant going into the shops and factories and workers' cafes. It also involved intellectuals assuming the jobs of workers. All this implied an interesting reversal of the experience of the circles. In this new phase, it was the radical intellectuals who were, initially at least, cast in the role of pupils. It was they who tried to emulate the workers on the job and in the cafes. They were now interacting with workers in places where the latter set the tone. Here the various norms and values pertaining to various aspects of the lives of workers strongly confronted those of the socialists. In short, the issue of who was to do the socializing and who was to be socialized was very much in doubt.

There was another aspect of the agitation campaign that contrasts with the experience of the circles. Jews in the circles, leaders as well as workers-students, generally were outside of the Jewish milieu. Other than the educational feature of the circle, there was little else that drew from or related to Jewish tradition. In this way also, the circle drew Jews away from the Jewish community toward assimilationism. But the situation was quite different during the period of agitation. Here, the radicals in their turn to the masses utilized the traditions and organizational forms of the Jewish community. In their organization of workers, the socialists built upon existing structures like guilds and mutual aid associations which already honeycombed the Pale. They also utilized religious forms in their ceremonies and political or labor activities. Thus, workers prior to a strike would take a solemn pledge to remain faithful to the strike, sometimes even using the same language as they did in the synagogue. Initiation ceremonies would be conducted in the spirit, if not the form, of a religious service. The melodies of songs written by socialists to arouse the labor movement among the Jewish workers were often taken from those heard in the synagogues. Even words associated with religion were adopted by the movement and utilized in a context similar to the religious one; that is, the word for excommunication became the term for economic boycott.[86]

The impact of this was to solidify the association between the radicals and the developing labor movement on the one hand and the Jewish people on the other. In their quest to bring socialism to the masses, the Jewish socialist assimilators found themselves inadvertently strengthening the cohesion of the Jewish community. Ironically, this happened at the same time that other forces, particularly urbanization, capitalism, and industrialism, were undermining the solidarity of the traditional Jewish way of life. They little suspected or desired that their activities would lead to the strengthening of the barriers that would separate them and their worker constituents from intimate contact with non-Jews. These Jewish nationals were unwittingly becoming a force for the cohesion of the Jewish community at a time when the other institutions of the community, particularly religion, were gradually becoming less capable of performing that function. This would be seen most clearly after the turn of the century when the socialists erected their most prominent organizational edifice.

THE USE OF YIDDISH

One of the principal centerpieces of this general development emanated from the socialists' decision to use Yiddish as the language of their movement. The medium of communication proved to be a central element in the new relationship and a vital factor in the spawning of a Jewish socialist movement. At the heart of the matter was the fact that the Jewish masses' language was Yiddish and the radicals' language was Russian. Once the die had been cast to go to the Jewish workers in their shops, streets, and cafes, the radical intellectuals had no choice but to use Yiddish. Thus, these Jewish socialist Russian-speaking cosmopolitan intellectuals, who only a short time earlier had been so contemptuous of this "jargon," now found themselves cramming to learn it. By adopting Yiddish, they set into motion a process that Yiddishized them and their movement in Russia and later in America.

It is important at this point to be cognizant of the status of Yiddish in the Russian Jewish community. Yiddish was the language of the Eastern European Diaspora. Originally it was a Middle High German dialect adopted by the Jews during their stay in Germany between the thirteenth and fifteenth centuries. Hebrew letters, words, and grammatical style were mixed in with it. Throughout the following centuries the vocabulary varied from area to area as words from local languages like Ukrainian or Polish were added on an unsystematic basis.

Throughout most of its existence Yiddish was primarily an oral language. Prior to the eighteenth century virtually the only books written in it were religious works for women, who were ignorant of Hebrew. In the nineteenth century the Hasidic movement, in its attempt to reach the masses, published its works in Yiddish. And in the same century the men of the *Haskalah* followed the same path, also increasing the store of Yiddish written material. By the mid-nineteenth century more secular and less serious works were published that gained a large audience. These were "soap opera" type novels or stories designed to entertain the Yiddish masses. In this period Yiddish lacked a rich and varied literature.

It was not a language associated with the educated members of the Jewish community. Although those with religious education would use it for everyday speech, Hebrew was reserved for dealing with the Torah and other things religious. The secularly educated viewed it with disdain. For them, it was a tongue of the streets, a language lacking in the more cultivated qualities. As Lucy Dawidowicz expressed it, ". . . unlike Hebrew, Yiddish possessed a mass culture before it attained high culture. The increasing vulgarity of that mass culture and its sub-literary productions elicited contempt for Yiddish among people with more refined literary tastes."[87]

It was not only the vulgarity of Yiddish that disturbed Jews of this strata. For those with higher secular education or those with aspirations to become socially mobile, Yiddish was an unpleasant obstacle or stigma. The identification of Jews with Yiddish inhibited their acceptance as peers by educated and cultured Christians. In their own quest for higher status, which usually meant assimilation, these Jews took great pains to put as much social distance between themselves and the Yiddish-speaking masses as possible. Many, indeed, conscientiously unlearned or forgot this "jargon." They also expected and hoped that over time Yiddish would die out as Jews became more integrated into their societies.

In the 1870s a few educated Jews in Russia had been concerned about the political fate of the Jewish masses from a very sympathetic and positive point of view. However, they chose to propagandize in Hebrew rather than in Yiddish. Yiddish for them was a dying language reflecting the rather sad experiences of an exiled people. In this, they anticipated the Zionist reaction to Yiddish a few decades later. In this decade, one of their number, P. Smolenskin via his newspaper, *Ha-Shahar*, or *Dawn*, realized the political importance of language in the Jewish people's struggle for dignity and a national existence. About Hebrew, he wrote: "It confers honor on us, girds us with strength, unites us into one. All nations seek to perpetuate their names. All conquered peoples dream of a day when they will regain their independence. . . . We have neither monuments nor a country at present. Only one relic remains from the ruins of our ancient glory— the Hebrew language."[88] The educated strata paid little attention to the growing popularity of Yiddish literature among the Jewish masses from the 1870s on. This, then, was the cultural legacy that the educated Jewish radicals inherited. There was little or nothing in their backgrounds from which they could draw to develop a positive feeling toward Yiddish. Initially they used Yiddish simply because it was politically expedient. The only thing positive about Yiddish as far as they were concerned was the fact that it was the mother tongue of about 97 percent of the Jews in Russia.

Their decision to learn and speak Yiddish had implications for communication far beyond that of learning the meaning of words. The workers were provided with the example of highly educated young men and women coming amongst them and struggling to learn their language. This action was probably almost as important for them as the message that these radicals preached. Unintentionally, by their embracing Yiddish, they reduced the social barriers that separated themselves as higher strata from the masses. In so doing, they facilitated communication with these people. Hitherto, these educated socialists had spoken to them, or at least to some of them, of a socialist society—an egalitarian society, which the masses would bring into being. But this message had been preached through a medium that implied something quite different. The use of Russian or Hebrew reflected a condescension and belittling of the very force that was being so highly praised. Now, for the first time, there was a basic congruence between form and content. This strengthened the masses' receptivity to the message as well as the social bonds between the Jewish radical intelligentsia and the Jewish masses. It was truly an historic moment for both.

The socialists' resolve to use Yiddish in their work with the masses was only the first step in the process of the Yiddishization of socialism. The next step followed from their realization that they were not very adept in their use of the language. They had been too far removed from it, and despite their efforts it would take time before they could become well-versed in it. The language was only one aspect of a larger problem. They also realized that they lacked an adequate appreciation and knowledge of the way of life of the common people which would be needed to work skillfully with them. To remedy this, the radicals sought out the help of an element in the Jewish community that was well-versed in Yiddish and well-acquainted with the sociology and psychology of the masses. It was largely from among the *polu-intelligent* or demiintellectual that the needed services were obtained.

The *polu-intelligent* was typically a former yeshiva student studying for a university entrance examination. He did this as an external student of a gymnasium, as the severe restrictions in the latter 1880s had barred the doors of the gymnasium to all but a very few Jews. In the late 1880s and early and mid-1890s, these students formed a large group that was called *eksternichestvo*. This group was to be the link between the Russian-speaking socialist leaders and the Yiddish rank and file.

There were some important differences between the *polu-intelligent* and the young socialists. First, the former did not have as expedient a view of their linguistic and cultural mission among the masses as did the radicals. The *polu-intelligent* tended to have a more intrinsically favorable view of Yiddish, some even being very enthusiastic about it. Second, they tended not to be very ardent socialists. Yet very soon after their recruitment into the movement, they found themselves in important and strategic positions thus tilting the movement in a more Yiddish direction then had been anticipated by the socialists.[89] The socialist leaders were aware of this but were not in a position to do anything about it. John Mil aptly summarized the situation: "The transfer from Russian to Yiddish opened wide the doors for an invasion of elements which hitherto had stood outside the movement or had been only weakly linked with it. . . . Their exact knowledge of the psychology, traditions, and customs of the Jewish masses enabled them to take up positions within the movement as translators . . . lecturers and agitators."[90]

Another factor was also responsible for tilting the movement in a more Yiddish direction. Because of a shortage of Yiddish books dealing with socialism and other subjects, the movement turned to Yiddish writers to remedy this situation. The radical intellectuals, concerned with in general and in the area of socialism in particular, found themselves in the position of writing and sponsoring the translation into Yiddish of Russian and Western works of literature and science as well as works on socialism. They also supported the writing of novels and stories in Yiddish containing themes dealing with the lives and conditions of the Jewish masses. By the mid-1890s the socialist movement was publishing the first Yiddish newsletters and newspaper in the czarist empire. By the turn of the century and immediately thereafter, the radicals discovered that their movement was one of the principal sources of Jewish culture and indeed a central fount of a Yiddish renaissance.

The success of the radical intellectuals in broadening the base of Yiddish culture had two consequences that they had neither planned nor desired. Much of the Yiddish literature—some of which had been sponsored by the socialists themselves—placed in the workers' libraries by polu-intelligent librarians was favorable to colonization of Palestine or was of a kind the socialists felt was too romantic, emotional, or mystical. Nor did this literature serve the end of social protest. The widespread popularity of these works, however, made it difficult for the socialists to dissociate them from the socialist cause.

In addition, by creating a richer and more varied Yiddish language and culture, the radicals were also responsible for helping to dissipate the stigma attached to it. As a result, Yiddish ceased to be the almost exclusive preserve of the Jewish working class and began to gain a broader appeal and acceptance throughout the other Jewish classes. As one of the popular writers they originally had claimed as their own wrote in 1910: "No single place, no minute in time, no class in our nation has an exclusive right to Yiddish. Everything, everywhere belongs to it." [91] But the radicals had never intended to unite the classes in the Jewish community. In fact, this unity undermined their mission as socialists, which was to divide the classes and foster class consciousness and conflict, not to foster Jewish consciousness.

They also found that they had undermined themselves in another related way. Again, contrary to their intentions, they had strengthened Jewish separateness. As Russified cosmopolitan socialists, they were deeply committed to a unified socialist movement that would encompass all nationalities. As Marxists, they believed that economic factors and class consciousness would eventually override national, ethnic, or racial distinctions. But in a short period of time, they had become the unwitting, but nevertheless key, instruments in the development of a vigorous and rich culture that served to keep Jewish masses separate and apart from their class counterparts among other nationalities.

As this general process was unfolding, however, the initial attitudes and feelings toward Yiddish on the part of the radicals were also being subjected to change. The conceptualization of Yiddish as primarily a tool was progressively eroded. In its stead, there grew the stance that Yiddish was a noble and worthy expression of a strong Jewish proletariat. This position was to be reinforced as a result of the bitter internecine political war with the Zionists in the latter 1890s and early 1900s. The Zionist attack on Yiddish as a doomed tongue and summation of a heritage of oppression and degradation strengthened the Jewish socialists' attachment to it. The confluence of all these factors shortly produced a socialist movement inextricably bound with Yiddish, a thoroughly Yiddish socialist movement.[92]

The emotional and political bond between Yiddish and socialism was soon to bring the movement full circle from its earlier association with assimilationism. The wheels were now set into motion that would carry the movement of Jewish socialists onto the tracks of separatism. Despite the continued obeisance to the long-range goal of a universalistic and egalitarian socialist society, the Jewish socialists, in their deepening affection for and immersion in Yiddish, as well as in their near-exclusive work with Jews, soon found themselves placed into a situation where their movement was to become a significant obstacle to the realization of their desired end. And it was Yiddish and their relationship to it that stood at the focal point of this development.

LEADER AND MASS LINKS

Until the socialists decided to go to the Jewish masses, they found the points of commonality, as well as bases for affection between themselves and the masses were quite limited. True, both the workers and the intellectual radicals were Jews and thus shared a similar history and heritage; but this Jewishness meant different things to each of the parties. Religion was one of the cornerstones of the Jewishness of the masses. Although by the 1880s many, particularly in the cities, could no longer be defined as devout, they still remained immersed in religious customs and regarded rabbis and Judaic laws as worthy of respect. The radicals, on the other hand, were a different breed of Jews. They were not immersed in religious customs nor did they view virtually any aspect of traditional Judaism with awe or respect. In this sense, they remained fairly consistent both before and after the decision to agitate among the workers. The culture of the masses was shaped by Judaism, Yiddish, and associational and institutional byproducts of their low-level occupations. Again, as we have seen, this was quite different from the culture of the radicals. For them, their culture was formed by Western secular values and ideas, Russian, and associational and institutional by-products flowing from socialism and their elevated educational status.

They did, however, share other things stemming from their common Jewish backgrounds. Anti-Semitism and national divisions within the czarist empire kept them confined against their wills in the same community. Radical Jews were probably more conscious of their victimization by these forces, for they had tried manifestly to overcome them, though without much success. Anti-Semitism and the parochialism of national feelings were both negative sources linking the fates and lives of the radicals and the masses. Negative forces, especially when they are also forces over which the targets have little influence, can prove tenuous sources of unity and common action.

The negativity can easily serve to foster self-hatred and, if sufficiently powerful, can produce internal divisions in the target community, as well as resignation and apathy. Also, there were numerous indications during the liberal years associated with the reign of Alexander II that when anti-Semitic barriers were lowered, educated and ambitious Jews, both radical and nonradical, would seize such opportunities to make the jump that would carry them beyond the boundaries of the community of their coreligionists. There is little reason to doubt that had these more liberal policies concerning Jews continued and become more widespread, increasing numbers of Jews would have moved toward assimilationism, thus weakening and fragmenting the strength and unity of the Jewish community.

The virulent resurgence of official and mass anti-Semitism in the 1880s and the firmness of national divisions in the czarist empire reversed this tendency and threw the socialists back toward the Jewish community and a Jewish identity. This time, particularly after the decision to work among the Jewish masses, they happened upon Yiddish. In addition to being the expression of the Jewish masses, it also had the virtue as far as the socialists were concerned of being an item unencumbered with religious baggage. Yiddish, then, was the one positive element upon which a Jewish identity could be constructed without having anything to do with religion. Their seizing upon Yiddish, together with their intimate association with the Jewish masses, provided them with both a source of positive Jewish identity for themselves and a cement that bound them to the Jewish masses.

The radicals' identification with and affirmation of Yiddish had implications beyond these immediate functions. As they used the language, wrote in it, and built upon it, these Jewish socialists forged the links that bound socialism to Jewishness. Through their affection for and work with Yiddish, they became the architects for a rich and vibrant culture that enriched the lives of the Jewish masses and strengthened a Jewish identity and sense of peoplehood. In so doing, these Jewish socialists found themselves in the position of reinforcing those aspects that separated themselves and their movement from the socialism that was emerging among the other nationalities in Russia at the turn of the century. Before, it had been the aversion of the other nationalities that had helped to keep the Jews apart. Now, thanks in large part to the efforts of the Jewish socialists, the very richness and attraction of a Jewish culture served as a positive polar force that increasingly confined the socialist movement they were creating into a Jewish orbit. Thus, by the end of the century, these Jewish socialists had created in Russia and then in America a movement that was as Jewish as it was socialist. Its most powerful and concrete form took expression in the General Jewish Workers Union in Russia and Poland, or the Bund.

THE BUND

The Bund was formed in Vilna in 1897 in the heart of the largest concentration of Jewish workers in the czarist Empire. It was an amalgamation of various Jewish socialist groups from throughout the Pale,
with the one from Vilna being the most important. The Bund was both
a centralized political organization and a mass movement with economic and political objectives. It was a structure that was at the same
time a political party and a labor union. Its membership was principally derived from two different strata in the Jewish community, intellectuals including the *polu-intelligent* on the one hand, and workers on the other. This was reflected in the social makeup of its 13
founders—five were intellectuals, and eight were artisans. The Bund
was an organization that was simultaneously located in Poland and
Russia. Finally, although committed to the cause of international socialism, it was an exclusively Jewish organization working among a
Jewish population at a time of rising national consciousness. It is
perhaps ironical that within a year of the Bund's founding, two other
organizations formally came into being, each of which represented
one of the two competing ideologies competing within the Bund. On
the Jewish nationalism side there was the World Zionist Organization
(1897) and on the international socialist end, the Russian Social Democratic Labor party (RSDLP, 1898). These organizations and the ideologies that they represented were to become bitter adversaries of the
Bund and its hope to combine within one body socialism and Jewish
nationalism.

Before continuing with our examination of the Bund, two observations should be made. One, the Bund emerged out of and enriched a
tradition of Jewish participation in radical causes. From the 1860s
through the near revolution of 1905, Jews were disproportionately
represented among the leadership and ranks of revolutionary movements. Jews were among the founding fathers of the populists and
were among those instrumental in bringing Marxism to Russia. Their
involvement as part of the rank and file may be gauged by various
police statistics. According to the files of the Third Division, or Russian secret police, Jews constituted about 6½ percent of those arrested
for political offenses between 1873 and 1877, a number that increased
to 14 percent from 1884 to 1890.[93] In 1903 Count Witte, the Minister
of Finance, complained in a conversation with Theodore Herzl that
while the Jews constituted a little more than 5 percent of the total 136
million inhabitants of Russia, they ". . . comprise about 50 percent of
the membership in the revolutionary parties."[94] And from 1903 to
1904, 54 percent of those imprisoned on political grounds were
Jews.[95] These figures are, of course, imprecise. But they do give an estimation, and their general consistency points to their overall, if not
specific, reliability. While it may be true that the police were more
likely to single out Jews for arrest and imprisonment, this should be

balanced by the fact that many Jews in no way considered themselves to be Jews. When they were asked their nationality by police and judicial authorities, these Jews would not identify themselves as such, preferring instead to proclaim themselves as Russian or some other national identity. In addition, the non-Yiddish speaking police had difficulty keeping Yiddish speaking radicals under close surveillance.

The second observation concerns Jewish participation in radical, socialist, and revolutionary movements after the formation of the Bund. The Bund did not have a monopoly on Jews who participated in such movements. Jews were to be found in the ranks of the Russian Social Democrats, the Bolsheviks, the Mensheviks, the Socialist-Revolutionaries, anarchists, and labor Zionists, as well as the Bund. Many of these, such as Trotsky, were to become bitter enemies of the Bund for various reasons. Although the Bund and its policies did not encompass all Jews who considered themselves to be radicals or who joined radical organizations, it was the one movement that encompassed the largest number of Jews and made the most significant impact on the Jewish community in Russia. The organizers of the Bund did not found this organization for the purpose of establishing a separate Jewish socialist organization. At the time of its founding, the Bundists generally regarded their creation as a subsection of Russian social democracy. In fact, during the first year of its existence, the Bund's Central Committee devoted much of its time and energies to building a united Russian social democratic party. The founding conference of the Russian Social Democratic Labor party in 1898 came about largely as a result of the Bund's efforts. It should also be noted that at the Bund's founding congress in 1897, the language spoken was Russian, and only one delegate there spoke in Yiddish.[96]

However, once again, regardless of the actors' intentions, the seeds for a uniquely Jewish socialist movement were present at the time of the Bund's birth. The factors producing this result were very much interrelated. First, as mentioned above, there was no general Russian social democratic movement in the 1890s to guide and advise the Jewish socialists, particularly the key Vilna Social Democratic group, the core of the Bund. This meant that the Vilna group and other Jewish socialist groups were left very much on their own. They had to chart out their own course and, very importantly, rely on their own resources.

The second factor was the most precious of their resources, responsive Jewish workers. The Vilna Group experienced success, or at least relative success, in their ventures among the Jews. Again, there was no conscious attempt to build a Jewish movement. Gradually and inexorably they moved in that direction. In 1894, after some debate, the Group utilized the anti-Semitic legislation of the czarist government to incite Jewish workers against the state. The attacks by Joseph Pilsudski and other leaders of the Polish Socialist party against their

Russian orientation also pushed the Group further into the arms of the accepting Jewish masses.[97]

By 1895 the ideologues of the group began to seek out intellectual and ideological justification for the pragmatic action in which they were engaged. Lev Martov, a leading figure of the Vilna organization and later of the Bund, developed a rationale that the Bund later also adopted as its own. Martov argued that the Jewish masses were in a very vulnerable position. Bourgeois Jews had either abandoned them or provided them with treacherous leadership. Also, they had no non-Jewish socialists to protect their interests and articulate their needs and demands. Consequently, Jewish socialists had to step into this void.

On a more abstract level, Martov contended that national states were important social forms whose existence socilaists had to recognize. The struggle for socialism could not be conducted without recognizing the interdependence of socialism and nationalism. Oppression and disabilities in the national realm impeded the development of the struggle in the arena of class. The Jews and their attitude toward their oppressed national status was his case in point. "A working class which passively accepts its inferior national status, such a working class will hardly be able to revolt against its inferior *class* status. Because the national passivity of the Jewish masses prevents the development of class consciousness, the task of awakening both the national and the class consciousness must proceed on parallel lines." [98]

The Bund's leaders went on to argue that the special problems of the Jewish worker demanded a special organization. As the Jewish worker suffered the double yoke of oppression as a Jew and as a worker, he needed an organization that would fight for both these interests, while at the same time it would not neglect its broader socialist responsibilities. Arkady Kremer, in the keynote speech at the founding conference of the Bund, dealt with the aims of the organization:

A general union of all Jewish socialist organizations will have as its goal not only the struggle for general Russian political demands; it will also have the special task of defending the specific interests of the Jewish workers, conducting the struggle for the civic rights of the Jewish workers and above all to carry on the struggle against the discriminatory anti-Jewish laws. That is because the Jewish workers suffer not only as workers but also as Jews, and we dare not and cannot remain indifferent at such a time.[99]

No general socialist movement nor one dominated by other nationalities, the Bund contended, could be relied upon to deal successfully with these specific Jewish problems. From the Bund's standpoint, a Jewish socialist organization did not imply the surrender of or even a deviation from the major long-term goal of all socialists—an international classless society. On the contrary, the Bund believed that through its work the attainment of that goal in which they deeply believed would be facilitated. Such an international society would not be realized if its component national elements entered as superordinate or subordinate to one another. A necessary prior condition, assuming the Bund's stance, logically had to be the equality of status for each working class nationality.

The Bund, at the founding congress of the RSDLP, tried to express in writing and formal organizational terms its position concerning the interrelationship of Jewishness and socialism and its conception of itself as a body joining together a particular social group in the context of a universal ideology. Thus, the first RSDLP Constitution contained the following unwieldy and unspecific sentence: "The General Jewish Workers Union in Russia and Poland enters the Party as an autonomous organization, independent only in questions which specifically concern the Jewish proletariat." [100] In its own newspaper, *Die Arbeiterstimme*, the Bund explained its concept of the relationship that obtained between it and the RSDLP. "It is clear that the 'Jewish Union' has no special privileges in the Party. The Party treats the 'Jewish Union' as it does *every* labor organization which defends the special interests of a particular nation . . . The Party does *not* desire that all workers in a united organization dance to one fiddle [emphasis mine]." [101] The Bund also pointed out that it required a measure of independence because of the need to carry on propaganda and organizational work among Jews in Yiddish and because of the special problems of the Jewish proletariat. The Bund, as asserted in the article, was the representative of the Jewish working class in the Party. [102] This formal relationship and the Bund's self-conception were not seriously challenged at the time but were very shortly to become the basis of a bitter conflict that drove the Bund out of the party in 1903.

BECOMING A JEWISH ORGANIZATION

In this period from 1898 to 1903, the Bund found itself constantly torn by the various forces coexisting within it. The dominant and most common expression of these internal struggles inevitably took the form of one between Jewish nationalism and universal socialism. These struggles were also very much related to events, new conditions, and constant challenges from within the Jewish and socialist communities. The overall weight of these pressures pushed them inexorably onto the path of a Jewish organization.

One of the first of these events occurred in 1898—most of the original Bund leadership was arrested, and the few who escaped this fate fled into exile. The Bund struggled to recover from this near fatal blow. In its battle for survival, it found a fresh source from which to draw new recruits: Jewish students, many of whom were studying abroad in places like Switzerland.

These students were part of a new generation. They differed from the older generation, as represented by the imprisoned Bund leaders, in several important respects. First, they were not ardent socialists. Second, they did not have a negative attitude toward Jewish nationalism. Indeed, this was a moving political force for them. Anti-Semitic policies of the czarist government, particularly the imposition of the strict quota system in schools, and the rising nationalism of other groups in the Russian and Austro-Hungarian empires stirred their own national consciousness. Although many were attracted to Zionism, others were repelled by this movement's politics. These young people wanted to do something about conditions in Russia, but the leaders of mainstream Zionism urged that Zionists not become involved in the politics of the country in which they resided. The organization's objective was to secure the cooperation or, at the very least, the neutrality of the Diaspora countries in order to be better able to attain its primary goal—a Jewish state. This was not an acceptable position for those Jews who felt that the conditions in Russia were intolerable for Jews. Because Zionism was flawed for them, they sought out other vehicles through which their Jewish nationalist feelings could be expressed.

This search led many to the Bund. For them the Bund's socialism was not the prime attraction. Rather it was the fact that the Bund was a meaningful force for Jewish civil rights and pride.[103] One of these students whose quest led him to the Bund wrote in 1899:

In order to win equal rights for Jews as a nation, it was essential to create or to mark off an independent revolutionary force. It was essential to put an end to the ancient passivity of the Jews. About the "Bund" we knew little. . . . Our idea of it was covered by mysticism. We not only respected it. We believed in it. We searched for the Bund and at the same time the Bund was searching for us.[104]

These were the Jews that the Bundists felt it necessary to recruit in order to stay alive. In order to attract them, keep them, and win them from Zionism, the Bundist leaders had to bend even more in a Jewish direction. Once in the organization, these bright, energetic, and nationalistic students moved into cadre and leadership positions, in part filling the void created by the mass arrests of 1898. In these posts, they allied themselves with the *polu-intelligent* to pressure the Bund to turn into an instrument for the expression of their primarily Jewish interests and concerns. The original or early Bundist leaders could not successfully resist this pressure. The Jewish workers in the Bund, the rank and file, were generally not troubled by this turn of events. Their socialism was still not that well developed as to cause them to object strenuously. Their own raised Jewish consciousness allowed them to be sympathetic to the direction in which the newcomers were moving the Bund.

At the same time as the *polu-intelligent* and new students, or nonworking-class elements, were ascending in the Bund between 1899 and 1901, the organization was losing its working-class base. One of the factors in the Bund's appeal to Jewish workers was the organization's leadership and militancy as a labor union organization. However, the years between 1899 and 1901 were ones of economic crisis in the Pale as well as in the Russian Empire. The Bund found it exceedingly difficult to wage successful strikes in such an economic environment, particularly in the face or rising unemployment. The Bund's inability to counteract increasing unemployment and falling wages cost it support among the workers.[105] Thus, in a very short period the elements in the Bund that were forces for socialism diminished while those that were more nationalistic grew in number and influence.

This turn of events was reflected in the contrasting actions of the Third and Fourth Bund Congresses of 1899 and 1901. At the Third Congress in 1899, the Bund decisively rejected the principle of Jewish nationhood and the demand for equal national rights for Jews. In 1901 the composition of the Bund had been decisively altered, and the influence of the new elements, particularly in the leadership, was felt. Although the Bund at the Fourth Congress did not explicitly call for equal national rights for a Jewish people, it did go very far in this direction. One of its key resolutions in this area proclaimed: "The congress holds that a state such as Russia, consisting as it does of many nationalities, should in the future, be reconstructed as a federation of nationalities with complete national autonomy for each nationality, independent of the territory in which it is located. *The congress holds that the term 'nation' is also to be applied to the Jewish people* [emphasis mine].[106]

The passage of that resolution symbolized the weakness of the Bundist socialists, the older leaders of the organization. Most were opposed to the notion of nonterritorial autonomy and Jewish nationalism. But they were unwilling to risk tearing their beloved Bund apart over the issue. The unity and growth of the Bund became for them the overriding consideration.[107] In this respect these older Bundists differed from Lenin, who was more than willing to split his organization in the quest for his ideological objectives.

The influence of these veterans and the organization's commitment to the ideal of the unity of the working classes were not entirely exhausted. Thus, in the context of the same resolution, the Bund appeared to draw back from pressing for national autonomy. Instead, the Congress resolved that ". . . for the time the struggle is to be carried on only against all discriminatory laws directed against Jews."[108] This was quite different from committing the Bund to promote Jewish nationalism.

In line with this apparent volta face, the Bund, in the form of a resolution, took the extraordinary step of issuing a warning to itself. In this resolution, the hazard of emphasizing special Jewish problems was highlighted. Such a policy, from the point of view of the resolution's sponsors, ran the risk of isolating the Jewish workers from their class comrades of other nationalities and at the same time pushing them closer to the Zionist camp. Thus, the Bund resolved ". . . to be careful not to fan the flame of national feeling, for that will only obscure the class consciousness of the proletariat and lead to chauvinism." [109] But the forces for Jewish separatism within the Bund were not content to let the matter rest. They pushed for a change in the official relationship of the Bund within the RSDLP that would reflect the Bund's evolving position on the nationality issue. This resolution stated: "Conceiving the Russian Social Democratic Labor Party to be a federated Social Democratic Party uniting all ethnic groups residing in the Russian state, the Congress resolves that the Bund, as a representative of the Jewish proletariat, would enter it as a federated part and directs the Central Committee of the Bund to implement this decision." [110] The adoption of this resolution and the premises underlying it set the Bund on a collision course with the RSDLP, particularly its Lenin-led *Iskra* faction.

THE BUND'S CLASH WITH THE RSDLP AND LENIN

Lenin and his men centered around the Party paper, *Iskra,* did not view the developments in the Bund with equanimity. Even before the Bund's 1901 congress, this faction had been vociferous opponents of the Bund. Their difference with the Bund was not on the order of tactics or timing; it was much more fundamental. The heart of it revolved around the very existence of the Bund and the Bund's conception of itself.

Lenin insisted that the Bund was constructed around a flawed premise—that a Jewish nation existed. There was no scientific basis for Jewish nationhood, he contended. The Jews were not a race; they lacked the two fundamental criteria necessary to constitute themselves a nation—a separate territory and a common language. Despairingly, but ironically and almost prophetically, he added: "All that remains for the Bundists is to develop the theory of a separate Russian-Jewish nation, whose language is Yiddish and their territory the Pale of Settlement." [111] Objectively, from Lenin's perspective, the Bund was stimulating the idea of nationhood among Jews at the same time that capitalism and industrialization were undermining the separate or insulated subeconomies that served as the economic base for national and ethnic distinctions. Lenin contended that the Bund, despite its formal objectives, was working against the best interests of the Jewish proletariat as well as the socialist movement. Lenin held the Bund guilty of strengthening the reactionary elements in the Jewish community, fostering a ghetto mentality, and isolating the Jewish workers from the common struggle of all proletarians.

At the same time, Lenin was very much aware of the problem of national oppression and anti-Semitism. For him, the struggle against national oppression and the battle for full and equal civil and political rights for all ethnic groups were integral elements of the socialist movement. He believed, however, that the only way in which these goals could be attained was through the victory of a united proletariat. The Bund, then, was delaying the eradication of anti-Semitism by weakening proletarian unity. It was not separateness and isolation that would benefit the Jews, Lenin argued, but assimilation. This, he believed, was the key to the Jewish question, and approvingly he quoted Karl Kautsky: "That [assimilation] is the only possible solution of the Jewish problem, and we should support everything that makes for the ending of Jewish isolation." [112] And then he added: "Yet the Bund is resisting this only possible solution for it is not helping to end but to increase and legitimize Jewish isolation." [113]

Lenin was not negative about things Jewish, nor did he wish to appear as if he were. There were, he contended, very positive elements in Jewish culture. However, these could only flourish when Jews were allowed to and did avail themselves of the opportunity to become assimilated. Thus, he pointed to the civilized world of Western Europe where, unlike Russia and Galicia, the Jews had been liberated from their enforced caste status. "There the great world-progressive features of Jewish culture stand clearly revealed: its internationalism, its identification with the advanced movements of the epoch (the percentage of Jews in the democratic and proletarian movements is everywhere higher than the percentage of Jews in the population)." [114] And again it was the Bund in alliance with the rabbis and Jewish bourgeoisie that blocked the Russian Jews from embarking on this progressive path by reinforcing their isolation. [115]

The Bund's battle with Lenin and its differences with the RSDLP came to a head in 1903 at the Second Congress of the party. By this time the Bund had grown accustomed to its independent role among Jews. Although it was in principle a constituent element of the RSDLP and bound by the programs and policies of the party's central organs, in actual practice the situation was different. Day-to-day independent political activities were more important than paper constraints. In fact, the Bund had grown so assertive and sure of its practical independence and monopoly in the Jewish field that in 1903 it criticized an RSDLP unit, in a city where the Bund had no organization, for infringing on its primacy among Jewish workers. This party organization had taken a position on anti-Semitism that differed from that of the Bund and had appealed directly to Jewish workers without mentioning or consulting the Bund. [116]

The Bund's conflict with the RSDLP was heightened by a set of events that took place shortly before the opening of the Party Congress which had the effect of strengthening the hand of the Jewish nationalists within the Bund. The infamous Kishinev massacre of April 1903, several months before the congress, was at the heart of these events. The enormity of the pogrom shocked and terrified the Jewish community and in the process fired up its collective Jewish consciousness. The students, a strata upon which the Bund relied heavily, were particularly incensed, and their Jewish nationalism rose in response. The Bund was swamped by the tidal wave of Jewish nationalism that swept over the Pale.[117]

The Bund itself could not help but respond to this rising force. Its sympathetic response was also motivated by an organizational concern. If the Bund did not react to the strong feelings of the Jewish masses and students, the Zionists most certainly would benefit at the Bund's expense in terms of numbers and prestige. Needless to say, the position of the nationalist element within the Bund was considerably strengthened by these developments. One of the organization's major actions won it the acclaim of almost all strata of the Jewish community. This was the Bund's formation and leadership of Jewish defense forces. The affection and responsiveness of the Jewish people bound the Bund ever closer to a Jewish identity and commitment.

There was yet another aspect of the situation flowing from the Kishinev pogrom that had a similar impact. Neither the RSDLP nor its leaders had firmly, clearly, and consistently denounced the pogrom or taken forceful steps to aid in the defense of the Jewish populace. Leon Trotsky, himself a Jew and a member of the *Iskra* group, defended the Russian socialists' reaction in terms very reminiscent of those of their counterparts in 1881. At a meeting of Jewish students shortly after the pogrom, Trotsky pointed out that the Russian socialists did fight anti-Semitism and cited as specific evidence a leaflet that had been published a few years earlier in his town, Nikolayev. But he added: ". . . there was really no need to fight anti-Semitism *specifically*. Anti-Semitism . . . was nothing but the result of the general unconsciousness of the wide masses. It was therefore necessary to make them conscious and then they would anyhow cast anti-Semitism away. To talk with them specially about Jews was superfluous."[118] This position, as well as the general lack of action by the party on behalf of Jews under attack by pogromists, could not but strengthen the resolve of the Bundists to act as independent agents with respect to the needs and interests of the Jewish people.

The Second Congress of the RSDLP, the arena in which the Bund put forth its demands, was, however, dissimilar from the First Congress. The Second, as opposed to the First, was in actuality the founding conference of the party, according to Isaac Deutscher. Between 1898 and 1903 a significant organization had been forged, with the *Iskra* group at its core, that owed virtually nothing to the work of the first conference. At the Second Congress Lenin and the *Iskra* group, implacable enemies of the Bund, were in the majority and dominated it. They also carefully prepared the battlefield for the confrontation with the Bund. At Lenin's behest, the Bund's request for a change in status was placed as the first item on the agenda.[119] In the course of debate the Bund spelled out the various aspects of the changes it desired. The Bund wanted the right to elect its own central committee and make policy affecting Jews. It also wanted the party to acknowledge its right to be the sole representative of the Jewish workers. It did not matter whether these were Jewish workers concentrated in the tens of thousands and having their own institutions, as in the Pale, or whether they were a mere handful. If they were Jewish, even if they did not speak Yiddish, the Bund demanded the right to a monopoly of representation of them within the party. Peoplehood or nationality and not geography or trade underlay the Bund's claim for organizational exclusiveness with respect to these workers.

Trotsky, encouraged by Lenin, responded vehemently. If only Jews had the right to represent and organize Jewish workers within the party, it logically followed, according to Trotsky, that non-Jewish members of the RSDLP were therefore barred from politicizing Jews. The fact that both Jewish and non-Jewish socialist organizers were comrades in the same party was of little consequence. Ethnicity and not politics was the key factor in the Bund's case. "This," Trotsky pointed out, "was an expression of distrust in the non-Jewish members of the party, a challenge to their internationalist conviction and sentiment." "The Bund," Trotsky exclaimed, "is free not to trust the party, but it cannot expect the party to vote no confidence in its own self." [120] Trotsky also stressed that the internationalist principles of the RSDLP prevented it from accepting the Bund's demands: ". . . to accept such conditions would mean that we acknowledge the bankruptcy of our political morality; it would mean committing political-moral suicide. The congress will not do this." [121]

Trotsky was correct. The Party Congress, led by Lenin, Trotsky, and their associates, refused the Bund's request for a new and special status. The granting of a federative status by the party would have been a de jure acknowledgment that the Bund was a special organ within the party coequal to its central executive bodies and thus a de facto independent organism existing within the body of the party. It would also imply that the party conference was in accord with the philosophical and national premises informing the Bund's request. Lenin and his supporters were unrelenting stalwarts of a strong centralized party. Lenin regarded this mode of organization as essential for the victory of the revolution in the czarist empire. Thus, the Bund could not be allowed in any way to compromise either the principle or the form of a cohesive centralized organization. Lenin summed up his position thusly:

The accursed history of tsarism has left us a legacy of tremendous estrangement between the working classes of the various nationalities which are oppressed by tsarism. This estrangement is a very great evil, a very great obstacle in the struggle against tsarism and we must not legalize this evil or sanctify this shameful state of affairs by establishing the 'principle' of the separateness of parties or 'federation' of parties. . . . The more we realize the necessity for unity, the more firmly we are convinced that a concerted offensive against tsarism is impossible without complete unity, the more obvious the necessity for a centralized organization of the struggle . . . centralism is essential for the success of the struggle of the proletarians of every nationality oppressed by tsarism against tsarism and against the international bourgeoisie which is becoming more and more united.[122]

He also went on to pursue the consequences of the Bund's demand for a federative status.

From the moment you demanded 'federation' instead of autonomy in matters concerning the Jewish proletariat, you were *compelled* to proclaim the Bund an "independent political party" in order to carry out this principle of federation *at all costs.* But by proclaiming the Bund to be an independent political party you reduced your fundamental error in the question of nationalities to an absurdity in a way which *inevitably and necessarily becomes the starting point for a change in the views of the Jewish Proletariat and of Jewish Social Democrats in general* [emphasis mine].[123]

For Lenin, the Bund's request for federation could only lead to its becoming a vehicle for converting both itself and the Jewish workers to the Zionist cause of a Jewish nation and thus separating the Jewish workers from participation in the unified revolutionary struggle.

The Bund attempted to counter these attacks. On a very pragmatic level, the Bundists pointed out that they were in the midst of a struggle with the Zionists for the allegiance of the Jewish masses. In order to compete effectively with this Jewish adversary, the Bund asserted that it needed the support of the RSDLP in the form of the party's recognition of the principle of equality among national groups.

On another level, the Bund contended that the argument that the overthrow of the czarist autocracy would inevitably lead to the solution of the Jewish problem had been overtaken by events, the most significant one being the rise of the Jewish masses. It was they who would be the instrument of deliverance from their oppressors. This did not mean that they would turn their backs on the working classes of other nations, the Bund added. The rise in national feelings among the Jewish masses would be paralleled by an accompanying heightening of the feeling of international solidarity as well. The two sentiments were interrelated, not contradictory, the Bund assured the RSDLP.

But the basis for the Bund's response was the issue of Jewish nationalism. This was at the heart of the controversy and was not a matter that could be compromised. As Vladimir Kosovski, the Bundist spokesman, asserted: "The Jewish working class is at the moment by virtue of language and psychology an individual national entity, and it is therefore as much entitled to National autonomy as any other nation."[124]

One more aspect of the struggle at the conference merits attention. The most vocal and visible opponents of the Bund at the conference were men of Jewish origin such as Martov, Trotsky, Akselrod, and Ginzburg. In fact, the resolution opposing that of the Bund's was introduced by Lev Martov, a former leader of the Bund, and seconded by 12 other delegates, all of whom were Jewish. And Trotsky publicly drew the delegates' attention to this fact. He pointedly added, on one of the rare occasions that he identified himself as a Jew,[125] that all the Jewish endorsers of this resolution, which included himself, ". . . while working in the All-Russian Party, regarded and still regard themselves also as representatives of the Jewish proletariat."[126] At this point a Bund delegate interjected: "Among whom they have never worked."[127] Later, Trotsky responded that: ". . . The claim of the Bund to a role of sole representative of the Jewish proletariat was opposed by my pointing to the fact that many Jewish comrades working among the Jewish workers have not joined the Bund, and yet consider themselves no less representatives of the Jewish proletariat as proletariat."[128]

It became clear to the Bundist leaders that they were engaged in a struggle within a struggle. Their Jewish non-Bundist comrades in the Party were challenging the conceptions of assimilationism versus nationalism, as well as the nature of the organizational structure of the RSDLP. As one prominent Bundist characterized it:

The contention between *Iskra* and the Bund was to a certain extent between assimilationists and nationalists-Yiddishists within the Jewish people itself. The struggle revolved around the question of whether or not the Jewish people in Russia would assimilate; whether there was a need to develop in the Jewish worker a separate Jewish culture, language, literature or no such need; and whether or not there was a need for a separate Jewish workers' organization in order to better guarantee the interests of the Jewish masses.[129]

It is interesting to note here an important distinction in the backgrounds of these two sets of Jewish socialist antagonists. Trotsky and his fellow Jews in the RSDLP and later in the Menshevik and Bolshevik factions generally had been reared in locations outside of or on the periphery of the Jewish community in Russia. The Jewish Bundists, on the other hand, either came of age in the very midst of the Jewish community or became active politically in those areas of the northern Pale where the Jewish proletariat was the most heavily concentrated.[130]

This type of background predisposed Trotsky and other Jewish RSDLPers toward an assimilationist position that, as adults, they typically assumed with great vehemence. For them, the ultimate solution to the Jewish problem would be an internationalist socialist society that paid no heed to distinctions between Jews and non-Jews. To hasten the establishment of such a society, it became necessary, in the view of these assimilationist socialists, for Jews to consider ethnic and religious distinctions between them and non-Jews as irrelevant. The Bund, in Trotsky's eyes, not only saw these distinctions as highly relevant, but, in addition, predicated its actions on distrust for non-Jews, regardless of whether or not they were socialists. This was an anathema to Trotsky. It was not until 1937 that Trotsky was to modify this position. Then, against the backdrop of the Nazi menace, Trotsky asserted that "even under Socialism, it might be necessary for the Jews to settle on a separate territory." [131]

The outcome of the various struggles of the Bund and the RSDLP at the congress was almost inevitable. Although the Bund eventually compromised and withdrew its request for a federative status as well as its insistence that other sections of the party seek the Bund's permission before addressing Yiddish-speaking workers in Bundist regions, this was not enough for the Iskra group. They wanted the unconditional surrender of the Bund. Even when the Bund agreed to be satisfied with a reaffirmation of its 1898 status, the Iskra group branded it as "outrageous." The Bund, then, had no other recourse but to leave the party. Lenin had been correct in his prophecy. The Bund was now a totally independent Jewish socialist party. [132]

This was not a status that the Bundists had actively sought. The Bund had wanted the RSDLP, as the major organizational embodiment of socialism in Russia, to provide its emerging Jewish identity with socialist legitimacy. Even as the Jewish component of its identity had grown stronger, the Bund still wanted to consider itself socialist and be considered by the organs of socialism as part of the universal movement. The RSDLP's decision had the effect of driving the Bund even closer to its accepting and responsive mass base among the Jewish workers. Lenin's prophecy, in part, was a self-fulfilling one.

THE JEWISH ATTRACTION

This mass base among the Jewish workers was the source of the Bund's strength. The Bund did not wish to weaken its bonds with this support even at the cost of injury to its internationalist socialist soul. To have appeared to subordinate its Jewish commitments and loyalty to that of Russian or abstract universal socialism put it in the position of jeopardizing its growing power and emerging leadership of the overall Jewish community. Even though the Bund rejoined the RSDLP in 1906, its withdrawal was a symbolic and concrete turning point. From 1903 on, as it intensively interacted with its mass Jewish base, the Bund became increasingly wedded to the cause of Jewish nationalism.

The Bund was also pushed in this direction by its Zionist antagonists. At the same time it was fighting with the Russian socialists, the Bundists were aware of the inroads that Zionism was making among the Jewish masses and students, its own cherished constituencies. The Labor Zionists in particular gave the Bund cause for concern because of the similarity of their ideology and their direct appeal to the Bund's sources of support. The Bund's response to the Zionist threat was two-fold. On the one hand it lashed out hard on ideological grounds. The attacks centered on the basic premises of Zionism and the political consequences that necessarily flowed from the pursuit of Zionist goals. The Jews, the Bund proclaimed, were not one people. Such a position ignored the important class divisions obtaining in the Jewish community. It served as a fig leaf for Jewish employers while they exploited Jewish workers. This unity theme of the Zionists inhibited the development of class consciousness among the Jewish masses.

The Bundists bitterly attacked the Zionists' call for a territorial solu-tion to the Jewish problem even as they themselves were in the pro-cess of formulating their own nonterritorial solution. The Zionists' ad-vocacy of a Jewish homeland was, in the eyes of the Bund, a form of escapism and surrender. It could only mean that Jewish workers had to despair of ever achieving full and equal political, civil, and eco-nomic rights in the lands where they were then located. By holding forth this utopian vision, the Zionists, according to the Bund, were deflecting the Jewish workers from mobilizing their energies to engage in the class struggle where they worked and lived. Ironically, much of the Bund's case against Zionism had the familiar ring of Lenin to it.[133]

At the same time the Bund held the Zionists guilty of weakening the common struggle for socialism that was being waged by various nationalities. The Zionists gave credence to the charge that the Jews were strangers or foreigners in Russia or Poland. It thereby isolated the Jewish workers' cause from that of his non-Jewish neighbors. From the Bundist point of view, this was undermining the basis for common understanding and common struggle between the Jewish and non-Jewish masses.

The Bund also objected to the Zionists' derision of Yiddish and to the prominence that they attached to Hebrew. Hebrew, as far as the Bund was concerned, was the language of the rabbis and a few vision-aries. The Zionists' attitude toward Hebrew symbolized their distance from the Jewish masses. Their contempt for Yiddish, the language of the masses and of their struggles, also symbolized in Bundist eyes their contempt for the actual situation of the masses. As one Bundist put it: "He who scoffs at Yiddish, scoffs at the Jewish people; he is only half a Jew." [134]

The Bund, however, could not rely solely on argumentation and the refutation of Zionist positions to protect its Jewish flank from this ad-versary. The Zionists had struck a very responsive chord among Jews. Also, they were not only stoking the fires of nationalism among Jews, they were being propelled by these forces as well. In order for the Bund to properly meet the Zionist challenge, it had to face the reality of the rising sentiment of nationalism among the Jewish masses and students. This basic issue had to be constructively dealt with if the

Bund was to maintain its standing. "It is ridiculous," the Bundists argued, "to say that this problem is of no concern to the Jewish masses. This is an argument that will convince nobody. On the contrary, the masses are too nationalistically inclined, and it behooves us Social Democrats to convince them that nationalism is not Chauvinism." [135]

The Bund's acceptance of the rising nationalist sentiment among the Jewish masses in turn legitimated and accelerated its own stimulation of that sentiment, much of it in ways that resembled those of their Zionist competitors. Like them, it increasingly emphasized the concern and pride that it had for the Jewish component of the workers' identity. Similar to the Zionists, the Bundists came to the position that the Jews were a nation. And, together with the Zionists, the Bund shared the belief that the solution to the Jewish problem revolved around the attainment and legitimation of the status of nation and the rights and privileges associated with it. But the Bund did not concur on a territorial format and it continued to persist in its allegiance to socialism.

The pressures, then, from both the Zionists and the Russian Social Democrats were significant factors in pushing the Bund toward a more discernible Jewish orientation. An even more significant factor was the existence of a mass political base and the Bund's ongoing interaction with it. Maintaining and nurturing this base largely determined the type of politics that the Bund pursued both inside and outside of the Jewish community.

THE POWER OF THE BUND

At the turn of the century and into the first decade of the 1900s, no other socialist or union organization in Russia, Jewish or not, rivaled the Bund in terms of the breadth and depth of its supporters. [136] However, the establishment of such a base as well as its maintenance and growth were like magnetic forces in pulling the Bund closer to a Jewish identity. The closer the Bund got to the Jewish masses and the more overtly and uniquely Jewish its themes and action, the larger and more responsive its Jewish support became. The Bund found that the national pride being evoked by the Jewish masses was redounding to the organization's benefit. The Bund's very triumph had set into motion a cyclical process in which the Bund became the captive of events, in many cases events that it had also precipitated. The enthusiasm of the Jewish masses for the Bund drew it deeper and deeper into the confines of the Jewish community. This did not result in the abandonment of socialism, but it did mean that the socialism the Bund was to advocate was very much one that had a Jewish brand to it.

The Bund, after struggling back from the mass arrests of 1898, experienced a rapid growth in membership and even greater growth in terms of communal influence. By 1900 it claimed a membership of 5600. Three years later the figure had risen to 30,000. And at its height in 1906, the Bund had 40,000 organized supporters. This growth occurred in the face of constant police intimidation and arrests. The number of Bundists arrested mirrors the membership growth curve—1000 in 1900; 2180 between 1901 and 1903; and 4467 in 1904.[137]

Another numerical indication of the Bund's influence can be ascertained from the number of meetings that it sponsored as well as the attendance at such meetings. From May 1901 to June 1903, the Bund organized 260 public meetings, with a total approximate attendance of 36,900. In the following year the number of meetings jumped to 429, with a total attendance of 74,162. There was also a similar pattern with respect to the number of leaflets it distributed. From 1901 to 1903 the number of leaflets passed out was 347,150. In the following year, the number almost doubled, to 686,000 pieces.[138]

The Bund also led and organized strikes among Jewish workers. Between 1897 and 1900 the Bund successfully conducted 312 strikes.[139] It was also an important organizer and stimulant of the numerous strikes that broke out from 1900 to 1904. During this period there were more than 1600 strikes among Jewish workers in the Pale. The number of strikers per thousand in these years was 240 for Jewish workers, a figure almost double that of their Russian counterparts. There were significant side features to these strikes. In the victorious strikes their benefits were short-lived. And the large majority occurred in shops employing less than 20 workers.[140]

The Bund's prestige in the general Jewish community rapidly ascended as a result of its role in combating pogromists in 1903 and 1904. In response to the Kishinev massacre in 1903, the Bund, as mentioned previously, organized self-defense forces and then exhilarated the Jewish community by leading a successful attack on a band of pogromists. In its actions and statements the Bund had tried to be careful not to intensify nationalist feelings that had already been raised by the pogroms. It realized that these sentiments would politically redound to the benefit of the Zionists, who were also organizing their own defense groups. But the Bund thought that it could forestall this by assuming a dominant leadership role in developing a militant opposition to the pogromists. The result was that it, and not the Zionists, was the recipient of mass adulation as the defenders of the people, and both the Bund and the Jewish masses were swept further along the road toward Jewish nationalism.

Even as this was occurring the Bundist leaders were trying to place the pogroms and the solution to the pogroms in a socialist framework. They wanted very much to resist the nationalist tides and maintain their links with their non-Jewish socialist brethren even in the face of the Kishinev massacre. Thus, very much in the socialist tradition, they put forth a resolution at their Fifth Congress, two months after

Kishinev, that stated: "The Congress . . . expresses its convictions that only the common struggle of the proletariat of all nationalities will destroy at the root those conditions that give rise to such events as Kishinev."[141] Their RSDLP comrades concurred but then built upon the Bund's own argument to attack it. Kishinev, they argued, demonstrated the pressing need for the development of proletarian unity, and this, not special efforts in the Jewish community, was the task to which the Bund should address its efforts.[142] Once again the RSDLP's negative reaction, coupled with a positive emotional response from Jews, pushed the Bund further from its universalistic commitments.

Despite or perhaps because of the disagreement with the Russian social democrats, the Bund's star was on the ascendance in the first half of the decade after the turn of the century. The Bund captured the imagination of the youth throughout the Pale. This was not limited to the older students of the gymnasium, yeshivas, and universities or the externs. It extended into the younger age groups as well. In 1903 a youth movement identified with the Bund emerged spontaneously. This movement was made up of primary school children and apprentices; in some instances, even ten-year-olds joined.[143]

The Bund reached its zenith in the first 10 months of 1905. Russia, in this period, had come alive with strikes and demonstrations in the wake of the Russo-Japanese War and more specifically the brutal assault on peaceful demonstrators carrying a petition to the czar on January 9, 1905. In the ensuing political and labor activity, the Bund, more so than its former comrades in the RSDLP, was successful in organizing strikes and demonstrations. The Bund seemed to be everywhere within the Jewish community. It reached into shops and areas previously untouched by any other political organization. It openly challenged and battled the hated police. Many had the feeling that the revolution was close at hand and that the Bund would be at the forefront in bringing it to Russia. "For thousands of Bundists and Bundist sympathizers," according to Henry J. Tobias, a leading contemporary historian of the Bund, "the exhilaration of political revolution, open and visible, and the personal participation in an heroic struggle made these few short months their moment in history."[144]

At the period of its greatest influence, it was quite clear that the Bund was operating in an almost total Jewish milieu. The Bundist leaders themselves were well aware of the broader political implications of this. Their assessment of why a revolution had failed to take place in Russia in 1905 focused on two factors: "the revolutionary passivity of the broad masses of the non-Jewish proletariat and the fact that [the Bund had] no permanent ties with them."[145] They quite correctly realized that the Bund, isolated in the Jewish community, would not be able to play a significant role in the broader revolutionary struggle.

COMMUNAL LEADERSHIP

However, even as these leaders were arriving at this conclusion, the remarkable events of the heady months of 1905 created an impact that pushed the Bund even further into the bosom of the Jewish community. At this period the Bund's influence and authority extended deep into the Jewish community. As the strife and demonstrations leading up to the abortive 1905 revolution grew in intensity, traditional governmental and Jewish agencies of social control and guidance experienced growing difficulty in functioning. In the Jewish community, the Bund began to operate in their stead. In this role, the Bund found itself involved in areas far removed from radical politics or union activity. One Bundist leader, writing in 1905, exclaimed:

The authority of the Bund . . . was very great, not only among the workers but among the great mass of the petit bourgeoisie and intelligentsia. It was regarded as some kind of mystical being with fear and hope. It could achieve everything, reach everyone . . . The word of the Bund was law. . . . Wherever an injustice, wherever an insult, even when it had no relation to the workers' movement . . . one came to the Bund as to the highest tribunal . . . It was legendary.[146]

Here, at the point of its highest prestige, we find the Bund accepting the mantle of communal rather than class leader. Again, the influence of the mass Jewish base and the need and desire of maintaining it shaped the political path of the Bund. The direction was clear. It was toward Jewish nationalism. Thus, in 1905, about seven months after the Bund realized the consequences of being isolated in the Jewish community, it formally incorporated cultural autonomy as part of its minimum program.[147] The Bund was now a cohesive force in the Jewish community, developing and bringing to maturity the tendencies that its agitator predecessors had initiated. In the process, the Bund undermined and weakened more traditional forces of communal solidarity; this can be seen most clearly in its battle with the rabbinate.

As enlightened socialists, the Bundists, like their immediate forebears, were hostile to traditional religion and to the rabbis. The Bund believed that these were forces that blocked the intellectual, social, economic, and political progress of the Jewish masses, and particularly their advance toward socialism. The Bundists saw the rabbis as active allies and colluders with the Jewish bourgeoisie, who worked to maintain the system of class exploitation while impeding the development of class consciousness among the workers.

The rabbis generally, for their part, were as hostile if not more so to the Bund than they had been toward the earlier Jewish socialists during the agitation campaign. They were very much aware of the fact that the socialists were undermining their influence and that of traditional religion among the Jewish workers. Deviation from orthodoxy was correctly seen by them as a necessary concomitant of the general move toward socialism by faithful and observant Jews. In response to this threat, rabbis often linked socialism to disrespect for religious traditions and to their authority as well as the state's, thus strengthening the bonds between all of these "sins." Thus, for example, in 1903 at Mezrich a special rabbinical proclamation declared: "Let it be known to the inhabitants of our city, that according to rumor there are many places here where young people hold meetings and assemblies, especially on the holy Sabbath at the time of the morning prayer. In each of these a young man has in his charge many students whom he teaches to abandon the paths of justice and law and go against the regime." [148]

Even the police concurred in the rabbis' assessment. In their sweeps in the Jewish community while searching for radicals, Jews caught smoking on the Sabbath were arrested. Such action was regarded as prima facie evidence of radicalism. [149]

Rabbis constantly reiterated that organized and traditional religion was on the side of authority, whether it was the czarist state or the Jewish employer. They would use their pulpits to attack the Bund for its promotion of strikes or to condemn the strikers themselves. At a meeting of rabbis in Cracow in 1903, a resolution was passed denouncing the Bund and calling upon Jews to shun the organization for its violation of the Torah, "which has told us to obey its laws and the decrees of the government where we reside." [150] The rabbis did not seem to realize that by their actions they were placing religion and themselves in the camp of the state and the employing class, two institutions that were identified with oppression and exploitation of the Jewish masses. Thus, Jews who were antagonistic to their employers over wages and working conditions or were hostile to the state because of its anti-Semitic policies were forced by the rabbis to link these hated enemies to religion. Even pride and strength in opposition to the forces of oppression were defined by some rabbis as "un-Jewish" behavior. In Minsk in 1902, after an anticzarist demonstration, one rabbi publicly declared: "How can we Jews, who are equal to crawling worms be involved in such deeds." [151] Thus, the rabbis inadvertently helped to identify courage and strength with their adversaries, the Jewish socialists.

The Bund, in conjunction with such unwitting allies, did have a measure of success in secularizing the Jewish community and thereby weakening religion as a force of cohesion. But this was not alone responsible for weakening religion. Rapid urbanization, the quest for secular knowledge, the spread of industrialism, and immigration also worked to break the cement of orthodoxy. The Zionists, too, also made their contribution to this process. It was the Bund, however, that stood as the vanguard in directly subverting the position of traditional religion as the sun around which the Jewish community revolved. [152]

This was an act of extreme significance for the Bund and the radi-

cals that would come after them, especially in America. The Bund in
its attack on religiosity and the institutions of Judaism was subverting
an historic force that had bound Jews together in the Diaspora. Religion had been the single most important positive source of unity
during the Jews' sojourn in foreign lands and particularly in Russia.
Jewish socialists prior to the formation of the Bund had not been very
much concerned about their attacks on the Jewish religion causing
Jews to abandon a Jewish identity. This was not the case as far as the
Bund was concerned. The Bundists, as opposed to earlier Jewish socialists, defined themselves as Jews and located themselves within the
Jewish community. The Jewish masses were their base. To have destroyed a significant source of Jewish identification without replacing
it with an alternative would have been political and organizational
folly. In order to preserve its unique constituency, the Bund, whether
conscious of it or not, had to find another source of unity and identification for Jews. And this alternative had to be one that was compatible with socialism as well as preferably being amenable to control by
the Bund. The Bund in itself partially served that function, but something else was needed. This was found in Yiddish.

THE IMPORTANCE OF YIDDISH FOR THE BUND

Yiddish and Yiddish culture appeared to fit the Bund's requirements.
It was a language and culture relatively free of religious overtones.
Yiddish was the natural expression of the Jewish workers. Yiddish
was a tongue and culture that the Bundists could elaborate and develop so that they would dovetail with the norms and values of socialism. Yiddish could also provide the base of a unified Jewish community that would allow the Bundists to argue their case for cultural
national autonomy in the new socialist Russia. Yiddish, indeed,
seemed the necessary alternative to religion, and the Bundists proceeded to wed themselves and their cause of socialism to it.

This solution was not without its costs. There were, in fact, at least
two major drawbacks. The first became increasingly apparent in the
years immediately after 1905. During this period the Bund found that
Yiddish was no longer uniquely in the domain of the Jewish proletariat. Nonradical Jewish intellectuals, as well as increasing numbers of
the Jewish bourgeoisie, dropped their principled opposition to this
language and began to approach it in a more positive manner. At the
Czernowicz language conference in 1908, Bundists, along with the
representatives of a broad cross section of the Jewish community,
joined together to pass a resolution in favor of recognizing Yiddish
along with Hebrew as national languages of the Jewish people.[153]

The Bund's very presence at the Czernowicz conference was symbolically quite important. Since 1905 this socialist organization had
refused to participate in meetings of Jewish groups in which it did not

have a dominant influence. The Bund's attendance at this language conference was the first deviation from this policy, reflecting the importance that it attached to Yiddish.[154]

Astute political leaders of the Bund saw the problem inherent in the identification of their organization with Yiddish. They realized that there was little that was inherently proletarian in Yiddish. Once it gained the approval and widespread usage by strata other than the working class, Yiddish had the potential of being a double-edged sword. Unity of the Jewish people based upon a truly common language and culture could easily obscure class divisions and impede the class struggle within the Jewish community.

These Bundist leaders realized that they could not prevent elements from other classes from building on the Bund's achievements in developing Yiddish culture in order to divert it to purposes other than those intended by the Bund. The Kovno language conference of 1909 further confirmed their fears in this regard. At Kovno the conference emphasized the aesthetic functions of Yiddish culture. The changing sponsorship of Yiddish periodicals and publications from 1894 to 1915, the year in which they were all suppressed by government edict, was another indication of this process. From 1894 to 1900 the Bund was responsible for 13 of the 15 Yiddish periodicals then in existence. Eighty-two of the 148 journals started between 1907 and 1915 could be described as bourgeois or conservative; the others were of general cultural interest. Of the total 261 Yiddish publications started during this 19-year period, the Bund by 1915 was responsible in absolute numbers for 54, or in relative terms, 21 percent. It should also be noted that there was no solid front within the Bund itself behind the position of the political primacy of Yiddish. Many Bundists also admired Yiddish from a largely aesthetic viewpoint. Thus, in a few short years, Yiddish was transformed from an overtly political and class medium into one that transcended class divisions and that was largely apolitical.[155]

The other major problem associated with the Bund's identification with Yiddish took longer to reveal itself. It revolved around the question of what would happen when the Jewish people, specifically its working classes, no longer spoke or used Yiddish. When this occurred what would happen to the Bund's unique constituency? The Bund had denied itself religion or race as ways of demarcating their Jewish adherents. The more successful the Bund was in socializing its members, the more the Bund relied on Yiddish as the major link between it and its mass base. When the Yiddish-speaking masses assimilated, as they would in Russia and America, and ceased to speak Yiddish, the Bund would then become generals without an army. Chaim Zhitlowsky, a socialist-revolutionary and Yiddishist, prophetically went to the heart of the matter: ". . . everyone must admit that the Yiddish language is the breath of life whose very inhalation renews the existence of the Jewish people. As long as Yiddish lives, there can be no doubt that the Jewish people will live." [156] One could also add to that not only the Jewish people, but Jewish socialism.

One way in which the Bund, and Jewish socialists later in America, responded to this situation was to erect schools and other institutions to perpetuate the Yiddish language and culture. This, in turn, increased their involvement with Yiddish and made them ever more dependent on it. Gradually, as we shall see later, the preservation of Yiddish language and culture became so significant that it evolved into an end in itself, supplanting the goal of Jewish socialism, for which it was originally designed to be a means.

From a broader perspective, it was not the Bund's reliance on and fostering of Yiddish that put it into a dead end. Its use of Yiddish as a major political vehicle stemmed in large part from the dearth of suitable alternatives or supplements. The occupational and industrial structure of the Jewish community did not lend itself to the building of a militant socialist revolutionary force. The Jewish masses, up to the revolution of 1917, were largely artisans and workers in small shops. They were located in industries far removed from those considered basic to an industrial society and basic to the construction of a class-conscious proletariat. When the revolution did come to Russia, theirs were not the work places that provided the foot soldiers. Instead, these came from the large factories involved in heavy industry, those that had barred Jews from their doors. [157] The Bund labored in the midst of an atypical proletariat whose occupational physiognomy had been distorted by anti-Semitism and its own religiocultural traditions. The Bund's reliance on Yiddish reflected their attempt to fashion out of ethnicity and culture what had been denied to them by structure. It was a valiant enterprise but one that had little chance of succeeding. Unfortunately, the Jewish socialists in America building on Bundist experiences also found themselves in a similar bind.

PERSONAL TRANSFORMATION WITHIN THE BUND

Before we turn our attention to the American scene, there is one further aspect of the Bund that merits attention. We have closely examined the Bund because of the impact that it made upon Jews and Jewish socialists in America. If one were to investigate the means through which the Bund had its most immediate and prominent effect, it would probably not be the tactics and policies of the Bund but the organization itself.

The Bund provided its adherents with a new and different world or way of life. Membership in the Bund literally entailed a personal conversion. New members were, in the words of a Bundist writer, expected to become ". . . different from what they had been." [158] Old attitudes toward religion, sex, or one's associates were to be put aside upon entrance. One leader spoke of it and the process in almost re-

ligious terms: "The Party was a Temple, and those who served socialism had to have clean hands, clean thoughts, pure qualities, and to be
pure in their relations with one another." [159] Commitment to the Bund
often entailed a break from previous forms and modes of existence.
For some this meant a break from their families and friends. The Bund
would reinforce this break in the case of its cadres by moving them
from one town to another. This would also serve to bind the activist
even more closely to the Bund. Relationships between the sexes were
on a more egalitarian footing inside the Bund than outside of it. In
short, family and tradition no longer served as guides for action and
for the instillment of moral virtues. In their stead was the Bund.

The Bund also provided its members with new sets of institutions
and structures, ensuring that its members' whole lives would be encompassed by the Bund. It was a movement that had its own educational classes, libraries, secret gatherings, demonstrations, and holidays. It had its own initiation rituals and ceremonies, including the
singing of the Oath, the Bund's anthem. It was a rich, full, and exciting world that required little from those outside of it. [160]

But perhaps most inportantly the Bund instilled pride in its members. They were new men, new Jews. They were different from the
traditional Jew. They were fighters and part of a moral and political
vanguard for great historical change. They had a mission that inspired
them and people who believed in them. This new consciousness was
seared in the bodies and souls of the Bundists who voyaged across the
ocean to recommence the old struggle on new soil. The Bund's greatest gift to the movement it inspired and helped to build in America
might very well have been this rich personal and organizational heritage. For those who came to America it was meaningful and important, but in the long run it was probably more important for them as
individuals than for the cause of socialism.

It is also important to note when they came to the United States.
The immigration of Jews from Russia to the United States reached its
highest points during the years in which the Bund was at the peak of
its prominence, around 1905. After the abortive revolution, a wave of
repression and pogroms hit the Jewish community and negatively affected the Bund as well. Thus, after reaching its zenith in terms of influence and members in 1905 and the early part of 1906, the Bund
declined. Within two years its membership shrank from a high of
40,000 to just a few thousand in 1908. [161] Many of its members, an
even larger number of supporters, and a yet larger number of Jews
whose lives it had touched were no longer available to it. They had
joined the great waves of immigrants to the United States, bringing
with them the actual and vicarious memories, as well as the traditions
of the Bund and Jewish socialism. [162]

CONCLUSION

The American Jews' relationship to the Left was originally forged in czarist Russia. There, in their confrontation with Russian capitalism, Jews first developed a large, concentrated, and culturally sustaining proletariat and thousands of socialist or socialist-oriented intellectuals. It was in Russia also that the first mass-based Jewish radical organizations were formed. In the process of immigration to America, many of the Russian Jews brought with them the political skills, organizational forms, and memories that emerged from their experience or association with the Jewish Left. These were the people who proved to be the major base and architects of a Jewish Left in America.

The experiences that shaped the Jewish leftists in Russia did not universally contribute to the building of a long-term nexus between Jews and socialism in the United States. In the czarist empire a heritage of anti-Semitism and a virulently anti-Semitic government had combined to channel the radicalism of Jews into a uniquely Jewish form. Though a source of difficulty, this form was generally not regarded as a significant problem by most Jews in or around the Jewish socialist movement. The overwhelming poverty and the highly proletarian composition of the Jewish community plus the confrontation with anti-Semitism produced a situation in which Jewish and socialist interests and goals were, at best, mutually supportive and, at worst, nonconflictive. In America, Jewish leftists were deprived of these foreign props that had allowed Jews in Russia the comfort of being Jewish *and* socialist. On these shores, political and socioeconomic conditions soon forced most Jewish Leftists to make a choice of being Jewish *or* socialist.

4 The American Roots

INTRODUCTION

The mass immigration of Russian and Eastern European Jews now permits us to change the venue of our discussion and analysis from the Old World to the New. The focus here will be on the factors and forces that affected the Jewish community from the 1880s until the eve of World War I and facilitated and motivated Jews to move to the Left. It was in this period that a significant prosocialist sentiment developed among American Jews. And it was during this time that the radical Jews constructed the organizations and institutions that formed the structural component of the Jewish Left subculture. These were socialist-led unions, radical fraternal orders, Leftist political parties, and newspapers and periodicals of and for the Left. (These organizations have also been collectively referred to as the Jewish labor movement by other writers, and this term will be used here as well.)

These several decades before World War I are crucial to the understanding of the relationship between the Jews and the Left in the United States. It was in this period that the foundation of the association that obtained throughout the rest of the century was laid. The sentiments, actions, and institutions of the Jewish Left and the Jews on the Left from the 1920s through the 1970s cannot be fully comprehended without an awareness and appreciation of the foundation that was erected before the Great War.

In this chapter we shall again identify and analyze those variables that contributed to the building of both a pro-Left sentiment among Jews and a Jewish Left subculture. Here, too, we shall see the importance of numbers, concentration, ethnic and occupational homogeneity, cultural insulation, and leadership. In America as in Russia these gave rise to a powerful, vibrant, and culturally self-sustaining Jewish working class—the primary force that underlies the Jews' relationship to the Left.

Also in this chapter as in the last, emphasis will be given to those factors that undermined the Jews' ties to the Left. In the United States, as in the czarist empire, the base of this relationship contained two significant flaws—one occupational and the other cultural. The occupational structure of the Jewish workers in America did not lend itself to the production of a classic Marxist working class. The marginal, small shop and the highly competitive and labor-intensive industries in which they were located could not be the mainstay of such a Jewish working class for any length of time.

The weakness in the occupational structure was compensated for by the strength in the cultural sphere. Yiddish—the language and the culture—was utilized by Jewish radicals to solidify and strengthen a Left-oriented Jewish working class. But the more reliant they became upon Yiddish, the more they and their followers became enmeshed in the Jewish community. And the more enmeshed in the Jewish community they became, as we shall see in subsequent chapters, the more susceptible Jewish Leftists became to nonradical Jewish pressures— pressures that continually worked to attenuate the Jews' ties with the Left.

In this chapter I shall concentrate on the interplay among the forces that predisposed the Russian and Eastern European Yiddish-speaking Jews to move to the Left and to erect a Jewish labor movement. At their peak these "causal" elements were able to produce a sturdy and viable network of associations, organizations, and institutions. These structures survived and functioned after the sources of their creation and strength had dissipated.

Finally, it is important to note that which this chapter is not emphasizing. I have given little attention to the ever-present forces in the Jewish community that regularly strove to pull Jews away from the Left. These countervailing forces obviously did exist even in the period at which the Jewish Left was at its height. One indicator of their presence was the failure of socialist parties to capture a majority of the immigrant Jewish votes in the years before World War I. However, these non-Left factors were not strong enough to prevent the Jews from becoming the ethnic or religious group most supportive of the Left in the United States.

Thus, I have chosen not to analyze the social bases of Jewish politics in America. Instead, I focus upon a particular segment of Jewish politics—the Left. In the process of so doing, other aspects must, perforce, get less attention. We now turn our attention to those elements that were conducive to and facilitative of the development of Left sentiments and organizations among Jews in the several decades prior to World War I.

NUMBERS AND POVERTY

Numbers were important to the Jewish Leftists for a variety of reasons, the most significant of which was the social support and reinforcement the members of this group provided one another. Numbers were also important in building organizations and institutions, as well as a popular sentiment.

The presence of several million Russian and Eastern European Jews in America in the early decades of the 1900s provided the Jewish Left with a large enough pool from which they could derive sufficient essential ingredients. There was enough to provide a leadership and a cadre, enough to erect their own organizations and institutions, and enough to serve as a constituency on which these Jewish leaders and cadres could concentrate their political efforts.

From 1881 to 1925 about 3½ million Jewish immigrants entered the United States. They were almost all Yiddish-speaking Eastern European Jews, with the overwhelmingly largest contingent, approximately three-quarters, made up of those from the Polish and Russian sections of the czarist empire. In the ten-year period from 1904 to 1914, a particularly important decade for our purposes, some 1,200,000 found their way to America.[1]

These immigrants, like others, were not a representative sample of the larger population from which they were drawn. They were younger, more secular, and more urban than the Jews who chose not to come. Also, particularly in the years after the Kishinev pogrom, they were disproportionately drawn from the most urbanized and industrialized sections of the Pale. These were precisely the areas most influenced by the Bund in specific and secular forces in general.[2] Thus, almost coincidental with the amassing of large numbers of people was the amassing of certain types of individuals who would provide the Left with sympathetic raw material.

The impact of their numbers was greatly heightened by their pattern of settlement. The great bulk of them landed and stayed in the North Atlantic States. In the period from 1899 to 1910, some 86 percent of the Jewish immigrants took up residence in this area, compared with 67 percent of their non-Jewish counterparts. The greatest number of Jews who settled in this region during this time could be found in New York State, where two-thirds of all Jewish immigrants chose to live. Nor were they spread out within the state, but, rather, were concentrated in New York City.[3]

In 1880 there were more than 80,000 Jews in New York City, representing about 10 percent of the total population. By 1915 their numbers had increased to 1,400,000, and they then constituted nearly 30 percent of the city's population. Almost three-quarters of all the Jews who immigrated from 1881 to 1911 immediately or soon after settled in New York City.[4]

Even within New York City the Jews were not widely dispersed. The Lower East Side of Manhattan, an area of 25 square blocks containing one eighty-second of the city's land area, became one of the earlier points of Jewish concentration. In 1892, 75 percent of the city's Jewish residents lived there. By 1903 the percentage had dropped to about 50 percent, but the total absolute number had increased. The population density for Jewish wards on the Lower East Side in 1900 varied from 433 to 651 per acre. Five years later, after a 14 percent increase in population for this total area, there were "Jewish" blocks within it containing from 1000 to 1700 people per acre. The Eighth Assembly District, located in the heart of the Lower East Side, averaged 730 people per acre. These Jewish sections were the most congested in New York City and probably in the entire world. In 1910, a year in which the Jewish labor movement reached its militant peak, the East Side, with about 542,061 inhabitants, also attained its height of density.[5]

The movement from the Lower East Side in the 1900s and 1910s was considerable. One study found that two-thirds of a sample of Jews living in this area in 1905 had left it for other parts of the city by 1915.[6] In 1916 only 23 percent of all New York Jews resided in the Lower East Side. Again, this was a considerable figure when translated into absolute numbers. Remember, too, that while the moving vans were transporting Jews from the area, trans-Atlantic steamers were depositing large numbers of Jews into the Lower East Side.

It is also important to note that departure from this section of the city should not be equated with dispersion. The Jews moved from the Lower East Side, but they did not stray very far. Instead they founded newer areas of Jewish concentration in New York City in such places as Brownsville, the East Bronx, Harlem, South Brooklyn, and Williamsburg. In 1918 almost three-quarters of the 1½ million Jews in the city lived in either the boroughs of Manhattan or Brooklyn, with the single largest area of concentration still the East Side.[7]

It should be noted that this was not a phenomenon unique to the Jews of New York City. Those that settled outside of this metropolis also tended to choose large urban areas such as Chicago, Philadelphia, Boston, Baltimore, and Cleveland. More than 90 percent of the Eastern European Jewish immigrants eventually settled in about 15 or 16 of the nation's largest cities. New York was the single most important.[8] And it is this city that shall be the primary setting for our account.

This urban or, more accurately, metropolitan pattern of settlement was in many ways an extension of the process that had begun in the Pale of Settlement in the latter decades of the nineteenth century. The move to New York or London or Berlin was part and parcel of the movement from rural to urban areas, from towns and villages to cities and metropolis.

The shift from *shtetls* and small towns of the Pale to Vilna and then to London or New York or Chicago was not solely a change in the size and density of living areas. It also involved a shift from locales where things traditional and sacred were important to new arenas where their sway was challenged and undermined by secularism. Movement to the cities and metropolises meant exposure to new ideas and new ways of conducting one's life. And it also involved close and intimate interaction with many people who shared the same problems and aspirations. These metropolises, the places to which the Eastern European Jewish immigrants were attracted, served as fertile soil for radicalism and socialist movements.[9]

The miserable living conditions of ghetto life in the New World also bred support and sympathy for the Left. The neighborhoods, apartments, and rooms that the Jewish immigrants (and others as well) occupied were dirty, unsafe, and overcrowded. Too many people in too small an area was one of the more negative aspects of life on the East

Side. In 1890 New York City's Tenth ward, located on the East Side, had the highest number of Jews of any ward in the city. Whereas the average number of persons living in a dwelling in a typical ward was 18, in the Tenth the figure was 38, the highest for the city.[10] A government report described the conditions of life in an overcrowded tenement on the East Side in 1886:

In the "Big Flat" were gathered, on a given day in 1886, 478 persons. . . . On the first floor were room for 14 families, and these were mostly occupied by low women and street walkers. . . . The hallways were "hang outs" for all the hoodlums in the neighborhood and after nightfall the lower floor was overrun with low women and young men who did not live in the house. . . . The Jews were principally engaged in tailoring, but there were some 54 peddlers in the building. Both tailors and peddlers were closely packed in very dirty rooms and lived upon poor and scanty food. The children were "very poorly clad". . . . Their food during the day was bread, no butter, and that was eaten by them in the hallway—they did not know what it was to sit at a table.[11]

Such circumstances could not help but bring disease in their wake. The incidence of consumption or tuberculosis rose among the poor and obtained the title of "proletarian sickness." The New York Health Department estimated that one out of every 17 inhabitants of the East Side, including men, women, and children, were infected by the "white plague." The intellectuals were the strata most heavily hurt by this disease.[12] Jews also suffered heavily from nervous disorders. The Jewish population in insane asylums was disproportionately greater than that for the Jewish population in the city as a whole.[13]

Crime and violence, as might be expected, were an all too familiar part of the East Side scene. Prostitutes, pimps, pickpockets, and petty hoodlums were a visible and troublesome element. Jews were largely the victims of the criminals. As the restraints of religion and the traditions lessened, many from the younger generation took to crime.[14]

This ghetto way of life was not solely a product of large numbers of poor immigrants pouring into a confined area. The filthy, overcrowded tenements of the East Side were also a function of human avarice. They represented to investors and real estate speculators lucrative investment opportunities. A combination of increased rents, a continual phenomenon, and reductions in maintenance, could bring handsome returns on one's investment.

The presence of crime and criminals was also not a "natural" phenomenon. An alliance between police, politicians, and criminals allowed it to flourish. A novelist described the mechanics of this alliance as seen through the eyes of a rising Jewish lawyer who was part of the corrupt Tammany machine:

There was keen competition for the pickpocket privilege of the Brooklyn Bridge terminal where swirling, pushing crowds made pocket picking easy and lucrative. Detectives were assigned to see that the regularly designated pickpockets operated without interference and to keep out poachers from this fine game preserve. Big Jim [Tammany leader] awarded the Brooklyn Bridge concession to my district. I divided it among four pickpockets. . . . A certain percentage of the pickings went to the guardian detectives and to the police inspector in charge of the Bridge district.[15]

The immigrant Jews were educated in the economic and political interests that underlay their miserable living conditions. Socialists and anarchists, as well as reformers, publicly and continually railed against the avaricious landlords and corrupt politicians and police. Socialist-led Jewish unions, in combination with other forces, did produce some reforms. These efforts, together with the abject circumstances of life about them shaped an atmosphere and a constituency among the immigrant ghetto Jews that was predisposed to socialism and reform.[16]

THE NETWORK OF CULTURE

The numbers and the residential concentration of the Eastern European Jews permitted and facilitated their building and sustaining a rich, varied, and unique culture. Yiddish, the language, lay at the heart of this culture called *Yidishkayt*. "This term signifies 'Yiddishness,' the moment and substance of devotion to cultural values associated with Yiddish." [17] *Yidishkayt* was a culture that at once differentiated and insulated the Russian and Eastern European Jews from surrounding cultures, including that of the German-American Jews. At the same time *Yidishkayt* and its differentiating and insulating characteristics provided the Russian Jewish radicals with a milieu that for a time was relatively cut off from leadership, values, and norms associated with "foriegn" or non-*Yidishkayt* cultures.

The German-American Jews and their culture, one might think, would have presented an early challenge to the establishment of a Yiddish-based culture. After all, the German Jews were coreligionists and, by the time the Eastern Europeans arrived in great numbers, were relatively well established in America. They had their own wealthy leaders and able professionals who could have provided experienced guides and leadership to the *yidn*, the Yiddish-speaking Eastern European Jews. Although they did try, their efforts were generally unsuccessful and they proved unable to prevent the Eastern European Jews from establishing *Yidishkayt* in America. The impotence of the German-Jews stemmed from strong animosity between the two Jewish communities, which we shall presently examine. This, in turn, was largely a product of a variety of important differences in the structure and culture of the two groups. Let us now focus briefly on the culture of the German-American Jews.

When the German-American immigrants came to America they

chose not to attempt to sustain a unique and vibrant Jewish culture. Instead, they preferred to identify and emulate the customs, manners, and even religious practices of their fellow Germans and later of middle-class American Christians. In this regard, they were very much the children of the Haskalah, the German-born Jewish enlightenment. But in the eyes of the Eastern European Jews, religious as well as nonreligious, this represented a crude aping of Gentiles and an attempt to curry their favor.[18]

The weakness of a uniquely German Jewish culture was not only a product of the German Jews' indifference to their culture, but also of their pattern of settlement. The German Jews, unlike their Eastern European coreligionists who followed them to the United States, did not concentrate in one or a few large urban centers. Instead, they dispersed.[19] Many went into the smaller cities and towns as peddlers and small tradesmen in order to seek their fortunes. This pattern in reflected in the Statistics of Churches in the 1890 United States Census. In this census, the government for the first and only time made a distinction between Reform (primarily German) and Orthodox (predominantly Eastern European) congregations. The data revealed that approximately 60 percent of the Reform congregations were located in cities of 25,000 or more inhabitants, compared with 85 percent of those of the Orthodox denomination. And although there were fewer Reform than Orthodox congregations overall, in part a function of the larger size of the individual Reform congregations, those of Reform Judaism were to be found in more states and in the less urbanized states such as Alabama, Arkansas, Indiana, and Mississippi.[20] In short, the Reform German-American Jews were spread too thin to establish and maintain a unique and vibrant culture, even had they desired one, which they did not.

This was not true for the Eastern European Jews. They desired to have such a culture and brought the building materials for it over with them on the ships. The mortar was made up of experiences in czarist Russia, traditions, and, of course, Yiddish. Their large numbers and concentrated settlements provided them with the manpower to build this culture in America and to staff the institutions needed to support it.

The orderly patterns of immigration that reinforced both their residential concentration and segregation also contributed to the strength of *Yidishkayt*. Their movement from the Pale and Europe to the large cities of America was neither atomized nor chaotic. Familial ties were a key factor in the immigration and settlement patterns of Jews, as well as other immigrant nationality groups. Once the earlier arrivals settled in America, letters soon began wending their way across the Atlantic, encouraging relatives to join them. From the other side's perspective, a relative in America meant that a family now had a safe harbor to which to repair in the event that life in Russia and Eastern Europe became too insufferable. It also signified that a familiar niche was available to them in the strange world known as America. About 80 percent of the Eastern European Jewish immigrants appear to have received some form of assistance from their American relatives in making their journey from the Old to the New World.[21]

This orderly trans-Atlantic resettlement was not just a family affair. Letters of encouragement and pleas for help were exchanged between those who had been lovers, friends, and neighbors in the old home-towns. Workers would also find jobs for their relatives, *lanslite* or landsmen, neighbors, and persons from their hometown or region, respectively, usually in their own shops or in places nearby. Jewish employers desirous of dependable labor often recruited from among their landsmen or those of their reliable employees. In such ways, families, neighborhoods, and towns would be transported almost intact and set down again in a tenement, block, or small neighborhood in a city in the United States.

This pattern of transplantation reduced the jarring impact of a new situation in a strange land for the recently arrived immigrants. Surrounded by loved ones and familiar faces who provided bed, board, and job contacts, the Russian Jewish immigrant was not bewildered and confused for long. In essence, he was not in America but in the midst of a reassembled Yiddish-speaking ghetto. This coherent and orderly movement had an important consequence for the adjustment of the individual immigrant and for the organization of the community. It helped the individual to adjust without having to come to grips with the American environment with any great haste. In terms of the community, it allowed and facilitated the organization of the immigrant community in such a fashion so as to minimize significant contact and assistance from "outsiders," Americans or *yahudim*. And the more solid and self-sustaining the Yiddish-speaking immigrant community, the greater the opportunity the Yiddish-speaking radicals had to vend their wares in an exclusive marketplace.

Two institutional factors, both of which rested on a highly concentrated, ethnically homogeneous population base, were largely responsible for maintaining a tightly knit, relatively self-contained Yiddish-speaking community. One of these was the extensive network of organizations and associations, sacred and secular, that the Jews erected in America. These included mutual aid societies, fraternal orders, educational and cultural organizations, and synagogues. In New York City almost every immigrant Jewish family by 1914 was, in some manner or another, involved in one of these organizations.[22]

LANDSMANSHAFT

At the core of this institutional network stood the *landsmanshaft*, the society of townsmen. The *landsmanshaft* was an organization that provided its members with a variety of services including religious, social, fraternal, educational, health, and mutual aid. Its membership was based primarily on kinship lines or common residence in a European *shtetl*, city, or region. The *landsmanshaft* was primarily a product of the Eastern European immigration and experienced its most vigorous growth during the years from 1903 to 1909. This was not a uniquely Jewish phenomenon. Other immigrant groups like the Italians and the Irish also organized mutual aid societies based on place of origin.

The *landsmanshaft* principle was embodied in various organizations. Even groups that were not formed on this basis found that when they reached a sizable membership, the members would begin to divide into subgroups based on ties of common geographical origin. This was true for radical organizations as well. Thus, in 1917 out of 3600 Jewish organizations, 1000 (or almost 30 percent) were of a *landsmanshaft* nature.[23]

Louis Wirth, in his classic work, *The Ghetto*, commented on the role and functions of the *landsmanshaft* among the immigrant Eastern European Jews:

. . . a stranger who is able to call himself a *Landsman* not only loosens the purse-strings of the first individual he meets, but also has access to his home. Not only do the *Lanslite* belong to the same synagogue, but as a rule, they engage in similar vocations, become partners in business, live in the same neighborhood and intermarry within their own group. A *Landsmanshaft* has its own patriarchal leaders, its lodges and mutual aid associations, and its celebrations and festivities. It has its burial plot in the cemetery. It keeps the memories of the group alive through frequent visits and maintains a steady liaison with the remnants of the Jewish community in the Old World.[24]

A Yiddish writer further elaborated on the importance of this central institution in the lives of the immigrant Jews:

Under the pressure of his initial wearying problems of transition, confused by his sudden jump from one world into another. . . . the Jewish immigrant created a social nest, the Landsmanshaft Society, which gave him a measure of social sureness and salved his pains-of-transition, returning to him at least a ray of his forsaken home atmosphere and serving him as a bridge between his past and his future life.[25]

The centrality of the *landsmanshaft* and the reestablishment of Old World residential patterns and interactions did have at least one initial negative effect upon communal solidarity. These factors did introduce and, for a while, sustain European town and regional rivalries in the New World. However, this proved not to be a long-lived problem. The common problems that they faced as ghetto residents, workers, and Yiddish-speaking Jews and the necessity to confront these issues jointly, diminished the saliency of these Old World differences.

It is also important to note that the *landsmanshaft* was very much a *de facto* working-class phenomenon. In the early decades of their existence, prior to World War I, they were almost exclusively filled by employees. It could be argued that this also reflected the dominant social class patterns of the immigrant society. But several decades later in 1938, when the Jews were no longer a predominantly working class group, 75 percent of the members of the *landsmanshaften* were workers. Most of them were employed in the needle trades.[26]

This meant that Yiddish-speaking workers were closely and continually interacting in a variety of different settings. They were sharing common experiences and problems in the context of their shops, neighborhoods, and voluntary, self-created organizations. The channels of communication for the sharing of commonly defined grievances was thus highly developed among them. The establishment and maintenance of the *landsmanshaften* and associated activities also gave the Yiddish-speaking workers experience in cooperating among themselves to achieve common ends. And it also implied that this immigrant proletariat was developing its own class subculture within the bosom of the Jewish community. All of these proved to be valuable preconditions or facilitating factors for the growth and development of Left organizations and of a pro-Left sentiment among the Jewish working class.

The second institutional factor that fostered the development of an integrated, relatively self-sustaining, Yiddish-speaking community and culture was the garment industry. This industry, which we shall consider in greater detail presently, was a Jewish industry. During the several decades of mass immigration, both the employers and the employees in the needle trades were predominantly Jewish. Physically, the shops and factories were generally located in Jewish residential areas. And during the years when hundreds of thousands of Jews annually disembarked in American ports, the industry's expansion allowed large numbers from each stream of new arrivals to find employment within it and within the confines of the Jewish community.

This industry performed a very important social and cultural function: It allowed Yiddish-speaking immigrants to live in their own economic world for several decades. It meant the minimization of their contact with outsiders, with the exception of German-Jewish employees early in the period. The garment industry thus served roughly the same function as an agricultural economy did for the Amish or the Mennonites. It tended to isolate and insulate a homogeneous community from the corrosive contacts and appeals of strangers by providing the community with a nearly self-sufficient economic enterprise. The Yiddish-speaking Eastern European Jews had not designed or created the garment industry for this purpose, nor did they actively work to strengthen this latent social function of the industry when Jews began to leave it and were replaced by Gentiles. However, regardless of their will, the industry did perform this function for a limited but crucial period of time. The garment industry also played another important cultural and community role: it generated funds. These were used to build and support social, educational, and cultural associations and institutions that strengthened the coherence of an homogeneous and insulated subculture within America.

YIDDISH

The basic mortar of this culture was Yiddish, the nearly universal language of the Russian and Eastern European Jewish immigrants. Its most important aspect, from which everything else flowed, was the fact that it was the language of the immigrant masses. Yiddish lay at the core of *Yidishkayt*. This culture, in addition to its unique language, also contained supportive institutions. The most significant among them were literature, the press, and the theatre. Yiddish, *Yidishkayt*, and the related cultural institutions together formed a homogeneous and self-sufficient culture for the immigrant Jews.

Jewish intellectuals played an important role in the building of this culture. Their presence in large numbers in America allowed them to develop and staff the various positions and institutions necessary to sustain a strong and viable culture. Their role as cultural architects and leaders was neither natural nor preordained. It largely stemmed from the fact that the Yiddish-speaking masses represented a large body of eager consumers for their ideas and talents. No other group in America was prepared to receive and accept them so readily. It was through this creative interaction between the Yiddish-speaking masses and their intellectual leaders that a flourishing *Yidishkayt* culture developed in America prior to World War I. *Yidishkayt* in America in this period was not neutral in terms of class orientation. Instead, it was largely a proletarian culture. This stemmed from the fact that it had been a people's culture in Europe. As we discussed earlier, the Jewish sacred and secular intelligentsia in Russia had been largely contemptuous of Yiddish as a language and culture up through the turn of the century. This meant that its most important carriers and transmitters were untutored Jews, who were also the Jews who formed the working and lower classes. They also were the people who immigrated to America in large numbers, bringing with them their beloved Yiddish.

Another factor that shaped Yiddish into a proletarian culture was the radical or socialist intelligentsia. Simultaneously in both Russia and America, Russian Jewish radical intellectuals came to the realization that it would be necessary to utilize Yiddish in order to reach the Jewish workers. In both cases, this purely utilitarian orientation was largely shed as the radicals become more deeply immersed in working with the masses and with Yiddish. They also began to develop an affection for *Yidishkayt*, and, within a very short period of time, these Jewish radicals had become the chief intellectual sponsors of Yiddish, nourishing, improving, cultivating, and developing it until *Yidishkayt*, under their tutelage, had become a rich and vibrant culture.

There were also intellectuals, in addition to the committed political radicals and socialists, who gave Yiddish a working class orientation. These were what might be termed "literary" socialists. They were Yiddish-speaking poets, essayists, novelists, and playwrights who dealt quite sympathetically in their works with the plight of the oppressed and exploited Jews. The daily struggles and tribulations of the Jewish worker were often the major theme of their literary efforts. The message conveyed in their work was the necessity for social justice for the Jewish working men. Shalom Aleichem, Sholem Asch, Jacob Gordin, and Morris Rosenfeld were among the leading lights of this talented group. It would have been difficult for these men not to have portrayed the Jewish poor and proletariat in less than a sympathetic way. Many of these "literary" socialists were either political socialists or persons who had had first-hand experience working in the sweat shops and living in crowded, dilapidated, overpriced rooms. Their artistic efforts reflected their own lives as workers and poor Jews.[27]

The social composition of their readers and public was also a factor in influencing their treatment of the Jewish laboring class. The consumers of their work were primarily Yiddish-speaking Jews from the working class. In America, they represented the only sizable body of consumers available to Yiddish writers. These Russian and Eastern European Jewish immigrants would not have spent their money or given their support to writers and artists who did not show them love, understanding, or respect in their work.

It is important to understand the nature of the creative interplay between the Jewish political and literary intellectuals on the one hand and their audience and public on the other in the shaping of a working class, prosocialist Yiddish culture. Intellectuals and literary men closely interacted with the Yiddish-speaking masses, principally through reading groups, classes, and drama troupes in which radicals and socialists played major roles. This relationship between culture and class was further solidified by the fact that so many of the political and literary socialist intellectuals were also laboring men.

The capstone to this whole process was the Yiddish press. Yiddish labor and socialist newspapers and periodicals, which moved into preeminence in this field about the turn of the century, did more than convey news. They functioned as educators and political agitators. This press helped the Jewish workers to read and improve their Yiddish. It gave them works of great literature by men such as Leo Tolstoy or Emile Zola, as well as the writings of comrades from their own shops. Articles from the fields of the natural and social sciences were also provided. Public events were analyzed from a socialist or worker's point of view. Readers were enjoined from the pages of these papers to join unions, participate in strikes and demonstrations, and vote for socialist candidates.[28] The Yiddish socialist press was also credited with strengthening the bond between intellectuals and Yiddish culture and, through that bond, between Yiddish intellectuals

and the Yiddish-speaking public. According to Samuel Niger, a leading authority on Yiddish literature and culture:

Attracting intellectuals previously alienated from the Jewish environment and
the Yiddish language to Jewish cultural activity was a substantial accomplishment. For this accomplishment we are indebted to the radical Yiddish press
and social ideas and ideals it propagated. Writers and speakers whose medium of expression had been Russian, Hebrew or German studied to become
Yiddish writers or speakers. Where once there had been an intelligentsia
without a people and a people without an intelligentsia, the Yiddish press
and the social movement it represented gave the intelligentsia a people and the
people an intellectual leadership. Both the intellectuals and the people benefited greatly. Creative individuals found an audience and the spiritually
thirsty masses found an opportunity to quench their thirst.[29]

It would be a mistake to leave the impression that the radical press
had a monopoly in the Yiddish-speaking community. There were Yiddish papers that did oppose the radicals and uphold traditional Orthodoxy as well as conservative politics. Indeed, the first daily newspaper printed in Yiddish in America, the *Yidisher Tageblatt*, or *Jewish
Daily News* (1885), was a conservative paper in matters of politics and
religion. Yet even these newspapers dared not risk alienating a predominantly working-class readership, and even as they opposed radicalism, the cause of the worker was treated from a generally prolabor
standpoint. Also, they could not avoid hiring, as writers and re-
porters, men of talent who were radicals and socialists.[30] Thus, almost
everywhere the Yiddish-speaking and reading workers turned, the
press in particular or to the culture in general, they found speakers,
writers, and artists who were sympathetic to their plight. And at the
vanguard of this culture stood the radicals and socialists. Their
weight in numbers and talent placed them in a preeminent position.
Although they had their critics and enemies within the Yiddish culture, their proworking class orientation was almost unassailed. The
power of the socialists in Yiddish culture prior to World War I is best
indicated by the *Forverts* or *Jewish Daily Forward*, a socialist newspaper founded in 1897. This paper, it was universally agreed, was the
premier journal and sociopolitical mentor of the East Side Jews.
   For a few short decades the creative interaction between the Left
and pro-Left intellectuals and the Jewish working class shaped *Yidishkayt* into a predominantly working-class culture. Thus, Yiddish-
speaking socialists and those sympathetic to socialism could create an
environment that was positive and receptive to socialism. Through
their pens and voices they could work, relatively unopposed, from
within *Yidishkayt* to make it a vehicle for the propagation of socialist
attitudes, values, and norms. They would have a limited period of
time before the corrosive forces of commercialism, Americanism, and
cosmopolitanism permeated their community's *Yidishkayt* shell.
   The very success that the Yiddish-speaking socialists were able to

achieve in creating an identity and mutual interest between socialism and *Yidishkayt* contained two especially significant and serious defects. One was that by concentrating on this Yidiskayt culture, the Jewish socialists were pushed into a situation that separated them from non-Jews. Second, the Leftist movement was built around a culture that was waning even at the height of the triumph of the Jewish Left. But these and other drawbacks were not apparent at the time. Jews and the Left in that period seemed to be almost natural allies. In the short run (actually a period of a very few years) the Yiddish-speaking radicals were indeed blessed with a highly favorable social context. Almost everything they needed to build a movement was available to them. However, unbeknownst to most of them, this constellation of favorable factors was not one that would survive for very long in America. The Jewish socialists reaped the benefits from an historically unique and short-lived situation.

THE GERMAN-JEWISH OUTSIDERS

The cause of the Left in the immigrant Russian and Eastern European Jewish ghettos in America profited from the antagonism and hostility that characterized the relationship between this community and the German-American Jews. Again, one might have expected the latter to have exercised a decisive leadership in the affairs of their immigrant coreligionists. This, however, did not prove to be the case. The attitudes, actions, religion, social class, and politics of the German-American Jews worked to bar them from playing such a role for a significant, but not lengthy, period of time. This, in turn, left the field of leadership in the immigrant community relatively open to indigenous elements, in the foremost ranks of which stood the Yiddish-speaking radicals.

These German Jews, in a remarkably short period of time after disembarking in America, had been exceedingly mobile. Within 20 to 30 years they had produced numerous millionaires, including, Joseph Seligman, Solomon Loeb, and Emanuel and Mayer Lehman. "It seems highly unlikely," according to the social historian, John Higham, "proportionately speaking, that in any other immigrant group so many men have ever risen so rapidly from rags to riches."[31] The mass arrival of Russian Jews was not a cause that warmed the hearts of the arriviste German Jews. These "Asians," to use their term, with their medieval garb and customs, threatened their newly acquired and not yet firmly established status. The Germans feared that the new arrivals would exacerbate the problem of anti-Semitism. And they were also worried about the financial burden that the pauperism of these immigrants might force them to carry.

Thus, their initial responses to the East European immigrants and to the prospect of continued mass immigration of these people were negative and hostile. Various spokesmen within the German-American community appealed to the East European Jews not to emigrate, assuring them that better days would soon be dawning in Russia. Other German Jews lobbied in support of legislation restricting immigration. A wealthy and more enlightened element among German-American Jewry, realizing that the Eastern European Jews could not be stopped, took a different tack. They developed and financed schemes to disperse the newcomers so that they would not be concentrated—and thus highly visible—in the few major metropolitan areas, especially New York City. These dispersion efforts had little success.[32] Israel Zangwill, a leading Jewish intellectual of the period, cogently expressed the cause of this failure:

On a misty summer day, New York is like a hell and I could never conceive how these poor Jews can bear the heat in the small, narrow rooms. Nevertheless, I have the feeling that, were I a Russian immigrant, I would give the following reply to the suggestion of moving away: No, I would say, here my soul at least finds satisfaction. Let your millionaires move to other cities, they possess so many resources. I possess only my Jewish atmosphere.[33]

Everything about the Eastern European Jewish immigrants seemed to arouse the enmity and contempt of their German-American coreligionists. This was symbolized in their cruel epithet, "kike," which they hurled at the "wretched refuse" of the Pale. The "uptowners" attempted to differentiate themselves socially from the "downtowners" in their own minds, as well as in the general public's. Even the richest and most well-established of the German Jewish families manifested this tendency. Thus Mrs. Solomon Loeb advised her children and grandchildren on the proper way to behave when on a train: "When traveling on a train for short distances, never hurry for the exit when it reaches your stop. People will think that you are a pushy Jew."[34] The dominant attitude of the "uptowners" toward less fortunate downtown coreligionists during the latter nineteenth century and the early years of the twentieth was summarized by Lloyd P. Gartner, a social historian of American Jewry:

The new immigrants were primitive and clannish, unwilling to take on American ways, insistent on maintaining "Asiatic" and "medieval" forms of religion and social life. "Culture" and "refinement" could not be found among them. They demanded charity as a matter of right without appreciation for what they received. They were unduly aggressive and assertive and embarrassed the painfully acquired good name of the American Jew. They had a disturbing penchant for unsound ways of thought, especially political radicalism, atheism, Zionism, and held to a form of speech which could not be called a language.[35]

No wonder, then, that many Eastern European Jews were not eager to accept these people for their leaders.

A key focal point of the antagonism between the Eastern European and German Jews revolved around their conception of Jewishness. One element of this was located in the religious sphere. Reform Judaism was the predominant religious orientation among the Germans in America. This version of Judaism contrasted with the Orthodoxy espoused by the Eastern Europeans. Reform Judaism in America was molded to conform to the middle-class status of the Germans and their assimilationist desires. Their services were dignified and conducted in German or English. They took place in temples that resembled the religious structures of their well-to-do Christian peers. In fact, some openly claimed that their Judaism was more a kin to respectable Christianity than it was to that practiced by the Russian Jews. The *Hebrew Standard*, one of the organs of the German Jews, proclaimed: "The thoroughly acclimated American Jew . . . has no religious, social or intellectual sympathies with them. He is closer to the Christian sentiment around him than to the Judaism of these miserable darkened Hebrews."[36]

The content of Reform Judaism befitted the heirs of the German-born Haskalah. Their Judaism was modern and rational. For them the principal carryover from the traditional religion was the moral laws. At the same time the German Jews were careful to strip from their Judaism almost all aspects dealing with the regulation of social behavior, such as in the choice of foods they consumed or the clothes they wore. Religion was relegated to one confined area of their lives and allowed them, outside of their temples, to be indistinguishable from the respectable Gentile middle class.[37]

The Eastern European immigrant Jews, "downtowners" in the parlance of New York City, returned the contempt and hostility of the German-American "Hebrews" or "uptowners," thus further polarizing the two communities. They were hurt and angry at the more well-established, self-proclaimed Jews who were so negative, condescending, and distant toward them. Rebuff at the hands of the German Jews, following the attempts to join their organizations and associations, reinforced the immigrants' anger. B'nai B'rith, for example, a national Jewish fraternal order, refused membership to Eastern European Jews on the grounds that they were unfit and "too uncivilized."[38] At the same time such action forced the East European Jews back into the womb of their own community where they erected and built their own uniquely Eastern European or Yiddish institutions, relatively free, for a time, from the influence of the *yahudim*-the Hebrew plural for "Jews" but used as a term of contempt by the Eastern Europeans for their German Jewish kinsmen.

The religion of the (New York) uptowners was singled out for special contempt. For both observant and nonobservant Russian Jews it symbolized the German Jews' attempt to ape and seek the favor of the Gentiles. The Yiddish socialists joined with their religious landsmen in heaping scorn and derision on the peculiar religion of the uptowners.

That which they do downtown to further religion and morality we might describe as ludicrous, were it not so tragic. Uptown *Yahudim,* who understand as much about the Jewish religion as an Irish *goy* understands about [a complex part of the Talmud]. . . . they are going to concern themselves with the religious problems of the East Side! Don't they know that a Hester Street teamster is a scholar and savant and an utter saint compared to the president of a Fifth Avenue Temple.[39]

The religious and nonreligious downtowners also had a different conception of their Jewishness. For the Orthodox believers, Judaism encompassed and directed all areas of their life, including costume and the foods to be consumed. This tradition as it was embodied in secular forms was also quixotically strong among the nonbelievers in the Eastern European immigrant community. It found a secular expression for them and, to a certain extent, for the observant Orthodox as well, in *Yidishkayt.* This Jewishness, too, pervaded all aspects of their lives and informed their identity as Jews. But Yiddish as a language and *Yidishkayt* as a culture were repugnant to the German Jews. The Yiddish theatre was denounced as "barbaric," and Yiddish was condemned as a jargon. Such a language and culture were regarded by the uptowners as contemptible relics of a past best forgotten. They feared that the major function of Yiddish and *Yidishkayt* would be to separate Jews from their Christian contemporaries and hold them up as objects of ridicule by Christian society.

In such circumstances, it was natural for the Eastern European Jews, when they founded organizations or associations in the political or economic fields, to make them into uniquely Jewish bodies. There were models available for them to emulate. This was what other immigrant groups, such as the Germans and the Irish, had done. Indeed, German-American Jews had even defended the right of these nationalities to take such action, while denying their Eastern European coreligionists this privilege. This tendency of the Russian Jews to form Jewish unions and political organizations was strongly attacked by the German Jews as it deeply offended their sensibilities and their feelings about proper Jewish behavior in the public sphere.

The German Jews wanted very much to be accepted as good Americans, who just happened to be of another religious faith. The Russian Jews were challenging this by acting as if Judaism was a nationality equivalent to those of the Irish or the Italians. The German Jews believed this image of the Jews as a nationality acting in an "un-American" and "clannish" manner would impede their acceptance (and assimilation) into American society. They publicly chastised their coreligionists for such insensitive and harmful behavior. Commenting on the efforts of Russian Jewish radicals to form unions among Yiddish-speaking workers exclusively, the *American Hebrew,* a prominent organ of German-American Jewry, railed in 1887: "We are Jews in the synagogues. . . . In the workshops we are and should be Americans."[40] And in 1896 on the occasion of the formation of an

Eastern European Jewish political club on behalf of the candidacy of William Jennings Bryan, a German-American Reform Rabbi was moved to comment: "My dear Russian brethren, who have done so much to cast a stigma on the Jewish name, are now adding this new sin to the long list of offenses which we are asked to stand responsible for."[41] In more restrained tones, another Reform periodical strove to educate Eastern European Jews ignorant of the ways of America: "The feeling of Jewish clannishness existing in the community will not die out until the Jews themselves cease to show symptoms of it, until, by their practice, they prove how they appreciate living in a country where civil rights have nothing to do with religious opinions and recognize that with regard to political affairs, they are only Americans."[42]

The German-American Jews, however, were not entirely hostile to their less fortunate Eastern European brethren. They did provide charity and relief funds. But in the first few decades after the beginning of mass immigration, such generosity did not perceptibly change the attitudes of the recipients and their kinsmen toward their German Jewish benefactors. The immigrants did not perceive the latter to be motivated by the religious obligation of zedakah, or true charity. The way in which the Germans administered their assistance also heightened antagonism between the two communities. One Yiddish newspaper commented on this:

In the philanthropic institutions of our aristocratic German Jews you see beautiful offices, desks, all decorated, but strict and angry faces. Every poor man is questioned like a criminal, is looked down upon; every unfortunate suffers self-degradation and shivers like a leaf, just as if he were standing before a Russian official. When the same Russian Jew is in an institution of Russian Jews . . . he feels at home among his own brethren who speak his tongue, understand his thoughts, and feel his heart.[43]

Even in this area the poor Eastern European Jews turned to one another and built their own charitable organizations to lessen their reliance on the benevolence of the German Jews.[44]

The differences and hostility between the two communities extended to other spheres as well. Differing economic interest reinforced the existing religious and cultural divisions between the Russian and German Jews. It was in the shops and factories of the German Jews that the Russian Jews found their first jobs. There they did not receive much charity. Instead, they earned low wages in return for 12 to 16 hours of daily labor in the context of unsavory working conditions. Until the Eastern European Jews displaced the German Jews as principal employers and major factory owners, a process that took several decades, the division in the economic world, as seen by Russian Jews, was relatively clear and simple. It was "we" versus "them," with "we" being Russian Jewish workers and "them" being German Jewish bosses.

Political party affiliations and the interests for which they stood also set off the *yidn,* or immigrant Yiddish speaking Jews, from the *yahudim.* The German Jews were predominantly Republicans. Of the two major parties, the G.O.P. was the one that seemed to be inimical to the concerns of the Eastern European Jewish immigrants. It was the party of the major business interests at a time when the vast majority of the immigrant Jews were workers. Also, and probably more important, the Republican party was the one in which the proponents of restricted immigration had the greatest influence.

In the earlier days of the mass immigration, Eastern European Jews had tended to accept the guidance of their German Jewish elders and support the Republican party. Their initial hostility toward the Irish-dominated Democratic party and their naive gratitude toward the political party of the particular national administration that had been in office at the time they arrived also tended to push them in this direction.

About the turn of the century, the immigrant Jews, particularly those in New York City, increasingly turned away from Republicanism. Except for occasional deviations, in the case of individual progressive Republicans such as Theodore Roosevelt, Jews in the early years of the twentieth century and, again, particularly those in New York City, voted increasingly for the Democratic and Socialist parties. These were the parties that the German Jews regarded with great hostility. They were also the parties that spoke most directly and immediately to the daily interests of the Yiddish-speaking community. It was the corrupt Tammany machine in New York City that provided needed goods and services to the immigrants in the form of apartments, coal, and food baskets. This welfare was given without the aura of condescension associated with the philanthropy of the German Jews. The Socialist party spoke to the ideals of the Yiddish-speaking immigrants and offered them the vision of a just society. The Republican party, on the other hand, the political organization with which the wealthy Germans were most closely linked, stood in opposition to the very parties that offered the immigrants material things for their bodies and ideals for their hearts.

The Jewish radicals among the downtowners utilized the various and overlapping animosities between their landsmen and the uptowners to consolidate their own position within the Eastern European Jewish community. In their bid for power and influence, they availed themselves of the opportunities that the German Jews provided. There were numerous occasions when the philanthropy of the German Jews coincided with their economic interests to the detriment of the needy Eastern Europeans. Thus, prominent charitable agencies provided strike breakers and cheap labor to employers. Some German Jews used their positions on boards of charitable bodies to obtain low-priced labor for their businesses. This was not always a consciously devious act on the part of the uptowners. They were capitalists who

154   JEWS AND THE LEFT

accepted the economic system and the situation of labor within it as givens. But despite the reasons or the motivation, the radicals were not sheepish about publicizing the cases and casting the German Jews in the most unfavorable light.[45]

In other instances the Jewish socialists benefited from the obtuseness of the German Jews in their attempts to uplift the downtowners. The most prominent example of this was the Educational Alliance. The German Jewish notables established this institution on the Lower East Side in order to educate, culturally enrich, and Americanize the immigrants. In the Alliance a multitude of classes and activities were organized to achieve these ends. Until the end of the first decade of the 1900s, however, they were conducted in English; Yiddish was generally forbidden within the walls of the Alliance. In one sewing class the students were encouraged to fine one another should someone be caught speaking Yiddish.[46] This policy was pursued in the midst of one of the world's heaviest concentrations of Yiddish-speaking inhabitants. Naturally, many persons enamored of, or immersed in Yiddish would be hesitant about enrolling in the classes of the Educational Alliance.

Radicals capitalized on this shortsightedness. They organized their own classes to educate and politicize the downtowners. Here, of course, the attitude toward Yiddish was quite different. Louis Marshall, a prominent German-American Jewish leader, commented on this to the leaders of the Educational Alliance: "We have permitted socialists to be bred right under our eyes. . . . Why has the immigrant not come to us and gone to the *Forward* [a Yiddish, then socialist, newspaper] which has its classes and schools . . . ? The *Forward* has had classes where people are spoken to in Yiddish."[47]

The radical downtowners continually fulminated against the German Jews, utilizing every real and imagined shortcoming of the latter as a club with which to strike them. They railed against the *yahudim* for their watered-down and hypocritical religion. They sharply made the connection that the very persons who preached reform, morality, and equality in the cloak of Reform Judaism were also the "bosses" who lived off the sweat of their immigrant coreligionists. The philanthropic and educational activities of the uptowners were depicted as part of a larger plan of the German-American bourgeoisie to establish economic and political hegemony over the East European American Jews. *Die Zukunft*, or *The Future*, a Yiddish-language socialist periodical, thundered out against the exploiting *yahudin*:

. . . they who were and continue to be strangers, who do not understand the spirit and do not know the actual needs of the Jewish population, they take upon themselves the right to be our mentors, our guides, our critics and chastisers. They want to control every branch of our life, our politics, our education, our press. . . . It is time that we considered and understood the character and significance of their favors. Whom are they doing a favor, themselves or us? . . . they do not mean it for our benefit, but they are guarding their own interests. . . . They, lacking intelligence and education, lacking true philanthropic feeling and a Jewish heart, want to control the entire life of hundreds of thousands of Jews. . . . Not only do they receive glory and honor because of their favors, but also practical benefits. They get the votes for their candidates. . . . They are our representatives and patrons! How is this coming to them? How much longer shall we allow people who have nothing in common with us . . . to be our counsellors and guides.[48]

Both the polemics and the reasoned attacks of the downtown radicals against the German-American Jews exacerbated those divisions that already existed between the two communities. The uptowners were the bosses, respectable citizens, watered-down Jews, and outside of, as well as opposed to, Yiddish culture. The downtowners were the mirror image. They were workers, anarchists, socialists, or Democrats, typically committed in various ways to the forms of Orthodoxy and very much immersed in *Yiddishkayt*.

The mutual hostility between the Eastern European and German Jews, while great, was not immutable. During times when Jews in Eastern Europe were attacked or threatened with physical harm, German American Jewish attitudes toward their Eastern European coreligionists did soften. In addition, even as diatribes filled the air, various elements within the two communities, including some socialists, moved toward bridging the gap that separated them. By the eve of World War I, a period of imminent danger to the Jews in Central and Eastern Europe, enough quiet spadework had been done to facilitate greater understanding and cooperation between them during and after the First World War. But again, in the decades prior to the War, it was hostility and mutual recriminations that generally defined the relationships between the uptowners and the downtowners.[49]

In the roughly three decades from the 1880s to World War I, our period of present concern, Jewish socialists found themselves in a favorable strategic position. They did not have to do combat with a powerful indigenous bourgeoisie. The wealthy and middle-class German *yahudim* were outsiders with respect to the Yiddish speaking Jews. And the middle class of their fellow *yidn* was not an effective opponent of the Russian Jewish radicals. Although increasingly numerous, and even containing some wealthy members, the Eastern European Jewish middle class was comprised, for the most part, of petty bourgeoisie, typically small-scale garment industry employers, tenement landlords, and small merchants. As a class they lacked the wealth and power to effectively combat the socialists in their midst. This Eastern European Jewish bourgeoisie also lacked the organization and solidarity that would have permitted them to inhibit or frustrate the establishment and growth of socialism in the large Eastern European Jewish communities. This particular drawback was largely a function of the highly competitive garment industry in which they were disproportionately located.[50]

The Yiddish-speaking socialists also benefited from a social handicap that the Eastern European businessmen in their midst imposed on themselves. These rising capitalists, in the process of ascending economically, would make changes in their social sphere so as to bring into balance as much as possible their social and economic statuses. This process involved moving out of the old neighborhoood and changing names, dress, manners, and speech patterns in order to project the image of an American or perhaps a German-American. Often Orthodoxy would be abandoned in exchange for Reform or Conservative Judaism or, in some cases, for no religion at all. As a result, the Jewish businessmen were weakened as a political force within their immigrant community.[51]

The unique overlay between class and culture was a related factor that accrued to the benefit of the socialists among the *yidn*. Yiddish culture in America became virtually a working-class culture for two principal reasons. First, as we pointed out earlier, the vast majority of the Eastern European immigrants were workers who spoke Yiddish and were part of the Yiddish culture.

Second, the socialists profited from the tendency of both the German Jews and the socially mobile Eastern European Jews, who used the German Jews as a model to remove themselves from the network of Yiddish culture. These mobile elements denigrated Yiddish and used it as little as possible. This gave the radicals who remained immersed in this culture an unparalleled opportunity to use it to their political advantage without having to face an influential indigenous class enemy within the boundaries and framework of *Yidishkayt*.

RELIGION'S WEAKNESS

The weakness of organized religion or Orthodoxy, a traditional foe, worked in the Jewish radicals' favor. The status of Judaism and the rabbinate in the several decades after the beginning of the mass immigration from Russia presented the Russian Jewish radicals with yet another unparalleled opportunity for leadership and influence in the immigrant Jewish community. The feebleness of organized religion and the dearth of strong rabbis among the Eastern European immigrants allowed the radicals in their midst to establish themselves, socialism, and their institutions as legitimate and preeminent forces within the Eastern European Jewish community as it was taking shape in America.

Two very important characteristics of the rabbis who emigrated from Russia to the United States helped the cause of the Left. One had to do with their quantity and the second with their quality. Relatively few rabbis came from Eastern Europe to America. From 1899 to 1910, 350 men gave their occupation as "cleric" to the United States immigration authorities out of a total of 1,074,442 Jews who entered America in those years.[52] The rabbis who did emigrate were generally not distinguished scholars or revered rabbis but rather those lacking in learning and prestige. For the most part, the highly educated rabbinate remained in Europe. "The absence of a religious elite," according to Charles Liebman, a sociological student of Judaism, "meant that the traditionalist immigrants were especially susceptible to a breakdown in religious consensus. To a greater extent than ever, the folk now set their own standards independently of the elite."[53] The radicals were able to use this religious leadership void and "breakdown in religious consensus" to their own political advantage.

This pattern of religious immigration was not limited to the clerics. The religious, particularly the very pious Jews tended not to emigrate in the pre–World War I period. Indeed, leading rabbis would warn the faithful in Russia to stay at home lest they endanger their commitment to the religion of their fathers. One even went so far as to declare anyone who immigrated to the United States to be a sinner.[54] A Russian Jewish immigrant who came to America in 1913 after first going to England, when asked why he did not proceed directly from Russia to the United States, replied: "It was easier. . . . To go to America was something out of the ordinary . . . afraid to go to America. Americans were apikorsim [free thinkers], they were atheistic. . . . To have somebody in America was to have somebody who was a convert."[55]

Those who did emigrate were disproportionately secular Jews, many of whom were socialists. However, the majority of the immigrants were believers. But their beliefs and commitment to traditional Orthodox Judaism were of a different nature and texture than those practiced in Russia. They were generally not willing to have their lives ordered by religious law and custom. The conditions in the New World did not facilitate the maintenance of this kind of commitment either. The need and desire to establish themselves and sink roots in a society where the values of capitalism held sway undermined obeisance to old customs and values. Thus, in 1912 a survey showed that 75 percent of Jewish workmen on the East Side did not cease their labors on the Sabbath. And in 1913, in the heart of the New York City ghetto, 60 percent of the Jewish storekeepers kept their places of business open on the traditional day of rest rather than lose desired sales.[56]

The immigrant children and young Jews seemed lost to Judaism. Little systematic effort was made to provide them with a Jewish education. In 1909 in New York City, about "three-quarters of the Jewish children of school age received no religious education. The quarter given some training hardly fared better. Incompetent teachers, shabby quarters and a sterile approach to education, combined to estrange many of the young."[57] And the Jewish immigrant community leaders in Chicago voiced similar complaints and fears for the "Jewishness" of their young.[58] After childhood the young men and women of immigrant communities, as their elders anticipated, were generally not to be found in the synagogues.[59]

It was true that the immigrants did establish numerous synagogues.

From 1890 to 1916, 1341 religious congregations were founded by Jews. Almost all were Orthodox and established by East European Jews. By 1917 there were 422 relatively permanent synagogues on the Lower East Side alone, and many more temporary ones usually appeared during the Jewish high holidays.[60] Membership in a congregation or attendance at religious services were not indicators of the depth of religious feeling and commitment. Many immigrants looked to their synagogues to satisfy other than religious needs. Synagogues provided the new arrivals with some sense of stability amidst all the change occurring around them. The fact that the large majority of the synagogues established on the East Side were *landsmanshaft* synagogues employing, when economically feasible, rabbis who were generally brought over from home towns or regions, attests to this function. In addition, many synagogues served as social centers and benevolent societies for their congregants.[61] The synagogue, then, was as much, if not more, a social institution of an ethnic community than a place for purely religious observance.

Given the nature of the synagogues and the type of commitment that the immigrants made to them, it was not an oddity for the same person who attended religious services to also vote a socialist ticket, full-heartedly belong to a socialist-led union, become a member of a radical fraternal organization, and faithfully read a socialist periodical. Synagogue attendance and religious observance, such as they were for many, did not cut one off from socialism. Observant Jews in America, unless provoked by thoughtless and crude attacks on their religion by radicals, found their religious beliefs not to be incompatible with socialist commitments.

This situation, as we have seen, did not obtain to the same degree in Russia. One major difference between religion, as it pertained to radical politics in the United States and Russia, was the role of the rabbinate. In Russia, even though weakened by the natural forces of urbanism and industrialization, as well as by competition with radicals and Zionists, Jewish clerics still had a measure of influence and prestige. They utilized this resource in their stuggle with the radicals. Rabbis in America were largely deprived of this source of strength.

THE RABBIS' PROBLEMS

There were various reasons for the weakness of the rabbis. One reason, as we noted above, was that they tended to heed their own advice and were reluctant to come to America. Those who did come were not men whose backgrounds and education demanded or merited great respect. Also, it should be noted that the Reform rabbis, who primarily served the German-American Jewish community, had so little influence on the East European Jewish immigrants that they could have been living in a different world, even though they were physically located in the same cities.[62]

But a more basic factor in explaining the weakness in the role of rabbi was structural and historical. The Lower East Side of the early twentieth century was too different from the nineteenth-century *shtetl* to support the traditional authoritative position of the rabbi. It was not only the situation in America or New York that undermined the rabbi's influence. Such tendencies already existed in the cities of the Pale in the late nineteenth century, but in the New World they were no longer tendencies but powerful forces. A contemporary historian succinctly outlined the basis of the rabbi's authority in the Old World:

In Eastern Europe, the rabbi's prestige and duties stemmed from his expertise as expounder of a code of religious law which regulated most of the civil life of the Jews. Scholarship (essential for the explication of the sacred laws) and instruction (the obligation of the scholar) were esteemed functions of the office. Arbitrator in all manner of disputes and overseer of public institutions, the rabbi was party to the major decisions taken by the community. . . .[63]

In the United States, religious law was of little importance in regulating the civil life of the Jews. The secular state and the tempo and needs of urban-industrial life performed this function. Also, the American government, unlike the earlier czarist government, never invested rabbis or other clerics with significant public authority. There was therefore little but tradition to give weight to the rabbis' opinions in the New World. But tradition in the absence of structural supports proved to be an ephemeral source of authority. And the traditions of the New World were not supportive of the rabbi, as they had been in the Old. America was much more a secular society than that of czarist Russia. Religion and religious differences were less important here. Ethnic differences, particularly during the periods of mass immigration, appeared to be more important. Thus, there was less historical reason to turn to the clergy for leadership on matters outside of their purview.

America lacked a tradition of popular and state anti-Semitism. In the nineteenth century czarist empire, the Jews, in response to such threats, had sought refuge in their traditional and religious communal institutions. They then strengthened and virtually sanctified them to enable these institutions to withstand the attacks from outsiders. In so doing, they elevated and reinforced the status and authority of the rabbis. The absence of a tradition of militant popular and official anti-Semitism weakened the rabbis' position among the pre–World War I Eastern European Jews living in America.

Finally, the rabbis in the United States had difficulty organizing themselves so as to present a united front that would have more effectively preserved, if not enhanced, their existing authority. This, too, was not as much a problem of will on their part as it was a factor rooted in the social structure of the immigrant community. Paradoxically, it also stemmed from East European Jews' desire to re-establish their religion in America. This meant that on the East Side alone 422 synagogues were formed shortly before World War I. "They represented a map of Russian-Jewish settlement with all of its sectional rivalries and regional peculiarities. . . . Though only a minority of the congregations had their own rabbis, staking out a hegemony under these conditions was difficult indeed. The rabbis' traditional, community-wide functions atrophied. They lost their independence and influence." [64]

The miserable experience of Rabbi Jacob Joseph in the United States was a vivid testimony to the rabbinate's sorry state in the decades immediately prior to World War I. In 1887 a group of East European immigrant synagogues on the East Side joined together to invite this rabbi to come from Vilna in order to fill the post of Chief Rabbi, one which they had created. Unfortunately, for him, he came. The Chief Rabbi soon found himself the object of attacks by radicals and secularists and the center of factional fights within the Orthodox community, all of whom objected to the attempt to establish a religious hierarchy in this country. Very few respected his authority, and he soon drifted into obscurity. His greatest popularity came in 1902 when the East Side turned out in large numbers to participate in and watch his funeral procession. [65]

The Eastern European Orthodox rabbis in America before World War I were trapped by a situation over which they had little control. And they were not very able to help themselves either, particularly in the way of organization. These men were unable and many more were unwilling to form a strong centralized organization. It meant that they lacked the means to supply the needs of congregations requesting the services of rabbis and the structure to ensure the authenticity of men who chose to practice the profession in America. Several attempts were made to found an authoritative body of Orthodox rabbis, one in 1898 and the other in 1902, but both attempts failed. In the absence of such an organization, scholarly and ordained rabbis from Eastern Europe found themselves in America competing for positions with "imposters." [66] In Newark, New Jersey, in 1924 the Jewish community of 60,000 to 70,000 persons had only three or four properly ordained rabbis. However, as the son of one of these men recalled, there were in addition: ". . . many fakers . . . who professed to be rabbis . . . a despicable crew of 'reverends' who were perpetually covetous of money and publicity . . . these fake rabbis had congregations. . . . It was not long before my father and his colleagues found themselves in a life and death struggle." [67] An observer of the scene around the turn of the century similarly wrote: "Rabbis in America are as thick as flies. . . . Whoever could get himself a silk hat, a white shawl around his neck, carry a cane or an umbrella in his hand and somehow piece together a sermon—he became a rabbi, a sage in Israel. For five dollars he would marry or divorce a couple, no questions asked." [68]

All of this could not help but demolish the traditional prestige and authority of the rabbi. In such a setting, amidst confusion, rivalries, and marketplace ordinations, the rabbis were in no position to challenge the radicals effectively. What is more, their own weakness and confusion afforded the socialists the opportunity to acquire a leadership role in the immigrant community surpassing theirs.[69] Despite the obvious differences between the two, there were some strands of traditional continuity in the sense that the new leaders were among the most educated and, in their fashion, "devout" segment of the Jewish community.

The rabbis, for their part, were cognizant of their situation and, to some extent, of the influence of the radicals among the immigrant East European Jews. Thus, although hostile to socialism, they did choose not to be as openly combative toward it as their counterparts in Eastern Europe had been. They also did not try, as did their fellow Catholic and Protestant clerics in the United States, to influence the labor movement among their communicants along conservative lines. In fact, from 1900 to 1915 perhaps out of sincere beliefs or the desire to keep and please a constituency, rabbis became almost preoccupied with the vision of social justice in their sermons. They preached that poverty was not a product of the will of God but, instead, was man-made and that labor had a right to organize to protect its interests.[70] Thus, in this manner, the rabbis indirectly legitimized the role of the Left among the Jewish immigrants.

It is instructive to contrast the organization and the attitude of the rabbinate in England with that of America relative to the relationship between religion and socialism. Jewish radicals in England were not able to attain as strong and as enduring a leadership over their East European immigrant coreligionists as did their counterparts in America.[71] One of the reasons for this centered on the rabbinate. In England the rabbinate was much more highly organized than in America. There, in the 1880s and 1890s the Federation of Synagogues was a powerful force that brought some semblance of order among Jewish religious organizations. English Jewry also had a Chief Rabbi, a position that New York Jewry tried and failed to establish in the 1880s.

Both the Chief Rabbi and the Federation of Synagogues in England were open and ardent foes of the radicals, even at the height of the latter's influence prior to the turn of the century. Rarely did they give any quarter in their struggle against their socialist foes. The religious leaders would accuse the radicals of being actual or potential Christian missionaries, a charge that had a measure of effectiveness among the Jewish masses. The Chief Rabbi openly espoused laissez-faire and even defended the sweatshops. In 1894 the appointment of a charismatic Eastern European rabbi, Chaim Zundel Maccoby, as Chief Rabbi strengthened the religious forces in their battle with the godless radicals.

The Chief Rabbi and the Federation of Synagogues were encouraged and guided in their opposition to the Jewish socialists by powerful and astute elements within the Anglo-Jewish community. One of the most notable personages in this regard was Sir Samuel Montague, a wealthy member of Parliament from Whitechapel, the area of Eastern European concentration in London. He clearly recognized the influence that organized religion could bring to bear in separating the radicals from the immigrant masses. Montague consciously financed and strengthened the Federation of Synagogues so that it might, in his words, "take the lead in combating this most serious evil [radical-atheists]."

The English Jewish radicals, as opposed to their American counterparts, had to devote much time and energy to combating their religious foes. This was time and energy drained from their political and union work. Also, their crudeness and inflexibility in this battle often alienated supporters and, more importantly, potential supporters who remained tied to some aspects of religious tradition and ritual. Most notable in this regard was the radicals' militant mocking of Yom Kippur, the most sacred holiday in the Jewish calendar. On this day they would hold Yom Kippur dinner balls and parade, openly and provocatively consuming food, in front of the synagogues filled with fasting Jews.[72] Their antireligious militancy made it very difficult for them to socialize intimately with observant Jews. It prevented the radicals from establishing the social rapport necessary to buttress their political message. Religious Jews found it difficult to coexist within the social world of the radical Jews. "It seemed useless to have religious Jews in [socialist] social clubs," one historian noted, "because such attempts invariably exploded with the lighting of the first cigarette on the Sabbath."[73]

A somewhat different situation existed in America. Here, the radicals were also anti-religious but not as fervent about it as the English Jews. Jewish radicals on this side of the Atlantic also made crude antireligious actions and statements. But these seemed not as numerous nor as continuous as was the case in England. Perhaps the difference in attitude and behavior was a function of the weakness of organized religion here and its reluctance to do open battle with the radicals. A feeble enemy does not merit much energy or attention.

In any case, the turn of the century marked a decline in the animosity that the radicals exhibited toward Judaism and religious Jews. Increasingly, socialists contended that "religion is a private matter." The leading Yiddish socialist newspaper called for respect for observant Jews. In America, Jewish socialists were more tolerant than their peers in England of their supporters who would march in their demonstrations, vote for their parties, read their literature, and then attend religious services, bar mitzvah their children, and fast on Yom Kippur.[74] Jewish radicals in the United States were more expedient than their brethren in England and more in tune with Lenin's contention that: "The unity of that genuine revolutionary struggle of the oppressed class to set up a heaven on earth is more important to us than a unity, in the proletarian opinion, about the imaginary paradise in the sky." [75]

In summary, the organized strength of the rabbinate in England and its active opposition to the Jewish radicals proved to be a key factor in frustrating the growth of radicalism among Eastern European Jewish immigrants. The Jewish socialists in London were never blessed with the presence of a weak, confused, and bitterly divided religious establishment as were their cousins in New York. This major difference between the two groups of Jewish radicals operating in the same immigrant milieu explains, in part, why, on the eve of World War I, Jewish radicalism was a spent force in England, while on this side of the Atlantic it was vigorously alive.

ZIONISM

The Jewish socialists in the United States were also fortunate with respect to the condition of another internal foe—Zionism. The Zionists in America barely existed as an organized force prior to 1914, and Zionism as an ideology was not in the same league, politically, as socialism as far as the immigrant Jews were concerned. Up to 1914 there were only 12,000 formal members of the Zionist movement, and the movement had never been able to raise more than $12,000 in any year. World War I and the danger that it represented to the Jews of Europe quickly changed this situation. Before 1914, however, Jewish socialists did not have to contend with competition from political Zionism for the loyalty of the immigrant Jewish constituency. [76]

LABOR

The occupational experiences, traditions, and characteristics of the Russian Jewish immigrants contributed to their receptivity to the Left in America. Once settled in the New World, many of the very same characteristics that had obtained in Russia took root with them in the United States. This unique combination of Old and New World conditions pertaining to the workplace helped to make the Jewish workers very important in the establishment of a Left or socialist force in the United States.

The Skilled Workers

The Russian Jewish immigrants, particularly those who came after the turn of the century, were predominantly skilled workers. From 1900 to 1925 approximately two out of three Jews arriving in America, primarily from Russia and Eastern Europe, who reported an occupation were placed in the category of skilled workers. [77] In this regard they were dissimilar from other Jews in Russia who did not emigrate and from other immigrant nationalities who did come to America.

The large proportion of skilled workers or craftsmen among the Jewish Russian immigrants indicated that they did not represent an occupational cross section of the Russian Jewish labor force. The percentage of craftsmen among the immigrants was higher than it was among the Jewish population of the Pale in 1897. They came from particular geographical areas and labor pools. These skilled workers were disproportionately drawn from those areas and provinces of the Settlement of Pale that had experienced the most rapid rates of industrialization and were, at the time of the emigrants' departure, the most heavily industrialized sectors. These were also the very areas where the Bund and other radical groups were the most influential.[78] Thus, when they settled in America they were already acquainted with industrialism and socialism from firsthand experience.

The large percentage of skilled workers among the Jews can better be appreciated by comparing it to comparable figures for other immigrant groups arriving in America at approximately the same time. Between 1899 and 1910, a period of extensive immigration, the percentage of skilled workers, again based on all those reporting an occupation among all the immigrant groups combined, was 20 percent. Among the non-Jewish Russians and Poles the percentage was 9 percent and 6 percent, respectively. Even if the comparison is made only with immigrants from relatively industrialized countries or areas such as England, France, Germany, or northern Italy, the proportion of skilled workers among the Jews is higher. It is the highest of any nationality group in this period.[79]

As artisans who were also Jews, these workers carried with them experiences and traditions that served them well when they were called upon to build unions and socialist organizations. They, more so than common laborers or peasant farmers, had a rich tradition of organization and mutuality behind them. These included their guilds, trade synagogues, mutual aid societies, strike fund organizations, and, most recently, unions. Contrast this experience and tradition with those of the southern Italian immigrants pouring into America at approximately the same time. As men of the soil, common laborers, and Catholics, their associational experience in Italy was limited to that of the mutual aid society. And in America, unlike their Jewish immigrant counterparts, this associational network did not spread. The southern Italians generally limited themselves to a few limited organizations or groups, especially those centering on the family and fellow townsmen.[80] Thus Jews, unlike Italians and similar immigrant groups, were used to working together, organizing, disciplining one another for the benefit of the larger group, and engaging in common struggle. Also important was the fact that these were usually their own self-created organizations and that they were generally democratic rather than authoritarian and hierarchical.

Not all of the Jewish artisans' heritage was supportive of unionism and socialism. These skilled workers also drew from a tradition of individuality and economic independence that had as its most concrete manifestation the establishment of one's own shop. This set of traditions did not necessarily undermine their mutual support and cooperation as artisan-employees. When their aspirations for self employment were blocked, the result could be anger toward the system that often was channeled into support of militant labor actions, if not socialism.

Occupational Distribution

Jewish skilled workers concentrated in specific occupations, reflecting their work experience in the Old World. Again, this degree of concentration can best be put in perspective by comparison with other nationality groups. From 1899 to 1914 the Jews comprised roughly 10 percent of the immigrants. Yet, in the same period: "They constituted 80 percent of the hat and cap makers, 75 percent of the furriers, 68 percent of the tailors, and bookbinders, 60 percent of the watchmakers and milliners, and 55 percent of the cigar makers and tinsmiths. They totalled 30 to 50 percent of the immigrants classified as tanners, turners, undergarment makers, jewelers, painters, glaziers, dressmakers . . . butchers."[81]

The possession of a particular skill, however, did not assure its immigrant possessor of a position in the New World where that craft could be applied. In some cases, such as blacksmiths, conditions on this side of the Atlantic were so different that there was little or no market for the skill involved. In other instances, as in the example of cobblers and bootmakers, mechanization and factorization reduced the craft to a near anachronism. In the building trades, the opposition of the non-Jewish workers prevented skilled Jews from plying that trade. In addition, the immigrant Jewish craftsmen were reluctant to enter labor markets that were geographically and socially distant from the ghetto. The Russian Jewish immigrant wanted to work and live close to his landsmen and coreligionists, where he could feel free to observe his religion and ethnic customs in a sympathetic Yiddish-speaking environment.[82]

Yet some of the immigrants could apply their Old World skills in a familiar and accepting milieu. The sheer mass of Jewish immigrants assembled in a limited area created a market for the services of "Jewish" craftsmen, such as butchers, bakers, and actors. However, the major provider of jobs that required the use of previous skills in the context of a Jewish milieu was the garment industry. Nearly half the immigrant Jewish craftsmen were in some way associated with the needle trades. This industry was the backbone of the economy and polity of the immigrant Jewish community.

The Needle Trades Workers

The garment industry was the single largest source of employment of all Jews from the 1880s up through World War I, the period of our present concern. In the 1890s approximately one-third of the Jews in the labor force worked in the needle trades. From the 1880s through World War I, Jewish workers constituted the single largest ethnic group in the industry. In this same period, and probably even today, Jews were the largest element among the employers as well.[83] It is also interesting to note that the clothing industry during this period, had the largest proportion of foreign-born among the ranks of employees of any industry in the United States. In 1910, 20 percent of all white male employees in industry were foreign-born. In the needle trades, the figure was 75 percent. This extremely high proportion was largely a function of the presence of Jews, together with other ethnic groups, particularly Italian, in this trade. The nearest rival to the garment industry, in terms of the proportion of foreign-born workers, was copper and iron mining—with approximately 66 percent.[84] These "immigrant" industries also served as the most important bases of support for socialist and radical movements.

The Jewish strength in the clothing industry, which encompassed men's, women's, and children's garments as well as caps, hats, and furs, was made even more pronounced by the concentration of the trade in New York City. In 1910, after a period of rapid growth, almost 70 percent of all women's clothing and nearly 40 percent of men's garments manufactured in the United States were produced in New York City. In the same year about half of all the factories in Manhattan were engaged in the manufacture of clothing goods. The needle trades employed over 200,000 workers, or close to 50 percent of the borough's industrial labor force. And about 75 percent of the needle trades workers in New York City in this general period were of Jewish origin.

Prior to World War I the garment industry was physically located in the areas of the most heavily Jewish residential concentrations. In 1900 approximately 80 percent of the industry located in New York City could be found in the small fraction of the borough of Manhattan below Fourteenth Street, or one eighty-second of the city's land area. This changed, particularly after 1920, when much of the productive facilities moved into the area between Eighth and Fifth Avenues, bounded by Forty-First Street on the north and Fourteenth Street on the south. However, for the period with which we are most concerned here, the garment industry was largely an East Side industry.[85]

The Jewish immigrants from Russia and Eastern Europe were attracted to the garment industry for a variety of reasons. One was their familiarity with the trade. Large numbers of Jewish men and women in Russia and Eastern Europe had acquired skill and experience in the altering and making of garments. Between 1899 and 1914 when they emigrated to America, it was only natural that they would choose to enter a trade in which they had experience. The religion of the employers in the garment industry was another important attractive feature. In the early decades of the mass immigration of Russian Jews, German Jews controlled the clothing industry, especially in New York City. In 1888, a prominent historian of the Jewish labor movement noted, "Of the 241 clothing factories in New York, 234 were Jewish firms. Similarly, Jews predominated in the processing of hides, furs and leather and the making of ladies hats and caps."[86] The immigrants felt more comfortable working for Jewish than for non-Jewish employers. Jewish bosses, even if they were Germans or *yahudim*, appeared to be more sympathetic to their religious customs and rituals than were their Christian counterparts. Once the Russian Jews had gained some experience with the industry in America, many of them also became employers. They then sought out their countrymen for employees. At the same time their fellow Russian Jews looked to them as sources of employment, as bosses who well understood the special customs and needs of Orthodox Jews.

It is important to note, however, that these workers often paid a price for the privilege of working for their "understanding" coreligionists. Abraham Cahan, speaking then as a socialist through the lips of his fictional character David Levinsky, a Russian Jewish clothing manufacturer in the novel *The Rise of David Levinsky*, makes this perfectly clear:

Three of my men were excellent tailors. They could have easily procured employment in some of the large factories where they could have been paid at least twice as much as I paid them. They were bewhiskered, elderly people, strictly orthodox and extremely old-fashioned as to dress and habits. They felt perfectly at home in my shop and would rather work for me and be underpaid than be employed in an up-to-date factory where a tailor was expected to wear a starched necktie and was made the butt of ridicule if he covered his head every time he took a drink of water. These, however, were minor advantages. The important thing, the insurmountable obstacle which kept these skilled tailors away from the big cloak shops, was the fact that one had to work on Saturdays there, while in my place one could work on Sunday instead of Saturday.[87]

The physical character of the work in the needle trades proved to be congenial to the Jewish immigrants. Although the labor was tedious and exacting, a powerful physical strength was generally not required. The Jewish immigrants, unlike their Italian and Polish counterparts, had not been conditioned physically by their experiences in the Old World to do heavy manual labor. The work in the garment industry was more suitable to the physical constitution of the Jews than was true of work in other fields open to immigrants, such as mining and construction. The rapid changes in needle trades technology in the latter decades of the nineteenth century had contributed to shaping the work to fit the Jews' physical abilities. "As mechanization routinized production," according to the historian Moses Rischin, "dexterity, speed, patience and regular habits became the prime work requisites. So endowed, undersized and underfed immigrants could compete without handicap."[88] This factor also facilitated the entrance of large numbers of Jewish women into the industry. By the turn of the century, more than half of the Jewish women in the labor force were employed in the needle trades. Jewish women were not the only females to find work in the garment industry in large numbers. Italian immigrant women, too, entered this industry in abundance.[89]

One of the most important necessary conditions in attracting Jews to the garment industry was the fact that they could find employment within it. It was going through a period of rapid expansion at precisely the same time that the Eastern European Jews were arriving in great numbers. The ready-made clothing industry in the United States antedated their arrival by only several decades. It was only after the Civil War that it could really be called an industry. The sewing machine had been invented in 1846 by Elias Howe. In the 1850s it was improved upon by Isaak Singer. The Civil War stimulated the growth of the clothing trades. The Union armies needed quick delivery of large amounts of ready-made clothing. It was then discovered that there were close correlations between the sizes of different parts of men's bodies. This allowed manufacturers to utilize fairly uniform standards of measurement, thus facilitating the use of machines and less skilled hands. The increasing utilization of improved machinery and work techniques further encouraged the factorization of the industry.[90]

At that point all that was lacking was a mass of workers with some skill, experience, or inclination to enter the garment trade. That is when the Jews arrived in force. The employment figures over a 70-year period indicate the relationship between the years of Jewish mass immigration and the expansion of the industry. In 1859 there were 5739 wage earners making women's and children's apparel in the United States. By 1879, shortly before the beginning of the mass arrivals, the figure had increased to 25,192, Two decades later it had more than tripled and was at 83,739. And 15 years after that in 1914, the number had more than doubled, reaching a high of 168,907, a figure that would not be surpassed until 1929. This pattern of expansion, although in a less accentuated from, characterized other branches of the ready-made clothing industry as well.[91]

There was probably an interactive effect between the growth of the industry and the mass arrival of Eastern European Jews. The long hours and high productivity of the Jews, aided by mechanization and the lesser importance of skill and experience as factors of production, reduced the cost of ready-made clothing. This discouraged people from making their own clothing and encouraged them to purchase such garments. The increased demand produced a need for a larger

work force, and such opportunity drew more Jews from Eastern
Europe into the American garment industry. As the figures for the garment work force and the value of the products of the garment industry
indicate, the cycle apparently reached its peak about 1919.[92]

New York City was the site where a great deal of this rapid growth
took place. Between 1880 and 1890 the number of men's clothing factories more than doubled, from 736 to 1554, while those manufacturing women's cloaks tripled from 236 to 740. In the same decade fur
shops quadrupled from 60 to 232. In 1880 there were 1081 factories
producing clothing in New York City and employing nearly 65,000
persons, or close to 30 percent of the city's industrial labor force.
Three decades later the number of clothing factories had increased to
11,172, and within them there were 214,428 workers, constituting
nearly half of the industrial labor force of the city. In 1913 clothing
factories and their work force had grown to 16,552 and 312,245, respectively.[93] In actuality, these figures underestimate the total number
of garment workers and do not give an accurate picture of the total
who had some experience in the trade. The official data gatherers simply could not collect accurate information either on the numerous
small shops hidden away in tenement flats or on small side streets or
on those who labored in their homes, particularly Italian women.
Also, their figures were not meant to reflect the high turnover that existed in the trade among workers and employers both. When these factors are taken into consideration in estimating the total number of garment workers and those who had worked in the industry, the figures
for New York City and the nation become considerably larger.

As Russian and Eastern European Jews poured into the garment industry from the boats that carried them to these shores, other features
that had attracted them earlier to this industry became less important
than the fact that it had become a Jewish industry. Jewish origin,
mixed with place of descent, increasingly became the major requirements for entry into the trade. This process was facilitated by the general reduction in skill requirements, which had been produced by
rapid mechanization and new work techniques.

In this period the garment industry began to mirror the map of Eastern Europe. This flowed from the importance of familial, *landslite,*
and landsman ties. Bosses and workers in individual shops recruited
and were sought out for employment by their landsmen. Soon individual shops and sectors of the industry were divided along landsmen
lines. Again, with the reduction of skill as a significant factor, industrial specialization and European home towns or regions almost coincided. Thus, Jews from a specific region outside of Minsk staffed the
children's cloak branch. Warsaw Jews made the purses. Those from
Puchevitz were the furriers. Over time this type of relationship spread
from single towns to linked communities and regions. Finally, it
evolved to an identity between a Yiddish-speaking Jew and garment
worker, as expressed in the term "Columbus tailor." It was a half jok-

ing appellation pointing to the fact that some Jewish immigrants who lacked tailoring experience before disembarking suddenly "discovered" this trade as they left the ship. Their ability to speak Yiddish gave them their entry into the needle trades industry.[94]

Thus, within a few short decades, hundreds of thousands of Jewish immigrants became garment workers. They worked in shops and factories that were crowded together in limited and specified areas of several major cities, especially New York City. These areas not only contained their places of employment but their residences as well. And, in both their work and residences, they were almost totally encapsulated within a network of Yiddish culture. All of this meant that the common grievances that they shared as Yiddish-speaking Jews, ghetto residents, and exploited workers could not help but be magnified and intensified, creating an environment and a populace ready to receive and embrace socialist programs and ideologies.

Homogeneity of Grievances and Skills

Let us now examine some of the grievances that these Jewish immigrants shared as garment workers. An objective observer would have thought the wages and working conditions of the needle trades employees, apart from any other aspect of the industry, would be sufficient in themselves to drive the workers to socialism. In these respects, the garment industry typified the worst features of industrial or quasi-industrial capitalism. The tenement flats, shops, and factories that harbored the needle trades were generally dirty, unhealthy, crowded, and unsafe. Often, in the case of small sweatshops, the employer's living quarters would serve as a shop as well. One typical shop was described by a trade unionist after an examination:

Dirt was piled up to the windows. Scraps of goods and dirt were strewn over the narrow filthy stairs. The first shop we entered consisted of a small room with two little grimy windows and a still smaller chamber which had formerly served as a bedroom, without windows. . . . Several sewing machines stood in the first room. It was so small that we had difficulties in approaching the operators, who sat very close to each other. Under the mantlepiece was the fireplace with a burning stove surrounded by flat-irons. The floors were filthy, littered with scraps of material. Several girls were sitting on the floor and working. . . . We went over to the small dark chamber where the pressers worked, but could not enter because there was no room for us. A few bearded men stood there pressing the kneepants, bathed in sweat. The room being totally dark, they worked by the light of a kerosene lamp.[95]

The reports of the state factory inspectors of Illinois and New York also recounted the dreadful conditions in which the garment workers labored.[96] Conditions were so bad among furriers that life insurance companies would not issue them policies. In 1911 a group of doctors hired by New York State found that: "Out of every ten fur workers, two had tuberculosis and two had asthma. Most of the remainder suffered from bronchitis, eye sores and skin disease . . . eight out of ten were suffering from occupational diseases."[97]

The wages in the needle trades were usually low. They were generally of such a nature that one family member alone could not adequately provide for the needs of the entire family. Necessity demanded that there be more than one wage earner in the family group. Prior to 1914 state investigators and welfare organizations estimated that the minimal annual budget necessary to sustain a family of three to four in New York City was between 800 to 876 dollars. For a single man it was about 500 dollars and for a single female 466 dollars. The annual earnings in the garment industry at this time were generally insufficient to place them within these minimal budget standards. Fifteen to 30 percent of the needle trades work force, those designated learners, earned between $3 to $6 per week. More than half received the munificent sum of $10 to $12 for a week's work. Thus, if the better-paid group worked a full 52-week year, the members of this group would earn from $520 to $640, a sum larger than the minimum budget for one worker but insufficient to meet the needs of a family with three or four members.[98]

But this calculation was a hypothetical one because it was a rare employee in the garment industry who worked a full year. The garment industry was very much a seasonal industry. There were usually two six-week periods of intense activity where work would be available for the asking, and overtime would be the norm. But during the slack period, which often lasted from three to four months, the majority of workers found it difficult to obtain employment in the industry. During the weeks in which work was available, the hours were long and hard, approaching 60 per week in the "better" shops. In the other shops the average number of hours per week was around 80. During the peak of the season, regardless of the nature of the shop, employees would work from 15 to 18 hours a day and sometimes even 20. The only limit in terms of hours became their physical capacity and need for sleep.[99] Jacob Riis described the scene among the East Side Jewish garment workers at the turn of the century:

Take a Second Avenue Elevated and ride up half a mile to the sweatshop district. Every open window of the big tenements, that stand like a continuous brick wall on both sides of the way, gives you a glimpse of one of these shops as the train speeds by. Men and women, bending over their machines or ironing boards at the windows, half naked. . . . The road is like a big gangway through an endless workroom where vast multitudes are forever laboring. Morning, noon and night, it makes no difference; the scene is always the same.[100]

The personal agony of the endless workday found expression in the poem "My Boy," written by a poet, Morris Rosenfeld, who labored as a pants presser:

I have a little boy at home,
A pretty little son;
I think sometimes the world is mine
In him, my only one.

But seldom, seldom do I see
My child in heaven's light;
I find him always fast asleep . . .
I see him but at night.
Ere dawn my labor drives me forth;
Tis night when I am free;
A stranger am I to my child;
And stranger is my child to me.[101]

Low wages and onerous conditions of work were not the only features of the garment industry that contributed to the garment workers' sense of class consciousness and receptivity to the Left. The level of skill and the hierarchical arrangements of work were two additional interrelated factors of the industry that also helped to move the workers in this direction. The decreasing importance of skill and the general leveling of the work hierarchy that followed in its wake produced a relatively homogeneous work force in the garment industry. This common occupational status by itself, and in conjunction with other commonalities involving the same people, facilitated the rise of class consciousness and a pro-Left sentiment among them.

The importance of skill as a factor in the production of garments was rapidly declining as the Eastern European Jews arrived in America. This was primarily the consequence of the joint effect of mechanization and the detailed division of labor. New and improved machinery and technological developments transformed a traditional skilled hand industry into a mechanized one by the turn of the century. At the same time the detailed division of labor, which accompanied the Jewish immigrants into America, made the skill of the craftsmen increasingly irrelevant in the ready-made clothing business. The custom tailor, skilled and familiar with all aspects of a garment, was pushed aside. In his stead there stood the semiskilled worker who was responsible for only one aspect or segment of the garment. The system had become so entrenched and routinized that the United States Industrial Commission could report in 1901 that, ". . . each particular division became a trade in itself. The machine operator did not know how to do pressing or basting, the presser could not do the work of others and so on." [102] The novice in the trade could now learn his dissected specialty in two to three months, whereas only a decade or so earlier it had taken a similar individual four to five years to properly learn the tailor's craft.[103] Although important pockets of skilled workers, especially cutters, continued to exist and be necessary, skill as a job requirement for the mass of garment workers was simply not important after the 1880s. This circumstance was not unique to the needle trades. Other industries at roughly the same period also followed this pattern. They included iron, steel, shoe manufacturing, meat packing, glass blowing, baking, and tobacco.[104]

The interaction between mechanization, the detailed division of labor, and cheap and abundant immigrant workers combined to make the garment work force largely homogeneous. Economic and prestige differentials, based on skill distinctions and experience, were generally wiped away. The skilled craftsmen, again with some important exceptions, found himself laboring beside and doing the same tasks as an individual three or four months new to the trade.

The leveling that occurred in the garment shops and factories of the New World ghettoes also had implications for status distinctions rooted in the Old World. The garment industry was a major employer and source of funds for immigrant Jews in a society that measured men on the basis of their ability to make money. Status differences based on Old World educational, religious, or occupational distinctions paled in comparison to monetary distinctions during the early decades of readjustment following their arrival. It was the garment industry that was the great leveler.

This process is insightfully portrayed in "Uncle Moses," a story by Sholem Asch. It is about a group of Jewish immigrants from Kusmin in the Pale who work together in a garment factory in Brooklyn. Their employer, a landsman, is called Uncle Moses.

Kusmin served its Pharaoh faithfully. Kusmin labored industriously, sewing coats, trousers, and waistcoats for people of whom it had not the slightest knowledge. All Kusmin sat upstairs in Uncle Moses' workroom. Reb Joel Hyman, the elder of the Kusmin House of Prayer; Izzy, the cobbler's assistant; Jankel, the women's tailor . . . Hyman, the barber surgeon . . . all of these men now worked for Uncle Moses . . . Uncle Moses made all the citizens of Kusmin equals. There were no more fashionables, no elders and no tradesmen, no Talmudic scholars and no dunces. There were no more cobblers . . . no barber surgeons, no tailors . . . all of them now served one god, all were doing the same kind of work—they were sewing trousers.[105]

This leveling process produced, within a short period of time, a large pool of Yiddish-speaking immigrant workers who performed common monotonous tasks, faced narrow job ladders, and shared a similar fate as garment industry employees. For the vast multitude of workers, individual differences in skill and experience were either largely nonexistent or irrelevant and, whatever the case, did not get translated into differential rewards in terms of pay, prestige, and conditions of work. (Payment by the piece, as we shall see, did result in some pay differentials and competition based on speed, but it was not that salient to compensate for the overall levelling process.) In such circumstances the idea of collective action as a means to improve wages, status, and working conditions grew increasingly meaningful for those who remained employees. Frederick W. Taylor, the early management theorist and efficiency expert, drawing upon his observations in other industries undergoing the same process around this period, soon saw the danger to management that ensued from a homogeneous group of employees. In 1905 he warned the captains of industry: "When employers herd their men together in classes, pay all of each class the same wages, and offer none of them inducements to work harder or do better than average, the only possible remedy for the men comes in combination; and frequently the only possible answer to encroachments on the part of their employees is a strike."[106]

The conditions in the garment industry, most particularly with respect to pay, did not conform entirely to the model that Taylor broadly stroked, as we shall see below. However, it did come close. In general, the nature and structure of the garment industry lent themselves to the combination and collective action that Taylor anticipated. This increasingly common response and outlook would not only be limited to strikes, as Taylor feared, but perforce would enter the ideological and political realm through class consciousness and a proclivity for socialism.

The decreasing importance of skill had other consequences that bore on the political situation of the garment workers. It reduced the significance of the craftsmen economically and politically. Their skill had been the basis of their leverage in the economic and political spheres. As mass production rendered skill obsolete, the importance of the individual in the manufacture of garments passed to the masses of workers as a group. Thus, important decisions as to economic and political action increasingly depended upon the actions and opinions of this body of workers.

The divisions and distinctions between the skilled and unskilled or semi-skilled workers in the garment industry in the United States become even more germane when placed in a more developed socio-historical context. When large numbers of Eastern European Jews began to enter the needle trades in the 1880s, they encountered the hostility of the cutters, who were generally non-Jewish Germans and Irish and were the most important group of skilled workers in the industry.

The hostility of the native cutters stemmed from a variety of differences between them and the Eastern European Jewish immigrants. First, they were highly skilled craftsmen who had organized themselves around the principle of craft separatism. From this vantage point they viewed the Jews as threats to standards and wages in the industry. They generally refused to cooperate with the lesser-skilled Jewish garment workers and also resisted the efforts of Jewish cutters, whose skill they tended to denigrate, to enter their organized ranks. Second, the differences that stemmed from skill and economic considerations were reinforced by ethnic distinctions. The cutters were largely of German and Irish origin. And, third, they tended to be political conservatives and, as such, hostile to the reformist and socialist sentiment that increasingly grew within the ranks of the immigrant Jewish garment workers.[107]

The enmity of the native cutters impelled the Jews to unite into a more unified and cohesive work force in order to defend their interests. There were two aspects to this striving toward unity. On the one hand, Yiddish-speaking Jews stood in opposition to their German and Irish enemies. On the other hand, a homogeneous work force opposed the skilled cutters. In this respect, the more skilled elements among the Jewish immigrants were, of necessity, forced to join ranks with the lesser skilled in opposition to a common enemy. This meant that the differences in self-interest, based on divisions of skill among the Jewish needle trades workers, were muted for a crucial period. The more skilled Jewish garment workers needed the cooperation of their lesser skilled fellow Jews. It also meant that the organizational experience and skills of the Jewish craftsmen would be employed on behalf of Jewish garment workers as a whole. And, again, all this was occurring against a backdrop in which skill was becoming increasingly less vital to production, thus elevating the significance of the mass of lesser-skilled or semi-skilled workers in economic and political terms.

The low skill requirements for entry into this Jewish trade had at least one additional significant political consequence. It allowed fairly large numbers of students, semiintellectuals, and intellectuals, many of whom had little or any work experience or skill, to become operatives in the industry. This afforded them the opportunity to become intimately acquainted with working conditions, while at the same time reducing the social distance between themselves and other workers. As a result, they gained a clearer understanding of the needs and interests of Jewish workers. This strata later provided a significant proportion of the leadership of socialist-led unions and political organizations.[108]

LEADERSHIP

We now turn our attention to leadership. After the early 1880s each new wave of Russian Jewish immigrants to the United States contained a progressively larger number of Jews who had been active in the socialist cause and labor movement in Russia. In addition to them, there were even more among the new arrivals whose lives had been touched and affected by these forces. The activists, together with those who had had some association with the Jewish labor movement, proved to be a crucial ingredient in transforming a potential constituency for socialism into a real one. Radical intellectuals had been among the first of the Russian Jews to emigrate to the United States in the 1880s. The most prominent among these political persons were the aforementioned members of the *Am Olam,* or Eternal People. It was from among their ranks that the leaders and organizers of the first socialist groups and newspapers in the Russian Jewish immigrant community were drawn.[109]

Limitations of Early Radicals

The Russian intellectuals' impact on this community, almost until the turn of the century, was somewhat limited for several reasons. One was their limited numbers. Another was that the bulk of the Russian Jewish radicals in the 1880s and 1890s were still committed to the struggle in Russia. Yet another important reason for their restricted level of influence among their fellow Jewish compatriots was the differences between them and the Russian Jewish community that was establishing itself in America.

These radicals were tied to Russian culture and politics. Things Russian had a positive association for them. They, more so than the nonradical Jewish immigrants, were acting in accord with a script conceived and drafted in Russia. The nonradicals had their own ties to Russia, but these were of a different quality. They were primarily concerned with the fate of family and friends and viewed Russian events from the perspective of the impact that they would have on loved ones and fellow Jews. They were more than happy to shake the dust of Russia from their clothes. Few, as we have discussed, dreamed of return. This was not as true for the radicals. For them, although their bodies were in America, their "spirits," as one of their number phrased it, "continued to hang onto Russia."[110] And, although there are no firm and reliable data pertaining to the rates of return of Jewish Russian radicals, there is some reason to believe that they returned to their homeland in much larger numbers, especially during times of heightened revolutionary activity, than did their nonradical fellow Jews.[111]

The Jewish radical emigres, although physically in the Russian Jewish community in America, were not emotionally nor spiritually a part of it. Their Russian ties and experiences were very strong and meaningful for them, especially in contrast to what their fellow Jews had to offer. They spoke Russian among themselves. Some, indeed, did not even know or remember how to communicate effectively in Yiddish. As far as politics was concerned, for the earlier arrivals in particular, events in Russia were more salient than those in the East Side. One Jewish historian of the early Jewish labor movement wrote of the youthful emigres of the 1880s: "Their heroes were the martyrs of Narodnais Volya [People's Will] . . . as late as the end of the 1880's, the pictures displayed at radical meetings on the New York East Side were often those of Russian revolutionaries executed after the assassination of Alexander II."[112]

Consider, for example, the case of Alexander Berkman, the Russian-Jewish immigrant anarchist. He arrived in the United States in 1888 at the age of 18, a former student whose mind remained filled with the ideas and images of the Russian nihilists and populists. As of 1892 he was planning to return to Russia to engage in politics there. However, this was changed by the dramatic clash between the steel workers and the Pinkerton Agency's armed guards during the strike at the Homestead, Pennsylvania, steel plant of Andrew Carnegie. Berkman, incensed by what had happened, vowed to kill Henry Clay Frick, the manager of the plant and the tactician in Carnegie's battle to crush the steel union. Interestingly, he did not seem moved enough by the plight of the Jewish garment workers, among whom he lived, to commit such a deed on their behalf. Berkman, on the way to kill Frick, recalled in his autobiography the thoughts running through his head:

In my mind I see myself back in the little Russian college town, amid the circle of Petersburg students . . . surrounded by the halo of that vague and wonderful thing we called "Nihilist." The rushing train, Homestead, the five years passed in America, all turn into a mist . . . and again, I sit among superior beings, reverently listening to the impassioned discussions of dimly understood high themes, with the oft-recurring refrain of "Bazarov, Hegel, Liberty, Chernishevsky, v narod To the People! [113]

Indeed while on the train he planned to use, after his arrival in Pittsburgh, the assumed name, Rahkhmetov—the hero of Cherinshevsky's immensely popular Russian nihilistic novel, What Is To Be Done? [114]

Russian radicals of Jewish origin who came to the United States before the turn of the century did not seem to regard their location within the Jewish working class immigrant community as being of major political significance. Struggles in Russia and among other nationality groups were often invested with more importance than those of their fellow Jews in America.

As products of Russian socialism, these Jewish radicals, until about the turn of the century, were largely assimilationist and universalistic in their outlook. Their vision of socialism did not include divisions along ethnic or national lines. In no way did they view it as part of their mission in the New World to form a Jewish socialist organization or a Jewish labor movement. In this feature they were very much children of their epoch, very much part of the Jewish radical tradition in Russia as they had known it.

Another characteristic that undercut their importance among their fellow Jews was their social status. They were generally educated young men who thought of themselves as intellectuals and emanated from bourgeois or petty bourgeois families. In Russia they had usually not engaged in manual labor. Also, their early socialist organizations, even though the term "workingman" was to be found in the title, were largely composed of persons like themselves, intellectuals from middle class backgrounds.[115]

Their class background, universalistic outlook, and Russian politi-

cal socialization coalesced with their youthful revolutionary ardor
and idealism to effectively separate them from their working-class
fellow Jews. One of these Russian radicals, trying to comprehend why
he and his fellows had not tried to organize Jewish workers in these
early years, wrote, "The necessity to organize Jewish workers, to raise
their material and cultural level, such an idea never occurred to us at
first . . . such kind of activity seemed . . . to be too commonplace,
not revolutionary enough."[116] Recall, too, that at this time their Russian and Jewish counterparts in the czarist empire did not regard Jewish workers as the best material for revolutionary movements. This
feeling had to have influenced those of them who came to America.

Changes After 1903

After 1903 this situation changed dramatically. The massive waves of
Jewish immigrants who fled Russia because of the Kishinev massacre
of that year and the events of following years possessed a distinctive
quality that differentiated them from the Jews of the pre-1903 immigrations. The new arrivals had been exposed to and had become a
part of the process of urbanization and industrialization in Russia.
Thousands had been involved in a Jewish labor movement. There
were also numerous intellectuals and political activists who had
served as cadres and leaders in radical and revolutionary movements.
After 1905, in the wake of political repression and pogroms, the
number of experienced activists and leaders coming to America increased further. Most prominent among the radicals and socialists
were the Bundists. This new immigration breathed fresh life into the
Jewish labor movement and provided it with a sizable leadership
cadre. These politicized immigrants joined radical fraternal orders,
increased the sales of socialist newspapers and periodicals, entered
unions, and infused the ranks of socialist and radical movements.
They breathed a revolutionary èlan into the East European Jewish
community. This was not only a phenomenon limited to New York
City, although this was their major point of concentration. It held true
for places like Milwaukee, Wisconsin, and London, England, as
well.[117]

The impact of these radical and left oriented immigrants was felt at
all levels of the Jewish labor movement. It was probably most visible
at the level of leadership in the intellectual, political, and union
arenas. In about two decades after their arrival, veterans of the Bund
had become presidents of three major needle trades unions and leading figures in the Communist and Socialist parties.[118]

The intellectuals, particularly the radical and socialist-oriented
ones, represented a significant proportion of the new wave of immigrants, exaggerating a tendency already present in Jewish immigration prior to 1903. In the 1880s young radical intellectuals had initially immigrated to the United States in scant numbers. More had

arrived in the 1890s, particularly via a London route. Many who had come from London were not the youthful, inexperienced types that characterized the members of the *Am Olam*. They were persons who had gained distinction or experience and had then looked for broader and more important stages on which to perform. Thus, the political intellectuals of the pre- and post-1903 immigrations, together formed a sizable force in the Jewish immigrant community.[119] In this regard, the Russian and East European Jews were distinctive. As Robert Park, the doyen of the sociology of ethnicity, pointed out, "Unlike other immigrant groups, the Jews brought their intellectuals with them."[120] Park actually overstated the case. They had brought their secular intellectuals; the religious ones stayed behind. And, although not all of the former were men of the Left, as a group they were definitely skewed in that direction.

The presence of radical and socialist intellectuals, as well as those oriented in that direction, was, needless to say, a boon for Jewish radicalism. It meant that the immigrant Jewish community itself would be able to meet the intellectual and cultural needs of its working classes. They would not have to rely on bourgeois intellectuals for intellectual leadership. There were, however, also conservative intellectual forces present in the ghettoes, and the Jewish masses were exposed to ideas opposed to socialism. The East Side and the other Jewish concentrations were not hermetically sealed off from these kinds of intellectual influences. But in relative terms the Jewish radical intelligentsia had more of an opportunity to disseminate their ideas and establish themselves as a legitimate presence in their community than did the radical intelligentsia of other ethnic groups. After 1903 the Jewish radicals' presence in large numbers, combined with their vigor and vitality and weakened competition, ensured them a major role in the shaping and protecting of the Jewish labor movement in America.

The influence of the activists and radical intellectuals among the new wave of immigrants was not entirely a product of their numbers, experience, and emotions. These were, of course, very significant factors, but there were others of a less obvious or dramatic nature that also contributed to their political potency. They differed from their pre-1903 radical predecessors in their class backgrounds and work experiences. There were more, in total number as well as in proportion, among the post-1903 socialists who were workers and worker-intellectuals. Recall that, prior to the latter 1890s, there were but few radical workers in the Russian Jewish community. It was only after the turn of the century that they existed in large numbers and were therefore able to serve as a pool from which emigrants, in sizable numbers, could be drawn. The situation with the intellectuals was similar as well. Prior to the mid- and latter 1890s, Jewish radical intellectuals in Russia had not worked alongside the Jewish proletariat in their shops and factories. In addition, the Jewish labor movement, particularly the Bund, in its process of expansion after the turn of the century, had recruited intellectuals, students, and *polu-intellectuals* from further down on the social scale than had previously been the case. All of this meant that when these types of radicals came to America they were much more in tune to the style, interests, and needs of Jewish workers than their predecessors, whose experience and backgrounds had tended to separate them from working class existence before their immigration.

The new radicals were also more "Jewish" upon their arrival than the old ones. In the Bund they had integrated or reintegrated themselves into the Yiddish-speaking community. While Russian culture and politics still influenced them, its potency, for reasons discussed earlier, was not as great as it was for their counterparts of a decade or two earlier. Thus, when the post-1903 group arrived, they did not have to work themselves back into the folds of the Jewish community or struggle with their Jewish identity. Nor was it necessary for them to learn Yiddish in America. All of this facilitated their integration into and their acceptance by the Jewish immigrant community in America.

These new radicals also did not have to struggle, as had their predecessors, over the issue of organizing a uniquely Jewish labor movement. This was not to say that doubts about this strategy were not still present or that the pre-1903 radicals had not modified their position over time. Again, it is a question of relative emphasis and experience. The post-1903 socialists, for the most part, had actively worked within the context of all-Jewish organizations and movements. Thus, they were more comfortable and more experienced in working in this milieu than their predecessors. Their view of Jewish workingmen as material suitable for union and radical organization was probably more positive than that of the earlier radical immigrants. By the time these socialists emigrated, Jewish workers in Russia had become more industrialized, and many had proven their mettle in labor and political struggles. The old view of Jewish workers as passive and petty bourgeois had, then, to some extent been dissipated for this group by these changes and events. Although time had not stood still for the Jewish immigrants and the radicals who came before 1903, Jewish workers in America, as we shall presently see, had not been as receptive to unionization and radicalization as had their counterparts in Russia. Thus there was little in the repertoire of the pre-1903 radicals to cause them to seriously challenge their traditional view of Jewish workers.

All of this meant that after 1903 Jewish workers found beside them in their work places and factories thousands of socialists, radical-intellectuals, and veterans of labor and revolutionary struggles. These were men and women who were sympathetic to their plight, shared their toils, and had faith in them. Thus, the recently formed Jewish working class had no farther to look than their own ranks for a pool of educated, experienced, and idealistic comrades to lead them in their union and political ventures in the New World. And the post-1903 radical arrivals were prepared to fill this role. This does not mean that all were seasoned revolutionaries. Many were not. A large proportion were youthful idealists without much organizational or leadership experience. But they did have the will and the desire to continue their struggle against autocracy and for socialism in their new setting. This was particularly the case after 1907 and 1908, the period of "black reaction"—the severe oppression of revolutionaries and their sympathizers, real or imagined—in Russia. The impact of the czarist repression on the new arrivals undermined their hopes of returning to Russia and led them to think of the United States as their permanent country. After 1908 these radicals became more deeply committed to the struggles and movements occurring in America, their new home.[121]

While the particular differences between the Jewish Russian radicals who came before and after 1903 are significant, it is very important to keep the larger context in perspective. The latter group came to the United States after having taken part, in various ways and at various levels, in a Jewish labor movement in particular and a revolutionary movement in general. Those who came during the years from 1881 to 1903 did not have the benefit of such involvements. It should be stressed that the post-1903 immigration extended into the early 1920s. This meant that the Jewish labor movement was not only receiving the veterans of the abortive 1905 revolution but also sizable numbers fresh from their combat in the revolutionary movements, centering around the opposition to the czar and crystallizing in the Bolshevik Revolution, which began in 1917.

It is also important to keep in mind the role and the attitude of the rank and file in the creation and promotion of its leaders. The large majority of the Russian immigrants before or after 1903 were probably not socialists or very active politically. However, there were many more in absolute numbers in the post-1903 waves whose lives had been touched by socialist political or trade union activities. They held positive feelings toward the socialists who had organized their unions and who had fought to improve the status of the Jews in czarist Russia.

The immigrant community in America had closely followed events in their former homeland. The exploits of Jewish revolutionaries, particularly Bundists, were prominently and positively communicated to the Russian Jews by their newspapers and periodicals, even the Orthodox and conservative ones. Russian and Eastern European Jews, in addition to emotional support for their heroes, also gave a great deal of financial assistance. Both the Bund and the Russian Social Democratic Labor party benefited from the contributions of Jews in America. The visits of legendary figures of the revolutionary movements to the New World, such as that of the Bundist leader Arkady Kremer in 1903, buoyed the spirits of the immigrants. Thousands would turn out to hear these demigods expound on the exploits and needs of the various revolutionary movements struggling against the czarist autocracy.[122] Thus, the climate in the immigrant community was very receptive to and appreciative of radicalism, which many naively equated with opposition to the czar. The specific features that formed and informed this public opinion were not as important as the fact that this receptive climate existed and was widespread. When these noble veterans of familiar movements came to live among their coreligionists in the ghettoes of the New World, they found a Jewish mass that was ready in various ways to receive, embrace, and be guided by them. This acceptance proved, as they started out in their political lives in America, to be a great asset that considerably facilitated their work.

The role and impact of the "revolutionary" wave was poignantly summarized by Joseph Schlossberg, an early leader in the Amalgamated Clothing Workers of America, a major Jewish needle trades union:

The spokesmen, the interpreters of our grievances, were drafted from our own ranks . . . they brought with them from the land of persecution high idealism and youthful enthusiasm. They were Socialists. The foundation and background of their socialism was the struggle against Czarist autocracy in Russia. We were all filled with the spirit of that sacred struggle, though we had not all participated in that struggle. Those people spoke for us, wrote for us and worked for us. Thus each of our gatherings, whatever the immediate object, was an occasion for spirited propaganda for social justice in the broader sense.[123]

The English Experience

The general importance of leadership in the formation of a strong Jewish labor movement can also be seen by contrasting the experience of the East European Jews in England with their experience in the United States. England was second to America in the number of Jewish immigrants it received from Russia and Eastern Europe. The British census revealed that in 1911 there were 106,082 Russian and Polish Jews on the island. The majority lived in the East End of London, the counterpart of New York's East Side. These East Enders also resembled their coreligionists on the East Side with respect to language, trades, and poverty.

A Jewish socialist movement did arise from this milieu in England, but it was a short-lived phenomenon that failed to take root. There are various reasons for this, but one of the most important was the ephemeral nature of the leadership. Eastern European Jewish socialist organizers and editors tended not to remain in England. In this respect they resembled many of their less political landsmen who sojourned for a brief time in England before continuing their journey to America. This, too, was a disruptive feature for the socialists who struggled to organize among the English Jewry. The radicals were drawn to

America by the wider fields of political opportunity available to them there. Everything about America was bigger and more impressive than England, and the challenge of making an impact in such a milieu acted like a magnetic force. This was particularly true for the best among them, who often were called to America by invitation of radical groups and periodicals desirous of proven talent. By the 1890s the pattern was set. "Emigration," according to a leading historian of English Jewish radicalism, "would continue to deprive London of a Jewish socialist elite who had served their political apprenticeships in the Whitechapel ghetto." [124]

Thus, while the East Side was accumulating leaders and activists in ever larger numbers, the East End was being drained of this element. By 1907 it was estimated that only about 200 Jewish socialists remained in England. Reduced in number and ability, the Jewish radical leadership in London, by the end of the first decade of the twentieth century, could no longer play an effective role. However, England's loss proved America's gain as far as Jewish socialism was concerned. For it was these double emigres who became the architects of the movement in the United States. [125] They, together with men and women like them who came directly from the radical parties and revolutionary movements of Russia, constituted a large and experienced vanguard that nurtured, educated, and organized a Jewish labor movement in America.

POLITICAL ALLIES AND POLITICAL CLIMATE

The cause of trade unionism and socialism among immigrant Jews—two closely interrelated phenomena prior to World War I—benefited from significant political allies and a supportive political climate. These allies and this climate provided the Jewish socialists with moral and political assistance as well as a socio-political context conducive to growth.

The Socialist party (SP), which we shall consider in greater detail below, was a primary source of support and encouragement for radicalism among Jews in the years prior to 1920. It is important to note that in 1912, or about a decade after the SP was founded, the party was a political force of considerable magnitude. A contemporary historian, James Weinstein, described it thusly:

During the decade ending with 1912, the Socialist Party of America enjoyed continuous growth and exerted a wide impact upon the political life of the nation. Starting with 10,000 members in 1901, the Party had grown to 118,000 by 1912, had elected some 1200 public officials . . . and was publishing over 300 periodicals of all kinds. In the labor movement, and in many of the reform movements of this period, Socialists held positions of prominence and won substantial followings. The steady growth of the Party filled many of its members with optimism. [126]

Such a Socialist party could not but give direct and indirect encouragement to socialist and prosocialist Jews. In short, such a Socialist party made it easier for Jews to become socialists.

Reformers

Jewish unionists and, to a lesser extent, Jewish socialists in the pre–World War I era also received assistance from non–Socialist party sources. The most important of these was the Progressive movement, a reform movement that lasted from roughly 1900 to the First World War. It included in its ranks liberal politicians, muckraking journalists, settlement workers, clergy, intellectuals, and university students. This movement also had a camp of fellow travelers that contained members, principally female members, of the nation's upper and upper middle class families.

These Progressives aided the growth of unionism and socialism among the immigrant Jews in a variety of ways. They influenced public opinion on behalf of the downtrodden and against the capitalist robber barons. In countless articles and books and in numerous speeches people such as Jane Addams, Ray Stannard Baker, Norman and Hutchins Hapgood, Robert E. Park, Jacob Riis, Charles Edward Russell, Ida Tarbell, Upton Sinclair, and Robert Wood informed the American public as to the miserable and exploited conditions of the poor, the immigrants, and the blacks. Their attacks and descriptions were powerful and were usually reinforced by some data or well drawn portraits of the suffering poor and exploited workers.

Progressives did not only limit themselves to describing and analyzing the abuses of urban industrial capitalism; they also advocated ways of solving or ameliorating the problems upon which they focused. Some called for legislative reform. City, state, and federal governments were urged to limit the hours of work, do away with child labor, force employers to institute safety procedures, and oblige tenement landlords to make their properties safer and healthier for their tenants. Others went beyond the framework of legislative reform and appealed to workers and immigrants to organize to help themselves. This group, which included Jane Addams, Gertrude Barnum, and Robert Wood, advocated and defended the right of workers to organize in unions to attain their desired ends and improve their lives and work situations.

The activities of these reformers were not limited to the writing of articles, making of speeches, and the lobbying of legislators. Those in the settlement house movement went to live among the poor and the immigrants in order to educate, uplift, and better their lives. In the course of such work, assistance to workers' struggles and growing unions was offered by some as a logical extension of the services that they were already offering. Settlement houses, such as Denison House and South End House in Boston, University Settlement and Henry

Street Settlement in New York, and Chicago Commons and University of Chicago Settlement provided facilities, advice, and encouragement to striking workers and to union leaders and organizers. The presence of these social workers and other middle class reformers on picket lines and at fund-raising activities for strikers was not an uncommon occurrence in those days.

The backgrounds of these reformers heightened their effectiveness in influencing public opinion and governmental leaders and "softening" them with respect to the need for reform and, perhaps, unions. On the whole, they were native American, Protestant, and came from families that ranged from middle to upper class. The settlement houses in the Progressive era attracted from ten to fifteen thousand university students and young graduates, many from Ivy League and Seven Sisters schools. Persons such as Eleanor Roosevelt and Frances Perkins did their stint in these settlement houses. And in the ranks of the fellow travelers of reform were persons who bore the names of America's wealthiest families such as Mrs. August Belmont and Miss Anne Morgan.[127]

Some of these converted to socialism; others became quite sympathetic to socialism. But by and large converts were relatively few in number. As a group, the reformers did not advocate the creation of a socialist America. They accepted the capitalist system as a given. Their desire was to improve and humanize it. Generally, these reformers chose not to involve themselves in issues bearing upon such basic socialist concerns as the redistribution of power or income. Instead, they focused on health, safety, and welfare matters and at various times were even able to enlist the financial and moral support of leading capitalists, who, for their own reasons, favored such "safe" reforms.[128]

The reformers did help, however, to make public opinion more receptive to the ideas of unionism and socialism. Their varied efforts on behalf of the poor, the immigrants, and the ill-treated workers made the general public more aware of the abuses that stemmed from unregulated and competitive capitalism. From this perspective, the reformers made the efforts of union and socialist organizers more understandable to the middle and upper classes and gave an aura of legitimacy and Americanism to unions and socialists. This meant that union organizers and their recruits could not as easily be stigmatized as evil doers and un-Americans, who were beyond the pale of respectability. They helped to create an atmosphere in which it was possible to join unions, which were more often than not led by socialists, and to vote for Socialists without becoming, in the eyes of the immigrant workers of the more fortunate native Americans, outcasts who were hostile to America and the established order.

The assistance that the reformers gave to the cause of unionism and socialism could be seen most clearly among the immigrant Jews in New York City, particularly during the wave of strikes that occurred in the garment industry between 1909 and 1916. WASP reformers and intellectuals tended to romanticize the Jewish immigrant more than immigrants from any other nationality.[129] The historian, Henry May, commenting about the attitudes of the pre–World War I young intellectuals, noted how impressed they were with the East Side Jews:

The Young Intellectuals went further than mere tolerance; they turned the conventional hierarchy upside down. Anglo-Saxons, repressed and bigoted, were at the bottom of the scale; at the top were the Italians, the Slavs, and above all, the Eastern European Jews of the East Side. Writers of Puritan ancestry, like Hutchins Hapgood, earnest radicals like Ernest Poole, found an endless satisfaction in the quarter's crowded streets. . . . On the East Side rebellious men could discover a fierce moral idealism like that they admired in the Russian novels, devotion to an ancient and highly traditional culture, and a struggle for progress against all odds.[130]

Later in writing about what they had seen and experienced, the Young Intellectuals provided their readers with a very positive and romanticized picture of the East Side Jews, who entered American fiction as ". . . the wise and saintly Talmudic scholar, the beautiful young garment worker hungry for life, the heroic union leader." [131]

The intellectuals and reformers and their allies in the clergy and the wealthier strata also aided the Yiddish-speaking Jews in more direct and more concrete forms. The municipal government and the state legislature were subjected to major lobbying efforts on behalf of reforms in the areas of work and housing among Jews and other immigrant groups. The reformers also came directly to the aid of Jewish unions, particularly those in which there were large numbers of Jewish females. This could be seen, for example, in the assistance given to the New York Women's Trade Union League (WTUL). "The League, financed by wealthy citizens and staffed by volunteer reformers, encouraged trade unionism among women workers." During strikes of women garment workers, the WTUL ". . . established a corps of voluntary pickets, women and girls from the upper-middle class to abet the strikers." The WTUL also aided the cause of these workers by reaching the ears and pocketbooks of New York's wealthier citizenry. In addition, the WTUL, sympathetic clergy, and concerned members from the middle and upper classes of New York City influenced editors and publishers of the major establishment papers and judges to adopt a more sympathetic position toward the Jewish garment workers and their struggling unions.[132] The climate that they created, as well as the specific assistance that they offered, helped these Jewish socialist-led unions to establish themselves and, in a less direct manner, aided the cause of socialism among the Jewish immigrants.

But the Progressive movement was not an unmixed blessing as far as the cause of socialism in the Jewish community was concerned. At the same time that these reformers were helping to legitimate socialism and make public opinion more receptive to its immediate objectives, they were also helping to make American socialism a reformist movement. Inside and outside of the Socialist party, middle and upper class reformers, as we shall presently see, were bringing the party closer to the position of the liberal wing of the Democratic party. As a result, the reformers inadvertently proved more helpful in bringing Jews to the Democratic party than to the Socialist party. But at the time such a defect within what seemed so important an ally was not appreciated by very many Socialists, Jewish or non-Jewish. The existence of political forces openly hostile to Jewish and working class interests made the Progressives look good by comparison.

NEGATIVE CONSIDERATIONS

Not all aspects of the Jewish community and of American society prior to World War I facilitated the rise of Jewish radicalism. In these very same years the cause of Jewish socialism inside and outside of the Jewish community was confronted with significant obstacles and enemies, which were responsible for keeping Leftist Jews a minority among their coreligionists. It is appropriate now to deal with the forces that were operating to negate the attraction of radicalism to Jews at precisely the same time that the pro-Left factors were having their major impact.

Bourgeois Politics

Although the power of the reformers and the Socialist party was on the rise after the turn of the century, at no time was radicalism or socialism a dominant political force among Jews or non-Jews. In the United States, overtly radical or militant parties on a national level received only a small minority of all votes cast during elections. This held true for the Populists, who came from American soil, and for the European-imported Socialist Labor party, as well as for the hybrid Socialist party.

As the Jews entered the American cities, from the turn of the century on, the two-party centrist political system appeared to be rather firmly entrenched. In New York City, the major locale of our study, despite occasional and noisy threats from reformers and Socialists, the Tammany machine generally dominated politics. This domination, despite some occasional exceptions, extended into the predominantly Jewish districts. From the late nineteenth century on, the Tammany Democrats were quite attentive to the interests of the ever-increasing number of Jewish voters. Jewish and other immigrants received the usual machine "services and goods," which included bags of coal and groceries and protection from seemingly arbitrary laws. Tammany was especially helpful to pushcart peddlers in their dealings with governmental authorities. Tammany politicians, Jewish and non-

Jewish, also never waivered in their opposition to the restriction on immigration—an issue close to the hearts of the recently arrived Jews. Tammany Hall was also the first party in New York City to nominate a Jew for Mayor—Nathan Strauss in 1894.

Neither of the major parties at the national level were basically hostile to Jews (despite some equivocation on the immigration question). The pragmatic Democrats and equally pragmatic Republicans came to the same conclusion with respect to Jews. Their growing numbers and urban concentrations made them too important to alienate. And catering to Jewish interests and sensibilities, as defined by the major parties, did not require significant structural changes in the parties or in capitalism.[133]

Thus, the immigrant Jews in America were not confronted with the narrow political choices that they had known in Eastern Europe. In the United States not only did radical parties compete for their favors, the bourgeois mainstream ones did as well. In this situation there was little cause for Jews not to accommodate themselves to the middle of the road American political system and also little reason for them not to adopt the conventional politics of those in whose midst they so peacefully resided. The reluctance of many to follow these conventional paths was in part due to foreign memories rather than rational calculations. In time pragmatic rationality would, as we shall see, triumph over political nostalgia.

A Different Kind of Anti-Semitism

The link between the Jews and the Left in America was also weakened by the fact that the degree of anti-Semitism in the United States was considerably less than it was in Russia. Anti-Jewish sentiment and actions were simply not as virulent, as pervasive, or as menacing here as they were in the lands of the czar. This meant that in America anti-Semitism, bereft of government support, was not a significant barrier to mobility, whether geographic, social, or psychic.

Jewish access to higher education in the two countries, from the 1880s through the early years of the 1900s, is one indicator of the different status of Jews in each society. In these years as noted previously the czarist authorities imposed harsh quotas to keep Russian Jews out of institutions of higher education. Jewish enrollments declined. In the United States there were no quota systems in these years (although they were instituted later). Jews in large numbers entered schools at all levels soon after their arrival from Eastern Europe. Between 1880 and 1889 Jews constituted 25 percent of the graduates from the City College of New York (CCNY). In 1902 the *Jewish Daily Forward* boasted in an editorial that, "About 90 percent of the boys there [CCNY] are Jews, most of them children of Jewish workers." Other sources also attested to the large numbers of Eastern European Jews in a variety of colleges in the 1900s and 1910s.[134]

Anti-Semitism was not totally absent from the colleges and universities in the United States in this particular period. But its character highlights the difference between the situation in America and Russia. At CCNY, the "Jews College," as it was popularly referred to, Greek letter fraternities barred Jews from membership in 1878. Similar events later occurred in other schools as their Jewish enrollments grew. But although Jews were restricted with respect to social intercourse, they were not, for the most part, denied access to the nation's colleges and universities.[135] In Russia the anti-Semitic authorities could, and did, deny them admission.

The basic point is that the comparative weakness of anti-Semitism in the United States undercut the conditions that facilitated the growth and maintenance of radicalism among Jews. In America, as compared with Russia, the Eastern European Jewish community was very early deprived of one of the external mainstays of its unique cohesiveness. And as this unity weakened so did one of the props that supported the Jewish commitment to socialism.

The relative weakness of anti-Semitism in the United States also affected one group that had played an important role in radical and revolutionary activities in the czarist empire. This group consisted of the bright, sensitive, and ambitious Jews whom the anti-Semitic czarist authorities penalized in two ways. They simultaneously blocked these Jews from leaving the confines of their community and frustrated their aspirations for social and economic mobility. We have already discussed the type of political response that this treatment produced in Russia.

The situation was different in the United States, where the bright and ambitious were able to move ahead. This mobility was directly injurious to the health of radicalism, particularly Jewish radicalism, in the United States because the numbers of frustrated and bitter Jewish youth were greatly reduced. And as the numbers diminished, so, too, did the supply of leaders, cadres, and activists of the Left.

It is important to keep in mind that in this discussion the comparative level and nature of anti-Semitism, as it existed in Russia and America in these several decades, is the focal point. Anti-Semitism was present in the United States in this period. Anti-Semitic individuals and groups did frustrate social and economic mobility for Jews. The immigrant Jews did suffer from the psychic pain inflicted by anti-Semites. But although examples of this could be found in the New World, they were more abundant and more harmful in the Old. Only two Jews were killed by anti-Semitic mobs in the United States, compared to hundreds in Russia.[136]

The anti-Semitism that existed in America did not prevent Jews, within a very short time after their arrival in the United States, from gaining acceptance by mainstream political parties and moving into positions of public trust. Samuel Gompers, an immigrant Jew from England, was President of the American Federation of Labor, a post he held almost continually from 1886 until his death in 1924. Others served as ward and district leaders, attained judicial posts, and ran as candidates for public office on the tickets of major and minor parties. In 1894, as mentioned earlier, Nathan Strauss was nominated by Tammany for the position of mayor of New York. In 1906 Oscar Strauss was appointed Secretary of Labor and Commerce, the first Jew to become a member of the President's cabinet. Although much of this acceptance was motivated by the need to cater to the growing political power of Jewish voters and men of wealth, the fact still holds that Jews, albeit not many, were accorded public recognition and official honor prior to World War I.

It is interesting in this regard to remark briefly again on the political behavior of the wealthy German-American Jews. "Our Crowd" had begun to experience the sting of anti-Semitism from their Christian peers in the 1870s. This pehnomenon continued to strike at them in the following decades, and they found it increasingly difficult to gain admission into the better resorts, private schools, and social clubs. ". . . by the end of the century Jewish penetration into the most elite circles in the East had become almost impossibly difficult." [137] Yet few, if any, of "this crowd" became Democrats, much less Socialists, as a result of their treatment at the hands of the Gentile establishment. Indeed, Herbert Lehman, one of the major political deviants among them, was considered a renegade for his affiliation with the Democrats. [138]

The role of government in fomenting or condoning anti-Semitism also played a role in shaping the political responses of Jews. Unlike the Russian government, which was openly and actively anti-Semitic, the United States government and the mainstream political parties neither provoked nor sanctioned anti-Semitism. The first time it appeared as an issue in national politics was during the presidential campaign of 1896. Populists, who had endorsed the Democratic nominee, William Jennings Bryan, included negative references to Jews in their speeches and writings. Bryan, however, publicly reassured the Jewish community that he and his party did not condone anti-Semitism, and this issue had little bearing on the outcome of the election. [139] Similarly, at the local day-to-day level, the Irish-American policemen's leniency toward their kinsmen who sporadically attacked their Jewish neighbors was a far cry from the official and unofficial encouragement and protection that the czarist authorities gave to the pogromist mobs in Russia. This contrasting reality of American life weakened the traditional association between anti-Semitism and the state and thereby reduced one impetus toward the Left among Jews in America. Jews in the United States, who were frustrated in their career plans or hurt by discrimination, could not as easily find the source of their difficulties in the offices of public officials.

The fear of state-sanctioned anti-Semitism, however, did not disappear overnight. For many, their recent and searing experiences in

Russia were engrained in their consciousness, creating a distorted prism through which they viewed events in America. Thus, police attacks on strikers became equated with cossacks' assaults. The radicals also did their best to vividly maintain the association between anti-Semitism and the authorities. They affixed the ultimate blame for prejudice and discrimination against Jews in America on the capitalists and their politico-economic system. But the obscurity of these links, combined with the considerably reduced level of oppression by authorities in this country, reduced the potency of their analysis and increasingly made it seem as if they were engaging in street-corner rhetoric. The Old World prism soon wore away under the pressure of time and events. Officer Mulvany, the policeman stationed in Rutgers Square on the East Side, simply could not be transformed into a representative of capitalist oppression, despite Emma Goldman's or other radicals' attempts to cast him in that role.[140]

American Anti-Radicalism

The Jewish immigrants also had special cause to eschew any involvement with or public support for radicalism in their new homeland. In the late 1880s, as they began to arrive in ever-greater numbers, labor unrest, in which non-Anglo-Saxon foreigners were highly visible, was used to stir up anti-immigrant sentiment in the country. In 1886 this sentiment was transformed into national hysteria against foreigners by the Haymarket tragedy. Several Chicago policemen were killed by a bomb at the scene of an anarchist-led meeting in Haymarket Square, Chicago. Many of the anarchists in the United States were foreign-born at the time, and, of the six men sentenced to death for the killing of the police officers, only one was a native-born American. Hostility toward foreigners and calls for the end to immigration continued and heightened in the 1890s, fueled by economic hard times and labor discontent in which foreigners again seemed to play a major role. Then, in 1901 President McKinley was assassinated by Leon Czolgosz, a reputed anarchist who, although native-born, was obviously of foreign extraction. This event and its handling by the press whipped up the citizenry's hatred and fear of foreigners and brought forth new calls for closing the nation's doors to this dangerous rabble.

The Eastern European Jews, with their strange garb, customs, and language, conformed to the stereotype of the strange and dirty foreigner, so unlike the English, German, and Scandinavians. They also harbored in their midst radicals and even anarchists, such as Emma Goldman. She was a Russian-born Jewish immigrant who by 1901 had achieved fame and infamy as one of America's leading anarchists. Her notoriety reached epoch proportions in the wake of President McKinley's assassination. Before Czolgosz had killed the President, he twice had had contact with Miss Goldman. This was enough for politicians and papers to accuse her of being the ultimate cause for the assassination, even though her meetings with Czolgosz had been brief and despite Czolgosz' vehement denials of her implication in any way. Soon Emma Goldman was transformed into a national menace, and her name was used by parents to frighten naughty children into obedience. In Rochester the local synagogue, in its attempt to dissociate Jews and Judaism from Emma Goldman, excommunicated her father, who was in no way sympathetic to radical ideas and who never got along with his daughter.

The immigrant Jews could not but be fearful. The hysteria against the hated foreigners threatened to cut off the principal refuge of their friends and loved ones still menaced by oppression in Eastern Europe; even their own position on this side of the Atlantic seemed less than secure. In the wake of the assassination and Emma Goldman's vilification, newspapers and politicians wildly talked of and advocated deportation. By 1903 it was no longer talk: Congress passed a bill that allowed for the deportation of immigrants who espoused dangerous views. All in all, this political climate was certainly not one that encouraged immigrant Jews to embrace, much less come close to, radicalism.[141]

Factors Within the Community

Finally, our quest for the sources of nonradicalism among Jews now leads us back to the same factors that contributed to their Left propensity. In each of the predisposing or facilitating factors there was some amount of slippage. Although organized religion and religious ties were weak in America, they did exist, and they were meaningful for numerous Jews. To this extent, religion either insulated them from radicalism or helped to attenuate their commitment to it. Although a disproportionate number of secular and urbanized Jews immigrated to the United States, there were also numerous Jews from smaller towns and *shtetls* still in the grip of conservativizing customs and traditions. Although Zionism was weak prior to 1914, it was present and had much latent support, which World War I would soon make manifest. But perhaps most important for our present concern was the experience of the immigrant Jews in the economic sphere. It is to this sphere, and particularly the garment industry within it, that we now turn our attention.

Objectively, the Jewish immigrants upon their arrival, as indicated earlier, lived and labored in crowded, unsanitary, and unsafe conditions. They received low pay in return for their long hours. But as bad as life was in the United States, it was generally better than the life they had left behind them in the czarist empire. In America at least they all had work, even if not all the time. Their efforts provided them with wages that allowed them to feed, clothe, and house themselves in ways that were, for the most part, better than had been possible in the Old World. Although they might have had high expectations, the contrast between their conditions of existence in Eastern Europe and America could not fail to impress them. In the words of one Jewish immigrant: "Even the slums of the day were beautiful compared to the living quarters of Lithuania. For example, even though the toilet was in the hall, and the whole floor used it, yet it was a toilet. There was no such thing in Lithuania. . . . Here there was running water. I saw horse cars and trolley cars and when I saw a cable car on Broadway, I thought America was truly the land of opportunity."[142]

Such attitudes and standards of judgment by "objectively" poor and exploited workers were not unique to Jews. Other observers have noted a similar phenomenon among Irish, Slovaks, Poles, Croats, Serbs, Magyars, Italians, and French Canadians. During their early years on American soil they were physically in the United States but psychically and socially not a part of it. They evaluated their present situation in America on the basis of standards in their homelands. In these comparisons America usually came out ahead. These immigrants, including the Jews among them, despite the nostalgia induced by separation from loved ones and familiar surroundings, were usually cognizant at one level or another of the more miserable conditions that existed in their homelands.[143] For example, one young Jewish immigrant, repelled by the harsh materialism and secularity of American society, dreamed of and planned to return to his native Slutzk in Russia, until a clear immage of the town flashed through his head.

Muddy, smelly courts and alleys. Dilapidated houses sunk into the earth, up to the windows leaning on wooden props like cripples on crutches. Inside, soot-covered walls, damp with mildew, a sooty oven in the corner of the house, belching smoke and sparks. . . . The sooty, sagging ceiling would collapse at any moment were it not for the supporting beams! . . . Startled, I rubbed my eyes as if trying to erase the traces of a bad dream. . . . I shivered; to such a horrid place am I going to return.[144]

Many of the non-Jewish immigrants came intending only to stay long enough to accumulate sufficient savings to buy land or a position in their home countries that would assure them a more satisfying life back there. In fact, many did return, particularly the Eastern Europeans and the Southern Italians. Given the rewards of the future in the old country, they were willing to endure exploitative conditions and apparent low wages while laboring in America's mines and mills. Despite long hours, many would volunteer for even more and for Sunday labor in order to fatten their bank accounts.

Such were the attitudes and standards of judgment among the newly arrived immigrants, the Jews included, that initially hardened them to the appeals of union organizers, anarchists, and socialists. Although objectively exploited and objectively categorized as proletarians, subjectively they had experienced upward mobility when they set foot in America and, in their mind's eye, they did not see themselves as laborers, but as landholders and small shopkeepers. This "false consciousness" could not and did not last too long. The longer they stayed and the more integrated into American society they became, the less meaningful became the differential between here and there, and the more meaningful their present life became. Several years of harsh reality as laborers in America and the realization that they would be staying helped them adjust their vision. As they grew older and sunk roots in the United States, they became more open to the appeals of unions and socialists.[145]

Surprisingly, the income of the Jewish immigrants served to tie many into the socioeconomic system that the socialists and anarchists railed against. Despite the low level of the average immigrant worker's wages, they were increasingly purchasing things that in Europe only rich men could afford. Pianos became more frequent. Phonographs abounded. Decent and better furniture appeared in bigger and better apartments. Such conspicuous consumption was made possible in large part by the immigrants' self-exploitation and the pattern of multiincome dwellers in a family. Whatever the cause, however, the physical results were evident. They were also evidence that the capitalist system in America did apparently reward effort. The noise from the pianos and phonographs made it difficult to hear the strident voices of the socialists.[146]

Then, there was mobility in its various forms—geographic, social, economic, and occupational. The solidarity and cohesiveness of the Jewish working class was constantly undercut, even at the height of its formation. In New York City, even as the Lower East Side became the area of concentration for Jews, many were already on the move to better and less crowded neighborhoods and apartments. Thus, between 1892 and 1916, as noted earlier, the percentage of the city's Jews living on the Lower East Side declined from 75 to 23 percent.[147] A government report on immigrants noted the Jews' rapidity of movement compared with other nationality groups. It went on to quote a popular observation, ". . . that from Hester Street [Lower East Side] to Lexington Avenue [uptown Manhattan] is a journey of about ten years for any given family."[148]

Geographic movement was only one type of mobility that weakened the solidarity of Jews. Economic and social mobility also played a major part in this process and in making the Jewish working class heterogeneous. In fact, even before they physically moved across the class lines, their patterns of expenditure and leisure pursuits indicated that in these areas they were, even as workers, conforming to middle-class values and traits. Thus, once the basic needs were provided, money would be saved for the children's education, as well as spent on the above-mentioned pianos and phonographs. Many would spend leisure time, when they had it, at concerts, lectures, dancing academies, and summer resorts.[149]

Socioeconomic mobility began to occur soon after the Eastern European Jews arrived in the United States. Longitudinal data for New

York City Jews in three successive decades from 1880 to 1910 reveal a high level of occupational mobility. In each 10-year period approximately 40 percent of Jewish blue-collar workers moved into a white-collar position.[150] In 1901 the United States Industrial Commission had come to the same conclusion. Commenting upon the economic mobility of the New York City immigrant Jews, it stated ". . . that the proportion is considerable and the rate rapid."[151] An analysis of the 1890 United States Census revealed that the predominantly New York and Jewish tailoring trade was largely a one-generation phenomenon.[152] This upward movement was so great and so steady that organization of labor unions among Jews in the 1880s and early 1900s could not be stabilized. As one historian of the early Jewish labor movement put it, "There appeared to be a correlation between the length of time of a Jewish union and the number of years the average Jew is in the trade."[153] One early Jewish labor leader rejoiced when his union lasted longer than five years.[154] If the organization of unions was difficult, so, too, was the development of class consciousness.

The Jewish workers in the garment industry, the principal employer in the Jewish community, were also affected by another type of mobility. The industry, during the time in which the immigrants entered in large numbers, was highly competitive, unstable, and marked by many business failures. This meant that the garment workers who remained in the trade were generally not employed by one employer in one shop during their years as employees. Instead, they had numerous employers and worked with different coworkers in a variety of settings during the course of their garment industry work lives. Each move required employees to take time to form new intimate social relationships that would foster trust in the evolution of a common response to common grievances flowing from a common boss.

The continual irregularity of long-term annual employment, flowing from the seasonal nature of the garment industry, also had a similar effect. For most garment workers a significant proportion of each work year was occupied in seeking other types of employment or other employers in the garment industry who had work, or living off savings and loans from relatives and friends. It represented time taken away from intimate interaction with familiar colleagues in the context of a known and familiar exploitative context. As such, it made the building of solidarity among employees in a given shop that much more difficult.

The observations of the social historian Stephen Thernstrom as to why socialism was weak among industrial workers in nineteenth-century America seems to be an appropriate summation of the impact that the various types of mobility had upon the development of a socialist consciousness among Jews.

The Marxist model of the conditions which promote proletarian consciousness presumes not only the permanency of membership in this class—the absence of upward mobility—but also, I suggest, some continuity in one setting so that workers come to know each other and to develop bonds of solidarity and common opposition to the ruling group above them. This would seem to entail a stable labor force in a single factory; at a minimum it assumes considerable stability in a community. One reason that a permanent proletariat along the lines envisaged by Marx did not develop in the course of American industrialization is that few Americans have stayed in one place, one workplace, or even one city long enough to discover a sense of common identity and common grievance.[155]

Yet even though these conditions of mobility held true for Jews, and probably for them even more than for others, it was among them that socialism in American attained one of its strongest bases of support.

One other special type of mobility also weakened the cause of socialism among Jews: the movement of the educated and the intellectuals, as well as those with administrative and managerial talent, out of the ranks of the workers, unions, and radical parties. The open and accessible institutions of higher education located in or close to the cities in which they lived and worked became a principal vehicle of mobility for the intellectually and professionally inclined, as the rather astounding aforementioned Jewish attendance figures suggest. The socialists themselves were quite concerned with this qualitative exodus from the shops and unions. The *Jewish Daily Forward*, during its socialist phase, openly attacked these upwardly mobile persons for deserting their fellow workers and comrades. "You have sold your birthright for a bag of lentils."[156] The personal columns of radical papers also offered testimony to the mobility of those who had succumbed to what the East Side called "the studying epidemic." There, in an ever-increasing amount of space, radicals and socialists who had moved from the shop floor to medical and legal offices would announce their readiness to receive clients and patients, even providing their office addresses and calling hours for their comrades and former work mates.[157]

Not all of these upwardly mobile radicals severed their ties with the socialist cause. There were many examples of professionals, most notably Morris Hillquit, who, after emerging from the shops, utilized their professional skills on behalf of needy workers and socialism. But such mobility eventually had to weaken the solidarity of and commitment to the working class and to socialism on the part of the mass of arrivers. There were those whose new positions in life did not lend themselves to the maintenance of former sentiments. These were the men who suddenly, after becoming employers and foremen, found themselves in adversary relationships with workers and former union comrades.

There were others whose new positions allowed them to make the break more gradually. The changing and improving life styles and new patterns of social and work relationships that flowed from their professions continually eroded their links with the cause of the workers. The fact that many of the professionals' initial clients and patients were drawn from their former comrades and coworkers may have helped them to maintain their earlier sentiments and attitudes. But as their manual work lives became distant history and as their circle of associates and friends, as well as clients, became more socially heterogeneous, their socialist ardor, bereft of significant social or economic support, eventually succumbed to the interests, demands, and life styles of their middle-class economic lives.

The Jewish brain drain, whether it came quickly or slowly after the attainment of a professional degree, was indicative of the fact that something was quite amiss in the Jewish labor or socialist movement, even at its height. This drain proved not that serious in the short run, prior to the First World war. Replacements for the defectors were continually forthcoming from the massive waves of the ever-arriving immigrants, particularly from the later and more radical waves. But the pattern of upwardly-mobile Jews defecting from socialism and labor unions was visible and established, nonetheless. And, it would be a pattern that the socialists would be unable to effectively cope with in the future, particularly when the immigration ceased after World War I.

It is important to add that the departure from the Left of those moving into the professions and middle class was not preordained. A large and well organized socialist movement with a well formulated and articulated ideology, a system of discipline, and a strong and supportive subculture could have prevented or at least inhibited the defection of the upwardly mobile. Unfortunately for the socialist cause, the socialist movement in America did not have these necessary attributes and thus could not effectively counter the appeals and opportunities offered to these mobile elements by capitalism.

AGAIN, THE GARMENT INDUSTRY

In order to understand more completely the structural factors that militated against class consciousness and socialism among Jewish workers, particularly with respect to social mobility, it is necessary to turn our attention once more to the garment industry. This was the preeminent economic force in the immigrant Jewish community, as well as the principal employer of Jewish labor. The nature and structure of the needle trades shaped and colored the attitudes and actions of Jewish workers and sharply influenced the type of unions and socialism that they spawned.

The first and probably most important feature of the garment industry in this regard was the opportunities for mobility that it offered in the years from the 1880s until World War i. Recall that in New York City the number of garment factories between 1880 and 1913 had increased from 1081 to 16,552, a growth of 15,471. This figure is probably an unrealistic minimum, because it did not take into account the many business turnovers and the smaller shops. But even if we accept the figure, for argument's sake, as a bare minimum, there were at least 15,471 additional factories that needed bosses, managers, foremen, and salesmen, as well as cutters and designers. All of these positions removed their occupants from the ranks of the unskilled or semiskilled garment workers. These figures also do not include the considerable numbers of white-collar jobs and professional positions brought into existence within the Jewish community by the expansion and maturation of the garment industry, as well as the increased purchasing power and changing life styles of the upwardly mobile garment workers.

The garment industry, particularly during this period of expansion, was so structured as to facilitate the constant growth and circulation of employing units. Hardly any major obstacles stood in the way of the many ambitious Jews who wished to establish their own shops. That most proved not very successful nor long-lived is not a very significant point. The significant factor was that it was possible to leave the ranks of the workers and to improve one's social and economic status. The impetus to avail themselves of such opportunities was reinforced by the unique occupational heritage of the Jews of Europe, that of the independent businessman and artisan. Whatever the individual or group motivation, an ever-increasing number of immigrant workmen seized the opportunity to leave the status of needle trades employee. An even larger number had their appetites and aspirations whetted by the constant visible evidence that it could be done.

One of the basic structural factors facilitating the realization of budding entrepreneurs was the fact that so little capital was required to start a shop. Fifty dollars often was the price that the ambitious worker paid for his trip from the working class to the bourgeoisie. This was certainly far less than the $1000 the aspiring homesteader needed to establish himself as a farmer in 1860.[158] The basic machine in the industry was the sewing machine. It was not an expensive item for the needle trades employers, especially when so many could and did require their workers to supply their own. Barring this, sewing machines could be rented cheaply by the week or month, remaining in the shop only as long as they were needed for available work. They were small, movable, and easy to operate, and they could be run either by foot power or by a cheap form of commercial energy.[159]

The nature of the industry or significant sectors of it worked against the advantages of large-scale production that characterized other branches of manufacture. There were too many important variables outside of the control of the industry that made mass production and heavy capital outlay for machines and work space prohibitive economic endeavors. Fashion was the most important of these factors. Fluctuations in popular taste prevented the production of large quantities of clothing prior to initial sales. This was particularly true in the case of furs, millinery, and women's high-priced dresses, cloaks, and suits. In addition to variations in fashion, many sectors of the garment industry were also highly sensitive to changes in the weather and the economic cycle. Longer periods of warm weather meant fewer sales of cold-weather clothing. Downturns in the economy meant large-scale postponement of purchases of new clothes. Given these conditions, it would have been folly for those in these sectors of the garment industry most affected by unpredictable and uncontrollable variables to invest large sums of money in machinery or factories.[160]

Labor posed no problem for the aspiring entrepreneur. The trans-Atlantic ships annually disgorged thousands of Jews, and Italians as well, who immediately sought employment in the garment industry. The cost of these workers to their employers was made cheap by their abundant numbers and by the large-scale use of work techniques that devalued the importance of skill in the construction of garments. Energy, motivation, and a certain level of manual dexterity became the necessary and sufficient requirements for entry of all but a few, such as the cutters, into the garment industry. And these requirements were easily satisfied by the hundreds and thousands of eager immigrant workers.

The confluence of such factors and conditions in the garment industry helped give rise to the contracting system, a phenomenon that became widespread after 1882. The contractor was a person who contracted with a wholesale merchant or manufacturer to make the garments that the latter desired. The merchant or manufacturer would supply the cloth or partially finished garments or bundles, and the contractor would provide everything else necessary to complete the job. This cut the fixed costs for the wholesaler or manufacturer. The contractor's major expenditure was for labor, but this expense was kept low by the intense competition for jobs, the low skill requirements, and the contractor's frequent employment of "self," which included the immediate family and the ever-present boarders. Capital was not significant either. The raw materials were supplied. The employees bought or rented the sewing machines and supplied their own needles and thread. Overhead was reduced by placing the shop in the contractor's own living quarters or in nooks and crannies of tenements. This not only reduced the cost of the workplace but, in addition, made the establishment less visible to government inspectors and union organizers.

Contractors represented only one, albeit significant, element in the garment industry. Small manufacturers represented another important segment of the trade. In many cases they were former contractors. These manufacturers could establish themselves with little capital once they were assured of buyers. Purchase orders were accepted as collateral by banks, a practice that allowed them to obtain additional capital for the purchase of raw materials and labor.

Large manufacturers were disproportionately present in certain sectors of the needle trades industry, such as undergarments, house dresses, and, to a lesser extent, men's clothing, where fashions were relatively stable or not very significant. In these product lines, manufacturers could more readily take advantage of the economies of scale and mass production. This made it difficult for those with limited capital to enter these sectors. Although there was diversity in the garment industry, and it did encompass large modern factories as well as small, almost medieval type, home work shops, the makeup of the industry was not as varied in New York City as it was in the rest of the country. In New York City, contracting was a major mode of production and remained a major component of the industry in the city through the 1920s and 1930s. However, overall, "In New York the production unit [was] smaller, the business easier to enter, the life of most establishments shorter and the industry most highly seasonal and competitive." [161]

Thus, as low pay, unsteady work, long hours, and poor working conditions were pushing the garment workers to the Left, the ease of entering the entrepreneurial ranks pulled them back. The needle trades proletariat was a heterogeneous group in terms of social composition and social values and attitudes. The actual and anticipated upward mobility impeded the development of working class consciousness. The presence in their midst of failed entrepreneurs, dreaming of a return to their previous status, undermined the workers' solidarity. The goal of owning one's shop, a prize that those in their midst were achieving all the time, gave them little incentive to develop a stable working class or socialist perspective. This anticipatory socialization (or previous socialization experiences in the case of the downwardly mobile) undercut their desire and ability to formulate a working class identity and take actions to defend the long-term interests of themselves as workers. The real or imagined ephemeral status of employees made them reluctant to take unnecessary risks to improve it. Conversely, the position of employer was a desirous one and one the worker hoped they would soon occupy. It seemed foolish, therefore, to take any action against the employer that would weaken or destroy his status and ability to function economically.

Such attitudes did not prevent garment workers from going on strike or making demands in militant forms for the improvement of wages or conditions of employment. But there was little that was intrinsically radical or socialist about such claims. The needle trades employees lacked the homogeneity and feeling of permanence as a proletariat class that would have permitted them to seriously disturb the interests of their employers as a class.

Let us briefly digress to compare and contrast the situation of the Russian Jews in America with their situation in czarist Russia with respect to the garment industry. In Russia, the garment workers seemed more radical and more supportive of a strong socialist movement. In the Pale, the Jewish needle trades employee was constrained in ways that were qualitatively different from those in America. In the empire, his status as a Jew prevented him from being a part of or taking advantage of industrial and capital growth. Jewish entrepreneurs and workers were forced to compete with one another in a small and shrinking market. Their religion was a stigma and a burden that penalized them in the business and civic spheres. But at the same time, it gave the Russian Jews, including to some extent the small employers, a common base upon which radicals were able to build.

The situation was different in the United States. Here, although anti-Semitism was present, it was not official policy, nor was it powerful as it was under the rule of the czars. Jews, both as businessmen and workers, were able to benefit from the industrial and economic growth taking place in the United States. The market for their goods and services was large and usually growing. Here the stigma of being a Jew was not as potent or as burdensome, and it did not seriously hamper opportunities for advancement in status and economic condition. Thus, one would expect that in America Jews in the garment industry would be less radical and less bitter than their counterparts in Russia.

Two additional interrelated structural features of the garment industry in the United States served to impede the development of class consciousness, union organization, and a prosocialist sentiment among the Jewish workers within it. These were the size and number of the independent employing units within it. Before World War I the clothing industry was unrivaled in terms of the quantity of independent employers and the small number of workers per employing unit. In New York City in 1913 there were 16,552 shops and factories in the needle trades business, and they averaged 18 employees per shop. These figures actually bias the average upwards because the smaller shops, particularly those of the contractors, were more likely to escape the surveyor's net. Again, in New York City, more so than in other cities housing a garment industry, there was a greater concentration of small shops.[162]

An industry characterized by a multiplicity of independent employing units, such as the needle trades, is not the most propitious ground upon which to build a union or socialist movement. First, there is the practical problem of organization. The more units, the more organizers and organizational efforts are required. In an industry in which a few firms provide employment for the large majority of the particular work force, a union can concentrate its organizational efforts and, after a few victories, establish itself as the union for the majority of workers. In a divided and scattered industry, many victories are needed before the same results can be obtained. There is some balance in these diverse situations. The larger employers are more able, economically and politically, to resist unionization than are the smaller ones. The smaller employers do not have the clout of the larger ones.

Once the smaller independent employing units are organized, the union, in this type of situation, is usually more effective than in the case of a concentrated industry.

Another related factor in a multiple-employer industry is that each employing unit represents an obstacle to the development of a sense of solidarity among workers in the industry. Their work situation tends to constrict the employees' sense of "we" concerning their mates in their particular workplace. It is more difficult for them to identify with large numbers of fellow workers in their trade who are employed by a multiplicity of employers. Such a situation, particularly in a marginal industry like the garment industry, facilitates the employers ability to manipulate their employees in their strategy of playing off one group of workers against another and in fostering the view of workers in competing shops as competitors. And when conflicts between workers and boss do occur, it is most likely to be seen by the workers as a conflict between one set of workers and one boss, as Marx suggested in *The Communist Manifesto*. They tend not to view it in a broader perspective—as part of a struggle between capital and a united proletariat.

The small size of the individual-shop work force in the garment industry intertwines with the fact of the multiplicity of employers in the industry. Work in a small shop is conducive to the growth of a bourgeois or petty-bourgeois mentality. The sociological rationale for this was well stated by Seymour Lipset, Martin Trow, and James Coleman, who were, in turn, informed by the insight of Karl Marx in this regard:

To the small shop-man the problems of the boss are more persuasive, and the chances for individual recognition and rewards through personal relations with the shop owner are felt to be greater than in large shops of even fifty or a hundred workers, where such direct and unmediated relations between employer and employee are not possible. . . . In the small shops not only are the foreman and owner closer to the worker as persons in their daily relationships, but also they are closer as statuses to which a small shop man can realistically aspire.[163]

Jewish employers in the garment industry played upon these personal feelings and sentimental commonalities in the small shops to further their employees' identification with them, rather than with a union or their fellow workers. The worker in the small shop lacked a supportive peer group that was large enough and significant enough to counterbalance the influence of the employer. In the little workplace, the boss's power, values, and norms were less capable of being challenged than in a larger arena. In the small shops workers had to exert much more courage and initiative to openly oppose their employers than was true of their counterparts in the bigger work arenas. It was not only open actions, it was also the feelings and attitudes that were important. It is more difficult, in the context of few supporters, to develop and express negative feelings and attitudes and then tie them into such abstractions as class conflict.

The highly competitive and decentralized structure of the garment industry also was not conducive to the arousal of a working class consciousness. Workers in the context of small competitive units in a highly risky business find that they, along with their employers, are engaged in competition. While their bosses compete with their counterparts for orders, they in turn compete with the employees of the other shops for work. The most common overt manner in which this was done was through wage competition. The workers would often succumb to their employer's plea and accept a voluntary reduction in wages in order to win orders for the shop and continued employment for themselves. They would thus put themselves in a position of a united front with their boss against other employers as well as against fellow workers in their same field. This type of competition, needless to say, did not foster or support the idea of community interest along class lines. Such a situation required tremendous insight and an ability to stand apart from one's own particular circumstances in order to overcome it. Garment workers, continually beset by periodic unemployment, uncertain wages, and the continual need to feed and care for their families, usually were not granted the time and energy to develop such sociological luxuries.

Jewish employers, particularly those in the smaller shops, consciously used a variety of tactics to foster a sense of commonality between themselves and their workers. Their primary aim was to secure a longer-working, lower-paid, more passive work force. Their efforts to build a mutuality of interest between boss and worker also was an obstacle to the evolution of consciousness along class lines for their workers. One of the more effective ploys revolved around the *landsmanshaft* principle. Employers purposely recruited as employees immigrants from their Eastern European hometown areas. They would then artfully play upon these *landsmanshaft* ties and appeals to develop a community spirit within the shop to further their own material ends. Let David Levinsky, the aforementioned fictional clothing manufacturer, explain the workings of this social control technique:

Everything bearing the name of my native place touched a tender spot in my heart. It was enough for a cloakmaker to ask me for a job with the Antomir accent to be favorably recommended to one of my foremen . . . an Antomir atmosphere had been established in my shop, and something like a family spirit of which I was proud. We had formed a Levinsky Antomir Benefit Society . . . which was made up, for the most part, of my own employees.

All this, I confess, was not without advantage to my business interests, for it afforded me a low average of wages and safeguarded my shop against labor troubles. The Cloakmakers' Union had again come into existence, and although it had no real power over the men, the trade was not free from sporadic conflicts in individual shops. My place was absolutely immune from difficulties of this sort—all because of the Levinsky Antomir Benefit Society.

If one of my operatives happened to have a relative in Antomir, a women's tailor who wished to emigrate to America, I would advance him the passage money, with the understanding that he was to work off the loan in my employ. That the "green one" was to work for low wages was a matter of course.[164]

This *landsmanshaft* tactic, together with the special consideration given to the religious observances and customs of the Orthodox immigrants, also functioned to impede the workers integration into the urban industrial American work force. This, too, had the consequence of interfering with the growth of an American working-class consciousness.

One other feature of the garment industry impeded the development of class solidarity among workers within it: the pervasive piece-rate system. The use of this pay system directly, although not entirely, counteracted the impact of a narrowing job ladder that was making the garment industry work force more homogeneous in terms of skill and outlook. Frederick W. Taylor had advocated the use of the piece-work, or piece-rate, system as a way of undermining the growing unity that the lessening importance of genuine skill was fostering among workers in such industries as steel. The Jewish garment manu-facturers had probably not read Taylor, nor were they probably consciously utilizing the pay system as a weapon in the class struggle with their employees. Whatever their motivation for using the piece rate system, the fact was that it was widely employed by them. The United States Industrial Commission in 1901 marveled at the way in which the immigrant Jewish workers took to the piecework system. It also speculated as to the reason that they did so:

One reason why piecework and high speed have become the framework of the contractors' shops is probably because the Jewish people are peculiarly eager to earn a big day's wages, no matter at what sacrifice. The Jewish workman is willing to work very hard for this and does not want to have it said that there is a limit to his earning capacity. It is the desire of the Jew to have his employ-ment so arranged that he can speculate and bargain upon his earning capacity and can make use of the seasons. Piecework gives him that opportunity . . . Usually he is anxious to accumulate money and open up a contractor's shop for himself or go into some kind of business. It is not for love of hard work nor because of lack of other enjoyment that the Jew is willing to work so hard, but for the sake of getting rid of work. . . . The Jewish immigrant is peculiar [compared to other immigrant nationalities] only in that he is not by nature a wage earner.[165]

The Commission's analysis was a perceptive one. It had touched upon one of the more important social control functions of the piece-work system. In addition to increasing profits and productivity, this system created divisions of interest within one shop or factory. Under it, an individual worker became the major determinant of his wages within boundaries established by his employer. This pay scheme encouraged workers to make their own private deals. Ambitious workers and those in need of money, which, of course, didn't exclude very many, were prodded by this system to conclude that individual effort would be more likely to produce a higher return than would collective efforts. In this way a community of interest between fast and slow, strong and weak, ambitious and apathetic, agile and not so agile was undermined and with it the basis for class solidarity.

The efforts of Jewish unions, and others, to abolish the piecework system and regulate and lessen the hours of work were viewed ambivalently by the Jewish workers. These laborers, including the author's mother, realized that if successful the unions would have the immediate effect of placing a limit upon their earning power and placing all of a firm's or shop's employees in the same or similar pay boat. Some did resist unionization on this score, and others, if unable, colluded with employers in under-the-counter arrangements to maintain the system. In any event, the piecework system among Jewish needle trades employees certainly did play a role in stigmatizing, although not in preventing, the emergence and growth of a working-class consciousness among them.

However, despite these obstacles built into the nature of the garment industry in pre–World War I America, socialist-led, predominantly Jewish unions did organize the industry. Jewish needle trades workers, as we shall see, became a major bulwark of socialism in the United States. The socialists and the unions were cognizant of some of the problems that these various obstacles represented to their long-term well-being and tried to abolish or ameliorate them. They were not totally successful. The resistance of these structural impediments to the attempts to eradicate them made the garment industry a precarious base for Jewish socialism. It meant that the needle trades workers would have to rely to some extent upon factors outside of their work situation for a sense of garment worker solidarity and class consciousness. Much of this sense had to rest upon the fact that they were Yiddish-speaking immigrants who shared similar experiences in the Old and New World and who lived close to one another in large numbers in a similar living situation within the context of a Yiddish cultural milieu. Again, this basis of unity was located outside the garment industry and conditions within it. It meant that when these external supports for worker solidarity weakened over time, as they would have to, the structures within the garment industry would have to bear more of the weight for this particular burden. This weight eventually proved too heavy a burden for the socialist led unions.

CONCLUSION

The Jewish immigrants' support for and attraction to the cause of socialism and the Jewish labor movement was being undercut at precisely the same time that it was reaching its pinnacle. Despite various obstacles, the cause and the movement did grow among Jews in the pre–World War I period. The combination of forces that existed in this period was powerful enough to override the obstacles and opposition to the establishment of a strong and intimate relationship between the Jews and the Left, a process that included several factors. First, there was the uprooting of several million persons in a short period of time who shared a unique and common religious and cultural background and heritage of oppression. Second, they came to live closely together in what evolved into their own social, cultural, and economic spheres in major urban centers under generally deplorable living conditions. Third, large numbers shared a common occupational fate in an industry characterized by severe exploitation. Fourth, there was an infusion of numerous intellectuals and radicals with experience in union organization and radical political activity. The peculiar condition of established Jewry in America and the weakness of organized religion enabled them to assume positions of leadership within this working class community. In short, in America for the first time in the history of the Jews, there was a large, concentrated, and culturally self-sustaining Yiddish-speaking working class led by indigenous radicals and informed by socialist values.

Such a constellation of factors and the class that it nourished reached their pinnacle in a short period of time prior to World War I. Afterwards they were on the decline, beset by structural factors and historical forces that were antagonistic to the development and maintenance of a socialist movement among Jews. But when it was at its peak, this class and its leaders threw up organizations and institutions that expressed and channeled their social and political ideals. It would be these organizations and institutions that would be accepted as legitimate by the community, that would sustain a radical (and later reformist) perspective among Jews long after the bulk of them had left the ranks of the proletariat. These were the radical fraternal orders, the Leftist press, Jewish trade unions, and Jewish units of the Socialist movement, which together formed and was called the Jewish labor movement. It is to the Jewish labor movement in the United States that we now direct our attention.

5 The Garment Unions

INTRODUCTION

The Jew's encounter with American capitalism in the late 1800s and the early 1900s set the stage for the development of a Jewish turn to the Left and a Jewish Left subculture. The structural component of this subculture was made up primarily of Left-led or oriented Jewish unions, labor fraternal orders, a press, and political parties. Together, these various organizations formed what is commonly known as the Jewish labor movement. This chapter will concentrate on the unions that were part of this Jewish labor movement.

Two basic positions will be set forth in this chapter. The first is that the Jewish unions in particular and the Jewish labor movement in general played key roles in developing a nexus between the Jews and the Left in the United States. The exploitation of Jews as workers and ghetto residents helped to form this tie. But the relationship needed an organizational form in order to sustain it for decades. It was the success and potency of these Left structures that nurtured the Jews' positive relationship to socialism in America. Their organizational vibrancy also protected this association for a time from the cumulative impact of the nonradicalizing events and the improving socioeconomic circumstances that eventually pressued so many Jews to foresake the Left.

The second argument advanced here seems almost contradictory to the first. It is that the very same components of the Jewish labor movement that fostered and consolidated a positive relation between Jews and the Left also undermined it. This negative role stemmed from the Jewish labor movement's Jewish interests and concerns and its confrontation with capitalism.

The Jewish labor unions—the subject of this chapter—came into existence with two souls—one Jewish, the other socialist. In the early decades of the twentieth century, each reinforced the other as the Jewish community in this period was largely working class and disproportionately prosocialist. However, with the passage of time and the accompanying improvements in the socioeconomic circumstances of the Jewish community, the Jewish and socialist souls no longer complemented one another. Closeness to an increasingly bourgeois and ethnically conscious community did not help the cause of socialism in the Jewish unions. The desire for success and organizational stability on the part of the Jewish socialist union leaders was the other major factor that weaned Jews from socialism. This desire led them to make accommodations with the capitalist system at the expense of their socialist allegiance. The decision to live within the boundaries of capitalism was made very early and led these Jewish union leaders eventually to the point where they became defenders of the status quo. In the process of this transformation, they also found it increasingly useful to stress their Jewishness and Jewish concerns.

THE JEWISH UNIONS

Our focus here will be on the Jewish garment unions. They were the largest and most important of the unions in this country, with a high percentage of Jews among their membership and a Jewish leadership. There were and are four principal Jewish needle trades unions: the International Ladies' Garment Workers' Union (ILGWU), the Amalgamated Clothing Workers of America (ACWA), the United Cloth Hat and Cap Makers' Union (later United Hatters, Cap and Millinery Workers' International Union (UHCMWIU), and the International Fur Workers' Union [later the International Fur and Leather Workers' Union (IFLWU)]. Most of our attention will be centered on the ILGWU and the ACWA, the unions in the women's and men's clothing fields respectively, and the two biggest of the four.

All of these unions shared certain features in common. They were involved with the making of clothing. Their memberships and leaders were largely Jewish. Their principal base of operations was New York City or, to a lesser extent, Chicago or metropolitan areas with heavy concentrations of Jews. And, until approximately 1936, these unions were generally headed by socialists or socialist sympathizers and, in the case of the furriers, communists.

The Jewish needle trades unions prior to World War II were the most important organizational and financial mainstay of the Jewish Left. They also constituted a major source of support for the non-Jewish Left as well during this period. Therefore, knowledge of their internal dynamics and political evolution provides an important understanding of how the relationship between the Jews and the Left evolved during these years.

One of the principal thrusts of this chapter will be to show how the interrelationship between the politics and "Jewishness" of these unions was crucially affected by the structure of the industry in which they were located. The economic nature and structure of the garment industry continually presented the leaders of the needle trades unions with a set of problems that had a major impact on both the unions' political direction and Jewishness. It is important to stress that the nature and structure of the clothes-making industry did not determine the ways in which the unions' heads behaved in the political and ethnic spheres, although they were major factors informing their decisions. But the leaders did have choices and options open to them. Their decisions as to how to respond to the garment industry in the context of capitalistic America led them from the path of socialism. It is also important to note that in this devolution from socialism these union leaders repeatedly came into conflict with many of their members whose socialist commitment was stronger.

THE EARLY YEARS

Efforts to organize Jewish workers, particularly needle trade employees, began in the 1870s and multiplied in the 1880s and 1890s, as increasing numbers of Jewish immigrants entered the American labor force. Jews in these decades were able to establish unions and did go out on numerous strikes. In fact, between 1887 and 1905 clothing workers, most of whom were Jewish, led the nation in terms of the percentage of workers in an industry participating in a strike. These workers proved better strikers than unionists, however, and most unions in the garment trades were short-lived.

The life of the needle trades organizations mirrored the seasons of the garment industry. At the beginning of a busy season, many workers were willing to strike, as they had the greatest bargaining power vis-a-vis their employers in this labor-scarce period. A union usually came into existence in conjunction with or in the immediate aftermath of a strike. However, after the strike was over or as the slack season approached, a union was found to be of little practical use. Members therefore ceased to pay dues and attend meetings. The union then would become moribund until the next major grievance or busy season.[1]

Despite the Jews' high rate of strike activity and propensity to form unions, albeit short-lived ones, it became part of the common wisdom of the time that Jews were not the proper human material with which to construct unions. Samuel Gompers, the English Jewish immigrant president of the American Federation of Labor, attributed it to their desire to ascend from the ranks of laborers to those of managers and professionals.[2] The prominent labor economist, Professor John R. Commons, writing for the United States Industrial Commission in its report of 1901, shared Mr. Gompers' viewpoint. He identified the entrepreneurial spirit of the Jew as the major impediment to their unionization:

The problem has been the nature of the Jew himself. The Jew's conception of a labor organization is that of a tradesman rather than that of a workman. In the clothing manufacture, whenever a real abuse arises among the Jewish workmen, they all come together and form a giant union and at once engage in a strike. They bring in 95% of the trade. They are energetic and determined. They demand the entire and complete elimination of the abuse. The demand is almost always unanimous and made with enthusiasm and bitterness. They stay out a long time, even under the greatest suffering . . . But when once the strike is settled, either in favor or against the cause, they are contented, and that usually ends the union . . . The Jew joins the union when it offers a bargain and drops it when he gets, or fails to get, the bargain.[3]

Commons was wrong and his view was a biased one. It is not necessary to invoke the entrepreneurial "nature of the Jew" to understand the causes for their failure to establish and maintain unions in these decades. Jews were not the only nationality to experience such difficulty. In fact, Jews were generally more successful in this regard than other immigrant groups or native Americans. In 1890 less than 3 percent of the workers in America were to be found in unions. It is interesting to note that the comparable figure for Jews in New York City in that year was roughly 12 percent.[4] The general point is that it was difficult for most groups of workers in the United States to organize and maintain unions in that period of history.

There were certain factors unique to Jews that inhibited the formation of unions among them before the early years of the 1900s. The Jews who immigrated before the Kishinev pogrom of 1903 were largely artisans and small tradesmen with the two statuses often intermingling in the same person. As noted earlier, they worked in small shops in Europe. Also, at the time that the large majority left Russia, the Bund had not been born, and sustained trade union activity among them was not a common feature of their lives. In short, their occupational background and experience were not conducive to the building of unions.

The Jewish immigrants, however, were not unique in terms of having an occupational background reputedly uncongenial to unionism. Although the peasant origins of the vast multitudes of Slavic and Italiam immigrants of the same period were different in many respects from those of the artisans or small tradesmen, these immigrants were also disinclined to enter unions. As the United States Industrial Commission aptly noted in 1901: "The fresh immigrant, who has for the most part been a farm hand, must first have a few years' practical experience . . . must have time to understand the conditions of the occupation and the objects of unionism."[5]

The occupations that the Eastern European Jews entered after they arrived in the New World, most notably that of garment worker, did differentiate them to some extent from their fellow non-Jewish immigrants who entered construction, steel, and mining jobs. The garment industry, as noted earlier, was not the most fertile soil upon which to build unions. The multiplicity of small and independent employing units as well as the ease of becoming an employer, manager, subcontractor, or foreman were some of the more important features that blunted the growth of unionism among the Jewish employees.

Another important factor centered around the issue of nationality. Immigrant Jews were not readily accepted as coworkers and less so as union brothers by other nationality groups in the garment trade. It was not only a case of prejudice alone. The Irish and Germans and others in the needle trades feared that the mass influx of Jews into the garment industry would inevitably cause the lowering of their wages and the deterioration of their working conditions. They therefore generally resisted working with or sharing their unions on an equal footing with the Eastern European immigrant Jews.

The immigrant Jews, for their part, were none too anxious to work closely in the shops and in the unions with other nationalities. They were aware of the negative attitudes and actions of workers and unionists in these groups toward them. The Jews also saw the others as competitors. And, in addition, there was a language problem. The Eastern European Jews spoke Yiddish, and this made communication with the non-Yiddish speaking workers in the garment trade quite difficult. Thus, language became another important barrier to cooperation in union activities between the Yiddish-speaking immigrants and those from other nationalities whom they found in the shops upon their arrival in the United States.[6]

There were also divisions among Jews in the garment trades in the 1880s and 1890s that inhibited them from working together in unions. Jews from Hungary and western Poland who sewed relatively expensive garments did not want to cooperate with their fellow Jews from eastern Poland and Lithuania who made cheaper clothing. They were so divided that even when a union was formed each had a separate branch. These divisions later began to crumble as Yiddish and socialism emerged as unifying forces.[7]

It took time for stable and permanent unions to take root among Jewish workers. Although there were unions earlier, it was not until approximately 1910 that Jewish unions became firmly established. By that time the large numbers of Jewish immigrants had made the garment industry work force into a predominantly Jewish domain. Also, the character of the immigrants had changed. After the Kishinev pogrom in 1903, each new wave of immigrants included ever larger numbers with trade union experience. There were also many among these newer immigrants who had led and been active in the building of unions and radical parties, especially the Bund. Changes had also taken place in the garment industry. It had become somewhat less chaotic and more settled and thus was more amenable to organization. The Jewish community, as we pointed our earlier, was by this time quite supportive of trade union efforts. Thus, in the period following the major organizing strikes between 1909 and 1912 the mainstays of the Jewish needle trades unions, the International Ladies' Garment Workers' Union, the Amalgamated Clothing Workers of America, and United Cloth Hat and Cap Makers' Union, and the International Fur Workers' Union were firmly established.[8]

SOCIALISM AND THE UNIONS

The unions that the Russian-Jewish immigrant established in the United States in the late 1800s and early 1900s were socialist unions. Typically, their leaders were socialists as were a large proportion of their members. Until the latter 1930s these organizations were among the most important institutional bulwarks of socialism in this country. It was also in this period that these unions nurtured a socialist commitment and subculture among their Jewish members in particular and the East European American Jewish community in general.

It is important to keep in mind, however, that at the same time these leaders and their organizations also accommodated themselves to the capitalist system. Once they had decided to participate in the American system, their commitment to the Left gradually but steadily weakened. In understanding this seeming paradox it must be kept in mind that these leaders and their organizations were not one-dimensional creatures. They were complex and responded politically to various forces and pressures in different and at times apparently contradictory fashions. Despite their increasing accommodation to capitalism throughout this century, these union heads and their organizations remained, along with the Jewish community in which they were located, further Left on the American political spectrum than most other comparable groups.

Jewish radicals were intimately involved in the building of unions starting with the early 1880s. Their most successful effort in this period was the United Hebrew Trades (UHT), founded in 1888. The UHT was a federation of unions in industries in which Jews predominated. The founders, organizers, and early officers of this federation were Jewish members of the Socialist Labor party. They were aided in their endeavor by Socialists from the United German Trades, the principal model for the UHT.[9] "The triple aim of the new organization," according to its first corresponding secretary, Morris Hillquit, ". . . was declared to be: (1) mutual aid and cooperation among the Jewish trade unions of New York; (2) organization of new unions; (3) the progaganda of Socialism among the Jewish workers."[10] In its platform the UHT explicitly committed itself to "the struggle against capitalist exploitation."[11]

The Jewish unions that the UHT helped to bring into existence and to survive were typically led by Socialists, many of whom had had some experience in the radical movements in Russia. Under their tutelage these Jewish unions grew in size and political strength. The leaders and large proportions of the members of these organizations were willing to devote a considerable share of their resources and energies to the socialist movement inside and outside the Jewish community.

The rapid growth of these unions after the first decade of the 1900s was impressive. In 1900 one of the largest of these, the International Ladies' Garment Workers' Union, commenced its existence with approximately 2000 members and a yearly income of $506. By 1908, after a precarious few years, it grew to 7830. A year later the ILGWU had over 58,000 members, and by 1918 there were 129,311 on its rolls. The rise of the Amalgamated Clothing Workers Association, or

Amalgamated, was even more spectacular. This largely Jewish men's clothing workers union emerged in 1914 as a result of a split within the non-Jewish United Garment Workers. In 1915 it had a membership of 38,000. Within three years the figure more than doubled to 81,000. By 1920 it reached a high of 177,000. Similar developments took place in the other smaller unions of the garment trade, such as the furriers, hatters, and glove workers. Non-Jewish unions also grew in this period, but their rate of growth was slower than that of the Jewish unions.[12]

By the end of World War I, the ILGWU and the ACWA were established economic and political forces. Owing to the growth of these unions, the clothing industry was one of the most heavily unionized sectors in the American economy. Fifty-eight percent of the employees in the garment industry were unionized in 1920, compared with 17 percent in 1910. In that same year, 1920, the comparable figure for all union members in manufacturing industries was 23 percent. Only the workers engaged in water transportation (longshoremen, seamen, etc.) surpassed the garment workers in the proportion who were union members. In their case, it was 86 percent. In less than a decade the clothing industry had moved from being poorly organized to being one of the most powerfully organized in the United States.

This feat and the role of the Jews and Jewish socialists in accomplishing it is even more remarkable given the fact that the clothing industry contained in relative as well as absolute terms close to the largest numbers of females outside of the clerical and service sectors of the economy. Its only rival in this regard was the textile industry, whose work force in 1910 and 1920 contained more females than the garment industry. But in 1920 the females in the garment industry represented a higher proportion of employees in their industry, 61 percent, than did their counterparts in textile, 48 percent. The percentage of unionized workers in the textile industry reflected the common wisdom about the difficulty of organizing heavily feminized industries. Only 15 percent of its labor force was organized in 1920, compared with 58 percent of the garment industry's. This disparity still holds when only the female workers in both industries are compared. In the needle trades, close to half of all women employed were members of unions, while in the textile industry the comparable figure was close to 10 percent.[13]

The difference in the degree of unionization between the two industries was not due to the number or proportion of females in each nor to the differences in the structure of the two industries, since both were characterized by a high proportion of independent employing units. The most salient distinction between the two industries bearing on the degree of unionization is the dissimilarity in the ethnic make-up of the labor force in each.

The Jews were the single largest and majority ethnic group in the garment industry. They were the mortar that socialist union organizers used to build a solid union structure. And, as described earlier, the major sectors of the industry were concentrated in Jewish and metropolitan areas, principally New York City. After 1903 the ranks of the garment workers were continually swelled by new immigrants who had had some contact with unionization before coming to America. In addition, among these new arrivals and also increasing in numbers over the subsequent years, there were Jewish radicals and Jews sympathetic to radicalism who were instrumental in building unions from among their fellow Jewish coworkers.

The labor force in the pre–World War I textile industry was neither dominated by a single ethnic group nor concentrated in metropolitan areas. The largest proportions of this work force were to be found scattered in various New England towns in which no one ethnic group predominated to the extent that the Jews did in New York City. The textile workers were not Jewish. The largest ethnic groups among them were native Americans, first- and second-generation Irish-Americans, and foreign-born Italians and Poles. The females among the native Americans and the Irish-Americans were, in the experience of union organizers, among the most difficult to organize. There was also considerable ethnic antagonism between these groups which was reflected during strikes. In the large and famous Lawrence strike of 1912, for example, the Irish and French Canadians scabbed en masse while their fellow Catholics among the Italians and Poles, particularly the former, did yeomen service on the picket lines. Few of these ethnic groups had had significant experience with unions or radicalism prior to entering this industry. It is also interesting to note that leaders of the textile workers' unions and strikes, unlike the garment workers, did not come from among a single ethnic group or from those who worked or had worked in the shops alongside them. In short, the divisions inherent in the structure of the textile industry were reinforced by the ethnic divisions in the textile work force.[14]

Socialism in general and the Socialist party in particular were the political beneficiaries of the strengthened needle trades unions. As they grew into powerful organizations after the first decade of the 1900s, these unions became among the most stalwart supporters of the socialist movement in the United States. In this period they openly declared themselves for socialism. Socialist clauses were written into their constitutions. Their conventions routinely passed resolutions endorsing socialism and candidates of the Socialist party. One ILGWU convention barred officeholders in the bourgeois Democratic and Republican parties from participation in its affairs. In 1912 the ILGWU wrote in the preamble to its constitution: "Resolved that the way to acquire our rights as producers and citizens and to bring about a system of society whereby the workers shall get full value of their products, is to organize industrially into a class conscious union represented on the various legislative bodies by representatives of a

political party whose aim is the abolition of the capitalist system." [15]
This closely paralleled a similar preamble in the Amalgamated's constitution. (Several years later both preambles were deleted.)

This support of socialism was not limited to verbal and written
statements at conventions and in constitutions. These unions gave
generous donations to the Socialist party and its youth affiliate, the
Young People's Socialist League. In elections for local, state, or federal offices, garment unions became the base of the Socialist party's
campaign machinery. It was the needle trades unionists who collected
contributions, canvassed, and dispatched poll watchers. They also
organized campaign rallies, invited speakers, and turned out the vote
on election day. In some SP locals, almost all the members were needle trades unionists. Although New York City was an important arena
for these activities, the garment unions performed similar political
functions for the Socialist party in Chicago, Philadelphia, Cleveland,
and other cities in which they were located. [16]

For their part, Socialists assisted the garment unions during their
time of need. During the important organizing strikes of 1910, for example, numerous branches of the Socialist party dispatched help in
the form of dollars and organizers while the party's paper, the New
York *Call,* vigorously defended the strikers. [17] By 1918 the mutual cooperation, affection, and assistance had progressed to such an extent
that a leading labor historian stated: "The needle trades' unions became synonomous with the Socialist Party. . . . the Jewish American
labor movement and the Socialist Party had consummated a successful political marriage." [18] Although the marriage partners were divorced in 1936, the garment unions through the 1920s and up to 1936
represented the bulwark of the labor contingent within the Socialist
party. [19]

The garment unions, however, did not only aid the cause of American socialism, they were also major institutional supports for the
cause of socialism among Jews. The relationship between the needle
trades organizations' and socialism among Jews was very similar to
the spider and her web. The unions were the institutional and financial corpus of the socialist web that encompassed many in the Jewish
community. One of the major strands in this web was the unions' material contributions. Socialist candidates and campaigns in Jewish districts in which the unions and their memberships were largely located
received significant monetary and manpower support from these Jewish unions. A significant number of the candidates who ran in these
districts were, in fact, Jewish Socialists who had had some kind of
prior special relationship to the garment unions and their officials.
Support from these unions became a necessary although by no means
sufficient condition for election to public office in these districts.
Such assistance brought into office Socialist assemblymen, aldermen,
judges, and one of the only two Socialist Congressmen (Meyer London, the union's attorney) ever to hold that office in the United States.

The garment unions were very much the foundation upon which Jewish socialism was built.

These Socialist campaigns, subsidized by the unions, also served to keep socialism and the Socialist party in public view and in the public consciousness. Elections were held infrequently. There were elections for mayor, aldermen, state legislators, governors, the House of Representatives, the Senate, and the Presidency. This meant that at least every other year there was some kind of election for public office. An election usually meant a campaign complete with public speakers, literature, parades, and numerous public meetings. Although the Socialist candidates usually lost, Jewish residents at least knew that socialism and the Socialist party prior to the 1920s was a vibrant force. Both the campaigns and the support given to them by the highly respected unions helped to make socialism an acceptable and legitimate force within the Yiddish-speaking community.

This tradition and this relationship managed to survive the break that many of the Jewish labor leaders made with socialism prior to World War II (as we shall see below). Even as they moved further from socialism and closer to the Democratic party, pockets of support for the older tradition remained among some locals, cadres, and leaders. To a far more limited extent garment union officials and funds continued to support through the post–World War II years socialist-oriented organizations and magazines such as the Social Democratic Federation, the *New Leader*, the League for Industrial Democracy, the Student League for Industrial Democracy, and the Students for a Democratic Society. Such assistance also continued the tradition of helping to maintain a relationship between socialism and Jews. Although these organizations were not officially Jewish, many of the members and leaders of these various socialist-oriented groups were Jews. Therefore, as late as the early 1960s, the increasingly moderate, reformist, Democratic, and anti-Communist garment unions and their subsidized organizations continued to legitimize and to serve as forums for socialist or quasi-socialist ideas and aspirations. These usually small and disproportionately Jewish groups, which were kept alive largely by the financial largesse of the Jewish needle trades unions, in turn helped to keep alive the idea of socialism in America. Indeed, one of the most important beneficiaries of this largesse in the 1960s was the Students for a Democratic Society (SDS), an organization subsidized by the League for Industrial Democracy.[20]

The needle trades unions also reinforced the relationship between socialism and the Eastern European Jewish immigrants in other than material ways. They assisted in establishing an identity between socialism and concerns close to the self-interest of Jewish workers. The efforts to abolish the sweatshops and child labor and to improve the economic and political status of women were rarely presented solely as ways to improve the material well being of the garment workers. Instead, the union leadership generally couched these campaigns in

terms of humanitarianism, social justice, and socialism, using socialist rhetoric.[21] The unions also championed issues that were of particular interest to their Jewish members. Thus, in 1912 the convention of
the ILGWU: ". . . opposed the Dillingham Immigration Restriction
Bill not only on the Marxist grounds of labor solidarity but also on the
ground that restriction 'intensifies national and race hatred' and that
the bill would, if enacted, 'prevent the victims of political, religious
and economic oppressions from finding a place of refuge in the
United States.' "[22] An organization led by and comprised of Jewish
immigrants who themselves had fled from oppression and who still
had relatives and friends and coreligionists living in fear of pogroms
could hardly be expected to take any other position. But, again, this
was done largely within the framework and rhetoric of socialism.

These Socialist union leaders gave their members and, through
them, their families, who constituted the bulk of the immigrant Jewish
community, the impression that only socialism and the Socialist party
were genuinely concerned with their lot as workers, Jews, and human
beings. No other parties or ideologies, especially capitalist ones,
seemed capable of addressing themselves to the material and ideal
needs and interests of this population. Thus, unionism, socialism, and
Jewishness were interlinked, reinforcing one another and extending
into other areas as well; for example, certain educational activities
were conducted under the auspices of or in conjunction with the garment unions. The intermingling of socialism, unionism, and education occurred even before the ILGWU and the Amalgamated were established. The predecessors of these and other unions in the needle
trades had combined socialism with education for their members before the turn of the century. In fact, the socialist-sponsored educational classes were often regarded as fertile recruiting grounds for
union members. Recall, too, that the Bund had also linked education
with socialism. These experiences and traditions, then, informed the
thinking of the union leaders as their organizations took root and
grew.

Socialists and radicals were involved in the educational activities of
the garment unions as soon as these unions instituted them. The first
head of the ILGWU and the ACWA's educational departments were
dedicated Socialists Juliet S. Poyntz and J. B. S. Hardmann, respectively. Local 25 of the ILGWU, the largest and one of the most radical
locals within that union, was an early major force in developing an
educational program for unionists. Many of the courses offered by the
garment unions were developed in coordination with the Rand School
of Social Sciences, the educational center of the Socialist party located on New York's East Side. This "socialist yeshivah," as it was
dubbed by the *Jewish Daily Forward*, established a relationship with
the Jewish garment unions that extended throughout the life of that
institution. (The financial generosity of the ILGWU helped to keep the
Rand School in existence for several decades.) In this "yeshivah,"

largely as a result of the cooperation between the Rand School and the Socialist-led Jewish Unions, prominent Socialists including Meyer London, Morris Hillquit, Louis Waldman, and August Claessen lectured before audiences of Jewish unionists. Even in those classes supposedly devoted strictly to educational matters, the Leftist instructors usually managed to squeeze in some discussion of Marxist principles.[23]

It was not only the exposure to socialist lecturers and teachers that buttressed socialism among the Jewish unionists. These various educational groups and forums that were sponsored by the unions or spontaneously developed within their framework served this end in a less direct but no less meaningful manner. They served as arenas in which Leftists within the unions could meet, interact, share ideas and grievances, and reinforce each other's commitment to socialism. In at least one case, the "Current Events Committee" of Local 25 of the ILGWU formed in 1917, the group became more radical than the ILGWU leadership.[24]

There were other union-sponsored activities and facilities that inadvertently helped to sustain socialism among Jewish unionists. The choral groups, amateur dramatic societies, vacation resorts, and cooperative housing projects that various needle trades unions financed or endorsed also indirectly served Jewish socialism. Again, they served as arenas and forums in which socialists and those sympathetic to the Left could interact and provide social reinforcement for the maintenance of a socialist perspective. These arenas also provided socialist and radical agitators with sympathetic or at least open-minded audiences. They also became increasingly important for the cause of socialism in the unions when the leaders began to direct their organizations along a more reformist or conservative path after World War I. While it is true that the nonclandestine activities and facilities of the unions were open to all members regardless of their political orientation, one can assume that the Left was the primary political beneficiary of them.

After World War I there were progressively fewer nonwork and nonpolitical party places where Yiddish-speaking and Jewish unionists and Leftists could interact. The tendency for Jews to leave their ghetto concentrations had been present before the war; but afterward it became even more rapid, and Jewish unionists participated in this exodus.[25] Even though other residential concentrations of Jews developed, they were not as large, or as densely populated, or as occupationally homogeneous as the ones that had been left behind. This meant that the union related contexts where Jewish workers could interact with one another took on added political significance.

These choral groups, vacation resorts, and cooperative housing projects were beneficial to the Left within the unions in a very practical way. As the union leaders became more conservative, they provided the Leftists with situations that were somewhat freer from the political and social control that these officials exercised in the more formal union settings. Needless to say, they were also places that were freer from the influence of the bosses and foremen present in the work place.

It must be assumed that those who organized and participated in these union events and facilities were not randomly drawn from the ranks of the union membership. It can also be assumed that certain of these environments were more conducive to a Left perspective than others. One of the best examples of such a union-sponsored environment was the Amalgamated's cooperative housing project in New York City. The primary organizers behind it were all Socialists. The project was financially aided by the largely Socialist Jewish Daily Forward Association, the board of directors of the then Socialist-oriented *Jewish Daily Forward*. Building began in 1926 on a site adjoining Van Cortlandt Park in the Bronx. By 1932, 4000 people were living in this cooperative housing development. (Later the Amalgamated built cooperative housing on the Lower East Side.) However, it was more than just a nice place for a Jewish union man to live. The Amalgamated apartments, operated according to the Rochdale cooperative principles, were the setting for a subculture composed primarily of Jewish needle trades' unionists that was, if not conducive to a socialist outlook, at least positively neutral toward it. "The Amalgamated apartments," according to the union's more or less official historian, Charles E. Zaretz, "afford their inhabitants a center for cooperative and educational activities." They housed a cooperative grocery, fruit market, laundry, and bus service. "The educational activities carried on in the buildings range from a kindergarten run for the children of pre-school age to Sunday morning forums for the discussion of current topics. Lectures, discussions and debates alternated by concerts, dances and other entertainments . . ." [26] The Jewish unionists who lived there and the cooperative world that they built helped to make the Amalgamated coop a bastion of socialism, albeit "right wing" or very moderate socialism.

SOCIALISM IN THE UNIONS

Before turning our attention to other parts of the Jewish labor movement, it might be fruitful to pause briefly and address the question: Why were these garment unions such a force for socialism in the first several decades of this century? What made these unions, more than most others in this country, so supportive of socialism?

The first, most obvious, and probably most important reason was that these unions contained a large number of socialists. From the inception of the unions, large numbers of socialists played important roles at various levels both inside and outside the unions in guiding them along a socialist path. In the early years of these organizations, virtually all of the Jewish leaders had come out of a socialist or radical background, particularly a Bundist one. The most prominent leaders of the garment unions after World War I were David Dubinsky of the ILGWU; Sidney Hillman of the Amalgamated Clothing Workers of America; and Max Zaritsky of the United Cloth, Hat, Cap, and Millinery Workers; and all were former Bundists. The most influential advisers outside of these unions were the Socialist editor of the *Jewish Daily Forward*, Abraham Cahan, and two of the leading Socialist attorneys in the country, Meyer London and Morris Hillquit, the latter a former shirtmaker.[27] One observer of the ILGWU commented: "From the time of the founding of the ILGWU until Dubinsky's election in 1932, being a Socialist was apparently a basic requirement for becoming president."[28] The leaders of the Italian garment unionists also were disproportionately drawn from men with radical backgrounds.[29]

This phenomenon was not limited to the top echelon of the unions. Socialists and other radicals were also found in other areas of the organizations, particularly among those involved in education, journalism, and organization. This tendency continued even after the top leaders made their break with socialism in the 1930s. One former Trotskyist recounted the heady days of the 1930s and early 1940s when he worked for the ILGWU as a low-paid field organizer:

Even though most of the Union's leaders had emulated Dubinsky in leaving the Socialist Party, the ILG was still a haven in those years for political nonconformists. Its devoted organizing and educational staffs included liberals and radicals from every section of the left except the Communists. . . . To be a union organizer was one dream of many young liberals and radicals during the 30's and early 40's; to be an ILGWU organizer, was almost more than could have been hoped for in even their wildest fantasies.[30]

This tradition remained alive in the post–World War II era, although it found a somewhat different expression. The atrophy of the Left parties forced the unions to seek cut organizers and future leaders from different reservoirs. Instead of the radical parties of old, they turned to other arenas believed to harbor youthful idealists, the most notable ones being, as mentioned earlier, Jewish college-student bodies. ILGWU recruiters went to such institutions as Brandeis University looking "for dissident or liberal or radical students who are willing to work for the ILGWU at rather low wages."[31]

Socialists were not to be found only among the officials. They were also present in large numbers in the rank and file of the garment unions. The growth in the strength of the unions and in their socialist militancy coincided with the recruitment of thousands of recent immigrants who had had some contact with radical and revolutionary parties and trade unions in Russia and Eastern Europe, especially the Bund. In the ILGWU, for example, these immigrants were influential in moving this organization closer to socialism. As the weight of their numbers and political convictions began to be felt after 1910, the ILGWU became more militantly class conscious in terms of its declared political positions.[32]

World War I brought a temporary halt in the influx of radicalized immigrants into the clothing unions. But with the end of the war, the influx resumed. From 1919 to 1924 more than a quarter of a million Jews, predominantly from revolution-torn Russia and Eastern Europe, immigrated to the United States. Many of them, especially the younger ones, like their prewar counterparts, had participated in revolutionary movements. Large numbers of these entered the needle trades unions, reviving their radical spirit. These post–World War I arrivals kept these organizations politically astir with their radical activities and rhetoric for years afterward. No other unions in this period acquired so many new members with the socialist proclivities of these newcomers.[33] One ILGWU official, in testimony before the United States Industrial Commission in the 1920s, explained that Jewish unionists appeared so radical because, "The great majority of them come from Russia; a large number of them have been engaged at home in fighting autocracy, in fighting ukases of the Czar, and to a great many of them obeying an order, even though the order comes from the union, is repugnant."[34] (Interviews with the unionists of this generation reveal that in the 1970s they are still on the left of the political spectrum and further left than the current union officials.)

The large concentration of radicals in the garment unions became the fulcrum of a dynamic process that fostered or prolonged the Left character of these organizations. Their sheer numbers made them into a constituency that the union leadership could neither ignore or alienate. But, these radicals and their sympathizers, as we shall presently discuss, constituted a major problem for these union officials, who became increasingly unwilling to act out their own professed socialist ideals in areas of substance, such as union democracy, level of wages, and labor-management relationships. Maintenance of their positions of influence in the organization and correct if not amicable associations with the larger and more efficient manufacturers superseded their idealistic commitments. The existence of the many Leftists and pro-Leftists in the rank and file, however, made it necessary to maintain at least a semblance of allegiance to socialist ideals.

The way out of this impasse was to find, whether consciously or not, areas in which the union leaders could demonstrate their allegiance to socialist values without jeopardizing their own organizational authority or relationships with employers. One solution was to emphasize their socialist commitments in areas that were largely of peripheral concern to the workers whom they led. This would allow these union leaders to show their colors to their rank and file and even at the same time reassure themselves that at some level they were indeed still true to their youthful idealism. Thus, it was socialist to support Socialist candidates for public office, particularly when they were "reasonable" Socialists like Meyer London. At the same time, such action was not very "costly." It was also socialist, humanitarian, and not "costly" to advocate and work for the elimination of sweatshops and child labor and to support the legal and political rights of women. These factors also played a role in the establishment of medical clinics, vacation resorts, and the cooperative housing project.

The social, educational, and health areas as well as Socialist electoral politics were the areas in which "socialism" was allowed to flourish. It was in these areas that the more radical elements could be situated and encouraged to act out their socialist faith. It was in these areas that the leadership could most openly show its socialist heart and its ties to the "good old radical days." In these ways the leadership could publicize their commitment to socialism and build their centralized organizations without having that commitment interfere with the core of union work, namely the relationship between employers and union employees and the relationship between the union leadership and members.

Even so cautious an approach, however, netted the garment unions and their leaders practical benefits from the socialistically inspired programs that they devised and made available to their members. These included union-sponsored and operated health, housing, vacation, and pension plans. These programs, generally operated and financed by national or international leadership, materially helped and enriched the lives of needle trades unionists while giving their unions national reputations as humanitarian and progressive organizations. At the same time, the programs functioned to bring stability to the unions and strengthen the hand of the central leaderships. These internal union social welfare measures gave the members concrete self-interested reasons for remaining in the organizations even when the unions were not able to deliver on higher wages and better working conditions. And the control of the funds for these programs as well as the actual operation of them by the central unions' offices weakened the locals' ties to their members while building those to the national leadership.[35]

Whatever the motivation of the unions' socialist leadership, their socialist and humanitarian activities, couched in socialist and humanitarian rhetoric, had to have an impact on the membership. These actions and this rhetoric throughout the 1920s and 1930s and to some extent after World War II reaffirmed the legitimacy of socialism as an ideal. The socialism emanating from the labor leaders may have been self-serving and of little practical importance in terms of wages, working conditions, and internal union operations; nonetheless, in words and actions, the unions' heads were publicly acknowledging the ideological supremacy of socialism over capitalism. Union members who were socialist or sympathetic to socialism when they joined found themselves in an organization that for decades encouraged them, if only through lip service, to maintain this commitment and attitude. In this respect, the garment unions were unique labor organizations in the America of the 1920s and 1930s and, to a lesser extent, the 1940s.

In the post–World War II years, the garment union leaders, as best exemplified by David Dubinsky of the ILGWU, did not renounce their own socialist past or the socialist tradition that informed the political past of their unions. Dubinsky and others could look back fondly and publicly on their socialist experiences even if they treated them as examples of youthful idealism or naivete. In the latter 1950s Dubinsky was still making speeches praising some of the great socialists of the nineteenth and early twentieth centuries. In the same period visiting socialists from abroad were invited as honored guests to the ILGWU's conventions.[36]

There was also another way in which the relatively large concentration of radicals and radical sympathizers in the garment unions fostered or prolonged the Left character of these organizations and their memberships. This stemmed from the fact that the very existence of such a membership encouraged Left parties to recruit and become active among the garment workers. From the point of view of these parties, it was largely a matter of economy. Radical parties throughout American history have rarely had substantial resources and have therefore had to choose carefully the areas to which their resources should be committed. The garment unions represented an area in which large returns could be expected. This type of reasoning informed the thinking of the Communist party in the 1920s when it chose the needle trades unions as its principal union arena. According to Benjamin Gitlow, the chairman of the Needle Trades Committee of the CP and the man in charge of the Communist drive within these unions, the party's decision was based on the fact that, ". . . the majority of members in these unions were the sort of foreign-born who had been for years under Socialist influence and hence attuned to our ideological approach . . . [and that the CP] already had some two thousand of our members scattered in these unions."[37] It should also be noted that the CP venture into the garment unions in the 1920s was not the first time that these unions had enjoyed the attention of a Left party other than the Socialist party. Between 1905 and 1908 the Industrial Workers of the World (IWW) had conducted a similar operation for similar reasons.[38]

One consequence of such Left attention was that the object, in this case the garment workers, became subject to considerable Left education, propaganda, and persuasion. Also, the source of this type of Leftism was not confined solely to the outside "raiders." The Socialist leadership in such circumstances was forced into a position of defending itself, in part by showing its own socialist colors. This all means that the garment workers in such periods became subjected to a continual and extensive barrage of appeals to socialism and socialist viewpoints and analyses. Such exposure is bound to have an impact.

The fact that the IWW and particularly the Communist party made significant inroads into garment unions is testimony to the political impact of these organizations and their Left ideologies among these Jewish unionists. At one point in the mid-1920s, the Communists and their allies gained control of New York City's ILGWU and International Fur Workers Union locals. Although they subsequently lost out in the ILGWU, the Communists and their allies did retain control of the furriers' union until the 1950s.[39]

Another related factor in explaining the exceptional relationship between socialism and the Jewish garment unions pertains to their history and importance within the context of the immigrant Jewish community. As noted elsewhere, Jews, more than any other immigrant group, brought their intellectuals with them to America. And Jewish intellectuals in larger numbers and proportions than others entered unions, particularly garment unions. They not only joined but participated in the building of these organizations. Thus, from the beginning Jewish intellectuals, or more accurately Jewish socialist intellectuals, played an important role within the unions. These pre-1900 pioneers established an important nexus between intellectuals and quasi-intellectuals and the unions.

The unions in this period, in part because of the numbers and activism of the intellectuals, became organizations of importance and prestige within the largely working-class immigrant Yiddish-speaking community. Therefore, the student, intellectual, or quasi-intellectual who decided to work for a union or become a union official had significant social support for this move. And those who entered the employ of the union from the shop floor were recognized as having taken a step forward. The major point here is that in the Jewish immigrant community, more than in other similar communities in the United States at the time, students, intellectuals, and quasi-intellectuals were making career choices, albeit not lifetimes ones in many cases, in favor of unions. Conversely, this meant that, at least at this point in their lives, large numbers of Jews were not becoming businessmen or professionals as were members of other immigrant communities, like the Italians.[40]

The consequence in terms of socialism and the unions is a fairly obvious one. The bright, the intellectual, and the energetic young men in the Jewish group who chose union work entered a status and a context in which they were expected to be Leftists. This was built into the definition of the role of union activist or official, even if many officials did deviate from it in actual practice in later years. Those among the Jewish and non-Jewish groups who became businessmen were not expected to be Leftists. Thus, the existence, the availability, and the community support for union work as a vocation attracted many to a status in which their socialist convictions and sentiments were reinforced or at least prolonged.

These, then, are some of the factors that help to explain why these

Jewish unions were so supportive of socialism during the early decades of the twentieth century. But it should be stressed that these socialist unions in these years were very much in tune with and an outgrowth of a Jewish immigrant community whose social structure and historical experience made it supportive of socialist institutions. It was also an interactive process as these socialist institutions like the unions reinforced the community's own socialist proclivities and sentiments.

SOCIALISM'S DECLINE

The garment union base of the socialist movement in America was a flawed base. At the very time that self-designated socialist union officials were espousing socialist ideals and supporting Socialist candidates, they harbored an even stronger commitment to pragmatism. Eventually this commitment was to take them out of the ranks of the socialist movement and into bourgeois mainstream politics entirely.

There were three interrelated factors that led these needle trades union leaders to develop this practical attitude and move away from socialism. One was that early in their careers these leaders had already come to the conclusion that the capitalist system would be a lasting and durable one. Acting on this premise, they chose to ensure their positions and the success (as they defined it) of their organizations by reaching an accommodation with the capitalist politicoeconomic system in general and the garment employers in particular.

The second factor leading to needle trades union leaders' conservative shift was the nature and structure of the garment industry. The basic instability that permeated the garment trades motivated these officials to search for ways to make it more secure, orderly, and stable. The means and allies that they used for this purpose took these union chieftains ever further from the socialist cause.

The third factor was the "Jewish factor." The Jewishness of the garment industry in terms of employers, employees, and union members made Jewish interests and the Jewish community things of significant concern for the union officialdom. Early in the life of the garment unions, their leaders recognized how important Jewish public opinion and the Jewish community were to the maintenance of their positions and the success of their organizations (again as they defined it). In these years a predominantly working-class and prosocialist Jewish community did render them assistance, and both the unions and the community reinforced each other's socialist commitment. But as Jews in America moved out of the working class and developed uniquely ethnic concerns, the garment union officials' close ties to organized Jewry and Jewish interests pulled them away from their earlier socialist commitment.

THE STRUCTURE OF THE GARMENT INDUSTRY

The decline of socialism within the garment unions was a direct result of their leaders' choices, which were informed and influenced by a variety of factors. Probably one of the most important of these was the nature and structure of the garment industry. It was the garment industry after all that provided the economic base for the unions' and the union leaders' positions of prestige and influence. It was the manner and ways in which these leaders decided to cope with the issues and problems emanating from the structure of the garment industry (and its location in the Jewish community) that eventually led to their severing their ties with socialism.

The garment industry, compared with others in this country, did not offer the most fertile ground for the development of strong unions, much less socialist ones. The socialists who headed the efforts to build needle trades unions in the late 1800s and early 1900s were confronted by several significant obstacles—obstacles that still characterize the industry today. The most important were: (a) a high degree of competition among a multiplicity of independent and relatively small employing units; (b) availability of raw materials and machinery free from ties to specific geographical areas; and (c) the needle trades labor force. As a labor-intensive industry, workers wages constituted one of or perhaps the major cost of production. The workers required to produce the garments were generally available in abundant numbers, as skill was not a major requirement for employment in the industry. All of these factors produced a constant and continual pressure upon employers to regard the cost of labor as the primary determinant of business life or death, success or failure.

The socialists who set out to organize unions in the garment industry were in a highly unenviable situation. The large number of small apparel employers, unlike the steel industry, made it costly for the unions to organize their workers or enforce contract provisions once they were organized. The relative unimportance of skill meant that the garment unions, unlike some of those in the building trades, had to rely primarily on its own resources to regulate the supply of labor—which was almost always abundantly available.

These very real structural features of the garment industry forced the socialist founders and organizers of the needle trades unions to make difficult decisions as to how best to unionize the industry and protect their own organizations. The decisions that they made, however, increasingly undermined their commitment to socialism. The actions of these men were not determined by the structure of the industry. They had the option to seek out socialist responses to their circumstances. These leaders could have reaffirmed their allegiance to socialism and tried to unionize and socialize the garment industry as part of a broad plan to make the United States into a socialist society.

If they had decided upon this alternative, many of their rank and file unionists would have supported them.

These officials, however, did not select the radical alternative. Instead, they chose to operate within the framework of the capitalist system. Once the capitalist environment was accepted as the norm, given the nature and structure of the garment industry, the needle trades unions' leaders inevitably had to subordinate their socialist ideals in order to deal with practical realities. This conservative decision also put them on a collision course with many unionists in their organizations who refused to compromise their Left principles.

THE CONCESSION

The concession that socialism would not soon triumph in America came relatively early in the history of the garment unions. It was made explicit in 1910 by Meyer London, a Socialist and future Socialist congressman, during the course of contract negotiations between the International Ladies' Garment Workers' Union and garment manufacturers. (London was the chief negotiator for the union.) This contract, it was recognized by all, would be the most important ever negotiated in the industry and could set the standards for union-employer relations for decades. In the bargaining sessions London, taking pains to point out to the manufacturers' representatives that the Socialists who led the ILGWU were reasonable men who were not bound by utopian or dogmatic socialist principles, assured them that: "We do not come to control your business; we do not come to control your trade. I, personally, would have liked to see a state of affairs where mankind should control everything in a cooperative effort but I realize in the year 1910 and in the cloak trade it is hardly possible of realization, and I have advised my clients and they have agreed with me in that view."[41]

This was not only a view held by London and his ILGWU associates. The same position was continually reiterated by Sidney Hillman, the head of the powerful Amalgamated Clothing Workers of America. Hillman, a Bundist in Europe and a man who defined himself as a socialist as late as the end of the 1930s, had long been a political realist. Since attaining the office of President of the Amalgamated at its founding in 1914, Hillman was continually concerned with tempering the socialist idealism of his more radical colleagues and rank and filers. The motivation for this trimming of his own (and other Amalgamated unionists') commitment to socialism was the desire to make the Amalgamated a more effective and a more responsible union. It was this motivation that led him to cooperate closely with employers. It was this motivation, too, that led Hillman to prevent the Amalgamated from endorsing the Socialist party in 1916, to delete the revolutionary socialist preamble in the Union's constitution in 1922, and to guide it toward an endorsement of Franklin Delano Roosevelt in 1936.[42]

Socialism for Hillman (and other garment union leaders as well) did not offer realistic guidelines for running a union in a capitalist society. In 1939 Hillman, while still a self-defined socialist, enunciated a long held position: "Labor unions cannot function in the atmosphere of abstract theory alone. Men, women, and children cannot wait for the millenium. They want to eat, mate, and have a breath of ease now. Certainly I believe in collaborating with employers! That is what a Union is for."[43]

On another occasion he explained: "Class collaboration does not necessarily conflict with a socialist position. It is simply making the best of what is indisputably a fact, that at least in this country we are likely to live for some time to come in a capitalist system, and it is just as well to get as much return as possible for the workers meanwhile."[44]

By the mid-1930s the number of avowed Socialists among the garment union officers reached a low point. This retreat stemmed not only from individuals making private choices in response to their particular circumstances but also from the decisions of the top leadership that were imposed on lesser officials. In 1936 David Dubinsky, Sidney Hillman, and Alex Rose, the heads of the ILGWU, the Amalgamated, and the Millinery Workers Union, respectively, formed the American Labor party in New York State for the purpose of increasing organized labor's support for Franklin Delano Roosevelt. Officers in these unions who did not voluntarily break their ties with the Socialist party to follow the policy direction of their chiefs were persuaded to take this course of action. Thus, for all intents and purposes socialism, or socialism as a force within the officialdom of the needle trades unions, was nearly dormant by the time World War II broke out.[45]

THE QUEST FOR ORDER AND STABILITY

Early in the organizational life of the garment unions, their Socialist leaders, in response to the circumstances that characterized the garment industry, made choices that took them on a path leading away from socialism. These decisions were made at the same time that these union leaders were espousing socialist principles and committing themselves and their organizations to the support of the Socialist party and its candidates for public office. Conservative options were selected, whether consciously or unconsciously, in the hope of bringing order and stability into a chaotic industry. These options also contributed to turning these unions into centralized and conservative organizations.

The rightward impact of these socialist unions' quest for order and stability was evident in the settlement that grew out of the ILGWU's 1910 strike. This was the greatest strike in the history of the ILGWU, the cloakmakers' "great revolt." This was the strike that literally "made" the ILGWU. From the settlement, labeled the Protocol of Peace, leading manufacturers and smaller ones as well agreed to recognize the ILGWU as the legal bargaining agent of workers in the women's clothing industry. This recognition was the single greatest gain that the ILGWU obtained from the "great revolt."[46]

In return for this and other benefits, the ILGWU demonstrated that the allegiance of its leaders to socialism and the Socialist party would not be allowed to interfere in any way with the operations of the union. In the Protocol of Peace, the Socialist union leaders and their chief negotiator, the Socialist attorney, Meyer London, sharply drew back from a class conflict and radical socialist position. It was in these negotiations, as cited earlier, that London announced that socialism was not on the ILGWU's agenda. The most concrete indicators of their reasonableness and of their willingness to abide by the rules of the game were these leaders' agreement to put aside the long cherished demands of militant unionists. The union solemnly agreed not to strike while the contract was in force and to forego a closed shop (a shop in which the employer could only employ union workers). Issues that arose during the life of the protocol were to be resolved jointly and peacefully. Instead of a strike, serious grievances were to be handled through a Permanent Board of Settlement—a body created by the protocol. This Board was to consist of three persons: one chosen by the ILGWU, one by the manufacturers, and the third chosen jointly to represent the public, or, more accurately, the Jewish public. The first head of this Permanent Board of Settlement, by unanimous and popular choice, was the liberal attorney, Louis Brandeis, a principal architect of the protocol.

The Jewish Socialist leadership of the ILGWU headed by President John Dyche and Secretary-Treasurer Abraham Rosenberg evidently believed that they and their organization had obtained a great deal in the protocol. Their victories, however, foreshadowed the weakening of a socialist commitment within the needle trades union officialdom. The protocol, for them, meant not only legitimization by the garment manufacturers; it also signified the first step of the union and management toward jointly stabilizing the industry. The settlement made partners out of these traditional adversaries.

The protocol also demonstrated the genuine concern that the ILGWU leadership had for its new partners, or at least some of them. Through the protocol and the negotiations for it, the ILGWU pushed the manufacturers, particularly the larger ones, to form and join manufacturers' associations. The ILGWU, indeed, felt so strongly about this that it refused in 1910 (and in other years) to come to terms with various employers who did not join a manufacturers' association in their respective trade. This strengthening of the "capitalist bosses" may have seemed odd behavior for Socialists. But it was not out of keeping with the mentality of union officials concerned with the problem of getting hundreds of small shops to abide by union wages and regulations. The ILGWU believed that a strong employers' organization would be helpful to the union by ensuring that its individual members lived up to contractual obligations. The Union then would have assistance in enforcing contracts. At the same time it indicated that the ILGWU (and the other needle trades unions that followed this example) was going to be a most cooperative partner with capitalist employers and thus an active sustainer of the capitalist system.

The protocol also strengthened the hand of the central leadership within the ILGWU, a long desired objective. The agreement was not between a local and an individual employer. It was between the ILGWU and the employers' association. The union and not locals within it became responsible for obtaining benefits and for enforcing the contract. A strong responsible centralized union was envisioned to work harmoniously with a strong responsible centralized employers' association.

In this light, a no-strike pledge did not represent much of a sacrifice as far as the ILGWU leadership was concerned. In their view, too many unnecessary strikes had been previously called. These strikes had drained the union's treasury in the past. Simultaneously, the strikes strengthened the position of the locals and shop units at the expense of the central organization. Individual shops and local strikes, from the perspective of the national officials, fostered close ties between members and local leaders and encouraged each to lose sight of the larger necessity to bring order and fewer strikes into the industry. By foregoing the right to strike, the national ILGWU officers in one stroke relieved their organization of a financial drain, buttressed centralized control, and improved their public image as reasonable men.

The leadership under Dyche and Rosenberg did their best to abide by the no-strike pledge during the life of the protocol. It refused to authorize a strike regardless of the provocation. The firing of individual union members for arbitrary reasons or even for the reason that he was an active unionist was never a sufficient cause for strike authorization. When unauthorized strikes were called in defiance of the wishes of the national office, the offending local or shop members would be disciplined. In at least one case, the national leadership dispatched scabs to break such a strike.

In the years in which the protocol was in force, the Socialist ILGWU officials demonstrated their willingness to pay a price for this cooperative arrangement. Unfortunately, however, it was their members and not they who bore the actual cost. Manufacturers who had agreed to abide by the protocol regularly evaded its provisions by sending work out to shops not covered by the contract. In some protocol shops, wages fell below the minimum agreed upon; union activists who protested were fired; and union membership fell. But no authorized strikes were called.

The rank and file objected to the costly compromises that their leaders were making in order to safeguard the union as an institution. As militant unionists and as socialists they decried the close cooperation between their officials and their bosses that seemed to produce so little practical payoff. To many of the workers in the shops, this was collaborationism and a betrayal of socialism.

President Dyche and his coterie in turn denounced the critics as being impractical idealists. Dyche believed that those who attacked his pragmatic politics saw the protocol "from the point of view of a Russian revolutionary."[47] These union members, the leadership felt, did not have an appreciation for the problems of maintaining a union in a field such as the garment trades. Many, if not a majority, of the ILGWU members refused to accept Dyche's position and logic. After four years of bearing the brunt of the costs under the protocol, the rank and file made its view known at the ILGWU's Twelfth Convention in 1914. A resolution calling upon the union "to repudiate the Protocol altogether as an interference with 'the historical mission of the working class to do away with capitalism' was only narrowly defeated."[48] But they did succeed in electing a new leadership that was more committed to socialism—Benjamin Schlesinger as president and Morris Sigman as secretary-treasurer—and a year later the protocol was abrogated.

The new leaders and the end of the protocol did not, however, indicate a major change in union policy. Socialist leaders in the ILGWU and the other needle trades unions remained convinced that their organizations' survival depended upon order and stability in the garment trades, which in turn, they believed, necessitated cooperation between labor and management. It was to these ends that the needle trades unions chieftains bent their efforts in subsequent years. And as they did so, the same conflicts between them and the rank and file erupted. Many garment trade unionists refused to surrender their commitment to socialism, particularly when the practical benefits for doing so seemed so minimal.

UNIFORM WAGES

The imposition of uniform wages throughout the garment industry became a major objective of the unions almost from the time of their establishment. Salaries, as noted above, in this labor-intensive industry represented a large, if not the largest, cost of production. As long as garment workers, whatever their reasons, were willing to work at varying rates for different employers, the garment industry would be characterized by severe competition and the attendant chronic insecurity for workers, their bosses, and their unions. The Amalgamated Clothing Workers of America, in particular, was very conscious of the need to equalize wage costs and thereby stabilize its own position as

well as that of the employers in the trade. As its General Executive
Board stated:

Early in our history as an organization we recognized that there were definite
limits upon our ability to improve and maintain wage and hour standards of
workers employed by a single manufacturer or in a single market, unless we
succeeded in raising the standards of all competing manufacturers and markets up to the same level. Thus, throughout our history, we have been confronted with the problem of stabilizing the clothing industry by taking measures to equalize the labor costs of competing manufacturers.[49]

A uniform wage policy was congenial to the interests of the larger
manufacturers, or "inside" manufacturers—those that encompassed
all phases of production. Lower wage costs were the principal weapon
in the arsenal of the smaller firms in their war against their larger
competitors. If the price of labor could be equalized, the larger employers, particularly those in men's clothing and other sectors less
prone to the vagaries of fashion changes, could utilize their larger
plants and more extensive machinery to gain an economic advantage
over their smaller rivals.

The unions' policy toward contractors or submanufacturers was informed by this need to establish uniform wage rates and again was
congenial to the interests of the larger employers. Ideally, the best policy with regard to contractors from the point of view of the unions
and, to some extent, the manufacturers as well would have been to
drive them out of business. The contractors typically paid lower
wages than the regular manufacturers and operated shops that were
less safe and less sanitary than those of the larger employers. As long
as they existed the larger manufacturers would be tempted to compete
with one another by sending part of their work to the lower labor cost
contractors. This would also generally mean taking work from a unionized work force and giving it to a nonunionized one, as contractors, far more than the large employers, were less likely to have union
contracts.

The unions, however, were never powerful enough to abolish completely the contractor shops. Instead, they tried to lessen their number
and regulate them. They utilized two major means to accomplish this
end. One was to try and make the larger manufacturer responsible for
the enforcement of union standards in the contract shops to which
they sent work. The second was to comprise a list of contractors acceptable to the union and force the manufacturers to deal only with
contractors on the approved list.

These provisos were to be built into the contracts that the manufacturers signed with the unions. If they were violated by the contractors,
the unions could then force the manufacturers to pressure the contractors to comply. But the more far-sighted manufacturers, which usually
meant the larger ones, did not need the threat of a union's club to see
the advantages that would accrue to them if all the contractors were

so regulated. If the unions were successful in this regard, they would be removing the significant source of instability in the industry and low-cost competitors as well.[50]

The garment unions, then, had good reason to favor the larger manufacturers. It was in their organizational and economic self-interest to do so. Although initially it was more difficult to organize the workers of a larger employer than a smaller one, more benefits accrued to the union from a relationship with the former once the workers were organized. It was easier and cheaper to police and enforce contracts with larger employers than with smaller ones. Employees in the smaller shops were more likely to be either intimidated by their employers or to collude with them in the violation of a union contract. Also, once under contract, the union could use the larger manufacturer as its agent in spreading union standards to other parts of the industry, such as the manufacturer and the contractor. And the unions also benefited by an economy of scale. One plant employing 1000 union workers required less of an outlay of union resources and personnel than did 10 factories each employing 100 workers.

All of these factors pushed the garment unions into an alliance with the larger manufacturers. At the time of the protocol, this alliance was somewhat tacit and cloaked in general and abstract terminology, but as time passed the alliance became more open and explicit. The Amalgamated, for example, provided loans and other types of help to some of the larger of the men's clothing firms. Both the Amalgamated and the ILGWU encouraged manufacturers to organize into associations.[51] Such as organizational form was in the common interests of both the larger employers and the garment unions. As Melech Epstein, writing from the point of view of the needle trades' union leadership, explained:

The association was usually controlled by the larger employers, who had a more permanent stake in the industry. They too came to realize that in the long run the union, by enforcing uniform labor standards, was a steadying factor in a cutthroat industry. As time went on, contact between the leading group of the association and the union became more and more mutually advantageous. The association kept recalcitrant employers to their obligations in the contract, while the union had many ways to back up the association against employers who refused to abide by its decisions. In trades with many hundreds of small industrial units, collective dealings between the union and the association facilitated reaching agreements as well as observing their terms. The paid executives of the associations also learned that it was in their own interest to maintain cordial relations with union leaders.[52]

In 1947 David Dubinsky, then president of the ILGWU, noted another way in which associations benefited the unions' interest. In that year in testimony before Congress, Dubinsky pointed out that his union had 90 contracts with associations that encompassed a labor force of 310,000 but 900 contracts with individual employers who were not part of an association and who employed 70,000 union members.[53]

PRODUCTIVITY STANDARDS

The garment unions also cooperated with employers by imposing on their members productivity standards that were designed to increase the efficiency and output of union workers. The explicit rationale behind these standards was to make the costs for employers who signed contracts with unions as competitive as possible with those for employers who would not recognize unions. As Sidney Hillman expressed it to his Amalgamated convention in 1920, "labor cannot destroy the house it lives in." [54]

The employers in the industry very much appreciated the efforts that the ILGWU and the Amalgamated were exerting on their behalf. Union officials were regarded as spurs to productivity. For example, one Baltimore clothing manufacturer, E. Strouse, in a letter to Sidney Hillman (October 3, 1919) complained that the local union representative was not visiting his plant often enough. "Asking that the representative visit once a day, Strouse noted that 'I have been trying to get more production for weeks and have been unable to do so.' Could you 'not do something that we might have him more oftener,' Strouse asked Hillman, 'because I feel that he is able to get for us what we want, better than we can ourselves and it is urgent from many angles, that we get our production.' " [55]

This concern for efficiency and productivity placed the unions in the same position as the employers vis-a-vis the workers. The rank and file, a largely socialist group, found that from about World War I on, their bosses were not the only group concerned with getting more work out of them. Now their own Socialist union leaders had adopted this goal.

THE CONSEQUENCES OF CLASS COLLABORATIONISM

The garment union officials' focus upon a uniform wage, increased productivity, and cooperation with the employers in the industry drew them ever farther from their socialist ideals. The adoption of these positions placed them into actual and potential conflict with their own members, particularly the more radical ones. Even as these Socialist officials were contributing to the coffers of the Socialist party and supporting Socialist candidates, they were actively disciplining Socialists and other radicals within their own ranks who disagreed with their class collaborationist policies.

One of the earliest indications of the consequences of pursuing a class collaborationist union policy was the degeneration in the quality of union officials. Once it was clear that a commitment to socialism meant little with respect to obtaining prestige or other nonmaterial benefits, they had no reason to use socialist principles as a guide for their own behavior.

In the absence of a meaningful socialist belief, these officials put up little resistance to accommodation with the capitalist system. Also, without such a commitment, they were less able to resist the pressures for cooperation with this system stemming from the daily and immediate demands of maintaining a union in a capitalist context. In such a situation, union positions became vehicles for self-aggrandizement, and their occupants in many cases became hacks.

Abraham Beckerman, a prominent Socialist party member, was one person who represented the low state to which socialism had fallen within the needle trade unions' officialdom. In the 1920s he served as General Manager of the Amalgamated Joint Board in New York City, the encompassing organization of all Amalgamated locals in the city, and gained a great deal of notoriety for his use of violence against internal union opponents. He was so successful at this that the *Jewish Daily Forward*, a fervent supporter of the socialist right or moderates in the needle trades, approvingly proclaimed: "Blessed Be Beckerman's Knuckles." Later Socialist Beckerman became closely associated with the infamous gangster Louis "Lepke" Buchalter. He and another Socialist ILGWU union official, Harry Cohen, were reputed to have lost their union positions for collaborating with gangsters. Eventually Beckerman was sent to prison. After prison, he reentered the garment trade but this time on the side of management. However, Beckerman did retain his ties to the Socialists and they to him. In 1950 he was honored at a banquet of veteran Socialists at which leading Socialists spoke on his behalf.[56]

Beckerman was not the only example of Socialist degeneracy in the garment unions. Knowledgeable observers and Socialist intimates of the leadership candidly expressed (usually in private) their negative assessment of the situation. J. B. S. Hardmann, a Socialist and official in the Amalgamated, unburdened himself about the quality of the New York City leadership of his union in the following manner in 1926: "[The Amalgamated New York leadership] . . . is not capable of delivering anything . . . [it] . . . is either lazy or incompetent or both."[57] In the same year Norman Thomas, then a rising star in the Socialist party, similarly complained of the lack of idealism among the New York City SP needle trade union officials. In a private communication to party leader Morris Hillquit, Thomas contended that the major force motivating these men was a negative anti-Communism.[58] At the end of the decade, another Socialist, B. Charney Vladeck, the managing editor of the *Jewish Daily Forward*, in a letter to his friend and fellow Socialist David Dubinsky, then acting president of the ILGWU, wrote: "My observations in our trade union movement in the last couple of years leads me to believe that the average union official has become a bureaucrat."[59]

The degeneracy of various officials was not the only product of the class collaborationist policy pursued by the needle trades' union officials. The demise of democracy in these organizations also could, in large part, be laid to the adherence to this policy. In order to make the partnership between labor and management work effectively, the union leaders believed it was necessary to have a powerful centralized organization. Strong leaders backed by such a structure could then more successfully impose uniform wages, higher production standards, and other unpleasant measures upon recalcitrant members (in their own long-range interests, of course). Limitations on the rank and file's ability to influence union policy became, as interpreted by union officials, almost a necessity for the operation of an effective organization.

Internal opponents, particularly if numerous and organized, represented a threat to the moderate or conservative leadership on a variety of levels. An opposition might be able to prevent the unions' officials from imposing their will upon recalcitrant members unaware of their best long-range interests. The lack of cooperation or obedience on the part of the rank and file could frustrate the leadership's plans to bring order and stability to the industry and at the same time reduce the willingness of the employers to cooperate with the unions' establishment. Opposition could also make the garment unions into unstable organizations, endangering their effectiveness and making the leaders' positions less secure. To ensure that these negative consequences did not come to pass, the heads of the garment unions took steps (as will be shown) to quash opposition. At the same time these steps also severely constricted the working of democracy in their organizations.

LEFT-WING DISSIDENTS

The garment unions, particularly the ILGWU (upon which we shall now focus), were unable to rid themselves of internal opponents or organized oppositional factions in the period from World War I throughout most of the 1920s. During these years the ILGWU and other needle trades unions were bedevilled by internecine warfare. The major disputants were various groups that were divided into two loose coalitions—the right and the left. The right consisted largely of right wing or conservative socialists, union bureaucrats, and their sympathizers. The left was made up largely of Communists, left wing or radical Socialists, anarchists, syndicalists, progressives, and their sympathizers.

The ILGWU hierarchy, led by right-wing Socialists, continually attempted to crush its left-wing opponents. From 1919 to 1921 the major radical threat came from the shop-delegate movement. The principal objective of this movement was to democratize and radicalize the ILGWU by reorganizing it along shop rather than craft lines. The ILGWU's response was to disqualify radical candidates from running for office and to arbitrarily divide the Local 25, one of the centers of this movement. These tactics did not bring an end to the ILGWU's internal political problems. In fact, if anything, they helped to exacerbate them. The largely Socialist or Socialist-oriented rank and file did not appear to approve of such nondemocratic use of union power. This arbitrary treatment of union dissidents also contributed to strengthening the already growing image of the union leaders as conservative bureaucrats, standing apart from their members.

It was not only the authoritarian and bureaucratic character of the leadership that troubled the rank and file. The ILGWU's membership was also disturbed by the failure of their leaders to protect them from increasing unemployment, lower wages, and deteriorating working conditions. The ILGWU, despite its close cooperation with the leading employers in the apparel manufacturing industry, was not able to preserve the gains it had obtained During World War I. The depressed state of the economy in general following the war and the growing importance of the wage-cutting jobbers and contractors in the industry, particularly in New York City, combined to undercut the ILGWU's ability to protect its members.

The leadership's response to these negative economic circumstances gave the left wing further ammunition in its campaign against the International. Rather than change its policy of cooperation and class collaborationism in view of the deteriorating economic position of the membership, the ILGWU's Socialist hierarchy reaffirmed its commitment to moderation and pragmatism. This policy did virtually nothing to help the beleaguered garment workers in the 1920s.

By 1925 the confluence of lower wages, higher unemployment, the union's conservative economic policies, and its authoritarian and insensitive rule combined to produce a majority for the left wing in the ILGWU in New York City. (These same factors also produced similar results in the Amalgamated and the International Fur Workers Union.) The central organizational focus of this opposition was the Communist-inspired Trade Union Educational League (TUEL). In the next several years a major struggle for control of the union took place between the right-wing leadership and the various radicals, militants, and Communists who backed the TUEL. A highlight of this battle was a 26-week strike of New York City ILGWU members in 1926.

The incumbent moderates and conservatives emerged victorious from this civil war. Although many of their left-wing opponents were forced out of the union and were later led out by the Communist party, a number remained and for decades thereafter challenged the leadership. Their reduced numbers, the obtuseness of the Communist party, and the frailty of the Socialist party, however, combined to limit their effectiveness. And after the late 1920s and early 1930s, they never again launched a serious effort to unseat the right-wing leadership.

The civil war of the latter 1920s v.·as bloody and costly in many ways. Each side was reported to have used violence and gangsters against the other. The right-wing, however, had more powerful allies and organizational machinery available to it than did the left wing, which helped to turn the tide in its favor. These included some garment manufacturers, the American Federation of Labor, Governors Smith and Roosevelt (of New York), the courts, and the police. The incumbents were also inadvertently assisted by the naivete and inexperience of their opponents and the dramatic shifts in policy of the Communist party, which disoriented its members and supporters.

The ILGWU's leaders' control of the machinery of the International was an additional and important factor in their triumph. This centralized control, which they had struggled to attain since the ILGWU's formation, allowed them to deliver telling blows to their left-wing opponents. Utilizing the power vested in their positions by the ILGWU constitution, the right-wing leadership suspended and expelled individuals and locals and barred left-wing delegates from conventions. The incumbents also amended the union's constitution to forestall the formation of organized opposition groups. In an amendment, which still stands, internal union groups, clubs, or caucases were forbidden except for certain short periods of time and in cases of exemptions granted by the General Executive Board. The "illegality" of these non-official internal groupings, of course, made it quite difficult for anything but a formal or paper democracy to operate within the ILGWU.

Not surprisingly the incumbents' control of the International itself stemmed from undemocratic procedures and antedated the Communist menace. These procedures can and probably were designed to frustrate the will of the majority of the members of the ILGWU. One of the most important of these was the method by which delegates were apportioned to the ILGWU's biennial convention. The convention is the highest authority in the ILGWU and its most important body. It is the convention delegates who elect the president, secretary-treasurer, and the general executive board. These officials have control over such vital union matters as authorization of strikes, contract negotiations, awarding of charters, and internal union discipline. The local unions select their own delegates, but their credentials must be approved by the convention. The number of delegates was not based on the size of the local. Smaller locals were alloted proportionally more delegates than larger ones.

The smaller locals that benefited from this arrangement tended to be allies of the right-wing ILGWU officers. Many of these were located outside of metropolitan areas in the midst of communities unfriendly to unionism and radicalism. In these circumstances, the smaller locals were very dependent on the ILGWU for support and for their existence. The smaller cutters' locals, which housed the most skilled and highest-paid members of the ILGWU, were also allied to the right wing. They did not wish to see their differential privileges taken away by a more egalitarian left-wing administration. Finally, a number of the smaller locals appeared to be paper locals—bodies whose major raison d'etre seemed to be the dispatching of proadministration delegates to ILGWU conventions.[60]

The larger locals, on the other hand, were generally less friendly to the central administration. Many, indeed, were centers of insurgency. They were located in metropolitan areas like New York City, where the climate was more positive to unionism and radicalism than in the smaller cities and towns. Their members were also more likely to be the lesser skilled and the lower-paid among the ILGWU rank and file. (The "Italian" locals, 48 and 89, in New York City represent the major exception to this generalization, as we shall see.)[61]

It is interesting to note that in the mid-1920s the Communists or the left wing of the ILGWU, the Amalgamated, and the International Fur Workers Union (IFWU) gained the support of a majority of the members of each union in New York City. But the right wing vigorously used its control over the machinery of the union to frustrate their rebelling New Yorkers, and only in the case of the furriers did the Communists win. A major reason for this is that between 80 to 85 percent of the furrier unionists were located in New York City. This was a much higher percentage than was true for the ILGWU and the Amalgamated. The IFWU central leaders, given the disproportionate weight of the New York Communist and pro-Communist locals in their organization, were not able to use effectively the same methods that their fellow Socialists and anti-Communists in the ILGWU and the Amalgamated used in their unions.[62]

The ILGWU that the right wing controlled at the end of the 1920s was barely viable as an organization. The internal civil war, the expulsions, and the predatory behavior of employers who took advantage of the ILGWU's weakness combined to leave the union in a sorrowful condition. The union was deep in debt, and its membership had fallen sharply. In 1931 the ILGWU reached a 23-year low of 19,897 members. Its future appeared to be very much in doubt in this period.

The ILGWU did, however, survive and it even prospered as an organization in subsequent years. But the way in which the leadership under Socialist David Dubinsky (acting president in 1929 and president in 1932) extricated the union from its precarious position indicated that the organization's allegiance to the principles of socialism and to the Socialist party was not going to be very durable. Money was borrowed from the banker Herbert Lehman and a few other German-Jewish notables. Large manufacturers acted as Dubinsky's silent partners in helping the union to reestablish itself. Assistance also came from the New York State governor's office and then from the FDR administration.[63] Obviously, none of these bourgeois friends of the Socialist-led ILGWU believed that they were strengthening the union's ties to socialism by their generosity. And they were right.

The socialist union leaders' class collaboration with the garment manufacturers may have proved beneficial to them and the employers, but there is reason and evidence to doubt that it was very helpful to most of the rank and file in the long or short run. In the decade from 1920 to 1930, the membership rolls of the garment unions atrophied.

The ILGWU, which had 105,400 members in 1920, lost about 60 percent by 1930. The Amalgamated membership's declined from 177,000 to 100,000 in the same period. The total membership in the clothing unions fell from 374,000 to 230,000 or a loss of 144,000 within 10 years. Real wages and the quality of working conditions generally followed the same downward pattern.[64]

The garment unions were not alone in suffering these reverses in this decade. Overall membership in unions in the United States during the same period fell from 5,048,000 to 3,393,000. The other unions were usually no more successful than those in the needle trades in holding onto previous gains in wages and working conditions for their members. All suffered the effects of the postwar recession in the early 1920s and that of the oncoming depression in the latter part of the decade.[65] It is therefore difficult to know whether any other policy that the garment unions might have adopted could have led to substantial benefits for their members. But we do know that by the end of the 1920s both the economic status of the needle trades workers and the socialist commitment of their leaders had sadly deteriorated.

THE FATE OF NEW YORK

The economic price that the garment workers had to pay for their unions' policy of class collaboration and industrial stability can be seen most clearly in terms of the clothing workers in New York City. This was where the largest number of clothing workers, garment union members, and garment employers were located in 1900, 1920, 1940, and in the postwar decades. New York City was the most important garment center in the country in the twentieth century and the major context in which the Socialist-led garment unions pursued their policies of cooperating with employers and bringing order and stability to the garment industry. The Amalgamated Clothing Workers of America, reputedly the most radical of the garment unions from its birth in 1914 until the early 1920s, was also one of the most aggressive in terms of following a policy designed to regulate and stabilize the garment industry, particularly that part of it located in New York City. In accord with the larger policy of regulating the industry, the ACWA, under the leadership of its president, Sidney Hillman, wanted very much to protect the competitive position of the New York market and employers. To do this Hillman believed that it was necessary to be firm in the application of a practice of uniform wage rates and to increase the efficiency and productivity of the New York garment factories. The ILGWU also shared this concern about the position of the New York market and was in general agreement with Hillman and the ACWA about how best to protect it.

In 1919 and 1920 the ACWA's New York City members gained firsthand knowledge of how the policy of protecting the garment industry in their city worked in practice. Some union members were forced by their officers to forego the opportunity to take jobs paying $5 to $10 higher than the standard union wages.[66] At approximately the same time the ACWA also actively encouraged New York clothing manufacturers to increase productivity through the introduction of more specialized machinery and a more specialized division of labor. This hurt the position of the skilled tailors and the slower workers and led directly to the reduction of the total number of jobs in the industry. The policy was defended as was that of uniform wage rates on the grounds that it would contribute to the long-term health of the garment industry in New York City and protect the competitive position of the New York City market, thus saving in the long-run the jobs of New York City workers and maintaining a relatively high standard in terms of pay and conditions.

This policy reaped few short-term benefits. The Amalgamated in the men's clothing industry proved unable to prevent work and jobs from leaving New York City and going to smaller cities and towns elsewhere in the country. The same phenomenon happened in Chicago, another important metropolitan base of the ACWA. In the period from 1923 to 1929, New York City lost more than 9000 jobs in the men's clothing industry, and Chicago, where the same policies had been applied, lost roughly 11,000. This was not a phenomenon caused primarily by the economic downturns at the beginning and end of the decade. In the same time span other areas in which the men's clothing industry was located gained in total number of jobs. In Baltimore, for example, the number increased from 7849 to 9363. In St. Louis, the total number of jobs rose by 624. The gains in these areas were indicative of the drift of the garment industry from the major unionized and Jewish metropolitan areas to the smaller locales where the union was weaker, and the number and proportion of Jews was fewer.

The internecine union warfare may have been a contributory factor. The Amalgamated undoubtedly was weakened by the struggles between the Left and the Right going on within it during the 1920s. Still, the potency of this factor must be questioned, particularly in relationship to the ACWA. First, the political struggle within the Amalgamated was never as bitter or as severe as it was in the ILGWU. Second, there was barely any civil war within the Amalgamated in Chicago, and more jobs were lost in Chicago than in New York.

The Amalgamated's policy was also not very successful in maintaining the wages and standards of its members in the New York City market, and the ILGWU was even less successful in this regard. In New York during the 1920s, the number of sweatshops increased. As the situation worsened in the early years of the Great Depression, it was not unusual for a garment employee in a dress shop to work from 55 to 60 hours and receive between $5.93 and $7.93 for this. This was in New York City, the most heavily unionized area of the garment industry.[67] The loss of jobs, the decline in wages and standards, and the rise in the prevalence of sweatshops in New York City by the early

1930s were in large part the results of the unions' policy of protecting the New York market through uniform wage rates, higher productivity levels, and cooperation with clothing manufacturers in stabilizing the industry.

The ILGWU under the leadership of David Dubinsky aggressively continued to pursue such a policy in the 1940s and into the post war years. It reached an almost ludicrous point when Dubinsky personally rejected a wage offer of New York City dress manufacturers because it was *too high*. "If I take it," Dubinsky protested to the industry's representative," . . . you'll have no money to give me next time because there will be no jobs left in New York." [68]

The policies pursued by the ILGWU and the Amalgamated have born bitter fruit for unionized garment workers in New York City. In 1963, for example, the average hourly wage of unionized needle trades employees was $2.39 per hour. A union member working at this rate for 40 hours per week over 52 weeks would earn $4,971.20, or $77 below the subsistence level in 1960 as calculated by the Bureau of Labor Statistics. But, not all ILGWU members earned the average hourly rate. In 1963, from 15–20% of these unionists earned less than $1.50 an hour. [69]

The failure of the policy of uniform or near uniform national wages and protecting the competitive position of the garment industry in New York City can be clearly seen by considering what has happened to garment worker jobs in New York City between the 1950s and 1970s. In this period wages in New York were depressed but not far enough to prevent the city and the New York region in general from losing jobs. Between 1958 and 1972 New York City lost 68,000 positions in the garment industry. Between 1950 and 1974 the percentage of all apparel workers in the nation employed in New York State declined from 34 to 15 percent. And in the same 24-year period, the percentage employed in the South increased from 17 to 44 percent. [70]

Historically, there were at least two ways in which New York's competitive position could have been safeguarded within the context of a policy of uniform wages. One would have been to have New York wages set the standard for the rest of the country, so that whenever the unionized garment workers in that city obtained higher salaries, the new wage rates would become the standard that the union would then try to attain everywhere else. The second would have been to try to ensure that New York City's union members' wages and benefits stayed in line with those of others elsewhere in the country. This would mean that the salaries of garment unionists outside of New York would then become the standard for the wages of the New Yorkers.

This second approach appears to have been the one that the garment unions generally followed. It proved to be a costly one for their New York members in particular and those outside of New York in general. The major reason for this was that the garment industry in New York was the most heavily unionized of any major area in the country throughout this century. Thus, it follows that the New York garment unionists were in the best position to have played a leadership role in raising the wage levels of the entire national clothes-making work force. Employers in sections such as the South, where the union was less prominent, simply did not have the same incentive to grant improvements in salaries and working conditions for their employees as did their counterparts in New York City. Thus, if the wages and working conditions of the needle trades' union members outside of New York became the standard for the application of a policy of uniformity, the logical consequence would be that the salary levels and terms of employment of all would drift to that of the lowest common denominator. The relative decline in the earnings of garment union employees in the post–World War II era and the increasing proximity between the hourly wages of production workers in New York City and Birmingham, Alabama, indicate that this is what did, indeed, take place.[71]

The pursuit of such a policy was injurious to the socialist idealism of the garment union leaders. In line with it, they were progressively transformed from aggressive champions of better conditions and salaries, as had been the case prior to World War I, to defenders of a declining uniform wage rate. The description of the ILGWU by the New York City Teamsters Union Joint Council with respect to its position on wages in New York City in 1963 is a sad commentary on how much this union had changed. In a letter to the Democratic majority of the New York City Council, the Teamsters wrote, "Surely you must or should know that the ILGWU has a vested interest in the perpetuation of exploitation, low-wage pockets, and poverty in New York City."[72]

Why did the garment unions' leaders not allow the wages and working conditions of their New York members to set the standard for the rest of the country? This course was open to them, but in order for it to have been effective, the unions would have had to organize the clothing workers throughout the country. For the unions were well aware, as noted earlier, that unless this was done, business and employment would flow to nonunionized areas where employers would have an economic advantage over their competitors who had to pay higher union wages. This had proved an obstacle to effective unionization of the industry before the turn of the century, when manufacturers moved plants and goods to avoid areas of union strength.[73] As Joel Seidman so aptly expressed it: "In so highly a mobile industry, with so much of the work easily learned, it is possible to maintain high standards only with complete national unionization, effective legislation, or both."[74] The garment industry, however, succeeded in extending into areas beyond the control of the unions throughout this century.[75]

THE COSTS OF A NATIONAL UNION

Had the garment unions strived to unionize the entire industry, such a policy would have required the devotion of tremendous resources and energy over a virtually never-ending period of time. Organization of the workers was only one aspect of the problem. Even if the unions had been successful in this regard, it would still have been necessary to check and inspect constantly places of employment for possible violations of contracts. The odds for success in such a venture never appeared very high.

It is reasonably clear from the evidence that the Socialist needle trades union leaders generally did not choose to invest inordinate resources and energy in organizing garment workers into unions outside of areas of Jewish population centers. This does not mean that no major efforts in this direction were ever made. In 1933 and 1934, for example, both the ILGWU and the ACWA launched extensive organizing drives in these types of areas. There were also campaigns conducted in individual cities, such as the Amalgamated's drive in Philadelphia in the late 1920s. These were apparently more the exception than the rule. (In 1976, when the ILGWU's membership had declined to the point where it represented 55 percent of the workers in the trade across the nation, the union had only 178 organizers on its staff.) It was evidently less costly in terms of the economic resources of the garment unions to attempt to bring about some degree of uniformity of wage levels through inhibiting their rise in heavily unionized areas than it was to try and unionize everywhere the industry was located.[76]

The flight of garment manufacturers and jobs from New York and other Northern metropolitan centers to areas like the South where the needle trades unions were not strong was costly not only to the workers but to these unions as well. Membership declined. As the percentage of garment workers in the South rose, the number of unionists in the ILGWU and the Amalgamated fell. Between 1960 and 1974, for example, the ILGWU lost about 10 percent and the Amalgamated 7 percent of its total membership. (Jobs and members were also lost because of the flight of the garment industry across national boundaries to places such as the Republic of Korea, Hong Kong, and Taiwan.) In 1974, although 44 percent of the nation's garment workers were to be found in the South, the Southern members of the ILGWU and the Amalgamated accounted for approximately 11 percent of each union's national membership.[77]

Economic factors, however, may not have been the only consideration in choosing between these two options. Embarking on a course of national unionization had other costs attached, political ones. These political costs could be viewed as deficits more from the point of view of the Socialist leaders than from the point of view of their organizations. These political deficits would emerge from the impact that an effective national unionization campaign would have upon the ethnic base of the Socialist needle trades' union heads.

The garment unions had been established and their Socialist chieftains had come to the fore in the context of a needle trades' workforce that was predominantly comprised of Yiddish-speaking Jews. Their common origin, experiences, language, and sympathy with a commitment to socialism had been the factors that compensated for the structural features of the industry that were so antagonistic to effective unionization. The ethnic homogeneity was the cement out of which the foundations of the garment unions had been constructed and out of which the political and organizational power of the leaders was also built.

The Jewishness of the needle trades' labor force was only one aspect of a larger Jewish factor that contributed to the power of the unions and especially their leaders. The pivotal role of the garment industry in the Jewish economy combined with its location in areas with heavily Jewish populations, particularly New York, provided the Socialist union heads with crucial political leverage. These two factors, together with a unified rank and file, helped to produce allies and supporters for the union leaders outside of the Jewish working-class and Left parties. Although this support from nonworking-class elements and institutions both in and out of the Jewish community may have been motivated more out of economic and political self-interest than ideology or humanitarianism, the end result—support or at least nonhostility—was more important than the reasons for it. These two factors—role in the Jewish economy and location in heavily Jewish areas—gave the unions' leaders access to public opinion, Jewish communal institutions, and political leaders inside and outside of the Jewish community that could be utilized to protect the unions' interests. The "unions' interests" were, of course, defined by their leaders, whose perception of these interests were mediated by their own.

The decision to turn the unions into national organizations would reduce the importance of the Jewish factor, one of the unions' most potent assets. It would mean that continual and major efforts at educating and politicizing non-Jewish workers would have to be made wherever garment manufacturers ran to escape from areas of union influence. This, of course, would require a great commitment of union resources. It would also be a much more difficult struggle because these workers were likely to be non-Jews and thus lack experience with unions and Left parties.

But the cost and difficulty of such a campaign were not the only drawbacks from the point of view of the union leaders' interests. The more successful these national efforts were, the more non-Jews would become union members. As their numbers and proportions grew, so would their desire to have leaders and officials from their own ethnic ranks. Thus, the Jewish leaders might find that the price for attaining good uniform wage levels and working conditions through a truly national union would be at the expense of their own personal positions of power and prestige. Needless to say, such a personal consequence would not have led them to devote much serious effort to the goal of broadening the base of their unions.

The deterioration of socialism and democracy within the garment unions as well as the poor wages and working conditions of the unionists and workers in the industry was a result of the decision of the leaders to adopt a policy of class collaboration. This was not a policy that was forced upon these men. This collaborationism led to a retreat from socialism because, as the radical research organization the North American Congress for Latin America expressed it:

In the framework of partnership, the union leaders' main concern is the capitalists' profitability, which is usually voiced as concern for the survival of the industry. They adopt, in part or in whole, concerns which are properly those of the capitalists and on many occasions become the agents for those concerns. Working for lower wages and longer hours, poorer working conditions and higher productivity become essential to insure a level of profits high enough to guarantee the survival of a particular capitalist or industry. . . . As long as capitalists have control over the means of production . . . trade unions will be constantly on the defensive. As one shop is being organized— or one industry, one region, one country—capitalists are moving on to another. Organizing the unorganized is therefore a never-ending task.[78]

This, unfortunately, is a good summary of the behavior of the Socialist garment unions' leadership in the twentieth century.

BOURGEOIS POLITICS

The structure of the garment industry and the ways in which Socialist union chieftains responded to it weakened their radical commitment in yet another respect. The balkanized nature of the clothes-making business and the mobility of the many small and independent firms made it quite difficult and expensive for unions to organize workers and regulate the industry. The cost of accomplishing these goals led these unions during their early and more socialist years to turn to bourgeois parties and institutions of the capitalist state for assistance.

The Socialist leaders in the early 1900s were quick to learn the benefits that could be rendered to them and their organizations through positive ties with municipal political organizations, even the much denounced Tammany Hall. When asked by their less expedient socialist members how working class militants could have friendly relations with Tammany Hall, the leaders pointed to the practical and positive fruits of these relations. It was through Tammany Hall that the unions were able to obtain police protection or neutrality during their picket and strike activities. Needless to say, the garment manufacturers also sought the same kind of assistance from Tammany.[79]

Tammany Hall, however, was not the only bourgeois political organization that was succored by and gave assistance to the socialist-led garment unions. In New York and Illinois, state legislatures passed legislation protecting the health and safety of the garment workers. The union heads learned very early that their ideological politics need not inhibit their practical politics when their real organizational interests were concerned.

They also learned another important lesson from their early experiences with municipal and state political and governmental bodies. This was the role that governments could play in labor management relations in the garment industry. Governments with the resources that they had available could more easily obtain results and enforce standards over a wide range of employers than could unions. It also seemed an efficient investment of the unions' own resources to utilize governments to do their work for them. Governmental legislative and decision-making bodies were relatively few, highly visible, permanently located, and susceptible to highly focused pressure. Garment employers on the other hand were many, not highly visible, mobile, and not always easy to pressure.

After the garment unions were established and became recognized entities following the wave of organizational strikes from 1909 to 1912, their Socialist leaders continued to look toward various governmental bodies for assistance. In this period, one which was to last for decades, the union chieftains broadened the scope and nature of the help that they wanted from governments. Now, in addition to health and safety measures, Socialists wanted a government controlled by their class enemies to increase their union rolls and regulate the garment industry.

This desire was not a foolish pipe dream. The garment unions obtained these political benefits from the federal government during World War I. In fact, the government willingly granted the unions their demands. It was war time, and there was a dire need for a large and continuing supply of uniforms for the troops. In order to ensure this goal, the federal government under pressure from the Socialist-led garment unions, particularly the Amalgamated, "insisted that workers be allowed to enjoy the rights of organization and collective bargaining, without discrimination because of union membership or activity. Firms that discharged workers for union activity were force to reinstate them under penalty of losing their government contracts."[80] Since the government did not have the ability to inspect all shops to ascertain the conditions of their operation, the unions were permitted to play the role of watchdog and trigger government action against nonunion firms or firms violating existing contracts. Given such support from the federal government, membership in the needle trades unions literally skyrocketed. The Amalgamated Clothing Workers of America and the ILGWU, the big two of the garment unions, grew in size from 139,300 in 1917 to 282,400 in 1920, a more than twofold increase in three years. Antiunion strongholds outside New York City such as Rochester capitulated before the onslaught of government-backed Socialist unions.[81]

It is interesting to note another facet of this warm war-time relationship between these Socialist unions and the United States government. On the surface, there appeared cause for animosity between these two bodies. The Socialist party very much angered the government by its antiwar stance before and after the United States entered the war. The needle trade unions were the financial and institutional bulwark of this antiwar party. The Amalgamated and the ILGWU were committed to socialism and the Socialist party in their constitutions. The Amalgamated, led by Sidney Hillman, had the reputation of being among the most radical of all the unions in the country. Yet, the United States government had a harmonious relationship with these very unions and particularly with Sidney Hillman. Why?

The answer, it appears, is that Sidney Hillman and these unions agreed to mute their advocacy of and support for socialism. Indeed, one historian went so far as to claim that "war contracts were used to buy off pacifist garment workers, particularly among the Amalgamated Clothing Workers."[82] There is no record of a deal between the government and these unions. But the historical record does reveal how politically neutral these unions became during the war. After the commencement of hostilities Sidney Hillman noted with pride in a letter to the New York Times (12/28/17) that his union had not called one strike. He also pointed out in this communication that, "The Amalgamated Clothing Workers . . . is not a pacifist organization. . . . Since the declaration of war we have cooperated with the government in every way by suspending our Union rules whenever the needs of the government required. . . . We have permitted overtime work, as well as work on Sundays, to speed up production." The Amalgamated unionists' patriotism was corroborated by a government official who observed that they had "remained loyally at work turning out uniforms as fast as machines can be put in for them to operate."[83] Hillman further demonstrated his cooperativeness by pressuring the Socialist editor of the Amalgamated's newspaper, Advance, to cease publishing antiwar editorials. At the Amalgamated's convention in 1918, Hillman successfully tabled a motion calling upon the union to officially endorse the Socialist party.[84] Also, the Amalgamated and the ILGWU, after the United States entered the war as a belligerent, purchased Liberty (war) Bonds despite the fact that the Socialist party opposed this and any other action by Socialists that aided the war drive.[85] All of this was to presage the way in which the Socialist-led garment unions would conduct themselves in the future—socialist rhetoric and non-socialist deeds.

After the war a change in administrations brought a change in the government's attitude toward the needle trade unions and other unions as well. The Republican administrations that followed that of

Woodrow Wilson were not very friendly to labor, but the Socialist garment union leaders were not totally bereft of friends in high places. New York's Democratic governor, Alfred E. Smith, for one, was sympathetic to the entreaties of the garment unions. However, economic conditions and political constraints limited the amount of actual assistance he could render. The garment unions also received some assistance in their efforts to organize the industry from Smith's successor, Governor Franklin Delano Roosevelt, and from Roosevelt's Lieutenant Governor, Herbert H. Lehman. Twice, once in 1929 and again in 1930, Roosevelt and Lehman intervened during strikes of the ILGWU to attain settlements favorable to the union.[86]

The return of the Democrats to national power in 1933 breathed new life into the relationship between the Socialist garment union leaders and the federal government. This relationship and the concrete benefits that the needle trades unions derived from it rivaled, if not surpassed, those obtained under the Wilson administration. The Roosevelt administration, anxious to stabilize the economy and to make it more rational, looked to unions for assistance. Through the National Industrial Recovery Act and other means, the New Deal, working with both unions and employers, helped to increase wages, lower working hours, and raise prices. But probably the biggest single benefit that these unions obtained from the Roosevelt administration was legal and political encouragement to increase their rolls. Between 1933 and 1934 the ILGWU's membership rose from 40,000 to 200,000 while the corresponding figures for the Amalgamated in the same period rose from 110,000 to more than 150,000. And as in the heady days of the Wilson administration, federal pressure was brought to bear against employers who were reluctant to sign contracts with the clothing-makers' unions.[87] One leading historian of the needle trades, Joel Seidman, observed that "Few unions in the American labor movement profited as much from the NRA as did the International [Ladies Garment Workers' Union], the Amalgamated and the Cap and Millinery Workers."[88]

THE SOCIALIST UNION LEADERS AS POLITICAL MODERATES

The seeking and the receiving of assistance from bourgeois politicians and parties could not help but moderate the socialism of the Socialist garment union leaders. The advent in 1932 of a liberal Democratic administration that was friendly to the needle trades unions carried home this fact. Sidney Hillman's overt arm-twisting of officials in his Amalgamated to resign from the Socialist party and David Dubinsky's resignation from that party in 1936 officially marked the virtual end of the decades-long tie between the garment unions and the Socialist party.[89] The unofficial demise, however, occurred earlier. Will Herberg, a social scientist close to the leadership of these unions stated, "that much of the socialism of the Jewish Socialist unions had, by 1933, become largely a mere sentimental vestige. By 1933, in fact, socialism . . . no longer bore any real relationship to the actualities of the labor movement." [90] And when the garment unions broke with the Socialist party, they left that organization virtually denuded of union support.

It is quite clear why the Socialist garment union leaders broke with the Socialist party and with Socialism. They, and through them their organizations, had become dependent upon the state for their well-being, and in practical terms in the 1930s that meant the FDR administration. These men were well aware of the importance to their interests of a friendly government. Sidney Hillman expressed this point of view in April 1936 in a talk to the General Executive Board of the Amalgamated:

We know that the NRA [National Industrial Recovery Act] meant the revival of our organization. . . . Anyone will agree that these things would have been totally impossible without legislation. Our condition, pre-NRA, was almost as bad as in all industry . . . there was a question whether we could have carried on as a successful organization for even another year. . . . We know that the defeat of the Roosevelt administration means no labor legislation for decades to come. . . . A change in the Administration raises a definite question whether the Amalgamated would have to fight completely on its own and not get the support which it enjoyed under the NRA. . . . I say to you that the defeat of Roosevelt and the introduction of a real Fascist administration such as we will have is going to make the work of building a labor movement impossible. [91]

David Dubinsky of the ILGWU concurred with Hillman and bluntly admitted: "When I resigned from the Socialist Party in 1936 it was purely for political reasons. We . . . wanted Roosevelt re-elected." [92] Dubinsky, for all practical purposes, had broken with the Socialists at least as early as 1928 when he indicated his preference for Al Smith the Democrat over Norman Thomas, the Socialist in the 1928 presidential election. [93]

These needle trades union leaders were not only breaking with the Socialist party and the ideology of their youth. They were not only aligning themselves with bourgeois politicians and parties. These union oligarchs were also commiting themselves to a new ideology—capitalism. Dubinsky clearly stated this in 1944 when he said, ". . . since that time [1936] I have come to the conclusion that socialism, certainly of the orthodox variety, will never work. Democracy is only possible in a society of free enterprise, and trade unionism can only live in a democracy. [94] Actually, Dubinsky was only expressing a point of view that had guided him, his predecessors, and his associates like Hillman in the conduct of their unions' affairs since the early days of the century.

The break between the Jewish garment union leaders and the So-

cialist party heralded the deepening involvement of the union leaders
with the more practical and relevent affairs of the middle-class parties. But they were hesitant for a variety of reasons to embrace quickly
and wholeheartedly the Democratic party, their apparent natural political home. Instead, the needle trades unions were primarily responsible for the creation, financing, and organizations of the American
Labor party (ALP) in New York State. This party was designed to be
the political vehicle that would help the hundreds of thousands of
Jewish unionists and their voting-age family members to make the
transition from socialism to the New Deal. Although most of the
leaders may have been aware of the practical benefits of becoming
New Dealers, they evidently feared that their followers had not yet
seem the light and were still tied to socialism. After all, their union
leaders had for several decades reaffirmed their socialism. These same
leaders had educated their members to be socialists, especially election-day Socialists. The union rank and file had for years been taught
by their Socialist mentors that the Democratic party was the political
organization of the corrupt big city machines and the Southern racist
bourbons. In view of the decades of this type of political education
and the members' commitment to socialism, it was deemed politically
wiser to make the transition from the Socialist party to the Democratic
party a gradual one.[95]

This, however, was not the only factor that lay behind the creation
of the ALP. The American Labor party provided the union leaders
with a political organization and a sizable constituency of their own.
To have jumped into the Democratic party and to have led their
members into it would have left them in the position of being generals
without an army. The ALP, on the other hand, was their political
army. It provided them with political bargaining power and leverage
to exact benefits for themselves and their unions.

The American Labor party did not represent the end of their political journey. Shortly afterwards, in 1944, the ILGWU, led by Dubinsky,
became the principal force in establishing and underwriting the Liberal party in New York State. The Liberal party was born as a liberal
anti-Communist organization with a liberal platform and image. It
was also in effect the political arm of the ILGWU.

One of its major functions was to protect the interests of the
ILGWU. It was able to do this more or less effectively for several
reasons. One, candidates nominated by the Liberal party gained
access to the union's treasury. Two, the party used its line on the
ballot in a very flexible manner, often delaying endorsing its own candidate for a particular office or else nominating one temporarily until
some kind of arrangement could be made with one of the two major
parties. Only then would it decide whether to nominate its own candidate or one from the Democratic or Republican party. And three, the
Liberal party and the ILGWU were believed to be effective mobilizers
of the Jewish vote in New York, a potent political force. In most elec-

tions, about one-third of the Liberal line voters were Jews, but in certain elections, such as the presidential election of 1960 and the United States Senate race in 1968, more than half were Jews, enough to swing the balance in a relatively close election.[96]

Thus, by keeping the garment industry in New York, the ILGWU and other unions managed to maintain a political base in New York. In this way, the garment unions were politically able to regulate the industry through pressue on the mayor of New York City, the governor of New York State, or the legislative bodies of the city and the state to ensure the industry's stay in New York. One consequence of such an interplay between politics, ethnicity, and union power was the Liberal party's opposition or failure to support a decent minimum wage for city workers in the early 1960s.[97]

The move away from socialism and the Socialist party to the American Labor and Liberal parties represented the culmination of a process, rooted in the nature of the garment industry, that began before World War I. The structure of the garment industry encouraged the Socialist-led unions to seek government assistance in their attempts to build their organizations. And once having done this and having obtained results, they were unable or unwilling to resist becoming enmeshed in alliances with bourgeois politicians and governmental institutions.

THE UNIONS AND THE SOCIALIST PARTY

It is important to take note briefly of the part played by the Socialist party in changing the garment unions' commitment from Socialism to the Democratic party. The first factor to be considered was the SP's policy toward trade unions, although in essence, the Socialist party did not really have a policy toward the unions. As it stated in its 1923 convention: "It is neither the right nor the interest of the Socialist Party to attempt to dictate to the unions concerning their internal affairs."[98] Norman Thomas reiterated this to the ILGWU in his letter to its convention in 1929: "We do not want a Socialist or Labor Party to run the unions."[99] In addition to this policy, or, more accurately, attitude, toward trade unions, the party lacked an organizational or sanctioning mechanism that would induce unions in its camp to follow its political line. All that the SP could do in this regard was either to exercise moral persuasion or, failing that, the ultimate action, expulsion.

This meant that Socialist union leaders were almost completely free from any Socialist party constraints in the running of their union affairs. They had no reason other than that of morality or sentiment to allow themselves to be guided by party positions in any area. In the case of the garment unions this meant, the leadership was free to pursue its interests in the ways it deemed most efficient and most pragmatic. Indeed, in 1933, on one of the few occasions that Norman Thomas took a critical stance toward the garment unions for the manner in which they conducted their internal affairs, he was soundly rebuked for his troubles.[100] In 1935, shortly after this incident, the garment-union-dominated New York City Executive Committee of the Socialist party reiterated its understanding of what constituted party-union relations:

First and foremost is the policy of non-interference in the internal affairs of trade unions. It has been the traditional position of the SP, nationally as well as locally, that the party, as such, will not attempt directly or indirectly, to dictate the internal policies of trade unions . . . or to organize for the purpose of controlling, dominating, or capturing them. There is nore more justification for the SP to interfere in the internal affairs of the trade unions than there is for such unions, as unions, to interfere in the internal affairs of the SP. . . . should there be a disagreement between the Socialist Party and a union, Socialist Party trade unionists should act in accord with the majority of their fellow unionists and not with the SP.[101]

The second factor concerning the Socialist party and the garment unions' drift from socialism was that the SP really could not do very much for the unions after World War I. The garment unions wanted to influence government policy and effect legislation that would regulate the garment industry and increase the strength of the unions. Prior to 1920 the SP in New York was a vibrant political force with the seeming potential to assist the unions in these goals. The party was strong enough to win elections in Congressional, aldermanic, and judicial races, sending, in 1917, 10 of its members to the state legislature as assemblymen, seven to the City Council, and one to a position as municipal judge. From 1917 through 1920 about 100,000 New York City voters in the various mayoralty, gubernatorial, and presidential elections held during this time cast their ballots on the Socialist party line. But after 1920 the party's fortunes declined, as did the number of voters it was able to attract. The election of August Claessens to the New York State Assembly in 1921 was the last victory for any Socialist running in New York.[102]

It was quite clear in this period that the Socialist party could not influence legislation except in an indirect manner. If the garment unions wanted help in the political arena, they would have to turn more directly to the bourgeois parties, which they did. Indeed, with the advent of the New Deal, the tie to the Socialist party was regarded more as a political liability than an asset. And Norman Thomas, the party's leading spokesman and electoral standard-bearer, found that after the New Deal, Socialist union leaders no longer praised him or invited him to their conventions. "There was a time," he wrote, "that I was much in demand by labor groups. . . . However, as the labor movement grew stronger and more deeply indebted to the New Deal it seemed to most of its leaders, including some ex-Socialists once inclined to deplore my relative conservatism, rather inexpedient to invite so prominent a Socialist as Norman Thomas."[103]

THE JEWISH CONNECTION

We now turn our attention to the third major factor, the Jewish factor, that contributed to the demise of socialism among the garment unions and their leaders. The development of these unions as Jewish unions, located within the bosom of the Jewish community, helped to foster a close association between the unions and the concerns of the Jewish community. Over time—decades and generations—this association proved detrimental to the socialist commitment of the garment unions and their officials.

Early Years

The early Jewish radical organizers of trade unions in the late nineteenth century were aware of the dangers to socialism inherent in the formation of Jewish workers' organizations. As cosmopolitan socialists educated in Russia, they believed that ethnically homogeneous unions would foster divisiveness and chauvinism in the working class and play into the hands of the bourgeoisie anxious to weaken working class movements. However, as noted earlier, they had little choice. The ethnic divisions and hostilities in the working class of America in the late 1880s, the barriers of languages and customs, and the presence of a mass Jewish working class caused these cosmopolitan socialists to put aside their principles and to organize all or predominantly Jewish, Yiddish-speaking unions.

The tension between their universalism and the Jewish make-up of their constituency was apparent from the first time that they tried to influence Jewish workers. The Propaganda Verein, or Propaganda Association, an organization of Russian Jewish radicals, many of whose leaders were former members of the Am Olam, issued a call for one of the first public meetings of Jewish workers on the East Side. It was to take place on July 7, 1882. The organizers wanted to alert and educate Jewish workers to the evils of strike-breaking and the need for labor solidarity across ethnic and national lines. But in the leaflet announcing the meeting, these purposes were not stated. Instead, the title of the leaflet proclaimed: "When will the persecution of the Jews cease?" and the brief contents dealt with the danger of increased persecution to Jews in Russia, Germany, and Hungary. It was obvious from this leaflet that the Propaganda Verein knew which issue would attract an audience.

In order to better ensure the success of the meeting, the leaders of the Propaganda Verein turned to the German-American socialists for assistance and speakers. This move was logical from their point of view. The Germans had a powerful labor and socialist movement in New York, probably the strongest in the city, with their own central body of trade unions, the Deutsche Vereinigte Gewerkschaften, and their own daily labor paper, the Deutsche Volkszeitung. Who better to educate Jewish workers to the need of labor solidarity than speakers from the German-American socialist community. This particular movement represented for the young Russian Jewish radicals the embodiment of wisdom and experience and a model worthy of emulation.

The speakers at this July 7th meeting included Germans, the Irish, and Russian Jewish radicals. They duly addressed their listeners on the need for labor unity, but they did it in languages that the Yiddish-speaking audience could not readily understand. Afterward, one member of the audience, Abraham Cahan, the future editor of the *Jewish Daily Forward*, approached the Russian-speaking chairman and asked: "If it [the meeting] is for Jewish immigrants, why are the speeches in Russian and German?" He then volunteered, although not a member of the Propaganda Verein, to deliver a lecture on socialism in Yiddish for this organization. Although contemptuous of Yiddish these well-bred Russian Jewish socialists did agree to Cahan's proposal.[104]

The first Yiddish lecture on socialism in the United States was delivered by Abraham Cahan on behalf of the Propaganda Verein on August 18, 1882, in a German beer hall on the East Side. Cahan followed this lecture by others and proved to be a popular speaker capable of attracting relatively large audiences. However, he was the only member of the Propaganda Verein to speak Yiddish in public. Despite his success, this initiative and opening was not pursued. The leaders of the Propaganda Verein did not fully realize the force that Cahan was tapping through his use of Yiddish to Yiddish-speaking workers.

The Propaganda Verein was one of several short-lived attempts by cosmopolitan or assimilationist Jewish socialists to organize Yiddish-speaking workers. Its efforts as well as those of the Jewish Workers' Verein, which was founded in 1885 and remained in existence for less than a year and a half, moved the Jewish radicals closer and closer to a Jewish-worker constituency. As they became more conscious of this, they began to develop the rationale that it might be necessary to first organize Jewish workers into exclusively Jewish organizations to facilitate their entrance into the mainstream of the American labor movement.

The United Hebrew Trades

This rationale was transformed into policy by the United Hebrew Trades (UHT), an organization founded in 1888. This was a federation of unions in industries in which Jews predominated. The model for it was the United German Trades in the United States, and German-American radicals assisted the UHT in its infancy. The founders and organizers of the UHT were Jewish members of the Socialist Labor party. Although they subscribed to a universalistic socialism that transcended national and religious barriers, these socialists were at the same time more pragmatic than their predecessors in the Propaganda Verein and the Jewish Workers Verein. These UHT organizers recognized the necessity of initially working within in all-Jewish setting.[105]

The UHT was a pragmatic response to the situation that existed among American labor unions in the late 1800s and early 1900s. The labor organizations that existed at this time were often divided along ethnic and racial lines. As the latest arrivals, the Eastern European Jews were not welcomed by other ethnic groups that had already established their economic control over a particular occupation. This was the case in the garment unions. The same situation also obtained among the painters, carpenters, butchers, bakers, waiters, and construction workers' unions.

The Jews' integration into the organized American labor force was also hindered by language and customs. Their inability to speak English, Bohemian, or the dominant language of a particular union impeded meaningful communication. The Yiddish language that they spoke and the Jewish customs that they observed insulated and separated them from other workers.

Given this set of circumstances, the Jewish radicals of the UHT had little choice but to organize Yiddish-speaking unions under the umbrella of the UHT. The first unions to be organized were the typographers, singers, and actors. After them came workers in various occupations, including the garment trades. By the end of 1914, or some 26 years after its founding, the UHT grew from a federation of three unions with fewer than 100 members to an organization with 111 affiliated unions whose membership numbered over 250,000. Virtually every major Jewish union in these years was in some way indebted to the UHT.[106]

Even as these socialist cosmopolitans were successfully establishing separate Jewish unions, they continued to look upon the UHT as a vehicle that would eventually unite Jewish and non-Jewish workers in integrated and (preferably) socialist unions. These integrated unions would, they felt, follow from the experience of the Jews in American unions and the economic strength that these organizations wielded. This position was also shared by the nonsocialist English-born Jewish president of the AF of L, Samuel Gompers. In principle an opponent of ethnically divided unions, Gompers was forced to come to the same conclusion as that of his fellow Jewish socialists. "I did not approve of organization along racial lines," Gompers contended, "but we all realized that to organize Hebrew trade unions was the first step in getting those immigrants into the American labor movement."[107]

The Jewish radical organizers of Jewish unions, however, continued to insist that their particularistic organizing efforts did not reflect their ideology. Their radicalism and socialism, they maintained, recognized no permanent divisions along racial or national lines. But their actions continued to be at variance with their ideology. The more deeply they moved into the field of organizing Jewish workers, the more loudly they insisted on their socialist universalism. In 1890 the UHT and the Jewish branches of the Socialist Labor party joined together to call for a conference that would lead to the founding of a Hebrew Labor Federation, a union that would encompass all Yiddish-speaking workers in the United States and Canada. The conference was convened under the slogan: "The world is our fatherland; socialism is our religion." In the declaration of principles of the Hebrew Labor Federation, the Jewish radicals summed up their position and tried to reconcile their particularistic actions with their universalistic ideology.

We have no Jewish question in America. The only Jewish question by us is the question of how to keep Jewish questions out of this country; and because only we, Yiddish speaking citizens, are able to work among Jewish immigrants, only because we speak their language and are acquainted with their lives, solely for that reason are we creating this particular Jewish body. The Yiddish language is our tool; to erase all borderlines between Jew and non-Jew in the world of labor is one of our aims.[108]

The Hebrew Labor Federation proved to be a short-lived union, but the Jewish socialists involved in the organization of Jewish workingmen, particularly those associated with the UHT, continued to subscribe to this position. Yet, even as they did so, they began to charter Yiddish-speaking locals in various trades. Being pragmatic, however, the socialists in the UHT also helped Yiddish-speaking workers to gain entrance into German-speaking unions when their number in a particular trade was not of a sufficient size.[109]

The mortar function of an ethnically homogeneous work force in the building of the garment unions should also again be stressed. The clothes-making industry, as we observed earlier, was highly unstable and offered little in the way of structural supports—such as large factories—for the building of a working-class or union consciousness. Given this situation, the common ethnicity, background, and language of the workers (as well as their common work situation) became a vital foundation for the construction of the garment unions. The builders of these unions might deplore, as did the principled socialists, such a state of affairs, but as union organizers they found it to be advantageous.

Once a predominantly Jewish workforce was defined as advantageous to the building of garment unions, these pragmatic socialist leaders would find it increasingly difficult to resist protecting and embellishing their particularistic ethnic base. Such action would then lead to the development of close ties with the Jewish community and to the leaderships' concern with Jewish issues and interests as concrete ways to secure the commitment of their constituency. Eventually, as the Jewish community changed from a largely working class and disproportionately prosocialist one into a middle class and pro-Democratic body, the Jewish ties of the socialist leaders helped to pull them from their commitments to socialism. All of this was not clear during the heady days when the Jewish unions were radical and young.

A fascinating aspect about this process was that it so closely resembled the experience of Jewish socialist union organizers in the czarist empire. They, too, as you will recall, reluctantly embarked on the organization of Yiddish-speaking workers into separate unions. American Jewish socialists, like their counterparts in Russia, soon found that they had developed a constituency. This constituency, comprised of separately organized Yiddish-speaking workers, provided them with a power base in the real world. In both cases, the Jewish socialist leaders became increasingly reluctant to weaken or alienate the population that constituted this base. Also, both groups of socialist leaders soon began to find themselves more sympathetic to things Yiddish that were technically outside the sphere of labor and socialism. Both were being drawn, despite their universalistic socialist origins and protestations, into a Yiddish milieu, a milieu on which they were becoming increasingly dependent.

Into the Jewish Community

This Jewish, or Yiddish, aspect of trade unionism and socialism among Jewish socialists in America was reinforced by Bundists. After 1905 many veterans of this movement came to America and joined the socialist-led Jewish unions and political parties as well. By that time the Bund had become much more accepting of Jewish separatism in the trade unions and socialist organizations, more so than the Jewish socialists of America, and the post-1905 Bundists emigrés reflected this orientation, further consolidating a tendency that was already underway.[110]

Once the practical shift toward a Yiddish-speaking worker base had been made, the socialist union leaders and their rank and file followers found it difficult to remain hostile toward other social strata in the Yiddish-speaking community. The heterogeneous and ever-changing social class composition of the Yiddish workers, particularly those in the garment trades, made a policy based on sharp class divisions and conflict a difficult one to pursue. There were too many real as well as desired ties between the Jewish unionists and the Jewish bourgeoisie to make a policy of class conflict attractive to the workers.

Once in positions of authority and responsibility, the socialist leaders of Jewish unions found that circumstances forced them to adopt a less hostile attitude toward the Jewish bourgeoisie. During times of severe economic hardship, their concern for their political base as well as the economic well-being of their Jewish charges led these leaders to seek material assistance, even charity, from the ostensible enemies of the Jewish working class within the Jewish community. During one such period in the 1890s, the *Arbeiter Zeitung*, the

Yiddish organ of the UHT, appealing to both the humanitarianism and the concrete self-interest of Jewish capitalists, openly and directly cried out for aid to the needy Jewish workers:

> Businessmen! Contractors! Capitalists! Forget now who you are and what you are! Forget your bitter feelings! Forget your old accounts—if your heart is not stone—be human! Help, help your workers, your customers . . . in their time of need! Help them to overcome their need—remember, one hand washes the other! They will again become your workers, your customers and your patrons and with their help you will retrieve the bread which you have cast out upon the waters.[111]

Such pleas rarely fell on deaf ears: aid was forthcoming from non-working-class and religious Jews. Such assistance from as well as the public appeals to the humanitarianism of these strata and classes made it difficult to later portray them as the dire and eternal foes of the Jewish working class even in the bitter strikes that were conducted in the next several decades.

The Jewish socialist union leaders were not the only ones who were constrained by circumstance from preaching and carrying out class warfare in the Jewish community. Jewish workers who, of course, were at the same time consumers, were numerically too important a group for other strata to alienate or antagonize. The many peddlers, small businessmen, and restauranteurs in the Yiddish world depended on the workers' purchasing power for survival and thus, as the socialists were aware, were favorably disposed to assist their working-class brethren in time of need. Also, during severe and widespread strikes, those businessmen whose livelihood depended on direct sales to their fellow Jews often found it in their interests not only to provide the workers with charity and credit but to exert pressure on their fellow Jewish capitalists to be more responsive to the union's demands. All Yiddish-language papers on the Lower East Side including the Orthodox press also realized where their self-interest lay and consistently posed as supporters of the Jewish workers. One Orthodox paper during the course of a labor dispute printed, free of charge, the union's statements while at the same time refusing to publish the manufacturers' position in the form of paid advertisements.[112]

The support that the Jewish socialist-led unions received from the Yiddish-speaking community, as well as the fact that a major reason for the existence of these separatist organizations was the language spoken by their members, could not but push these leaders and their organizations further toward a Yiddish and a Jewish community orientation and commitment. In order to protect their leadership positions and the integrity of their separatist unions, things Yiddish and Jewish would have to become a more important focus for the leaders of these socialist unions. Whereas the use of Yiddish was once viewed as an unpleasant expedient necessary to reach workingmen who understood no other language, again, as in the case of the Bund, it would soon be transformed under pressure of events and organizational necessity into a value in its own right. It was not long before these unions, in the words of J. B. S. Hardmann, the Educational Director of the ACWA, "became the home . . . of Yiddish poets, artists, and novelists." [113] And Jewish leaders were sufficiently astute to realize that the more the unions, rather than groups external to the unions, satisfied the cultural needs and interests of its membership, the more committed its members would be to the union.

The establishment of unions limited to Yiddish-speaking workers was the first step in the process that led to the creation of an identity of interest between Yiddish and Yiddish culture on the one hand and Jewish unions on the other. It was not the logic of internal dynamics alone that led to this development. Events such as the reaction to the Kishinev pogrom and the influx into the unions of large numbers of Bundist and Bundist-influenced "Yiddishists" after 1905 heightened the Yiddish or Jewish consciousness of the Jewish unions and pushed them further and faster toward a Jewish commitment. Whether or not the Jewish socialist architects of these unions found this occurrence desirable was not a very relevant consideration—there was not much that they could do to seriously oppose this process of Yiddishization.

Other Jewish considerations also tempered the radicalism of these leaders and their organizations. One was the accelerating process of Yiddishization that resulted in the development of a community orientation in addition to a class orientation. This was probably not viewed as a potential source of conflict of interest at the time in which Yiddish was closely associated with the Jewish working class. However, as Yiddish transcended this identification, helped in part by unions and the socialist Yiddish press who sponsored and provided platforms for Yiddish artists and men of letters, and became a community property, the unions' commitment and indeed dependence on Yiddish could not but inhibit their class radicalism. Yiddish was linking them into aesthetic alliances and worlds of meaning together with the Jewish bourgeoisie, the religious Jews, and other nonworking class strata of the Jewish community and it was these elements that increasingly shaped and defined the nature of the Jewish community.

Jewish Bourgeois Allies

The Jewish bourgeoisie, particularly its wealthier segments, was one quarter from which assistance was sought and obtained. This positive relationship between the Socialist garment unions and sectors of the Jewish middle and upper-middle class became apparent in the years from 1909 to 1912, the period in which the needle trades unions launched their major organizational strikes—the strikes that led to their firm establishment. It should also be emphasized that in these years the garment unions were also aided by non-Jewish middle and upper-middle class individuals and groups including Progressives, liberals, and "do gooders." Some of the best examples of aid given to the garment unions by nonworking-class Jews and non-Jews occurred during the International Ladies' Garment Workers' Union's cloak-maker strike of 1910.

The "Great Revolt," as this strike was popularly known, literally made the ILGWU. The major issues in the strike were union recognition and the closed shop. The economic impact of the strike on the Jewish community in New York City was enormous. The major income-producing industry within the immigrant Jewish community was crippled by the strikers, and few within the Jewish economy could escape its effects. Without wages, Jewish workers could not buy goods or pay their rents. Although the small businessmen and landlords were willing to extend credit to the strikers, they could not afford to do so indefinitely. The strike also occurred during the garment industry's busy summer season, and the longer it lasted the fewer the number of garments available for sale in the nation's dress shops. This meant the removal of another source of income from the Jewish community.

The small businessmen and landlords began to side with the strikers. They were not only motivated by economic self-interest but were also influenced by the synagogues and the Yiddish-language press, labor as well as nonlabor, who took positions on behalf of the strikers. Finally, concern for the welfare of the strikers, many of whom were relatives and friends, also played a role. Thousands of strikers had been forced to seek charity and donations in order to feed, clothe, and house themselves and their families.

Eventually a settlement was reached when Jews outside of the Yiddish immigrant community, largely German Jews, entered the dispute. They, together with the forces already marshaled on the union's side, enabled the strikers to reach a settlement. Though it was not all that the unionists desired, it was, on the whole, one that was favorable to the union and to the cause of unionism in the needle trades.[114]

Some observers have speculated that the German-American Jews entered the dispute on the side of the immigrant Yiddish-speaking strikers because they were moved by the economic hardship of the strikers and their community. Others have suggested that they were motivated by a desire to protect the Jewish image, including their own, from being scarred by labor strife. Whatever their motivations, the nature of their economic self-interests facilitated the role that they played in the settlement. Their economic position did not dictate an alliance with their social and economic inferiors among the Jewish garment manufacturers. These outsiders were primarily bankers, financiers, lawyers, and large retailers. Thus, they were generally located outside of the Yiddish immigrant economy. However, even they, particularly the large retailers in their midst, were not immune to the effects of a large, long, and bitter strike of garment workers. In

any case, Jacob H. Schiff, the senior partner of the prestigious investment firm of Kuhn, Loeb and Company and the head of the American
Jewish Committee, a political arm of the German-American Jewish
community, exerted pressure on the garment manufacturers to adopt a
more conciliatory position, one more favorable to the union's demands. His influence, and through him the group that he represented,
soon prevailed. The settlement, labeled the Protocol of Peace, appeared to be so prounion that one cynical observer was moved to comment: "Demands that the Schiffs would have opposed in industries in
which they were interested, they were ready to have the cloak industry accept." [115]

The Socialist union leaders, for their part, welcomed the intervention of the Yiddish-speaking bourgeoisie and, after initial suspicions
were calmed, that of the German patricians as well. The unionists
wanted a way out and were willing to accept help from any quarter,
including the much maligned *yahudim.* The efforts of the German
Jews on their behalf, while not totally dispelling the heritage of mutual suspicion and hostility, did spark the beginning of a process of
conciliation between the Socialist labor leaders and this group. In the
years after the protocol, these two groups found areas of common concern about which they shared a common outlook, areas generally related to Jewish concerns. Both groups strongly opposed the growing
influence of Zionist organizations in the Jewish community after
World War I, and both shared an anxiety about anti-Semitism.

The best example of the way in which mutual interests and sustained efforts bridged the differences between these Socialist unionists and the wealthy German Jews can be seen in the relationship between the financier Herbert H. Lehman and the Socialist B. Charney
Vladeck. The relations between the two grew out of their mutual interests in Jewish affairs. They became so friendly that Herbert Lehman
in December 1929 was more than pleased to write a letter of recom-
mendation for Vladeck's son to Columbia University. Later, in 1930,
Vladeck felt comfortable enough to ask Lehman, then Governor of
New York, to intervene in a labor dispute in North Carolina on behalf
of the aggrieved workers. Interestingly and revealingly, Vladeck based
his appeal for Lehman's intervention on the fact that he was a prominent Jew and that the employer involved in the dispute was also a
Jew. The employer, Mr. Bernard Cone, Vladeck told Lehman, had expelled his workers from their jobs and homes for affiliating with an
AFL union. This action, Vladeck contended: ". . . opens a new field
for anti-Semitic agitation. . . . I feel that Mr. Cone ought to be told by
someone of influence that not only as a citizen but also as a Jew (particularly as a Jew), he carries a responsibility which he cannot take
lightly." [116]

In 1929 the leaders of the German-American Jewish community
demonstrated their friendliness to the cause of Jewish unions in a very
direct and concrete fashion. In that year the ILGWU was deeply in

debt and on the verge of not being able to function. At that crucial point the ILGWU's president, Benjamin Schlesinger, requested and obtained a loan of $100,000 from the pillars of the German Jewish establishment, Julius Rosenwald, Herbert H. Lehman, and Felix M. Warburg.[117] Assistance, common interests, and relationships of this kind contributed to the muting of the Socialist union leaders' class hostilities. They also significantly diminished their intracommunal class hostility and helped to make these Socialists more broadly Jewish in their orientation. And it was the Protocol of Peace that served as the initial vehicle for the development of amicable relations between the immigrant Socialist unionists and the wealthy German-American Jews.

ZIONIST INROADS

World War I marked a turning point, or at least hastened a process, in the evolution of the Jewish labor leaders' attitudes toward their Jewishness and in their position in the American Jewish community. The war, as with other crises affecting Jews, stimulated a rise in the Jewish consciousness of American Jewry in general and the Eastern European Jews in particular. Many of the major battlefields were located in areas of Jewish population centers. These areas were also the hometowns and birth places of many in the Eastern European Jewish immigrant community, and large numbers still had close relatives and friends living there.

This growing feeling of solidarity with their fellow Jews was heightened by the British government's issuance on November 2, 1917, of the Balfour Declaration. The declaration stated that: "His Majesty's Government views with favour the establishment in Palestine of a national home for the Jewish people." It appeared to be a major step toward the creation of a haven for oppressed and threatened Jews. President Wilson's support of the Balfour Declaration encouraged even more American Jews to identify themselves openly with the cause of their coreligionists and in the process raise their Jewish consciousness.

The socialist and heavily Bundist influenced and oriented Jewish labor leaders were deeply troubled by this growing feeling of Jewish identity and solidarity among their union members and among the Yiddish-speaking community in general. First, it ran counter to the universalistic socialist ideology to which they still felt committed. They recognized that such sentiments could transform their constituents into Jewish chauvinists. Second, and closely related to this, they feared that their bitter foes, the Zionists, would become the major political beneficiaries of the emotionalism stirring the Jewish community. The soaring increase in the rolls of Zionists underscored their fears. In 1914, on the eve of the war, 12,000 in America were officially registered as Zionists. After four years of war and the issuance of the

Balfour Declaration, the figure rose to 144,235, and this was only the tip of what probably was a mountain of support for the Zionists.[118]

The Jewish labor leaders, who themselves were not strongly unified on the issue of the Jewish question, found themselves being pulled closer and closer to a Jewish, as opposed to socialist, position by the tide of events and the sentiments of many of their union members. This was reflected in their attitude toward the American Jewish Congress. The American Jewish Congress, which convened in 1917, was a Zionist-initiated idea to create a congress in which all sectors of the Jewish community in America could arrive at a consensus on vital matters concerning Jews, particularly those in war-torn Europe. Although the Congress did not pursue strictly Zionist positions, it did serve as a way for the Zionists to make political inroads into the Jewish community. The socialist labor leaders at first opposed the call for them to join the Congress, which they knew would be Zionists dominated. But eventually they became members. This signified not only the overcoming of their qualms in cooperating with Zionists but also their acknowledgement of the prominent role of the Zionists in the wider Jewish community. Henceforth, it would be increasingly difficult for them to remain silent on or apart from issues affecting Jews as Jews.[119]

This shift was also evident in the formation and proceedings of the Congress of Jewish Labor, which was held in early 1919 in New York City. Stirred by events abroad and the need to counter the Zionist-influenced American Jewish Congress, the Jewish Socialist labor leaders joined together with Labor Zionists to call their own congress. The Socialist labor people constituted the majority at this meeting. The two major items on the agenda, which did not deal exclusively with issues pertaining to Jewish workers, were the protection of the rights of Jews and the Balfour Declaration. These were matters of a broadly Jewish concern, but the Congress of Jewish Labor felt compelled to deal with them.

In the course of the congress, the question of Palestine could not be avoided. The Zionist conception of Palestine as a national home for the Jewish people was an anethma to the Jewish Socialists, particularly those who came out of the Bund. However, despite the life-long animosity to this idea, Jewish Socialists, including recent Bundists, came within a hair's breadth of passing a pro-Zionist resolution on Palestine. This heretical act was not consummated but came close enough to indicate that a major shift in the position and ideological orientation of the Jewish labor leaders was in fact taking place.[120]

The depth of this inroad of pro-Zionist or Jewish nationalist sentiment within the garment unions can also be gauged by a resolution passed at the ILGWU convention of 1920. This resolution expressed the union's gratitude to the British Labor party for its efforts on behalf of "a national homeland on the ancient Jewish soil of Palestine." In the same resolution, the convention congratulated the British Labor party on its electoral achievements. The resolution in effect symbolized that the Jewish concerns of the ILGWU were not to be treated as independent from the union's socialist interests.[121]

The Socialist Jewish labor chieftains, however, continued to remain vocal foes of Zionism throughout the 1920s. But even as they voiced their opposition to this ideology, they were being converted to a pro-Palestine perspective. They were unable to divorce themselves from the affairs of Jewish labor unions in Palestine. In 1923 Zionist-oriented Socialist Jewish labor leaders founded the National Labor Committee for Organized Jewish Labor, which came to be known as *Gewerkschaften* (from the Yiddish for United Hebrew Trades). The first head of this organization was Max Pine, the Secretary of the United Hebrew Trades. The *Gewerkschaften* was supposed to be a purely philanthropic device through which Jewish unionists could contribute to the welfare of the Jewish labor movement in Palestine. It soon grew in size and influence as more and more Jewish labor unions chose to affiliate with it and participate in its yearly fund-raising campaigns. By the early 1940s the *Gewerkschaften*, which was renamed the National Committee for Labor Palestine in 1936, had become a major operation of Jewish labor. Its convention in 1944 was attended by representatives from over 1000 organizations, primarily labor unions. And an additional 2000 took part in the annual fund-raising campaign of that year.

In addition to being a charitable organization, the *Gewerkschaften* was successfully used by the Zionists to make Jewish unionists and their leaders more familiar with and sympathetic to not only the Histradut, the Jewish labor federation of Palestine, but with many other aspects of Jewish life in Palestine. As this occurred, the Socialist labor leaders and their members were drawn further into a Jewish identity and into a spirit of commonality with the other classes and strata that comprised the Jewish community.[122]

THE NAZI MENACE

The rise of the Nazis and their threat to Jews in Europe in the 1930s, like earlier Jewish crises, pushed the Jewish Socialist labor leaders closer to a Jewish identity and to the Jewish community. The case of the Socialist and union activist Morris Goldovski exemplifies the not atypical reaction of this category of individuals. He recalled the impact that the Nazis had on his Jewish identity and politics:

. . . "pious Jews prayed to G-d in the synagogues and requested all Jews to fast. . . . [though a non-believer] I acquiesced with the pious Jews' appeal and I, too, fasted for solidarity's sake," he admitted with some chagrin over his own past "assimilationist tendencies." He found a renewed sense of national identification superseding the formerly exaggerated universalism, growing "more convinced that Jews must have their own homeland," a cause he espoused by participating in the Histradut and Labor Zionist campaigns.

. . . In the wake of the Holocaust, Goldovski and others would recall with pain the tragedy of the Nazi era. . . . "We still performed the routine duties of union work . . . but heart and mind were preoccupied with the travails befalling the Jewish people and also the democratic and socialist world." [123]

The increasing concern and interest of Jewish Socialists and Socialist union leaders with Jewish issues was also reflected organizationally. The ILGWU, for example, in its conventions called public attention to the plight of the Jewish people. Though deep in debt, the ILGWU also donated in 1931 $5000 to help Jewish refugees from Hitler. The reasoning behind this gift was very significant. Aid for these people, according to President Benjamin Schlesinger, took precedence over union needs. "This kind of obligation has to come first," he told his somewhat reluctant secretary-treasurer, David Dubinsky. "We must be a responsible part of the community." [124]

Several years later, guided by the same objectives, the leaders of the ILGWU and other Jewish unions organized the Jewish Labor Committee (1934). Its major public commitments were the instigation of a boycott against German-made goods, the dispatching of relief to Jews and others in need in Europe, and a battle against bigotry. In 1938 the Jewish Labor Committee joined together with virtually every major Jewish organization outside of the Communist orbit in order to more effectively coordinate efforts to save Jewish lives and promote Jewish political interests. [125]

The goal of saving Jewish lives and in other ways defending Jews from Nazis and other anti-Semites is, needless to say, a noble and worthy one. But the issue here is not whether it was worthy or unworthy. The issue is whether or not the way in which this goal was pursued promoted a Jewish identification at the expense of a socialist commitment. I contend that the manner in which the Jewish unionists responded to the goal of helping their endangered fellow Jews in Europe pushed them closer to the Jewish community, which in essence meant a bourgeois directed community, and at the same time pulled them further from their already frayed socialist commitments.

One could even conjecture that had these Jewish socialists and ex-socialists unionists organized effectively as socialists as well as or instead of as Jews the odds of attaining their cherished goal might have improved. There were non-Jewish socialists such as Norman Thomas who fervently spoke out in favor of rescuing European Jews by opening the doors of America to them. But, instead of aligning themselves with socialists like Thomas and strengthening his position, the Jewish union leaders beseeched their friend and political ally, President Roosevelt, to save Jewish lives by admitting them to the United States. The results of these and other supplications are too well known for further comment. Energetic demands as socialists or as Jews could not have produced worse results.

A HEIGHTENED JEWISH IDENTIFICATION

In the 1930s and after Jewish Socialist union leaders began to be increasingly "Jewish." More and more of their energies and concerns were devoted to matters of a broader Jewish interest and less to issues dealing solely with Jewish labor. By the mid-1930s these Jewish unions had become Jewish interest groups as well as labor organizations, and their leaders had evolved into power brokers in and for the Jewish community.

Ironically, this growing identification of Jewish Socialist union leaders as Jewish interest brokers was reinforced by the American labor movement. Both the American Federation of Labor and the Congress of Industrial Organizations gave recognition to these union chieftains as spokesmen and protectors of Jewish interests. The universalistic Socialists who had founded and guided the destinies of the Jewish unions found in their later years that history had played strange tricks with them. They had achieved their life-long ambition of moving themselves and their organizations into the mainstream of the American labor movement. But as they did so, they found that their influence in this broader movement and in national politics as well rested in large part on their traditional Jewish-worker base and on their position in the influential prolabor Jewish community. The paradox was heightened by the fact that their potency in American labor and politics rose during the period when their unions' memberships were becoming progressively less Jewish in composition.[126]

The emergence of this new role and heightened Jewish identity coincided with the decrease in the proportion of Jews in their unions. By 1934 the proportion within the ILGWU fell to less than half. A similar trend could be observed in the Amalgamated. In 1937 it was estimated that less than 40 percent of this union's members was Jewish.[127] This decline in the ranks of Jewish garment unionists reflected the decline in the numbers and proportions of Jewish blue-collar workers in general and the increasing size of the Jewish white-collar and business strata.

The numbers and proportions of Jews in the garment work force and unions declined much faster than the numbers and proportions of Jews who were garment manufacturers. In the Northeast, particularly in New York City, the employers remained predominantly Jewish. Thus, by the 1930s and more so thereafter, the union officials shared more ethnic and background experiences in common with the manufacturers than with their own union membership. Indeed, not a few union officials like the aforementioned Beckerman became employers. Even familial ties were not unknown, the current ILGWU president, Sol C. Chaikin, for instance, has a son who is a dress manufacturer. (Jewish unionists may have kept their sons from entering the shops as workers, but there does not seem to have been that great an injunction against their entering as employers.)

It is difficult to believe that this ethnic commonality between union leaders and bosses did not have a practical impact upon the policies that the union officials pursued. The common use of Yiddish, or at least Yiddish expressions, eating the same ethnic foods together, attending the same communal functions, health clubs, and sharing a host of viewpoints on issues bearing upon Jewish concerns had to soften the demands that the Jewish leaders would make upon their employer counterparts.

The way in which some Jewish employers consciously utilized their Jewishness in attempts to get favorable treatment from Jewish union officials is exemplified in the following account. In 1941 Paul Jacobs, a Jew and a socialist and an ILGWU organizer, went to a small upstate New York town in order to form a union among non-Jewish workers employed by a Jewish employer. In the process, he and the employer met. " 'You're the union organizer, aren't you?' 'That's right.' 'You're Jewish too, aren't you?' 'Yes,' I [Jacobs] answered. 'Why do you ask?' 'Listen,' he said. 'Why do you want to make *rishis* [Yiddish for trouble] and stir up these goyim about the Jews? What do you care about these dumb goyim, anyway?' " [128] In this particular episode, the union official did not respond to this overture and became very angry with the manufacturer. But in this case he was young, idealistic, and had socialist principles. It probably would have been different if the official was older, cynical, and committed to the principles of the free-enterprise system. (It is, however, difficult to obtain evidence to document this assertion.)

Increasingly over time the garment union officials had less with which to defend themselves against the informal leverage of commonality of ethnicity and background exercised by the employers. The informal pressure that their employees might have used as a counterweight diminished in effectiveness or potential effectiveness. A black, Puerto Rican, female, and Christian membership simply could not match the Jewish employers in terms of the number of informal pressure points accessible to them. This meant that the largely non-Jewish union members had to rely strictly on formal measures to make the leaderships be responsive to their needs and interests.

The garment union leaders were also constrained in their ability to resist informal pressure from fellow ethnics in the ranks of management by the pragmatic and self-interested strategies they had adopted earlier in their careers. If Jewish manufacturers in the greater New York area were confronted with harsh demands, they might have either closed their shops or moved them to areas of the country in which the garment unions were weak. This, for reasons cited above, would not have helped the unions. Thus, it was to the unions' benefit (as their leaders saw it) to assist the Jewish manufacturers (and others as well) to remain in the New York metropolitan area. Once these union officials had compromised to this extent, they had less with which to resist compromising on other fronts as well, including being cooperative with their fellow ethnics on the other side of the bargaining table.

It is important to keep in mind the structure and make-up of the Jewish community toward which the Socialist union leaders were moving in the 1930s. By the 1930s, it was no longer a predominantly working-class entity as had been the case prior to World War I. In the several decades that the Eastern European Jews had resided in America, they experienced considerable occupational, educational, and material mobility. Also, the Jewish bourgeoisie were more important both in numbers and influence than had earlier been the case. It was the Jewish middle class increasingly from World War I on that defined the essence of the Jewish community. Thus, when the Jewish Socialist leaders moved close to such a community in the 1930s, they were moving toward individuals and groups that would give these labor chieftains socialist identities and commitments little support. It was their Jewish identities and commitments that now counted. Socialism from this perspective probably represented to both the union heads and their Jewish community peers some sort of irrelevant youthful baggage.

The Jewish Socialist labor heads' growing pro-Palestine orientation in particular and their concern and interest with things Jewish in general were factors that were relevant to the maintenance of their power bases—their unions, which performed an organizational function similar to Yiddish. The Jewish union chieftains and their organizations had benefited from Yiddish in the first several decades of this century. The Yiddish language had been a source of cohesion and solidarity for the Jewish unionists and their leaders. Yiddish defined them and separated them from other Americans. It also allowed them to maintain a Jewish identity without working for it or insisting upon it. The decline of Yiddish among American Jews weakened the bonds of solidarity and the sense of uniqueness among Jewish workers.

The universalistic Socialist labor chieftains should have welcomed the decline of Yiddish. After all, they had commenced the organization of Jewish workers as an entity distinct from other workers quite reluctantly. Yiddish was merely going to be an expedient and unpleasant vehicle through which to reach these workers, who understood no other language. In the 1920s, 1930s, and 1940s, however, with Yiddish rapidly declining, they had an opportunity to assimilate their membership and their organizations into the mainstream of the American labor movement. As time went on it would be easier and easier to transform their unions into American, as opposed to Jewish, unions.

These union leaders did not do this. They did not utilize the opportunity that the atrophy of Yiddish gave them. Instead, as the usage of Yiddish waned and as the percentage of Jews in their unions declined, the heads of the unions chose to become more identified with Jewish matters and concerns, again principally in efforts to aid the *yishuv*, the Jewish community in Palestine.

This pattern was very similar to the one followed by the nonobservant Jew, who, while in the midst of a large Jewish urban ghetto, did little to affirm his Jewishness but who, upon moving into a suburban residential area with few Jews, changes his behavior. In the new situation he is more likely to be observant, more likely to seek out fellow Jews to associate with, and more likely to take the trouble to be Jewish.

However, it is not necessary to utilize a sociopsychological interpretation to understand the behavior of the Jewish trade union heads. The diminution of Yiddish also meant the weakening of the base upon which their power lay. As leaders of Jewish needle trades unions, they were granted a special status by other Jewish leaders, the powers of the American labor movement, and the city, state, and national politicians. Recall, too, that the use of Yiddish had helped build a unified labor movement in an industry that was fundamentally unstable and torn by intense competition. The building of a Jewish identity and consciousness at a time when Yiddish was declining enabled them to have, for a time, the benefits that Yiddish had given them.

This exchange was not made without cost. The cost was their commitment to socialism. Again, this was not the only factor that weakened their commitment. There were other forces at work pushing in the same direction. But the more they worked at being Jewish, the more they emphasized ethnicity and the conception of a unified Jewish people. This could not help but diminish their allegiance to socialism.

These various pressures that led the Jewish socialist unionists from socialism and toward a Jewish identity did not crystallize suddenly. They were present before and particularly after these unions were established before World War I. Dedicated universalistic socialists at the heads of these unions did not surrender this commitment overnight. Yiddish-speaking socialist unionists did not quickly come to the position that they were no longer part of a broader unified struggle to bring socialism to America. On their journey from universalistic socialists who happened to be Jewish and speak Yiddish to Jewish liberals and reformers, they at the same time built and maintained structures that contributed to the maintenance of socialism in the Jewish and larger American community.

THE POLITICS OF ETHNICITY

These Jewish Socialist garment union heads were very much aware of the role of ethnicity in politics. In the latter nineteenth and early twentieth century, they had acquired first-hand knowledge of how a union hierarchy utilized an ethnic base to maintain itself in power.

Socialists in the women's and men's clothing unions had to fight conservative entrenched union oligarchies resting upon non-Jewish ethnic groups such as native Americans, Irish-Americans, and German-Americans in order to establish their own socialist-oriented unions. These non-Jewish oligarchies in their fight for power had even used anti-Semitism as a weapon to keep Jews out of their unions' positions of power.[129]

The best illustration of how ethnicity and anti-Semitism were utilized against Jewish radicals in the garment unions can be seen in the United Garment Workers of America (UGWA). The Amalgamated had in fact come into existence in 1914 in part because heads of the United Garment Workers of America, then the only extant recognized union in the men's clothing field, had refused to give leaders and representatives of Jewish garment workers positions of influence and authority commensurate with the numbers they represented. At the UGWA Convention in 1914, the leadership of this union when challenged by delegates from Jewish workers, particularly those from New York City, told its supporters: ". . . that it was their duty, as decent American women, to stand by their general officers in their struggle against the Jews, who were trying to put Jewish officers in the place of non-Jews."[130] The UGWA leadership was so successful in its tactics that these Jewish delegates left to form a rival union in 1914, the ACWA.[131]

Several years later the UGWA leadership in an apparent change of heart or policy did admit Jews to its General Executive Board (GEB) and did hire Jewish organizers. But despite these actions, the UGWA was not able to compete successfully with its rival in the men's clothing industry, the Amalgamated, among Jewish workers. One of the major reasons for this failure appears to have been that the Jews on the UGWA's GEB and the Jews hired as its organizers differed from the Jews in the shops. The former were all German Jews while the latter were predominantly Eastern Europeans. Cultural differences, it would seem, were more telling than religious commonality in the organization of a union.[132]

The Socialist (Russian) Jewish needle trades union leaders when in power proved not averse to using ethnicity to insure their own positions. Consciously or unconsciously, ethnicity was utilized as a lever to stay in power, even as the union leaders proclaimed their allegiance to socialism and to the Socialist Party. It is, however, very difficult to maintain a commitment to an ideology that purports to promote equality and a more equitable distribution of power in society while at the same time holding organizational power on the basis of the support of one ethnic group in a multiethnic organization. This disparity between espoused ideology and political reality became even more pronounced when that ethnic group constituted a numerical minority of the membership. The manner in which ethnicity and Jewishness were utilized in New York City and in the headquarters of the garment unions is indicative of why the Socialist Jewish leaders were reluctant to embark actively upon a campaign to make their unions into truly national organizations.

The Italians

The position of the Italians within the ILGWU from its inception provides a good illustration of the way in which ethnicity figures into union politics.[133] At the time the ILGWU was founded, Italians were the second largest ethnic group employed in the making of women's garments. By 1910 in New York City they represented about one-third of all such workers, and in some specific trades such as the cloak-makers and shirtwaist-makers their numbers approached 40 percent. Yet in the same year and in the same city, only a small handful of ILGWU members were Italian, and all of the officers were Jews. This phenomenon, it should be noted, was not unique to Italian immigrants in the garment industry. Italians, in general in this period, with some notable exceptions, had low rates of participation in unions in America.[134]

A significant cause of the disparity between the size of the Italian work force and union membership in the needle trades can be traced to their experience in Italy, their culture, and the nature of the Italian-American community around 1910. The Italian immigrants in this period were overwhelmingly from southern Italian peasant families. From 1899 to 1910 approximately 84 percent of Italian immigrants were from southern Italy. Virtually nothing in their experience in southern Italy prepared them to accept unionism much less radical unionism. In this respect they were quite similar to the Jewish immigrants who entered America and the garment industry in the latter nineteenth century.

The situation was almost the reverse for northern Italians. In the early 1900s their rate of unionization, according to the United States Immigration Commission, was the highest for any of the 14 foreign-born nationalities surveyed—40 percent. In this respect, they outdistanced the Jews, with 21 percent organized. By contrast, the rate for southern Italians was 10 percent.[135] The experience of the northern Italian workers, who came from industrial and urban settings and had had some degree of participation in or contact with unions and radical movements, similar to that of the post-1900 Jewish immigrant, obviously made them more receptive to unionism after they emigrated. This was true whether the destination was America, Argentina, or France.[136]

The inhibiting role of culture and historical experiences was heightened among the southern Italians in the garment trades owing to the very high percentage of women in their ranks. While it is true that a large majority of the Jews in the garment industry were also women—about 70 percent—Jewish females were not as restricted by their families, community, and culture in dealing with unions or worldly affairs.

Organizers complained that Italian women, who were more retiring than their Jewish sisters, permitted the Jewish girls to control the unions . . . and hold meetings in the Jewish quarter late at night. Italian parents, who objected to their daughters keeping late hours, refused to permit them to participate in unions. . . . In short, the traditional position of the Italian girl in the community was a deterrent to organization.[137]

Differences between the nature and structure of the Italian-American and Jewish-American communities during this period also contributed to the low Italian union-participation rates. Unlike the Jewish community, there were scarcely any significant leaders or institutions that encouraged Italians to join unions or radical parties. On the contrary, the organized Italian community generally took a negative attitude toward unionism. This community, unlike the coexisting Jewish one, was predominantly in the hands of a conservative-oriented bourgeoisie.

It was not only cultural and community factors, however, that accounted for so few Italians being in the ILGWU. Other factors overlapped and interacted with these to produce this outcome. Prominent was the attitude of the union and its Jewish members to the Italian garment workers. Prior to 1910 the ILGWU gave very little of its resources or attention to the issue of organizing Italians. "In fact," according to social historian Edwin Fenton, ". . . the word Italian does not appear in the ILG convention proceedings until 1910."[138] Since the trade unions made little effort to enroll Italians, the Italian workers had little reason to overcome cultural obstacles to become members.

The ILGWU's attitude and behavior toward Italian garment workers evidently appeared reasonable to this union's leaders at the time. Until 1910 the ILGWU was neither very stable nor financially solvent. Its meager resources were invested almost totally in the constituency most likely to support the union—the Eastern European Jews.

Tension and a lack of understanding between the Jewish unionists and the Italian workers also inhibited the ILGWU from actively organizing Italians. It was not easy for a Jew and an Italian to communicate. The Jews spoke Yiddish and to a lesser extent English. Few Italians, on the other hand, particularly the sheltered Italian females, spoke either language. The language problem, the traditional behavior of the Italian females, and the different mores and customs of their Jewish coworkers forestalled the development of interethnic friendships. Thus, the ILGWU did not have an informal basis of Jewish-Italian solidarity upon which to build.

Whereas the grounds for understanding and friendship between Italian and Jewish garment workers were not substantial, the bases for hostility between them, particularly on the part of Jewish workers, were. Italians helped to drive Jewish wages down. They were willing to work for less money than their Jewish counterparts. The animosity between the two groups was also fueled by te behavior of Italian workers during garment strikes. They scabbed. Jewish workers also scabbed, but the Italians who did so were more numerous and probably more visible. Prior to 1910 few Italian communal institutions criticized this form of behavior.

Paradoxically, the grounds for animosity were also the bases for the Jewish ILGWU leaders' attempts to organize Italian workers. The former realized that the union could not hope to be very effective in the industry if the Italians remained unorganized. Nonunionized Italians would exert a continual downward pressure on wages and break strikes. Self-interest and self-preservation called for the Jewish ILGWU officers and activists to bring Italians into the ILGWU.

From 1910 on the ILGWU, in cooperation with socialists in the Italian community, launched major efforts to enroll Italians. These proved relatively successful. In 1912 of the approximately 60,000 ILGWU members in New York City, 20,000 were Italians and 35,000 were Jews, with the rest scattered among other nationalities.

It was at this point that the politics of ethnicity in the union came to the fore. Although Italians had about a third of the members, every local in the City was headed by a Jewish president. The only positions in the ILGWU occupied by Italians were those of business agent and organizer, and these were very few in number.

The Italians soon began to demand representation in the officialdom of the ILGWU in numbers that reflected their proportion in the union. These demands remained unrealized because of the unwillingness of Jewish office holders to share power and because of the numerical distribution of Italians within ILGWU locals. Although a third of the union members in New York City were Italian, in every local in the city they were outnumbered by Jews. Without control of a local, they did not have much of a chance to gain significant positions within the ILGWU other than those doled out by Jewish incumbents.

The Italian ILGWUers responded tō this situation by arguing that at least some locals be divided along ethnic lines to bring in Italian-controlled locals. The Jewish Socialist ILGWU leaders raised strenuous objections as Socialists and democratic unionists to this proposal. Ethnicity was for them a valid or legitimate axis along which any union and especially their union should be divided. They contended that the only legitimate divisions in a union could be on universalistic grounds such as occupational specialty—cloakmaker or dressmaker—occupational skill—cutter—or geographical location. These divisions did not take into account the race, religion, or nationality of union members and thus were not as divisive as the particularistic ones. This was a principled position. It was also a position that reinforced Jewish domination of the ILGWU.

The Italians were not put off by such a self-serving principled position. In the face of the Italian pressure, the Jewish Socialist officers began to give way—but very, very slowly. Their first concession to these southern Europeans was the branch system. The branch system did not represent much of a concession on the part of the Jewish Socialist leadership as it had little meaning as far as power in the International or the particular local was concerned. The Italian branches did not provide Italians with access to policy-making positions in the ILGWU locals, the New York City Joint Board, or the International's General Executive Board. In fact, within the branches Italians were completely dependent on Jewish officials for funds to pay branch officers, secretaries, and for literature. All money requests as well as editorial policy for the branch papers had to be approved by officials in the locals or the Joint Board—which meant non-Italian Jews.

It is not cnly the lack of power commensurate with their numbers that fueled the demands of Italians for more equitable representation. They were also incensed with the use of Yiddish at local and joint board union meetings. This was not only a symbol of their subordinate position, it was also a cause as well. Many Italian ILGWU members who did not understand Yiddish simply stayed away from union meetings rather than sit for hours without understanding what was going on. The absence made it easier for the Jewish officers to stay in power and set policy.

By 1919 the Italian ILGWUers finally succeeded in gaining for themselves charters and the control of two locals, Local 48 (Cloakmakers) in 1916 and Local 89 (Dressmakers). In the first years of their existence, each of these locals encompassed all Italian-speaking ILGWU members in New York in the cloakmaking and dressmaking trades. Later they were granted jurisdiction over all Italians in these trades (except the cutters) regardless of whether they spoke English or Italian. Local 89 eventually became the single largest local within the ILGWU, while Local 48 (numbered in honor of the Italian revolt of 1848) attained a position of third or fourth largest. These two locals retained their ethnic distinctiveness and through this their control over access to well-paying garment jobs into the 1960s. They functioned as Italian locals even though as nationality locals they were illegal under the provisions of a New York State law of 1945 and the federal government's Civil Rights Act of 1964.[139]

It is also interesting to observe that in these decades two Italians played important roles in the decision-making of the ILGWU. They were Luigi Antonini and Salvatore Ninfo, General Executive Board members. The reason for their prominence was that each had his own ethnic base as president of an ILGWU Italian local—Ninfo with Local 48 and Antonini with Local 89. Real power continued to rest with Jewish officers who predominated in the locals, joint boards, and in the international headquarters as well.

This policy of concentrating Italians into a few large locals may have proved quite rewarding to the individual Italians who headed them and probably even to the members of these locals. But at the same time, it facilitated the control by Jewish Socialists (and later former Socialists) over the New York City Joint Board, the International's General Executive Board, and the union's presidency and top offices, the most important offices and bodies within the ILGWU. This control stemmed from the fact that raw numbers of members were not the major determinants of who became a joint board or GEB member or International president. Each of these positions was filled under a system of nonproportional representation that favored smaller locals over larger ones, a situation that still exists today.[140]

Thus, by concentrating the Italians into two large locals in New York City, the Jewish and (until the mid-1930s) largely Socialist leaders ensured their hold over the International and the New York City Joint Board. As the number of Italians in the rank and file of the ILGWU continued to surpass that of Jews in the 1930s and 1940s, this political-legal arrangement forestalled the Italians' coming to power in the International. By the latter 1940s Italians could claim of all positions of real importance in the union's hierarchy only three of the 23 members on the ILGWU's General Executive Board.

It is not possible, on the basis of the evidence available, to state that the Italian leadership of the ILGWU made a deal to forego claiming power commensurate with the numbers of Italians in the union. (Of course, it is possible that Italian ILGWUers did not consider ethnicity to be a factor in voting for their officers and representatives. But in view of their past political behavior in the ILGWU and their electoral politics outside of the ILGWU, this does not seem much of a possibility.) In addition, the Italian leaders did not just refrain from challenging the Jewish incumbents; they were, on the contrary, among the staunchest supporters of the Jewish right-wing Socialists and the Dubinsky forces that controlled the ILGWU from the 1920s on. In this regard it is interesting to note that Local 89, the power base of Luigi Antonini, was formed by taking some members from Local 25, which in 1919 was the most radical local in the ILGWU.

The following account of a garment union meeting in the 1920s makes clear the way in which ethnicity was used as a device to maintain incumbent leaders in power. It is based on the verbatim notes of a prominent Socialist and the Amalgamated's first director of education, J. B. S. Hardmann. Although the union in question is not named, from Hardmann's description it can only be a local of the ILGWU or the Amalgamated.

The General Executive Board of one of the large needle unions is in session. Committees appear requesting that the dissolved Italian Local A3 be restored and that the members who had been transferred to the respective trade locals—pressers to pressers, operators to operators, etc.—should be again united in the old A3. The reason that had been given for dissolution was disorderly conduct of business and factional fights. The argument for restoration is that organization by language makes for homogeneity, members feel at home and are more active. Against that, the opponents of restoration argue: "We are an American organization, we should speak the language of the country. . . . Noisy meetings, several speaking at the same time. . . . Public opinion about us is disturbed . . ." The hearings are over. The Board is in closed session; only one spokesman of the pleaders for restoration is sitting in. The president [of the local] asks him: "Phil, let's not kid ourselves here. Language is not the issue. What is?"

The spokesman answers: "Yes, Brother President, no kidding. *Our share in the leadership of the organization in the city is the issue* [italics mine]. It is not because our people talk loudly or gesticulate unduly that our charter was revoked. *When we are in one local with all our people together we count for something; but scattered over the whole place, we do not. Yes, we want our clear share of the leadership* [italics mine]. Time was when we were not so many. We are now very many—most of the lot in fact. There was a time when we didn't know the language, and we had no leadership. That is no longer the case. We speak the American language and we have the leadership." The "official" Italian member of the Board asks: "But aren't our people being treated fairly?" [The reply] "We don't like that 'being treated' thing. We want to be doing the 'treating' ourselves." [141]

Blacks and Puerto Ricans

In the post–World War II era, the black, Puerto Rican, and female members of the ILGWU have experienced the greatest disparity between positions of influence and authority and number of union members. By 1967 these two groups constituted approximately 33 percent of the unionists in the ILGWU. Yet no person from either ethnic group held a local manager's post or a vice-presidency. At the same time the International's General Executive Board contained only one Puerto Rican and no blacks. Eight years later this representation of blacks and Puerto Ricans on the General Executive Board was equalized so that it included one from each group. It should also be noted that only one member of the General Executive Board in 1975 was a female, despite the fact that 85 percent of the ILGWU's membership is made up of women. [142]

The ILGWU leaders are very aware that members of these groups have few positions of authority and influence within the union. In a candid interview in June 1975, the current president of the ILGWU, Sol Chaikin, admitted that there was a lack of Hispanic, black, and female leaders in his union. Chaikin attributed it to a lack of motivation on their part to participate in union affairs and administration. The women, he claimed, were too involved with their families. But with the blacks and the Hispanic members the reasons were different.

When my father joined this union, he really felt he wanted to build a better world. He had a social vision. This was true of thousands who came into this union, but it was not true of blacks and Hispanics until recently. . . . The last generation of blacks and Hispanics did not come out of Czarist Russia or Middle European countries, places of social ferment. But the young blacks and Hispanics have participated to a much greater extent in social change, and it is this group we're going to look to for our new generation of leaders. It will happen, I'm convinced.[143]

Motivation stemming from a proper background may indeed be a major factor in explaining the paucity, to use Chaikin's word, of black, Hispanic, and female leadership. But even if the ILGWU president is wrong in his socio-psychological assessment, the blacks, Hispanic, and female members should prove to have in their ranks hundreds of highly motivated individuals, the chances of the ethnic and sexual composition of the leadership changing are very slim. Owing to the ILGWU's constitutional provisions pertaining to eligibility for the union's presidency and General Executive Board, at least as of 1968, a black and Puerto Rican, no matter how highly motivated, had as much chance of becoming president of the union or a member of the General Executive Board as the proverbial camel had of getting through the eye of the needle: "As a result of the restrictive requirement, *no more than four or five nonwhite persons are eligible for the General Executive Board and virtually none at all for the top leadership positions.*"[144]

THE RISE OF NONWORKING CLASS JEWS

Bureaucratic obstacles were not the only device that assured the concentration of power in the hands of a white and Jewish leadership. Control over the channels that led to leadership positions and the people who had access to them was also important. In the early decades of the ILGWU, most of the leaders who came to the fore, such as David Dubinsky, appeared to have had some experience working in a garment shop. Virtually all of these were also Socialists or members of other radical parties; and virtually all were Jews as well.

By the latter 1930s and early 1940s, it became increasingly apparent that shop experience was no longer a formal or informal necessity for admission into the channels leading to positions of power and influence in the union. As work experience declined in importance, the leadership grew more reliant on other sources to fill union posts. These were radical parties, particularly the Socialist party, and the colleges. Interestingly, these sources also supplied the union with Jews while at the same time the number and proportion of Jews on the shop floors were declining.

Organizers, for example, were largely drawn from the radical movement and the colleges. Paul Jacobs, an ILGWU organizer in the early 1940s, notes that virtually all of the organizers hired with him were from the radical movement, and at the same time they were virtually all Jews. He also goes on to point out that in the same period all of the local ILGWU staff in Harrisburg, where he worked, was Jewish even though the garment labor force in that area was predominantly non-

Jewish. The current president of the ILGWU, Sol Chaikin, also started out as an organizer in the early 1940s. He did not have any experience as a garment worker, although his father and mother did work in the shops. Chaikin was recruited into the ILGWU after completing Brooklyn Law School.[145]

By the latter 1940s and early 1950s, the ILGWU was leaning more heavily on educational sources for future officials and leaders. These included colleges such as Brandeis University. In 1947 President David Dubinsky of the ILGWU commented on the reasons for this: "In the earlier years of the ILGWU our leadership element was nourished chiefly in the traditions and idealistic atmosphere of the old-time radical and Socialist movement. That reservoir has gradually become exhausted."[146] To replace this exhausted source Dubinsky advocated that the ILGWU establish its own school to train future leaders. In accord with his desire, the ILGWU Training Institute was established and opened its doors in May 1950.[147]

The requirements for entry ensured that those who used this channel as a source of mobility within the union were going to be largely white and Jewish. A student had to have at least a high-school education and be able to support himself during the one-year course of study. Of the 37 accepted for the first class, 18 were graduates of a university, and 11 others had had some college education. Only 10 were ILGWU members, and a majority were Jewish.[148]

It would be a mistake to regard as a sign of ethnic favoritism the ILGWU's reliance on sources that produced largely Jewish candidates for responsible union positions. Although ethnic favoritism may have played a role, another factor was also operating. The persons recruited through these sources, as opposed to those from the shop floor, were more likely to be dependent for a successful union career on the officials who selected them than would a worker emerging from the ranks. The latter might have a constituency of his own among fellow workers and unionists in the shop or factory from which he came. Those selected by the union's leadership were much less likely to have such a constituency and potentially independent power base for their careers. Thus, by utilizing nonwork arenas such as colleges to find future leaders, the former Socialist Jewish union chieftains appeared to be recruiting persons who would be more amenable to their guidance, and at the same time more likely to be white and Jewish, than would be the case if they relied on the rank and file. Also, Jews, particularly those with college backgrounds, were not as likely to develop an identification with a largely non-Jewish, noncollege educated membership as would non-Jews from the ranks.

One could argue that an ethnic groups' interests in a multiethnic organization like a union or a political party or even a government need not require for their protection that positions of power in that body be allocated in accord with their numbers. It is theoretically possible that the needs and concerns of an ethnic group in such a multiethnic body could be more than adequately met without their having their own ethnic brethren in influential posts. Conversely, ethnic representation, as Mayor Dailey's black congressmen and ward leaders have shown in Chicago, is in itself no guarantee than an ethnic group's interests will be satisfied.[149] The key factor appears to be the responsiveness of the leadership and the representatives and the construction of a political system within the organization that assures a high degree of responsiveness.

The ILGWU leadership, however, does not appear to have been very responsive to the needs of its black and Puerto Rican members. The lack of political representation for these groups within the ILGWU has been costly for them and their interests. These groups are disproportionately located in the lowest paying job categories in the garment industry. In 1963 almost 20 percent of the ILGWU members in New York earned less than $1.50 per hour. Virtually all of this 20 percent were blacks and Puerto Ricans. Lack of representation has penalized these groups in another area: the area of domestic donations. Between 1959 and 1961, when the proportion of Jewish ILGWU members approximated that of blacks and Puerto Ricans together, the union donated $18,750 to black and Puerto Rican causes and $140,000 to Jewish ones.[150]

History and changing economic circumstances had combined to severely test the socialist and liberal commitment of the Jewish leaders of the ILGWU and the other garment unions. They had come to power as Socialists in unions whose members were predominantly Jewish, as were they. However, even as they came to power, the number and proportion of Jewish workers in the garment industry was declining. The industry itself encouraged Jews to leave the shop floor. It was relatively easier in the garment business to move from employee to employer than was true for most any other industry. On the other hand, the children of the Jewish garment workers tended not to follow in their parents' footsteps. The availability and attraction of middle-class occupations such as teacher, social worker, and professional, as well as clerk, drew them away from the employ of the garment industry. Eventually the Jewish Socialists and ex-Socialists found themselves presiding over unions in which there was a minority of Jews among the rank and file. The manner in which they dealt with this change in the ethnic composition of their organizations proved not to be one informed by the principles of socialism.

CONCLUSION

This analysis of the Jewish union has stressed two points. One, Jewish unions officered by Jewish Socialists and filled with largely prosocialist and Jewish rank and file played an important role in fostering and building a positive relation between Jews and the Left in America in the early decades of this century. These unions through their educational courses, internal propaganda, cooperatives, and open and considerable support for Left political candidates and parties encouraged Jews, both members and nonmembers, to be and to support Leftists. These unions not only promoted the cause of socialism among Jews, they also promoted it among Americans. They were among the principal institutional bulwarks of the Socialist party for decades.

The second point emphasized in this analysis is that these very same leaders and institutions undermined the Jews' ties to and support of socialism. This negative role was the product of decisions of Socialist union heads as to how best protect the interests of their organizations within a capitalist society. The instability of the garment industry—their major industrial base—heightened these leaders' concern for the viability of their unions and motivated them to seek ways to bring order and stability to both the garment industry and their organizations. In this quest, these Socialists made the assessment that socialism would not triumph. Survival and organizational effectiveness, they concluded (either consciously or unconsciously), depended upon close cooperation with and the assistance of employers, bourgeois political parties, and other agencies of the capitalist society. Soon these socialists became transformed into exsocialists and supporters of the capitalist system.

This metamorphosis was also aided by their location in the Jewish community and the use they made of ethnicity. As cosmopolitan Socialists, the organizers and heads of the needle trades unions deplored the fact that their organizations had to be largely Jewish ones. Ethnic divisions among workers and their unions were regarded as obstacles to the development of a working-class consciousness and opened them to chauvinist appeals. Owing to the character of the garment industry, however, the ethnic base became the most effective one on which these socialist leaders built and developed their unions. In the process of accepting and relying upon this ethnic base, the labor chieftains became increasingly dependent upon the Jewish community as well. As they did so and as the community became more bourgeois and more concerned with ethnic interests, the leaders and their organizations were drawn from their earlier socialist commitment.

It is also apparent that ethnicity was utilized (whether consciously or unconsciously) as a political device to ensure that power remained in the hands of the Jewish Socialist (and later ex-Socialist) leaders. The usage of ethnicity in this way could not help but undermine the commitment of these men to a political creed that demanded high universalistic and democratic standards of its adherents. This indeed was one important result.

It is important to stress also that many Jews (and others) in the rank and file of these unions did not approve of the conservative direction taken by their leaders. In the first three decades this disapproval gave rise to serious conflicts between the memberships and their officials.

These conflicts were based on practical differences that had ideological associations. From their perspective, the workers and union members could not ascertain the long-range benefits that their leaders' class collaborationism offered them. It contravened their own commitment to socialism and the public statements of the labor chieftains as well. Their leaders had indeed helped to educate them on the virtues of socialism and the basic evils of capitalism. The practical benefits gained from a policy of accommodation in terms of wages and working conditions proved to be intermittent and usually short-lived. What exacerbated the situation even further was that the less socialist the leadership became, the more oligarchical and authoritarian they also became.

Thus, the contribution of the garment unions and their leaders' to the partnership between Jews and socialism was a mixed one. There is no doubt that they played a very important role in sustaining and nurturing this relationship. There is also no doubt that they played an important role in weakening and undermining this relationship. It proved difficult for these men to hold to their youthful idealism in the face of the imagined opportunities and benefits of cooperation with what appeared to be an invincible capitalist system.

6 The Fraternal Orders and the Press of the Jewish Left

INTRODUCTION

The primary focus of this chapter will be the Jewish labor fraternal orders and the Left or pro-Left Yiddish-language press. These, together with the Jewish unions and radical parties, constituted the institutional core of the Jewish labor movement and the Jewish Left subculture.

A two-fold objective underlies the discussion and analysis of these: First, to elucidate the manner in which both institutions built and nurtured a Jewish Left subculture and in the process developed close and positive ties between Jews in America and the Left; second, to demonstrate and explain how these very same institutions weakened and attenuated these ties.

The guiding theme of this chapter is that the rooting of Left institutions in one ethnic group—in this case the Jewish community—proved subversive to Leftist goals and purposes. Totally supported by and enveloped in the Jewish community, neither the Left press nor the fraternal orders proved capable of resisting the ethnic pulls of their readers and constituents. Concern with organizational viability during decades in which the number of permanent working-class Jews declined and Jewish national sentiment increased pressured these institutions to broaden their base and orientation. No longer were they able to successfully exist as institutions appealing only to working-class and Leftist Jews. In the new context, they became more Jewish and less radical in their orientation, particularly as the Jewish community toward which they were orienting themselves at the same time became increasingly more bourgeois in terms of its composition, leadership, and political values.

This metamorphosis was also furthered by the decline of the Left parties after World War I and their adoption of policies that conflicted with Jewish interests. These developments in the Left made the Jewish Left institutions even more dependent upon Jews while at the same time forcing these organizations to make choices between their socialist allegiances and Jewish constituencies. The end result in the most prominent cases was a conscious (or unconscious) decision in favor of a Jewish orientation. This choice either led, sometimes dra-

matically, sometimes gradually to a decline in these organizations'
ability or willingness to promote socialism among Jews.

LABOR FRATERNAL ORDERS

The radical Jewish labor fraternal orders that did so much to orient
Jews to the Left in the early decades of this century emerged from an
immigrant Jewish working-class community honeycombed with all
types of fraternal and mutual-aid associations. Prior to the emergence
of the radical orders at about the turn of the century, their predecessors were typically apolitical. The vast majority were affiliated with a
synagogue and took the form of a *landsmanschaft*—that is, membership based on location of residence in the old country. Although
generally sympathetic to labor, due in large part to their overwhelmingly working class memberships, these fraternal and mutual-aid associations did little to further the interests of the fledgling unions or
to manifestly arouse working-class consciousness.

The orientation of these societies began to change with the arrival
of large numbers of more secular and more politically aware Jewish
immigrants after the turn of the century. These new immigrants
stirred and aroused the *landsmanschaften*. Pressured by demands for
greater political involvement and action on behalf of unions and radical parties, splits began to occur, resulting in the formation of two or
more *landsmanschaften* from the same town or region. The divisions
were along political or religious lines, for example, conservatives
against progressives and the Orthodox against the freethinkers. The
newer landsmanschaften retained the social and mutual-aid functions
of the older societies while tending to leave aside their more religious
and frivolous orientations. To these functions the emerging labor orders added or stressed others. One was secular education, because of
the greater importance that the Yiddish laboring masses attached to
education; another was the maintenance and propagation of
socialism.

The three largest and most important of these labor fraternal orders
to emerge from the newer immigrants were the *Arbeiter Ring*, or
Workmen's Circle (WC), the *Yiddisher Nationaler Arbeiter Farband*
(later called *Farband*, or the Jewish National Workers' Alliance), and
the Jewish section, later Jewish People's Fraternal Order, of the *Internationaler Arbeiter Ordn*, or International Workers' Order (IWO). The
first WC branch was founded in 1892 and in 1900 various branches
came together as a national labor fraternal order guided by a nonsectarian socialist ideology. The *Farband* was established by the Labor
Zionists in 1912 and was a vehicle for the expression of their unique
ideology. The IWO came into existence in 1930, largely as a result of a
political struggle and division within the Workmen's Circle, and from
its earliest days assumed a position and outlook close to that of the
Communist party. The IWO was a multi-ethnic organization, with its

Jewish component being the largest and most important. While also concerned with politics, all sold insurance and provided concrete monetary benefits to members and their families in cases of need.

Each of these fraternal orders tried to create a social milieu for its members and their families. To this end they sponsored schools, summer camps, choruses, dramatic societies as well as the usual fare of lectures, dances, dinners, and testimonial affairs. A primary function of these groups and events was to provide a social world in which Left or progressive Jews could meet, interact, and strengthen their political commitments. The more inclusive and extensive this social world, the less would be the need for and contact with the corrupting and seductive social milieu of the bourgeoisie or religious Jews.[1]

THE WORKMEN'S CIRCLE

The biggest and most important of the Jewish labor fraternal orders was the Workmen's Circle. From its earliest days the WC was closely identified with the Socialist party. Its officers were Socialists, and it openly espoused the virtues of the Socialist party (SP). The WC also had intimate ties with the Jewish unions, particularly those in the needle trades, and the Jewish labor press. The WC succeeded early in carving for itself an identity as the third branch of the Jewish labor movement, along with the unions and the SP.

The Workmen's Circle quickly addressed itself to two pressing needs of Jewish radicals and progressives around the turn of the century. One was to provide socialists and unionists an alternative to the existing nonradical or religious-oriented fraternal orders and lodges. Yiddish-speaking Jewish Leftists and those secularists sympathetic to the Left needed a social organization of their own to provide them with friendship, mutual aid, and moorings in a strange society. These immigrant Jewish radicals and unionists, similar to their less radical counterparts, had come out of a milieu in which they were used to such organizations. Too long bereft of one of their own political complexion in the New World, they and their families had found it difficult to take part in associations in which their politics were continually subject to challenge. The Workmen's Circle and its component branches provided them with the alternative they had been seeking.

This alternative, however, was not totally at variance in organizational features and functions with the nonradical fraternal orders of the immigrant community. Most of the WC branches in the larger metropolitan areas were established around a landsmanschaft core. Like the other immigrant associations, residence in the Old World and the Yiddish language formed much of the cement on which the Arbeiter Ring built its foundation. This fact did not change very much in the succeeding decades. Shortly before World War II more than half of the WC branches in the New York area, its primary area of concentration, continued to be *landsmanschaft* branches. So even though the WC differed from its counterparts in terms of ideology, it was linked with them, and in the process linked its members with theirs, through their reliance on the *landsmanschaft* principle and Yiddish. This commonality would, in the future, contribute to the Workmen's Circle's evolution into a Jewish interest organization.

The other pressing need of Yiddish-speaking immigrant radicals addressed by the Workmen's Circle was for a fraternal order in which Jewish radicals of different political views could cohabit. At the time in which the WC was established, the Jewish Left was made up of various warring camps of socialists and anarchists. The order's founders believed that the WC could be an umbrella organization of the Jewish Left in which there would be no place for internecine political warfare. Instead, the WC would serve as a neutral social and educational arena in which the competing factions could intermingle and learn to cooperate in the interest of furthering the class struggle. This meant, however, that there was a built-in mechanism within the WC that would constantly push it toward seeking out the lowest common political denominator on the Left. This same mechanism would over time also push it along a path toward moderation and liberalism and away from a firm socialist commitment.

The WC soon began to grow into a powerful organization. There were several key ingredients that produced this success. One, it appealed to a unique and growing market for members. Two, it had no real competitors in its field. And three, it offered good health and death benefits. By 1915, 15 years after its establishment as a national labor fraternal order, its membership had increased from 872 in 1900 to 49,913 in 1915. Three years later the figure was more than 60,000, making the Workmen's Circle one of the largest and most influential orders in the American Jewish community.[2]

The Workmen's Circle owed much of its growth to the post-Kishinev waves of Jewish immigrants. Similar to the experience of the Jewish trade unions, these new members were drawn from ever-expanding pools of new arrivals who had had some contact and experience with trade unions and radical organizations, particularly the Bund. (Bundists had established their own fraternal order in the United States but in a policy change in 1907 dissolved it and joined the WC en masse.)[3] By the 1920s former Bundists represented a majority of the rank and file and an even larger majority of the organization's activists. In fact, at the national level, they held virtually every office of importance in the Workmen's Circle.[4]

In the first decade of its existence, the WC forged a role for itself as the "Red Cross" of the Jewish labor movement. In a sharp departure from the practices of its nonpolitical or nonradical predecessors and competitors, the WC consciously and formally took politics into account in granting assistance. Struggling Jewish labor unions learned that the WC could be counted on for financial help. Such support became larger and more varied as the WC grew and matured. It included help in organizing unions and in boycott campaigns against nonunion products. Jewish radical groups in the United States and abroad, particularly in Russia, also benefited from the pockets and treasury of the WC and its members. This aid was not only limited to Jewish organizations—the Socialist party was also a recipient. Like the Jewish unions, the WC mobilized its members to participate in the campaigns of Socialist candidates. In 1914 it proved instrumental in the election of the Socialist Meyer London to Congress. London, it should also be noted, was the WC's legal counsel.

The Workmen's Circle commenced its existence as an unabashedly radical organization. In its first declaration of principles adopted by its first convention in 1901, the WC stated: "The spirit of the Workmen's Circle is freedom of thought and endeavor towards solidarity of the workers, faithfulness to the interests of its class in the struggle against oppression and exploitation."[5] "Its spiritual object," the declaration continued, was to bring: ". . . on the day of their [the workers'] complete emancipation from exploitation and oppression. Thus, the Workmen's Circle intends to be a factor in hastening the time when the ideal of freedom and equality, not only in political but also primarily in economic matters, shall be realized."[6]

This radical commitment extended beyond the declaration of principles. It was also built into the requirements for membership. Before becoming eligible for membership, the prospective joiner had to pledge that: (1) he would join a union in his trade if he were not already a member and (2) he would vote only for working-class parties, which at that time meant the Socialist and Socialist Labor parties. In its first year one member was expelled for supporting the Republican party. In subsequent years thousands of members were expelled, many of whom were later reinstated, fined, or in other ways penalized for supporting nonsocialist candidates and parties and engaging in activity deemed detrimental to the cause of unionism. After 1920 the organization was guided by the policy of supporting candidates of parties "who stand for political freedom and economic equality." In point of practice, meant the Socialist party.

At the same time as it committed itself to Socialism, the Workmen's Circle adopted a hostile stance toward organized religion, particularly Judaism. In fact, the organization was originally conceived as a nonsectarian association, and one of its founding members was a non-Jew. One branch of the Circle was dissolved after the leadership found that its members had organized a *minyan* (group of 10 men required for Orthodox Jewish prayer services) for the High Holidays. Such action and feeling toward Judaism was in accord with the cosmopolitan socialism that guided the leadership and activists of the Workmen's Circle.[7]

In the decades after World War I, the Workmen's Circle experienced increasing difficulty in maintaining both its commitment to socialism and its hostility toward Judaism and Jewish nationalism. However, even as its allegiance to radicalism slackened, it still remained a major institution within the Jewish community, which acted to maintain links between the Jews and the Left. By 1925 the WC had attained a membership of more than 87,000 and had assets of more than $3 million. It was one of the largest and wealthiest organized Jewish bodies in America. Membership within it conferred some degree of status among Eastern European–born Jews. Thus, its policies and actions carried weight among its members and the Eastern European Jewish community.

WORKMEN'S CIRCLE MEMBERSHIP

Year	Number of Members (to nearest thousand)	Average Age
1900	872	
1915	50,000	
1918	60,000	
1924	83,000	35.9
1925	87,000	
1930	71,000	
1932	70,000	
1941	72,000	48.1
1969	53,000	55.3
1972	52,000	
1976	57,000	

Sources: Minutes of the Workmen's Circle in Workmen's Circle Paper, YIVO Institute of Jewish Research, New York, New York; American Jewish Yearbook; The Inner Circle, February, 1977.

In the 1920s and to a decreasing extent in the decades thereafter, the leaders of the WC wrote and spoke out on behalf of socialism. Virtually all of the major figures in the organization were themselves Socialists, a tradition that lasted into the post–World War II era. Until 1940 the Workmen's Circle routinely continued to endorse and work for the election of Socialist party candidates. Even after its break with the Socialist party in 1940, it continued to have close relations with the Jewish Socialist Farband and financially assisted the Rand School. At its 46th convention in Detroit in May of 1946, the WC still proclaimed its allegiance to and faith in socialism: "The Convention proclaims its strong belief in socialism and will help strengthen the forces which can create a mighty socialist movement in this country."[8] Later, as it drifted further from this commitment, the organization became a significant force for liberalism in the Jewish community. In the 1950s and 1960s the leadership took strong stands in favor of civil rights, government-sponsored medical programs, federal aid to education, foreign aid, and welfare programs, while clearly enunciating its opposition to McCarthysim and fascism.[9]

The policies and actions that the Workmen's Circle pursued within its branches in the 1920s and 1930s gave practical support to the position of its leaders in shoring up the members' allegiance to unionism, particularly Jewish unionism, and to the Socialist party.[10] In these decades members were penalized for joining the Democratic or Republican parties, failing to join unions, or for taking actions that the leadership deemed hostile to union principles. Members were even punished for bringing one another into capitalist courts in order to resolve grievances between themselves. The penalties invoked against such political deviants included fines, suspensions, and expulsions.

The use of the ultimate sanction, explusion, for such political transgressions declined after World War I. The ruling by the New York State insurance authorities that no one should be denied benefits because of political affiliations and the changing class composition of the membership, as we shall see, made widespread use of this penalty for this category of offense too costly. But such deeds did result in fines, denial of the right to hold any office within the organization for a specified number of years, and the transference of the errant member from his branch to a membership-at-large status. In particularly offensive cases, explusion was still utilized.

The Workmen's Circle appeared to have stricter socialist standards for its members than did the Socialist party for its formal adherents during the 1920s and early 1930s. On several occasions branches of the Socialist party appealed to the Workmen's Circle to take no action against Socialists in its ranks who had enrolled as Democrats in order to help their businesses. In 1931 the secretary of the WC was moved to state in his annual report that whereas his organizaiton had expelled persons for engaging in antiunion activities, the Socialist party had allowed the same individuals to continue their membership within the party. He contrasted the disparate ways in which the cases were handled and commented that "our organization always acted in accordance with the principles of the Socialist Party," with the implicit meaning being that such was not the case within the SP.[11]

CHANGING CLASS COMPOSITION

It is important to note the political impact that the WC had upon its nonworking class members. Their involvement in this organization subjected them to a continuing pro unionist and prosocialist influence typically not present in their economic lives outside of the WC. In addition, through them the Workmen's Circle was able to project a pro socialist and pro unionist orientation into the increasingly bourgeois Jewish community. Of course, this type of political impact over the long run could not help but wane as the WC's membership became increasingly middle class in composition. But, in the short and medium run, which in practical terms meant decades, the WC was able to perpetuate and strengthen a type of political orientation among Jews that was not congenial to their economic self-interests.

This change in the homogeneous working-class character of the WC took place amidst a Jewish population that was becoming more middle class in the 1920s; increasingly thereafter this tendency within the organization became even more marked. This was particularly so in the nonmetropolitan areas where the membership of whole branches was entirely or predominantly middle class in composition. The reasons for a nonworker remaining in or joining an essentially working-class organization like the Workmen's Circle were varied. The insurance and death benefits were an attraction. The educational, social, and cultural affairs offered under the auspices of the WC were another incentive. And sentiment, nostalgia, and friendship patterns undoubtedly played their role.

Membership in the Workmen's Circle, particularly for those in largely non-Jewish areas, was also a way of maintaining an identity as a secular Jew. In the confines of the branch, isolated or semiisolated Jews could relax as Jews and feel comfortable in speaking Yiddish with one another. Also, one can speculate that for the Jews who had left the major metropolitan areas, the political outlook of the WC combined in some way with the other aspects of the organization that provided a Jewish identity. For them, the WC was a body that combined Yiddishness and radicalism. In many places with a small Jewish population, the Workmen's Circle became for the "comrades" as its members were called prior to the split in 1930, the institutional source of their Jewish identity. In these areas, lines were sharply drawn in the Jewish community between those who belonged to the local synagogue and those who joined the Workmen's Circle. As a result, the secular and radical aspects of the WC become the features that most distinguished it from the synagogue and thus most likely to be stressed by the WC members in these small communities.

In addition, WCers outside of the major metropolitan areas were more likely to have their socialist positions strengthened by the official pronouncements and organizational literature than was true for their fellow members in the metropolises. In the smaller cities and towns, the WCers were very reliant on the official literature to inform them as to what was transpiring within the Workmen's Circle. Given the fact that Socialists were always in the top leadership and most likely to control the public information and image of the organization, those WCers most dependent on the order's publications for news and views of the WC were being exposed to a socialist perspective. Those most dependent on such publications were typically WCers in the small cities and towns. Members in the big cities like New York, on the other hand, were much more aware and part of the informal and generally conservatizing compromises that increasingly moderated the policies of the organization. It took time, however, before such moderating trends were reflected in the official publications, which meant that members in the hinderlands were being exposed to the older, more socialist Workmen's Circle for a longer period than their metropolitan peers.

In such circumstances, for these WC migrants from the metropolitan areas to become less radical or significantly less radical would mean to become less Jewish. Their animosity toward Judaism, which brought with them as WC radicals into the small towns and cities, was reinforced by the subsequent divisions and distinctions between branch and synagogue, which they helped to maintain. Therefore, secular Jewish businessmen in the less populated areas of Pennsylvania, New York, Ohio, New Jersey, and the South who wanted to retain their Jewish identity had few resources available to help them in this endeavor other than the WC. It would seem likely then that they would be willing to utilize the radicalism of the WC as they interpreted it as one more prop for their Jewish identity. This interpretation makes it easier to understand why, as one knowledgeable historian phrased it in referring to this type of WC membership: ". . . this steadfast loyalty to the radical beliefs of their youth is a striking peculiarity of the Jewish middle class." [12] It should be noted that a disproportionate number of the more radical members of the WC were former workers outside of metropolitan areas. [13]

Whatever the reasons, however, a sizable number of middle-class Jews, including those in the larger metropolitan areas as well as in the towns and smaller cities, found themselves in an organization that propagated pro-socialist and prounion values. These factors not only characterized the values of the WC but its norms as well. The Workmen's Circle and various of its branches apparently expected its middle-class friends to adhere to the order's values and norms in the course of their business affairs. For example, WC employers were expected to hire union labor and facilitate the unionization of their shops. In another example, during a widespread strike of weavers in Paterson, New Jersey, in 1924, Workmen's Circle members in Paterson who owned their own weaving shops were persuaded to cease working in order to help the strike. Those who did not comply were fined. In these circumstances, the middle-class Jews' membership in and allegiance to the WC offset or counteracted to some extent the political interests of their class position.

One should also note that the socialist element and emphasis within the WC did not steadily wane after World War I. Historic events such as the Depression and its impact on the Jewish community, particularly its working class, would at times reinforce this element and aspect. Also, in the latter 1930s and early 1940s, Bundists—

active Socialists—fleeing from Europe joined the WC after their arrival and stiffened its socialist as well as anti-Zionist resolve.

EDUCATION: JEWISH AND SECULAR

Young Jews were another strata that the Workmen's Circle attempted to bring into a socialist environment. The order was concerned about this group not only in terms of its attitude toward socialism but because the organization needed young members in order to survive. In its quest to reach youth for the organization's sake as well as that of socialism's, it created various groups and facilities for the purpose of properly socializing them for membership in the socialist fraternal order and for retaining their commitment within it once they were adults. To this end the WC established schools, summer camps, youth groups, choruses, and dramatic clubs. The schools, however, were at the heart of this network.

The first Workmen's Circle School was established in New York City in 1906. By 1911 more schools had been set up in New York as well as in Chicago and other metropolitan areas. In this year in the greater New York area alone, the student body numbered about 1500. These schools were not designed to substitute for public schools. Classes were only held on Sundays. They were, however, designed to propagate socialism among Jewish youth, primarily the children of immigrant Yiddish-speaking Jews belonging to the Workmen's Circle. Interestingly, during this five-year period, the language of instruction in these schools was English, and there were no Jewish subjects in the curriculum.

These early schools failed, in large part because of the absence of Yiddish and Jewish content. Even radical Jewish parents wanted their children to learn Yiddish and know something about their people. The nature and place of Yiddish and things Jewish in the schools were to become major points of contention in the Workmen's Circle between the assimilationists on the one hand, and various types of nonassimilationists on the other.[14] (We shall explore this further below.)

In 1918, after a period of uncertainty and debate, the Workmen's Circle once again began to establish schools. Similar to the earlier ones, these were not designed to serve as substitutes for public school. Classes were held in the afternoons. Again, similar to the ones that operated in the period from 1906 to 1911, the propagation of socialism and socialist values was regarded by the WC as a prominent goal of the schools. But the schools established in 1918 and afterward differed in a very important regard from their predecessors. These WC educational institutions now gave considerable emphasis to Yiddish and Jewish subjects in the curriculum. This emphasis was to grow with the passage of time.[15]

The Jewish and the socialist missions of the Workmen's Circle schools in the early post–World War I years was reflected in the goals adopted for them at the organization's national convention in 1920. One of the primary objectives of these schools this body asserted was: "To bind the Jewish worker's child to the Jewish working class, and prepare him to carry on the struggle of his parents for a better world." The other major goals cited by the convention were: "To develop among the children the feeling of uprightedness, love of the oppressed and respect for the fighters for freedom [and] . . . To develop idealism and the effort to accomplish great deeds, which is necessary to every child of the oppressed class in his striving for a better order."[16]

Although the schools of the WC, as well as the parent body, were not able to maintain this emphasis on socialism, the decline of socialism in the education of young Jewish children was a gradual process. Young students throughout the 1920s and 1930s were exposed to socialism, but in an increasingly moderate and humanistic form. They also had some awareness of the Jewish labor movement and participated into the latter 1930s in May Day celebrations with labor and socialist groups. There were few other schools in America of the 1920s and 1930s in which young people received such an exposure to socialism. In fact, the WC's Educational Committee complained in the early 1930s that they had difficulty obtaining socialist books for children in the United States because there were so few in existence.

It should be stressed that the ties built by the Workmen's Circle schools between their students and socialism were not only a product of formal education. The daily experience in the classrooms of the WC made the students cognizant of the fact that socialism lived outside of their family. The schools provided evidence that the Jewish community (or at least segments there-of) believed socialism to be important and legitimate. The approximately 75,000 children who attended these schools between 1918 and 1934 were able to reassure one another over the years that their families' adherence to socialism was not unique.[17] In short, the Workmen's Circle educational institutions provided social support along with formal education in the attempt to instill some socialist or socialist-oriented values and principles in the students.

Even the site of at least one important Workmen's Circle educational institution attested to the order's closeness to socialism in the pre-World War II years. The organization's *Mittel Shuleh*—a secondary school—in Manhattan was located in the same building that housed the Socialist party's Rand School. This location had more than symbolic significance. *Mittel Shuleh* students at times ventured into the auditorium of the building to hear socialist orators like Norman Thomas, Algernon Lee, and Harry Laidler. This undoubtedly had an influence in creating among the eavesdroppers an allegiance to socialism or at least to very liberal values.

After World War II socialism continually declined within the schools. Yet in 1946, in the process of reformulating the schools' objectives, socialism found a place on the list as one of the major objectives. Although socialism rarely appeared as such in the classrooms after the latter 1940s, liberalism and humanism did have a relatively prominent place in what had become predominantly Jewish schools. The emphasis on a concern for social justice and equality then was justified on the grounds that these were important factors or conditions for Jewish well-being in the modern world. Thus, under this ideological rationale the Jewish students in the WC were exposed, along with Yiddish and Jewish subjects, to views and perspectives that were friendly and sympathetic to the labor movement, civil rights, civil liberties, and oppressed peoples. Throughout most of America during this postwar period, these were subjects and attitudes that were not at all common in other educational environments. Nor were there many classrooms in the United States, other than some in the WC, that had portraits of Karl Marx on their walls.

By 1950 the WC's educational system contained 92 schools, including kindergartens, elementary schools, and some high schools, and about 37,500 Jewish students at all levels and for various amounts of time received a Workmen's Circle education. In these years, as with the parent body, the class composition of the students changed. The percentage of workers' children in attendance declined, and after World War II the student body was largely made up of the sons and daughters of nonmanual workers, most of whom did not belong to the WC. They saw in the WC schools a means to provide their children with a secular Jewish education.[18]

This change in the class composition of the students' parents was one factor leading to the decreased emphasis on socialism and politics. But, as with the parent organization, middle-class persons in the schools were exposed to positions and perspectives that were sympathetic to socialism and later to labor, civil rights, civil liberties, and oppressed peoples. Such subjects and the attitudes that accompanied them helped to keep alive (particularly in the cold-war era) links in the Jewish community, even if only sentimental in character, between Jews and the Left.

MODERATION AND JEWISHNESS

The decline in the Workmen's Circle commitment to socialism paralleled a similar decline within the Jewish needle trade unions. Prior to World War I the WC had been firmly aligned with socialism and actively assisted the Socialist party and its candidates. After the war the WC's ardent allegiance waned. This decreasing commitment to the Left took place at the same time as the Workmen's Circle developed a more favorable attitude and position toward Jewish concerns and identities. The sources of its transformation from a radical labor fraternal order with Jewish members into a Jewish fraternal order with liberal sentiments and a socialist heritage were its Jewish base and, once established, the way in which it chose to maintain its organizational viability.

The organization's relationship to Yiddish and Jewishness was not a significant issue in the early years of the order's existence. Until about 1915 cosmopolitan and, perhaps, assimilationist Jewish socialists were firmly at the helm of the national organization. As cosmopolitan socialists they viewed with hostility anything that smacked of nationalism, which they defined as Yiddish and Yiddish culture, a feeling of special allegiance to the Jewish community or people, Judaism, and Zionism. Indeed, the very establishment of the Workmen's Circle raised their political anxiety. They did not wish to see an all-Jewish fraternal order established. As one of their number, stated at the organization's national convention in 1915 during the heat of a debate on the Jewish character of the WC schools: "[The convention should] establish once and for all that the *Arbeiter Ring* is not a Jewish institution." [19] The aforementioned non-Jewish Socialist Sunday schools of the WC were concrete testimony to the orientation and the power of the cosmopolitans in the order. Of these early leaders, a later and none too sympathetic Workmen's Circle official wrote: "For them, Jews are not a people and Yiddish is not a language." [20] The great fear of these early cosmopolitans was that if and when the Workmen's Circle embarked on a path leading to a positive relationship to Jewish nationalism or Judaism, such a route would take the WC away from socialism. They were correct in their assessment.

By 1915 the leadership and the policies of these universalistic Jewish socialists was seriously contested. Their rivals in what can be loosely termed the "Jewish faction" had become too numerous and their objections too strenuous for them to be contained by the cosmopolitan socialists. The entrance en masse of Bundist-influenced immigrants was the key factor that turned the tide against the old leadership.

Prior to the Bundists' appearance on the scene, those WC members who desired a more Jewish content in the organization were motivated by a combination of lingering tradition and sentiment. Politically and intellectually it was not too difficult for the cosmopolitan socialist intellectuals to deal with them. The Bundists, however, were different. They were socialists with bona fide credentials. They had a well-developed intellectual and political position. From the Bundists' perspective, Jewishness—which in essence meant Yiddish and Yiddish culture—and socialism were not in conflict but supportive of one another. Given the numerical and political strength of the Bundists and the numbers and sentiments of their allies among the "sentimentalists," it was only a matter of time before the Jewish faction would become the dominant one.

The year 1916 marked the ascendancy of this Bundist-inspired Jewish faction. Then, for the first time in the order's existence, a majority of delegates to the national convention endorsed the position that WC schools should combine socialism, Yiddish, and secular Jewish subjects in the curriculum. Shortly thereafter the Workmen's Circle became transformed into one of the most influential propagators of Yiddish culture in the United States. The order began an extensive Yiddish publishing campaign. It brought out books in Yiddish on political economy, history, and natural sciences. The WC also sponsored Yiddish lecturers on various subjects who were dispatched on national tours. And Yiddish choruses were also established.

All of these endeavors brought the WC closer to a Yiddish and Jewish identity. Recall, too, that they were taking place as the WC's membership was rising. Newer immigrants, among others, were being attracted to an ever more Jewish fraternal order. Once again, as with the Bund in Europe and the Jewish needle trade unions in the United States, a dynamic interaction between a Jewish organization and a Jewish constituency was set into motion, pushing that organization ever more toward a Jewish identification. As the Jewish identification of the WC became more powerful, its association with socialism attenuated.

It is also important to recognize how the emphasis upon Yiddish added to the growing dilemma of the Workmen's Circle—a dilemma of which they were sometimes unaware—from the 1920s on. The *Arbeiter Ring* had come into existence as a socialist fraternal order drawing from a Yiddish-speaking worker base. As such, it was a different kind of fraternal order from the other types in the Jewish community at the time. The others, largely nonpolitical, were divided on the one hand into those that had a religious orientation and a membership of Orthodox Jews and on the other into those that were American or assimilationist in orientation and whose affairs were guided by middle-class Reform or Conservative Jews. The most notable example of this kind of fraternal order was the B'nai B'rith. The Workmen's Circle, by contrast, working class in composition, and socialist, was hostile, or at least not very sympathetic, to religion. What made it Jewish was the fact that its leaders and members were almost entirely Jewish and Yiddish-speaking. (Even during its militant cosmopolitan stage Yiddish was the primary language of discourse at its meetings.)

This was to be the heart of the organization's dilemma after World War I. Realistically, it had little choice but to stress its Yiddish commitment. It could not become an *American* radical fraternal order because there was no call for one between 1900 and 1930. The other radical or labor fraternal orders that did exist in that period were largely made up of one ethnic group, the Finnish one being the most notable example at the time. The Yiddish-speaking members of the WC would not have been comfortable in, nor would they have joined, or remained members of an American or multiethnic radical fraternal order. If the WC had become significantly more positive toward religion, it would have lessened its distinctiveness vis-a-vis the religiously oriented fraternal groups whose members were also largely Yiddish-speaking workers sympathetic to the labor movement. Emulation of the middle-class Jewish fraternal orders was also out of the question. The WC was an immigrant workers' organization, and its policies and programs had to reflect that fact in order for it to maintain its viability. Also, once the WC had commenced its life and grown in strength and resources on the basis of a rather clearly delineated and unique population base, the impetus would be to guard and protect that base. And its base was the secular, radical Yiddish-speaking workers.

There seemed little reason to worry about membership size prior to 1924. The organization, almost from its inception, had experienced a continual growth. Boats from Europe seemed constantly to bring new members. But the flow of immigrants had slowed to a trickle during World War I. After a brief period of revival from 1921 to 1923, immigration laws barred the entrance of masses of Jews to the United States and thus to membership in the Workmen's Circle. The diminution of immigration meant that the WC had to seek its members from among those Jews residing in the United States. Without substantial new immigration of Jews, the organization would soon have to recruit American-born Jews into its ranks. It took little imagination to understand that the American-born in particular and the foreign-born in general who were increasingly acclimating themselves to America would grow to find themselves at odds with or uncomfortable in a Yiddish fraternal order.

By the 1920s the Workmen's Circle had established a unique identity as well as a unique constituency. It was not in a position to adapt readily to changes in its environment. It was a Jewish labor fraternal order that served a Jewish working class clientele, but the only feature that made it Jewish was its Yiddish character. If it did choose to become an American or English-speaking organization, it risked alienating its oldest members, the heart of its body. But if it did not become American and English-speaking, the organization risked annihilation. Yet if it did become American, what would give it its Jewish identity? As with the Jewish unions, a Jewish interest or identity appeared to be an important factor in maintaining the allegiance of and attraction for Jews to the order.

The major way out of this dilemma appeared to be an emphasis on secular Jewishness, which in effect meant Yiddish and Yiddish culture. If the ships would no longer bring Yiddish-speaking immigrants to augment its membership, then the WC would have to resist the

Americanization of its constituency in the United States. The WC became, as noted above, one of the major defenders and promoters of Yiddish, Yiddish literature, and Yiddish culture on the North American continent. In this way, its Yiddish-speaking constituency would be preserved, and its Jewish identity left intact.

Such a course had implicit within it a political cost to its socialist identity. There was nothing inherently proletarian about Yiddish. The seeming identity between Yiddish and the working class was limited to a few short decades in the United States. Similar to the Bund, the *Arbeiter Ring* together with the Socialist Yiddish newspapers did a marvelous job of embellishing and refining Yiddish through its publications, lectures, concerts, and dramatic groups. The WC and its Yiddish Socialist allies in Eastern Europe and America succeeded in making this language and culture acceptable to the Jewish bourgeoisie and intellectuals. And as it became a people's language, it lost its identification as the tongue of a class. As this process unfolded, the Workmen's Circle's emphasis on Yiddish became a lode-star carrying it into the realm of Jewish consciousness and nationalism and away from Jewish socialism.

THE SCHOOLS

The WC *shules* and the change in emphasis between Yiddishness and socialism that had occurred within them since 1920 offer the best examples of the political cost to socialism that the WC paid for its identification with and dependence upon Yiddish and secular Jewishness. The establishment of Yiddish schools, as mentioned above, had originally been opposed by the cosmopolitans in the organization on the grounds that they would eventually become vehicles for Jewish chauvinism. At the 1916 convention at which Yiddish schools were approved, the majority tried to allay these fears and reassure the universalistic socialists. First, the majority stressed that socialism would not be made subordinate to Jewishness in the schools. Radicalism was to have the major emphasis. Second, it argued the Bundist position that the two factors were mutually supportive.

This Jewish majority also invoked other defenses of its position that indicated how important the Jewish or Yiddish issue was to them. The Yiddish schools or *shules* of the WC, it contended, would attract the children of the working-class Jewish parents away from the *Talmud, torahs, and heders* (religious institutions). Indeed, parents in the Workmen's Circle were quite concerned about their children's Jewish identity. Some had even wanted the order to provide bar mitzvah lessons in its schools. Mixed in also with the issue of Jewish identification was one of familial continuity and solidarity. The report of the Educational Committee of the 1916 convention spoke directly to these emotional feelings:

Our children are growing up alien to our language, to the ideals and customs of our people. They look down upon the majority of our people . . . as an inferior culture. Occasionally, their attitude is that of contempt . . . our children should be acquainted with the immense treasures of Jewish culture, old and new . . . that they may be able to continue to create its culture. . . . This education must be free from the spirit of *Atah Behartonu* (the Chosen People) and from Chauvinism.[21]

Recall, too, that the members were aware of the failure of the WC's earlier venture in schooling where the schools had taught socialism but ignored Yiddish.

The Yiddish *shules* were to become a prime instrument in the WC's endeavor to survive as a Jewish organization. These schools and other parts of its cultural and educational program were to be the front line of the order's defense against Americanization. The schools would ensure the existence of an American-born generation of Yiddish-speaking Jews, or so it was hoped, and the survival of a Yiddish Workmen's Circle when the immigrant generation died out.

At the time of the 1920 convention when the schools were established and generally accepted, they were given the mandate to propagate both socialism and Jewishness. The latter, however, was given less priority than the former. It was still a period when the schools' supporters and administrators saw no inherent incompatibility between socialism and Jewishness. This outlook was given expression in one of the leading goals of the schools: "To bind the Jewish worker's child to the Jewish working class." This particular aim touched upon another future problem: It was not only a future generation of Yiddish-speaking Jews that concerned the Workmen's Circle; it was a future generation of Yiddish-speaking working-class Jews. The order had cut out a mighty task for itself, much too large for it in fact. It had not only to resist the Americanization of the immigrant Jews and their progeny but also the movement of its own membership into the middle class, a development that World War I had helped to hasten.

By 1927 a perceptible shift in emphasis had taken place. Yiddishness and Jewishness now were given greater emphasis than socialism. The shift in this direction continued unabated in the following years. By 1937 the WC's educational leaders were proudly and unashamedly pointing out ". . . the national value of our school." Socialism still had a place in the curriculum, but now the official motto of the schools was "the Jewish child to the *Jewish people*." The aim of binding "the Jewish worker's child to the Jewish *working class*" [emphasis mine] was now to be found only in the memories of the "friends" and the historic records of the *Arbeiter Ring*.[22]

By the end of World War II, the development of Jewish consciousness and Jewish nationalism had become the major raisons d'etre of the school system. The 1946 WC convention placed the organization's stamp of approval of what already had occurred and made explicit that the schools should now place: ". . . emphasis on the sense of a *Jewish People*, to which the child's adherence should be developed, and the concept that this People was one though distributed through many lands. It was regarded as desirable that the Jewish child regard his personal destiny as bound up with the destiny of this Jewish people." [23] Socialism was not abandoned but consigned to a minor supporting role. It presence as a general ideal toward which the children should strive was justified on the grounds that socialism was necessary to make the world safe for the free survival of the Jewish people and their culture.

In about 30 years time, the emphasis had completely reversed. The schools' major mission had become the perpetuation of the Jewish culture. The elevation of the Jewish factor in the WC *shules* from the early 1920s through the post-World War II era can be ascertained in part from the nature of the holidays that the official curriculum expected the students to celebrate. In 1920, they were four: Passover, Purim, Hanukkah, and Lag B'omer. All of these had a national or personal connotation to them. By 1958, the WC students were expected to celebrate all Jewish holidays, including those like Rosh Hashana and Yom Kippur which were primarily religious in nature. [24]

CONSERVATIZING PRESSURES

The schools' movement in this direction and the reasons for it mirrored, perhaps in a more accentuated form, the similar changes that had taken place in the organization. The most notable structural change that underlay the shift toward a more Jewish emphasis was the alteration in the origin and class makeup of the student body over time. At the time of the *shules'* establishment, the students had been almost entirely children of European-born, working-class members of the *Arbeiter Ring*. By 1934, the proportion emanating from middle-class homes had increased and only slightly more than half were children of parents who belonged to the Workmen's Circle. After World War II the students were predominantly children of American-born Jews, the majority of whom were neither in the working class nor the Workmen's Circle. [25]

A similar change in the class composition of the membership, although much less accentuated, also took place over these same years. In fact, as early as 1924 a factory owner had attained a position on the National Executive Committee of the WC, its highest executive organ. (He subsequently was expelled for antiunion activities in connection with the functioning of his factory.) [26]

Coincidental and perhaps overlapping with the changing class composition of the Workmen's Circle was another change in the nature of the membership that did little for the organization's ties to socialism. This change emanated from the increasing numbers of Jews who were attracted to the WC on the basis of factors other than socialism. As B. Charney Vladeck, a prominent Jewish Socialist, explained: ". . . as long as the WC was not very strong, people joined not only for the benefits but for the higher purposes as well. Now, however, the Workmen's Circle is a secure place for insurance and other practical services, with the result that there gravitates to it a mass of people remote from radical and social purposes."[27]

The growing numbers and influence of the middle class and benefit seekers in the WC and the schools made it increasingly difficult to pursue an activist working-class policy such as striving toward economic equality, which had been one of the organization's earliest aims. Instead, the socialism of the WC became blander, less focused, more abstract, and more humanistic—in short, more congenial to middle-class sensibilities and interests. The maintenance of an emphasis on socialism under such circumstances would become an issue that would divide the membership and eventually cause the departure of many of the middle class from the organization and the schools.

The order could ill afford to lose such people or, for that matter, any of its members in quantity. After the mid-1920s it soon became quite clear that the WC was not a growing organization. A Left-Right split in the 1920s had resulted in the departure of several thousands, and, probably more important, the era of mass immigration of Eastern European Jews had come to an end. The importance of these two factors—one political and the other demographic—can be seen in the membership statistics of the WC. In 1925 it reached its peak with more than 87,000 after years of almost continual growth. From that point on the organization's growth stagnated and then began to decline. By the 1930s its rolls had stabilized at from 70,000 to 72,000 members.

But it was not only a question of raw numbers. Organizational stability and, in the long run, survival depended upon the recruitment and retainment of middle-class Jews. Although the large bulk of Yiddish-speaking immigrants were still workers in the 1920s, increasing numbers were entering or aspiring to enter the middle class, and this was even truer for their children. The WC was hard put to ignore this development and the need to recruit from among the younger and more middle-class population. The nearly constant increase in the average age of the membership was a stark indicator of what the future held in store if the WC did not reach this group.

In such circumstances, a change in policy and orientation seemed the only way in which the WC could retain its organizational viability. The question then became which of its major two defining characteristics would it modify—Yiddishness, or Jewishness, on the one hand, or socialism on the other. The substantial alteration of both would mean the obliteration of its organizational identity. It would also mean that its distinctiveness vis-a-vis other fraternal orders, such as B'nai B'rith, in which socialism and Yiddishness were not given emphasis would be substantially reduced. Socialism, rather than Yiddishness, if there was to be a choice, appeared to be the more likely candidate for alteration for several reasons.

First was the aforementioned increase in the number of Jewish bourgeoisie in the membership and in the Eastern European Jewish community, as well as those who joined because of the benefits. All signs in the 1920s indicated that this growth would be a continuing phenomenon. Second was the exodus in the 1920s of the more radical "friends." This stemmed from the battle within the order between the Socialists and their sympathizers, or the right wing, on the one hand and the Communists and their allies, or the left wing, on the other. This struggle mirrored the one that was taking place in the garment unions at the same time and often involved the same people. By the end of 1929 when the final split occurred, more than 10,000 had exited from the organization. (Not all of these were left wingers; some were those who had become disheartened with the continual political bickering and infighting.) One of the most serious casualties in this battle were the *shules*. In 1926 the left wing captured the vast majority of the *shules* and took them along when the final break occurred. (The educational system was later rebuilt.)

Actually, the split between the left and right wings of the organization only exacerbated a rightward drift evident in the organization before World War I. The order became increasingly less severe in sanctioning or weeding from its ranks members who did not or would not maintain a firm allegiance to socialism. This meant that the numbers of those within the WC who deviated from such a commitment would grow, as it did in the 1920s and 1930s. The use of expulsion for enrolling in or voting for candidates of the Democratic and Republican parties had also decreased prior to the war. The decision of the insurance authorities of New York State that the WC risked losing its right to issue insurance if policy holders were deprived of benefits because of political-party affiliations made the order less willing to use this ultimate sanction for such deviations. This meant more nonsocialists in the membership. (Expulsion was not totally abandoned despite the ruling with respect to insurance and policy holders. The WC, like other organizations, knew how to evade the spirit of legal or formal restraints although adhering to their letter.)

In the 1920s and 1930s an ever-growing number of cases concerning members' association with the Democratic and Republican parties as well as antiunion activities were brought before the National Grievance Committee of the National Executive Committee, the WC's ultimate arbitrator of disputes. In many of the cases, the political deviant defended himself on the grounds that he was ignorant of the organization's stricture against supporting Republican and Democratic candidates or parties. As the number of instances of such political violations grew over the years, the penalties imposed by the branches and the National Grievance Committee became less severe. Such a relationship between offenses and punishment was symptomatic of the order's inability to adhere to a socialist position.[28]

The Workmen's Circle's commitment to Yiddish and secular Jewishness, in contrast to its allegiance with socialism, became a less divisive issue in time. One of the last major debates on the order's Jewish and Yiddish orientation occurred in 1931. Interestingly and curiously, the editor of the largest Yiddish-language daily in the world, Abraham Cahan of the *Jewish Daily Forward*, was the loudest and more prominent critic of the WC with respect to the role that Yiddish and Jewish concerns were playing in the WC. Focusing on the schools, Cahan argued that their Yiddish orientation inhibited their students from entrance into the cultural mainstream of American life. And, echoing the cosmopolitan contention of a decade or so earlier, he charged that the Jewish and Yiddish emphasis of the WC curriculum diverted Jewish youth from socialism. But by the mid-1930s such attacks and such debates had subsided. The rising Hitler menace muted the voices of the assimilationist critics while stirring the nationalism of the WC members and the entire American Jewish community as well.[29] Yiddish was now a symbol of pride and unity. For the Workmen's Circle it was also, in this context, a means by which it could maintain close links with its Jewish constituency.

There was a political consequence, however. As Yiddish and a positive attitude toward it no longer differentiated working-class from nonworking-class Jews in the order or in the community, an organization that was so closely tied to and identified with Yiddish found it increasingly difficult to pursue politics that were negatively regarded by an ever-growing sector of its Yiddish-speaking membership. It was much easier to avoid the divisive issues centering around socialism and stress the unifying factor of Yiddish.

The departure of the left wing gave greater political weight and influence to those tendencies and elements within the order that were moving it toward moderation, in effect, eliminating from the organization a more radical pressure group. Coincidentally, this exodus also heightened the already important position of the leadership of the needle trades unions' leaders within the Workmen's Circle. The leaderships of both organizations had always been close. In fact, many, such as Abraham Baroff, the first provisional secretary of the WC and later general secretary of the ILGWU, were officers in both the WC and their respective unions. This type of relationship was not limited to the top officeholders of these bodies. Many, if not most, of the Workmen's Circle friends, particularly in the larger metropolitan areas, were also members of garment unions. In fact, during and after the Left-Right battle in the WC, the needle trades union leadership did its best to recruit its unionists into the Workmen's Circle. All of this meant that through the 1920s and 1930s, the political attitudes and views of the rightward moving garment-union chieftains, who had fought their own battles with their more radical opponents, became increasingly the attitudes and views that informed the direction of the Workmen's Circle.

In the 1930s the rightward shift was also facilitated and hastened by the policies and programs of the Democratic and Socialist parties. The WC's leadership, similar to the garment union leaders, found the style and policies of FDR's New Deal to be generally to their liking. Concurrently, areas of differences with the Socialist party arose. The Workmen's Circle officially broke its lifelong association with the Socialist party in 1940 over the issue of the party's opposition to America's entrance into the war against Hitler.

By the latter 1930s and early 1940s, the nonsocialist course of the Workmen's Circle was clear. The Arbeiter Ring, especially after Hitler's advent to power, moved increasingly to become a Jewish interest group. It successfully drew close to the organized Jewish community—a community that had kept it at arm's length owing to the order's youthful radicalism. A deemphasizing of socialism and an emphasis on Jewish interests accelerated the Workmen's Circle's intergration into the bourgeois-dominated Jewish community.

The Circle's position on a national homeland for the Jews also softened, bringing the organization closer to the position of the Jewish mainstream in America. Although officially adhering to the position that it was non-Zionist—a position it still claims today—the Workmen's Circle enthusiastically supported Israel and contributed millions of dollars through the United Jewish Appeal and the purchase of Israeli bonds. In fact, its stance vis-a-vis a Jewish homeland had moved so far that in the post–World War II decades, the order could comfortably cooperate at various levels with its former Zionist rival, the Farband, the fraternal order of the Labor Zionists. The two organizations agreed to share one teachers' seminary for instructors of their respective schools. They also used some of the same books in both educational systems. And in some instances they shared the same members as well.

After World War II adherence to socialist principles was neither a formal nor an informal requirement for membership and good standing within the Workmen's Circle. The drive for membership focused on quantity. The order, for example, advertised among Jews for family circles and cousin clubs to affiliate. Facilities for bar mitzvahs were also brought to the Jewish public's attention. Also, in the quest to survive as a Jewish fraternal order, the Workmen's Circle sent out to the Jewish community mass mailings that were followed up by specially trained "membership-insurance counsellors." These counsellors were taught to attract Jews into the WC in part on the basis of the insurance benefits that would become available upon membership.[30] Even the socialists within the order were forced to appeal to Jewish interests to influence the behavior of their fellow WC members. Thus, in an attempt to increase the circulation of the Left-leaning periodical the *Call* a group of Workmen's Circle socialists wrote to their brother members, "We feel that you would look forward eagerly to read your weekly copy of the Call as anxiously as you anticipate your morning lox, cream cheese and bagel sessions."[31]

In the 1960s and the 1970s the Workmen's Circle was a respected member of the Jewish community in America. Although it continued and continues to advocate liberal and humane positions on the issues of the day, the Workmen's Circle radicalism has been consigned to the dustbin of history, resurrected only to show how rambunctious the order was during its stormy youth. The transition from a radical and antinationalist labor fraternal order into a Jewish and liberal one was not, it should be stressed, a change that was planned. It happened because the Jewish community became increasingly bourgeois and nationalist. The WC would have been unable to maintain its viability as a popular organization among Jews had it maintained its socialist identification.

THE COMMUNIST-ORIENTED SUBCULTURE

The International Workers Order (IWO), or the *Internationaler Arbeiter Ordn*, formally came into existence as a radical labor fraternal order (and mutual-benefit society) in 1930. It was largely a product of the Left-Right split within the Workmen's Circle. The IWO was closely associated with the Communist party, and many of its leaders were undoubtedly Communists. The IWO, however, was not the first experience that Jews further to the left of the WC had in erecting the framework of a socialist milieu. Prior to its emergence Jews whose politics were closer to those of the Communist than to the Socialist party had built various groups and institutions similar to those found within the Workmen's Circle.

One of the earliest of these was the Jewish *Freiheit Gesang Ferein*, or Freiheit Chorus. The Freiheit Chorus was formed initially by Jewish leftists associated with the newspaper, the *Freiheit*. In 1923 it was formally established in New York City. Shortly thereafter the number of such singing societies increased to 16 and were to be found in virtually every city that had a considerable Yiddish-speaking population. The Freiheit Chorus, whose name changed to the Jewish People's Choruses during World War II, survived into the 1950s. The Freiheit Chorus was politically under the influence of the Jewish section of the Communist party, although many of the individual chorus members were not themselves Communists.

The *Freiheit Gesang Ferein* was not an isolated phenomenon. After it was organized similar singing societies associated with the Workmen's Circle and the Labor Zionists were also developed and similarly spread throughout Yiddish-speaking communities in the United States. Also, in the Communist-party orbit, nearly every foreign-language grouping had its own chorus or musical unit. In fact, it was not until 1933 that the first English-language chorus associated with the Communist party came into being. But of them all, the largest and most famous was the Jewish *Freiheit Gesang Ferein.*

The Freiheit Chorus served several political functions. For the chorus members themselves, it served the important function of bringing together their love for song, their affection for Yiddish, and their radical political orientations. In the context of the Singers Society, each of these aspects reinforced one another. The Freedom Singers also performed a similar function for their audiences. Yiddish-speaking radicals found in the Freedom Singers Society an enjoyable social outlet in which they could hear with pleasure songs in Yiddish dealing with a radical or labor theme. The existence of these choruses made it less necessary for Yiddish-speaking radicals to venture outside their political social milieu for the satisfaction of social needs. This meant less contact with nonradicals and more interaction with fellow radicals. The end result was the strengthening of their ties and commitment to radicalism.

The chorus's function of binding Jews to radicalism or a radical perspective was most evident in the towns and cities outside of the major Yiddish-speaking population centers. Jews who migrated to such areas were largely businessmen. In the 1920s and 1930s their social position as well as their small numbers and the fact of their Jewishness precluded their membership in unions, their formation of radical parties, or their joining of existing radical groups, which were few and far between in their environments. In such circumstances, the Freiheit Chorus became a convenient, expedient, and pleasurable way to retain contact with Yiddish radicalism. Even as their own radicalism became more of memory than a reality, the choruses were a constant reminder and social reinforcement, sometimes the only one, that served to link them and their families to a radical perspective. The Communist party benefited from these links as well. Although the Freedom Singers and their audiences in the towns and smaller cities were generally not members of the party, the choruses stimulated not only sentimental links with radicalism but financial contributions for the coffers of the party, its affiliates, or various campaigns as well.[32]

The Communist party became well aware of the various benefits that it and radicalism received from the Freiheit Chorus and its counterparts in other language sections. It gave its own (perhaps inflated) assessment of their ideological function in the *Daily Worker* of January 17, 1934: "The chorus is one of the most popular mediums for reaching the masses. The capitalist class through the churches . . .

use this medium for lulling the workers. The revolutionary movement uses it for rousing the workers against their oppressors."

THE COOPS

Another social structure associated with the Yiddish-speaking Communists illustrates the importance of institutions in the building of a radical subculture. This was the cooperative housing project, the United Workers Cooperative Colony, or as it was popularly known, "the Coops." This was built in the late 1920s on Allerton Avenue in the Bronx and at the time of its completion contained about 750 apartments that housed several thousand people. The inspiration and the leadership for the Coops came from youthful immigrant Yiddish-speaking Jewish workers who were Communists or pro-Communists and who had had previous experience in cooperative endeavors in the United States. The *Morning Freiheit*, then a Yiddish-language Communist newspaper, provided some financial assistance and much of the publicity necessary to bring the Coops into existence. (By 1945 the Coops were no longer cooperative housing. Financial exigencies caused their sale to private owners.[33])

The Communists and their supporters did not have a monopoly on cooperative housing projects in this period. Other Left Jewish groups also had their own or at least lived in cooperative housing where their political position was the dominant one. The Amalgamated Clothing Workers Association sponsored a cooperative housing project in which Socialists were the leading political element. The Labor Zionists also had their own, the Farband Houses. Each of these cooperative housing endeavors strengthened and perpetuated the Jewish Left subculture. The Allerton Avenue Coops, however, the focus of our discussion here, was probably the best known and the most overtly political of them all.

The resident population of the Coops, particularly in the earlier years of its existence, was very homogeneous in ethnic and social-class composition as well as in its politics. The tenants were almost all immigrant Yiddish-speaking working-class Jews. The vast majority were trade unionists, generally members of the garment unions. Politically they were largely Communist or pro-Communist. The weight of this concentrated homogeneity, by itself, would probably have sustained over time a strong consensus as to political ideology, values, and norms. But the production and maintenance of such a consensus was not left solely to the normal social processes that would have evolved from this kind of population. Conscious political decisions, policies, and political substructures within the Coops reinforced the natural homogeneity so as to better ensure the existence of a Communist-oriented subculture.

The very process of becoming a tenant was something that combined unofficial election with official selection. The public reputation of the Coops in the 1920s and 1930s ensured that most who chose to live there would bring with them a positive political orientation. A pro-Communist tenant-selection committee and Board of Directors made this process of self-selection a less fallible one. This does not mean that political deviants were absent from the Coops. There were among the tenants individuals who voted for capitalist parties, but their numbers were small, and their public profile was generally quite low. Those political deviants who did become known, particularly when they were Communist renegades such as Lovestoneites or Trotskyists, experienced a great deal of public censure, and in some cases they moved out.

Organized activities and organizations abounded within the Coops, and almost all of them had some political content, which in essence meant a Communist or radical content. The biggest and most important holiday celebrated by the Coops' residents was May Day. On this occasion hundreds of children and their parents would turn out to march in the big parade to Union Square. As one participant remembered it: ". . . the kids from the Coops had their special place, singing, chanting slogans, marching with pride behind our own bands and our own banners." The following day, in notes to the public schools explaining their children's absence on May 1, the parents typically wrote: "Please excuse my daughter/son for being absent on May First. It was a worker's holiday." [34] Along with participation in the May Day festivities, Coops residents would also involve themselves in nearby strikes and demonstrations for liberal and progressive causes. These included the struggles to save Sacco and Venzetti, the Scottsboro Boys, and the Spanish Republic as well as more local ones to prevent evictions and to integrate municipal swimming pools.

The organizations within the Coops ran the gamut from children to adult, from literary to sports, and from scientific and cultural to overtly political. There were choral and drama groups, dance workshops, string ensembles as well as various committees that sponsored lectures. In all of these, radical politics played some role. In the choral groups, Left songs and Red Army songs would be sung. Even while engaging in sports activities outside of the Coops, athletic teams from there would make their politics known. For example, while playing basketball, the Coops players would wear shirts emblazoned with the slogans "Free Tom Mooney" or "Free the Scottsboro Boys."

The Coops also housed the largest schools of the International Workers Order in the nation. In these *shules* the students would learn Yiddish as well as radical and labor history and politics. The Coops also had its own Communist party groups for young people commencing with the Young Pioneers who started its members on the road to the Communist party by inducting children at the age of eight.

In this milieu, children and adolescents did not regard political radicalism as something to hide or be ashamed of. It was part of the value system of their social world—a world populated by family, friends, and adults who were proud of their politics. Thus, probably nowhere else in America but in the area of the Coops could a five-year old have the following dialogue with his public school teacher: " 'I see you live in the Coops. Are you a Communist?' " " 'Sure,' " he replied, drawing himself up to his full five year height. " 'I've been a Communist for a long time!' "[35]

In the Coops it took no special effort for a young person coming of age to be a Leftist, which in the 1930s and early 1940s generally meant a Communist or a pro-Communist. The youth who adopted this political orientation were not rebels or deviants. They were conformists with respect to the world that mattered to them, a world that met their social, cultural, and emotional needs—the Coops. As one Coop resident reminisced: ". . . it created a sectarianism beyond belief, and a false sense of security for far-out ideas. . . . In a sense, it was an artificial island, an illusion to live here. You could make your whole life revolve around the Coops."[36] And, as another asserted: "We in the Coops were convinced that we were the mainstream, and it was only after we moved out that we found what the real world was like."[37] In the Coops becoming a Communist then was not a blow in the conflict of generations but instead an assertion of generational continuity.

The following description by a person I interviewed, a former resident, of his boyhood years in the Coops illustrates the social and political processes that operated to produce and maintain Communist conformers:

At the age of 8, I, along with many of my friends, joined the Young Pioneers, the children's section of the Communist Party. At the age of 15, you graduated into the Young Communist League. All of my friends were in the Young Pioneers. Within it, we had a social club and hockey team. I was the goalie for my team. We also had our own publication.

There was a library in the Coops and as you might expect it was a radical library. We attended a nearby public school, PS 96, and when it came to May Day the school would empty out as all the kids would be marching with the Young Pioneers in the May Day parade.

His case also illuminates the mechanisms that came into play when a political deviant appeared in the community, even when the deviant was 12 years old. These mechanisms surfaced in the case of our informant when, at the age of 12 with the guidance of his older brother, he proclaimed himself to be a Trotskyist.

When I formally announced myself as a Trotskyist to my friends in the Young Pioneers, these twelve year old kids behaved as Stalinists, just like their parents. I was cut dead. They did not talk to me and they would have nothing to do with me in school. Needless to say, I could no longer be on the Young Pioneers' hockey team. I had no friends. I was friendless. Later, when I and several others tried to distribute Trotskyist literature in the Coops, the literature would be torn from our hands and we would be chased or beaten up. Adult Trotskyists were forced to move out of the Coops if they were found out.

I should also mention the reaction of my aunt to my conversion. We loved each other dearly especially her as she had no children of her own. When I became a Trotskyist and told that to my loving aunt she took my pictures off the wall and stopped talking to me, her twelve year old nephew that she loved so dearly. And she never spoke to me again after that.

Another activist who spent part of his boyhood in the Coops also remarked on the social pressure to conform to the appropriate ideology. In his case, some Coops neighbor women overheard him talking about Trotsky in a noncritical manner. Upon hearing this, they quickly went to his mother, as in other communities they might have if overhearing a child's plans to shoplift or commit truancy, in order to warn her of the bad attitude of her son.

The Coops residents, both children and adults, had a political impact upon those who lived outside of the cooperative. They made their neighbors more open to and more receptive of radicalism by helping them to resist evictions and by opening apartments in the Coops to those whose finances left them without a place to stay. In the public schools the large number of Coopniks and their unabashed radicalism influenced and swayed their fellow students. One Jewish Leftist, interviewed as part of this study and a resident of the Coops, attributed his own shift to the Left to the contact and communication that he had had with many of the ideological classmates from the Coops.

Radicalism within the Coops waned by the latter 1940s and 1950s. This diminution of radical politics was largely due to forces outside of the cooperative housing project. One should also note that after 1945, when it was no longer a cooperative, the residents had no official influence over the selection of new tenants. It is reasonable to assume that the newcomers were therefore less committed to the Left than were the older residents. However, even though the Coops did not produce Communists in the 1950s and 1960s to the extent they had in earlier decades, the population in this housing project did contain some Leftists and, in the 1960s, New Leftists as well. Coopniks also continued to involve themselves in struggles on behalf of unions and blacks. In 1977 the city of New York took official recognition of the Coopniks' contributions in this regard and on the occasion of the 50th anniversary dinner of the projects designated that day as Workers Cooperative Colony Day.[38]

THE INTERNATIONAL WORKERS ORDER

The International Workers Order (IWO) was another fraternal order that augmented the institutional infrastructure of the Jewish Left. The IWO came into existence in 1930. Its founders were former left-wing dissidents from the Workmen's Circle. Their politics were those of or close to those of the Communist party.[39]

The IWO, though founded by Jews, quickly became a multinational fraternal order. The non-Jewish foreign language and foreign-born fraternal groups that became a part of the IWO generally were linked to or associated with the Communist party. Jews, however, throughout the slightly more than two decades of the IWO's existence constituted the single largest nationality. From 1930 through 1942 almost all of the Jewish IWO members were located in the English (language) Section, the biggest section and in the Jewish (Yiddish language) Section, the order's second largest unit. In 1942 the Jews from the English Section joined with those in the Jewish Section. In 1944, the Jewish Section was reorganized and took the name, Jewish People's Fraternal Order (JPFO). From that point until the formal dissolution of the IWO in 1954, the JPFO was the largest unit within the order. The Jewish membership in the IWO was at its peak in late 1947 when it reached about 60,000, approximately one-third of the entire order at the time.

The IWO served as a central focus of a Jewish Left subculture. Similar to its rival, the Workmen's Circle, the International Workers Order sponsored lectures, classes, choruses, dramatic groups, and social events. The order, like the WC, also operated or endorsed Yiddish-language schools and a number of summer camps for adults and children. In fact, most of the Jewish Section's (later JPFO) schools, teachers, and camps in the early years had formerly been part of the Workmen's Circle. They had been captured from the WC in 1926 by left-wing dissidents who had brought them into the IWO when it was organized four years later.

The relationship between the International Workers Order and Communism and the Communist party was similar in ways to the pre–World War I relationship between the Workmen's Circle and Socialism and the Socialist party. The promotion of Communism, the struggle of the working class, and the eradication of ethnic and racial prejudice figured prominently among the goals of the IWO. In most cases the policies and public positions of the IWO on the issues of the day were very similar, if not identical, to those of the Communist party. One resolution of the 1938 convention of the IWO, for example, stated that ". . . the Convention considers sympathy with and support of the Soviet Union a natural function of every member of the Order." Communist party members and in many instances Communist party leaders such as Earl Browder belonged to the International Workers Order. Conversely, many of the leaders of IWO such as General Secretary Max Bedacht were Communists.

The nature of the IWO's origin and its links to the Communist party caused it to be a more radical fraternal order than was the WC in the 1930s and 1940s. First, the initial IWO members were left-wing members of the Workmen's Circle. This meant that those who remained in the WC were the more conservative members. Second, the respective political ties of each fraternal order made a difference. The WC's identification and alliance was primarily with the right wing of the Socialist party and with Socialists en route to becoming (or who actually were) non-Socialists. The IWO's ties, on the other hand, were with the Communist party. Although the CP was not consistently socialist in its politics, it was still more socialist than the right-wing Socialists and ex-Socialists. Thus, the IWO members were pulled to the Left by this political connection. A third factor pushing the IWO in this direction was its rivalry with the WC. In the process of staking out its own identity and competing for a similar constituency, the IWO, in its earlier years especially, emphasized its radical politics.

The IWO's membership, however, was not limited to Communists. Non-Communists did belong although it is difficult to ascertain with any degree of accuracy the proportion of the members that they represented at any given time. As had been true for the WC, the principal attractions for non-Communists as well as Communists were the low-cost medical and life insurance programs that the IWO offered and its active fraternal life. It is important to note that not all Communists in the leadership of the IWO viewed these benefits solely as lures for the naive. Prior to the advent of Social Security in the latter 1930s, these Communists considered ". . . the development of the most effective fraternal insurance a duty of revolutionary leadership." In accord with this position, the IWO actively campaigned in the 1930s for federal social insurance programs. It was their position also that: "The supplying of fraternal life and fraternal benefits is the basic purpose of the Order. An approach to the problems of leadership in the Order which makes it appear that the supplying of fraternal benefits and fraternal life is merely an excuse for the organization and not its purpose will shut the door of the organization to the broad mass."[40] It is interesting to point out, however, that in 1951 Rubin Salzman, general secretary of the JPFO, credited the order's low-cost insurance rates with attracting many members.[41]

The various links between the IWO and the Communist party became the weapons that state and federal authorities and the media as well utilized to kill the order. In 1947 it was placed on the Attorney General's list of subversive organizations. In 1950 the state of New York petitioned the state supreme court requesting the liquidation of the IWO on the grounds that it was a Communist-dominated organization. After a lengthy court battle the IWO lost.

In 1954 it was liquidated, and all of its assets were seized. Ironically, prior to this the United States government had, owing to legal measures taken by the order, removed its name from the Attorney General's list. The stripping away of its charter to sell insurance was the last and fatal blow suffered by the IWO. This fatal blow had been preceded by others that had developed in the period of anti-Communist hysteria in the late 1940s and early 1950s. At one point after the order was taken off the Attorney General's list, Eisenhower's At-

torney General Herbert Brownell threatened IWO members with deportation. Such attacks led to a decline in membership—annual membership went from 163,802 in 1948 to 135,769 in 1951—and were
climaxed with the above mentioned coup de grace. It should be noted,
however, that even after the formal demise of the IWO, various
members in the larger cities carried on its tradition by organizing independent cultural clubs and by operating Left-oriented Yiddish
schools.[42]

The IWO provided a social world for its Jewish (and non-Jewish)
members in which Communist and Left ideals were a central ideological focus. To the extent that IWO members could meet their social,
cultural, and educational needs and interests within the order, they
were insulated from contaminating contact with bourgeois social institutions, and their interaction with nonbelievers was limited. Immersion in such a social world, as in the Coops, facilitated the acceptance by the members of Left ideals and ways of interpreting the
world.

The Communist leadership of the International Workers Order was
well aware of the political benefits that could be derived from the construction of such an enclosed social world. In a memorandum entitled
"Guiding Policy for the Communists in Their Leadership and Work in
the International Workers Order," the author(s) state:

An effective club life . . . makes these masses seek in the Order not only protection through insurance but also friendship, social life, entertainment, advice on daily problems, information and so forth. Such an effective club life
makes it possible to draw into the activities of the Order the whole families of
members. In the organizing and guiding of the life and activities of these
masses of men, women, youth and children lies the tremendous possibility of
Bolshevik work presented to the Communists as the leaders of the Order. We
can influence and educate the masses; we can overcome their mutual prejudices which capitalist education has generated in them through racial, religious or political miseducation; we can make these masses an active force in
the struggle for progress and class consciousness. . . . An internal life and activities based upon the broadest possible mass policy will make the Order an
instrument to break down among the masses fear of or prejudice against Communist leadership. It would instead establish confidence in that leadership
and enable it to teach the masses in the Order to think and to act progressively.[43]

The Jewish Communists, particularly those who spoke Yiddish,
within the IWO were probably more of a self-contained or insulated
group than their Socialist counterparts within the Workmen's Circle.
The latter, by the middle to late 1930s, were becoming more moderate
in their views, more accepting of and acceptable to the Jewish middle
class, and more receptive to American life and institutions. Those associated with the IWO, on the other hand, generally differed with
their Socialist peers on all of these points. Conversely, this meant that

members of the IWO were likely to be more estranged from the general Jewish community than were the WC friends.

Also, the IWO was to some degree influenced by Communist norms concerning interaction with nonmembers. The party expected that such interaction was to be kept to a minimum and strongly encouraged its members to choose their friends and even their spouses from among fellow believers. A marriage between two Communist party members was referred to as a "progressive marriage." There were also what might be termed "progressive divorces," where political differences figured in the dissolution of marriages. Actually, activists in both the CP and the SP were very likely to have politically homogeneous circles of friends and marriages. It almost naturally followed from their degree of political commitment and their lack of time and energy to maintain meaningful social ties with nonbelievers. But the CP buttressed the normal social processes with a quasi-official stance on the issue of non-CP interaction.

The Communist party's social policy made eminent sense from a sociological point of view. Once the social life of a believer, regardless of the nature of the belief, is totally encapsulated within a network of fellow believers, departure from the church or party is made much more difficult. Withdrawal, whatever else the cost, entails the loss of friends and isolation. One Jewish member of the Labor Youth League (LYL), a Communist party youth organization, described the impact of the social cost of leaving the party at the time of the trial of Rudolph Slansky, the Jewish Communist party leader of Czechoslovakia, in 1952 and 1953. When he began to raise doubts about the trial and his commitment to the CP the anxiety concerning his social life mounted. "I was fearful in a way because I had built a whole life around it, almost all my friends were in the LYL and I had built my whole life around it. I knew what would happen if I continued to raise serious questions about it [the Slansky trial]. I would lose all my friends."

He was right. Ostracism of apostates was standard Communist policy. After all, the party in non-Communist countries had few other sanctions that it could bring to bear against such people. To have allowed the party faithful to retain social contact with those who departed would have lowered the cost of leaving and created doubts about their own membership. In many instances marriages would dissolve when one spouse left the CP and the other did not.

Shunning former members was not limited to social contact, it also extended into the economic realm as well. There were many in the Communist party who owed their livelihoods to the Communists. These were often small businessmen and professionals whose clientele contained a significant number of party members and sympathizers. Quitting the CP meant for them a severe economic sacrifice. The same was also true for those functionaries and writers who were employed by the Communist party.

The social walls around the Yiddish-speaking Communist party members in and around the IWO were thicker than those of the English-speaking members. Their immersion in Yiddish culture effectively cut them off from American life. Their adherence to Communism tended to separate them from nonparty members in the Yiddish-speaking community, making them socially dependent upon the Communist party and Yiddish-speaking Communists and Communist sympathizers. The small businessmen, professionals, writers, and others who relied upon Communists and pro-Communists in the Yiddish community for their jobs were also more closely tied to the party than their English-speaking peers. The FBI, according to one informant, was forced into the role of an employment agency for Yiddish-speaking members who were contemplating leaving the party. In order to help them, the FBI would canvas the Yiddish community for persons and businesses willing to give them employment.

It was not surprising then to find in the 1940s and the subsequent decades that Yiddish-speaking Communists were among the party's most faithful followers. Their immersion in a Yiddish Communist subculture had produced a rather loyal following for the party in general and for Yiddish Communism in particular. The role of ideology and politics, however, in the post–World War II era was undoubtedly subordinate to the decades-long social network that they had forged. And the IWO was a central institution in this network and Yiddish radical subculture.[44]

This was not the only way in which the IWO benefited the Communist party. Funds from the IWO and its members proved helpful in the maintenance of various CP institutions. One of the major beneficiaries of the IWO's largesse was the then-Communist Yiddish daily, the *Morning Freiheit*. From 1944 through 1946, for example, the IWO paid the *Freiheit* $35,140 for advertising. It also purchased in the same time period $31,651 worth of advertising from the *Daily Worker*. These expenditures, it should be noted, were entirely legal. Yiddish-speaking members were also encouraged to subscribe to the *Freiheit*. The IWO also sponsored fund-raising appeals for the Scottsboro boys, for antiwar campaigns, and for training persons to fight in the Spanish Civil War. This type of financial support to the Communist party and its related organs and campaigns provided one of the most important grounds for New York State's illegitimate liquidation of the order.[45]

THE IWO SCHOOLS

The IWO's influence, however, was not solely limited to the immigrant Yiddish-speaking generation, although this was its most important base. Similar to the Workmen's Circle, the IWO developed institutions to reach and socialize the American-born generation to its ideological perspective. It was well aware of the necessity to counteract the inroads of capitalist ideology among the younger generation. It was quite explicit concerning the political function that its youth groups were to perform. "The children's groups of the IWO represent a collective effort of our organization to help the individual parent members to solve the problems of developing their children into conscious members of the working class." [46] This ideal, however, was to become progressively more difficult to realize as the number of its members, particularly the number of its members' children in or en route to the middle class, continually increased. The most important of the vehicles that the order established or encouraged to perform this important political socialization function were schools and summer camps.

The IWO had an extensive school system. At one point in the 1930s, there were about 100 elementary and three secondary schools within it. In 1943 it added the School of Higher Jewish Education, *Kursn*, to the system in order to provide Yiddish teachers for the schools. In 10 years Kursn produced 62 graduates. The enrollments in the other schools of the IWO varied. At the height of their popularity in the early 1950s the IWO *shules* had an enrollment of between 6000 and 7000. [47]

The (Jewish) IWO schools in several respects resembled those of the Workmen's Circle, particularly those that existed during the WC's most radical period. The IWO schools emphasized Yiddish and deemphasized religion, as did those of the Workmen's Circle. The IWO schools in the 1930s and 1940s, however, gave more emphasis to labor and radical politics than did their counterparts established by the Workmen's Circle.

The socializing role of the *shules*, particularly as they interacted with other institutions of the Jewish Left, was clearly exemplified in the life of a former leading Communist, who was interviewed for this study. His parents had been active in the Jewish revolutionary movement in Russia. After coming to the United States, they were not active in politics. However, they did read the *Freiheit*, belong to the left-wing of the Workmen's Circle, and send their 11-year-old son to a left-wing *shule*.

I dare say that my original contact with the left wing, socialism and ultimately the Communist movement came from the fact that I was a pupil in the left wing Yiddish shule. I went on to the secondary school, a middle shule in Harlem until I was about 14 or there about. And I suppose my entry into the revolutionary movement, and I say that somewhat jocularly, was when I became an officer of the children's committee for miners' relief [there] in 1927 at the age of 14. That's where I trace the origins of my revolutionary career.

In 1950 the Jewish People's Fraternal Order of the IWO, for practical political reasons, formally dissociated itself from the *shules*. (If they were JPFO assets, they ran the chance of being seized by the State of New York. Also, in this period it was not wise to be formally associated with an organization considered by the media and govern-

mental authorities to be Communist or Communist-dominated.) They
continued to function, however, operated as independent entities by
groups made up of parents and others, who were usually former
members of the JPFO concerned with the secular, Jewish, and radical
education of Jewish children. Such activity had the unintended consequence of maintaining them in an organized Jewish Left context.
Under this new arrangement the *shules* now became known as "progressive Jewish schools." The formal dissociation of the JPFO from
the administration of the schools did not reflect itself in a sudden
change in policy. Enrollments were also not significantly affected, although they were already on the decline. As of 1959, however, there
still were 80 progressive Jewish schools in existence.[48]

The position of Yiddish and Jewish subjects in the curriculum of
the IWO schools initially correlated with the position of the Communist party and the influence of the more universalistic or cosmopolitan
Jewish socialists affiliated with the left-wing of the WC, and later with
the IWO, as well as the CP. The Communist party, however, was not a
monolithic party with a consistent policy on Jews and Jewish issues
(as we shall soon see). There was considerable fluidity as positions
fluctuated and as various teachers and administrators pursued their
own policies with respect to Jewish issues. Those who taught in the
schools, many of whom were hold overs from the Workmen's Circle's
educational system, were quite concerned about a place for Yiddish
and Jewish subjects in the curriculum.

One Communist, who was a pupil during the early years of the
shules' existence, commented in an interview on Dec. 28, 1974 on the
emphasis and type of Jewish education that he received:

It was secular in that they weren't narrowly parochial. They prided themselves on their internationalism and on the fact that there couldn't be a Jewish
solution to Jewish problems. They followed the Marxist theory of more universal solutions, socialist solutions. . . . They were concerned with maintaining a bilingual tradition in this country of a Yiddish culture side by side with
the predominant American or English language culture. There was much emphasis on the work of Peretz, Sholem Aleichem, and other founders of Yiddish literature and poetry. They placed a very definite left wing stamp on the
Jewish part of the culture and on the politics that was expressed and conveyed in the education.

The situation became more consistent after 1936. The Communist
party, which had hitherto been antagonistic to specifically Jewish concerns, changed its policy. Jewish cooperation in the struggle against
fascism was needed. After this, Yiddish and things Jewish in the
schools had the endorsement of the party and became more clearly a
dominant focus within the schools. This orientation was clearly expressed in the declaration of Moissay J. Olgin, the editor of the Yiddish Communist paper the *Morning Freiheit* to the Yiddish Cultural
Congress in 1937:

We are of one mind on the type of Jew we wish to see as a product of the Yiddish school. We wish to see a healthy Jew, a Jew who feels himself at ease in his Jewish background, a Jew to whom nothing Jewish or human is alien, a Jew who won't fall into the snares which lurk in the works of certain false prophets—the trap of national gloom or the trap of national arrogance.

We wish to see a proud Jew who is capable of resisting the assimilator with his shabby coin of practicality and the nationalist with his shabby "thou art chosen" banner. We wish to see a Jew who . . . will know how to link the progressive forces of the Jewish people to the progressive forces of all other peoples in the same country or in other countries in the struggle for a better, more humane life and who will, at the same time, remain a Jew, a son of his people, a fighter for the future of his people.[49]

It is interesting to note in Olgin's comments the stress that the term "Jewish people" received and the neglect of the term "Jewish working class." This emphasis was not peculiar to Olgin, who was the leading Yiddish-speaking Communist in the Jewish community. It was also reflected in the declaration of the fifth conference of IWO schools held in 1936. Here, too, the "Jewish people" and its heritage was emphasized and made part of the aim of the IWO's educational system: ". . . the past of the Jewish people is ultimately bound up with our present interests; the history of the Jewish masses is our history. . . . We must acquaint the Jewish child with his people's past, bring to light every possible and significant element in Jewish history, and hand them over to the child as his historical inheritance."[50]

This emphasis on Yiddish and the Jewish people continued and grew stronger in the following years. Traditional Jewish holidays entered the schools in a secular Jewish populist garb. Passover, Purim, and Chanukah were three of those that gained early admission. Each of these lent themselves to an interpretation in which the Jewish people, and not Jewish workers or peasants, could be exemplified as struggling for national liberation against a foreign enemy and not against a Jewish ruling strata or class. Creative minds soon found ways to secularize and popularize other less combative Jewish holidays. Thus, with respect to Rosh Hashanah, the Jewish New Year, it was stated that: "The traditional blowing of the shofar [ram's horn] was the clarion to rally for the liberation of the Jewish people from their oppressors."[51]

The schools also dealt with issues that gave the students a Left perspective. These included the American labor movement, American politics, international affairs, and civil rights. But these subjects were considered from a Jewish as well as a Left perspective. The administrators and teachers wanted to impress upon the students at least two facts: One was the identity between the Jewish heritage and the Left. The second was the existence of a community of interest between Jews and other suffering groups. Rosh Hashanah, for example, was shown to have a Left symbolic meaning for more than just Jews. "The *shofar* blowing of the laboring masses will drown out the trumpeting of the temporary ruling interests of the earth." Notice, however, that the reference was not made to Jewish laboring masses or to Jewish ruling interests. The general objectives of these Yiddish progressive schools were summarized in a 1954 editorial in *Jewish Life*, a periodical with close ties to these schools: "The schools develop in the children a kinship with Jewish and non-Jewish laboring masses and with the history and progressive culture and traditions of the Jewish people. The children acquire an elementary knowledge of Yiddish. They are taught to identify their interests with those of the Negro people and other oppressed groups." [52]

The schools, however, were doing more than building links between Jews and oppressed groups. They were also building a Jewish identity and a sense of community among Jews, which included the secular and radical Jews on the one hand and religious and nonradical Jews on the other. It seemed that despite their differences in political orientations, the development of the Jewish question in the Workmen's Circle schools, in the JPFO, and in the progressive Jewish schools ran parallel to one another, with the latter schools being a decade or so behind.

The JPFO, and later the progressive Jewish schools, wanted to remain Jewish and radical after the war and into the cold war period. But political pressures, social changes, and organizational dynamics made it increasingly difficult to maintain a balance between the two. The cold war motivated attacks on the IWO, and the mood in the United States made it difficult for the schools to be open and concrete about radicalism. Also, the JPFO and progressive schools appeared to be attracting an increasing proportion of middle-class Jewish children. This was also an inhibition against hewing too close to a class-conflict line in the schools as was also the case in the Workmen's Circle schools.

Conversely, it was easier as well as more necessary for the JPFO and progressive Jewish schools to stress Jewish identity and interests rather than radical ones. In the America of the cold war era, Jewish private schools were more likely to survive than were radical ones. Jewish parents with children in the progressive Jewish schools as well as well as those Jews concerned with and involved in their administration generally did not want their charges to be without a Jewish identity. These schools also had a vested organizational interest in maintaining a Jewish character. Without it, they would lose their uniqueness and claim to the patronage of a unique clientele. They then would be forced to compete for funds and students on a more open market with other private, nonsecular, and progressive schools that were just beginning to dot the landscape in the 1950s.

The issues then arose as to the nature of a Jewish identity and interests in post–World War II America. Yiddish could no longer carry the burden it once had in this regard, but it was not jettisoned. There was too much in the way of sentimental ties to do this. Other things Jewish had to supplement the role of Yiddish in providing the schools with a Jewish identity.

The experience of the Washington, D.C., Jewish Children's School, one of the largest of the Jewish progressive schools in the late 1950s, illustrates the ways in which these schools came to grips with the dilemma. It also is an example of the way in which the progressive schools' radical heritage found expression in cold war America. This particular school, like all of the progressive Jewish secular schools, according to Dr. Alfred Henley, the Director of the Washington, D.C., Jewish Children's School, had an important mission to play in terms of unifying the Jewish community. They were simultaneously to attract the secular Jews back to the Jewish community and reinforce the religious community's social conscience. The schools and their pupils, he contended, had to place themselves within the bosom of the Jewish community. "Our children," Dr. Henley stated, "must learn tolerance in the special sense that they feel at ease with fellow Jews wherever they meet or worship, whether this be in the B'nai B'rith or a synagogue." To further this end, the older students were taken to the B'nai B'rith building to conduct a Passover seder as part of their extracurricular activities. Jewish history was given a heavy role to play in the building of a modern Jewish identity. It was also seen as a way of retaining the traditional association between Jewishness and secular political values, values in this case that were not radical but liberal and humane. Also, the link between them and the Jewish people was no longer made around the vehicle of social class but of something uniquely Jewish in nature that was devoid of class implications—namely, anti-Semitism. "The chief goal in our own secular schools," according to Dr. Alfred Henley, "is to arm our children with those lessons of Jewish history, both ancient and modern, with which they can defend themselves and the democratic traditions of all other Americans. The main spur to gaining this knowledge is the prevalence of anti-Semitism." [53]

The politics in these schools, as exemplified by the Washington, D.C., Jewish Children's School, were far more liberal and humanist than they were radical. Students were now instructed on issues and problems with which any well-meaning liberal could feel comfortable. The class struggle and social revolution were replaced by the questions of poverty and peace in America. And accompanying them were subjects dealing with the plight of the Negro as well as anti-Semitism and life in Israel.

The political role of these schools in post–World War II and cold war America, however, should not be underrated. It was true that they were no longer the radical institutions of socialization they had been in the past, but in comparison with other socializing agencies in the United States of that period the progressive Jewish schools were among the only places in which young people were being exposed to many controversial issues from a perspective that was both positive and sympathetic. The schools also kept alive the traditional link between Jewishness and social justice. While the link of radical party and program that tied the two together was missing from the curriculum, the attitudes engendered in such an environment exposed the students, particularly those from Jewish middle-class families, to a point of view discordant with their class position and with the dominant political perspective in American life. It also tended to make them more receptive than their Jewish and non-Jewish peers who did not attend these progressive schools to liberal and Left ideals and concepts.

SUMMER CAMPS

Another institution that functioned along lines similar to the IWO and the progressive Jewish schools was the summer camp. The IWO was not the only labor fraternal order to operate summer camps. The Workmen's Circle and the Labor Zionist Farband did too. (Other nationalities such as the Germans also had Left-oriented summer camps.) But those associated with the IWO accommodated more persons and were generally more radical over a longer period of time. The camps and resorts of all the Jewish labor fraternal orders were attended by children, adults, and families, but they were most frequented by children and adolescents. It is also important to note that large numbers of those who attended, adults and particularly youngsters, had no formal ties with the order that ran the camp or resort. Indeed, for many these summer places of enjoyment represented their first and, in some cases, major or sole involvement with a Jewish Left or Left institution.

The initial period of the establishment and growth of these summer camps and resorts was in the 1920s. These were the years in which Jewish incomes were rising along with statuses. Jewish workers and former workers as well found themselves in a better financial position to take vacations and send their children to summer camps. At the end of the 1920s, such camps and resorts were to be found near major Jewish population centers around the country, with the largest concentration being close to the New York City metropolitan area.[54] These summer encampments played a significant political role for young and older Jewish Leftists and had a political impact upon the non-Leftists or those on the fringe of the Left who attended them. Politically, as apart from other consideration such as relative costs, the camps were attractive to Jewish Leftists. They guaranteed a summer respite in a congenial political and Jewish environment. Jewish workers and Jewish Leftists could be assured that in them they could find their brand of politics and Judaism.

They were another social institution in which Jewish Leftists, whether Communist, Socialist, or Labor Zionist, could meet together as a group, freely interact, share ideas and opinions, and openly reinforce each other's Jewish Left political allegiance. This type of function became increasingly important with the passage of years. As Jewish Leftists moved out of the ranks of the working class or away from densely populated Jewish working-class neighborhoods, the social arenas in which they could meet and interact became fewer in number. This was particularly true during the bitter cold war period of the late 1940s and 1950s.

The Jewish Left summer camps and resorts also played a particular role for the wealthier workers and middle-class Jews, whose numbers increased after World War I. Their day to day economic pursuits and interests no longer tied them to a Left political commitment. In an increasing number of such cases, youthful experience and idealistic sentiment were the only reasons they remained loyal to the political Left. In the context of the camps and resorts, however, realistic economic considerations could be put aside, at least temporarily, and freer rein given to the expression of Left and Communist ideals and songs. Here sentiment was buttressed by social support, and consequently these more affluent Jews remained somewhat longer in the sphere of the Jewish Left than would have otherwise been the case.

The camps and resorts also had their political effect on many Jewish non-Leftists who attended them for various reasons, including cost, physical proximity, and rumors of freer sexual standards. Regardless of what drew them to these places, once there they were exposed to Leftists and a Left political environment. Undoubtedly there were some who were converted by such an experience. But there were probably many more who simply returned to their homes and jobs with a favorable attitude toward the Left. Such persons and their attitudes helped the Left to maintain itself in the Jewish community in the 1930s and in the post–World War II years. Their presence and views inhibited the ability of anti-Leftists to isolate and stigmatize the more committed radicals in the Jewish community in these decades.

The Jewish Left summer camps for children were important institutions of political recruitment and socialization. More Jewish youngsters came into contact with them than with the *shules* of the various orders. The most famous and probably the most important of these camps was Camp Kinderland in New York State. This camp had originally belonged to the Workmen's Circle. In 1926 the left-wing of the Workmen's Circle had captured it along with many of the *shules*. Afterward it moved into the orbit of the IWO.

The administrators of Camp Kinderland made a conscious effort to inculcate the campers with Left and progressive Jewish values. Similar to the IWO *shules*, Camp Kinderland and other camps like it, wished to educate and socialize its charges so that they would acquire both a Jewish and a Left identity. Yiddish was viewed as an important means of linking the two and was consequently stressed. Thus, the daily life of the campers as well as the waiters and counsellors, most of whom were former alumni of IWO camps, was filled with stories, songs, poems, lectures, and games designed to make the children aware of their Yiddish-progressive heritage and the struggle for social justice that united Jews with other people. Yiddish poetry and folk songs dealing with the political and social conflicts of the immigrants were recited and sung. Activist needle trade unionists came to tell of the conditions in which the Jewish unions fought to gain a foothold. Non-Jewish Leftists and Communists also spoke of their lives and movements. Blacks active in the civil rights movement and left-wing entertainers, both Jewish and non-Jewish, such as Morris Carnovsky, Paul Robeson, and Pete Seeger entertained as well as politically enlightened their camp audiences.[55]

The long-time director of Camp Kinderland, Elsie Suller, expounding on the activities, goals, and philosophical underpinning of her camp in the 1960s stated:

Camp Kinderland introduced them to the Jewish heroes of our American past, the Colonial Period, the Revolutionary War, the Abolitionist movement, and the labor movement. No Kinderland camper will equate "two sides" in the Civil War. Kinderland continues to transmit these progressive Jewish values to its children. . . . "Shnell Loifen Di Reder," "Mein Rue-a Platz," "Ich Hob A Klein Yingele," "Solidarity," "Joe Hill." When the campers sang these words they were reliving the early struggles of their *zeides* and *babas* (grandparents) in the needle trades movement of 50 years ago.[56]

Its philosophy is a secular humanist one. Camp Kinderland would be faithless to our society today if it did not have among its campers Negro children and on its staff Negro staff members and on its program Negro freedom traditions, and of course our own Jewish freedom traditions. In Camp we can influence the children who will be the future committed ones, where we can teach them this secular humanist point of view. We cannot, as Jews, be faithless to our society today. We must be committed and every day in these two precious summer months, 24 hours a day, we try to invest our children with this kind of conscience, with the understanding that there cannot be a commitment as a Jew unless there is a commitment as well to brotherhood.[57]

Camp Kinderland and other children's camps in the IWO tradition did achieve some success. The alumni of these camps who were interviewed uniformly spoke of the positive impression that the camps made upon them. For many, their first and most important contact with the Left was made in these camps. Also, in the 1950s and 1960s these camps provided them with their first real contact with Yiddish culture. In the post–World War II period, camps such as Camp Kinderland became for these individuals virtually the only place outside of their families where they gained a knowledge of and sympathy for a Left and a Yiddish Left tradition. In this respect, the Jewish community through these alumni retained a tie and a sympathetic attitude toward the Left. Camp Kinderland, as with other institutions of the Jewish Left that reached beyond a Left constituency, succeeded to some extent in keeping a progressive tradition alive among Jews. For a limited period of time, it was also successful in counteracting the pressures emanating from the socioeconomic composition of the post–World War II Jewish community that pushed it further and further from its Left heritage. Many of the alumni of these camps were later important figures within the New Left.

The summer camps made another more direct contribution to the Jewish and American Left, particularly to the New Left. They were the major nonfamilial institutions of the Jewish Left that attracted and socialized young Jews to a Left role. Their role in this regard was accentuated after World War II and during the McCarthy period. In these years, as we shall see, the Jewish community was becoming more dispersed and more middle class. Consequently, the neighborhoods, political parties, and unions increasingly became less effective as radical agencies of political socialization. The repression and closed atmosphere of the McCarthy era further stifled the expression of radicalism within these organizations as well as in Jewish Left families. In this period the camps' traditional role in assembling large numbers of Left Jewish youngsters in a context where their values and outlooks could be openly expressed and supported was highlighted.

The camps' Left socialization function was not limited to children of the Jewish Left. Campers who did not come from such a background also became attracted to the Left as a result of their camp experiences. This type of contact within a legitimate Jewish social institution in which the Left campers, counsellors, and administrators set the dominant tone was the first important step for many on the road toward becoming a member or an activist within a Left or Communist organization. This process was described in an interview on Dec. 29, 1974 by one such activist from a relatively apolitical family who traced the beginning of his involvement in the Left to his first camp experience at the age of 11: "It had a profound influence on my life. I liked the way people related to each other. I liked the spirit that was involved. I became friends with the kids, a lot of whom came from Red families. I got caught up with them and then one thing led to another."

One former member of the Labor Youth League (LYL), a post–World War II Communist youth organization, informed a 1956 New York State legislative committee investigating Communist indoctrination and training of children in summer camps that he joined the LYL at the suggestion of his counsellor at Camp Kinderland. It did not seem out of the ordinary in the context of a bunk that was divided into groups named Paul Robeson, Henry Wallace, and Anna Pauker (former Foreign Minister of Rumania). Another excamper, who went on to become a leading Communist, remarked on the political role of his fellow campers prior to World War II: "Through the camp I became acquainted with young people, children who were involved in the more straight away Communist children's movement, the Young Pioneers." He continued to associate with them outside of Camp Kinderland and two years later became a member of the Young Communist League.[58]

SUMMARY OF FRATERNAL ORDERS

The IWO (JPFO) and its affiliated groups played an instrumental role in the construction of a Jewish Left subculture. It was not alone in this endeavor. The other Yiddish labor fraternal orders, the Workmen's Circle and the Labor Zionist Farband, and their auxiliary organs also contributed to this end. There were differences in emphasis between the three orders, particularly between the JPFO-IWO on the one hand and the WC and Farband on the other. The latter two became less radical and more a part of the Jewish mainstream more quickly than did the IWO. This was particularly noticeable after World War II. But there remained even then a great deal of similarity. All three could be placed on the liberal-to-Left end of the American political spectrum. And all three remained concerned with issues of social justice, which informed the character of the subculture that they built.

The other defining features of that common social world were Yiddish and Jewishness. Regardless of their political differences and their initial stances toward Jewishness, a considerable convergence took place. All of them strongly desired to retain a Jewish character and implant a sense of Jewishness into the subculture that they were building. As we have seen in the case of the Workmen's Circle and the IWO, it became increasingly difficult to prevent their radical and Jewish emphases from working at cross purposes with each other.

THE LEFT NEWSPAPERS

The Jewish Left press, along with the labor fraternal orders and the unions, was an integral part of the Jewish labor movement in America in the early decades of this century. This press played within the Eastern European Jewish community in the United States a crucial role in shaping public opinion and attitudes toward socialism. Through deeds as well as words, it supported and strengthened other institutions of the Jewish Left as well as those of the American Left. The end result of its efforts was to create a climate of opinion that made socialism an acceptable and legitimate ideology within the American Jewish body politic.

Like the other institutions that comprised the Jewish labor movement, the Jewish Left press arose from an immigrant Yiddish-speaking working-class base and found that the issue of Jewishness had to be considered along with socialism. As with the fraternal orders, its establishment as a strong Jewish organizational entity dependent on a Jewish constituency for support set the Jewish Left press on a path that gradually and steadily led it to a position in which Jewish interests and concerns blunted its commitment to socialism.

Jewish Daily Forward

The major exemplar of the Jewish Left press and of its political and ethnic evolution is the *Jewish Daily Forward*, or *Forverts*. It was founded in New York City in 1897 as an independent Socialist daily newspaper. Within a decade the *Forverts* became the nation's largest Yiddish daily, attaining a circulation of close to 72,000. By 1917 it had established its preeminence as the most important Yiddish newspaper in the country and one with the largest circulation in the world—nearly 200,000. It was also the largest Socialist daily in the United States, second only to the English-language weekly *Appeal to Reason* as the most widely read Socialist periodical in the country prior to 1920.[59]

The establishment and growth of the *Forverts* was largely a product of both the increase and change in the character of the Jewish immigration that began to take place about the turn of the century. Prior to that time Yiddish-language periodicals, socialist or otherwise, had a difficult time gaining acceptance. German-American Jews discouraged publication of such periodicals. Their general view of these, as expressed in their English- and German-language publications, was one of contempt. The *American Israelite*, an English-language organ of German Jewry, for example, in its evaluation of a Yiddish periodical, stated: ". . . this jargon amuses the masses and makes mock of Judaism. There are many writers of trash in this country and there is no need of this Babel of idioms to render us ridiculous."[60] The German-American Jewish community and its press did not want the Yiddish-speaking Jews to establish any institution that would hinder their Americanization.

The German Jews were not the only Jews who were less than enthusiastic about a Yiddish-language press prior to 1900. Several strata within the Russian and Eastern European Jewish community in the United States had similar feelings about this kind of publication. Many of the pious and religiously educated Jews felt that it was more profitable to study the Bible or Talmud than to exert effort on a paper that was more German than Yiddish in nature. The secularly educated among the Eastern European Jews regarded Yiddish as jargon and preferred to read Hebrew or German publications.

Another obstacle that stood in the way of the establishment of a Yiddish-language press was the literacy level and cultural traits of the masses. Many were illiterate or barely literate in Yiddish. Also, these earlier immigrants were closely attuned to an oral tradition. The older Jews from the small towns of the Pale, according to the publisher of the first Yiddish daily in the United States, the *Yiddishes Tageblatt*, ". . . did not have the slightest need for a newspaper and its functions. They loved to hear the news, that is, from one who read aloud. To read for themselves, and every day at that, did not even enter their imagination."[61] Abraham Cahan, the *Forverts'* editor, voiced similar complaints in the 1890s about the reading ability of the Jewish immigrant workers: "Many of our workers could barely read unvocalized Yiddish texts. Not only did we have to teach them in our writings how to think, we also had to teach them how to read our writing."[62]

The first Yiddish-language daily newspaper to emerge from this milieu and survive was the *Yiddishes Tageblatt* or *Jewish Daily News* in New York City in 1885. The *Tageblatt* was not the first Yiddish-language periodical to be published in the United States. Several had preceded it, but those that survived only did so as weekly or monthly publications. The *Tageblatt* was a daily newspaper. In other respects, however, it resembled the Yiddish-language press as it was then constituted. It had an Orthodox orientation as did virtually all other institutions that the Eastern European Jewish community built prior to the 1880s. Politically, as befitted an institution associated with Orthodoxy, the *Tageblatt* was conservative and a supporter of the Republican party.

The Yiddish-language labor and Left press began to emerge in the latter half of the 1880s. It, too, began with weeklies struggling for existence. In 1894 the first Yiddish Socialist daily, the *Abendblatt*, or *Evening Journal*, made its debut. The *Abendblatt* along with the weekly *Arbeiter Zeitung* and the monthly, *Zukunft*, both of which preceded it, were essentially the organs of the Yiddish-speaking section of the Socialist Labor party. These, however, were not the only Yiddish-language publications to espouse socialism and radicalism to the Jewish masses.[63]

The emergence of this kind of press coincided with the increasing numbers of Yiddish-speaking immigrants who began to arrive in the United States in the 1890s. Different from the typical immigrant of the 1870s and 1880s, these men and women came from the larger towns and cities. They had higher rates of literacy and appeared to be more interested in culture. They were also more secular and less bound by the constraints of Orthodoxy and tradition. They were people who had gained some experience in the larger shops and factories of the Pale. And toward the end of the century, there were in their ranks workers who knew something about unions and radical parties. However, they lacked leadership and an organized means of communication that could counter those Orthodox and German-American Jewry. This leadership and means of communication were soon found among the young Russified intellectual Jewish radicals. They came from men such as Abraham Cahan, a member of the People's Will and the *Am Olam*.[64]

These political and literary radicals reluctantly and gradually began to realize that these newer immigrants in particular and the Yiddish workers in general constituted their special audience and potential constituency. As the fledgling Yiddish-language labor press began to develop and interact with this growing audience-constituency, more of the Russified Jewish radicals became attracted to both this press and these people. As Samuel Niger, one of the leading Yiddish men of letters in the United States, expressed it:

Attracting intellectuals previously alienated from the Jewish environment and the Yiddish language to Jewish cultural creativity was a substantial accomplishment. For this accomplishment we are indebted to the radical Yiddish press and the social ideas and ideals it propagated. Writers and speakers whose medium of expression had been Russian, Hebrew or German studied to become Yiddish writers and speakers. Where once there had been an intelligentsia without a people and a people without an intelligentsia, the Yiddish press and the social movement it represented gave the intelligentsia a people and the people an intellectual leadership.[65]

Yiddish, for these cosmopolitan socialist journalists and writers, was initially just a convenient and expedient vehicle for reaching the masses, who understood little else but this language. Socialism was the message and Yiddish the medium. Soon these labor journalists found it necessary to become concerned with the medium in two important and interrelated respects. First, they had to make Yiddish into a more Yiddish language capable of being understood by the Yiddish workers and public. This entailed removing many German and Russian words and phrases. The stress was to be on the shaping of a language that the common man could easily understand. Secondly, they realized that the literary level of the Jewish masses made it necessary for them to educate the Jewish workers in Yiddish. Thus, similar to the Bund, the Jewish Left press became a major educator and propagator of Yiddish and Yiddish culture. This press became a school for the Yiddish-speaking masses, who found in its pages new ideas, literature, and discussions about the social and natural sciences. Again, similar to the Bund, these Yiddish publicists wanted not only to make the masses more adept in Yiddish and convert them to socialism but also to raise their general level of culture. Socialism was not to be for the ignorant as far as the Jewish Left papers and periodicals were concerned.

Shortly after the turn of the century, the Jewish Left labor press was established. It was by then an educational and political force of significance within the Yiddish-speaking immigrant community that challenged the hold of Orthodoxy and the maintenance of the status quo. It soon reached beyond the boundaries of the dedicated few in the radical parties and struggling unions. It became, more so than any other institution with the possible exception of Orthodoxy, a mass-based community institution.

The *Jewish Daily Forward* soon after it appeared became the major carrier of the tradition that had grown out of the short experience of the Jewish labor press that had preceded it. Building upon and embellishing that tradition, the *Jewish Daily Forward* went on to become the leading Yiddish-language newspaper in the country. The *Forward's* future preeminence, however, was not evident at the time of its birth in 1897. It came into being as a result of a factional fight within the Socialist Labor party; its founders were among those who lost in the struggle. This meant that the paper lacked the endorsement and support of the SLP. Worse yet, it had to compete against the more established Yiddish labor daily, the *Abendblatt*, the Yiddish voice of the SLP, while at the same time bearing up under the attacks from this paper and Daniel De Leon, the head of the SLP, who were determined to drive the *Forward* out of existence. Compounding this was a lack of funds that made its survival quite precarious in the first few years. But the *Forward* did survive and prosper.

A prime reason for the *Forward's* survival and growth was the numbers and the nature of the Jewish immigrants who poured into the United States after the Kishinev pogrom and the abortive Russian revolution of 1905. As described earlier, these new immigrants were more secular and politicized than their counterparts of earlier years. In the *Forward*, they found a special newspaper that spoke to their various needs and interests and in them the *Forverts* found the mass readership that it had been searching for.[66]

The editorial policy of the *Forward* as shaped by its first and long-time editor, Abraham Cahan, also contributed to its prosperity. The *Forward* as conceived by Cahan was to be a socialist journal different from its predecessors and rivals. It was to be flexible and nondogmatic in its approach to politics and religion. It would contain human interest stories and features that had little or nothing to do with socialism. Not everything in the paper was to be interpreted from a socialist point of view. A Jewish perspective would also be given legitimacy. This was to be a formula for success.

The *Forward* had been born with a mandate to further the cause of socialism, the unions, and the class struggle. But the definition of what constituted the correct form of socialism, an appropriate union, and a legitimate class struggle was primarily decided by Abraham Cahan. This was made perfectly clear in an early policy statement published in the *Forverts* on April 21, 1901:

Inasmuch as there are various trends within the socialist movement itself, the *Forverts* will remain an organ for the free discussion of all the views arising from the common belief in socialism.

However, the *Forverts* will support that socialist movement which will under the prevailing conditions, prove itself to be the best; that is, which will more reflect the free flexible principle of the *Forverts*.[67]

It soon became clear that the principal criterion that guided Cahan and his subordinates in the operation of the newspaper was not socialism but success as measured by circulation figures. Cahan was able to put this kind of stamp on the *Forward* because of his editorial brilliance and autocratic nature. The structure of the ownership also facilitated his ability to pursue such a policy. The *Forward's* founders, mainly because of their experience with the Socialist Labor party, organized the paper so that it would not in the future fall under the control of any political party. They created a corporation called the Forward Association which was the official owner of the newspaper. Membership in the Forward Association was limited to persons who: (a) belonged to a union, (b) adhered to the principles of democratic socialism, and (c) gained the approval of the Association's admission's committee. In practice, this came to mean that membership in the Forward Association was limited to those who gained the approval of editor Cahan.

Cahan quickly guided the *Jewish Daily Forward* to a leading position within Jewish journalism. By 1907 it was the leading Yiddish language daily in New York City if not the world. By 1910 the *JDF*'s annual circulation was 122,000, a figure that represented almost 40 percent of all readers of Jewish papers in New York. In the early 1920s the figure approached a quarter of a million.[68]

It would be misleading to suggest that the success of the *Forward* was attributable to the socialist policy of the paper. The *Forward* was more than a socialist newspaper. Its columns and editorials, unlike those of its socialist predecessors and competitors, were open to human interest and sensationalist concerns. The *Forward* also differed from other socialist or anarchist Jewish newspapers in its attitude toward Judaism. In its pages religion was not attacked. Instead, respect was accorded the positive feelings about Orthodoxy held by many within the Eastern European Jewish community in America.[69]

The brand of socialism that Cahan offered to the readers of *Forward* was undoubtedly also a factor in the attraction of readers. The *Forward's* socialism was generally moderate, pragmatic, flexible, and lacking in the stridency that characterized other Yiddish-language radical papers. The position of the *Forward* with respect to socialism was aptly summarized by the literary critic and social historian Irving Howe as follows: "The socialism of the *Forward* was a loose, enfolding creed, with many virtues, many sins. If it showed little theoretical sophistication during the years before the First World War, pretty much the same was true for American socialism as a whole."[70]

The socialism of the *Forward* was subject to much criticism by socialists who were less moderate and less pragmatic than editor Cahan. Cahan's consistent rejoinder to these critics was to point out the necessity of reaching as many people as possible and reaching them with a socialism that they could understand and be willing to accept. The more Jews who read the *Forward*, according to Cahan, the more the doctrine of socialism would be permeated throughout the entire community. Other Yiddish socialist and anarchist papers may have been more faithful to doctrine than the *Forward*, but their circulation was miniscule while that of the *Forward* was massive by comparison.[71]

In the first two to two and a half decades of this century, the *Jewish*

Daily Forward was a major force within the Jewish community linking that community to socialism, albeit a somewhat watered down socialism. There were several means by which the paper bolstered the socialism of Jews. Perhaps its most important contribution in this regard was to legitimate socialism and the idea of socialism as a respectable ideology among American Jews. The *Forward* accomplished this first by becoming a popular mass newspaper, whose views on issues, events, and personalities became the most widespread, if not the dominant, ones in the immigrant community. And these views, it should be stressed, were, in the earlier decades in particular, socialist ones. The Yiddish readers of the paper learned to see and understand their life in America through, if not red, then at least a pink lens.

The second way in which the *Forward* legitimated socialism was to boldly fill a leadership and educational vacuum in the immigrant community. The traditional leaders and teachers, primarily the Orthodox rabbis, were, as discussed earlier, not in a good position to offer the immigrants meaningful advice on how to cope with conditions in the New World. Cahan and his writers assumed the responsibility for guiding and educating the immigrant community in a variety of spheres. This guidance and education, again particularly in the pre–World War I years, had a decided socialist character. The immigrants were taught not to scab during strikes. They were admonished to become citizens and vote for socialist candidates. However, even in the noneconomic or nonpolitical spheres, socialism often played a role. Many plays, poems, and books were reviewed and evaluated not only on their artistic merit but also on their relationship to socialism. Invariably those works that were deemed to have both artistic and socialist, or prolabor, merits gained a positive review. And a positive evaluation in the *Forverts* usually was a guarantee of success. This power, in turn, meant that writers and playwrights would then be tempted to add to or stress in their work a socialist or prolabor dimension. The cumulative result was that the *Forverts* became able to influence politically not only the readers of its pages but also those who attended plays and read poetry and novels.

Its influence even extended to other Yiddish-language newspapers in such a way that the *Forward's* socialism and socialist perspective became even more entrenched in the immigrant community. One way this occurred was through emulation. Other editors tried to emulate the *Forward* in hopes of stumbling on its formula for success. Although its politics and political viewpoint may have been not the aspect most chosen for purposes of emulation, it was not always easy to avoid bringing it along with some other feature. Another way was through fear. Other newspapers became reluctant to make open and prolonged attacks on the *Forverts* as it moved into a position of ascendancy. They feared the loss of readers and advertisers. The *Abendblatt's* demise in 1902 could be attributed in part to its intemperate attacks on the *Forverts.*

The *Forward* directly influenced the way in which the American immigrant Jewish community saw the world and understood its problems. It did this by opening its pages to the writings of leading figures in the socialist and labor movement, both Jewish and non-Jewish, from all over the world. The list of such contributors included Leon Trotsky, Leon Blum of France, Edward Bernstein and Karl Kautsky of Germany, Ramsay MacDonald and Philip Snowden of England. The leaders of the Bund such as Mark Lieber, Vladimir Medem, and Raphael Abramovitch made known their views to American Jewry through the columns of the *Forverts*.[72]

One of the best illustrations of the power of the *Forverts* with regard to political opinion within the Yiddish-speaking community occurred in 1917. The *Forverts*, then at the height of its popularity and influence as indicated by its circulation figure of approximately 200,000, advocated a noninterventionist policy with respect to the United States and World War I. This was in accord with its support of the Socialist party's antiwar St. Louis Manifesto. The *Forverts*' position was so influential in the Jewish immigrant community that other Jewish groups and newspapers dependent on a Yiddish-speaking population base were hesitant to openly oppose the *Forverts* on this issue. The Labor Zionists, for example, who supported President Wilson's war policy, feared introducing a resolution in favor of the President's war policy for fear of provoking the *Forverts*. Similarly, Robert Maisel, Director of the AFL-inspired and controlled American Alliance for Labor and Democracy, in a letter to Samuel Gompers, the President of the AFL, bemoaned the fact of the *Forward's* ability to impose its war policy on the Jewish community: "Fear of the daily *Forward* plays a big part in the Jewish newspaper situation. . . . I have talked to many people and had information from many sources and I can see no way to break the ice except through ownership of a Jewish paper. . . . No Jewish paper at present has the backbone to stand up and fight the *Forward* and its anti-Americanism."[73] (Later the *Forverts* changed its position on the war and American intervention.)

The *Forward's* contribution to socialism among Yiddish-speaking Jews was not limited to the shaping of public opinion. It played a major role in building a Socialist party organization on the East Side and molding the Eastern European Jews into a Socialist constituency. It advocated socialism in its columns. It instructed its readers on how to register for and vote in elections. The *Forverts* organized and heavily financed the campaigns of Socialist candidates. Its very office building became the center for Socialist rallies and organizational meetings. Virtually every Socialist who won election to a public office in a district containing a sizable Yiddish-speaking population owed his triumph to the efforts of the *Forverts*. "The *Forward* is more than a newspaper," as one leading Socialist of the day pointed out. "It is an organization which controls the Socialist Party in those districts where it has a strong following, the officials of the Jewish labor unions and kindred organizations, and the labor press. Within its own sphere of influence it wields a power as great as Tammany Hall in its dominion."[74]

Its impact as a Socialist organization was not only felt in electoral politics. Virtually every Socialist-led Jewish needle trades union that was established or grew to prominence in the first two decades of the 1900s was deeply indebted to the *Forward*. Many of the more prominent organizers and leaders of the Jewish unions in this period were socialist writers for or staff members on the newspaper. They included such men as Joseph Barondess, Max Pine, Morris Hillquit, and Benjamin Schlesinger. Often the *Forward* planned and organized strikes, including the major ones that led to the establishment of the unions. During strikes the *Forward* made innumerable contributions to assist the unions and the strikers. It would also deny advertising pages to any shop on strike, while at the same time castigating recalcitrant or particularly exploitative employers.[75]

The *Forward's* socialist ardor began to cool after 1920, although it still continued to support the Socialist party and its candidates. Indeed, the *Forward* was the SP's financial mainstay. Until 1929 it contributed $500 each month, and it is believed by some historians that the party could not have survived without this assistance. Additional sums of money were given for election campaigns and special needs of the party. In 1934 Norman Thomas begrudgingly admitted that his party was heavily dependent on the *Jewish Daily Forward* for its operations.[76] This financial assistance, however, was not limited to the English-speaking parts of the Socialist party after 1920. The *Forward* gave funds and other types of support to maintain institutions that formed part of a Jewish socialist subculture. These included radio station WEVD in New York City, the magazine *New Leader*, the League for Industrial Democracy, the Rand School, and various summer camps. These were not exclusively Jewish institutions, but most of their leadership and readership or clientele were Jews from the New York City area.

In 1936 the lifetime relationship between the *Jewish Daily Forward* and the Socialist party was severed by the paper led by Cahan. This, however, did not end the *Forward's* association with socialism. After the break Cahan and the daily were instrumental in the organization and financing of a new, more moderate, Socialist organization called the Social Democratic Federation. The SDF was made up largely of right-wing Socialists who had left the SP about the same time as the *Forverts*. About three-fourths of this new Socialist organization's members were from New York City and its environs, and presumably an overwhelming majority were Jews.

In the same year Cahan and the *Forward* also played an important role in the formation of another political party: the American Labor party of New York State. Although it was not a socialist party, many Socialists and disaffected Socialists were among its founding

334   JEWS AND THE LEFT

members and early supporters. And although it supported the candidates of the bourgeoisie parties, the ALP was generally considered to have a very liberal political orientation. Again, similar to the SDF, most of its leaders and supporters were Jews from the New York City metropolitan area.

The *Forward* continued its drift from socialism to liberalism during World War II and afterward. In this postwar period it remained a liberal organ. In 1957 the paper was asked to return to the fold of the Socialist party, but it refused. Its major and overriding focus after the war was with Jewish concerns and interests.[77]

The *Jewish Daily Forward*, in the post–World War II era, was no longer a potent political force or a prime molder of Jewish public opinion. Although still the leading Yiddish-language journal in the country, its readership by 1950 had declined to 79,719. Ten years later the paper's circulation had fallen to less than 65,000. Those who read it were primarily older, Yiddish-speaking Jews whose day in the sun as political activists, like that of the *Forverts*, had passed.

The *Forward* had made its major contribution to developing a close relationship between Jews and the Left during the first three and a half decades of its existence, particularly the first two decades. Its major role in this regard could be divided into two related categories. One, the *Forward* was a part of as well as a builder of a vibrant Jewish Left subculture. Two, it was a socialist molder of Jewish public opinion. Although the paper had started life as the political voice and expression of a narrow strata of working-class conscious Jews, it soon became a communal institution that reached beyond a working-class base and into the Jewish middle class as well. In both of these respects, the *Forward* was able to shape a socialist milieu and public opinion that kept not only Jewish workers within a Left arena but many nonworking-class Jews as well. The *Forward*, then, was another institutional vehicle that helped to keep American Jewry on the liberal to Left end of the political spectrum through the 1930s, even as the interests emerging from its changing class composition were pulling it in an opposite direction.

The *Jewish Daily Forward*, like the needle trade unions and the Workmen's Circle, developed a more Jewish emphasis as it grew less committed to socialism. As with its partners in the Jewish labor movement, the root causes of its transformation from a Jewish newspaper with a Socialist focus into a liberal daily with a Jewish emphasis was its Jewish base and the *Forverts'* concern for its organizational viability.

This shift in the balance between Jewish and socialist concerns was presaged in the very early years of the *Forward's* existence. One reason that the paper had been able to survive in its fight with the *Abendblatt* and the Socialist Labor party in its first five years was because of the differences in the way the two labor journals dealt with Jewish issues and concerns. The two prime examples of this in these years could be seen in the difference in the way the two papers treated the Spanish-American War (1898) and the Dreyfus affair (1898–1904). Both of these issues interested and agitated the Jewish community in the United States. Jews had had a historic hatred of Spain dating back to the Inquisition and the expulsion of the Jews from Spain in 1492. Colonel Dreyfus of the French Army was a Jew whose religious origin was used to falsely incriminate him as a spy. His case had stirred up considerable anti-Semitism in France.

The *Abendblatt*, a Yiddish-language daily of the Socialist Labor party, refused to play up the Jewish aspects of these two issues. With respect to the Spanish-American War, it stressed the imperialistic motivation of the American government's interest in Cuba. With respect to the Dreyfus affair, the *Abendblatt* thought Dreyfus the man and Dreyfus the Jew to be of minor importance compared with the larger issues involved.

We cannot join in the trumpeting of all Jewish papers, who are of the opinion that because Dreyfus is a Jew, they must shout that he is innocent, that he is a victim of intrigue by the enemies of Israel. . . . From the depths of our hearts we wish success to Emile Zola in his unceasing endeavors to expose the injustices committed by the military. Not so much to free the unjustly accused man, Dreyfus. Oh! How can you compare a single instance of the wrongs suffered by one man from capitalism and its main support, militarism, with the wrongs that millions of workers suffer day and night.[78]

The *Forward*, in contrast, stressed the Jewish angle of both stories and gained readers at its rival's expense.

The appeal of the *Forward* to Jewish interests and concerns can also be seen in the March 16, 1902, issue of the paper. This edition was the first in which Cahan had complete authority. The lead article or editorial entitled, "Send your children to college if you can, but don't let them be disloyal to their own parents and brothers!" written by Cahan extolled the fact that hard-working Jews sent their children to college. This, he indicated, was a function of the dedication of the Jewish people to education.

You don't find many German, Irish or Italian children in City College. About ninety percent of the boys there are Jews, and most of them are children of Jewish workers. . . . The Jew undergoes privation, spills blood, to educate his child . . . it shows our capacity to make sacrifices for our children (perhaps this is one of the reasons it is so hard to make the Jews disappear), as well as our love for education, for intellectual effort.[79]

This emotional tribute to the Jewish people it must be remembered came from the pen of a Socialist, an assimilationist Socialist.

The *Abendblatt's* general position on Jewish matters alienated Jewish readers or potential readers. It felt, as did the SLP under DeLeon, that to concern itself with specifically Jewish matters or to express

Jewish feelings would be to encourage bourgeois Jewish nationalism. This paper, guided by its vision of cosmopolitan and scientific socialism, also attacked the religious faith and customs of Orthodox Jews.[80]

Editor Abraham Cahan, an atheist and cosmopolitan socialist, significantly deviated from the *Abendblatt* and traditional socialist practice on this matter. In the pages of the *Forward*, Jewish faith and religious customs were, as briefly noted above, treated with respect. Antireligious Socialists and anarchists were publicly admonished, even in the *Forward's* earliest years, to refrain from attacking Judaism. "Freethinkers, Don't Be Fanatics" was the title of one early editorial. In another instance, in 1909, Jewish freethinkers were given advice as to their behavior on Yom Kippur, the holiest day of the Jewish calendar, and one of the holidays that Jewish anarchists used to mock publicly via Yom Kippur balls and the eating of ham sandwiches in front of synagogues.

On this day, he [the freethinker] should not flaunt himself in the eyes of the religious people. There is no sense in arousing their feelings. Every man has a right to live according to his beliefs. The pious man has as much right to his religion as the freethinker to his atheism. To parade one's acts that insult the religious feeling of the pious, especially on Yom Kippur, the day they hold most holy, is simply inhuman.[81]

This attitude toward religion was unprecedented among Jewish radicals at the time. Fellow Socialists on the staff and on the Forward Association were highly critical of Cahan's position. They did not feel that the demonstration of such respect and tolerance for religion did much to further the cause of socialism. Cahan's response was that it increased the circulation and thereby spread the socialist message to those it had previously not reached. Religious Jews and Jews who were still tied to Judaism and its customs by ties of family or sentiment were most prominent in this category.

Cahan and other Socialists as well were concerned about not placing themselves and their cause at odds with the Jewish religion as the Jewish anarchists had so clumsily done. The alienation of those who had some ties to Judaism would deprive socialism of many potential recruits. It would also deprive the *Forward* of potential readers. The *Forward's* advocacy of respect and tolerance was one way of demonstrating that religion and socialism were not fundamentally hostile to one another. Cahan and his paper took the lead in moving beyond this point to demonstrate that Judaism was compatible if not supportive of socialism as they defined and interpreted it. On the pages of the *Forward* and in the mouths of its staff, socialism became a secular form of Judaism. Thus, Cahan in an ode to socialism in 1910 cited the parallels between this secular religion and Judaism:

The spiritual cheer which this ideal creates . . . is a divine reward . . . a reward that Judaism promises the righteous in the world to come but which laboring humanity attains in this world. [The Law of Moses was invoked on behalf of striking workers.] Thou shalt not withhold anything from thy neighbor, nor rob him; there shall not abide with thee the wages of him that is hired until morning. So it stands in Leviticus. So you see that our bosses who rob us and don't pay commit a sin, and that the cause of our unions is a just one.[82]

The Socialist party's Rand School was lyricized by the *Forward* at its founding in 1906 as "the socialist yeshivah . . . where the rabbis and teachers of our movement are being prepared."[83] Moses himself was depicted as the first walking delegate because of his leadership in the strike against the Egyptians.[84]

These attempts to link Judaism together with socialism were not unique to Cahan and the *Forward*. But he and his paper were among the pioneers in this regard. These appeals to Jewish religion and tradition and biblical terminology seemed to be attractive to the Yiddish-speaking masses who had not made a total break with religion, even as they embraced the causes of socialism and unionism. It was also a way of establishing the legitimacy of socialism within the immigrant Jewish community—a community that, while not overly religiously observant, still accorded some measure of respect to traditional Judaism. For Cahan and the *Forward*, this policy had the additional function of increasing readership.

However, it is inconceivable that this linking of socialism and Judaism bore only positive fruits for socialism. If Judaism and things Jewish legitimized socialism to the religious and quasi-religious, did not the Judaized socialism that the *Forverts* preached legitimize and sustain religion or religious sentiments and a Jewish identity among the socialist believers and near believers? In any event, as the number of religious and quasi-religious subscribers multiplied, a Socialist newspaper guided by the axiom of *Nothing Succeeds Like Success* would find the pressure to represent the Jewish interests of this bloc of readers difficult to resist.[85]

The religious or near religious Jews, however, were not the only nonsocialist Yiddish-reading groups that Cahan and the *Forward* wished to reach. It was his aim to attain as broad and as large a readership as possible. One way he succeeded in achieving this goal was by consciously modeling the *Forverts* after the successful yellow journals of Pulitzer's *World* and Hearst's *American*. Thus, he made entertaining and light features a staple of the *Forward*. These included human interest stories, reports of murders, the serialization of romantic novels, and the gossip about the lives of famous people.

The most famous feature in this category was the *Bintel Brief* (Bundle of Letters). This was a column containing selected letters from readers, who wrote to the *Forverts* for answers to their problems. Each letter would be accompanied by a reply as to how best to cope with the problem. Most of the letters and replies published in this column had little to do with socialism. They fell mostly into the categories of family problems and difficulties with the opposite sex and were largely related to or caused by the difficulties of adjustment to life in the New World.[86] The *Bintel Brief* was also used to soothe and attract the older, more religious generation who were having difficulty with their more secular and radical children in America. So when a radical and freethinker inquired about whether he should get married in a synagogue for the sake of his bride's parents, the editor responded: "The advice is that there are times when it pays to give in to old parents and not grieve them. It depends upon the circumstances. When one can get along with kindness it is better not to break off relations with the parents."[87]

These types of light features angered Cahan's more orthodox socialist compatriots and writers on the *Forward*. On two occasions he even resigned, and at other times he threatened to resign because of this type of opposition. Cahan, however, was victorious in pushing through his point of view. These features did attract readers for the *Forward*, and, confronted by circulation figures no other Yiddish-language socialist newspaper had ever before approached or dreamed possible, his socialist critics on the *Forward* either begrudgingly accepted his viewpoint or resigned.

Cahan attracted other sectors of the Yiddish-speaking community through his concern with Yiddish and Yiddish culture. He simplified the Yiddish used in his paper so that the man in the street could easily read it. This involved censoring the German and Hebrew words and phrases that other papers used to make Yiddish seem more respectable. (Yiddish men of letters severely denounced Cahan for going too far in his popularization of Yiddish. They felt that his policies would lead to a jargonized Yiddish devoid of sophistication or cultural richness.[88]) One result of Cahan's simplification of the Yiddish used in the *Forward* was to attract Jews who had never before or with any great regularity read a newspaper.[89]

Cahan also opened up the *Forward* to some of the best of the Yiddish writers and essayists. Men like Morris Rosenfeld, Abraham Reisin, Sholem Asch, Isaac Bashevis Singer, and I. L. Peretz wrote for this paper at various times. But not all of these literary men were committed socialists, and increasingly the *Forward* published articles and essays by these and other grand men of Yiddish letters that had little to do with socialism and the struggle of the laboring man. This, while adding to the total of *Forward's* readers also augmented the number of nonsocialist subscribers.[90]

The *Forward* did not wish to exclude or alienate from its subscribers even the Jewish capitalists and landlords, provided, of course, they were decent and correct thinking people. Thus, the *Forward* accepted their advertisements, provided they were not involved in a labor dispute. Socialist tenants were advised that insofar as capitalism would not soon be collapsing, it would be best for them to cooperate with honest landlords. One indicator of its own acceptance of the capitalist system and admiration for the United States as well was its advertisement for a 10-cent Yiddish translation of the American Constitution. The *Forward* referred to it ". . . as the little torah . . . the highroad to citizenship, employment and success." And as if to demonstrate how broadminded and nondogmatic it was, the *Forward* publicized the foibles of workers and their political representatives admitting as it did in one editorial, "We idealize the working class a bit too much."[91]

Editor Cahan's concern with and success in obtaining a mass-circulation Yiddish-language newspaper ensured that the paper would be flexible and pragmatic in its approach to socialism. At the same time the broader and more heterogeneous the readership became, the more difficult it was to resist developing a more Jewish orientation and focus. Yiddish, Yiddish culture and a Jewish identification appeared to be the common denominators least likely to antagonize any sizable segment of the paper's readers. Yiddish-speaking socialists after all were expected to be flexible, broadminded, and tolerant of other people's feelings and beliefs. Or at least this is what Abraham Cahan expected of them. Cahan and the *Forverts*, it should be emphasized, were not the only Yiddish socialists and Yiddish-language socialist periodicals moving in a Jewish direction. There were others, but Cahan and the *Forward* were among the most prominent who led the way.

Cahan and other Yiddish socialist intellectuals and their publications were, at the turn of the century and in the early 1900s, affected by a rising tide of immigrants and events that heightened their Jewish interests and concerns. In Eastern Europe, the Bund as well as the Zionists and other Jewish groups were developing and encouraging a Jewish identity and Jewish interests among socialists and radicals who had been previously hostile or oblivious to such concerns. And underlying it all were the pogroms and anti-Semitic actions of the Russian authorities and the lack of a significant response by non-Jewish socialists in Russia or elsewhere. All of this was closely observed and closely felt by the Eastern European Jewish-born intellectuals and radicals in America.

Then in 1903 the Kishinev pogrom occurred. No other single event to date had such an impact on the Yiddish-speaking world. It greatly accelerated the process of the Judaization of the Jewish and Yiddish-speaking intellectuals and socialists on both sides of the Atlantic. One prominent Jewish socialist in the United States in speaking about the political impact of Kishinev upon the Left-leaning Jewish masses in America, stated: "This was a veritable nationalist epidemic. . . . The radicalism of the Jewish masses practically disappeared before the nationalist wave."[92] The impact of Kishinev upon the cosmopolitan Jewish socialists could be clearly discerned in David Pinski and his work. Pinski, writer and dramatist as well as a former staff member of the *Abendblatt* and a literary editor of the Socialist Labor party's weekly, the *Arbeiter*, was deeply shocked by the Kishinev pogrom. After it he moved toward a more nationalist position and eventually became an ardent Labor Zionist. His drama, *Familie Zevi*, which was conceived "At the open grave of the Kishinev victims," gave expression to the change in his political and ethnic stance. One of the characters, Leon Zevi, a Jewish cosmopolitan socialist and antinationalist, represented a generation of radical intellectuals on their way to a new identification when he stated: "My way was the way of self negation, while all around me Jews followed the way of self liberation and self affirmation—Jews full of strength, full of courage, of powerful will and gigantic faith." [93]

Cahan and the *Forward* sailed along on the crest of this nationalist wave. They, after all, had little reason to resist it. The growth of a Jewish consciousness and a Jewish interest did not violate the flexible and continually evolving socialist tenets of the man who controlled the *Jewish Daily Forward*. Also, this rising nationalist sentiment undoubtedly reflected the sentiments of a large majority of the paper's readers. And Cahan was generally quite responsive to the feelings of the *Forward's* subscribers, particularly on those issues where so many felt so strongly.

The paper, as discussed above, did not abandon its socialist commitments in the pre–World War I era. Even after Kishinev the *Forward* continued to advocate and work for socialism, and Cahan himself remained for many years one of the leading Socialist personalities in America. This allegiance to socialism in this period was presumably a matter of principle and youthful revolutionary experience for Cahan and the other Socialists associated with the *Forward*. Such a political position was also congruent with the interests and sentiments stemming from the dominant socioeconomic makeup of the Yiddish-speaking population in New York, the *Forward's* readership base. This population before the war was made up largely of workers. Even as nationalist currents rose among them, much positive feeling for socialism remained. In addition, their leading organizations and institutions were the Socialist-led unions and labor fraternal orders. And these were leaders and organizations with whom Cahan and the *Forward's* staff had many close, intimate, and overlapping relationships.

It is important to stress that in most of the first two decades of the twentieth century, outside of some cosmopolitan Socialists, there was little significant opposition to the view that a Jewish interest was highly compatible and overlapping with that of a Socialist view. The post-Kishinev waves of immigrants, which contained large numbers of Bundist as well as Zionist-oriented Yiddish-speaking workers, intellectuals, and political activists, greatly strengthened this position while simultaneously diminishing that of the older antinationalist universalistic socialists. [94]

Cahan and the *Forverts* also became increasingly receptive to the concept of a mutuality of interest between Socialists and Jews. This had, in fact, been the largely implied position of the *Forverts* since its inception. However, even though the paper had assumed a position more markedly sympathetic to Jewish interests and concerns than any other previous Yiddish-language socialist publication, Cahan had not completely broken from his cosmopolitan origins after launching the *Forverts*.[95] But the daily's structure and broad base in the Yiddish-speaking community meant that it had to be responsive to rising trends and popular currents if it wanted to survive as a mass-circulation newspaper. Consequently, the *Forverts* was not going to place itself in a position of opposing a rising tendency that sought to harmonize Jewish and Socialist interests, Cahan's personal feelings notwithstanding.[96]

This responsiveness to this particular pressure as well as to the changing socioeconomic composition of the Yiddish-speaking immigrant community can be discerned in the different ways in which Cahan and the *Forverts* handled the 1908 and 1910 Socialist Congressional campaigns in the East Side's Ninth Congressional District. In 1908 the candidate was Morris Hillquit, a prominent Jewish Socialist who was among the leaders and founders of the Socialist party of the United States. In this campaign Hillquit, speaking in Yiddish to his largely Jewish audiences, told them that as Congressman from the Ninth District, "I will not consider myself the special representative of the Socialist Party and the interests of the working class of the country."[97] The *Forverts* endorsed this non-class and non-socialist position, but Hillquit lost the election after being roundly attacked in the Yiddish press for his lack of concern about Jewish matters and interests.

In 1910 the *Forverts* and Meyer London, the new Socialist Congressional candidate, took a different, broader approach. Now the Yiddish Socialist paper and the Yiddish-speaking Socialist candidate were willing to be more appreciative of and sympathetic to Jewish concerns and interests than had been the case in 1908. The difference, however, was not only limited to the Jewish sphere. The Socialist candidate and the Socialist paper were also more appreciative of and sympathetic to the nonworking-class Jews in the district. The reason for this change in emphasis was not difficult to discern. The number of small businessmen and professionals, along with those who saw little incompatibility between Jewish and Socialist interests, was on the rise. Consequently, the *Forverts* depicted the 1910 candidate, London, as being the representative of the East Side in contrast to the 1908 candidate, Hillquit, whom it portrayed as the representative of the "working class." And in the 1910 campaign, in pursuit of this overall change in orientation, the *Forverts* published an interview with an East Side storekeeper who claimed that:

As a businessman I will work and vote for Meyer London. Our interests demand this. . . . The honest businessman must have someone who will take his part, [someone] the politicians will fear. . . . When Meyer London will be elected he will be under no obligation to anyone. As a citizen of the East Side he will be in a position to accomplish a great deal. . . . When Meyer London is elected to Congress he will be the spokesman of the Jewish Quarter.[98]

No such interview or viewpoint had been expressed by the Forverts in the 1908 campaign; this time the Socialist candidate won the election.

The Forverts continued to be guided by a pragmatic conception of socialism and a concern for Jewish interests in the succeeding years. These two emphases did not, however, remain in a static relationship to one another. The changes and events that were occurring inside and outside of the Jewish community could not help but keep the relationship between the two in a state of flux. But as time progressed the Forverts began to place more emphasis on its Jewish orientation and become more practical about the socialism it continued to support and advocate. Again, its very success in becoming a widely read daily rooted in the Yiddish-speaking community supported this transition. It was this mass circulation that was responsible for Forverts' economic and political power.

The desire to protect this position and its role within the Jewish community led the Jewish Daily Forward to compromise its socialist principles. One such compromise occurred in 1917. As the United States moved closer to involvement in World War I, the informal and formal pressures upon antiwar dissidents, including the Jewish Daily Forward, grew. In response to these forces, the Forward, while formally subscribing to the official antiwar and anticonscription policy, began to soft-pedal its stand on these matters. On October 5, 1917, the United States postal authorities warned the paper of an impending revocation of its second-class mailing permit. Cahan's response to this threat was to enter into a deal arranged and mediated by the paper's attorney, Louis Marshall, a leader of the German-American Jewish community. According to the terms of this arrangement, Cahan pledged not to attack the government on war-related issues. According to Marshall, the socialist editor kept his word even though at the same time the Forward openly supported Socialist antiwar candidates for political office.[99] It was the conclusion of one historian that: "Marshall's intercession had the effect of locating the Forward in the Jewish community more firmly than in the socialist community." [100]

Cahan's wish to maintain the economic and political position of the paper was perforce an act that committed him and the Forward to the Jewish community, the basic source of circulation, advertisements, and money. At the same time the lack of a strong commitment to a basic body of socialist principles virtually assured that the Forward would become an increasingly Jewish newspaper. This general stance made it difficult for the Forverts to resist pulls away from socialism, pulls that grew ever stronger after World War I. Two of the most important of these were the increasing middle-class makeup of the Jewish community and the emergence of a Communist movement in the United States.

In the first case, the increase in the rate of social mobility among the Eastern European Jews and the general rise in their standard of living made it ever more difficult to pursue policies based on the interests of the working class. The Eastern European Jewish working class in America during World War I and into the 1920s was becoming an ever-diminishing proportion of the Eastern European Jewish community in the United States. And many of those who remained within it were living better in these years than ever before in their lives. The *Forverts* simply could not afford blithely to ignore this development in its editorial and political policies. The improving socioeconomic status of the Eastern European Jewry and their children in America became a constant prod pushing the *Forverts* toward liberalism and away from socialism.

The other factor was the emergence of Communism in the American and Jewish communities. Briefly (as this shall be considered in greater detail later), the Bolshevik Revolution of 1917 directly and indirectly produced splits in the Socialist parties around the world, including the Socialist party of the United States. Left-wing Socialists in many instances broke with their respective parties to form some version of a Communist party with concrete or sentimental ties to the Communist party of the Soviet Union. Jewish left-wing Socialists in the United States were no exception.

The major consequence of this split among the Jewish Socialists was to push the *Forward* toward a more moderate and a more Jewish position. This was in turn a result of two related developments. One, the left-wingers and more radical elements on the *Forward* staff such as Moissaye Olgin and Paul Novick either quit or were fired for their political views. This meant that the *Forward* and the Forward Association were suddenly without a significant internal left-wing pressure group and thus less capable of resisting pressures both from within and without for a greater movement toward moderation. Two, the split led to the formation of an organized left-wing, later Communist, force opposed not only to the Socialists who remained within the Socialist party but to the *Forward* also. This eventually led in 1922 to the creation of a Yiddish-language daily closely associated with the Communist party called the *Freiheit*, or Freedom. The existence of an organized enemy on its left that had in its arsenal a daily that competed for a still important segment of the *Forward's* readership led the *Forward* to seek allies on the right. It was to the right-wing Socialists and liberals that the *Forward* turned for its natural allies in the struggle with the left-wing Socialists and Communists.[101]

The *Forverts* also turned to the Jewish community and its organized forces for support in the struggle with this enemy on the left. The *Forverts* drew even closer to its traditional allies in the needle trades unions and the labor fraternal orders, who were themselves going through a similar left-versus-right struggle. The *Forverts* as part of its battle also utilized a Jewish appeal. It tried to wrap itself in the mantle of Jewishness while at the same time striving to place its left-wing foes beyond the bounds of the community. For example, one editorialist who wrote in both the *Forverts* and its subsidized socialist weekly, the *Zukunft*, accused the Jewish radicals of stirring up anti-Semitism by their political activities: "If the Jewish revolutionary would steadfastly remember his responsibility for the sufferings of his people, he would be more tactful and take better account of the conditions surrounding him; he would then not clamor for the impossible, as our Jewish revolutionaries now do." [102]

The criterion of evaluating political action primarily on the basis of its effect upon Jews was increasingly to become the way in which the *Forverts* guided and judged its own actions and those of other groups and parties. The *Forverts* in this regard showed more tact and assumed more responsibility for the Jewish people than did the Jewish revolutionary. But, of course, the ultimate determinators of what was good for the Jewish people and what was tactful and responsible behavior were Abraham Cahan and the *Forverts*.

This posture was clearly revealed in the actions of the *Forverts* and the allies that it sought in the 1920s and 1930s. In 1922 Abraham Cahan, then still a Socialist, supported conservative Samuel Gompers for the presidency of the AFL, despite the fact that his opponent, John L. Lewis, was more liberal. He believed that opposition to Gompers would be injurious to the interests of the ILGWU. [103] It was this type of reasoning and this quest for responsible allies that led the *Forverts* in subsequent years to support moderate and right-wing Socialist leaders in the Jewish needle trades unions and in the labor fraternal orders in their struggles with left-wing Socialists and Communists.

By the early 1930s the *Forverts'* formal break with socialism and the Socialist party was imminent. In 1932, for example, while still defining itself as a socialist newspaper, the *JDF* tacitly endorsed Herbert Lehman's candidacy for the New York governor's office while formally supporting his Socialist party opponent, Louis Waldman. Support for socialism and the Socialist party no longer seemed good for Jewish interests as defined by the *Forverts*. The liberal reforms of the New Deal and its assistance to the revival of the needle trades unions converted Cahan into an early supporter of FDR. This was a major factor that pulled Cahan and the *Forverts* away from the Socialist party.

There was also a push factor. The Socialist party and particularly its major spokesman, Norman Thomas, began to do things and adopt positions that Cahan and the *Forverts* thought to be injurious to Jewish interests. Norman Thomas's attacks in 1933 and 1934, for example, on the *Forward's* union allies for corruption and conduct unbecoming principled unions gained him the enmity of the *Forverts* and the accusation that he was endangering the entire Jewish labor movement. The adoption by the Socialist party in 1934 of a militant Declaration of Principles presaged the final break that was to occur in 1936. After 1934 the *Forverts* continually attacked Norman Thomas and his allies in the Socialist party. They were variously accused of being cheap politicians or Moscow stooges. Thomas also experienced great difficulty in getting the paper to print his views on socialism.[104] He did, however, indicate what he thought of Cahan in a letter to B. Charney Vladeck on August 3, 1934: "I believe that Cahan exercises a highly autocratic and hurtful degree of power in the Socialist and Jewish labor movement, not merely because of the Forward's circulation but because of its power over the money bags."[105] Then in 1936, for the first time in the history of the *Jewish Daily Forward*, the paper endorsed a Democrat for president, Franklin Delano Roosevelt.[106]

The *Forverts* continued its drift to the right and toward becoming a "Jewish" daily in the following years. More and more it appeared to be guided in its editorial policy by two major considerations: sales and Jewish interests. After World War II it became an ardent supporter of Israel and an even more implacable foe of Communism. The Communists, both domestic and international, were depicted as the major enemies of the Jewish people and of Israel as well as of the United States and the free world. Those who knowingly or not sympathized with Communism or advocated policies that the *Forverts* interpreted as being similar to or supportive of the Communists were also attacked. By the 1960s the *Forverts* had become an ardent defender of the United States' involvement in Vietnam.[107]

It also continued to retain intimate relations with the established leaders of the Jewish needle trades unions and the Workmen's Circle as they also drifted from socialism. More and more, these organizations tended to be equated with the Jewish community. Therefore, criticism of them became, in the *Forverts'* view, attacks on the Jewish community and the Jewish people, regardless of the creditability of the criticism. Thus, when an article appeared in *Harper's* in 1963 criticizing David Dubinsky of the ILGWU for his autocratic running of the union and for his policy of being too accommodating to the interests of garment employers, the *Forverts* blasted the critic, Paul Jacobs. One of the major points, as far as the *Forverts* was concerned, was that Jacobs had ignored the role that Dubinsky and the ILGWU had played in the Jewish Labor Committee, an organization that had fought the Nazis. As the *Forverts* pointed out: "It is a shame that it had to be a Jewish young man that spreads such stuff and suppressed the fact that the JLC helps a group that lost six million people, slaughtered by the German Nazi beasts."[108] Here Jacobs the ILGWU critic is nearly transformed into Jacobs the Nazi supporter.

One of the more salient of the indicators marking the *Forverts'* own transformation into a Jewish organ in the postwar period was its attitude toward Orthodox Judaism. Continuing a tendency that had been with it since the beginning, the *Forverts* became increasingly respectful of Orthodox ritual and customs. It also added two Orthodox rabbis to its staff. And when one of these rabbis criticized the Union of American Hebrew Congregations for attempting to establish a non-Orthodox synagogue in Israel, the *Forverts* did not repudiate him. Instead, it tried to be understanding of the delicate situation and the feelings of the various parties. The *Forverts* obviously did not wish to antagonize the feelings of the Orthodox rabbinate and Orthodox Jewry at this point in its existence.[109] The *Jewish Daily Forward*, then, after World War II had come full cycle. It now was a Jewish daily paper supporting narrowly conceived Jewish interests. But before this development it had along the way educated and bound several generations of Jews in the United States to a socialist perspective.

The Freiheit

The *Jewish Daily Forward* was not not the only socialist-oriented Yiddish-language daily to be published in post–World War I America. There were two others. One was the short-lived *Di Tsayt*, the organ of the Labor Zionists. It began publication on August 29, 1920, and went out of business on April 26, 1922.[110] The other paper, which is still in existence today, was the *Freiheit*. The *Freiheit*, which commenced its journalistic existence on April 2, 1922, was one result of the left-versus-right split in the Jewish Socialist Federation. Originally, it was operated by Jewish left-wing Socialists and Communists. Later the paper became an unofficial organ of the Communist party, although officially it was operated by the Freiheit Association (similar to the Forward Association).[111]

The *Feiheit* and the *Forverts* were similar in several significant ways. Both were Yiddish-language dailies based in New York City. Each regarded the Yiddish-speaking workers as its special constituency (although the *Forward* more than the *Freiheit* sought a broader and more varied readership base). This was reflected in their circulation figures. At no time did the *Freiheit's* circulation significantly challenge that of the *Forward's*. In 1930, the year of the highest annual circulation of the *Freiheit*, it reported a circulation of 64,500 (a highly suspect and probably inflated figure). The *Forward* in the same year reported a figure of 175,000. The *Freiheit*, like its arch rival, became the nerve center of a Yiddish Left subculture (or perhaps subsubculture). It too became the hub of a variety of kindred organizations and activities among Yiddish-speaking Jews. These included choruses, reading groups, orchestras, dramatic societies, and summer camps. The *Freiheit*, like the *Forverts*, provided a platform and an outlet for some of the best Yiddish literary talent in the United States. Again, like the *Forward*, the *Freiheit* gave journalistic and financial support or subsidies to groups, organizations, and political parties that had a political viewpoint similar to its own. The aforementioned

Coops are one notable example. And it too was intimately involved with a Yiddish-language fraternal order, the IWO, and unions or, in some cases, parts of unions in areas of Jewish concentrations. Whereas the *Forverts* was close to the International Ladies' Garment Workers' Union, the *Freiheit* was an intimate of the Communist-led furriers' union.

Inspite of all these similarities, important characteristics differentiated the two Yiddish-language dailies. Organizationally and politically the *Freiheit* did not have the independence and autonomy of the *Forverts*. The latter was always an entity separate from the Socialist party. The *Freiheit*, on the other hand, was virtually a party enterprise from the 1920s through the mid-1950s. Thus, in these decades the Communist party had far more influence over the *Freiheit's* management than the SP ever had over the *Forward*. For example, the Communist party removed the editor Moissaye Olgin from his position for a period of time. The Socialist party could never have done that to Cahan. Basically, the crucial difference between the two papers (when both were linked to their respective Left parties) was that the *Freiheit* staff regarded themselves as Communists and were usually willing to accept CP guidance and discipline while Cahan and his staff, although Socialists, from the very beginning cherished their independence.

The political and organizational differences between the two newspapers, however, did not preclude nor prevent the *Freiheit's* moving from the Communist party orbit and metamorphosing toward a Jewish, albeit a radical Jewish, orientation. The *Freiheit* in every decade from the 1920s through the 1950s found itself in a situation of having to choose between the Communist party and the Jewish community on issues where both took strong and contradictory positions. In the early decades the paper continually opted for the Communist side and continually antagonized at least a portion of its Jewish constituency. Eventually, the *Freiheit* reached a point where an important decision had to be made. Was it to be solely a Communist newspaper proclaiming party policy to Jews with little if any base in the Jewish community, or was it to be a newspaper that was reflective as well as part of a segment of the Jewish community? Over a period of years the *Freiheit* chose the second alternative, or, in other words, to be a Jewish newspaper independent of the Communist party. Thus, the *Freiheit*, like the *Forward*, found that viability as a newspaper with its own base was more important than ties to a particular Left party. The *Freiheit*, again not unlike the *Forward*, found that it could not alienate the Jewish constituency upon which it rested. The decision taken by the *Freiheit* staff over time that eventually led it toward a Jewish orientation and independence from the Communist party did not occur in an historical or political vacuum. Two factors in particular influenced its decision-making process. One was the shifting policies of

the Communist party, particularly on issues of concern to Jews, and
the other was the growth of national sentiment within the American
Jewish community.

The metamorphosis of the *Freiheit* and the role that these factors
played in this development can perhaps best be ascertained through
tracing the positions that the *Freiheit* took on the *yishuv*—the name
for the Jewish community in Palestine prior to 1948—and on Israel. It
was on these subjects that the newspaper came into the most serious
conflict with both Jews and Communists. And it was the *Freiheit's*
stance on Israel that, in large part, led to the final break with the Communist party.

From 1922 to 1929 the *Freiheit*, although anti-Zionist, had never attacked the *yishuv*. The Jewish community in Palestine was treated as
an entity separate from the Zionist movement. When the *yishuv* was
mentioned in the paper, the *Freiheit* would usually demand that the
Jews in the Holy Land be granted proper minority rights by the British
who controlled Palestine.

In 1929 the *Freiheit's* treatment of the *yishuv* changed dramatically.
This reversal of policy was in accord with the Communist party's relatively new hard-line ultra-Leftist policy. The occasion as well as the
vehicle for the *Freiheit's* adoption of a hostile stance with respect to
the *yishuv* and Jewish nationalism was an Arab assault on Jews in Palestine in which scores of Jews died. The paper's initial response was a
very careful and balanced one. It labelled the atrocity a "pogrom,"
meaning an assault of anti-Semites upon Jews, and placed most of the
ultimate responsibility upon the British imperialists. A portion of the
blame was also alloted to the Zionist leadership for its anti-Arab policies.[112]

This multifaceted position satisfied no one. Jews were embittered
because Zionists or fellow Jews received some of the blame for the
shedding of Jewish blood. The CP was angered because the *Freiheit*
placed the Arab onslaught in the context of a pogrom while grossly
understating the role of British imperialism and Zionism's cooperation with it. The party strongly urged that the *Freiheit* rectify its position, which it described as ". . . hardly, if at all, different from the
stand of the Jewish nationalist, Zionist and the capitalist press."[113] It
then demanded that the *Freiheit* print the Communist party's stand on
the violence in Palestine. The paper complied publishing the following: "The roots of the revolt of the Arabian masses are to be found in
the economic exploitation of the Arab peasantry, whose land has been
expropriated by British imperialism through the reactionary Jewish
Zionism . . . The establishment of a Jewish country in Palestine is the
fig leaf of British imperialism in its land-grabbing aggression . . .
And the Zionist movement is willingly and knowingly lending itself
to this mission."[114]

The *Freiheit* did not limit itself merely to printing this declaration.
The declaration was supplemented with articles and editorials de-

nouncing the Zionists. It also turned the tables and accused the Zionists of organizing pogroms against the Arabs. Editor Moissaye Olgin now placed the ultimate responsibility for the spilling of Jewish blood on the Zionists: "You [the Zionists] are playing with the blood of misled people. . . . You are out to satisfy your nationalistic robbery instincts at the expense of an alien people on an alien land. . . . The blood will fall on you. . . . You are murderers." [115]

The Communist party's declaration and the *Freiheit's* campaign against the Zionist "murderers" aroused the wrath of the Jewish community. A boycott campaign was launched against the *Freiheit,* and it was almost driven into bankruptcy. In Chicago, its offices were attacked by crowds of angry Jews. Its spokesmen who went around the country to defend the paper's and the CP's position found themselves confronted by hostile Jewish crowds.

This type of reaction was not limited to non-Communist Jews. Yiddish-speaking Communists and Communist sympathizers were also hurt and embittered by the new stance on Palestine. This conflict between Communist loyalties and Jewish sentiments was expressed in a letter to the *Freiheit:* "Everything that you write about the Zionists is true. But, for Heaven sake, it is Jews who are being beaten . . . Zionist colonies, why not say Jewish colonies . . . Jewish blood is being shed . . . I beg of you, don't justify the shedding of Jewish blood." [116] The conflict was so great that a distinguished group of Yiddish writers who had previously written for the *Freiheit* publicly broke with it. And in the aforementioned meetings convened to present the *Freiheit* viewpoint to Yiddish-speaking audiences, spokesmen considered it the better part of wisdom to select guards for protection from among non-Jewish Communists. (In 1957, the *Freiheit* reevaluated its position and once again labelled the Arab assault as a pogrom.)

The *Freiheit* survived. The principal reason for this was that it had established a hard core of Yiddish-speaking supporters. Even though many of them might disagree with the paper's position on issues concerning Jews, there were many other areas on which there was considerable agreement. In addition, once they withdrew from support of the *Freiheit* and remained Communists or pro-Communists, there was nowhere else they could comfortably turn. The *Forverts* did not represent a viable alternative even though it was a prolabor and non-Zionist Yiddish-language newspaper. By 1929 the *Forverts* had earned the animosity of the *Freiheit* and its supporters on a host of issues. One failing by the *Freiheit* was insufficient reason to forget the *Forverts'* history of opposition to groups and issues to which these Yiddish Communists and pro-Communists still felt committed.

Also, it was not simply a question of agreeing or disagreeing with the viewpoint of a newspaper. The *Freiheit,* as mentioned earlier, stood at the center of a network of Yiddish proletarian institutions. In this subculture, the Yiddish Communists and pro-Communists found a world that offered them identity, meaning, friendship, and understanding. It was simply not possible for them to forsake the Freiheit and retain membership in this subculture. The fate of fellow Jews in the yishuv and elsewhere concerned them as Jews. But their own fate as total persons in the everyday world of the Yiddish Communist-oriented subculture was of even greater concern.

The Freiheit's stance on Zionism and the yishuv was the first but by no means the last time that it antagonized some of its constituency and the Jewish community on a Jewish issue. Its defense of the Nazi-Soviet pact in 1939 and its belated response to news of Soviet attrocities against Jews also proved controversial and costly. (These issues and events will be examined in greater detail within the broader context of Jewish and Communist relations elsewhere in this study.) Still, the Freiheit survived and maintained the allegiance of a core of followers.

The allegiance of this group was retained not only because of their involvement in and affection for a Freiheit-inspired subculture. It was due to other factors as well. Many in this group did not deeply disagree with the Freiheit in its reaction to the handling of these issues. Furthermore, there were many other issues on which the Freiheit and its readership basically agreed. And very importantly, the Freiheit and the Communist party in the years after 1929 did not remain consistent and implacable foes of the yishuv or other interests and matters concerning Jews. From 1936 to 1948 the Freiheit and the Communist party as well as the Soviet Union took approaches to primarily Jewish matters that warmed the hearts of Communists and pro-Communists in the Jewish community. The campaign against anti-Semitism, the advocacy of Yiddish culture, and the support for the creation of Israel, were prominent examples of the Freiheit and the Communist party's ability to promote a pro-Jewish point of view.

The Freiheit also did not wish to alienate American Jewry or offend the Jewish sensibilities of its supporters. Although its readership did not compare in size with that of the Forverts, and although it did not aspire to be a broad-based mass circulation Yiddish-language daily, the Freiheit still did not want its influence to be restricted to the 20,000 or so readers that it had during the 1930s. The Freiheit wanted to be able to make some impact in the Jewish community beyond the circle of its subscribers. The paper's editorial staff realized that continued hostility toward the yishuv and Jewish concerns would cut it off from the Jewish community and also be a source of tension with committed followers as well.

In 1936 the Communist party's new position on Jews and Jewish culture, stemming from its desire to gain allies—even bourgeois Jewish allies—in the struggle against fascism, allowed and encouraged the Freiheit to be more responsive to the interests and concerns of its Jewish base. At the same time this policy change allowed and encouraged the Freiheit to seek new readers among Jews beyond its traditional circle of support. In 1938, at the 19th Convention of the New York State Communist party, the *Freiheit's* editor, Moissaye Olgin, expressed his concern about the *Freiheit's* and the Communist party's relationship to the Jewish community and even admitted the past mistakes that both had made in this arena:

Comrades . . . We managed to alienate the Jewish masses. More than that, we managed to convey. . . . that the Communists are hostile to the Jewish national aspirations. We fought Zionism, which was correct but . . . we forgot that many progressive elements. . . . were Zionistically inclined. We forgot also that the craving, the desire for nationhood is not in itself reactionary. We conveyed the impression that the Jewish people . . . in Palestine are our enemies and we are theirs.[117]

In the next decade, with the major exception of the Hitler-Stalin Pact in 1939, there was scarcely an issue pertaining to Jewish matters over which the Communist Party and the Jewish community were at odds. This congruence between its two souls, however, meant that the *Freiheit* staff and its readers had little armor with which to resist envelopment by the rising tide of Jewish consciousness and nationalism. Hitler and the Holocaust accentuated the Jewish identity of Jews on the *Freiheit*, in the Communist party, in the Jewish Left subculture, and in the American Jewish community. The sentiment in favor of a Jewish national homeland in Palestine at war's end among American Jews was overwhelming. And the least opposition to this concept came from the pool from which the *Freiheit* drew its supporters, the Yiddish-speaking blue collar workers. A 1945 Roper Poll revealed that 11 percent of American Jews were opposed to the establishment of a Jewish state, but among blue-collar Jews the percentage was six percent and among those who spoke English either brokenly or not at all the figure was five and eight percent, respectively.[118] The breadth and the depth of Jewish feelings on this issue demanded that the *Freiheit* favor the establishement of a Jewish state in Palestine. Fortunately for the *Freiheit*, the Soviet Union was a champion of this position in the immediate postwar years. Thus, the *Freiheit* could freely and positively respond to both its Jewish consciousness and base on the one hand and the guidance of the Communist party on the other. This, however, was one of the last times that the *Freiheit* found itself in so fortunate a position on a matter of importance pertaining to Jews and Jewish interests.

After the establishment of the state of Israel in 1948, the Communist and the Jewish attitudes toward it began to diverge. This divergence, which grew larger over time, place the *Freiheit* in a difficult position. It was forced to chose between its Jewish and Communist constituencies and bases. By 1952, when it became clear that the Labor government of Israel was formally abandoning its policy of nonalignment and moving closer to the United States, the *Freheit* developed a position that allowed it to continue to reach out simultaneously to both the Jewish and Communist camps. Editorially the paper distinguished between the people and the state of Israel on the one hand and the government on the other. The people and the state received the support and good wishes of the *Freiheit*, whereas the government of Israel was attacked for its pro Western policies.

In 1956, the reactions of the Soviet Union and the United States Communist Party to Israel's attack on Egypt in combination with France and the United Kingdom subjected the *Freiheit's* general policy on Israel to severe strain. It became increasingly clear that the paper would soon be in the position of having to alienate either Communists or Jews. It also became increasingly clear that the *Freiheit*, in the making of unpleasant choices, was not going to alienate its Jewish supporters or its own Jewish soul.

The movement of the *Freiheit* from the Communist camp and toward a pro-Israel orientation was perceptible in the wake of the Suez War. The paper was not as condemning of Israel as either the Soviet Union or the American Communist Party. Though critical of Israel, the *Freiheit* took the opportunity after the war to express its open solidarity with the people and the state. In the December 2, 1956 issue, editor Paul Novick wrote an editorial entitled, "Israel Is Here To Stay!" In it he tried to show his pro-Israel sympathies and at the same time indicate the linkage that existed between the paper and a Communist position. The *Freiheit*, at this time, did not wish to place itself beyond the Communist pale. Novick pointed out in the editorial that the *Freiheit* was guided in its attitude toward Israel by two premises:

1. That the birth of Israel was a great historic event. Israel came into existence in the midst of a progressive anti-imperialist struggle, with the help of socialist states and the fact that the United States and the Soviet Union joined hands in favor of its formation.

2. That the State of Israel must be safeguarded and protected, and that once and for all it must be made perfectly clear that Israel is here to stay.

He concluded by again differentiating between the people and the state of Israel on the one hand and the government on the other. "We say that the people of Israel must not be punished for the deeds of Ben Gurion. The life of the state of Israel must be secured."

This editorial by Novick is indicative of how "Jewish" the *Freiheit* was becoming. On earlier occasions, when there was some divergence between a Communist and Jewish line, the paper would have come down heavily on the Communist side and provided its Jewish constituency with a Jewish rationale or reason why it should concur. This time the situation was reversed. The Communists were now the ones to whom the ideological sop was being served. The other interesting aspect of this piece was that the only major conceivable threat to Israel's existence in 1956 had to come from the Soviet Union. It was the Soviet Union that armed Egypt and that threatened to invade

Israel during the war. The *Freiheit*, then, through this editorial, was placing itself clearly in the pro-Israeli camp while at the same time giving credence, however inadvertently, to the long-held position of its bitter enemies in the Jewish community that the Soviet Union represented a significant threat to Jewish interests. It should also be noted that this Jewish attitude toward Communist Russia had been reinvigorated and greatly exacerbated by the revelation earlier in 1956 of Stalin's heinous crimes against Jews and Jewish institutions in the USSR.

This movement toward a more "Jewish" orientation continued after 1956. By the time of the next Arab-Israeli war in 1967, the *Freiheit* found itself directly opposed to the line of the Soviet Union and the American Communist party with respect to Israel. The party and the USSR took the position that Israel was the aggressor in the latest war and should return all captured territories to the Arabs. The *Freiheit* countered by contending that Israel had waged a war of self-defense and that Israel did not have to return all of the conquered Arab lands. (It should be noted that even at this time some members of the *Freiheit's* editorial staff still were arguing in favor of the Communist position.) There was little room for compromise between these two stands. The differences over the war and the ways to bring peace to the Middle East were primary factors in Novick's expulsion from the Communist party and the final break between the party and the *Freiheit* in 1968. The paper and its staff, according to the CP's leading expert on Jewish affairs, Hyman Lumer (whom I interviewed), had "more and more adopted the line of the Zionists on the question and abandoned the line of the Communist Party."

The clash over Israel, although quite important in itself, was part of a larger issue—the Jewish issue—on which the *Freiheit* and the party grew to hold increasingly divergent views and eventually led to the final rupture in relations between the two. In addition to Israel, one other *causus belli* within the context of the Jewish question was the assimilation of Jews. The *Freiheit*, through its editor Paul Novick, was charged by the party as being opposed to the assimilation of Jews. Not only did the party feel that Novick was against assimilation in general, but it charged him with being opposed to assimilation in the Soviet Union. Novick was accused of attacking the Soviet Union's policy in this regard as a policy of forced assimilation.

Paul Novick was removed from his seat on the party's National Committee and then expelled for his "crimes" revolving almost entirely around the Jewish question. An interesting but revealing sidelight to his expulsion was the manner in which both the *Freiheit* and the Communist party dealt with it after the event. Neither chose to publicize it in America until 1977. The *Freiheit* evidently did not wish to alienate or antagonize those among its supporters with strong ties to the Communist party. And the party, for its part, most likely did not wish to alienate or antagonize those among its members who sympathized with the Freiheit on the Jewish question. The CP did, however, publicize the expulsion outside of the United States and finally in this country on May 12, 1977.

One of the last major salvoes in what has become an almost open war between the Freiheit and the CP was hurled by the latter in the party paper, Daily World, on May 12, 1977. In an article that was actually a reprint of the statement of the party's Central Committee, the CP formally and openly denounced the Freiheit on a variety of charges centering around the Freiheit's handling of Israel and Soviet Jews. The former Communist editors of the Yiddish-language paper were accused among other things of: ". . . persistence in exploiting and distorting for opportunist reasons healthy national sentiments among Jewish People, particularly among Jewish workers, in a way which supports the reactionary nationalistic position of Zionism. . . ."

Thus, the Freiheit was no more able than the Forverts before it to resist the growth within it of a Jewish identity and interest. In both cases, each had severed their long-term relations with their respective Left parties largely because of differences stemming from Jewish interests. The cause of these developments was the same. Both were Yiddish-language dailies rooted in a Jewish community. Both the Freiheit and the Forverts wanted to have a political impact of their readership and on the Jewish masses. Consequently, each had to be responsive to the felings and interests of its Jewish supporters and to some extent of the Jewish community that lay beyond them. This need to be responsive and sympathetic to Jewish concerns made the Freiheit an the Forverts, in a sense, captives of events and developments that affected their constituents and the Jewish community from the 1920s through the post–World War II era. The most important of these was the growing middle-class status and heightened standard of living of the Jewish community on the one hand and the rise of a nationalist or pro-Israel sentiment fostered by the Holocaust on the other. These particular developments eventually place both the Freiheit and the Forverts on a collision course with their respective left-wing parties.

It should be noted that the Freiheit did not become as reformist in its policies as the Forverts either before or after its break with the Communist party. It remained and continues to be a prolabor and, in general, a proradical newspaper. The primary reasons for this appear to be the greater ideological commitment of the Freiheit staff, as compared with that of the Forverts', to socialism and the political character of the Freiheit's constituency. The Freiheit established an intimate relationship with Jewish individuals, workers, and organizations that stood further to the Left than did those who supported the Forverts. If it had moved too far to the right, the Freiheit would have overlapped with the Forverts and lost much of its uniqueness. Once this political distinctiveness had eroded too far, there would have been little reason for its constituency to maintain its allegiance. And once it overlapped too much with its rival, the *Freiheit* would have found itself competing in the same general marketplace with the *Forverts* for readers and supporters. Given the economic power and the popularity of the *Forverts* among the Yiddish-language population, the odds against being successful in this competition appeared slim.

CONCLUSION

Labor fraternal orders and a Left press erected on American shores in the early decades of this century formed a significant part of the institutional core of a Jewish labor movement and Jewish Left subculture. These fraternal organizations and their offshoots and the labor newspapers were the vehicles through which thousands of Jews for decades developed loyalties and commitments to the Left in the United States.

These institutions shaped the Left political orientation of their members and readers in various ways. First, they were political socialization agencies. The fraternal orders and especially the labor press politically educated their constituents and influenced the way in which they viewed and understood politics. Second, they insulated their constituents from politically contaminating contact with bourgeois individuals and institutions. Jews through the Left fraternal groups and newspapers could fulfill many of their educational, social, and cultural needs. This meant that there was little necessity for them to go beyond the boundaries of their Leftist-oriented social world. Third (and very close to the second), these organizations facilitated continual contact between Leftist or pro-Leftist individuals. Continual interaction with like-minded persons socially reinforced the Left propensities of the individuals who belonged to the fraternal orders and their organizational subsidiaries.

The Leftist fraternal associations and the press, however, with the passage of time moved from a radical to a Jewish orientation when the radicalism was either moderated or consigned to an historical waste bin. The key levers that moved them in the direction were their all-Jewish constituencies and concern for organizational viability. The diminution in the size of a Yiddish-speaking working class led those fraternal associations and newspapers that desired to be relevant or successful to seek a broader based constituency from within the Jewish community. This in turn moderated and "Jewishized" the orientation of these institutions in two ways. First, to attract and maintain as well as augment a readership and membership heterogeneous in terms of class and religion it became necessary to adopt a political line and position congenial to this new constituency. Second, the more broadly Jewish and less socialist these institutions became, the more susceptible they were to developments within the American Jewish community, such as a rising ethnic consciousness, that further hastened their movement from secular radicalism.

The political metamorphosis of the Left fraternal orders and press was neither rapid nor consistent. The various component parts of these institutions moved from socialism at different speeds over time. Some retained their radical orientation into the post–World War II era, and a few continue to do so up to the present day. It was these latter institutions or subinstitutions, the remnants of a once powerful Jewish Left subculture, that produced and nurtured radicals and radical-sympathizers among American Jews into the period of the New Left and still continues to perform this role for the small numbers of Old Jewish Leftists that are politically active in the 1970s.

7 Down from the Heights: Post-World War I Developments that Weakened the Jewish Left

INTRODUCTION

During the pre–World War I years, the various factors that worked against the Jewish community's tie to the Left, although present, were not full-blown. The large and concentrated self-contained Yiddish-speaking immigrant working class community, with its large complement of socialist intellectuals and leaders, was then a subsociety strongly predisposed to the Left. After World War I the factors that had contributed to a close tie between the Jews and socialism atrophied, while those that had mitigated against such a relationship became stronger. In this chapter we shall examine the various changes and forces that helped to undermine the nexus between the Jews and the Left in the post–World War I decades.

IMMIGRATION

One of the most important changes that adversely affected the Jewish Left in the post–World War I period was the rapid decline in immigration. The Yiddish-speaking immigrants from Russia and Eastern Europe had been a constant source of reinforcement for the relationship between the Jews and the Left in the United States. They had more than compensated for the Jews that left the factory floor, quit the old Jewish neighborhoods, stopped speaking Yiddish, and ceased voting for Socialists. The newer immigrants were Yiddish-speaking workers, many of whom were fresh from contact with radical trade unions and revolutionary movements. In America, disproportionately, they were manual workers, thy lived in the old Jewish neighborhoods, and they supported the parties of the Left.

The year 1921 marked both the recommencement of mass Jewish immigration following the wartime lull and the end of such large-scale immigration as well. From 1915 to 1920 a total of 79,921 Jews entered the United States, compared to 138,051 in 1914 alone. In 1921 the figure rose to 119,036. From 1922 to 1924 the average anual number was about 51,000. For the rest of the decade the yearly average dropped to approximately 11,000. From 1931 to 1938 the annual average fell even lower, to about 7,000.[1]

This pattern was not unique to Jewish immigrants. The immigration laws of 1921 and 1924 were designed to limit the number of Europeans coming to America's shores. And the laws served their purpose. European immigration declined from 652,364 in 1921 to 148,366 in 1925.[2] These laws, however, were not oblivious to national origin; they were drafted so as to insure that immigrants from "better stock or northwestern Europe would outnumber the "inferior" peoples from Southern and Easten Europe. One of the "inferior" groups specifically aimed at were the Jews. Congress did not want great waves of "unassimilable," "filthy," and "un-American" Jews inundating American shores.[3]

The cessation of large-scale Jewish immigration meant that the role of the foreign-born within the American Jewish community would soon diminish. Indeed, even before the restrictive laws had been passed, the 1920 census recorded that native-born Jews outnumbered those born outside of the United States.[4] Henceforth, the American-born and those who had first come to the United States as youths would increasingly determine the political direction of the American Jewish community. This cessation of mass immigration, also meant that the role of Eastern European influences and experiences in the politics of immigrant Jews in America would soon diminish. As they became more acculturated and as their children matured on the soil of the United States, it would be American conditions and the experiences of life in the New World that would become the key factors in the shaping of Jewish political attitudes and behavior.

This situation did not augur well for the Jewish Left or the Left in general. From 1912 on it was the immigrants who provided the primary source of Socialists in the United States. In 1919 they had been a majority within the Socialist party. At the birth of the Communist party (following the split in the SP in 1919), the foreign-born made up approximately 90 percent of the members of that organization. It was not until 1936 that the CP would be able to claim that a majority of its members were native Americans. And this was at a time when approximately 87 percent of the population in the country who were 21 years of age or older were native born.[5]

History provides another example of the fate of a Jewish Left in a western capitalist country, the United Kingdom, when Eastern European immigration is restricted. The Jewish Left flourished there during the period of mass immigration from 1903 to 1906 and in the few years immediately thereafter. Then Parliament passed the Alien Act in 1905, which limited the number of Jewish immigrants, in the years between 1906 and 1914, to an annual average of from 4000–5000, or half of the 1905 figure. In 1914 new legislation virtually terminated the admission of Jews into the United Kingdom. Without new recruits, activists, and leaders plus losing established leaders and cadres to the United States, the Jewish Left in the United Kingdom rapidly faded after 1914.[6]

SOCIOECONOMIC CHANGES

Prior to 1920 the Jewish Left had received its strongest support from Yiddish-speaking Jews located in the working class, in unions, and in crowded ghettoes. It was precisely these traditional Jewish Left constituencies that decreased and weakened the most after World War I, as the result of upward economic and occupational mobility and horizontal geographical mobility.

Occupational Mobility

During the pre–World War I years, a majority of Jews in the United States were classified as industrial workers. They were largely concentrated in the needle trades in a few major urban areas. After the war the Jewish community in America became increasingly a white-collar and middle-class community.[7] During the 1930s, surveys of Jews in various towns and cities, although fraught with methodological problems, suggest that Jews were then largely occupying white-collar positions. And, within the nonmanual category, they were increasingly moving from the clerical, sales, and small proprietor occupations to ones higher on the socioeconomic ladder, particularly the professional occupations.

The trend in this direction was interrupted during the Depression but rapidly resumed after World War II. A focus on the professional category allows us to more clearly see this movement. During the 1930s, roughly 11 percent of employed Jewish males could be classified as professionals. Shortly after World War II, approximately 15 percent could be so classified. By 1957 the figure was 20 percent; and 15 years later, the percentage of professionals among Jewish men in the labor force was 30 percent. The meaning of these statistics becomes sharper when placed in a comparative context. In each of these time periods, the Jewish percentage of professionals was roughly twice as large as that for American males as a whole. Also, as might be expected, the rise in the percentage of professionals was accompanied by a decline in that for sales and clerical occupations, the categories at the lower end of the nonmanual scale.[8]

On a national level, the Jewish working class became an even smaller minority of the Jewish community after World War II. Several years after the war, surveys of Jews in various locales indicated that between 4 and 25 percent were in manual occupations. In 1957 data indicated that throughout the country there were approximately 20 percent of employed Jewish men in blue-collar positions. (The 1934 and 1957 estimates used different definitions and data bases.) By 1972 the figure had declined to about 10 percent, while the comparable figure for all American men in the labor force was in excess of 50 percent.[9] It is quite clear then that on a national level the Jewish working class in America was a short-lived phenomenon. It reached its height in terms of numbers and political importance prior to World War I, after which it rapidly declined. But, for our purposes, the developments within the Jewish labor force cannot be limited to the national scene. The Jewish working class played its major political and economic roles in a few large urban centers, particularly New York. It is there that the relationship between the Jews and the Left was the strongest and most important. And it is in New York City in particular that most of our attention in this study is directed.

The Jewish working class did not decline as rapidly in the major metropolitan areas as it did in the smaller cities and towns. In New York and Chicago in the early 1930s, about a third of the gainfully employed Jews were industrial workers. Two decades later the percentage of blue-collar workers among Jewish males had not declined appreciably. It was approximately 30 percent in 1952 and remained about this size in New York City in the early 1960s.[10] The maintenance of a sizeable working-class population in New York City after World War I is an important factor for our purposes. It was this concentrated working class that served as the base upon which the structure of the Jewish relationship to the Left rested. However, closer examination of this metropolitan Jewish working class indicates that it was not the best base for any movement intent on becoming a major influence in national or state politics. Although large, it was only a minority of the Jewish labor force in New York City. This was true as early as the 1920s. Its size continually diminished over the years, as noted above, until it reached about the 30 percent mark. Thus any political group or party within the Jewish community that limited its appeal and concern to manual workers was destined to play a minor role, even in New York City.

However, it was not only a matter of size. The constituent elements and the factors that shaped this metropolitan Jewish working class are also important with respect to the role of the Left. Two notable and interrelated features of the New York City Jewish working class were age and ethnicity. The Jews in blue-collar work in New York City after World War I were disproportionately older and foreign-born compared to their coreligionists in nonmanual occupations. Thus the Jewish working class in the post–World War I decades represented the past rather than the future.

Let us briefly examine the reasons for this. The most obvious appears to be that the Jewish working class was not replenished. There were two major ways in which this New York City group of workers could have grown in size. One was to recruit Jewish workers from outside the city's boundaries. The other was for the Jewish workers to produce children who followed in their occupational footsteps. Neither condition obtained for the Jewish working class in New York City or anywhere else in post–World War I America. (The Hasidic Jews who came after World War II represent something of an exception, but they are not directly relevant to this discussion.)

The most important source of outside recruits before the war were the Eastern European immigrants. Legislation of the early 1920s, however, insured that the constant streams of immigrants to the ranks of the workers, unionists, and Leftists prior to the war were reduced to rivulets afterwards. The cessation of mass immigration in the early 1920s meant that the Jewish working class in America, in order to survive or grow, would have to reproduce itself or gain recruits from the downwardly mobile.

The children of Jewish workers did not follow their fathers into the working class in significant proportions in either New York City or the nation as a whole. As early as 1900, the trend was discernible among the children of the immigrant workmen. The younger generation sought paths leading to white-collar occupations. Even during the Depression the percentage of non-working-class American-born Jews, starting their occupational lives was appreciably higher than that of their father's generation.[11] Data gathered from New York City in 1950 and 1952 indicate that the percentage of blue-collar workers among the foreign-born Jews is about twice as high as it is among those born in the country.[12] A study based on United States Census materials from 1950 also confirms this same tendency on a national scale. The study indicated that whereas 48 percent of the Russian-born (largely Jewish) males in the labor force were blue collar workers, the comparable figure for those males born in the United States with one or both parents from Russia was 32 percent.[13]

Jewish working-class parents did not encourage their children to pursue working-class occupations. They generally wanted their sons and daughters to have better occupations. This was reflected in a popular story that circulated in the garment district during the Depression:

A machine operator asked his boss, a *landsman*, to take in his young son, just out of school, as a floor worker. "Moishe," said the boss, "why a floor worker? There is an empty sewing machine near you. Take your son and teach him the trade." "Not on your life, Sam," was the heated reply. "If I teach him to operate the machine, he will remain a cloak maker and I don't want that. But, as a floor worker, he will go to night college and become a somebody."[14]

Even children from Socialist workers families were admonished not to enter the working class. One such individual, Harry Roskolenko, a prominent writer, recalled his mother's words to her children: "Don't work for others, work for yourself. Don't be like your father, a wage slave . . ."[15]

It is important to realize that more than just a movement away from the working class was involved. Jews were also leaving the unions— important sources and sustainers of Leftists. In the ILGWU, for example, the percentage of Jews steadily declined. In 1924 they constituted 64 percent of the membership, by 1934 they represented less than half, and in the 1940s, only about one-third.[16] The white-collar occupations to which the Jewish working class and their children were moving were, with some notable exceptions, not receptive to unionization. This movement out of the unions and working class was facilitated by structural changes that were occurring in America. In each decade of the twentieth century, beginning in 1900, the percentage of males in white-collar positions increased. In 1900 it was 18 percent; in 1910, 21 percent; 1920, 25 percent; 1930, 29 percent; 1940, 31 percent; and 1950, 37 percent. Anerican-born Jews as well as first generation Jews than had positions available to them outside of the working class.[17]

The core of the Jewish working class in the United States in general and in New York City in particular was made up of foreign-born Jews. Although many of this group who started their working lives as manual laborers subsequently rose to white-collar positions, most of the Yiddish-speaking immigrants who began as blue-collar workers apparently finished their occupational careers in this same broad category.[18] The data for Eastern European Jews in Boston are the most precise in this particular regard. In this city in 1910, approximately 75 percent of these foreign-born Jews were in blue-collar occupations. By or near the end of their working lives, this percentage had declined to 51.[19] The less precise data for New York City and for the nation also suggest that a majority of the Eastern-European-born Jewish immigrants were manual workers at the beginning and the end of their work careers.[20]

This core group of foreign-born Jewish workers represented a major base and source of continuity for the Jewish Left in the first several decades of the twentieth century. This group, however, was not as substantial or as homogeneous as the data seem to indicate. It is necessary to stress that the best of the available information about their careers does not provide a picture of occupational changes during their working lives. That is, we do not have the longitudinal data that would shed light on intragenerational occupational mobility. The cross-sectional data that we do have to work with masks the considerable changes that took place in the occupational careers of this immigrant generation. We do know that there was a relatively large amount of movement back and forth between the blue- and white-collar categories, particularly during the 1930s. This phenomenon was most pronounced in the garment industry.

This phenomenon suggests that at any moment in time during the 1920s and 1930s, many immigrant Jews who were in the working class in fact were not part of it in sentiment. In 1925, for example, the

General Executive Board (GEB) of the ILGWU singled out as a major source of its problems those members who had left to start their own businesses and then returned when they did not succeed. When they returned to the union, the GEB noted, these failed entrepreneurs brought with them, ". . . the psychology of a boss, regarding the Union as the cause of their failure. And, they are relentless enemies of the Union, trying to harm it whenever possible." [21]

This movement between white- and blue-collar occupations was not the only occupational change that took place within the immigrant working-class group, particularly in the strategic garment industry. As the decades passed, an increasing number of such immigrant Jews became concentrated in the more skilled and high-paying jobs within the manual labor category. In the garment trade, they were disproportionately cutters and designers.[22] The Jewish men who held these positions tended to become increasingly less socialist over time. For example, Local 10, the cutters' local of the ILGWU and the home base of David Dubinsky, was one of the most important opponents of the Left within that union. In the early 1960s, while other locals comprised of less skilled workers became largely black and Puerto Rican, Local 10 retained its predominantly Jewish character, apparently by preventing members of those groups from gaining entrance.[23]

Thus the socioeconomic working-class base of the Jewish Left after World War I became smaller and weaker. The large and powerful Jewish working class that had provided so much support to the Left prior to World War I was a short-lived and essentially one-generation phenomenon. By the 1920s the immigrant Jewish community was no longer as heavily influenced by a vibrant socialist-oriented working class. As the Jewish community became increasingly middle class and white collar in composition, its economic self-interest no longer led it in the direction of supporting the Left.

Educational Mobility

It is also important to examine another facet of socioeconomic mobility, educational mobility. The enrollment of large numbers of young Jews in colleges and professional schools in the post–World War I era sapped the strength of the Jewish Left. Again, as with occupational mobility, this tendency had been apparent before the war but accelerated afterwards. In the years after World War I the bright and ambitious young men of the Jewish community, whose counterparts had been denied access to higher education in czarist Russia and impeded from gaining higher education in the New World by the economic necessity of providing for themselves and their familits after arriving there, could take advantage of the institutions of higher education open to them in the United States.

The data on Jewish enrollments in American colleges and universities prior to World War II is fragmentary but internally consistent. The

364   JEWS AND THE LEFT

data indicate that Jews were disproportionately represented among the nation's student body and that their enrollment during the post–World War I years markedly increased from what it had been in the prewar years. In 1915 Jewish students constituted about 3 percent of the total enrollments in the 534 colleges surveyed. Four years later, in 1919, they constituted about 10 percent of all students in the 108 institutions surveyed. This rise in enrollments immediately after the war was however, not only a Jewish phenomenon. The number of students in higher education in the United States rose markedly between 1915 and 1920 (441,000 to 598,000).[24] But, as one historian expressed it: ". . . second generation Jews (who, unlike the Catholics, had no colleges of their own) stood out more and more as the most numerous and successful ethnic minority invading the campuses."[25] In fact, the Jews were so successful that colleges and universities instituted quota systems to minimize their numbers. The quota system did not reduce overall Jewish attendance at postsecondary institutions, but it did limit their numbers at the more elite private schools of the East and at the medical schools.[26] However, one of the better surveys conducted in the interwar period revealed the 105,000 Jewish students in the 1319 institutions surveyed was approximately the same in 1935 as it had been in 1919, 10 percent. This may, however, have been a function of the Depression. In any case, the total number of students was an impressive figure.[27]

After World War II the number of Jews attending institutions of higher education rose to about 200,000. By the early 1960s the figure had increased to about 275,000. These numbers, when compared with the total number of Jews in the college-age cohort (ages 18–24), reveal that higher education had become the norm for Jews in this age bracket. The proportion of Jews in the college-age cohort who actually attended an institution of higher education ranged from about 60 percent in the 1950s to between 70 and 80 percent in the early 1960s.[28]

Another way to examine educational mobility is to compare the educational accomplishments of native-born to foreign-born Jews. A study conducted in New York City in the early 1960s indicates that 22 percent of foreign-born Jewish males had attained some college education or went further. The comparable percentage for native-born Jewish males, which includes second- and third-generation males, is 62 percent, a difference of 40 percentage points. The contrast is also striking when only those who had graduated from college and gone on to graduate or professional schools are compared. Nine percent of the foreign-born Jews are in this category, compared to 38 percent of the native-born.[29]

Both the Jewish and non-Jewish Left suffered because the American colleges and universities were so open to Jews. Access to higher education deprived the Left of numerous leaders, cadres, and activists. For the Jewish Left in particular, the mass enrollments broke the nexus between the Jewish intellectual and the Jewish worker that had originally been forged in czarist Russia. After World War I in the United States, Jewish intellectuals and, to a lesser extent, Jewish youth, soon disappeared from the factory and shop floors. The colleges and universities were the channels by which those who entered were able to move out of the working class and away from working-class politics.

Students and Radicalism Before World War II

That does not, however, mean that all who were in or exposed to higher education were or became non-Leftists. American colleges and universities did harbor and produce radicals among their student bodies at various periods after World War I and World War II, but, in small numbers. From World War I until the beginning of World War II the combined *student* membership of the two largest Left youth groups (the Young People's Socialist League and the Young Communist League), probably did not exceed 12,000 in any given year. For most years, the average was far smaller than that. Actually, this was almost a self-fulfilling prophecy, as both the Communist and Socialist parties did not consider the campuses appropriate arenas to politicize or to recruit from until the mid- to latter-1930s. They tended to regard college students as lost to the cause of the proletariat.[30] The Depression did not change this situation appreciably as far as student membership in Left parties and organizations was concerned. In 1934, at CCNY, then predominantly Jewish, an investigating committee appointed by the official alumni group (the Associate Alumni), reported that ". . . less than one percent of the total student body belonged to radical organizations."[31] Several years later various national surveys indicated that the percentage of radicals among students at large was not much in excess of 2 or 3 percent.[32]

Students did move toward the political left of the spectrum in the 1930s. In 1932, for example, a national student survey reported that, for the first time, the majority no longer favored the Republican party but did support Franklin D. Roosevelt and the Democrats. Large numbers also took part in antiwar activities during this decade. In 1934, 25,000 students reportedly took the Oxford Pledge to refrain from participating in a war. A year later about 185,000 students took part in a demonstration for peace. In 1936 approximately 200,000, or 20 percent of the nation's student body, went out on strike against war. Twenty thousand joined the American Student Union, a coalition of Communists, Socialists, and liberals, which was an antiwar organization throughout most of its existence.[33] Such activities should not be taken as valid indicators of a commitment to the basic reorganization or restructuring of American society, much less to revolution. Generally, the most popular political organizations and activities that had a radical bent involved opposition to the oncoming war. There is, however, nothing that is intrinsically socialist in opposing war. In the

1930s the Left did not have a monopoly on this stance; even right-wing isolationists opposed any preparation for armed conflict, albeit for different reasons. It was easy for students to identify an antiwar position with Leftist politics. The Left, particularly the Communists, the largest group on the Left, focused much of their energies on the issues of war and peace. The Young Communist League and Communist cadres within student political organizations made these issues a central part of the political agenda for students throughout most of the period of the student movement of the 1930s.[34]

It is easier for the Left to build a student movement around an issue such as peace than it is to build one around a class-related cause. For the most part, nonclass issues do not cause such deep divisions or intense opposition as do class issues. College students in the United States are generally either from the non-working-class or on their way to middle class positions. It is thus difficult to mobilize a significant number of them for any extended period to oppose either the class or the interests of the class from which they originated or to which they are moving. By focusing on such issues as peace, civil rights, or civil liberties the Left can more easily mobilize students, but such issues are not central to the essence of the Left. The Left's dilemma in working with American college students is that, after World War I and up to the present, it has been effective in reaching them on only nonclass issues. Of those it has reached on this basis, relatively few have been able to make the shift to support the Left on economic issues central to socialist positions. An associated problem is that, once the particular dramatic event that has given rise to student concern passes, as in the case of Sacco and Venzetti in the 1920s, student support for the Left and its front organizations subsides.[35]

In the 1930s, for the vast majority of students who participated in them the strikes against war and membership in the American Student Union or other similar groups, represented the furthest Left they would go in their political lives. These probably were the only radical gestures of their lives. The description by Joseph Freeman, a Jewish student at Columbia University at the time of World War I, of his peers at that time is quite appropriate as a description of the subsequent careers of students "radicalized" by war or war-related issues of two decades later: "But little came of their brief enthusiasm for the social revolution. And the war the boys grew up to be good Republicans and Democrats. One 'anarchist' became a district captain for Tammany Hall; a 'socialist' took over his uncle's shoe factory in Massachusetts; a 'syndicalist' became a federal attorney."[36]

The Jewish university students of the 1920s and 1930s were politically both similar and dissimilar to their Christian counterparts. The Jews were similar in that only a minority of them were members of Left or left-front organizations. They were different in that relatively more Jews were politically active and involved in Left or left-oriented organizations. The colleges with large Jewish enrollments in the

1920s and 1930s, such as CCNY, Hunter College, University of Chicago, Temple University, and the University of Wisconsin, invariably contained the most activists, liberals, and Leftists. (This was not only true of these decades; it continues at the present time.)[37] In the generally quiescent 1920s CCNY, the college with the largest Jewish student body in the country, was not that much of an exception from the norm. Relative to other campuses, however, it had a more radical political environment. The most prominent embodiment of this radicalism was the Social Problems Club, which was "captured" in the early 1920s by a score of Communist students. Under their control, it grew from about 20 members to several hundred and became, in the words of Herbert Zam, who organized the Communist takeover and later became leader of the Young Communist League, ". . . an indoctrination center for Communism among native-born students."[38]

It is necessary to put this situation in perspective. Not all of the members of the Social Problems Club were Communists. Even though the Communists may have controlled it, they did not want the club to become strictly a Communist adjunct. Even if all the members of the Social Problems Club were Communists in particular or leftists in general, they still would constitute a numerically small minority of the CCNY student body. This factor is probably the most interesting. Here, in a student body made up largely of Jews, many of whom came from working-class families associated with unions and radical organizations, the Left in the 1920s could claim the allegiance of no more than a relative handful. The student career of Morris U. Schappes, later a Communist leader of the CCNY faculty in the 1930s, illustrates how the most likely student candidates for the Communist Party could attend the college in the 1920s and not be attracted to the movement. Schappes came from a working-class Jewish family. His father was a union activist and a man of radical political inclinations and sentiments. At CCNY from 1924 to 1928, Schappes, however, was not a radical and did not join the Social Problems Club, although he did attend various lectures that it sponsored. His major motivation was to hear particular speakers who were usually not very radical. He also went to hear nonradical orators who spoke at forums at Cooper Union or at a nearby branch of the New York Public Library. His was more a quest for knowledge than for politics. At CCNY he won an essay prize in the English Department for an essay that was a positive assessment of Mussolini's fascism.[39]

American students became more politically active in the 1930s, initially in response to the Depression and then in response to the rise of fascism and the growing threat of war. Once again, Jewish students were disproportionately active and disproportionately represented in Left organizations and movements. In 1929, even before the Communists seriously turned their attention to the campuses, Jewish students from CCNY formed a significant segment of the leadership and cadres of the Young Communist League, which had its headquarters in New

York City.[40] Shortly thereafter, as the nationwide student movement began to blossom, the organizational infrastructure that underlied it was largely peopled and moulded by Jewish students. The Student League for Industrial Democracy (Socialist), the National Student League (Communist), the Young People's Socialist League, the Young Communist League, and the American Student Union (mixed) were generally led and officered by Jewish students, especially those located in, or originally from, New York City.[41] One of the principal leaders of the student movement of the 1930s was James Wechsler, a Jewish student who attended Columbia University in this period. He notes in his account of the movement that ". . . a large number of those who inaugurated the left-wing student movement . . . were Jews."[42]

A poll taken at CCNY in 1936 at the height of the student movement reflects the extent of leftist sentiment within this school's predominantly Jewish student body. Out of 2,206 ballots in the presidential straw poll, 23 percent went to the Communist candidate, Earl Browder; and 12 percent went for the Socialist standard bearer, Norman Thomas. Thus more than a third of the students favored the presidential nominees of the Left. In the same poll, 20 percent of the students voted for Franklin D. Roosevelt on the American Labor party, a liberal left-oriented New York State political party. Altogether the CCNY preferences indicate that more than half of the students in 1936 could be considered as at least favorable to the Left. This figure was significantly higher than at any other campus in America.[43]

The Communist party and, to a lesser extent, the Socialist party were the organizational beneficiaries of the effervescent student movement. In the 1930s students and recent college graduates were perhaps the single largest source of new members in the Communist party (the largest Left organization of the period) and the Socialist party. One report on Communist party membership in those years indicated that the majority who joined were between the ages of 18 and 23 and, disproportionately, these appeared to be Jewish students, student drop-outs, or recent graduates. Many of those who entered the CP in the 1930s fresh from college rose to positions of importance within it. Most notable in this regard were the Jews who had been students at CCNY and Brooklyn College who edited and wrote for the *Daily Worker*.[44]

Again, it should be stressed that our attention is now focused on a minority within a minority. The majority of Jewish students in the United States in the 1930s did not join a Left party or organization, either during their college days or afterwards. Even in those colleges where the Left had its highest number and proportion of members and sympathizers, most notably CCNY, the period of major force was rather limited, generally running from about 1934 to 1938 or 1939. In those years at CCNY, one former student activist estimated that the Socialist students numbered between 35 and 40, while the largest Left group on campus, the Communists, had a membership of several hundred. The annual total enrollment at CCNY during this period was about 6000. It therefore seems reasonable to assume that in terms of membership, the Left encompassed about 5 percent of the student body at its height among the students at CCNY.

By the end of the 1930s the Left (for reasons we shall examine below) was a spent force among Jewish as well as non-Jewish students. At CCNY in 1940, four years after the poll in which almost one-quarter of the students selected the Communist candidate as their choice for president, the percentage was now reduced to less than 5 percent.[45] Many, if not most, who had joined the Communist party during the 1930s while students or soon after leaving college had abandoned it by 1940. One study estimated that most who did leave the Communist party did so before their twenty-third birthday.[46] The longevity of the party career of the aforementioned James Wechsler is typical in this regard. Wechsler joined the CP in 1934 while a student at Columbia. By 1937, at the age of 22, he had severed his relationship with it.[47]

What were the factors that produced this minority of Jewish student leftists and also the larger, but still minority, of Jewish students with Left proclivities in the 1930s? The answer to this question will enhance our comprehension of the processes at work among the majority that did not become leftists or active Left sympathizers. This becomes an important consideration because of the large proportion of Jewish youth who were enrolled in colleges in the interwar years and afterwards.

Communism in particular and the Left in general seemed to have their greatest appeal among Jewish students when the colleges, together with the economy, were not able to fulfill their expected mobility functions. The Jewish students of the Depression decade much resembled their late nineteenth-century ethnic counterparts in czarist Russia and in the exiled student colonies of Europe. They were more similar to them than they were to their fellow Jewish students in America who preceded them to the colleges (or to those who came after). The most significant characteristic that they shared with their Russian forebearers was the blockage of their socioeconomic mobility and their belief that their mobility was stymied. Those who attended college in the mid-1930s had little reason to be optimistic about their job prospects after college.

Before the Depression (and afterwards as well) access to college had virtually assured Jewish students that they would gain entrance into a white-collar or professional position. During the Depression, the economic contraction, in conjunction with increased enrollments among Jews, severely reduced the objective and perceived ability of the institutions of higher education to channel these students into the middle class and better paying jobs.[48] A brilliant student who obtained a civil service job as a security guard at the Statue of Liberty was regarded as an object of envy by his peers. In short, these students had little reason to believe that their association with higher education would make an appreciable impact on their working lives in the foreseeable future. They had little reason to conform to middle-class patterns or to forsake a working-class identity or an allegiance to an ideology or political party that oriented itself to the working class. The *Student Review*, the organ of the New York Student League, an organization largely comprised of Jewish Communist students, presented this point of view quite explicitly in the early 1930s: "The years spent in universities . . . were . . . only wasted years. A social order which involves this waste . . . is sick . . . Like the workers, we have nothing to lose." [49]

This Jewish student generation of the Depression also shared with its fellow Russian Jewish predecessors another related characteristic that pushed both student groups toward the Left—anti-Semitism. The desired and expected positions in the occupational world and professional schools to which their academic merit should have given them a relatively wide access were perceived as being largely denied to them, not only on the grounds of the overall economic crisis, but also because they were Jews. Though many of their number were successful in obtaining admission to professional schools and white-collar and professional jobs, the nature of such success only increased their bitterness. It was a secondary or alternative success. For example, many of those who were admitted to dental and pharmacy schools originally desired and expected to go to medical schools. Those few who were hired by colleges as faculty members were given the lowest and most insecure positions in the faculty hierarchy. Jews who made it through the best or good law schools found that their salaries and careers began on a lower monetary or status level than their Gentile counterparts. James Wechsler, in his attempt to explain the presence of a disproportionate number of Jews in the left-wing student movement focused on the traditional double yoke—anti-Semitism and restricted economic opportunity:

. . . Jewish students reacted to the economic crisis in greater numbers than did others because of the burden of that decline, in its inception, fell most heavily upon them. Even in times of comparative prosperity, they did not enjoy many of the benefits which accrued to their Christian colleagues; they were barred from jobs because of their religion, professional schools systematically rejected their applications. . . . If there is an "instinctive" radicalism among certain sections of the Jewish community, it is the product of centuries of economic torment, lessened in degree, but not in kind, in this country. [50]

It was not only the similarity of predicament with their predecessors in late nineteenth-century czarist Russia that moved Jewish students in America toward the Left in the 1930s; it was also the characteristics they shared with their immigrant parents during the pre–World War I period of mass immigration that pushed them in this direction. The Jewish students in the 1930s, like to their parents, were a homogeneous mass, concentrated in large numbers, sharing a common cultural and political heritage as well as a common source of oppression. They, too, were insulated from the outside world in their residential as well as college ghettoes.

The Jewish students in New York, our major area of concern, were homogeneous in several key aspects. They were not only Jewish but, more specifically, they were largely second-generation Jews from Eastern European family backgrounds. In 1938, 80 percent of the parents of the freshman class at CCNY were foreign-born, with the majority coming from the former czarist empire.[51] Most parents, it can be presumed, were either blue-collar workers or low-income entrepreneurs of small businesses. Wechsler claims that this was the socioeconomic composition that largely defined the student activists,[52] were also relatively homogeneous with respect to academic accomplishment. During the Depression the free municipal city colleges of New York attracted more applicants than they could accommodate. Consequently, objective standards of admission were raised in order to "legitimately" limit the number of students who gained admission to manageable proportions. The result was to produce a very bright and highly motivated student body who soon came to realize that their mental abilities would not lead to professions or professional positions commensurate with their intellectual achievements.[53]

These Jewish students, with their shared grievances and common backgrounds, were also concentrated in New York City. In various ways, this was the product of Depression conditions. The relative lack of job opportunities had increased enrollments. The financial plight of their parents limited the range of schools to which Jewish students could apply largely to the free or relatively free municipal and state schools close to home, most notably the free municipal colleges of the New York City. The quota restrictions at the private colleges were also a factor. As a joint consequence of all these variables, the majority of Jews in institutions of higher education in the 1930s was to be found in New York City. In 1935, for example, 53 percent of all Jewish students in the country attended school in that city.[54] Most of those students were probably enrolled at the municipal colleges—CCNY, Hunter, and Brooklyn. These colleges then took on the aura of the pre–World War I Jewish lower East Side ghetto, complete with the politiking of Jewish leftists who were politically sagacious enough to realize that the student bodies of these schools offered them opportunities similar to those offered by the working-class Jewish ghettoes of an earlier day.

The Depression also fostered within these students an identification with their home environments, largely located in Jewish ghettoes that were smaller, but still not that dissimilar, from the lower East Side, particularly during this period. In New York City the majority of the Jewish students were commuters, traveling each day to and from their family's home. Thus college attendance did not represent a major break from their home environment. This constant contact with family and neighborhood made them highly cognizant of the devastating effects of the Depression. The economic crisis had slowed or halted Jewish economic and geographical mobility. In many cases, such as the father of John Gates, who was a Communist student in CCNY in the 1930s and later editor of the *Daily Worker*, it pushed a middle-class father back into the ranks of the working class.[55] One communist student, commenting on the economic condition of his classmates and their families in 1933, observed: "None of the students come from wealthy homes. Now things are getting worse. I have known students in my classes who ran up enormous absence records because they couldn't get carfare to come to school. There are many who go to classes hungry. The extent of unemployment among parents must be startling. Most of the students either work or look for work."[56]

Many leftist students came from Socialist or socialist-oriented home environments and were politically experienced leftists or predisposed in that direction by the time they arrived at college. This was not only a function of a Left family environment but also a function of growing up in a large and densely populated Jewish neighborhood containing many Left or pro-Left Jewish workers. This type of background also affected the more numerous nonleft Jewish students. The visible and open presence of various Communist, Socialist, and Trotskyist speakers and organizations in their home areas made them familiar with the Left before college. Thus, when they attended institutions of higher education, they tended to regard the Left as a natural and legitimate presence in their collegiate political arena. It therefore was not as stigmatized at Jewish colleges as it was at non-Jewish ones.

For those who were leftists while in school, particularly the activists, the colleges held out few, if any, practical reasons abandoning their Left politics. In fact, many Jewish Communists either scarcely attended classes or quit prior to graduation in order to more effectively pursue their political careers. Work on behalf of the Left appeared more ideologically and emotionally rewarding than did concentration on classroom studies. One prominent Jewish Communist (who left the party in 1956) described what motivated him to drop out of CCNY in the early 1930s:

Those were, as Edmund Wilson writes of the Hoover years, "desperate days when nothing worked." There was a vacuum of ideas and of action which the Communists were trying hard to fill. They alone seemed to have a program. . . . The Communist movement was the locomotive of the future, capitalism only a convulsive dying gasp. Only the Communists were able to infuse youth with idealism, missionary zeal and a crusading spirit. With these, they invoked a willingness to undergo any hardship, to sacrifice life itself if need be, for the cause of the socialist revolution. I now attended classes only enough to collect my scholarship money. Any conflict between school hours and my political activity was resolved in favor of the latter.[57]

The student role, within the context of an apparently collapsing capitalist economy, offered little in the way of immediate or future rewards, compared to stopping the eviction of workers from their apartments, organizing for the Communist party, or fighting the fascists in Spain. Next to the seamen and longshoremen, students and dropouts, particularly those from Jewish backgrounds, made up the largest occupational group to fight in Spain.

Another related factor in shaping the Jewish students' commitment to the Left was the existence in their midst of a significant and organized reference group. These Jewish leftists were present in sufficient numbers in schools like CCNY to set the political tone among the students. Their numbers gave assurance to one another and helped to legitimize their politics to themselves and to potential recruits. It was not only their numbers, it was also their quality. Those who were attracted and became involved with the Left, especially those who rose to leadership positions as student leftists, were not the campus odd balls. They were generally the brightest, most precocious, and most dedicated students. There were also enough of them with experience to organize and maintain political clubs, such as the Social Problems and the Socialist clubs. These were organizations generally led and operated by the more committed Left students. At the same time, they attracted many more who were primarily Left in sentiment. The clubs facilitated and encouraged sustained and selective interaction among these like-minded students, thus reinforcing their commitment to socialism. They also helped to crystallize the political thinking of their members and for some, like John Gates, transform them from a vague proleftist into solid Communist party activists.[58]

It is again necessary to bear in mind that the Left students in these colleges were not isolated or stigmatized deviants. They existed in the midst of predominantly Jewish student bodies that were largely liberal and pro-Left in their feelings. There were virtually no conservatives in their midst throughout a good part of the Depression. In the aforementioned 1936 straw poll at CCNY, for example, less than 4 percent of the student voters cast their ballots for the Republican candidate, Alfred Landon.[59]

This Left and pro-Left sentiment and activity of Jewish college students in the 1930s was largely a product of the Depression. This economic crisis interrupted and interfered with the pattern of geographic and socioeconomic mobility that Eastern European Jews and their children had established in the 1920s. The Depression had also prevented the colleges from performing their usual function of channeling students into respectable and acceptable middle-class occupations. When the economy of the country was not in a lengthy downturn, as was the case in the 1920s and in the several decades following World War II, Jews were socioeconomically mobile; a college education did appear to have a practical payoff. In these periods the Jewish (Marxist) Left on the campuses played a considerably dimin-

374 JEWS AND THE LEFT

ished role. The improved economic situation following the Depression also dissipated the ghetto characteristics of the Jewish student bodies. In the following decades improved family finances and a weakening of anti-Semitic barriers facilitated the movement of Jews from colleges and universities in the New York City area. The addition of Queens College to New York City's college system in 1937 had also, to some extent, taken the pressure off the other three colleges. By 1946 the percentage of Jewish students attending school in New York City was down to 50 percent; nine years later the percentage was reduced to 38 percent; by 1963 Jewish students in New York City accounted for less than 28 percent of all Jews in institutions of higher education in the country.[60] Their dispersion and mobility, as with that of their parents, also further removed them from the Left institutions and milieus of New York City. As with their parents, the same process led to an attenuation of ties with the Left.

In short, the Depression was very much an aberrant period, during which Jewish students were figuratively, if not literally, proletarianized. The economic crisis reinforced the various ties that bound these students to their working-class families and working-class neighborhoods. It was only natural that in this period there should develop among them an ideology and political commitment that reflected their proletarianized status. Once this economic abberation had passed and economic growth resumed, Jewish students resumed the social, economic, and geographic mobility that the Depression had interrupted, and they drifted away from the Left. But, as we shall see, even in more prosperous times, Jewish collegians were to remain disproportionately more Left and liberal than their non-Jewish peers. (This will be considered in more detail in the discussion of the New Left.)

The various Depression-related factors were, of course, not the only ones that explained the relationship of the Jewish students to the Left. The politics of the Left, as it related to Jewish needs and interests (as we shall presently see), was also an important factor in shaping the Jewish students' responses to radicalism, as well as those of their parents. The economic conditions have been emphasized here, not only because they are important but also because they had more of an impact upon Jewish students, both as students and as Jews, than noneconomic ones. The noneconomic factors, of course, affected them in both of these roles, but they appeared to be more salient with respect to their Jewish identities. As such, we shall then consider this aspect when we examine the relationship between the Left parties and the Jews.

The Loss of the Intellectuals

In essence, the 1930s was the last time that educated young Jewish men were barred en masse from access to desired positions. After

World War II opportunity beckoned. Jewish intellectuals found all types of opportunities open to them—in publishing houses, universities, and law firms.[61] As they turned toward successful or at least professional careers, they also turned away from radicalism. The Left was now largely but certainly not totally deprived of an element that had supplied it with leaders, activists, theorists, and journalists.

It was not only such success that facilitated the rightward drift of Jewish intellectuals after the 1930s. Such movement was the result of a variety of interacting factors. Probably as important as career opportunity was the fact that significant sectors of American society accepted Jews. Their Jewishness was no longer a stigma. After the Holocaust, the levels of anti-Semitism diminished, particularly among those groups who were most likely to interact with Jewish intellectuals.[62] Their acceptance was also facilitated by their acculturation. By the 1950s men like Norman Podhoretz, the current editor of *Commentary*, had (purposely) lost much of their immigrant, ethnic, and working-class veneer. They mastered the English language and successfully invaded cultural domains that WASPs had long monopolized as their own.[63]

This acceptance by America was more than reciprocated. Jewish intellectuals, along with their non-Jewish peers, after World War II halted their private and public cultural and political war with this country. "[M]ost writers," according to the *Partisan Review* in 1952, "no longer accept alienation as the artist's fate in America; on the contrary, they want very much to be a part of American life."[64] The "most writers" that the *Partisan Review* likely had in mind were in the main Jewish writers of a former radical inclination. These were largely the ones who edited as well as wrote for this formerly radical magazine. And Norman Podhoretz, speaking for his generation, also gave witness to the acceptance of America. "American society," he declared in 1957, "seemed on the whole a reasonably decent environment for the intellectual."[65]

It was probably not difficult for Jewish intellectuals to call a cease fire and join hands with the former enemy—American society. Much earlier in the century Abraham Cahan, as a representative of his generation of Jewish intellectuals, had more than once made known his desire to accept and be accepted by America. His successors and intellectual progeny were more fortunate than he. The lowering of barriers to Jews permitted them to finally offer to the United States their long held gift of approval.

World War II made it almost a necessity that these Jews show their gratitude toward what by now was their native land. It was the might of America that brought to a halt the greatest menace the Jews had ever known. As one Jewish intellectual and former radical expressed it (to me in an interview): "If it were not for the United States, I might have been a bar of soap."

The politics and policies of the Left, as we shall see in greater detail

376 JEWS AND THE LEFT

in Chapter 8, were also factors that contributed to the Jewish intellectuals' flight into the mainstream. The Communist and the Socialist parties' waffling on the war issue prior to American involvement, at a time that Jewish lives were in immediate danger, did little to endear either organization to these Jews. The onset of the Cold War, the Communist party's and the Soviet Union's hostility toward Israel after 1952, and the revelation of Soviet atrocities against Jewish intellectuals and Jewish culture cleared the boards of any gratitude toward the Soviet Union that might have lingered from its role in World War II. The pursuit of Jewish interest, whether defined in terms of Israel, Judaism, or Jewish acceptance, dictated that in the choice between the Soviet Union and the Communist party on the one hand and America (and the Democratic party) on the other, the decision could not go in favor of the USSR and the United States Communist party.

Regardless of the reasons for the rightward movement of American Jewish intellectuals after the Depression, the important fact is the movement itself. The Left lost a strata that had contributed to its potency, particularly in the case of the Jewish Left before World War I. Whereas once the Jewish intellectuals had taken to their mimeographed pamphlets and soap boxes to carry the message of the Left to Jews and non-Jews, after World War II the situation was much different. Now these same types were utilizing mass periodicals and prestigious university platforms to send a different kind of political message to the Jewish and non-Jewish communities. This time the beneficiary of their efforts was not the Left; it was mainstream America. As expressed in the pages of *Commentary* in the 1950s, according to Norman Mailer, "one got the impression that the United States of America, for all its imperfections . . . was the best society a human nature . . . was likely to build."

Geographic Mobility: Dispersion

Occupational mobility was not the only kind that was injurious to the Jewish Left. Geographic mobility also sapped its strength. As the Jews dispersed from their intial areas of settlement and then from the second areas, the solidarity and cohesiveness of the Jewish working class was weakened. This was an important structural base of the Jewish Left. In New York City the process can be most clearly observed. Prior to World War I the Lower East Side was the major area of concentration for Jewish immigrants in general and Jewish workers in particular. Even in this period, as noted earlier, Jews, including Jewish workers, were moving from this large ghetto. But the heavy influx of new Jewish immigrants to the Lower East Side in this period maintained it as a primary point of Jewish residence. In 1910, despite the out-migration, this district reached its height in terms of the total number of Jewish residents, approximately 350,000.[66]

Before World War I the lower East Side was not only an area of Jewish residential concentration, it was also the district in which the garment industry was located. As noted earlier, this meant that there were also large numbers of Yiddish-speaking immigrant garment workers who lived and labored close to one another. Even the industry was on the move shortly before the war. It was shifting into areas north of the old ghetto's northern boundary line, 14th Street in Manhattan. Both of these trends accelerated during the 1920s. Jews and the garment factories moved out in rapid numbers. However, the considerable growth of the clothing industry and the influx of large numbers of Jewish immigrants into it had, to a large extent, provided replacements on the Lower East Side for those who had departed. After the war the situation changed, and the garment industry's shift from the Lower East Side was quite apparent in absolute and relative terms. In 1917 the number of garment workers employed south of 14th Street in Manhattan was 84,000. This represented 43 percent of those employed in the needle trades in Manhattan. In 1922 the figure was 47,000, which represented 29 percent of the industry's labor force in that borough.[67]

It was not only the shops and factories of the garment industry that left the Lower East Side. Many of those who labored within them changed their place of residence and abandoned the district. In 1923 about 25 percent of the members of the International Ladies Garment Workers Union and the Amalgamated Clothing Workers of America who lived in New York City resided in or near the Lower East Side. Although we lack comparable data for the earlier years, one can assume that the proportion who lived there then was considerably higher than 25 percent. By 1950 the proportion had diminished to 5 percent.[68] The nearly simultaneous decline in the number of workers employed in the garment shops and factories on the Lower East Side and in the number of needle trades' unionists living there does not mean that they were moving their residences closer to their place of employment. In 1922, for example, the clothing industry had slightly over 161,000 workers physically employed in places located in Manhattan. At the same time, only 41,299 members of the Amalgamated and ILGWU had their places of residence in Manhattan. Even if we take into account the fact that the New York City membership of these two unions in this year was not coterminous with the aforementioned 161,000, the disparity between that figure and 41,299 is suggestive. A possible explanation is suggested by a survey that questioned a sample of the members of these unions about why they had moved. Only 13 percent cited "more convenient to place of employment" as the reason.[69]

This process of separating the work place from the residence was not limited to the Jewish garment workers. It was a phenomenon that came to characterize Jewish members of the labor force in the 1920s and the 1930s. After World War II it was accelerated. Jews flocked to the "bedroom" communities of Queens and the suburbs outside New

York City and other major urban areas. The process, as it affected the Jewish garment workers, is important. When they were concentrated into restricted areas, as on the Lower East Side, the needle trades' workers constituted a core group within the larger Jewish working class. As their numbers declined and they moved further from one another and further from their places of employment, the numerical and structural factors that had combined to shape them into a working-class-conscious community also receded. After the decline of the Lower East Side concentration, in no other place in the United States did there exist a community in which masses of Jewish workers in the same industry lived so close to each other and their work places.

The demise of the Lower East Side as an area of Jewish and worker concentrations did not mark the end of Jewish population centers in the greater New York City metropolitan area. As this area of settlement fell in terms of number and density of Jewish residents, other areas experienced an increase in the size of their Jewish populations. In the 1920s and 1930s Brooklyn and the Bronx, which had attracted Jews even before the war, continued to do so even faster afterwards. Between 1917 and 1927 the number of Jewish residents in the Bronx more than doubled, from 211,000 to 420,000. In the same period, Brooklyn's Jewish community increased by 229,000, reaching a total of almost 800,000. By contrast, Manhattan's Jewish population fell from 696,000 to 465,000 in the same 10-year period. After World War II, this population shift became even more accelerated, with the most discernible movement being toward the borough of Queens and to the outlying suburbs. Indeed, by the latter 1960s more Jews resided in Nassau and Suffolk counties on Long Island than in any single borough of New York City.[70]

This phenomenon of movement from the first immigrant area of settlement was not limited to Jews in New York City in particular or to Jews in general. In Chicago, Boston, Providence, and Minneapolis the same kind of shift took place. The Eastern European immigrant Jews were not content to dwell in their original neighborhoods and districts.[71] Other immigrant groups also moved from their first areas of settlement in America, although none appeared to leave so quickly or in so great a proportion as the Jews.[72]

If we continue to focus on the Jews of the greater New York City area, the most important for our purposes, we can ascertain some significant features within the post–World War I migration that have implications for the relationship between the Jews and the Left. Most discernible was that the postwar migration was more varied than that which took place before the war. In Brooklyn, for example, the Jews who had flocked there in the earlier period largely settled in such areas as Williamsburg and Brownsville. Afterward many went not only to these sections but also to places such as Borough Park, Bensonhurst, and Coney Island. A similar sort of pattern characterized the postwar migration to the Bronx. Even within Manhattan, as the total Jewish population declined, areas such as Washington Heights and Riverside Drive gained sizeable numbers of Jewish residents.

The Jews were not randomly dispersing from the Lower East Side ghetto. They were moving into newer ghettoes. All of these areas were at least 40 percent Jewish in population and some, such as Coney Island and Brownsville, were over 90 percent Jewish. This development also occurred in other parts of the country.[73] The new ghettoes differed from the older ones in that they contained better housing and the residents tended to journey further from their homes to their places of work than was true in the older ones, particularly the Lower East Side. The total Jewish population was more dispersed. In 1916, 82 percent of the Jews in New York City lived in 13 definable sections. By 1925 a comparable percentage resided within 17 sections.[74] The exodus of immigrant Jews and Jewish garment workers from the Lower East Side and the dispersion to other areas in and around New York City significantly undermined the structural base of the Jewish Left in the greater New York area, its primary center of concentration in the United States. This did not mean that the remaining Jews on the Lower East Side no longer contained leftists in their midst. The sizeable number of votes for Socialist, Communist, and progressive candidates—from the 1920s into the 1930s—that were cast by Jews continuing to reside there testifies to the continued existence of leftists.[75] Also, the Jews who moved and concentrated in other areas in these decades did not necessarily jettison their leftist principles and beliefs on their journey from the Lower East Side. A sizeable portion of the Jewish Left survived the trip to the Bronx and Brooklyn as memoirs, interviews, voting statistics, and the location of Communist party community clubs reveal.[76] However, after World War I, none of these communities could duplicate the circumstances that prevailed in the prewar Lower East Side ghetto. None had as many Yiddish-speaking workers. None had so large a concentration of workers in the same industry. None were as culturally and economically self-sufficient as was the Lower East Side in the first 15 years of the twentieth century. In short, none were as capable of supporting a Jewish Left superstructure in as meaningful a fashion as the immediate pre-World War I Jewish community on the Lower East Side.

The Jewish Left was cognizant, at least on an overt political level, of the consequence of the population shift from the Lower East Side. As early as 1908 Jewish Socialists complained that too many radicals were leaving this area for nicer quarters in Brownsville and the Bronx. This, these politicians realized, had the affect of diluting the radical character of the Lower East Side and, specifically, lessening the chances of electing Socialist candidates. One Yiddish periodical at the time sadly observed: ". . . the moving vans move out the radicals."[77]

There were several features of this geographical mobility that bode ill for the fate of the Jewish Left. One was associated with the social characteristics of the movers and of the nonmovers. There appeared to be a fairly consistent pattern that characterized the original population shift from the Lower East Side to the second areas of settlement and those that characterized the shift from the second to the third areas of settlement. This pattern was peculiar not only to the immigrant Jews of New York City and their progeny but also to Jews elsewhere in the United States. Generally after such moves, those who remained behind tended to be the older Jews. The younger Jews were more likely to move out to newer neighborhoods.[78] This meant that the Left, if it were to survive as a significant political force, had to be as geographically mobile as the Jewish population. If it remained rooted primarily in the older area of settlement, like the Lower East Side, it would be condemned to a marginal existence and identified as an immigrant political phenomenon. To escape from this fate the Socialists and Communists in the post–World War I decades had to not only move with the shifting population but also develop a base among the younger and more Americanized Jews. This group was moving into areas that were less receptive to the Left than the Lower East Side. The new neighborhoods were less populated and more heterogeneous in terms of class and language than the older ones. The newer the area, the more likely it was to be predominantly residential and one from which the occupants commuted to work. These areas were less insulated from the outside world and more American than the older ones.

The nature of the organization of the Left also increased its vulnerability with respect to geographic dispersion. From the 1920s through the post–World War II period, the major parties of the Left, the Communist and Socialist parties, were organized primarily around neighborhoods and communities as opposed to factories and shops. Thus, when neighborhoods changed or when leftists moved, the party structure was shaken. It had to be reestablished in the new community.[79] There appears to have been little effort exerted by leftist organizations to influence where a member or supporter moved to.

The underlying reason for this geographic mobility also had negative implications for the Left. This movement reflected the growing prosperity of the immigrant community. This was not only a characteristic of those who were leaving the working class; to some extent it was also true for those who remained workers.[80] The reasons these workers actually gave for their move indicate that practical considerations were not a major factor. According to the responses of Jewish members of the Amalgamated and the ILGWU who had lived on the Lower East Side and then left in the early decades of this century, relatively few moved in order to "lower their rental costs" or to find "living quarters close to their jobs." Only 7 and 12 percent, respectively, cited these as their reasons for leaving the Lower East Side. The two most important determinants were the quest for "better housing" and for a "better environment for their children." Roughly 75 percent cited the former and more than 50 percent gave the latter as their reasons for the move.[81]

This more prosperous immigrant community and their native-born progeny who were able to find better jobs and better housing could not offer a secure base for a political movement guided by an egalitarian and industrial-worker-oriented ideology. The economic changes that were taking place in the immigrant Jewish community would have to make an impact on the manner in which it related to the Left and also on the Left that was located within it. This dual impact was going to be one that weakened the Left.

THE DECLINE OF YIDDISH

The horizontal and vertical mobility of the immigrant population and its children was not the only factors that weakened its cohesiveness and insularity in the post–World War I decades. Another was the change that was taking place in their principle medium of communication—Yiddish. As the years passed, the use of Yiddish was overtaken by English. Yiddish was the primary language of the immigrant Jewish community before World War I; but it was more than a language. It was a culture and a medium that bound the immigrant Jews together while simultaneously insulating them from significant contact with the non-Jewish world. During this period Yiddish and yiddishkeit was very much proletarian-oriented and heavily influenced by leftists of various stripes. Again, the (then) socialist *Jewish Daily Forward* was the leading Yiddish language paper in the country and, for a period of time, the leading socialist daily as well. English and the English-language media had less of a radical orientation. Although there were English-language radical papers and journals in the United States after World War I, their numbers and total circulations were miniscule compared to that of the nonradical press. Even among those papers within the orbit of the Communist party in the 1920s, the foreign-language papers combined had a far larger circulation than the English language *Daily Worker*, the key paper of the central leadership. In fact, in the 1920s the Yiddish language *Freiheit* had higher sales than the *Daily Worker*. (This was also true in the 1950s.) It then logically followed that the more Jews read and spoke English, the more accessible they would become to the political ideas and influences of the more conservative English-speaking world. Therefore, the more inroads that English made into the Eastern European Jewish community, the less likely it was that the Jews would retain their commitment to the Left.

Various statistics indicate the inexorable rise of English within the Eastern European Jewish community in America. In 1910 in the largely immigrant first-generation American Jewish community, over 90 percent of all foreign-born Jews spoke Yiddish. By 1920 it was clear that the younger American generation was going to be an

English-speaking group. In 1920, 62 percent of the combined foreign-born and their children were listed as giving Yiddish as their mother tongue. By 1960 the percentage had declined to 17 percent.[82]

This same trend can also be seen for the readership of Yiddish-language dailies over time. In 1917, a year in which the Jewish Left was at or near its height, the total circulation of these papers reached an all time high of about 750,000. About 70 percent of the Yiddish readers were located in the New York metropolitan area. Ten years later, in 1927, the total national readership of the Yiddish press had declined to 535,000—a drop of almost a quarter of a million readers. In 1944 the figures for total readership reached 425,000, and by 1960 it was down to 140,000. During the same period, the readership of the *Jewish Daily Forward* went from about 200,000 to 64,000. The *Freiheit* also suffered a similar fate, its readership declining to 8,000 by 1960.[83]

The decline in the circulation of Yiddish-language dailies occurred during decades in which the readership of English-language publications aimed toward Jews in America were on the increase. In 1910 the circulation figure for these publications was 205,000. Ten years later it had increased to 372,000, and by 1940 this readership totalled 794,000. By 1960, or in two decades, this number more than doubled reaching 1,826,000.[84] This phenomenon of the increased readership of English-language Jewish newspapers and magazines had political meaning. These publications were predominantly and decidedly nonradical and sometimes even antiradical. In 1957, for example, the independent radical monthly *Jewish Life* (later *Jewish Currents*), the only English-language radical publication aimed at a Jewish audience, had a total circulation of 1800. In earlier years, it had reached a circulation as high as 9,000.[85] This meant that those Jews reading English-language papers emanating from the Jewish community were consistently being exposed to nonradical and conservative points of view and interpretations of issues and events.

The decline in the use of Yiddish was not a phenomenon that affected all Jews in America. As might be expected, it varied with respect to age and generation. The foreign-born and the older Jews were more likely to be members of households where Yiddish was spoken. The younger and the American-born were more likely to be distant from Yiddish. Yiddish useage also intersected with geographic and social mobility. Those who left the first and second areas of settlement, those who moved up the socioeconomic scale, and those who went on for high school and college educations were more likely to be nonconversant with Yiddish.[86] This linguistic development was frought with important implications for the Jewish Left. Yiddish and *yiddishkeit* had been very important to its growth and strength. These had been among the major implements used in constructing a base among Jewish workers and their families. It was also via Yiddish that the Jewish Left attracted persons concerned with maintaining a Jewish identity. Now the Jewish Left was faced with the fact that its foundation was being eroded.

One way in which the Jewish Left responded to this situation was to attempt to perpetuate the useage of Yiddish among working-class and socialist-oriented Jews. The various Yiddish-language schools of the Workmen's Circle and the International Workers Order (IWO) became the principle embodiment of that attempt. The decline of Yiddish, however, could not be stopped or reversed. The pressures toward anglicization emanating from increasingly widespread Jewish involvement in American secular education in particular and from the greater acculturation and integration of Jews into American society in general were too powerful.

The Jewish Left was, especially in the wake of the cessation of mass immigration of Yiddish-speaking Jews, confronted by a harsh reality. If it did not branch out beyond a Yiddish-speaking base, it was doomed to become a minor and increasingly anachronistic presence on the fringe of both an Americanized Jewish community and an Americanized Left community. It was therefore necessary for the various Jewish socialist parties and organizations to follow the young, the native-born, the American-educated, the economically mobile, and the English-speaking out of the first and then the second generation ghettoes. At some level the Jewish Left must have realized that its prospects for success among such Jews were not very promising. Some sectors of the Yiddish-speaking Jewish Left refused to engage in this chase and were more or less content to grow old and weak ensconced in the security of their Yiddish-speaking world. (See Chapter 8 for further discussion of these organizations.)

The change in the numerical balance and importance between Yiddish and English after World War I also opened up an old dilemma that Yiddish had papered over but not eliminated. The Jewish Left in pre–World War I America and Russia had reached a position of strength and eminence because of its Jewish constituency. Whether desired or not, the Jewish aspect of the Jewish Left had been a major factor in the recruitment of this constituency. Yiddish in this respect was convenient, and it was a politically acceptable alternative to two other principal means of expressing a Jewish identification, religion and nationalism. These two were, however, anathemas to almost all socialists. Yiddish and *yiddishkeit* thus allowed the Jewish Left to identify itself as Jewish to its constituents and at the same time pass muster as a socialist movement.

The gradual and consistent demise of Yiddish then raised, or reraised, significant issues that not many within the Jewish Left were comfortable in dealing with. If the Jewish Left were to remain concerned with attracting Jews, a substitute for Yiddish had to be found, but one that did not foster religiosity, nationalism, or separatism in the Jewish community or within its own membership. Such an alternative was exceedingly difficult to find. (In the latter 1930s, as we shall soon discover, Communists found their Jewish vehicle—anti-Semitism.)

There was another path that the decline of Yiddish opened to the Jewish Left—the opportunity to put aside the Jewish component of their constituents and appeal to Jews only as workers or American workers. Indeed, from the perspectives of cosmopolitan socialists, Jewish workers were only proletarians with a different religious and historical background. From this point of view it was only a matter of time before occupational, industrial, and other secular forces in American society would make that distinguishing background an irrelevant one, thus facilitating the integration of Jewish and non-Jewish workers in the same Left parties and organizations.

Ideologically the argument of the cosmopolitan socialists was an appealing one. It probably always had a certain appeal regardless of when it was advanced. However, it ran into conflict with certain organizational and political considerations, especially after World War I. To go the route indicated by the universalists would mean the dissolution of the Jewish Left, including its various organizations and institutions and its unique constituency. In this eventuality, leaders and activists within the Jewish Left would be deprived of their special community base—a base that had given them much of their authority and their positions of influence within their respective political parties. Many such leaders were unwilling to dissolve or surrender the foundation that had made them important. In the conflict between radical ideology and an organizational base, being important appeared more preferable than being correct, particularly in the context of a powerful capitalist society in which the chances for revolution were dim.

In actual practice, after the World War I, the Jewish Left and the American Left, which increasingly was absorbing it along with American-born Jews, did not develop a consistent or well-thought-out response to the demise of Yiddish. Various alternatives were explored and some pursued only to be later dropped. It was not until 1937, for example, that the then foremost party of the American Left, the Communist party, via its New York State branch published an ongoing journal, *Jewish Life*, directed specifically to English-speaking Jews. (It lasted only 18 months.) Until that time the CP had been content to reach Jews through the *Morning Freiheit* and the pages of the non-ethnic-oriented *Daily Worker*. The Socialist party, on the other hand, remained dependent on the *Jewish Daily Forward* to reach Jews into the mid-1930s. The SP, however, never developed an English-language publication aimed specifically at Jews (see Chapter 8 for further discussion).

In summary, no Left party adequately came to terms with the situation created by the gradual demise of Yiddish. The need to define the character of the Jewish community in the United States and the relationship of Jewish Leftists to the Left and to the Jewish community was one problem that many were not anxious to deal with, especially directly, either as individuals or organizations. It would have forced them to confront the fact that there were increasingly fewer characteristics in the American Jewish community that lent themselves to a Jewish identification with or support of the Left.

CONSOLIDATION OF ORGANIZATIONS

Communal Organizations

The ties between Jews and radical movements in the United States were also adversely affected by the rise and consolidation of ostensibly nonpolitical organizations within the Jewish community. These philanthropic and communal organizations performed important political functions. They provided the means through which bourgeois and nonradical Jews exerted their influence and passed the values on to the Jews. And as their potency grew, that of the radicals waned.

Pre–World War I Jewry could not be characterized as disorganized. Jews in this period had their religious congregations, landsmanschaften; various mutual aid societies; unions; and labor fraternal orders. But these organizations, especially those not associated with socialism, tended to be localized around a delimited geographical area within a city or around Jews with a common occupation or place of origin in Europe. These organizations also mirrored the division of the community. The Eastern European Jews and the German Jews were further divided by a multiplicity of organizations into various groups, which separated the Orthodox from the nonreligious, the Zionists from the non-Zionists, the leftists from the nonleftists, the traditionalists from the secularists, the assimilationists from the nonassimilationists, Galicians from Lithuanians, and Rumanians from Poles.

The leftists had benefitted most from this multiplicity of communal organizations. The weakness of the religious groups and the barriers against the German Jews had provided them strategic opportunities to develop their own organizations and recruit widely among the immigrant Yiddish-speaking and largely working-class Eastern European Jews. It was the leftists in the period shortly before World War I who had the largest, most inclusive, and most centralized institutions—the unions and the labor fraternal orders. Organizationally, the Jewish labor movement represented a major deviation from the typical form of Jewish organization that had preceded it in Europe and America. The others typically were formed around a Jewish religious identity reflecting, in large part, the way Jews had been defined and treated in the Diaspora. These other organizations, typically congregations and communal bodies, were generally led and controlled by some combination of the rabbinate and wealthy Jewry. As we have observed in nineteenth-century Russia, various forces—including urbanization, industrialization, capitalism, together with the enlightenment and growth of a Jewish working class—had helped to break the organizational hegemony of these traditional institutions and the strata that controlled them. As they weakened and as the Jewish working class grew, the Jewish labor movement made its appearance. This movement was not led or controlled by the rabbinate or the wealthy. It was one of the first major organizations within Eastern European Jewry to eschew a religious identity. In its stead the labor movement implicitly fostered a secular Jewish consciousness, while explicitly utilizing class as the basis of its organization. Throughout much of the pre–World War I period, the Jewish labor movement and its leaders did not acknowledge overtly the supremacy of the abstractions— Jewish community or Jewish people.

In America the Jewish labor movement benefitted from the mass migrations. As noted above, the rabbinate and the wealthy were not able to reestablish their organizational control over the immigrant Jewish community. This largely working-class population turned mainly to its own leaders and its own organizations for support and guidance. This was an aberrant situation in terms of world Jewish history. Even in the period of its greatest strength, around World War I, there were already indications that the Jewish labor movement's organizational preeminence among Eastern European Jewry would be seriously challenged. The challenges were important and did have implications for the future. The basis with the most potential for eroding the status of the organized Left was a Jewish consciousness. Jewish crises and need stimulated the emergence and growth of organizations that rivaled and then later surpassed the organized Jewish Left with respect to leadership and influence in the Jewish community. These same factors also stimulated a desire for unity in the fragmented Jewish community and for organizations that would fulfill this need. As such, these crises directly challenged the bases upon which the organized Left was erected.

The felt need for some type of communal organization gained expression in the wake of the worsening predicament of the Russian Jews in the early 1900s. The Kishinev pogrom of 1903 and the dramatic rise in the number of immigrants that followed heightened the sense that the Jewish community in America had to make some kind of organized responses to deal with these problems. The American Jewish Committee, formed by wealthy German Jews in 1906, represented their response to these crises and problems. This movement toward community organization was strengthened in 1908 after the New York City Police Commissioner publicly charged that the Jews, who made up one-quarter of the city's population, constituted one-half of its criminal population. The response to this charge and to the other problems of the immigrant community led to the formation of the Kehillah in New York City in 1909.[87]

The *Kehillah* was designed to be the communal organization of New York City Jewry. Its purpose was "to further the cause of Judaism in New York City, and to represent the Jews." [88] One of its principal moving forces and first head was Rabbi Judah Magnes. He made explicit what he believed the *Kehillah* would do for Jewish unity: "wipe out invidious distinctions between East European and West European, foreigner and native, Uptown and Downtown Jew, rich and poor; and make us realize that the Jews are one people with a common history and with common hopes." [89]

The time was not yet ripe, however, for such unity within such a communal organization. Prominent members of the rabbinate were willing, as were the leaders of German American Jewry, but the Jewish labor movement was not. The organized Jewish Left viewed the *Kehillah* and the thrust for Jewish unity that it embodied "as a plot by clerics and philanthropists to dominate Jewish communal life." [90] Abraham Cahan stated the Jewish socialists' opposition to participation: "No more ground exists today for bridging the deep distinctions of class interest, class consciousness and origin that [existed] for thousands of years until now. On the contrary, the differences today are even greater because of the progress of free thought and especially [because of] the class struggle and political antagonism." [91]

The radicals' suspicions of the motivations of the Jewish notables in pushing for Jewish communal bodies had a real basis to them. Both the formation of the American Jewish Committee and the support for the *Kehillah* were in large part motivated by the notables' desire to check the spread and the influence of radicalism among Jews. Astute men like Louis Marshall, a prominent attorney and leader of the German Jewish community, recognized that if he and those like him did not shape the politics of the Jewish community, the radicals would then have the upper hand in doing so.[92]

In any event, the direct approach to communal organization as embodied in the *Kehillah* failed, and in 1922 it ceased to exist. But attempts to form communal organizations and to coordinate policies affecting Jews did not die with it. These took other institutional forms, the most important of which were the philanthropic organizations. These agencies, with their directors, boards, and professional social workers, proved much more dangerous to Jewish radicals and Jewish radicalism than the *Kehillah*. It was primarily through these charitable bodies that the middle class and wealthy Jews gained ascendancy over the Eastern European Jewish community and its American progeny.

Philanthropic Organizations

Prior to World War I efforts had been made, with varying degrees of success, to bring some unity and order into the field of philanthropy. Generally, it was the wealthy and acculturated German Jews who tried to organize this area on a rational and systematic basis. The initial federations in Boston and Cincinnati that coordinated a variety of philanthropic efforts on a municipal level owed their birth largely to German American Jews. Eastern European Jews, however, tended to draw back from active cooperation in these endeavors, especially in New York City. The class, ethnic, cultural, religious, linguistic, and political differences between these two Jewish communities formed a barrier limiting such cooperation.[93] The obstacle to unified philanthropic endeavors was, however, overcome. In the surmounting of this barrier the Jewish bourgeoisie gained an important means of influencing and directing the politics of Jews in America. The control of *communal* philanthropic organizations gave these people the means with which to contain and weaken the Jewish Left.

Wartime-Induced Cooperation

The Jewish crisis of World War I moved Jews in America toward unity and simultaneously provided the rationale and legitimation for wealthy Jews to move into those positions of authority previously denied to them. The concern for the safety and well-being of relatives and friends in Europe located in the paths of opposing armies prompted the Eastern European Jews in America to seek ways of assisting their loved ones. In this search they brought into being Jewish charitable agencies for overseas relief (no permanent ones existed prior to 1914), that permitted religious, bourgeois, and radical Jews to learn to actively work together. In the process of so doing, the radicals gave their traditional Jewish foes opportunities for political gain; and the Left's adversaries made use of these opportunities.

Initially, the wartime crisis did not appear to be sufficient to overcome the usual divisions and animosities. In October 1914 the Orthodox Jews brought into being their own agency, the Central Relief Committee for the Relief of Jews Suffering Through the War (CRC). Several weeks later the Reform Jews, under the aegis of the American Jewish Committee, formed their own overseas relief organization, the American Jewish Relief Committee for Sufferers from the War (AJRC). Socialist leaders held back. They were opposed to cooperation with the religious and the German Jewish notables and were also opposed in (socialist) principle to giving charity. The socialists wanted funds to be given for the rebuilding of organizations and institutions of working class life, as opposed to individual handouts.

Jewish public opinion, however, soon made it known that old and now seemingly irrelevant rivalries had to be put aside in the interest of effective relief efforts. The first move toward communal unity in the sphere of overseas assistance occurred in late November 1914. It was then that the wealthy German Americans of the American Jewish Committee and the Orthodox Eastern Europeans agreed to coordinate their efforts through one body, the Joint Distribution Committee (JDC).

Later the Zionists also recognized the efficacy of cooperating within the framework of the JDC.

The Left and labor leaders in the Eastern European American Jewish community, however, continued to refrain from participation in any relief organization in general and the JDC in particular. But by 1915 both these positions were reversed. In August 1915 the Left, labor, and liberal leadership brought into being the People's Relief Committee for Jewish War Sufferers (PRC). Three months later they took the PRC into the Joint Distribution Committee. Thus, for the first time in contemporary American Jewish history, the Orthodox, the German Americans, and the Left were all working together for a common Jewish end.[94]

What had caused the Left to reverse itself? Pressure from their constituents grew rapidly and became too insistent to ignore. Rank-and-file Jews in the unions, labor fraternal orders, and Socialist party refused to be bound by a policy that prevented them from helping their people in Europe. In ad hoc fashion, as individuals and as groups, they began to collect charitable contributions and cooperate with the relief agencies of the Orthodox and German American Jews. The heads of the Jewish Left were then confronted with two choices: They could remain firm and watch their constituents desert them on this issue, watching their supporters participate without political guidance and leadership in organizations dominated by antiradicals; or they could change their stance on the issues and participate as a coherent body in the JDC. They eventually chose to do the latter.

The cooperation between the Jewish leftists around the PRC and the JDC extended for a time beyond the war's end as they continued to hold joint fund-raising drives. In 1924, however, the PRC dissolved. Although various members of its constituent elements, such as the *Jewish Daily Forward* and the Workmen's Circle continued to send money to favorite overseas projects, overseas relief was largely in the hands of the JDC.[95]

Politically and organizationally, the Jewish Left paid a price for cooperating with Jewish nonradicals and antiradicals. The Left demonstrated by its actions that there was indeed common ground for cooperation with the Jewish bourgeoisie and the Orthodox—concern for the fate of Jews. A Jewish crisis had succeeded in overcoming the barrier to organizational cooperation between the socialists and the bourgeoisie. Once the Jewish Left had indicated to its members and supporters that its traditional adversaries within the Jewish community merited legitimacy and respect, it would be difficult to convincingly recast them in their old roles as class villains, as the Left tried to do in later years during periods of labor-management strife.

Prior to this with nonradicals and the Jewish middle class cooperation, the Left had, primarily through the vehicle of the PRC, demonstrated that fund-raising drives could also be vehicles for political organization. During those collection efforts, the Left had emphasized mass participation and turned out thousands of volunteers. When the PRC merged its fund-raising activities with those of other Jewish organizations and with the JDC, such mass drives were ruled out. Shortly thereafter the PRC disappeared entirely. After 1924 the Left no longer had its own instrument for collecting and distributing funds among Jews. It had voluntarily denied to itself a way of mobilizing its supporters and influencing other Jews. Thus the Jewish organizations that collected and distributed money and those that also amassed influence and authority within the Jewish community were almost entirely led by nonradicals and antiradicals.

Perhaps of more importance was that the wartime crisis and the charitable cooperative endeavors that sprang up in its wake moved the Jewish Left closer to a Jewish communal identity, as opposed to a Jewish class identity. The Jewish base upon which it rested responded to the crisis as largely a Jewish crisis. These leftist constituents literally forced their leaders to define the situation in the same set of ethnic, as opposed to class, terms. This cooperation also gave thousands of Jewish leftists and their supporters practical experience in intimately associating and cooperating with Jews from other classes and strata in a common Jewish enterprise.

This response of the Left was in accord with the increased communal consciousness that the war had spurred among Jews throughout the United States. At the same time the Jewish labor movement, by its actions, was also contributing to this tendency, particularly among its own constituents and among the Eastern European American Jewish community from which they were drawn. Its behavior in this direction was not limited to the area of relief. In 1917 the Jewish Left agreed, although reluctantly, to participate in the broad based American Jewish Congress.[96] Organizationally the Jewish labor movement, by strengthening the Jewish communal consciousness through its own participation in Jewish communal bodies would eventually harm its own special interests given the fact that this consciousness was one increasingly dominated by non-leftist Jews. The organizational cooperation of the Jewish Left in Jewish affairs eventually redounded to the benefit of the Zionists and the Jewish middle class.

The character of this war and postwar cooperation was another important factor in weakening the Jewish Left. The experience in the relief work indicated that Left Jewish leaders, in the context of joint organizational endeavors with other sectors of the Jewish community, especially German American Jewry, were willing to assume a somewhat subordinate role. For a short period before the formation of the PRC and even afterwards, Left Jews indicated by their behavior that they had no principled opposition to following the lead of the wealthy Jews. This was an important precedent.

Rise of Federations

This spirit of community and the striving for a common purpose remained within the arena of philanthropy following the war. It also helped to bolster the movement toward a more unified and centralized means of dealing with charity than was true before the war. After the war and into the early and mid-1920s, Eastern European and German Jewish philanthropic bodies in various cities including New York, Chicago and Baltimore, began to join together in philanthropic federations. The federation movement symbolized the growing unity within the American Jewish community. At the time some believed it to be more than symbolic. The first executive of the newly created New York Federation for Support of Jewish Philanthropic Services (later the New York Federation of Jewish Philanthropics and hereafter referred to as the Federation), I. Edwin Goldwasser, declared in his 1918 report: "The entire community has been welded into a solid unit. There is no division of uptown or downtown nor any other sort of division within the Federation."[97] This description was somewhat premature. It would be decades before the divisions within the Jewish community were eradicated. Goldwasser was correct in his unstated assumption that charity work and the federations were going to be the principal means through which this unity would be attained. By the mid-1920s another leading Jewish social worker, Maurice B. Hexter, cogently commented on the way in which charity had contributed to the cohesion of the Jewish community:

Our charitable work has been one of the chief factors in maintaining and strengthening the solidarity of the Jewish community. We have no organized church. Each of our synagogues is a separate unit. That which has most bound our people together has been our shoulder to shoulder work in the cause of philanthropy. Our repeated charity drives have been our great social events, using "social" in the best sense of that word. They have developed among us feelings of affection and comaraderie that have been more impelling perhaps than those derived from any other source. The collateral by-products of our fund gathering efforts, whether they have manifested themselves in drives, or otherwise, have had a stimulating effect on communal endeavor.[98]

The growing unity that was reflected and stimulated by these developments was harmful to the interests of the Jewish Left. The principle of unity was not the troublesome factor. It was the character of this amalgamation and the directing forces behind it that were so negative. The Jewish Left in Eastern Europe and in America was not opposed to bringing unity to the ghettoes, filled largely with workers and petty traders. In this case the Left was setting the tone for this unification, which was based on class as well as common religious origin. The unification that had taken place during the war and was taking place in the 1920s was different. The community was now wealthier and more heterogeneous in terms of class. The organizing impulse did not give priority to socialism but rather to a sense of Jewish consciousness and a spirit of Jewish community. The non-Left bourgeoisie were the ones who now were setting the tone.

The Jewish Left was now in a difficult position. Its members and supporters were all Jews who lived mostly in the Jewish community. They could not be insulated from the currents swelling around them. The more that they were part of an environment that emphasized Jewishness, the more likely they would be to develop a heightened sense of their own Jewishness. Indeed, the Left had contributed to this by the nature of its all-Jewish organization. The Left's cooperation with the non-Left Jewish organizations during and after the war indicated to its members that cooperation and coordination of efforts with fellow Jews, as Jews, was not unprincipled behavior. But now in the postwar years it was becoming increasingly clear that the more cohesive and "Jewish" a community became, the more difficult it would be for the Left to hold its members and to adhere to a socialist position.

This increasing consolidation of the Jewish community, particularly in the philanthropic sphere, also carried with it a more immediate negative consequence as far as the Jewish Left was concerned. It gave the Jewish middle- and upper-middle-classes an access to a leadership role among Eastern European Jews. Prior to the war the various divisions between the largely working-class Eastern European American Jewish community and the predominantly middle-class German American Jewish community had curtailed the latter's influence among their Eastern European coreligionists. The Left, as we have already seen, made good use of these barriers to build its own position within the immigrant ghettoes. The combination of the weakening of these barriers and the movement toward unification now gave the wealthy German Jews and the Jewish middle class entry into what had been the near preserve of the Left—the Eastern European groups. The most prominent vehicle in this incursion was philanthropy and the philanthropic federations.

Philanthropy and the organizational efforts that built it played an important role within the Jewish community. Even after the wartime crisis was over, and despite the increasing prosperity of the American Jews, charitable donations did not decline to their prewar levels but remained quite high. In 1925 donations totalled over $11 million, compared to approximately $1.66 million in 1916.[99] Fund raising became a more integral part of Jewish life. Collection drives, however, involved much more than raising money for worthy causes. They were also platforms that reached throughout the Jewish community to present views and opinions designed to mold public opinion. One of the major aims of fund raising was to foster the development of Jewish consciousness and communality because that was what the middle class and professional men who controlled them wanted them to accomplish. The Zionists were among the most adept at using fund-raising drives to get across their point of view. The Left, on the other hand, largely ignored this area. When it did participate, it did so on a fragmented basis or on behalf of essentially non-Left causes, particularly the Jewish groups in Palestine.[100]

The most organized and adept form of fund raising was conducted by the philanthropic federations. This had been one of its major purposes. The federations were also one of the major means through which the Jewish middle class gained a strategic and directing position within organized Jewish life. Whether by design or by accident, the Jewish middle class had found in the federations a potent way to exercise its power within the Jewish community without having to openly seem to be doing so. The philanthropic federation allowed them to skirt the open political issues that had been raised by the Left over the Kehillah.

The organized potency of Jewish middle class was intertwined with that of the federations. Originally this form of organization was conceived as a more rational and efficient centralized means for collecting and distributing funds within the Jewish community. In line with this, the role of the federations in shaping the policy of the agencies for whom they collected funds was supposed to be a sharply limited one. The federation did not have a mandate to interfere with the autonomy of the agencies that it serviced. Soon after the federations became operative as bodies encompassing the Eastern European and German Jewish charitable agencies within their scope, it became evident that the federations were not going to be confined by their original mandate. The control of funds and their more rational and centralized administrative apparatus enabled the federations to transcend the early limitations that had been placed upon them. The mechanics of this operation were succinctly stated by an historian of the federation movement, Harry L. Lurie:

There was no initial provision for the federation as a central planning agency. The terms of agreement between the federation and the beneficiary agencies called for a basic guaranteed minimum for each agency and left to the federation as a whole the disposal of surpluses. Since the guaranteed minimums represented the amount of funds raised in the initial year of organization, the federation soon had a considerable amount of additional funds to distribute. . . . Through its budgetary processes, research studies and other procedures, the Federation in New York, as in all other cities, became an important factor in the growth and development of services. Shifts in programs, mergers of agencies, discontinuance of outmoded services and other progressive developments which had occurred can be credited to the federation.[101]

The rise in the power of the federation coincided with the expansion of its concern to matters outside the area of charity. The more wealthy and settled Jewish community of the post–World War I era required far less immediate philanthropic services than its prewar predecessor. This situation facilitated the entry of the federations into other arenas of organized Jewish life, in which both directly and through example, they established priorities, developed programs, built institutions, and generally influenced the direction, orientation, and shape of the Jewish community in America. The federation's influence and authority and that of its related and affiliated agencies continued to grow throughout the decades between the 1920s and the 1970s.[102]

The general direction and orientation of these federations motivated programs and policies that were inimical, at various levels, to the interests of the Jewish Left. The federations strove to mold the Jewish community into a more cohesive community that would ideally be located within the mainstream of American life and be accepted as an integral part of American society. Class consciousness, class conflict, and socialism were not going to be defining characteristics of this Jewish community if the federations had their way.

The persons who established the policies in the federations and the related agencies and the professional staff that implemented them could not be expected to contribute to the strength of a Jewish Left or of any other type of Left in America. From the early decades of the twentieth century until the present, those who sit on the various policy-making boards of the philanthropic agencies, especially the federations, have been drawn from the more successful ranks within the Jewish bourgeoisie. Their class interests alone place them in opposition to socialism or anything that speaks of radicalism.

The process by which these federations and the philanthropic leaders attain and retain their positions also gives them the opportunity to pursue policies and programs in accord with their middle-class values and norms. Typically these people are not elected to their offices. They reach their decision-making posts through a process of self-selection or selection by influential middle-class peers. In either case, the Left played little if any role in the process. There is no electorate to whom these leaders are responsible. And, if they are responsible to any constituency at all, it is most likely one that is made up of wealthy donors—that is, to persons from the same or a higher class than their own.[103]

Jewish Organizational Strength

The importance of the federations and their leaders should not be allowed to entirely overshadow other significant developments in organized Jewish life after World War I. The federations were part, a leading part, of the organizational expansion and consolidation of the

Jewish community. The postwar Jewish community in America was more thoroughly organized than the one that had existed before the war. This was reflected not only in the growth of philanthropic federations but also in the increase of other organizations. The largest growth occurred in the most numerous of Jewish organizations, the local congregations. In 1917 there were approximately 1901 such congregations in the United States. By 1927 the number had risen to 3118, an increase of 1217 congregations in the 10-year period. There was also an appreciable growth in the numbers of organizations in the educational, cultural, and social spheres during the same period. In the latter 1920s American Jewry had become a highly organized body. Near the end of the decade, the community was honeycombed by at least 17,238 separate organizations.[104]

The character of these postwar organizations, as well as their number, merits our attention. In the 1920s and 1930s, as in the Federation, the members of these organizations became more heterogeneous. Groups that had originally catered to constituencies that mirrored the divisions within the Jewish community, acquired memberships that now tended to cut across those traditional divisions. Thus the B'nai B'rith, a German American Jewish fraternal order that had been reluctant to admit Eastern Europeans before the war, was unable to resist their mass entry afterwards. In 1925 the B'nai B'rith elected its first Eastern European president, and since then all succeeding presidents have been from that background.[105] A similar intermingling occurred within the religious citadel of the German Jews, Reform Judaism. By the latter 1920s the membership of this denomination in the major cities was evenly mixed between Eastern European and German Jews.[106] Even the landsmanschaften could not resist this tendency toward heterogenity. The 1920s and 1930s witnessed a growth in the number of nonlandsmen within them, as Galicians joined with Lithuanians, Russians joined with Roumanians, and the native-born joined with the foreign-born. By the latter 1930s about 30 percent of all the members of the landsmanschaften were not landsmen. This was particularly true at the leadership level, where organizational ability and knowledge of English appeared equal to, if not more important than, place of birth.[107] In the Workmen's Circle, as noted elsewhere, the proportion of nonworkers and nonsocialists in this previously working-class socialist fraternal order increased also. Correlated with this development (and in part caused by it) was the increasing tendency toward organizations that were broad in scope and responsibility. Smaller, previously independent or autonomous groups, similar to philanthropic agencies, moved toward merger and affiliation with larger federations. In some cases a national organization emerged whole without benefit of local antecedents, such as the American Jewish Congress did in 1917. Between 1916 and 1925 the number of national Jewish organizations of all kinds virtually doubled. By 1927 the

American Jewish community's network included 59 citywide federations and 164 state and national bodies.[108]

At the core of these national organizations and the federations, which in effect constituted the organized Jewish community in America, stood a small handful of individuals and families. They were the elite of the wealthly American Jewry. This concentration of power and authority was most clearly revealed in a post World War II study of the leadership of major Jewish organizations. The structure of control that this study uncovered was essentially a summary of the developments that had been occurring for decades: ". . . in eight *major* national Jewish organizations . . . 28 individuals occupied a total of 108 directorships, and four families held 31. One family occupied 11 directorships, and another eight, and another seven. One man held seven posts (his wife held eight), another six and four persons five positions each." All of these interlocking directorates were held by persons "conspicuously identified" with local federations and welfare funds. "The implication drawn is obvious but instructive," according to political scientist Samuel Halperin: "the millions of dollars collected in the community for various causes were dispensed by the 'arbitrary wishes' of a few wealthy individuals."[109] There is little need to add that these few wealthy individuals were not likely to be even mild supporters of or sympathizers with the Left in general or the Jewish Left in particular.

These developments and the factors that underlie them were of great import for the Jewish Left. The Jewish labor movement had achieved a powerful and preeminent position within the Eastern European Jewish community before 1920, in large part because it was the most effectively organized segment within this body. The Left had benefitted by the semianarchic condition that obtained among the newly arrived immigrants. Its most serious organizational challenger at that time had been the fragmented and disoriented synagogue. This was not the case after 1920. The Left was now challenged by a variety of organizations, and it found itself having to seriously compete for members and influence among the Eastern Europeans. The competitors included secular organizations as well as reinvigorated religious bodies.

The competing organizations, like the philanthropic federations, were generally headed by middle-class or religious Jews. They were not all necessarily anti-Left, but they were largely non-Left in their politics. This meant that the more contact the Eastern European American Jews and their children had with groups outside of the Left, the more likely these Jews would be to lose or weaken their attachments to the Left. The more organized and the more coordinated the Jewish community became, the greater would be the power and the influence of the middle-class Jews who headed and staffed this organizational network. The increasing number and rising prominence of these middle-class-dominated organizations and their non-Leftist leaders among Eastern European Jews in particular and American Jews in general was largely the result of the aforementioned socioeconomic and demographic changes taking place among American Jewry. The decline of large-scale immigration during the war and its virtual cessation in the early 1920s diminished the flow of socialist-oriented Yiddish-speaking workers. It also brought a period of stability that allowed more systematic organization to take place. At the same time, the dispersion of the Jews from their areas of first settlement, their movement toward and into the middle class, and the decline in their use of Yiddish eroded the barriers that had separated them from the influence and authority of both the German American and the American middle class.

Organizationally the breaching of these barriers had occurred at a most inauspicious time, as far as the Jewish Left was concerned, for at least two reasons. First, internally the Jewish Left was having many political and organizational problems. The bitter internecine warfare between the Jewish Communists and the Socialists in the 1920s and the troubles of the garment industry weakened the institutions of the Jewish Left at precisely the same time that its opponents were growing stronger. Second, the 1920s were a period of significant decline in the strength of the American Left in general. Toward the end of this decade the American Left was no longer a significant presence on the American political stage. This was more true for the American than the Jewish Left (as we shall see). Thus the more contact that immigrant Jews had with America and the more Americanized they became after World War I, the more likely it was for them to come under the organizational influence of the non- or anti-Left.

Organized Judaism

After World War I the Jewish Left was confronted by a stronger traditional enemy—organized Judaism. Prior to the war, as discussed above, organized Judaism had been in disarray. The widespread immigration of secularists and the relative failure of rabbis and the more learned and pious to follow suit had made it difficult for organized Judaism to effectively adapt to the strange new environment in America. The Left had taken advantage of this condition of its religious rival to attract supporters and build its institutions from among the Eastern European American Jews. But by the end of World War I organized religion among the immigrant Eastern European Jews appeared to be adjusting to its American environment and showing signs of strength. One indicator was the aforementioned growth in the number of congregations, which increased from 1769 to 3118 to 1927. By 1937 there were 3728 congregations in America, 3900 in 1952, and approximately 4200 by the early 1970s. In New York City there was a similar trend: The number of congregations rose from 843 in 1917 to 1044 in 1927 to 1330 in 1937.[110]

Those figures become more meaningful when placed in context. When compared with population growth, a revealing pattern appears in the pre–World War II years. During the decade 1907–1917, the number of Jews in the United States increased by 90 percent. This was largely a function of immigration. The corresponding growth of synagogues in this period was only 8 percent. The relationship was reversed in the next 10-year span. From 1917 to 1927 the Jewish population increased by 25 percent, and the number of religious bodies increased by 64 percent. This pattern was repeated in the following decade but was not as pronounced. From 1927 to 1937 the percentage growth for population was 12 percent and that for congregations was 20 percent.[111]

After World War II the raw numbers of people and religious bodies were more stable. But this situation masks an important development that took place in those years. Although the number of congregations remained relatively similar, a great deal of turnover was taking place. The older and smaller religious bodies were closing their doors and being replaced by newer and larger ones. The postwar building of synagogues was the most prodigious in American Jewish history.[112] It seems quite clear, then, that the end of Jewish mass immigration and the stabilization of the Jewish community in America was beneficial to organized Judaism, at least in terms of congregation growth and consolidation. The figures for congregations underestimate the growth in the importance of organized religion among Jews after World War I. The numbers do not take into account the other organized bodies that the congregations directly or indirectly spawned, such as brotherhoods, sisterhoods, youth societies, and study groups. In 1927, for example, the number of congregation-related organizations of all kinds (7137) was twice as great as the total for congregations by themselves. Together they constituted a majority of all Jewish organizations in the United States and were by far the groups that involved the most Jews.[113] This combined figure for religious bodies and their affiliated organizations is a more valid indicator of the influence of Judaism in organized Jewish life than the number of congregations itself. It suggests that following World War I, organized Judaism in America was very much alive. America, then, was not as hostile an environment for Judaism per se, as had originally been assumed by the Orthodox rabbinate. (However, if only Orthodox Judaism is considered, that assessment may not have been entirely wrong.) Indeed, the more Americanized the Jewish population became, the stronger grew its commitment to some form of organized Judaism. By 1971, according to a prominent sociological analyst of American Jewry, Marshall Sklare, "The American synagogue [was] . . . by far the strongest agency in the entire Jewish community."[114]

The involvement of the synagogue in the secular affairs of American Jews was no accident. Many rabbis desired it, as did numerous Jewish laymen. They wanted the synagogue to become the center of organized Jewish life; on the whole, they were generally successful in bringing this about. A leading sociologist of Judaism in America, Charles Liebman, commenting on this aspect of the role of the synagogue, noted: "It provides recreational and educational facilities, lectures and art classes, social outlets and golden age clubs and a meeting place for other non-synagogal Jewish organizations in the area. It raises funds, not only for its own needs but for Jewish philanthropic purposes as well. The synagogue based campaign provides a major source of funds for federations of Jewish philanthropies and for assistance to Jews abroad, particularly in Israel." [115]

That type of involvement and use of the synagogues may have been disturbing to religious purists but not to others beyond their ranks. The Jewish secular groups (other than Leftist ones) generally found such an arrangement quite to their liking. The synagogue and the rabbi legitimated their activities and the goals of their organization in the eyes of the Jewish and non-Jewish community. Neither the religious authorities nor the Jewish secular leaders envisioned their groups as being in competition with one another for members and influence within the Jewish community. Membership in the secular groups that were related to or involved with the synagogue was not conceived of as excluding membership in the religious body. On the contrary, "Most members of the major communal organizations are synagogue members. Indeed Jewish organizational membership tends to be a supplement rather than an alternative." [116]

The active relationship between the synagogue and the secular activities of Jewish organized life benefited not only the secularists but also organized Judaism. It became a way in which the synagogue and the rabbi could move to the center of life in the community, a position that certainly could not be achieved solely on the basis of religious activities and functions. The persistently low level of Jewish attendance at services indicated that reliance on religion alone would consign the rabbi and the synagogue to the periphery of the Jewish community. If holding meetings within the synagogues and having rabbis participate or officiate at them conferred legitimacy upon the activities of the secular organizations, this also strengthened the position of the rabbi and organized Judaism. This type of secular involvement aided the development of a sense of Jewish consciousness and community. It blurred the lines between the sacred and the secular. Donating money to a Jewish secular charity drive, nominally headed by a rabbi, playing basketball in a synagogue, or attending a lecture on modern dance in the same hall in which the torah was located became ways of demonstrating to oneself and to the community at large that one was a Jew. This development appeared to satisfy, if not please, almost everybody but the ardent secularists.

The Jewish Left was, of course, among the ardent secularists. The Judaicizing of the Jewish community and the strengthening of the role of organized religion was not a positive development from its point of view. The Left could not readily meet in a synagogue or request that a rabbi officiate at one of its gatherings. Even if it desired to take such actions and was able to find a willing rabbi, these actions would act to legitimate and buttress the position of organized Judaism, especially among the Jewish Left's ordinary rank and file. (However, when there were overriding considerations, the Left would turn to rabbis and congregations for legitimation or for the opportunity to reach out beyond its members and active sympathizers. During the period of the united front, for example, the Communist party was more than willing to overcome its inhibitions and hostility to religion in order to obtain the support of a rabbi or a synagogue.) To refrain from contact with organized Judaism (while other political groups, including the Zionists were involved with it in various ways) placed the Jewish Left at a tactical disadvantage. There seemed no acceptable solution to this problem. The Left was in a bind. The more the Jewish community was Judaicized and the more the religious authorities were strengthened, the worse its own position became.

The synagogue was not the only aspect of organized Judaism to become more important after World War I. The rabbinate also grew more influential. Prior to the war the rabbinate, as noted earlier, rabbis were relatively few in number, disorganized, and disoriented by life in the New World. All these factors had reduced their Eastern European status in the eyes of the immigrants. The situation began to change during and after the war. Their numbers increased, and growing proportion of them were men who were either born or reared in the United States. American seminaries began to produce rabbis for American congregations in relatively substantial numbers. In the five years from 1918 to 1922 these institutions graduated 118 rabbis. In the following five years, from 1923 to 1927, 168 matriculated.[117]

The public status and the communal importance of the more Americanized rabbis appears to have been greater than that of their pre-war, foreign-born counterparts.[118] Rabbis trained in America were, for the most part, men who acquired a secular college-level education along with their clerical training. They increasingly looked, dressed, and spoke like middle-class American gentlemen or proper Protestant ministers. The rabbis became more familiar and involved with the world around them and with secular issues that concerned their congregations.

The position of the rabbinate inside the Jewish community also benefitted from the changing public definition of Jews. In the prewar years the Jews had been considered a people, a race, and a religious group. Afterwards, the latter conception evolved as the most dominant one. Such a definition was very functional for the Jews, as it facilitated their integration into American society and their public acceptance as formal equals to major Christian denominations.

Organized Judaism also became a vehicle through which the middle class and the non-Left was able to penetrate the Eastern European

American Jewish community, especially the second generation within it. In this regard, its primary cutting edge was Conservative Judaism, which arose in America in the early 1900s. It was specifically conceived as a way of breaking the hold of traditional Orthodoxy among the Eastern Europeans and a means of Americanizing both them and Judaism. At the same time a by-product, an almost necessary by-product, of this movement was the elevation of the status and authority of the Americanized Jewish middle class among the Eastern European Jews and their children.[119]

The men who supported the development of Conservative Judaism were the wealthy leaders of the German American Jewish community, men such as Jacob H. Schiff and Lewis Marshall. Ironically, they were largely affiliated with Reform Judaism. However, as the major chronicler of Conservative Judaism, Marshall Sklare, points out: "The philanthropists recognized that Reform had little appeal to the immigrants. They felt that a modified Orthodoxy, stripped of ghetto characteristics, would be the type of Judaism most suitable for the Eastern Europeans.[120] In pursuit of this aim, these philanthropists gave their monetary and moral support to the development of this movement. The most concrete and probably most important expression of this support was embodied in the Jewish Theological Seminary, originally founded in 1886 to train rabbis in America. But it had not been able to function effectively. In 1901 the more astute leaders of German American Jewry reorganized and revived it for their purposes. They provided it with funds and imported a prominent European scholar, Solomon Schechter, to serve as its head. It was their hope that the Jewish Theological Seminary would become the citadel from which flowed the leaders and rabbis of "a modified Orthodoxy." In this regard, their hopes and monetary investments were rewarded.

Conservative Judaism did make substantial inroads into important segments of the Eastern European community. Orthodoxy did not prove to be adaptable to the new conditions. It was too closely tied to traditions as they had evolved in the Eastern European environment. As the Eastern European Jews in America became more acculturated and more mobile socioeconomically and geographically, Conservative Judaism seemed more attractive. It was a form of Judaism that kept many of the forms of Orthodoxy with which they were familiar but was also more modern and more American without being as deviant as the Reform Judaism of the German American Jews. Conservative Judaism became, in time, the most popular of the three major denominations. By the early 1970s the number of American Jewish households affiliated with Conservative synagogues was about the same for the combined figure of those associated with Orthodoxy and Reform.[121]

The growth and development of Conservative Judaism was inimical to the interests of the Jewish Left for various reasons. Perhaps most important, it was more formidable a foe than Orthodoxy. Before World

War I the organized state of Orthodoxy in America and the Eastern European traditions that surrounded it proved beneficial to the Jewish Left. Organizationally Orthodoxy was weak and torn by various problems. And because the overwhelming majority of the members were working-class Jews, the ability and desire of the Orthodox rabbinate and lay leaders to effectively function as a politically conservative influence among the Eastern Europeans in the United States was tempered. Unlike the situation in the Pale, Orthodoxy was not a serious organizational or political competitor to the American Jewish labor movement before World War I.

At the same time, however, the traditions and spirit of Orthodoxy were quite helpful to the Jewish Left. There were major sentimental and emotional features within the Eastern European Jewish community in America that helped to make it a cohesive community. But, these traditions also served to insulate this community, to some extent, from the influence of the German American Jews and American society. The Jewish Left, as previously noted, used this factor to its advantage.

The developing Conservative movement, particularly after World War I, altered this situation. It was better organized than Orthodoxy and had leaders who were more familiar with American conditions. Conservative Judaism was more capable of competing with the Jewish Left than was Orthodoxy. Its most effective area of influence was not among the Eastern European masses but among their children and the more Americanized among them.[122] This was precisely the population that the Jewish Left had to reach if it had any hope of remaining as a political force within the American Jewish community. Conservative Judaism also provided a force through which the Jewish middle-class and American middle-class values were able to debilitate the insulating barrier fostered by the traditions of Orthodoxy. Conservative Judaism, of course, was not the only factor in weakening this barrier. Nevertheless, it was important because it was doing so via the religious and cultural areas. Before the Conservative movement had established itself, the political influence of the Jewish middle class in the Eastern European American Jewish community had been diminished by the religious hegemony of Orthodoxy. And the Reform affiliation of the German American Jews inhibited them from playing what should have been a natural leadership role.

The middle class within the Eastern European community, particularly the more Americanized segment within it, were in a different situation, but one that had similar consequences with respect to their political influence in the religious sphere. For many, Orthodoxy was not a religion commensurate with their higher status and degree of acculturation. It was tainted with the aura of the Old Country. There were too many associations between it and poverty, medievalism, and irrationality. For this group, Reform was one alternative; breaking with Judaism was another. Politically each option redounded to the benefit of the Jewish Left. It removed a segment of a potentially influential group from the Eastern European community. Even if this Jewish middle class decided to remain within the bounds of Orthodoxy, the Jewish Left had some reason for optimism. This class would then be part of a weak organization in which the majority would still be working class.

Conservative Judaism, from the standpoint of the Jewish Left, represented an unwelcome alternative. Affiliation with it kept the Americanized Jewish middle class within organized Judaism and the Eastern European Jewish community. Membership within the Conservative movement, as opposed to Reform Judaism, did not signify a major break with this community. Conservative Judaism was better organized than Orthodoxy, while not suffering from the same factors that inhibited Orthodoxy in the political arena. Politically, Conservative Judaism proved injurious to the interests of the Jewish Left within the Jewish community in a variety of ways. First, it was an organized force within this community that the Left did not control or influence. Second, it gave the Jewish middle class strategic access to authority among Eastern European Jewry. The men who moved into the leadership positions within the Conservative movement were not petty traders and owners of small businesses. They were people who were among the most successful of the foreign-born and their children, such as professionals and owners of large- and medium-sized businesses. Such people were not as reticent as their less successful counterparts in Orthodoxy in promoting their political aims. Regardless of their open politics, their presence and position within an organized body of Judaism helped to spread middle-class examples, values, and general influence throughout the Eastern European Jewish community.

Conservative Judaism, through its lay and religious leaders, provided a more direct political threat to the Left because of the support that Conservative Judaism gave to Zionism. Of the three denominations, Conservative Judaism was the most ardently pro-Zionist. It gave the Zionist movement funds, leaders, and a major base within the Jewish community. The Zionists were the major foe of the Jewish Left.[123]

All the post–World War I trends associated with organized Judaism proved harmful to the Left, not only those associated with Conservatism. The elevation of the status and influence of the rabbinate and religion in organized Jewish life was detrimental to the Jewish Left. This was not primarily due to the overt hostility of organized Judaism toward the Left, although this cannot be disregarded as a factor. In fact, the rabbis as a whole tended to hold more positive attitudes with respect to socialism than the clergy of any other religious denomination in America prior to World War II.[124] Yet even during the Depression a majority within the rabbinate accepted the capitalist system as given. Generally the rabbinate and organized Judaism eschewed direct involvement in political affairs and controversial social and economic issues.[125] When they did enter the political arena, either directly or indirectly, the beneficiaries of this intervention were most likely to be the various opponents of the Jewish Left, particularly the Democratic party and the Zionist Organization of America. Rabbis, spearheaded by the Conservatives among them, were among the most important sources of support for the Zionist movement in America.[126]

Fundamentally the major damage that organized Judaism did to the Jewish Left stemmed from its relative success. Even though a majority of the Jews in America in any given decade of the twentieth century did not choose to affiliate with a synagogue, it still proved to be a resilient institution and was recognized by many of the disaffiliated as a legitimate corporate embodiment of the Jewish people. This post–World War I success of organized Judaism meant that the Jewish Left had to contend with a more formidable opponent than had previously been the case. Essentially, organized Judaism was in a zero-sum competitive relationship with the Jewish Left. The more success that organized Judaism had in attracting or influencing Jews, the less the Left was capable of achieving with that group. One indicator of this can be discerned in the various studies of Jewish political opinion and behavior. They suggest that the more involved Jews are with their religion, especially if they are Orthodox, the less likely they are to be liberal or Left in their politics.[127] Isaac Deutscher, in his classic essay "The Non-Jewish Jew," also arrives at similar conclusions from the opposite side. After considering the lives of prominent Jewish radicals, such as Leon Trotsky and Rosa Luxembourg, he contended that the radicals were most likely to emanate from those who broke with or were separated from organized Judaism.[128] The rising influence of organized Judaism, especially in the newer areas of Jewish settlement, then was highly prejudicial to the interests of the Jewish Left in America after World War I.

ZIONISM

The most serious direct political challenge to the position of the Jewish Left from within the Jewish community came from the Zionists. The competition and the antagonism between the radicals and the Zionists had been a constant feature of Jewish political life since the latter nineteenth century. This competition and hostility between the two groups was exacerbated by the fact that both regarded the Eastern Europeans in America, as well as in the Old World, as the primary target of their political activities. Zionist organizations and sympathizers were present in the United States prior to World War I, as we have already pointed out. They were relatively few in number, and they were politically a minor force among the Eastern Europeans, especially when compared to the Jewish Left. Their influence within the Jewish community was delimited not only by the opposition of the socialists but of the Orthodox and the affluent as well, each, of course, for their own separate reasons. That Zionists' best efforts were in the smaller cities and towns outside the great Jewish population centers testifies to their limited overall influence within the American Jewish community. It was in places such as Newburyport, Massachusetts, Milwaukee, and Baltimore that the Zionists were most successful.[129]

This situation changed dramatically after the outbreak of World War I. The concern for the safety and welfare of the Jews in Eastern Europe engulfed the immigrant Jewish community in America, who were tied to the Eastern Europeans by bonds of friendship and blood, as well as by religion. And the bulk of the Eastern European Jews were located in the paths of the contending armies. In such a context, the familiar appeal of the Zionists fell on more receptive ears.

The Zionist cause was also aided by other foreign factors, most notably the Balfour Declaration. On November 2, 1917, the British foreign secretary, Arthur James Balfour, wrote: "His Majesty's Government views with favour the establishment in Palestine of a national home for the Jewish people and will use their best endeavours to facilitate the achievement of this object." Here, for the first time, a major world power endorsed and legitimated in the non-Jewish society of nations, a Zionist goal for the solution to the Jewish problem in Europe.

The endorsement of the Balfour Declaration by President Woodrow Wilson provided a further boost to the Zionist cause. Wilson's public support made it easier for the immigrant Jews to become Zionists, or at least Zionist fellow travelers. It significantly reduced, at least for a short time, the anxiety that identification with Zionism would open the Jewish community to charges of dual loyalty that anti-Semites could then exploit. The pro-Zionist action of the President of the United States had now undercut the potency of such accusations. Wilson's endorsement also directly stimulated the growth of Zionist sentiment among the American Jews. If the president of the United States believed that the Zionist cause was worthy of support, why should average Jews withhold theirs. To become a Zionist or to give financial assistance to Zionist organizations could be interpreted as following the leadership of the president.[130]

An additional factor that spurred the growth of Zionist support and sentiment among the Jewish masses was the ascension of Louis D. Brandeis to the most prominent leadership post within the Zionist movement. Brandeis was an eminent lawyer and a major public figure when he became the president of the Provisional Zionist Committee in August 1914. His action provided further legitimation to Zionism and encouraged many to follow his lead. It was not only Brandeis that encouraged this tendency. It was also the character of the lieutenants that he gathered around him and the eminence of others whom he helped to attract to Zionism. These included Felix Frankfurter, then a Harvard Law Professor; U.S. Circuit Court Justice Julian Mack; the philosopher Horace M. Kallen, and the wealthy Nathan Straus. Collectively these men changed the public face of Zionism. Now the Zionist cause was led by men who were powerful and respected in both the Jewish and non-Jewish worlds. No longer was American Zionism to remain the " 'eccentric pasttime' of a few Reform rabbis, the scholars of the Jewish Theological Seminary, and a handful of laymen. . . ." From a small, decentralized, peripheral group in Jewish society, the Zionists now quickly developed into a cohesive political group with the best political connections of any Zionist party in the world. Brandeis, Frankfurter, and Rabbi Stephen S. Wise enjoyed official access to the leaders of the Wilson administration, including the president himself.[131]

These factors produced unprecedented support for Zionism in the Jewish community, the most tangible being the rise in formal membership in various Zionist organizations. Before 1914 membership had never risen much beyond 12,000. By 1918 the number of officially declared Zionists reached about 175,000, which does not take into account the large number of other Jews who did not join a Zionist organization but gave financial support to the movement. It was quite clear that by war's end a dramatic shift in sentiment had taken place among American Jewry. The Zionists were now a major political force within the American Jewish community with which the Jewish Left would have to seriously contend.

The growth of Zionism in response to the Jewish crisis emanating out of World War I was not a unique occurrence. Earlier in Eastern Europe, as well as in America, about the time of the Kishinev pogrom, Jewish crises typically resulted in an increase in the number of recruits and converts to Zionism. The Zionists, more so than the Jewish radicals, were adept at turning Jewish difficulties to their advantage. This pattern did not end with World War I. It was to continue and become even more pronounced in the 1930s and 1940s, and the Left and Jewish Left were to prove relatively ineffective in doing anything about it.

The highwater mark of Zionism in America for several decades was in 1918. It receded in the 1920s and early 1930s. Membership in the major official Zionist body, the Zionist Organization of America (ZOA) steadily declined, from 149,235 in 1918 to 56,838 in 1919. By 1922 the ZOA rolls had declined to 18,481, and in 1932 membership reached its nadir with 8484.[132] This decline was due to various factors. First, the termination of the war had brought with it the end of the immediate threat to the safety of the Eastern European Jews. As was so common in Jewish history, the conclusion of a crisis dampened the flames of Jewish consciousness and nationalism. Second, the outbreak of the Red Scare in 1918 and 1919 and the rise of anti-Semitism in the 1920s created a climate of opinion that made membership in a Zionist organization seem a risky venture. Jews became anxious not to provide any support for claims that challenged their loyalty. Third, there was a good deal of internecine warfare within the Zionist movement. Various factions and cliques struggled with each other for leadership positions and over the direction of the movement. This disillusioned many members and led to resignations as well as to a decline in the number of new entrants.[133] The Zionist movement, however, did not die. Although the Zionist organizations weakened, Zionist influence within various sectors of organized Jewry remained firmly implanted. Zionist activists, or at least active sympathizers, were to be found in virtually every important Jewish organization. Synagogues, rabbinical associations, fraternal orders, and Jewish labor unions contained persons who were willing to influence their colleagues on behalf of Zionism.

The most important areas of Zionist activity after World War I was fund raising for Palestine. Even as organized Zionism was declining in the 1920s, the ZOA succeeded in raising almost $15 million for that cause. The Zionists were interested in gaining more than money from these charitable drives. They used fund-raising drives to gain access to various Jewish organizations and institutions and to shape public opinion to accept Zionist goals and future political action. Their use of fund-raising activities, their own as well as others, for political ends was an ingenious way of furthering their interests. This was, of course, as we noted earlier, not unique to the Zionists. Non-Zionists and the Jewish Left had also used fund-raising for political purposes. What made the Zionist use of this device so unique was their tenacity and persistence over so long a time period. Few Jewish organizations could or would raise objections to collecting funds for the welfare and health of Jews in Palestine. Once the principle was accepted, it became difficult to oppose the means by which the fund-raising activities were carried out or prevent the Zionists, the principal organizers of these campaigns, from reaping political benefits. A political scientist, Samuel Halperin, described and analyzed the political function and consequences of Zionist fund drives as follows:

Utilizing platforms provided by fund raising occasions and exploiting genuine humanitarian impulses, Zionists were able to persuade American Jews of the desirability and practicability of their program. Eventually, the demands, if not the motivations, of "non-political" fund raising organizations and "political" Zionist groups became virtually indistinguishable. . . . Broadening their popular base by infiltrating and influencing already existent associations by erecting new umbrella organizations (such as the National Conference for Palestine), Zionists added "educational content" to the ordinary philanthropic appeals of saving Jews and helping the poor unfortunates. In this way, ever larger portions of American Jewry came to view Palestine Zionistically— not in terms of mere temporary disaster, but rather as a "long-range and permanent solution to the Jewish problem." In this way, too, the deep conflicts dividing the Jewish community, which had defied all previous efforts at communal organization, became sufficiently controllable to permit Zionists to mobilize and channel public opinion into political action. . . . Within the arena of fund raising for "worthy causes," Zionists were also able to convert, or at least to overpower, the philanthropically disposed objectors who, had they not been neutralized or corralled in some type of joint endeavor with Zionism, might have organized effective obstruction to the further advance of Zionist influence. . . . Finally, the various institutions and the gradually developed annual "habit" of American Jews giving to Palestine eventually produced sufficient unity of thought to permit political action.[134]

Zionism reaped the fruits of these efforts in the 1930s and 1940s. American Jews, in response to the mounting crises affecting Jews, came to accept Zionism and the solutions it suggested as an almost natural way in which to deal with them. Each series of major foreign crises heightened Jewish consciousness and communality, which the Zionists had helped to build. The Arab attacks on the yishuv in Palestine in 1929 and in 1936, Hitler's continuing assault on German Jewry following his ascension to power in 1933, the British restriction on immigration to Palestine later in the 1930s, the Nazi attempt at a "final solution" during World War II, and the battle for Israel in the late 1940s were used by the Zionists to further strengthen their own position and the role of Zionism in the Jewish community. The growth of organized anti-Semitism in the United States in the 1930s also redounded to the Zionists' benefit.[135]

The consequences for Zionism of these Jewish crises and the work of the Zionists in shaping Jewish responses to them can be ascertained in various ways. Financial contributions for the welfare of Jews in Palestine provides us with one way of gauging Zionist and pro-Zionist sentiment. This was the principal and most immediate concrete way in which the Jews reacted to those events. The total amount of all contributions to assist Jews abroad and the total number of Jews contributing soared. The amount given through the principal Zionist channel, the United Palestine Appeal (UPA), which sometimes ran joint campaigns with other agencies, also rose dramatically. From 1901 to 1930 the UPA, or its Zionist components or predecessors, raised a total of approximately $14 million. During years from 1930 to 1939 the figure was $8 million. From 1940 to 1945 the UPA raised over $42 million. In 1948 alone, the UPA funds totalled approximately $75 million, which was more than it raised between 1901 and 1945. It should be stressed that the UPA was not the only fund-raising channel for Palestine Jewry. There were numerous others whose experience paralleled that of the UPA in these years.[136]

Membership in Zionist organizations was another way in which American Jewry reacted to the crises. In 1932 the ZOA's rolls had declined to their all-time low of 8484. By 1939 the rolls had increased to 44,453; and in 1945, at the end of World War II, membership was 136,630. In 1948, as the struggle for a Jewish state reached its height, the ZOA reported a membership of approximately 250,000. The Hadassah, the women's branch of the ZOA, also experienced a similar expansion over these years, growing from 27,349 members in 1932 to about 243,000 in 1948. At this time the membership in specifically Zionist groups in the United States was greater than that of any non-Zionist organization, apart from the synagogues.[137] By the end of World War II, the distinction between Zionist and non-Zionist Jewish organization was more apparent than real. Virtually every Jewish organization of any significance was committed to the establishment of some form of Jewish state in Palestine. Zionism had succeeded in accomplishing what no other movement or ideology had ever done in the American Jewish community. It had united American Jewry around its program, at least central aspects of it. No other movement or political tendency within the American Jewish community in the immediate years after World War II was either effectively capable or desirous of directly challenging the Zionists. Any organized body that did so risked losing the support of its Jewish members and sympathizers. Even the Communist party, the long-time foe of the Zionists, ran candidates for electoral offices in Jewish districts on campaign platforms that stressed their support for a Jewish state in Palestine.[138]

A Roper poll made public in November 1945 clarifies the extent of the Jewish community's support for the Zionist goal of a Jewish state in Palestine. In this poll a national cross-section of American Jews was asked to choose one of two conflicting statements that reflected their views:

1. A Jewish state in Palestine is a good thing for the Jews; every possible effort should be made to establish Palestine as a Jewish state or commonwealth for those who went to settle there;

2. Jews are a religious group only and not a Jewish nation; it would be bad for the Jews to try to set up a Jewish state in Palestine or anywhere else.

Of all the Jewish respondents, 80 percent chose the prostatehood statement compared to approximately 11 percent who designated the antistatehood statement.[139]

The magnitude of support for the Zionist position expressed in the poll was unprecedented. The results become more impressive when the internal construction of the poll is examined and the historical timing of it is considered. The poll posed the two statements in their most extreme form so as to "require respondents to vote on the most stringent form of the issue and thus give the results a higher indicative value." Therefore, instead of using the vague and more popular term *homeland*, the poll used the word *state*. That only 9 percent of the respondents were "undecided" was remarkable for a poll of this nature. Thus, it revealed that when confronted with the choice in its most stark form, American Jews were quite prepared to opt for the Zionist solution to the Jewish problem.[140] Furthermore, as impressive as the figure of 80 percent is, it probably did not represent the height of Jewish support for a Jewish state in Palestine. The poll was conducted before the full extent of the Nazi slaughter had become known and before the major campaign and physical struggle to establish the state of Israel had commenced. Unfortunately, such a national survey of Jewish opinion was not repeated at a later date. The pattern of growth in both financial contributions and membership in Zionist organizations from 1945 to 1948, as well as the results from at least one local survey (Baltimore) taken immediately after the state of Israel had been established, suggests that more than 80 percent of American Jews in 1948 favored a Jewish state in Palestine.[141]

The growth and influence of Zionist organizations and the impressive strength of Zionist feelings within American Jewry were major factors in driving the Left to the periphery of the ideological and political Jewish marketplace. One reason and perhaps the most important one was that the rise of Zionism fostered and reflected the waxing of a Jewish consciousness and a sense of Jewish communality. Zionism and pro-yishuv activities before 1948 (and pro-Israel ones thereafter) became a major centripetal force within American Jewry, particularly for nonreligious Jews and those only peripherly involved with organized Judaism. For this group, which constituted a large proportion of the Jews in America, Zionism became both a way of expressing their Jewishness and a conduit back into the Jewish community. Zionism also became a primary vehicle for the Jewish community's reinvigoration. As early as 1904 leaders of Conservative Judaism had envisaged such a role for Zionism. They viewed Zionism as a means of securing Jewish immigrants to Judaism after they had become Americanized. This position proved to be prescient. Rabbi Mordecai M. Kaplan, an eminent, sociologically oriented Jewish scholar and the founder of Reconstructionism, surveyed some of the evidence of the close and mutually rewarding relationship between Zionism and Jewishness in the early 1930s:

Of especial significance, from an educational standpoint, is the extent to which the Zionist movement has reclaimed Jewish womanhood and Jewish youth for an interest not alone in the rebuilding of Palestine, but in all matters Jewish. The Hadassah organization is noted for its success in arousing thousands of American Jewish women to a sense of responsibility to the Jewish people, no less than for its effective health work in Palestine. Young Judea . . . Junior Haddassah and Avukah . . . have rendered invaluable service in cultivating in American Jewish youth a loyalty to the Jewish people and its heritage. . . . If it were not for the structifying effect of the interest in the upbuilding of Palestine the work of the communal centers, synagogues, philanthropic and educational institutions might have gone on, but it would have become soulless and spiritless. As evidence of Zionism's power to supply Jewish life with new inspiration and vigor, we might point to the fact that Jews who had become totally alienated from Jewish life have for the first time found themselves spiritually and are giving the best of their thought and energy to the Palestinian movement.[142]

Thus as Jews, the Jewish community, and Jewish problems came to the fore as objects of concern and focal points of the outpouring of energy and emotional commitment, other interests and loyalties, including leftist ones, had to wane.

The various policies and actions of the Zionists in promoting their cause and in responding to Jewish crises also gave them important political advantages vis-à-vis the Jewish and American Left. The way in which the American Zionist leaders defined and shaped their movement provided them with significant leverage in Zionism. As it was defined and molded by Justice Brandeis and other leaders, it became, within an American context a philanthropic expression of Jewish consciousness rather than a vehicle for Jewish nationalism. In 1897 the basic and authoritative principles of Zionism were put forth in the Basle Platform of the First World Zionist Congress in Switzerland: "Zionism seeks to create for the Jewish people a home in Palestine . . ." Louis Brandeis shifted the emphasis in the definition of Zionism for American Jews: "Zionism seeks to establish in Palestine, *for such Jews as choose to go there* and their descendants, a legally secured home where they may live together and lead a Jewish life" [emphasis added]. Brandeis' definition came to be the one that defined the character of Zionism among American Jews.[143] This formulation allowed American Jews to be comfortable in becoming or supporting Zionists. As Brandeis had formulated it, Zionism was a means through which American Jews could express their support, financially and politically, for *other* Jews who chose to live in Palestine. This land, according to the American version of Zionism, would then become *their* home and not a home for *the Jewish* people.

While this essentially "philanthropic" version of Zionism may not have pleased the more orthodox Zionists who controlled the movement in other parts of the world, it did appear to be congenial to the American Jewish community. Few American Jews, despite the efforts of various Zionist groups who differed with Brandeis' position, chose to go to Palestine. In 1928 Chaim Weizmann, then president of the World Zionist Organization, noted that the United States had yet to send one solitary pioneer to Palestine. Although this may have been an overstatement, more reliable statistics covering the period from 1919 to 1945 show that only 8057 Jews from America emigrated to Palestine, which constituted about 2 percent of the total Jewish immigration during those years. American Jews were obviously more willing to send their dollars to Palestine than their children.

This philanthropic formulation served the cause of Zionism within America quite well. It did much to reduce the charge of dual loyalty. As defined by most of the American Zionist leadership, it allowed Jews to be Zionists and to feel fully loyal to the United States. This version of Zionism also facilitated American political and social leaders in giving their public endorsement to the movement, further legitimizing Zionism in the eyes of American Jewry. Such legitimation also encouraged Jewish membership in and support of what was now an approved movement.

On those grounds, the Jewish Left was at a disadvantage compared to the Zionists. Its ideology—Marxism and the class struggle (for those groups within it who remained committed to the latter notion)—was not as benign as that of the Zionists and certainly not as susceptible to public endorsement from prominent persons in American society. The pronouncements of the Left (even when moderated), appeared too divisive and harsh for an upwardly mobile Jewry that was increasingly desirous of being accepted into American society. The Jewish Left, primarily the Communists within it, was not as able as the Zionists had been to relieve itself of the burden of dual loyalty or, even worse, of fealty to a non-American power. Zionists, for example, were never investigated by the House Committee on Un-American Activities. Zionism had proved much more successful than the Left in establishing its American bona fides, which gave the Zionists another advantage over the Left in appealing to American Jews.

Both the Zionists and the Communists gained support from American Jews as a result of the way each responded to anti-Semitism in the United States from the middle 1930s through the 1940s. However, the Zionists appeared to be the major beneficiary. Anti-Semitism attacked Jews as Jews and thus heightened their feelings of Jewishness. Zionism represented a direct and a Jewish way of responding to it, as compared to the more indirect, diffuse, and traditionally less Jewish way the Left responded to anti-Semitism. One informed observer has commented on the relationship between Zionism and anti-Semitism in the United States during this trying period: ". . . Challenged as it was in ethnic and religious terms, the 'will to live' of the Jewish people brought about a massive revival of nationalistic sentiments. To many Jews Zionism seemed like the natural, long-range solution to perennial anti-Semitism. With its appeals for Jewish auto-emancipation and self-respect, Zionism was thus able to fill a patent void in American Jewish life.[144]

In the 1930s and 1940s Zionism was also advanced and accepted by many Jews as a means of "normalizing" the Jews' status in America. It would put them on the same basis as other immigrants who showed concern with the homelands they or their parents or grandparents had left. Hannah Arendt put forth this position in a direct, almost aggressive, form: "A vital interest in Palestine as the homeland of the Jewish people is only natural . . . [and] needs no excuses in a country where so many national splinter groups show loyalty to their mother countries. Indeed, a Jewish mother country might thus rather tend to 'normalize' the situation of Jews in America and be a good argument against political anti-Semitism."[145]

The increasing receptivity of American Jews to Zionist positions and arguments strengthened the Zionists' organizational and opinion-forming influence within the Jewish community. As its stock rose in these spheres, that of the Left declined. The Zionists' organizational clout within organized Jewry in the 1930s and 1940s not only limited the sphere in which the organized Jewish Left could operate, it also weakened the working-class and pro-Left identity among Jews that had sustained the Jewish Left. As the seemingly interminable Jewish crises continued and as Zionism became ever more legitimate and respectable, organizationally the Zionists went from strength to strength. According to Samuel Halperin,

The more Zionism came to be accepted by American Jewry, the more difficult it was for any given group to resist its demands. Success in one sector of the Jewish political world facilitated victory in other sectors. Groups began to use their Zionist affiliation as a weapon against their rivals. . . . As Zionism became increasingly respectable in the Jewish community, a "bandwagon effect" could be observed. . . . Zionism was viewed as a "Jewish badge of honor" and a prerequisite for community leadership and eminence. Zionist leadership, in turn, exploited these successes to enhance further its standing among American Jews and to influence recalcitrant groups to adopt a more pro-Palestine posture.[146]

In addition to other consequences for the Left and Leftists, this situation did not bode well for working-class and pro-Left Jews who were or became involved in Jewish organizations outside the exclusive preserve of the Left. Such participation meant that they would increasingly find themselves in bodies in which they were interacting with or following the leadership of Zionists. In such circumstances there would be little, if any, reinforcement for a Left or pro-Leftist identity but, rather, pressure to adopt one that was Zionist or pro-Zionist. Consequently there had to be an erosion of a Left commitment or propensity from those involved with such groups. Nonmembership in Zionist or Zionist-oriented groups did not mean that Jews in the Jewish community were invulnerable to Zionist pressures. From the middle 1930s through the 1940s, Zionism generated a climate of opinion that blanketed the Jewish community, which significantly influenced Jewish political attitudes, opinions, and behavior. Zionism also set the terms of the discussion of and debate about ways in which Jews should respond and deal with the various threats affecting them and their coreligionists abroad. In this climate even committed Leftist Jews experienced difficulty in resisting Zionist and Zionist-oriented appeals to the Jewish side of their identities.

The Zionists' hegemony over Jewish public opinion was the result of not only years of preparation and their ability to profitably respond to events but also the nature of the action and response of the Jewish Left to the crises affecting Jews. Generally the Jewish Left offered no real competition to the Zionists on this ground. It was not willing nor able to present a major Left alternative to the position of the Zionists. The Bundist or Bundist-oriented Socialists and former Socialists grouped around the Jewish Labor Committee and the *Jewish Daily Forward* were not so committed to socialism by the mid-1930s as to be able to offer a full-blown version of the traditional socialist response to Zionism. Instead they harped on specific points or some vague abstractions on which there were differences between them and the Zionists, but then generally went along with their traditional foe on concrete action that the Zionists had largely initiated and designed. This, however, was no substitute for a developed counterpolicy, which the Jewish Labor Committee did not possess.[147] Similarly, the Jewish Communists after 1936 hurled fewer and fewer open challenges at their long-time and hated foe, the Zionists. The Jewish Communists, after the launching of the policy of the united front in 1935, began to take greater care in their public treatment of Zionism. They were well aware of the extent of pro-Zionist sentiment within the Jewish community. The spokesman for the Jewish Bureau of the Central Committee of the United States Communist Party stated that "There is no doubt that the Zionist propaganda has succeeded in influencing thousands of workers and toilers, as well as a section of the leadership of certain mass organizations which were coming our way on the question of the united front and the people's front."[148] The CP, it is clear, did not wish to alienate the many Jews who felt positively toward Zionism by continuing its vigorous, bitter, and sometimes crude attacks on the movement.[149]

Impelled by this political motivation, the CP's public treatment of Zionism and Jewish nationalism underwent a change—it became hesitant to label Zionism "as a chauvinist movement" and "a breeding ground of fascism,"[150] as had the New Masses of February 19, 1935. By 1938 Moissaye Olgin, a leading Jewish Communist, told his party comrades: "We fought Zionism which was correct, but in fighting Zionism, we forgot that many progressive elements of the Jewish people were Zionistically inclined. We forgot also that the craving, the desire, for nationhood is not in itself reactionary, although Zionism is reactionary."[151] By 1943 Alex Bittelman, the general secretary of the Morning Freiheit Association and a leading CP theoretician, while still claiming to reject Zionism, referred to it as "only one tendency among many in Jewish social life—a tendency which has its own philosophy on the nature of Jewishness and which conducts its own policy as a party on the question of Palestine."[152] Bittelman, as the CP's leading spokesman on Jewish matters, also took public note of the areas and issues on which the Communists and the Zionists were in agreement. He even complimented the Zionists for their efforts on behalf of the Jewish people and openly declared that there were Zionists in the Morning Freiheit Association. Bittelman went so far as to publicly chastize the Jewish Labor Committee, the Forward, and the Bundists for their continued hostility toward Zionism. Before the end of World War II Bittelman was urging Jewish Communists and Jewish Zionists to unite in a common struggle for victory.[153] This newly declared attitude toward Jewish nationalism did not end with the war. In 1948 in a Congressional by-election in a largely Jewish district in the Bronx, the Communists actively conducted a pro-Jewish statehood campaign in favor of the candidate of the American Labor Party, Leo Isaacson. (He won.)[154]

The powerful and emotional appeal of Zionism and Jewish consciousness against the backdrop of continued threats and attrocities to the Jews of Europe and Palestine dominated the Jewish community in the 1930s and 1940s. It made major inroads into the former bastions of the Jewish Left—the Jewish working class and the Eastern European American Jewish community. Given the failure of leftist Jews to construct and articulate a counter force to the Zionist arguments and positions and Left's seeming approval of various Zionist actions and policies, one could scarcely have expected their less-tutored constituents and supporters to resist the appeal of Zionism and Jewish consciousness that accompanied it. It was not only the less-tutored and vaguely Left Jews who proved susceptible to Zionist notions and a heightened Jewish identity. In the context of the impending and then actual holocaust, long-standing Left objections and alternatives to Zionism appeared either irrelevant or burdensome. Even Leon Trotsky, a militant anti-Zionist and a man who had suppressed or repressed a Jewish identity throughout most of his life, reversed his long-held position on the issue of a Jewish state because of the Nazi menace to the Jews. As early as 1932 Trotsky had become convinced that Hitler actually intended to destroy the Jews. The only way the Jews could avert annihilation, in Trotsky's view, was a Jewish state. After the menace had passed, this Jewish state, as Trotsky envisioned it, would join with other Socialist states to become part of a World Socialist Federation.[155] Isaac Deutscher, the noted European Jewish Marxist intellectual and long-time opponent of Zionism, spoke for many like-minded persons of his political generation when he wrote for an American audience in 1954 that "I have, of course, long since abandoned my anti-Zionism, which was based on a confidence in the European labor movement. . . . If, instead of arguing against Zionism in the 1920s and 1930s I had urged Jews to go to Palestine, I might have helped to save some of the lives that were later extinguished in Hitler's gas chambers. For the remnants of European Jewry—is it only for them?—the Jewish State has become an historic necessity."[156]

Deutscher's sentiments were also shared by Jews whose adult lives had been involved with the Communist movement in the United States. One such was Bittelman, a major figure in both the Jewish and non-Jewish camps of the Communist party for decades. In his unpublished autobiography written during the early 1960s, he criticized the role that he had played in the 1930s: "I should have fought not only against fascism and war, but also for the honor and survival of the Jewish people. I should have fought the Nazis, not only as an anti-fascist and a Communist, but also as a Jewish national revolutionary, and urged other Jews to do likewise." Bittelman then went on to describe the lesson that he had learned from this failure to behave like a Jew during the time of his people's greatest trial: "Jewish Communists, Socialists and social progressives must now learn that the best service they can render the cause of social progress, of Socialism, of internationalism and true patriotism, is to prepare and lead the Jews everywhere to fight for Jewish survival." [157]

Those statements could be considered the retrospective expressions of an embittered old man who was expelled from the Communist party in 1960 at the age of 70 for having aligned himself with antiparty revisionists. These same sentiments have, however, been echoed by others, whom I have interviewed. It seems clear that the growth of a Jewish consciousness within Bittelman and other Jewish Communists was spurred by the various attacks on Jews in the later 1930s and 1940s, culminating in the Holocaust.

Such a development within individuals cannot be understood only in terms of primordial ties and ethnic feelings brought to the fore by awesome events. It also has to be understood in terms of broader organizational and political terms. The rise of a Jewish consciousness and the preeminence of Zionism in the American Jewish community were interactive phenomena. Both fed off the realistic menace to Jews. It was the Zionists, much more than the Communists, who harnessed the response to the events and the heightened Jewish consciousness to serve their organizational and political ends. Again, the absence of an organized counterforce by the Left to the Zionists and the failure of the Left to publicly articulate a developed alternative to the Zionists' position on the Jewish question meant that seasoned Leftists, even ardent Communists, were without much social and political support in resisting the forces that called forth their Jewish consciousness. Given this context, as their Jewish identities reemerged or became more defined, their leftist ones weakened or were made vulnerable.

This development was exacerbated by continual contact with Jewish workers and the Jewish community in general. It was difficult for the Jewish leftists, Communists included, to work among the Jewish masses and not be influenced by the depth and breadth of their Jewish (national) consciousness during the latter 1930s and the 1940s. The Jewish working class and other sectors of the Jewish community in which the Left had made or desired to make inroads were increasingly becoming more Jewish in terms of their identities and interests, which either took primacy over or seriously challenged their class identities and interests. The concrete expression of these Jewish interests and identities was increasingly determined by the positions and formulations of the Zionists. Jewish Left activists who had to work or relate to such Jewish groups and masses could hardly help being affected by the sentiments and being drawn into the orbit of the Zionist-molded Jewish consciousness.

However, it was more than an individual dilemma and a question of cross-pressures; it was also an organizational dilemma of the Left which, by the end of the 1930s, largely meant the Communist party. During this period, the CP could not afford to launch major frontal attacks on Zionism or Jewish nationalism or, later, Israel without risking the loss of support from American Jews who were deeply committed to those Jewish forces and phenomena. But, to ignore the Zionist and pro-Israel sentiment would mean tolerating a force that potentially and eventually would further separate the Jews from the Left. Even the expedient of riding with the tide of Jewish nationalism, as they had done in the Isaacson congressional campaign, had its longrange drawbacks. Such action placed the Communists in the position of endorsing the reinforcing Jewish nationalism or Zionism. It strengthened the Jewish identities and interests of their constituents and prospective constituents in the Jewish community, as well as those of Jewish party members. This, in turn, meant that when the policies of the PC were no longer congruent with Jewish nationalism, the CP would find itself in a weak and vulnerable position among American Jews. In short, the revivified Jewish consciousness and sense of communality that the Zionist movement fed and spawned, forced the Jewish Left and leftist Jews into a political relationship with the Jewish community that was to prove costly to the historical ties between the Jews and radicalism.

THE IMPORTANCE OF ISRAEL

After the state of Israel was established in 1948, the Zionist movement declined (as did the Old Left as embodied in the Communist party). There instead arose a potent emotional and political commitment to the new Jewish state. By the mid-1960s, and especially after the Six Day War of 1967, support for Israel was virtually the single most important factor in defining one as a Jew and a member of the Jewish community.

This development was not entirely natural. There is no doubt that the American Jewish community's collective guilt about and memory of the Holocaust made it receptive to supporting Israel. This inclination was, however, also fostered and furthered by the policies and activities of American Jewish educational, religious, social, philanthropic, labor, and political groups. Increasingly since 1948 they brought Israel and things Israeli toward the center of their organizational lives. The government of Israel and various Israeli institutions and groups also did their part in building close ties between themselves and American Jews. The capstone to this whole process was the all-too-frequent Israeli military crises. Threats to Israel, especially those in 1967 and 1973, called forth from American Jews a tremendous surge of support for and emotional identification with the Jewish state. For example, In 1967, contributions to the United Jewish Appeal were almost four times greater than in 1966.[158]

After the state of Israel was established, it became increasingly clear that the growth among American Jews of a pro-Israel identification would be injurious to the interests of the Left. First, this phenomenon, like Zionism, diminished the importance of class distinctions and other ideologies such as socialism that separated one Jew from another. The Left among Jews traditionally suffered whenever the Jewish community was united around a Jewish interest or concern. And, in the 1950s and especially in the 1960s, a pro-Israel sentiment and identification did unify Jews and provide them with a common Jewish interest and common Jewish cause.

Second, Israel for the first time in modern Jewish history gave Jews everywhere a Jewish nation to be concerned about. Prior to its formation, Jews as "rootless cosmopolitans" (an epithet coined by Soviet Communists) were relatively free to pursue universalist ideals and ideologies such as socialism. Other ethnic groups around them had to contemplate the costs to their nation and national interests before they could consider being as universalist as the Jews. After 1948 Jews in America as well as in Israel became more like other peoples in that they now felt forced to add national concerns and interests to their political perspective. Thus the odds in favor of Jews being as free to be universalistic and Left declined after 1948.

Third, the policies of Israel and the attitudes of other governments toward it were, after 1948, factors in attenuating the ties between the Jews and the Left in the United States and in other western countries. Initially, it did not appear that Israel would threaten these ties. In fact, there even seemed reason to believe that the new state might even strengthen and revivify the Jews links to the Left. Domestically the most powerful forces in Israel were the labor movement and Socialist or socialist-oriented political parties. The socialist kibbutz was a prominent institution in Israeli society and the source of much of that country's leadership. Internationally Israel came into existence with the strong support of the Soviet Union. Arms, which were crucial to the Jewish state's survival, came from Czechoslovakia.

But within a few short years after its birth, Israel could no longer count many friends among the nations in the Soviet bloc. In 1952 the Israeli government officially abandoned its policy of nonalignment and tilted to the West. Both Communist and Third World countries denounced it as an agent of imperialism. After 1952 the western capitalist nations were the only sources that the Jewish state could rely upon for necessary military and economic assistance. In fact, Israel even tried to become a member of the North Atlantic Treaty Organization. Conjointly with this development, the socialist sectors of Israeli society became less significant.

These new circumstances—ones that still prevail—placed many Jewish leftists and proleftists in conflict. Their political ideology inclined them to be hostile to the leading capitalist and imperialist powers. But as Jews concerned about Israel's survival, it was difficult not to view with at least some favor those same nations who now were the only guarantors of the Jewish state. That the major threats to Israel came from Arab organizations and states strongly supported by Communist and Third World countries espousing various brands of Marxism put additional pressure on the ties of many Jews to leftist movements. This pressure was, in the 1960s and 1970s, exacerbated by political pressure from various Jewish organizations, on the one hand, and radical ones, on the other. Their conflicting policies and public stances made it exceedingly difficult for a leftist Jew to be favorable to both radicalism and Israel's survival as a Jewish state.[159] (See Chapter 8 of this book for a more detailed discussion of this issue with respect to both Old and New Leftists.)

The political configuration of Israel's allies and enemies also contributed to the development in American Jews of a hostile attitude toward the Left. The verbal threats and denunciation of Israel by the Soviet Union, the Third World nations, and American radicals and their attacks on the United States as the major ally of Israel made it difficult for the Left to reach into or even retain its level of ties in the American Jewish community. In the era of the New Left, representatives of organized American Jewry made it very clear—the Left and New Left were inimical to Israel's existence. From this perspective, to give radical movements any sympathy or quarter was to endanger Israel.[160]

Finally, the elevation of Israel to the center stage of American Jewish life in turn reinforced the position of the non-Left strata among American Jews. A connection or an involvement with fund drives to help Israel or Israeli institutions became almost a sine qua non for leadership in the American Jewish community. Those whose Jewish political position benefitted from such an association were generally the important donors, the fund raisers, and the officers of Jewish organizations, in other words, the wealthy and the professionals.[161] Such leaders would not likely be receptive to leftist appeals or concerns.

In sum, the emergence of Israel as a state and the difficult international position in which it found itself shortly thereafter contributed in a variety of ways to pushing American Jews toward the right. As a leading American Jewish intellectual and moderate socialist, Irving Howe stated: "The authority of Israel within the baroquely structured milieu of organized American Jewry became enormous, sometimes decisive, and despite the moderately leftist tilt of the Israeli government, its impact upon American Jews was necessarily conservative."[162]

NONCONSERVATIZING TENDENCIES

So far we have generally been dealing with factors that contributed to the attenuation of the positive relationship between the Jews and the Left after World War I. The stress given to those elements that debilitated this association might lead to the impression that after World War I there was little remaining to sustain it and that after the war the Jews continually and inexorably moved from the left to the right of the political spectrum. This was not the case. Ties between the Jews and the Left constructed before 1920 and encased in significant institutions did remain intact. Also, there were new conditions and new situations after World War I that helped to strengthen this ethnic community and the socialist movement.

Before we turn our attention to these newer and reinvigorating factors, it is important to briefly pause and stress the continuing contribution of the pre–World War I socioeconomic and institutional bases to Jewish–Left ties. These bases, as noted above, were weakened by post–World War I developments, but they were not totally undermined. Although the large working-class ghetto of the Lower East Side did loose large numbers of its Yiddish-speaking residents, many stayed behind. Of those that left, considerable numbers moved into newer, smaller Jewish ghettoes. While a relatively large proportion of Jews did leave the working class, many (especially in the larger cities like New York) continued to do manual labor. Although religious and non-Left organizations did grow, some Jewish leftists remained beyond their reach. Prominent leftist institutions, such as the Workmen's Circle and the ILGWU, did move away from this political orientation after the war, but the change was gradual. Even in the post–World War II period, such institutions continued to provide a home for Jewish leftists and proleftists. Other Jewish Left institutions, such as the International Workers Order and the Furriers Union, retained a marked leftist character for decades. Thus, although there was considerable change in the socioeconomic, demographic, and institutional structure of the post–World War I Jewish community, there was also substantial stability. This stability, coupled with the firmness of the basic Left institutions and with inertia, sustained the links between the Jews and the Left after World War I, albeit in a weakened form.

ANTI-SEMITISM

The bonds between sectors of the American Jewish community and socialism were not entirely based on factors from the past. One of the post–World War I developments that strengthened these ties was the waves of anti-Semitism that swept America at various times in the 1920s, 1930s, and early 1940s.

Anti-Semitism, as we have previously observed, was no stranger to America's shores. Although present before World War I, it was not potent, especially when compared to the anti-Semitism in czarist Russia (and in Rumania)—the referent points for the Eastern European Jews in the United States. Prejudice and discrimination against Jews in the United States did not seriously interfere with their geographic and socioeconomic mobility. The relative weakness of American anti-Semitism contributed to the decline in cohesiveness among the Eastern European Jews while facilitating their acculturation and sentimental attachment to America and their socioeconomic advancement—all of

which weakened their allegiance to the Left. The growth and spread
of anti-Semitism during World War I and in the succeeding decades, however, reversed or slowed some of the conservatizing tendencies.

The Nature of Anti-Semitism From World War I to World War II

Before describing and analyzing the ways in which anti-Semitism in
the interwar years bolstered the ties between Jews and socialism, it
would be useful to breifly look at the dimensions of anti-Semitism
during this period. Anti-Semitism became a significant problem for
Jews, especially Eastern European Jews in America, during the World
War I. The war caused Americans to look with suspicion and hostility
at foreigners and foreign-speaking persons on American soil. They
were suspect as possible spies or subversives or as persons whose
ideas, language, and customs detracted from the unity needed to wage
a successful war. In order to reduce this burden, foreigners were expected and felt obliged to demonstrate not only their loyalty to the
war effort but also their loyalty to America. Things foreign were to be
dispensed with as quickly and as thoroughly as possible—to be replaced by things American. Foreigners and so-called hyphenated
Americans (foreign-born Americans with supposedly dual political
loyalties) were, according to nativists and the public opinion they
dominated, expected to somehow disappear and be resurrected as 100
percent Americans. Although this nativist cloud fell over Jews and
other immigrant groups, Jews became the object of special attention.
Prior to America's entrance into World War I, the Russian Jews, the
Irish, and the Germans in the United States had ardently opposed the
Allied effort because of their hostility toward czarist Russia. After the
American declaration of war on April 6, 1917, the immigrant Jewish
community, compared to the other immigrant groups, contained significant elements who refused to become ardent supporters of the
Allied cause. This lack of total public backing for the war by the Jews
gave reinforcement to anti-Semitic feelings.[163]

But what was even worse, from the point of view of American pa-
triots, was that the Jews also harbored outright opponents of the war;
and these antiwar Jews were also atheistic radicals. A major focal
point of Jewish antagonism toward the war and the resulting public
hostility was Morris Hillquit's New York City mayoralty campaign in
1917.[164] The Hillquit campaign embodied all the elements that the
prowar public and its leaders associated with Jews. It could easily be
conceived as part of a Jewish conspiracy against the United States,
given the general atmosphere of the time. The candidate was a Russian-born Jew and a leading Socialist who had been instrumental in
drafting the Socialist party's antiwar St. Louis platform. His strongest
backing appeared to be the Yiddish-speaking Jews, particularly those

concentrated on the Lower East Side. Meyer London, the Socialist representative of these Jews in Congress, was one of a handful who had voted against war with Germany. Hillquit was also endorsed and strongly supported by the most prestigious and popular Yiddish-language newspaper in the United States, the socialist-oriented *Jewish Daily Forward*. From the perspective of the prowar groups and the anti-Semites, the campaign had all the hallmarks of Jewish conspiracy against the United States. This view was supported by the timing of the campaign. It was conducted after April 6, 1917, the date on which the United States formally became a belligerent. There was no tolerance for any expression of antiwar sentiment, no matter how noble or pure its motivation. The campaign also coincided with the triumph of the Bolshevik Revolution in October 1917. As the Bolshevik Revolution appeared to be led by Jews and was enthusiastically greeted by Jews in the United States, it became relatively easy for anti-Jewish groups to label all Jews as Bolsheviks intent on destroying America from within.

Hillquit's defeat and the growth of prowar sentiment among the Eastern European Jews did not bring this war-engendered anti-Semitism to an end. Jews were still considered to be dangerous aliens and Bolsheviks. At one point, leaflets and speeches in Yiddish became suspect merely because of the foreign language and not their content. There was at least one case in which Jews were arrested for distributing subversive literature on the grounds that it was written in Yiddish. In New York, police agents attending political meetings on the Lower East Side reported to their superiors the radical content of Yiddish speeches, despite the fact that few of the agents understood the language. If it was delivered in Yiddish, the presumption that it therefore was radical.[165]

The end of the war brought no respite to those feelings about Jews. If anything, hostility increased. The German menace had now been superceded by the Red menace. Against the backdrop of the Bolshevik Revolution abroad and the eruption of labor strife involving large numbers of foreign-born workers, Jews became linked in the public mind with radicals. The first major labor strike after the war was launched by the garment unions, which were dominated by Jewish Socialists. Then there were the deportation proceedings against Emma Goldman and Alexander Berkman, the Russian-born Jewish anarchists. Jews thus appeared to be prominent among the supporters and leaders of the Socialist party and, what was even worse from the standpoint of the American public, of the largely foreign-born Communist parties in the United States as well. Where once Jews had been dangerous and disloyal for their apparent aid to imperialist Germany, now they were an unpatriotic menace because of their radicalism.[166]

Subversion was not the only charge leveled against the Jews in the generally bigoted atmosphere of the 1920s.[167] They were also accused of being a financial menace to America. Jewish bankers, it was claimed, were out to control the American economy. Jews were both bomb-throwing, bearded Bolsheviks and money-grasping Shylock bankers. These themes were picked up and broadcast throughout the United States. The single most important propagator of the notion of the Jews as a universal menace was Henry Ford. Through his widely distributed newspaper, the *Dearborn Independent* (circulation 600,000), Ford continually attacked the menace of the international Jewish conspiracy from 1920 to 1927. Ford's direct and vulgar attacks were buttressed by other leading Americans, who, however, tended to be somewhat more circumspect in their attacks on Jews in particular and non-Nordic foreigners in general. Racist books, articles, and editorials in the guise of scientific objectivity "educated" the American public about the biological inferiority of the Eastern and Southern Europeans, as well as the Asians and Africans, and about the threat these people were to the racial foundation of the American nation. In 1921, for example, Vice-President Elect Calvin Coolidge wrote in the periodical *Good Housekeeping* that "biological laws show us that Nordics deteriorated when mixed with other races." [168] Similar views seeped through the pages of the major novels of the 1920s. [169]

A survey of racial attitudes conducted in 1926 testifies to how well the American public was educated on the subject of race. In this study 1725 native-born Americans, overwhelmingly from Northern European origins, were asked to give their reactions to seven different forms of social contact—including marriage, membership in same social club, and employment in respondent's occupation—with members of 40 different racial groups. When ranked in descending order of preference for the seven types of contact, the rankings revealed a social hierarchy with Northern and Western Europeans at the top, the Eastern and Southern Europeans somewhere in the middle, and the Africans and Asians at the bottom. German and Russian Jews were generally found between the twenty-fifth and twenty-seventh rankings, with those from Germany accorded a higher ranking. It is also interesting to note that non-Jewish Germans were generally ranked ninth and Russian non-Jews, seventeenth. Both German and Russian Jews were ranked lower than Italians, Poles, Roumanians and, Armenians. [170]

This racist hierarchy was not only held by the American public and opinion leaders but also by those who influenced and controlled immigration policy. The immigration laws that Congress drafted after World War I reflected this racist thinking in that preference was given to prospective immigrants from Northern and Western Europe (non-Nordics) over those from Eastern and Southern Europe (non-Nordics). The Jews were also singled out for special consideration by those who affected immigration policy. Shortly after the war, in the wake of renewed waves of Jewish immigration, the House of Representatives' Committee on Immigration specifically used anti-Semitic contentions as a major factor in its attempt to permanently bring to an end the era of mass immigration of any people to the United States. In the early 1920s, the committee cited and endorsed the views of anti-Semitic American consuls, the officials abroad who were responsible for approving the prospective immigrant's request for authorization to enter America. According to these consuls and the Committee on Immigration, "America faced an inundation of 'abnormally twisted' and 'unassimilable' Jews—'filthy, un-American, and often dangerous in their habits.'"[171] In 1924 Congress passed and President Coolidge signed a restrictive immigration law incorporating the racist views of some of the leading thinkers on the subject, which closed the gates of America to any future mass immigration of Jews or non-Jews.[172]

These were not the only doors to close or partially close to Jews during the 1920s. The more prestigious colleges on the East Coast and the medical schools throughout the nation also felt it necessary to limit the numbers of Jews they admitted. Columbia University, for example, in a two-year period reduced the proportion of its Jewish students from 40 to 22 percent. Similar action was taken by New York University, Harvard University, Dartmouth College, Rutgers University, and others. The barriers of the medical schools were more formidable than those of the undergraduate colleges. The medical schools, whose enrollments had diminished from more than 28,000 in 1904 to less than 20,000 in 1927, did not wish to have a large proportion of Jews among their student bodies. A comparison between the successful and nonsuccessful applicants from among Jewish and non-Jewish CCNY graduates in the latter 1920s reveals that among the Jewish graduates the proportion of those who applied and were successful in gaining admission to medical school dropped from 50 to 20 percent during this period. The proportion of successful Christian applicants among these CCNY graduates varied between 70 and 80 percent. Consequently thousands of aspiring Jewish medical students reluctantly turned to careers in dentistry and pharmacy in the face of the anti-Semitism that put the medical schools beyond their reach.[173]

Employers of white-collar labor should also be added to the list of those who were interested in barring Jews during the 1920s. In the postwar era native-born Jews and upwardly mobile foreign-born Jews sought positions outside the scope of the traditional Jewish areas of the economy (e.g., the garment industry), as they acquired high school and college educations. They wanted to become white-collar workers—clerks, insurance agents, stenographers. Employers of white-collar labor who had been reluctant to hire Jews prior to World War I were even more reluctant afterwards: "By the end of the 1920s one informed estimate indicated that Jews were excluded from 90 percent of the jobs available in New York City in general office work."[174]

Jews also experienced difficulties in the area of housing. Although they moved from the old ghettoes during the 1920s, they found that they were not welcome in previously non-Jewish neighborhoods. Even in New York City, Jews were confronted with restrictive devices and Christian hostility in their quest for new homes and apartments. In sections of Manhattan and Queens, for example, Jews had to battle for the privilege of living next door to non-Jews.[175] A popular history of the 1920s, *Only Yesterday*, by Frederick Lewis Allen aptly summarized this situation: "The Jews fell under the suspicion of a majority bent upon an undiluted Americanism. . . . The Ford attack, absurd as it was, was merely a manifestation of a widespread anti-Semitism. Prejudice became as pervasive as the air . . . and all over the country Jews felt that a barrier had fallen between them and the Gentiles."[176]

There appears to have been some abatement in the level of anti-Semitism in the latter 1920s and early 1930s. But then two developments helped to revive anti-Semitism after this period. One was the Depression; the other was the rise of international fascism. In the climate generated by the impact of the economic crisis and the example of the fascist powers, as well as the fear of war with them, anti-Semitism again became pronounced. Some 200 or more rightist movements sprang up, most of which were decidedly anti-Semitic. Thousands joined organizations such as the Silver Shirts, the Black Legion, Father Couglin's National Union for Social Justice and his Christian Front, as well as many other anti-Semitic groups. Hundreds of thousands of Americans were continually exposed to anti-Semitic arguments, contentions, and "facts" through such media as Father Couglin's national broadcasts and the Reverend Gerald B. Winrod's periodical, *Justice*. As the threat of war with the fascist powers became more of a reality, respectable personages such as members of Congress and the popular hero, Charles A. Lindbergh, singled out Jews as one of the major groups pushing the United States into an unnecessary war. The outbreak of World War II and the end of the Depression that followed in its wake did not bring a decline in anti-Semitism. If anything, the war exacerbated racial and religious frictions, and anti-Jewish feelings became more intense and widespread.[177]

Public opinion polls of the latter 1930s and early 1940s indicate that anti-Semitic attitudes had become quite extensive during this period. In 1938, when asked by the pollsters "Do you think the Jews have too much power in the United States?", approximately 41 percent of the American public replied in the affirmative. In 1942 this figure increased to 51 percent and rose to 58 percent in 1945. In 1939 roughly two-thirds of those polled thought that Jews had objectionable qualities and half believed that Jewish business people were less honest than non-Jewish ones. In 1937 more than half of the American population indicated that they would not vote for "a Jew for President [even if he] . . . was well qualified for the position."[178] Charles Herbert Stember, a social psychologist familiar with the various polls and surveys, concluded that ". . . over half of the population during the 1930's and 1940's seems to have thought of Jews as greedy . . . perhaps one-third . . . considered them 'pushy,' something like one-quarter subscribed to some notion of clannishness among Jews, and another quarter to ideas of Jewish grossness." [179]

As in the 1920s, anti-Semitism in the latter 1930s was not limited to attitudes and feelings. It also found expression in the economic arena, particularly when competition for jobs was most fierce. According to social historian John Higham, "economic discrimination peaked during the Great Depression. Colleges rarely hired Jewish faculty; private schools virtually never. . . . In New York it was generally understood that a Jew stood no chance of getting a white collar job if a non-Jewish applicant was available." [180]

Political Responses to Anti-Semitism

The growth of anti-Semitism did not directly or indirectly buttress Jewish support only for the Left. It did not produce a uniform political response from American Jewry. Some turned to the Democratic party for assistance. Many turned toward Jewish nationalism or Zionism as a more direct and Jewish way of dealing with this ethnic and religious hatred. Still others turned to or reaffirmed their allegiance to the Left.

It was not only through the reactions of individuals that anti-Semitism aided the cause of the Left among Jews. There were various ways in which anti-Semitism prove to be a "negative" ally of the Jewish radicals. First, it slowed or impeded the economic and geographic mobility that undermined the foundations of the Jewish community's support of the Left. Racist-inspired retrictions either prevented or retarded many Jews from leaving their old neighborhoods or manual and petty trades occupations. In this manner anti-Semitism shored up those aspects of the Jewish community which had played so important a role in developing a Jewish working-class consciousness in the pre–World War I years.

Anti-Semitism, in the form of the quota system, also contributed to the building of a similar type of radically-oriented Jewish community—the "Jewish" colleges of New York City, most notably CCNY. In the absence of restrictions against Jews in other colleges, the number and character of the Jewish students who attended CCNY in the 1930s might have been quite different. There would have been more dispersion to other schools. There would have been fewer Jews at CCNY who felt that they were there because their Jewishness prevented them from going elsewhere. In the absence of rigid quotas, CCNY in the 1930s would not have been so filled with Jewish students who shared not only a sense of common grievance but also other characteristics, including a socialist background.

Anti-Semitism had a pro-Leftist impact upon those who managed to break through the barriers and *objectively* improve their position. However, the educational and economic goals that they managed to attain after struggling with anti-Semitism were often lesser ones than originally expected or less rewarding than those attained by non-Jews with similar or lower capabilities. Thus those whose grades and test scores should have gained them admission to medical school had to avail themselves of dental and pharmacy colleges as less than satisfactory consolation prizes. Even at CCNY, Jews who managed to gain academic posts there when no other college would hire them soon found that their religious background significantly interfered with their chances of promotion.[181]

The condition of the Jews, particularly during the mid- and latter-1930s, conformed to that which social analysts such as Alexis de Tocqueville and Karl Marx believed to be highly conducive to radical and revolutionary activity. The discrepancy between what is and what ought to be has proved to be a powerful political force in a variety of historical settings, including the French Revolution and the United States civil rights movement. Its potency for radical political action is heightened within a group that believes itself to be relatively deprived and that is confronted by circumstances that make this feling less tolerable. One such circumstance occurs when a group conforms to society's rules of the game for getting ahead and then finds that society violates its own rules and prevents it from attaining its just rewards. Another circumstance occurs when a group whose objective social and economic position has been on the rise is confronted by a new situation in which such improvement is either slowed, impeded, or reversed for seemingly arbitrary and capricious reasons.[182]

In the mid- to latter-1930s the Jews, particularly the younger, more ambitious, more educated, and more acculturated, could be generally characterizd as a relatively deprived group confronted by both of the aforementioned aggravating circumstances. This group was no longer as likely as were their prewar predecessors to contrast their position in America with their less fortunate counterparts in Europe. The more Americanized the Jews became, the more likely they were to use American standards, ideals, and reference groups to assess their own position. As anti-Semitism became more pronounced within the context of the Depression these Jews found cause to feel "aggressively" relatively deprived, no matter how "better off" they were economically or socially than Jews in Europe or Germany. Once again, as in nineteenth-century czarist Russia, young, ambitious and educated Jews found themselves constrained by a double yoke—anti-Semitism and restricted economic opportunity—that blocked or impeded their mobility and denied them their seemingly just deserts because of an accident of birth. Like those in czarist Russia, many Jews in such circumstance turned to the Left as a way of striking back. One stereotypical but not uncommon embodiment of the way in which Jews responded is the radical or pro-Leftist Jewish dentist who turned to the Left after being denied entrance into medical school because of his religion.[183]

Non-Jewish Contextual Factors

Non-Jewish contextual factors also have to be taken into account, as noted earlier, when considering the reasons for anti-Semitism moving the Jews in a leftward political direction. In modern European history, with some exceptions, anti-Semitism has been associated with the political right and Christianity. The classic example of this configuration of forces was nineteenth- and early twentieth-century czarist Russia. Conversely, the Left has generally been the political force most sympathetic to the plight of the Jews and the political organization most receptive to Jewish participation. Given this set of friends and foes, it seemed natural for Jews, when confronted by anti-Semitism, to turn to the Left.

In the mid-1930s and into the 1940s in the United States, this traditional line-up generally obtained. The Right, particularly the Christian Right associated with such clergy as Father Coughlin and Reverend Gerald Winrod, was anti-Semitic; the Left was largely either not anti-Semitic or else actively opposed to the Right. Christian America as embodied by Charles A. Lindbergh, the *Saturday Evening Post,* the Hearst newspapers, and the State Department, seemed blithely unconcerned about the fate of the Jews abroad and, by implication, those in the United States. Conversely, liberals and the Left opposed the enemies of the Jews—Hitler and the fascists—and strove to open America's gates for Jewish refugees. Given these conditions, it appeared only natural that Jews should move or be predisposed to the Left.[184]

Another factor that must be considered when dealing with the political direction of the American Jews' response to anti-Semitism is the character of the political organization or force that directly works at wooing their support during an anti-Semitic period. In Eastern Europe during the latter nineteenth and early twentieth centuries, the two most active political contenders for the allegiance of the Jews were the Left (principally the Bund) and the Zionists (including their left wing, the Labor Zionists). The situation was both similar and different in the United States. In the 1920s, it was the Zionists who made the most concerted effort to capture Jewish political support. Their efforts were so successful that they were able to influence, as well as seize, the political initiative away from the Socialist Jewish labor movement. The Communists, the other major (and later more important) party of the Left, appeared relatively indifferent to Jewish problems and actually hostile to the Jewish community in Palestine.[185] In this context, it was more natural for Jews to move toward Zionism in reaction to anti-Semitism.

This situation did not change appreciably until 1936. Until then the Zionists were the most active political group appealing to Jews on Jewish issues. Franklin D. Roosevelt and the New Deal made great headway among Jews in this period, but not because of their direct appeal to Jews qua Jews. The New Deal, as we shall see, garnered the support of Jews because of its general liberalism and reformist economic policies, as well as its wooing of Jewish labor leaders and their organiztions. After 1936 (as we shall see in detail below), the Communist policy toward Jews did change. From this date until 1948 the Communist party, now the largest single organization on the Left, made a concerted effort to reach Jews, using Jewish problems and issues (particularly anti-Semitism). The Communists did their best to place themselves in the vanguard of the struggle to combat anti-Semitism. Their position was also strengthened by Communist Russia's public concern for Jews and its opposition to Hitler, except for the 10 months between August 1939 and June 1940 when the Nazi-Soviet pact was in force. This post-1936 effort of the American Communist party did obtain results among Jews. The Communists, by virtue of their vigorous reaction to anti-Semitism and their expressed concern about other Jewish problems, did succeed in causing many Jews to adopt a Left or a more pro-Left position.[186] This *relative* Communist success among Jews was not only a function of the ardor with which the Communist party and the Soviet Union wooed this group, it was also a function of their perceived power, vis-à-vis other groups, to effectively cope with domestic and foreign threats to Jews. From the latter 1930s through the early 1940s, the Communist party did appear to grow in number and influence. More important, the party basked in the reflected light of the Soviet Union, which, throughout most of this period, was the most important declared foe of the Nazis.

THE SYMPATHETIC WHITE COLLARS

The rise of anti-Semitism was not the only interwar development to counter the Jewish drift from the Left. A special type of occupational upward mobility was another. Although the movement of Eastern European Jews and their children from the working class to the middle class eroded the traditional occupational base of the Jewish Left, not all who quit the working class moved into jobs in which a Left allegiance was anathema. Many Jews, particularly during the Depression, found themselves in middle-class positions that facilitated or encouraged the maintenance of a Left orientation. Those white-collar and professional positions that were most supportive of such a political orientation included teacher, social worker, sales clerk, librarian, writer, and professor. Although these middle-class positions did not lend themselves as strongly as the working-class ones to the development of a vibrant institutional Left subculture, they did provide an occupational buttress to the association between the Jews and the Left after World War I. The movement of many Jews into these occupations was one of the few post–World War I developments that allowed the Left to reach the young, the native-born, the acculturated, and mobile Jew.

The leftism and the support for leftism associated with these white-collar jobs was largely a function of the dynamic interplay between the political character of the Jewish incumbents and the nature of the positions that they chose to enter. The character of the work involved in these jobs and the material and social rewards given to the incumbents of these positions have, at various periods of history, predisposed those who held them to be more receptive or less hostile to the appeal of the Left than persons in other middle-clas occupations. This predisposition became more pronounced during a time of socioeconomic crisis, such as the Depression, when the capitalist system appeared to be incapable of meeting basic socioeconomic needs and not able or willing to provide appropriate social and material rewards for its social workers, teachers, professors, writers, and librarians. This predisposition became even more pronounced when the incumbents of such positions were Jews who brought with them their leftist political baggage.

There are various factors intrinsic to and associated with many of the middle-class positions that the Jews entered in the interwar period which account, in part, for their leftist proclivities—aside from the politics brought to them by their incumbents. One of the most important is the various ways in which they resemble working-class occupations—either in pay, prestige, or condition of employment. Thus the movement from semiskilled or skilled blue-collar job to sales clerk, teacher, or social worker need not entail a significant shift in political values from those held by the working class.

Such middle-class white-collar occupations as teacher, social worker, and librarian, in being similar to working-class jobs, have political consequences. They are salaried and thus dependent positions, which cast their occupants into the role of employee in an employee-employer relationship. Also, as service-oriented positions, they do not necessarily provide opportunity or a direct interest for their holders to economically benefit from the exploitation of others connected with their work. (In practice an under certain circumstances, social workers and teachers have used their positions and relationship with the poor to improve their own status. But the point here is that, compared to occupants of middle class positions in the private profit sector, such tendencies are not as pronounced.) The incumbents of these middle-class positions do not have to suppress or control workers in order to obtain economic rewards or to improve their own economic position. In short, not only are there similarities between these white-collar jobs and working-class occupations, but probably as important, the former also have no direct economic conflict of interest with the working class. Objectively there is little that is intrinsic to the nature of the dependent, service-oriented middle-class position that would cause its incumbent to adopt a political stance fundamentally different from that of a person in the manual labor force.

The proclivity toward the Left is also reinforced by the character of the clientele that this middle class serves and the nature of the services that it provides. In the large cities in which most Jews lived and worked in the interwar period, those Jews who taught school or did social work generally serviced individuals from the working class or the poor. The contact between these professionals and their clients was not based on pecuniary motives but, rather, on an ideal that emphasized noneconomic motives. The mandate of these professionals was to help those whom they serviced without any expectation of direct economic benefit from them. Given this clientele and informing service ethic, these dependent and service-oriented middle-class professionals could not help but develop a sympathetic awareness for the plight of the poor and the working class to whom they gave professional assistance. Such sympathetic awareness feeds into a Left or pro-Left political position that favorably regards action or policies to ameliorate such conditions.

There is also another type of pro-Left dynamic working in the case of the so-called intellectual occupations that the Jews entered (such as writer, librarian, and professor). It has been argued that intellectual occupations predispose their incumbents toward the Left because of the inherent conflict that obtains between those who are involved ideas, ideals, and creativity and those who hold economic and social power and maintain the status quo. According to a leading political sociologist, Seymour Martin Lipset: "Intellectuals are . . . more likely than persons in other occupations to be partisans of the ideal, and thus to criticize reality from the standpoint of the ideal. The need to express the inner logic of their discipline or art form also presses intellectuals to oppose the established leadership that prefers continuity to change." [187] This association between intellectuals and the Left was also a function of another aspect of the intellectual's role and status. This is the aspect that flows from the perceived discrepancy between their professional status and intellectual acumen on the one hand and their social prestige and material rewards on the other. As Lipset expressed it:

. . . a major source of American intellectuals' political leftism derives from their seemingly almost universal feeling that they are an underprivileged group, low on the ladder of social recognition (prestige), income and power, as compared with businessmen and professionals. . . . This low self-image encourages professors and, I would suggest, other intellectuals as well to pursue the same political path as other "deprived" groups the world over—to support those political parties that attack the existing distribution of privilege. [188]

In addition to understanding the specific occupation-related factors, it is necessary to keep the larger socioeconomic context in mind. In the 1930s large numbers of children of Jewish immigrants were pouring forth from high schools, colleges, and professional schools, seeking white-collar and professional jobs. The Depression decade was a difficult time for most newcomers trying to land white-collar jobs or establish themselves as a professional. The number of high school, college and professional school graduates increased appreciably during the 1930s, while the number of professional and white-collar positions remained fairly static. In 1930 there were about 667,000 high school graduates. By 1936 the figure was a little over 1,015,000; by 1940 it had reached almost 1¼ million. In 1930 the graduates of the undergraduate colleges, graduate schools, and professional schools totalled almost 140,000. Six years later the total was approximately 165,000, and by 1940 it reached over 216,000. Thus, in the 10-year period from 1930 to 1940, there had been a 54 percent increase in the total number of graduates from institutions of higher education. By contrast, the increase in the number of white-collar positions held by men in the same 10-year span was 870,000, a growth of approximately 9 percent. This was the smallest increase in absolute numbers as well as in percentage that had occurred in any previous decade in the century.

The situation was comparable within those specific fields that college-educated Jews strove to enter. Between 1930 and 1940, the number of physicians increased by about 12,000, while the number of dentists decreased by 1100. There was also an absolute decrease in the figure for pharmacists in the same span, from 84,000 to 83,000. The largest professional field for the upwardly mobile working-class Jews was elementary and secondary school teaching. Nationally, from 1930 to 1940, there had been some expansion in this area—with the total increasing from 854,000 to 875,000. This was not a very substantial increase and was the smallest, both in absolute and percentage terms, in the twentieth century. There were years during this period when the total numbers decreased, such as between 1932 and 1934, when the figure declined from 871,000 to 847,000.[189]

Success in attaining a professional or white-collar position during the Depression did not ensure the incumbent a comfortable financial existence. From 1930 to 1940 the average annual earnings of college teachers and independent professionals, such as lawyers, physicians and dentists, declined—while that for public school teachers, low to begin with, remained fairly static.[190] The financial situation of Jews in these occupations was worse than that for their Christian colleagues—Jewish professionals tended to earn less.[191] This was due not only to discrimination but also to "the fact that few of the Jewish professionals had gone to good schools, many were foreign-born, and few inherited the established practices of parents and relatives."[192] When Jews entered the professions and the white-collar positions it was at a time of economic contraction, and they tended to be disporportionately concentrated at the bottom of their occupations in terms of income, prestige, and security.

This context exacerbated those leftist proclivities inherent in or associated with the dependent, service-oriented white-collar jobs and the intellectual positions that upwardly mobile Jews tended to enter. The addition of Jews from working-class, union, and radical backgrounds to this mix created an even more leftist tendency. While there were not many doctors, dentists, and lawyers in the Communist party, those who were, were generally Jews. A good portion of them were novices who had problems starting their careers, attaining status, and earning a reasonable income.[193] The most prominent organizational expression of this combustible mixture was the Left or Left-oriented white-collar trade unions that emerged in fields with significant numbers of Jews and which were generally located in areas of Jewish concentrations, particularly New York City. Most prominent among such unions were those representing elementary and secondary school teachers, college professors, social workers, and retail clerks.[194] These militant unions did not encompass the majority of the white-collar employees in their respective trades nor the majority of the Jewish workers within them. But their memberships did tend to be disproportionately Jewish.

One of the earliest of these white-collar unions was the New York City Teachers Union, organized in 1916. Its founders were largely Jews, leftists or liberals with ardent prolabor feelings. The union attracted 600 of a teaching staff of 20,000 in its early years, and it reached its height in the latter 1930s when membership rolls went to about 6500 (out of a total of approximately 35,000 New York City school teachers). In the 1930s, after this union became Local 5 of the American Federation of Teachers (AFT), it was the single largest local, with from 20 to 25 percent of the national membership. It should also be noted that the proportion of teachers in the AFT in New York City was considerably higher than the national average. In 1936 there were over 870,000 classroom teachers in the United States; only about 15,000 of them were in the AFT.[195]

There was little doubt about the Left politics of the Teachers Union, as Local 5 was also known. During the 1930s it supported the loyalist government of Spain and was actively involved in various struggles against anti-Semitism, fascism, and racism. It was also in the midst of the 1936 campaign to force CCNY to reinstate 13 professors including a Communist faculty member who was also the leading member of its own college union. In 1944 the Teachers Union was expelled from the AFT on charges of Communist domination. It subsequently became affiliated with the United Public Workers, which, in turn, was expelled from the CIO on the grounds of Communist domination in 1949. A year prior to that, the Teachers Union had been one of a very few unions in the country to endorse the presidential candidacy of Henry Wallace. Between 1951 and 1956, 38 teachers, largely members of the Teachers Union, were illegally dismissed from their positions by the New York City Board of Education on grounds of Communist influence. (Some 20 years later, they were all officially reinstated when the Feinberg Law, the statute that empowered the Board to fire them, was declared unconstitutional.) Many more quit rather than testify before various investigative bodies concerning their politics, past and present. Those discharged included many officers and former officials of the Teachers Union, including the president, a former president, the secretary, and the chairman of its Academic Freedom Committee. Virtually all of the officers and probably most of those fired for political reasons were Jews.[196]

The political coloration of the Teachers Union can be understood as the product of the interaction of various factors. First, the very size of the New York City teaching staff made it (and continues to make it) more amenable to unionization than staffs in smaller educational systems. As we have noted in earlier discussions, large numbers of employees concentrated in delimited work arenas have traditionally fostered a sense of class consciousness and a readiness to organize as collectivity on the basis of common grievances stemming from a common employer. Second, many Jews became New York City teachers. This was particularly true during the Depression when there were few other white-collar alternatives available. Generally these Jews were from working-class, trade union, and radical backgrounds. This meant that they were familiar with, if not disposed positively toward, unions and radical politics. Third, the difficulties involved in commencing a career as a teacher in New York City during the Depression were such as to predispose them toward Left politics and Left unions: ". . . they often found themselves unemployed, were forced to take poorer positions as substitutes and found discrimination in their efforts to get better jobs."[197] Typically they were to be found clustered at the bottom of the teaching hierarchy, low in status, security, and pay and with little hope for advancement. Fourth, by the time that large numbers of Jews became New York City teachers, there was a Left union organization ready and willing to recruit them. They did not have to build a union from the beginning. It was there, complete with a staff of Left and Left-oriented organizers and officers and a Left tradition. Given the overall socioeconomic context and the specific context of the New York City school system, as well as the nature of the human material that they had to organize, it is not difficult to see how the Teachers Union achieved the level of success that it did. One might ask why they were not even more successful.

Another example of a largely Jewish and Left professional union was the Association of Federation Workers (AFW)—which later evolved into Local 19 of the United Office and Professional Workers of America (UOPWA). The AFW and Local 19 were not the only social service unions, but they were the largest and the most prominent. The AFW was the first social workers union to be formed in this country (1932). It drew its membership largely from the Jewish social work employees of Jewish social service agencies. Initially limited to New York City, the AFW and unions like it spread to such other cities as Boston, Philadelphia, and Detroit. There, too, the membership was largely Jewish—again, drawn predominantly from Jewish social service agencies. The New York AFW, however, remained the largest and most important concentration of social worker unionists.

In 1937 the New York AFW helped to organize the UOPWA and then joined it and became Local 19 of that CIO union. This example was followed by some social work unions and groups in other cities. By 1939, there were some 3000 members of social service unions in the UOPWA, with 65 percent of them in New York City. Local 19 and other UOPWA social service locals, like their earlier counterparts, were primarily made up of Jewish social workers employed by Jewish social service agencies.

The AFW, Local 19 in particular, and other social work unions (and locals) were Left organizations in general. Radical social workers were largely responsible for their formation. A large proportion of their members were leftists or proleftists. A significant core of the leadership and the membership of both the AFW and Local 19 were in all probability Communists. They may even have contained a higher proportion of Communists than any other existing trade union in the United States. In 1950 the UOPWA and Local 19 were expelled from the CIO on the grounds of Communist domination. In 1951 the Jewish Philanthropies of New York withdrew its recognition of Local 19, using the same charges as the rationale for its action.

The reasons for the radical proclivity of these Jewish social worker unionists are similar to those of the teachers discussed earlier. First, New York City in the 1930s contained the largest number of privately employed professional social workers. This was the result of the numerous social service agencies sponsored or supported by the Federation of Jewish Philanthropies. Second, virtually all employees of such agencies were Jews. Many of them came from families and neighborhoods with a tradition of radical or union activity or from colleges where leftists had been relatively prominent. In large part, they were second-generation Americans and, in their families, first-generation white-collar workers. These social workers were therefore close to the Left tradition and ambience of the immigrant generation. Third, although as social workers they were professionals (but clearly low status vis-à-vis other professions), they were treated, especially during the Depression, more as industrial workers. They were forced to deal with salary reductions, layoffs, work overloads, and arbitrary treatment by employers. It was the interplay among all of these factors that prompted these social workers to adopt a Left political orientation.[198]

CCNY Professors

The Left and the pro-Left activities and organizations of the teaching staff at CCNY in the 1930s provides the most vivid example of the consequences of joining Jews from working-class and union and radical backgrounds with an intellectual profession in the context of a worker-boss relationship. During the Depression the CCNY faculty was reputed as having one of the largest and most influential Communist party collegiate units in the United States. It also contained, in all probability, the largest number of Jews of any college faculty in the country. In both these respects it was rivaled by its counterpart at Brooklyn College.[199]

The Jews of the academic staff of CCNY throughout much of this decade were very much akin to proletarians. (The appellation of "proletarian intellectual" would not be far from the mark.) They were overwhelmingly concentrated at the lowest ranks—teaching fellows, tutors, and instructors. Their full-time annual wages ranged from $600 to $2400 per year. Like industrial workers, they had no guarantee of employment, as they worked on the basis of yearly contracts. Regardless of the number of years that they taught, tenure was almost entirely beyond their expectations. Tenure was reserved only for full professors and the chance for their promotion to such an exalted status was quite remote.[200]

The authority and power relations of these lower echelon faculty, in relation to their employer, was also quite similar to that of unskilled factory hands. Through the middle 1930s all power was vested in the president of the college, who was reputed to be an autocrat. One tutor at CCNY at the time described the situation as follows:

When I joined the English Department the structure of the college was completely autocratic. The president appointed everybody, everybody on the teaching staff, everybody on the janitorial staff. Heads of departments were appointed by the president. There was no curriculum committee of the college. There was no curriculum committee in any department. There was no way in which an individual instructor or teacher could make his voice felt unless he could persuade the head of his department to persuade the president.[201]

The politicization and radicalization of the Jews among this intellectual proletariat was also heightened by the rise of fascism and the anti-Semitic Nazi menace. This international situation gave rise, in 1935, to the organization of the Anti-Fascist Association of the Staff of City College. Jews and Communists, particularly Jewish Communists, were instrumental in the formation of this organization. The Anti-Fascist Association became another means of strengthening the position of the Left on this largely Jewish campus. It was also a vehicle for promoting a Left orientation and viewpoint among the faculty concerned with the Fascist threat. All of these factors—labor background, status, working conditions, and the rise of fascism—against the backdrop of the Depression would have been enough to foster a heightened leftism among the Jewish faculty at CCNY. In 1934 they had given rise to the formation of an official Communist party unit at the college.

It was not until 1936, when a major incident occurred that directly played on all of these Left-inducing factors, that large numbers of the staff shifted to a pro-Left stance: In April 1936 Morris U. Schappes, a tutor in the English Department, and 12 other staff members of similar rank were arbitrarily fired. These 13 academics had virtually no warning of their dismissal prior to being officially notified. Schappes, a popular and highly regarded teacher, as well as a Communist, had taught at CCNY since 1928. He received his notice on the way to his nine o'clock class. Politics, rather than academic competence or economic necessity, appeared to be the reason for dismissal, as all of the 13 had been active in the Anti-Fascist Association, the Instructional Staff Association (an organization that Schappes and other Communists had helped to organize), and the College Teachers Union. The animosity of the college's president, Frederick B. Robinson, toward these groups was well known at that time. The dismissal notices in this environment stirred a major protest. It spilled over campus and academic boundaries to involve labor unions with whom Schappes and his associates had amicable ties. Mike Quill's Transport Workers Union and Joe Curran's National Maritime Union protested against President Robinson's action, as did the New York City Central Trades and Labor Council. Robinson soon reconsidered, and all 13 were informed that they would be retained by the college.

The arbitrary dismissals and the victory of the 13 staff members, as a result of the multifaceted campaign in their behalf, motivated many of their fellow faculty to join the organizations with which they were associated. The Instructional Staff Association, the Anti-Fascist Association, the College Teachers Union and the Communist party unit at CCNY all grew in size and influence as a result of these actions. More and more faculty began to realize that their only hope against arbitrary administrative action was through the organizations that leftists and proleftist faculty members had helped to forge.

The Left did not rest upon its laurels. Strengthened by the triumph over President Robinson and the increase in membership and influence within which it wielded direct and indirect leadership and authority, leftist faculty continued to concentrate on the two issues to which the lower echelon academic staff and the Jews among them would be most responsive—working conditions and fascism. By 1939 their campaign for a more democratic structure and increased job security had born fruit. Many of their goals were attained. Elected faculty committees now became instrumental in the appointment and promotion of their peers. The academic staff selected their own department chairmen and curriculum committees. Tenure was granted to anyone with three consecutive years of service, regardless of rank. The Left, particularly the Communists, gained even greater influence and prestige as a result of these reforms. By 1939 its authority on campus was probably at or near its peak. In that year, the Anti-Fascist Association, together with the National Student Union chapter on campus, demanded that the college administration sponsor a demon-

stration at the school during class time to protest the Naxi invasion of
Czechoslovakia. The administration concurred. This demand, much
less the administration's concurrence, would have been unheard of
only a few years earlier. Morris U. Schappes spoke at the rally as the
designated representative of the faculty.

The Left did not have much time to enjoy its popularity and power.
The Nazi-Soviet pact of August 1939, followed by the Communist
party's even-handed denunciation of the Fascist Axis and the Allies as
imperialist aggressors, proved to be a costly blow to the influence of
the Left on the campus. The Jewish faculty were quite concerned
about the fate of their fellow Jews at the hands of the Nazis. They
could not accept the line that the British government, locked in mortal combat with the fascists, was to be scorned as much as the German
regime. When a state legislative committee investigating subversion
descended on the campus in 1940 and when the New York City Board
of Higher Education suspended 35 faculty and fired 6 others for non-
cooperation with the committee or "for neglect of duty and conduct
unbecoming a member of the staff," the Left found few faculty who
would rally to its cause. It was not only the Left's stance on the war
and toward the allies that produced this reaction. The very success of
the Left in ameliorating the causes of work discontent had also reduced the militancy of the faculty. Ironically, the two major issues
that the Left had successfully ridden in its effort to gain the support
and allegiance of the disproportionately Jewish faculty now had
turned against them. The lower ranks of the faculty were no longer
that similar to industrial proletarians, and the Left was no longer in
the vanguard in the struggle to combat the Fascist menace that threatened Jews. The Jewish faculty at CCNY now had little cause to identify with the Left. Their occupational, religious, and ethnic interests
now pushed them away from the Left and toward the liberal mainstream.

Sympathetic White Collars in the New Left Era

The Jewish white-collar contribution to Jewish Left ties did not end
after the Depression and World War II. Although the widespread and
nearly continuous upward socioeconomic mobility of American Jewry
in the postwar decades was generally injurious to such a linkage from
the past, there were selected aspects to this mobility that were not
nearly so negative. In the post–World War II decades certain types of
white-collar Jews thrown upward in the wave of Jewish mobility inadvertently or consciously provided a certain amount of support for the
relationship between some Jews and what is called the New Left.
(Before proceeding further it should be stressed that the following
does not represent a detailed analysis of the varied and complex relationship between the New Left and American Jews. This will come in

Chapter 8. Here the emphasis is on one specific element—the occupational status of the parents of the members of the New Left.)

This association between sectors of the Jewish white-collar strata and the New Left can be ascertained by an examination of the socioeconomic composition of Jewish and non-Jewish New Leftists in the 1960s. In this period New Leftists—variously defined—were eagerly drawn from the colleges and universities and from the middle class. In the early to mid-1960s, they were most likely to be found at the more intellectually elite colleges and universities, from among the upper sectors of the middle class, and from among the upper class. The evidence of studies dealing with individual campus protesters, members and officers of the Students for a Democratic Society (SDS), and national samples of self-identified New Leftists throughout the 1960s suggest that Jews among these various types of New Leftists were disproportionately drawn from the elite schools and from upper middle-class families. Their fathers tended to be doctors, lawyers, and college professors.[202]

Those high white-collar professional positions were precisely those that Jews increasingly occupied in the post–World War II decades. (The relatively wealthy entrepreneur—that is, owner of or partner in a business as opposed to corporation executive—were another of these positions.) The war, for example, dates the entrance of Jews en masse into the faculties of American colleges and universities. The Jewish professors, however, were only a more dramatic indication of the general expansion of the numbers of Jewish professionals in the 1950s and 1960s. At the end of the 1950s, as noted earlier, Jews in this category constituted 20 percent of Jewish males in the labor force. By the late 1960s the comparable percentage was 30. In both periods this proportion was approximately two times greater than that for non-Jewish males in the labor force.

The relationship between parental professional status and New Left membership or identification on the part of the son or daughter among Jews is a complex one and is the product of the interaction of several variables. An interpretation of this association involves dealing with the political baggage that Jewish incumbents of professional status bring with them, the aspects of that position that have or can have pro-Left political consequences, and the political appeal of the New Left in the context of the times.

First, given the relatively greater historical involvement of Jews with the Left, as well as the history of negative treatment by those who dominated or controlled access to professions, the probability is higher for Jews than for non-Jews that they will bring with them to their professional positions a liberal-to-leftist political perspective or a greater sympathy and openness to Left and New Left ideas and ideals. Given that parental politics is the best single predictor of a young person's politics, it should then logically follow that the college-age children of such liberal-to-Left professionals should themselves tend to be liberal-to-Left on the political spectrum and New Leftists.

A variety of different studies and reports dealing with New Leftists and their professional parents tended to be more liberal and Left than their non-Jewish peers. There are also studies that indicate that Jewish professionals in general tend to be more to the Left in their politics than their non-Jewish peers.[203]

Fortunately, there is a major study of one kind of Jewish professional—professor—that provides information about the political baggage of such an individual, his current politics, and the political involvement of his college-age children during the era of the New Left. This study is based on a large national survey (60,028) of American professors in 1969. Its findings provide explicit support for the contention that political heritage is an important factor in explaining the propensity of the children of Jewish professionals to be part of the New Left. Initially, Jewish and non-Jewish faculty were asked, "What were your father's politics while you were growing up?" Almost 50 percent of the Jews responded Left or liberal. The comparable percentage reported by their Gentile peers was 15. They were next asked about their own politics. Here 75 percent of the Jewish, as opposed to 41 percent of the non-Jewish faculty, identified themselves as being Left or liberal. Finally, the combined impact of this political heritage upon their children could be observed via responses to questions about these youngsters' politics. "Among those faculty with children of college age," according to the authors of this study "a majority (56 percent) of the Jews report that their children have 'been active in civil rights, anti-Vietnam, or other demonstrations,' as contrasted with little more than one-fifth (22 percent) of the Gentile professors."[204]

Ideal and real attributes of the professional role can also lead its incumbent and his children to either be supportive of liberalism and socialism or at the very least not very hostile. Ideally, the professional's code of ethics enjoins him to put aside pecuniary and other selfish interests. Instead he is asked to emphasize humanist and altruistic values and do his best to further societal well-being. The values promoted by such a code are or can be interpreted as highly compatible with those of socialism and incompatible with those of capitalism. One would assume that a liberal-to-Left incumbent of a professional role would choose to do somewhat more than pay lip service to the more "positive" of his profession's ethics.[205]

In addition, the manner in which a professional typically earns his income can also facilitate a liberal or prolabor perspective. Usually the professional in his occupational role earns his income or the bulk of it through his own efforts. He does not have to enter into a conflict or potentially conflict situation with employees over the level of the wages and the share of the profits.

The ideology of the New Left throughout most of the 1960s was also another factor in attracting the sons and daughters of professionals to its banners.[206] In this period little stress was put on Marxist notions of class and class conflict. Instead the stress was placed upon humanism and the adherence to ethical values. The New Left's vanguard force, its agency for change, was not the proletariat. It was, instead, man-at-large exercising his potential for growth. As the leading organization of the New Left, the students for a Democratic Society expressed it in the Port Huron Statement of 1962: "We regard men as infinitely precious and possessed of unfulfilled capacities for reason, freedom, and love." The enemy as far as the New Left was concerned was not the capitalist class but the large impersonal bureaucracies that appeared to stifle human initiative and creativity.

These conceptions and values, resembling as they did the professionals' ideals, were those that the Jewish (and non-Jewish) children of the professionals and upper white-collar strata could find appealing. This new radical movement, unlike its predecessors, did not force them to define their parents' class and the class toward which they themselves were moving as a significant enemy. For Jews especially the identification of the bureaucracy as the principal object of hostility could not but touch a sympathetic nerve. After all, it was the private bureaucracies of the large corporations that had long barred Jews and closed to them one route to upward mobility. This indeed was one reason why the Jews produced so many professionals and entrepreneurs.[207]

The New Left's choice of civil rights and peace as issues around which to mobilize its forces was also something that the children of the bourgeoisie could find nonthreatening. These issues, like the antiwar movement that stirred Jewish (and non-Jewish) students in the 1930s, did not divide people along class lines. They were societal and human issues and divided people into the "good guys" and the "bad guys." From the position of the comfortable Jewish middle class located in the suburbs and gilded ghettoes, no immediate interests were threatened in attacking racists and war mongers. There was nothing personal about these enemies to prevent the sons and daughters of the Jewish professional strata from acting out their morality on the political stage. (Later in the latter 1960s and 1970s, when the New Left did become more radically Marxist and more concerned with issues of class and class conflict, it lost many of its middle-class members and supporters.)

Also, in the 1950s and 1960s the feebleness of the Old Left, a more Marxist Left, was another factor that facilitated the commitment of Jewish and non-Jewish students from professional and upper white-collar homes to the New Left. In the absence of a strong political force from the (Old) Left, students were, in a sense, free to roam over to the Left side of the political spectrum. It meant that they could define what was Left. It meant that they could define what were the concerns and objectives of the poor, the minorities, and the workers. These could be defined in ways that did not challenge their class interests or their parents'. And, the debilitated character of the Old Left also meant that there was little danger that New Left ideas and actions would actually lead to a real revolution.

Thus not all that the Jews experienced after World War I and World War II drove them from an association with the Left. The anti-Semitism of the interwar period and the sympathetic white-collar strata produced by a confluence of upward mobility and a special Jewish location in the labor force helped to preserve, or at least not to challenge, the traditional links between the Jews and the Left.

SUMMARY

History, when all the various factors are weighed, was not kind to the special relationship that the Jews and the Left had established prior to 1920. Almost as soon as this relationship appeared to be firmly in place it was beset by events and developments that caused it to atrophy. Restrictive immigration laws deprived the Left of Yiddish-speaking working-class recruits from Eastern Europe to replace the upwardly and outwardly mobile Jewish workers who constituted the backbone of the movement. Prosperity and geographical dispersion also undercut the structural sources of the support for the Jewish Left in the Jewish community. And the more American and more middle class the immigrants and their children became, the less committed they became to a Left political perspective.

The post–World War I years also witnessed the rise of organized challengers to the Left from within the Jewish community. Religious bodies, philanthropic federations, and Zionist groups became stronger after the war. These organizations, with their middle- and upper-middle-class leadership, strengthened the potency of nonleftist forces among the immigrant Jews and steadily chipped away at the structural and ideological base of the Jewish Left. These organizations and their bourgeois leaders had, by the 1930s, moved into a position whereby they, in essence, defined the Jewish community and the issues of import to it. As Jews who were leftists became "more" Jewish in the wake of crises (or evolution of their life cycle) it was this nonradical organized community that influenced the content and outlook of their revivified Jewish identity.

The creation of Israel and its existence as an independent nation in the context of a Cold War also weakened Jewish ties to the Left. American support for and Soviet and Third World opposition to this Jewish state since about 1950 made it extremely difficult for Left and pro-Left Jews with any favorable feelings toward Israel to retain their level of commitment to this kind of politics.

Not all developments, however, had a negative impact on the fortune of the Jewish Left. The rise of anti-Semitism after the war and in the 1930s, while injurious to the interests of the Jews as a whole, did prove helpful in strengthening the ties between this group and the

Left. The bitterness and the blocked mobility, especially in the context of the Depression, ensuing from the actions and attitudes of anti-Semites reinvigorated this waning association and enabled the Left to reach for a time the more assimilated second generation. Also, some of the white-collar positions that this generation managed to obtain, particularly during the Depression, did not force their Jewish incumbents from working-class and pro-Left backgrounds to break from the Left tradition and environment that had nurtured them. Jewish social workers and teachers, for example, found a Left perspective compatible with their professional positions. A similar development occurred in the post–World War II era. But in this case it primarily involved the children of professionals—higher status professionals—and the Left (here the New Left) was not a very Marxist movement.

Finally, the ongoing role of the institutional infrastructure and subculture developed by the Jewish Left should be stressed. Although weakened by all of the conservatizing developments and internecine political warfare, they continued to function for decades after World War I. This structure and culture continued to nourish and insulate Jewish leftists and their progeny, albeit in diminishing numbers, despite the forces pulling Jews from leftist politics.

8 The Left Parties' Treatment of Jews and Jewish Issues

INTRODUCTION

The major thesis underlying this chapter is that political parties, especially leftist ones, played an active role in shaping the relationship between Jews and socialism in the United States in the late nineteenth and twentieth centuries. The actions and policies taken by Left parties on Jewish issues and on matters concerning Jewish interests, whether advertent or inadvertent, affected the degree and level of support that they received from Jews. When the parties took positions viewed by Jews as being positive on matters Jewish, more Jews joined them or gave them psychological, moral, and electoral backing. Conversely, when these radical parties took what most Jews considered to be negative stances on Jewish interests, Jews withdrew their support.

There is, of course, no one-to-one relationship between the "Jewish" actions and policies pursued by leftist parties and the degree and extent of support they receive from Jews. Political behavior and social life are more complicated than that. Leftist parties, as we shall see, have not always been consistent in their treatment of Jewish issues. The seemingly contradictory actions within relatively short periods make it less likely that Jews would respond quickly to the latest stance of these parties. Coincident with this, Jews, like other political actors, are constrained by inertia and tradition in terms of how and when they respond to the actions of particular parties. Also, Jews, like members of other ethnic groups, do not enter the political arena solely as Jews. In their consideration of political action, they also take into account nonethnic and, particularly, class identities and interests. Finally, the stigmatization and repression of socialist parties in the United States throughout much of the period under consideration also confounded the relationship between Jews and these organizations. In this situation, regardless of what these parties did with respect to Jewish concerns, there would always be some, who, out of fear, would refuse to join or give them financial or electoral backing.

It is also important to insert a methodological caveat here. The nature of the data used precludes a systematic test of the hypothesis that leftist political parties' actions affected Jewish political attitudes and behavior. But the available evidence seems to indicate that this is historically the case.

Again, it is my contention that the policies and tactics of the parties of the Left significantly influenced whether Jews would be attracted to or repelled from them. The manner in which these parties dealt with Jewish issues, interests, and sensibilities affected the degree of support or opposition they got from Jewish members and from sectors of the Jewish community at large.

This chapter will also be concerned with the internal and external factors that shaped the socialist parties' attitudes toward and position on Jews and Jewish issues. These organizations were not always free to or desirous of courting Jews. Leftist parties that hoped to be a national force were aware of the costs associated with an identity as a Jewish or near-Jewish organization. The existence of anti-Semitism in the United States and in the Left parties themselves, in addition to the multiethnic composition of the American society, gave these socialist bodies cause and a justification for caution in their dealing with Jews and Jewish issues. Anti-Semitism aside, reliance upon or too close an identification with one (or even a few) ethnic group(s) in multiethnic America was a formula for political disaster for any party with national ambitions.

The disproportionate support of Jews placed the Left parties desirous of being both American and universalistic in a bind. Socialist principles were not supposed to be bent on behalf of particularistic ethnic considerations. Similarly, the desire to be accepted as American induced them to give short shrift to expressions of ethnicity and to place low or negative evaluations on those things that facilitated the labeling of these parties as foreign or Jewish. The dilemma that constantly confronted Left strategists, Jewish and non-Jewish, whether conscious of it or not, was how to reach out to non-Jewish ethnic groups and to second- and third-generation Americans, while not alienating their already committed adherents—the Jews. This dilemma was never satisfactorily dealt with by the Left parties or by leftist Jews.

REFORMISM

The Left parties' attitude toward and position on reform, while not directly related to Jewish concerns, was a factor of considerable importance in affecting the relationship between Jews and the Left in the United States. It is my hypothesis that socialist parties were more successful in attracting Jews to their standards when they put forth programs and platforms that were more reformist than radical or revolutionary. Conversely, when more militantly socialist positions were stressed, Jews in the United States were less likely to be leftist. In addition, when bourgeois parties stole or borrowed reformist planks from Socialists, the Jewish allegiance to the Left typically diminished, if not in ardor, than at least in numbers.

Unfortunately, this thesis is not readily amenable to testing. Adequate comparative and quantitative data necessary to prove or disprove it are lacking. One of the major problems along these lines is demonstrating that the reaction of Jews to reform or revolutionary socialism was significantly different from that of non-Jews. The imprecise data that is available in the form of autobiographical and biographical statements, election returns, and Left party membership statistics, as well as other fragmentary evidence, however, does appear to indicate that Jews were attracted to the Left during times when it stressed reform and repelled from it when it was more revolutionary.

There is also another difficulty that must be addressed prior to commencing a discussion and analysis of the Jews' relationship to the Left as mediated by reformism. This particular problem centers around the meaning of reformism within socialism.

The meaning and the import of reformism to the socialist movement has engaged the attention of theorists and activists from Marx to the present. (The detailed intracacies of the complex discussions and debates need not concern us here.)[1] Broadly (and perhaps crudely), reformism can be defined as a process of accommodation by socialists to the capitalist system. This involves a *disproportionate* emphasis on tactics and means that are not in themselves threatening to capitalism at the expense of socialist tactics and goals that do threaten the system. Thus reformism is implicit or explicit when socialists *disproportionately stress:* (a) electoral politics over working-class action; (b) organizational politics over the politics of mass mobilization; (c) education over action; (d) the necessity to build a multiclass constituency over a working-class one; and (e) immediate demands for political or economic reforms, such as shortening the work week or the election of judges, over the more long-ranging and general goals of the abolition of the private ownership of the means of production. Reformism also typically involves muting a concern with class conflict and revolution. Instead, class conciliation or a peaceful form of class struggle takes the place of class conflict; and evolution, as opposed to revolution, is heralded as the way socialism is to triumph.

It is important to note that advocacy of elements of reformism (as described above) by a socialist individual or organization does not mean, ipso facto, that the advocate is a reformer. Such a designation requires an investigation into what is stressed and what is not stressed and whether reform is treated as distinct from revolution. Karl Kautsky, a major theorist in the German socialist movement of the late nineteenth and early twentieth centuries, distinguished the reform socialist (or social democrat, as reformists were often labeled) from the revolutionary in the following manner: "Those who on principle reject political revolution as a means of social transformation, and who seek to restrict that transformation to the measures that can be obtained from the ruling class, are *social reformers*, however opposed their ideals may be to those of the existing order. . . . What distinguishes the social reformer from the revolutionary is not that he advocates reforms but that he deliberately refrains from going further."[2]

The Socialist Labor Party Reformers

The 1886 New York City mayoralty election provides the first vivid example of the attraction of reformism to Jewish socialists. In this election, the socialists in the Jewish Workers Verein (JWV), in conjunction with the Socialist Labor Party (SLP), backed the candidacy of Henry George, a nonsocialist reformer, and worked for him within the framework of the United Labor Party (ULP), a nonleftist party. These radicals were well aware that George and his campaign organization did not see themselves engaged in a mission to promote socialism. The ULP, for example, was primarily the creation of the nonsocialist element among organized labor in New York. And Samuel Gompers, then president of the American Federation of Labor (AFL), and by no means a socialist, was a leading force in George's campaign.[3]

Why then did the Jewish and non-Jewish socialists support him? Abraham Cahan, then a member of the JWV and the SLP and an active George campaigner, made clear the socialist view on the ULP's nominee: "Although George continued to talk about the single tax and the land question, most of his followers, including the socialists, disregarded this. He was supported in spite of his theories and because of his purity of purpose and honesty as contrasted with the corruption of the other parties. As far as the socialists were concerned, the important thing was that George was the candidate of the working class."[4]

As the campaign became more heated and as George's chances of actually winning rose, the socialists increasingly put aside their political objections to throw themselves into the electoral struggle. This campaigning did much to temper the purism of the Jewish socialists and anarchists who actively participated in it. Ambivalent feelings about the nonsocialist aspects of George and his program were repressed. The radicals also ventured beyond their principal constituency, the working class, to organize and appeal to storekeepers and peddlers. At the same time the Jewish leftists became less dogmatic. Instead of calling for revolution or preaching about the forthcoming fall of capitalism as in earlier years, they revealed an awareness of practical political dynamics and a long-term dimension. "Do not lose your courage, worker, if George is not elected mayor," declared the *New Yorker Yiddishe Volkszeitung*, the organ of the Jewish SLP members, prior to election day. "You are now just beginning to develop among your ranks an independent political force and it takes time to carry out a political revolution, as it takes time to change the entire social system and to abolish wage slavery."[5] The Jewish Leftists did not entirely abandon their socialist commitments while working for George's election. They reasoned (or perhaps rationalized), primarily among themselves, that his major notion—that of a single tax on land—could be interpreted as a variant of the position advocated by Karl Marx in the *Communist Manifesto*. Furthermore they argued that the campaign could be viewed as a means of breaking the hold of the two major capitalist parties on the working men of the city. These leftists held, whether George won or lost, that the working class of New York City would be impelled further down the road to socialism because of the issues raised.[6]

All of these socialist-based arguments may have had some degree of validity; but compared to the nonsocialist aspects and lessons of the campaign, particularly as viewed from the perspective of the not-so-astute Jewish immigrant masses, they must have seemed a bit distant and somewhat hazy. The nonsocialist facets were much more direct and obvious. The George campaign provided the vivid example of ardent socialists working arm in arm with nonsocialists on behalf of a reformer. Why should a politically unsophisticated person then believe that there was significant difference between reformism and socialism? Concurrently, the prospects for George's victory and the immediate practical benefits and reforms that would follow in its wake educated the Jewish community to the rewards that could be obtained through participation in electoral and reform politics. Once the Jewish working class, the natural constituency of the Jewish socialists, learned this lesson, how could their socialist leaders resist following them and avoid increasing involvement in the politics of reform, the politics of capitalism?

It was not only the politically unsophisticated immigrant Jews that the George campaign lured toward reformism; it also attracted the radicals who participated in it, as evidenced by the experience of Abraham Cahan, who was far from being a highly knowledgeable socialist. But at the time there were in America only a handful of Jews who were more versed in Marxist and anarchist doctrines and literature than he. Cahan, although aware of George's shortcomings as measured by a socialist yardstick, became convinced that the campaign had its virtues: "I realized that it [the campaign] had served to intensify the propaganda against capitalism and corruption and crooked politicians. It seemed to me that even a child could perceive that more had been accomplished with this kind of propaganda than with the anarchist propaganda of the deed."[7] Cahan remained a radical for the next several decades, but his radicalism became increasingly moderate as he became more appreciative of the reforms that could be obtained through participation in the electoral and capitalist systems.

Whatever doubts and questions that the George campaign may have raised in the minds of the Jewish radicals concerning their socialist faith, they were not sufficient at that point to cause them to abandon their European-imported faith. Soon after George's defeat in the 1886 election George and reform were abandoned as false gods. The socialists prepared themselves to reenter the electoral arena, but this time it would not be in the role of junior partner in a reform coalition. Now they would show the electorate their true socialist colors. The results, as measured by the number of votes, were not encouraging. Socialists running under their own banners and principles did very poorly among Jews. In 1888 the SLP received 182 votes in the Lower East Side's Eighth AD. Two years earlier in the same AD, George's vote had been 2671. In fact, it would not be until after 1910 that the vote for Socialist candidates in Jewish districts rivaled or surpassed that which George received in 1886.[8]

It was not long before many Jewish and German SLP members lost their taste for militant socialism. This shift in taste was accelerated by the rise of Daniel De Leon to the leadership of the SLP in the early 1890s. Guided by De Leon, the SLP adamantly opposed any tacit or overt alliance with reformist groups or parties. De Leon's vision of socialism did not include compromise: "We have to emphasize as strongly as possible the vital aim of the revolution—the overthrow of wage slavery. We also must emphasize just as strongly, that everything which is less than the abolition of wage slavery, all 'improvements,' are gains for capitalism."[9]

De Leon's vision of socialist purity eventually led him and his party into an attack on nonsocialist trade unions, particularly the American Federation of Labor (AFL). In his view the AFL not only did not advance the cause of socialism but it also actively blocked workers from moving in this direction. The AFL leadership, De Leon contended, through compromises with employers and a narrow focus on immediate economic improvements for its members, functioned as the labor supporters of the capitalist system. The concessions that nonrevolutionary unions obtained from employers were in De Leon's colorful language: "banana peelings under the feet of the proletariat."[10] The only type of union organization capable of overthrowing the capitalist system, De Leon believed, was one that was both industrial and revolutionary—an organization that made no concessions to capitalists.

After failing to capture the craft-based AFL, De Leon brought into being a rival labor federation, the Socialist Trade and Labor Alliance (STLA, or Alliance) in 1895. This was an heretical act for orthodox socialists, in that it violated the principle prohibiting dual unions. Dual unions, many socialists believed, weakened organized labor's strength by dividing it into competing camps. The STLA was to be a revolutionary union, the embodiment of De Leon's dream. It was not going to be a labor organization that concerned itself with diversionary issues such as shorter hours or better working conditions. It was instead going to be concerned only with the attainment of socialist revolution.[11]

Initially, the Jewish SLP members were not alienated by De Leon's militancy and attack on reformism. In 1894 Cahan publicly endorsed his leader's attack on reformist parties and unions. There was near unanimity, for at least a brief period, with De Leon's trade union policy. Jewish unions were, in fact, one of the important core elements in the STLA.[12]

This support for revolutionary socialism proved to be short-lived. The principle reason for this disaffection was the issue of dual unionism. When it became clear that De Leon's union policy meant breaking with the AFL plus abandoning the struggle to improve wages and working conditions through the medium of immediate economic demands, Jewish and other unionists lost their ardor for the STLA. By 1898 most of the Jewish and German unions had withdrawn from De Leon's federation and sought admission into the AFL.

This shift of Jewish socialists from revolutionary socialism and dual unionism to a reformist position had actually been presaged by the wording of the platform of the first Yiddish socialist daily in the United States, the *Abendblatt* (1894). The Jewish socialists in charge of the paper announced that although they were principled socialist opponents to the American capitalist system they were at the same time democrats and evolutionists. The term "evolutionist," according to the historian Melech Epstein, "marked a new phase in their political thinking. The Socialist Revolution was still the leitmotif of their propaganda, but it was becoming more like a prayer, dutifully repeated, but hardly affecting the daily affairs of those who pray."[13] And it was their daily affairs—especially those related to the needs of their unions and to their own integration into American society—that continually diluted their foreign-born revolutionary fervor.

The leading opponent of De Leon's revolutionary policies within the SLP was Morris Hillquit. He and his supporters, many of whom were also Russian-born Jews from New York, took strong exception to the establishment of a union organization that rivalled the AFL and argued that a dual union would weaken the entire labor movement through internecine warfare. They also contended that the STLA undermined the growing influence of socialists within the AFL, which, they argued, contained the bulk of American unionists and that therefore socialists should focus their energies there.[14] This position was also no doubt shaped by the assistance that fledgling Jewish unions either received or desired from the AFL.[15]

By the latter 1890s De Leon's vision of revolutionary socialism as principally embodied in the position of dual unionism and his highly autocratic personal style provoked multiple expulsions and departures from the SLP. Immigrant Jews with reformist tendencies were among the most prominent to take leave of the SLP, such as Abraham Cahan, Meyer London, Max Pine, Louis Miller, and Morris Hillquit.[16] These were the men who either were or would be the most prominent leaders of the Jewish labor movement. They were also men who Daniel De Leon described as "The moral, physical, and intellectual riffraff from Russia."[17]

The Socialist Party Reformers

The Socialist party, shortly after its formation in 1901, was for the next several decades the political embodiment of socialism in the United States. The script for the reformist-oriented Jewish socialists was virtually the same as it had been in the SLP. Indeed, many of the principal actors such as Hillquit, London, and Cahan were the same. The New York branch of the SP (along with the one in Milwaukee) was during most of this period a principal center for reformist or *constructive* socialism.[18] Radical sociologist Charles Leinenweber described the New York City Socialist Party as ". . . a reformist party— its platform, such as it existed, a shifting, uncertain collection of proposals for municipal ownership of utilities and transport, for better housing, and for cheap bread, milk, fuel and ice; its leadership, staunch believers in the electoral process and the parliamentary road to socialism."[19]

The New York SP grew and prospered in the years before World War I, when reformism became its dominant orientation. The SP gained more members, supporters, and voters from among immigrant Jews when it stressed practical reform than when it emphasized revolutionary socialist principles.[20] Political scientist Lawrence Fuchs, in his discussion of Jews and the Socialist Party, claimed that "The reform plank as its platform may have been its best vote getter. Socialists won more supporters by denouncing local corruption than by casting visions of the millenium . . . the Socialists talked as much of honest elections and new bath houses as they did of government ownership of railroads and international justice."[21]

These visions of the socialist millenium as factors attracting the immigrant Jews to socialism should not be totally disregarded. The loftiness of socialist ideals, even when espoused by conservative Socialists, helped to inform and shape a needed moral community for the immigrant Jews of New York's ghettoes. To newcomers in a strange and often hostile environment, whose own sense of community had been shattered by forces in the Old World and the uprooting that accompanied the mass migration, acceptance into the moral community fashioned by the Socialists was undoubtedly appealing. This was also a socialist community that contributed to their sense of worth and dignity, commodities that were not plentiful in the sweatshops and crowded tenements.[22] Moses Rischin, in an important history of the Eastern European Jews in New York City prior to World War I, summarized in idealistic forms the emotional appeal and impact of socialism upon these immigrant Jews: ". . . the appeal of socialism lay in its universalism, in the moral majesty of its social critique, in the messianism of a message that welcomed all men, regardless of race or creed, into the community of mankind. The impressiveness of its learning, the spirit of brotherhood that it communicated, the optimism and ethical appeal that promised 'an enlightened and blessed time,' were irresistible."[23]

It would, however, be a mistake to equate this idealistic socialism with reformism. It would also be a mistake to leave the impression, as Irving Howe does in his influential *World of Our Fathers*, that Jewish socialism was characterized largely by dreamers and moderates. There were militants and revolutionary Socialists among Jewish Socialist party members. New York Jewish Socialists (as noted in Chapter 2) were very prominent in the leadership and rank and file of the left wing Socialists who quit or were expelled from the party in 1919. There were Jews in the SP and in unions who very much endorsed the principle of class conflict in word as well as deed. In their bitter and hard fought strikes to build socialist unions and retain them, Jewish workers in and out of the SP demonstrated to their employers and to their union leaders as well that they were not always willing to be reasonable and accommodating. By their actions they also demonstrated that radical or revolutionary socialism was by no means an anathema to them (see Chapter 5).[24]

Many Jewish unionists and SP members were alternately reformers and radicals. Many were also uncertain about what it all meant. Relatively few Jewish workers in the first two decades of the 1900s seemed to know what socialism was all about, apart from the vague and often beautiful ideals espoused by socialist street corner orators. Writer Harry Roskolenko, in reminiscing about his socialist, garment union member, immigrant father, commented: "When we talked about Socialism at home, it was more through the use of symbols than from actual knowledge. Had my father read Marx? He'd heard of him. Had he known any Socialists in Russia? A few." Socialism for his father, Roskolenko observed, was the Yiddish socialism of "East Broadway [the location of the *Jewish Daily Forward* and the Workmen's Circle], his sick and death benefit society, his membership in the Union."[25]

The leadership of the New York SP was generally more consistently reformist than the rank and filers in the first several decades of the century. Hillquit, London, and Cahan had a national reputation as opponents of radical and revolutionary socialism. It is, however, interesting to observe that in election campaigns for public office neither Hillquit nor London were consistently reformers. In appealing for support to Jewish voters both of these moderates (and lawyers) at times gave their audiences reason to believe that they shared a belief in revolutionary socialism. In 1914, for example, London, whom Howe describes as a responsible and judicious socialist and member of Congress, exclaimed to a largely Jewish crowd: "We shall not rest until every power of capitalism has been destroyed and the workers emancipated from wage slavery."[26]

Reform socialists like Hillquit, the SP's leading theoretician, were in part responsible for the vagueness and confusion that the Jewish masses had about socialism. The message that Hillquit preached as a three-time SP candidate for Congress (from heavily Jewish districts in 1906, 1908, and 1920) was a very mixed one. On the one hand, Hillquit publicly subscribed to the belief that capitalism would fail and socialism would triumph. Class struggle, he contended, would play a role in this development. On the other hand, Hillquit argued, it would not be revolutionary action that would cause the demise of capitalism. Instead, the fall of this system would come about largely due to the natural evolution of capitalism. As it matured, capitalism would lay the groundwork for the victory of socialism.

In Hillquit's scenario, the working class was given a limited supporting role in the defeat of capitalism and the advancement of socialism. He did not urge them to mobilize as a militant force to engage in a revolutionary class struggle but enjoined them to educate themselves and focus their efforts on behalf of socialism in electing Socialists to public office. In the struggle for socialism, workers were also cautioned by Hillquit to break no existing laws and cooperate with understanding elements outside of the working class, such as intellectuals and members of the petty bourgeoisie. It was probably confusing to immigrant workers to hear about the class struggle and the need to abolish wage slavery from the lips of a successful corporation lawyer, a man who was very much a well-groomed and well-spoken American gentleman. In fact, in Hillquit's 1906 campaign for Congress, "the business integrity and stability of an attorney already worth $100,000 were emphasized." [27]

The reformists' control of key institutions also helped to cool the revolutionary ardor that periodically swept through the Jewish masses. Hillquit and his backers had a firm hold on the New York SP organization. Cahan was the autocratic ruler of the socialist *Jewish Daily Forward*. And their allies and reformist counterparts usually held important leadership positions in the garment unions and the Workmen's Circle.

It would be a mistake, however, to leave the impression that the world of Jewish socialism in the early decades of the twentieth century was divided between scheming reformers in positions of power and revolutionary masses continually foiled in their quest to overthrow the system. The world of Jewish socialism was more complex than that.

Reformist socialism did have an appeal to the Jewish masses. Jewish workers as would be true of any workers appeared to be very much appreciative of the immediate benefits that their Socialist party mentors and legislators helped to deliver. Few seemed willing to forego the improved health and safety measures on the job or the bath houses that socialist reformers either directly or indirectly helped to bring into being.

It is important to clarify here the issue of reforms and reformism within socialism. The advocacy of immediate improvements in the health, safety, and standard of living of working and poor people does not differentiate reformist from radical or revolutionary socialists. The difference between these two socialist wings is that the reformists typically concentrate on the attainment of reforms as virtual ends in themselves and only vaguely or abstractly make the connections for their constituents between these reforms and the achievement of a socialist society. The radical socialists, on the other hand, push for reforms both as a good in itself and as a means of educating their constituents to the fundamental limitations of capitalism. For these socialists the advocacy and attainment of reforms are ways to raise the socialist consciousness of workers and the poor and increase their realization of the more fundamental reforms that could be offered to them under socialism. Radical socialists keep the connections between immediate social and economic improvements and the ultimate triumph of socialism in the forefront of their appeals to their constituents.

The dominant orientation of the leaders of Jewish socialism was reformism. The nature of the election campaigns of the Socialist candidates in Jewish districts in New York indicates that these campaigners believed that votes could best be garnered through the advocation of reform socialism. A cursory examination of the issues stressed and the votes won during the election campaigns in Jewish districts after 1910 when the wave of socialism was advancing indicates how appealing moderate and practical socialism was to Jewish voters. In Jewish sections of New York City the number of votes Socialist candidates received rose as Socialist campaigners, in the words of one labor historian: "subordinated revolutionary ideology to promises of immediate social reform." [28] In the 1914 election that first sent the East Side's Meyer London to Congress, the *Jewish Daily Forward* (then considered a stalwart of socialism and the Socialist Party) never advanced one socialist argument on his behalf, even though it was his most powerful backer. [29]

The 1917 elections in New York City, spearheaded by Hillquit's mayoralty bid, probably represent the high-water mark of Jewish electoral support for socialism. But in these elections the issue of socialism was very much subordinated to other considerations by the Socialist candidates. Hillquit focused primarily on the issue of the war and the necessity of keeping the United States out of the conflict. Another principal feature of his election efforts was his attack on the high cost of living and on the rising food prices. His campaign was eventually referred to as the "Peace and Milk" campaign. [30] As for socialism, according to the prominent lawyer and leader of the German American Jewish community, Louis Marshall, "[that] has been entirely eliminated from the Hillquit propaganda." [31] In fact much of the advocacy for traditional SP causes, such as the municipal ownership of public utilities came from Tammany Hall, which hoped to undercut Hillquit's support through such measures.[32]

The target of the Socialist campaign efforts in the New York Jewish districts helps make it clear why moderation and practical reform was stressed. The Socialists were not only appealing to the working class but to other classes and strata as well. In 1910 Morris Hillquit publicly argued that "Our principal efforts must be directed towards the propaganda of Socialism among the workers. . . . But they should by no means be limited to that class alone . . . the ultimate aims of the movement far transcend the interests of any one class in society and its social ideal is so lofty that it may well attract large numbers of men and women from other classes . . . [the workers] are by no means the only class which has a direct economic motive for favoring a change of the existing order.[33] In Meyer London's campaign for Congress that year, a considerable effort was made to secure the votes of small businessmen and professionals.[34] One writer in the Socialist *New York Evening Call* commented that in this campaign the London forces had appealed to "everything except the class consciousness of . . . workers."[35] An appeal to the class consciousness of the workers, as well as a stress on nonreformist socialism, would obviously lessen the chances of gaining the votes of the nonworkers.

This type of campaigning was not peculiar to New York Jewish Socialists. Other Socialists running in non-Jewish districts also ran reformist campaigns. The nominal head of the Socialist party, Eugene V. Debs, realized that such electoral efforts, even when successful, did little to advance the cause of socialism. Commenting on the electoral victories in 1910 of Socialists in Schenectady and Wisconsin whose campaigns were very similar to those in New York City, Debs thought that "In each case . . . the candidates had won because they had deserted their principles. They had been elected by reform votes, not by Socialist votes." Later, writing in the same vein, Debs bitterly accused the Party of housing ". . . not a few members who regard vote getting as of supreme importance, no matter by what method the votes are secured and this leads them to hold out inducements and make representations which are not at all compatible with the stern and uncompromising spirit of a revolutionary party."[36] This reformism, Debs believed, was rooted in the fact that the Socialists who gained public office and the Socialists who led the party were drawn from non-working-class elements. They were ministers, lawyers, and editors and not the organization's blue-collar members. This assessment, with the exception of ministers, aptly fit the New York City Socialist electoral candidates and party leaders.[37]

The New York City Socialists who downplayed socialism and blurred the distinctions between reform and socialism while running for office did not do this only as an election-day expedient. These actions reflected the developed belief of such leaders as Cahan, Hillquit, London, and Waldman. These men, although from working-class backgrounds and usually with experience as blue-collar workers, represented the editors and lawyers whose influence in the party worried Debs. They and the local SP organization that they headed were major forces for moderation in the national party. Their socialism was essentially pragmatic, evolutionist, and reformist. It was this vision that inspired them on the election stump, in the halls of legislatures (for those who won elective office), and in the deliberations of the Socialist party. It was such men (particularly Hillquit), backed by their powerful New York organization, who spearheaded the attacks that forced the left-wing militants to leave the party in 1913 and again in 1919, when their beliefs and influence proved too challenging to that of the reformist right wing.[38]

The limitations of reformism in terms of benefits derived by the Socialist party can also be discerned in the area of unions. In New York, by the end of 1913, Socialist union leaders, with the assistance of the Socialist party (and the action of masses of needle trades workers) finally established, secured, and legitimated the Jewish garment unions. In a brief period several hundreds of thousands of primarily Jewish needle trades workers found their way to these labor organizations that held forth the promise of (relative) job security, higher wages, and better working conditions. Despite the efforts of the Socialists that had gone into making these unions a reality, the SP, aside from an increase in votes on election day, appeared to gain very little. As the numbers of union members in these Socialist-led and Socialist-inspired unions dramatically increased and approached about 400,000, the number of SP members in New York in no way grew by the same proportions. From 1908 to 1912, approximately the years of the organizing strikes in the garment trades, less than 1000 Jews entered the SP as new recruits.[39]

It is, of course, possible for a union member to be a socialist and have a highly developed sense of class consciousness without being a member of the Socialist party. Undoubtedly there were some of these in the garment unions. Undoubtedly there were also unionists who felt that their membership in a Socialist-inspired and officered labor organization was tantamount to being a Socialist. But, in the midst of a stable capitalist system, it becomes difficult to hold onto such an identity without a meaningful tie to a Socialist organization. An insightful Socialist writer sadly commented in 1913 on the state of socialism within the garment unions in the *Jewish Daily Forward*: "The outside world assumes that Jewish Unions are Socialist, but a closer look will show that it is far from the truth. The Union member listens to a Socialist speech, reads a Socialist article, is imbued with the Socialist spirit, but what is Socialism he doesn't know. And the first reform breeze carries him away from us. . . ."[40]

The Socialist-led organizations that were the core of the SP in New York—the unions, the *Jewish Daily Forward*, and the Workmen's

Circle—did not, however, choose to mobilize their members and supporters on behalf of revolutionary socialism. After 1919 the leaders of
these organizations, generally reformist to begin with, continued to
drift farther and farther to the right. The furthering of the immediate
interests of their organizations as ongoing entities in a larger capitalist
system (as we have seen) caused the leaderships to develop ever-
increasing ties with bourgeois elements in and outside of the Jewish
community.

The SP suffered as a result of this process. First, the Jewish worker
or intellectual who might have moved toward socialism was deprived
of political guidance and not provided a meaningful option to the political status quo. Second, the radically inclined Jewish worker (or intellectual or petty bourgeoisie), in moving toward socialism, now had
to surmount the obstacles presented by not only the capitalist system
but also the conservative socialists. In the 1920s and 1930s those who
desired to become socialists in New York had essentially two alternatives available to them. If they joined the Socialist party, which relatively few did, they had to "leapfrog" the central institutions of the
party. The other alternative that many more pursued was to throw in
their lot with the Communist party.

By the mid-1930s it was quite clear that the established New York
Jewish wing of the SP had become too conservative for both the national SP and the New York branch. The entrance of younger and
more militant elements into the national and New York Socialist parties, despite the opposition of the Old Guard—as the right-wing Jewish (and non-Jewish) Socialists were called—helped to turn both the
national and the New York Socialist parties toward a more militant direction. Unable to hold the drift toward militancy or to expel their
radical opponents as in 1913 and 1919, and at the same time attracted
by the policies and successes of the New Deal, moderates and conservatives drifted from the party and finally broke with collectively in
1936.

The Old Guard's departure virtually finished the SP as an effective
political organization. Although the numbers of defecting moderates
were significant, more important were the organizations that they took
with them. Prominent among these were the *Jewish Daily Forward,*
the needle trades unions, and the Workmen's Circle. Together these
had constituted the organizational and financial backbone of the SP
throughout the interwar years. Without these organizations and the
moderates, membership in the SP by 1938 had declined to a near all-
time low of 7000. By the end of the decade the party barely had sufficient funds to maintain a skeletal national office.[41]

Many of the members and organizations that formed the Old Guard
were Jewish in character. There were also non-Jews in its ranks. These
included those from Jasper McLevy's Connecticut organization, Pennsylvania Dutch from Reading, and Finns from the Finnish-language

federation. But the bulk of the Old Guard was made up of Jewish individuals and organizations, many of whom had been at the heart of the Jewish labor movement.

Outside of the SP these disaffected moderates moved to embrace FDR and the New Deal. Some took this step directly, via membership in the Democratic party. For others it was a slightly more indirect process. Those who still chose to identify themselves as Socialists organized the Social Democratic Federation (SDF) in 1937. Still others formed the American Labor Party (ALP) in New York State in 1936. Both the SDF and ALP, regardless of minor ideological differences, shared the same major political goal in their early years—the election or reelection of FDR and support for the New Deal.

These two organizations also had a largely Jewish membership. Each was also financially and organizationally dependent on the needle trade unions and on the *Jewish Daily Forward*. And, very important, each was only a temporary way station for Jews en route to the Democratic party.

The Communists and Reform

The Communist party was not dissimilar from the Socialist party in terms of the positions and policies that attracted Jews. Generally the CP acquired more Jewish members and supporters when it stressed moderation and reformism than where it encouraged socialist militancy. Reformism, however, was not always on the CP's agenda.

The United States CP had only limited success in gaining support from virtually any sector during its hard line Third Period (1927–1935). This policy was urged on the party by the Soviet leadership of the Communist International (Comintern). It was informed by the view of Soviet leadership that the latter 1920s were to be years that would usher in a period of recurrent capitalist crises. These crises, in turn, would present the working class under the aegis of the Communist parties (in their respective capitalist nations) with unparalleled opportunities to attain power. To prepare themselves for this eventuality, these various Communist parties were expected to divest themselves of reformist and moderate tendencies. There was to be no compromising with capitalism. The Third Period was going to be a bitter struggle of "class against class" led by a lean and militant Communist vanguard.

The United States Communist party, did not deviate from the new line. In the field of union activity, the party, in a reversal of traditional policy, withdrew its faithful from established unions to form their own (dual) revolutionary labor organizations. The Socialist party—the major competitor for the allegiance of the working class from the Communist party's point of view—was villified as the party of social fascists, and its meeting were broken up by Communist militants. Communists in America were going to lead the class struggle unencumbered by any ties that might force them to compromise their Marxist sectarianism.[42]

The radicalism of the Third Period did not strengthen the CP—using numbers here as the key indicator of strength. From 1925 to 1930, the party, never large to begin with, suffered a net loss of 8500 members, declining from 16,000 to 7500. The hard line of the Third Period had to be a significant factor in accounting for this decline (although the available data do not allow us to weigh its impact with any great precision).

The decline was halted in 1930. From this year until 1935, membership increased. In 1935, the last year of the Third Period, membership reached about 30,000. The difference in the 5-year periods before and after 1930 was not so much in party line, although this was becoming more flexible by 1935, but in national economic circumstances. After 1930 the impact of the Great Depression was felt through the land. It was the Depression that recruited Communists. It was the Depression that made these prospective Communists more sympathetic to the CP's hard line. Still, one wonders how many more would have come into the party after the turn of the decade had the American Communist leadership abandoned its Third Period position.[43]

The CP's abandonment of the militant sectarianism of the Third Period and the adoption of liberal and reformist positions after 1935 did indeed produce dramatic results. In the approximate 10-year period from 1935 to 1945 (with the exception of the period of the Stalin-Hitler pact, 1939–1941) the United States CP adhered to the policies of the Popular Front (or United or People's Front) first publicly enunciated at the Seventh Congress of the Communist International in 1935.[44] These new positions plus the Depression and (then) the war against fascism were largely responsible for a dramatic increase in membership and influence of the American Communist party. By the end of the 1930s, the party, together with its youth wing, numbered about 100,000. Roughly a quarter million persons passed through the party in the same period. In addition there were almost a half million individuals in organizations close to or aligned with the CP. Communists were also key factors in organizing unions, unemployed councils, youth and Negro groups, and other organizations.[45] These years—1935–1939 and 1941–1945—were also the years during which the CP achieved its greatest success among Jews. (Reformism, however, was not the only party factor responsible for its success among Jews in particular or others in general.)

Communists, in following the line of the Popular Front, embarked on a quest for "a united front of all working class organizations against fascism, and a popular front of the working class with all other anti-fascist forces."[46] To achieve this goal Communists, reached out to non-Communists and to classes outside of the working class, put aside the strident tones and radical positions of the Third Period and, instead, lowered their voices and advocated reformist policies. The struggle for a socialist America was subordinated to the fight against fascism abroad and reaction at home.[47] Earl Browder, the CP's general secretary, enunciated this new line in December 1936:

> Although the toiling majority of the population are not ready to struggle for socialism, they *are* ready to defend their democratic rights and living standards against the attacks of reaction and fascism. . . . We can organize and rouse them—provided we do not demand that they agree with our socialist program, but unite with them on the basis of their program which we make also our own. . . . Everything that organizes and activizes the working class and its allies is progress toward socialism. . . . This is the fundamental conception that underlies the revolutionists' understanding of the fight for the People's Front.[48]

In 1942, when the struggle against fascism was on in earnest, Browder went even further in deemphasizing the importance of socialism: "The CP has completely subordinated its own ideas as to the best possible economic system for our country . . . to the necessity of uniting the entire nation, including the biggest capitalist. . . . *We will not raise any socialist* proposals for the United States, in any form that can disturb this national unity."[49] Several years later Browder publicly took the goal of a socialist America off of the CP's agenda when he exclaimed: "We frankly declare that we are ready to cooperate in making capitalism work effectively in the postwar period."[50]

During the period of the Popular Front (again with the exception of the Stalin-Hitler Pact years), the CP was in effect a left-wing extension of the Democratic party. FDR, whom the party had earlier attacked in harsh terms, became transformed into a near hero. In 1936, although it ran its own presidential ticket, the CP objectively supported FDR. In the campaign the party focused much of its energies on attacking FDR's opponents, the Republican Landon as well as the Socialist Thomas. In 1944, the CP enthusiastically worked for FDR's reelection.[51]

The success that the CP experienced as a liberal and reformist organization set in motion a dynamic that locked it even further into this position and made it ever more difficult for Communists to openly and aggressively advocate socialism. Party cadres and activists found themselves in unions and other organizations surrounded by large numbers of new recruits who were attracted to the groups by the liberal and reformist positions these Communists were advocating. The very number of these recruits, the fear of alienating them, and the desire to gain even more members combined to make Communists ever more willing to push for reform and deal with socialism later.[52] CP officials writing in their own internal publication, the *Party Organizer*, complained about this trend: "Our industrial units to a great extent have remained pure and simple trade union groups. As a matter of fact, many of our Communists who are members of trade unions do not know the Party and its role as a revolutionary force in the political life of the community."[53]

George Charney, a leading functionary active in the 1936 campaign, described the process of liberalization from his own experience: "As the [1936] campaign progressed our primary emphasis to defeat Landon gained popular favor and I found it difficult to counsel a vote for Browder. . . . Neither could we, on the hustings, rest on a negative case. The realities of the political conflict compelled us to adopt a more constructive attitude toward Roosevelt and the liberal trend in the Democratic Party."[54] If a sophisticated party cadre could be so moved, what then would be the reaction of the average member of the CP?

The emotional appeal in working within a party that was honest and focused on humanist, liberal, and reformist goals was considerable. The extent to which new Communists during this period were properly socialized as socialists, however, is a matter that is still being debated.[55] Charney, for one, did not believe that the people in the branches he was familiar with were getting much of a Marxist education. But for him this did not seem to represent much of a problem compared to the "emotional return" both recruits and cadres were getting for their investment in a nonsectarian party: "The branches were alive because the people were alive, and if most had but a dim notion of Marx or of socialism, they had a strong conviction that the party represented a new form of human brotherhood that combined faith and a militant struggle for a better world. Indeed at times I could sense that communism had meanings and attractions as the spiritual extension of the Judeo-Christian ethic."[56]

The desire to become relevant and a respected political force was also unleashed by the United Front. In the 1920s and early 1930s the CP had been confined to the fringes of American political life and was a small Left party overshadowed by the SP on the left of the national political spectrum. When the CP became more liberal and moved closer to the Democratic party, its fortunes improved. By the mid-1930s its membership exceeded that of the SP. Soon afterward the CP became the most preeminent force on the Left while the SP evolved into the role of minor gadfly barely able to keep itself alive.

The CP was far from being a major political party. In its quest for a position of influence in American life, the party turned to elections and the Democratic party. The CP was no stranger to electoral politics before the United Front. It had run a variety of candidates for national, state, and local offices since the early 1920s. However, these elections were generally not invested with great importance and certainly did not loom large in the party's overall strategy.

After the United Front the situation changed. Elections from the mid-1930s on began to play an increasingly important role in CP life and strategy. As Charney observed: "Our work in industry still had priority but the center of gravity shifted to the community and the election cycles. For the first time the party designated legislative representatives in Washington and Albany. . . . Socialism belonged to the future, inevitable, of course. . . . What mattered was the present, and in the present, the elections.[57]

As elections became more important, so did the CP's relationship to the Democratic party. Although the CP used several election vehicles in the latter 1930s and 1940s (including its own organization, the ALP, and the Progressive Party), the Democratic party was the primary focus of its activities. It was the party of the majority and the ruling party of the country. If the CP was to be relevant and influence America's policies, particularly those concerning foreign affairs, the easiest and most direct way of accomplishing this would not be through some minor third party but through the Democratic party itself. Even as the CP ran its own candidates and supported those on third party tickets, the primary object of its election concerns after the mid-1930s was the Democratic party. The CP celebrated after the 1936 presidential elections even though their own candidate, Earl Browder, had received about 80,000 votes—some hundred thousand less than Norman Thomas. But it was not Browder's votes that mattered. What really counted was Roosevelt's near 28 million ballots. According to Charney: "We rejoiced in the victory of Roosevelt, for it was a victory for the people and we had played a part in it. We rejoiced because the party had achieved status as a recognized political force in the country."[58] After the war and after Browder's downfall in 1945, his successor, William Z. Foster, the veteran hard liner, did not abandon the electoral strategy of focusing on the Democratic party.[59]

In order to be relevant and influential in the Democratic party and the nation, according to the logic of the United Front, the CP wanted to build its own numerical base. To do this the party could no longer afford to concentrate exclusively on the American working class. Scarcely any strata or class except the most damnable capitalists fell beyond the scope and (benevolent) interest of the CP. Professionals, small businessmen, and members of the white-collar strata discovered that they were no longer the *enemy* of the CP but individuals and groups whose welfare appeared to deeply concern the former vanguard party of the working class.[60] In Sunnyside Gardens, a middle class suburb of Queens, New York, the party campaigned on issues like sewage problems, mortgages, and other ills of the small home owner.[61] This reformist CP wanted not only the support of these people as voters but also to recruit them into the party as members. In line with this, special professional units were established within the party to facilitate the professionals' entry into and involvement with the organization. CP functionaries went so far as to put aside their proletarian garb, mannerisms, and customs in favor of those of the middle class. They wore suits and ties, traveled by Pullman sleepers, and, like proper bourgeois gentlemen, helped their wives on with their coats.[62]

TREATMENT OF JEWS AND JEWISH ISSUES **463**

The appearance of an ever-increasing number of white-collar and professional workers among new recruits indicated that the party's appeal to the middle class had borne fruit. From 1935 to 1941 the proportion of members from this class increased from 10 to 44 percent. This percentage decreased after 1941 due to the fact that the labor force from which the Communists recruited became more heavily blue collar in composition, a result of the move to heavy war production and the drafting of nonvital, mainly white-collar, workers. By war's end, the proportion of party members in professional and white-collar occupations remained substantial—at least 30 percent. (The significance of this figure grows when it is understood that an additional 25 percent of the membership at the time were classified as "housewives.") In the 1940s, possibly earlier, the American CP was unique in the international movement in terms of the large proportion of those within it who were not industrial workers.[63]

This situation did not change much in the latter 1940s and early 1950s, when party, which was on the decline, did not enjoy much success in recruiting among workers in such major industries as steel, longshoremen, garment, and trucking. It did best among white-collar and professional persons: ". . . the main areas of . . . growth [in New York City] were in the West Side, Washington Heights and the Village—among the middle class. . . . Instead of a lean, proletarian profile, we presented a figure of middle class, middle aged fat."[64]

Those middle-class members whom the liberal CP successfully attracted to it were not a representative cross-section of their class. A disproportionate number of the persons from this socioeconomic background who moved into the CP's orbit were Jews. This can be ascertained in a variety of ways. One way is through residence of CP members. In the latter 1930s and 1940s the party was comparatively most successful in its recruitment attempts in areas of Jewish concentration. In New York City, the West Side, Washington Heights, and the Village had large Jewish populations. The same sort of pattern holds when membership data for New York State as a whole and California are considered: From the latter 1930s on, the New York and California CP units were the largest in the national party, with New York alone accounting for 51 percent of the membership by 1951. In both states the membership was concentrated in the largest cities, New York and Los Angeles—two municipalities with disproportionately large Jewish populations. At the same time, these were the state organizations with the lowest proportion of industrial workers in its ranks, only 29 percent in the New York party and 38 percent in the California unit in 1946. Conversely, each state organization had a high proportion of members who were employed in white-collar and light (as opposed to heavy) industries, occupational areas of Jewish concentration in the two states. In these same years New York and California also led other state units of the party with respect to the percentage of Jews among their members. It therefore seems safe to assume that significant numbers of Communists were Jews in white-collar and professional positions.[65]

There are also other grounds to support this assertion. A plurality of the intellectuals and writers who moved toward the party in the 1930s were Jews. The two intellectuals who played a major role in sheherding their peers into the sphere of the CP were Michael Gold and Joseph Freeman, sons of Yiddish-speaking immigrants.[66] Intellectuals and writers were joined in this trek, as we mentioned earlier, by teachers, social workers, and clerks who, like the intellectuals, were disproportionately Jewish.

Why Reform?

The attraction to reformism by leftist or leftist-inclined Jews in America stems from the interplay of a variety of factors. The most important of these are the quality of the experiences that they had as Jews and as economic men in czarist Russia and the United States. In examining this experience it is important to focus on that of the Socialist leaders that emerged from the ranks of the leftist Jews. These were the men that provided political direction and ideological spectacles through which their constituents viewed their world. It is in the interaction between leaders and followers within the context of Jewish and American social, economic, and political structures that much of the explanation for Jewish reformism can be found.

Earlier we detailed the factors that facilitated and led Jews toward socialism. In Russia around the turn of the century and in the United States in the early decades of the twentieth, poverty and misery, coupled with the appropriate structural and historical conditions, had been sufficient to propel a significant minority on the road to socialism. But in the United States these socialist propellants proved neither as harsh nor as long lasting as those of czarist Russia, and the Jewish movement toward socialism predictably diminished. Reformism was a means by which Jewish Socialists, who would not or could not abandon their deeply felt political commitments as Socialists, came to grips with the new and for them more positive economic, social, and political realities existent in the New World. Reformism became a way station on the route toward membership in the bourgeois polity.

The occupational base upon which Jewish socialism was built in Russia and the United States was not a solid one. By itself, this foundation—made up largely of artisans, petty entrepreneurs, and workers in small shops in highly competitive and marginal industries—did not facilitate the development of a strata receptive to revolutionary socialism. In the Old Country, financial distress and the pervasiveness of a pernicious anti-Semitism had combined with this occupational structure to bolster the Jews' commitment to socialist movements. At the same time these other forces, particularly anti-Semitism, obscured the weakness of the Jewish occupational base as a factor inducing a socialist allegiance in its own right. Ber Borochov (as we noted in Chapter 3) was aware of this problem. So was Trotsky, who argued that Jews did not make the best Bolsheviks or revolutionary socialists. This stemmed from the reasons behind why they were drawn to socialism. In Trotsky's view, the Jews' embittered national feelings were more salient than their class experiences in prompting them to become socialists. For him class was the primary factor in the development of a true, or revolutionary, socialist.[67]

In the United States the comparatively lower level of anti-Semitism meant that the Jews' occupational structure would carry most of the burden of moving them toward socialism and of sustaining that commitment. But, in the absence of "Russian allies", the Jews' occupational structure (and mobility experiences) could not in itself carry this political load. One consequence of this set of circumstances was the receptivity among Jews to reform socialism in the United States.

Reformism and the drift from socialism among Left Jews was largely the consequence of the absence of a large, two-generation working-class Jewish proletariat in America. This absence was in turn due to the expanding American economy and the opportunities available to Jews to move out of the working class. The garment industry—the single most important employer of Jewish workers—did not foster the growth of such a proletariat. The numerous strata of small shopkeepers, peddlers, and successful former needle trades workers meant increasingly in the decades between 1910 and 1930 that there were fewer in the Jewish community receptive to messages aimed solely at an industrial proletariat. In such circumstances it became difficult for Left parties and politicians who wished to be relevant within American Jewry to preach revolutionary socialism.

The interrelationship between class and ethnic experiences and a predisposition toward reform socialism can be seen most clearly in the cases of the early leaders of Jewish socialism in the United States. Many of them, as noted earlier, were persons whose economic mobility in Russia had been frustrated because they were Jews. Their Jewishness became the cause of their involuntary entrance into the working class. They did not, however, spend much time as workers in Russia or the United States.

One of the consequences of their ethnically induced downward mobility apparently was their definition of and attitudes toward socialism. The socialism of these emigres tended to be emotional and lacking in clarity and consistency. One social scientist described them in the following terms: ". . . even the veterans were vague as to the ideological content of their radicalism. Thus Cahan admits that 'I had no exact grasp' of socialist doctrine, and if this was true of a 'circle' participant it was certainly true of the vast majority of other intellectuals. Khayim Spivakovsky (Spivak), a participant in the Am Olam movement, informs us that the Russian Jewish intelligentsia brought

with it 'no clearly defined political, social and economic views.
. . . ' " [68] Similarly, Hillquit admitted that in his early years in the
United States "I already considered myself a Socialist, but my socialism was largely emotional and sentimental. My notions about the philosophy and practical program of the movement were quite vague." [69]

It is not, of course, necessary to be well-versed in Marxist theory to
be a socialist. The conditions of work have made socialists out of
many workers ignorant of Marxist texts. The issue here transcends
that of knowledge about a complex theory.

The uncertainty and vagueness that young Jewish radical intellectuals felt about socialism stemmed, I contend, in large part, from the
factors that moved them toward this ideology to begin with. For these
young men, the nature of their experience as proletarians did not appear to be significant in impelling them toward socialism. Typically,
they were not proletarians for any appreciable period, either in Russia
or in the United States. More important were the associated factors of
anti-Semitism and blocked social mobility. Their ideology reflected
their life situations, not their proletarian statuses.

The way in which they came to socialism in Russia made these
reluctant proletarians vulnerable to conservatizing influences in the
United States. The comparative freedom, economic opportunity and
relative acceptance as citizens and individuals challenged the socialist commitment of these "blocked mobiles" almost as soon as they
stepped foot on American soil. For example, Cahan, in describing his
early years in America—a period in which he was a fervent Socialist—wrote:

I longed to persuade myself that by distributing socialist leaflets I would be
leading the life of a Russian revolutionary in the United States. The word
"leaflet" had a sacred sound. It was "forbidden fruit" even though it was not
forbidden. . . . What kind of socialism could it be without conspiracy. . . . I
felt America's freedom every minute. I breathed freer than I had ever breathed
before. But all the time I was saying to myself, "All of this is a capitalist
prison." And the confusion in my brain was compounded by the fact that in
the first few months in America I worked like a slave at my first jobs.[70]

It was difficult for the untutored masses to embrace revolutionary
socialism in the United States when their socialist tutors and leaders
were embracing America. In Russia, Vladeck, the prominent Socialist
party activist, had been a daring Bundist organizer with Bolshevik
sympathies. In America this man prayed in gratitude for his adopted
homeland in front of Independence Hall.[71] How militant could the
Jewish masses be when one of the early journals of the Yiddish-speaking Socialists, *Naye Welt* (*New World*) could write in 1909: "These
two words, *Naye Welt*, express the program of the new magazine. . . .
We will study the *Naye Welt*. . . . America is the future country of
the Jews. . . . America has given the Jews everything, equality and
opportunity." [72] The Eastern European Jewish leaders and influentials

in the Socialist party benefitted from America's largesse in terms of their occupational attainments. Many of them, including Cahan and Hillquit, had risen from the shop floor to professional status. These mobile men were, according to De Leon, the source of the opposition to him. As he viewed it, the *weltanschauung* of the rightists who opposed him was informed by "the changing angle of vision of the former workingman who had become bourgeois."[73] De Leon was not alone in locating the source of reformist opposition in Left parties in a bourgeois cohort. Later Debs, Foster, and Trotsky were to come to the same conclusions with respect to those they accused of being rightist in their respective parties—Socialist, Communist, and Trotskyist. It was probably not by the workings of chance that a disproportionate number of the reformists that they railed against were Jews from bourgeois backgrounds or Jews who held professional positions.[74]

Trotsky's analysis of Jewish socialists in America in 1940 was very similar to the analysis he constructed of Jewish socialists in Russia decades earlier. His position on Jewish socialists in America was stimulated by the state of the Socialist Workers Party (SWP), an avowedly Trotskyist party. The SWP in the 1930s was (1) a small organization of about 200; (2) a disproportionately Jewish party, especially so in its leadership; and (3) a body characterized by considerable internecine warfare. Trotsky attributed many of the problems that plagued the SWP to its heavy concentration of nonproletarian members, particularly the nonproletarian Jews concentrated in New York City. In the midst of a factional fight, which was largely between midwestern non-Jewish "workers" led by James Cannon and New York Jewish "intellectuals," Trotsky took up the cudgels against the latter:

The party has only a minority of genuine factory workers. The non-proletarian elements represent a very necessary yeast. . . . But . . . our party can be inundated by non-proletarian elements and can even lose its revolutionary character. The task is, naturally, not to prevent the influx of intellectuals by artificial methods, but to orient practically the entire organization toward the factories, the strikes, the unions. . . . You have, for example, an important number of Jewish non-worker elements in your ranks. They can be very valuable yeast if the party succeeds by and by in extracting them from a closed milieu and ties them to the factory workers by daily activity. I believe such an orientation would also assure a more healthy atmosphere inside the party. . . . If we seriously establish such a general orientation we will avoid a great danger—namely, that the intellectuals and white collar workers might suppress the worker minority, condemn it to silence, transform the party into a very intelligent discussion club but absolutely not habitable for workers . . . it was absolutely necessary in order to cleanse the atmosphere of the party, that the Jewish petty-bourgeois elements of the New York local be shifted from their habitual conservative milieu and dissolved in the real labor movement.[75]

In the course of this controversy the New York faction—led by Martin Abern and Max Shachtman, two Jewish non-proletarians—

responded by obliquely charging Trotsky and his allies with helping to spread anti-Semitism: "'An 'anti-New York' propaganda is spread [by the Cannon-Trotsky faction] which is at the bottom catering to prejudices which are not always healthy." To which Trotsky angrily replied:

What prejudices are referred to here? Apparently anti-Semitism. If anti-Semitic or other race prejudices exist in our party it is necessary to wage a ruthless struggle against them through open blows and not through vague insinuations. But the question of the Jewish intellectuals and semi-intellectuals of New York is a *social*, not a *national*, question. In New York there are a great many Jewish proletarians but Abern's faction is not built up of them. The petty-bourgeois elements of his faction have proved incapable to this day of finding a road to the Jewish workers. They are contented with their own milieu. . . . Shachtman will perhaps recall that . . . I advised the National Committee to move away from New York and its atmosphere of petty-bourgeois squabbles for awhile to some industrial center in the provinces.[76]

Foster, in his struggle against the largely Jewish Lovestoneite faction of the CP in the latter 1920s, was also accused of anti-Semitism. He, too, apparently blurred the distinction between Jewish and petty bourgeois background. In a word-of-mouth campaign against the Lovestoneites, the Foster group, which included Alexander Bittelman, charged that: "Lovestone, Bert Wolfe, Willie Weinstone were COLLEGE MEN-bourgeois . . . [And] that they were JEWS. . . ."[77]

The underlying sociological verity that Trotsky, Foster, Debs, and De Leon were obliquely alluding to was the socioeconomic character of the Jewish community in America, which had provided the context from which Jewish socialists emerged. America had not provided a fertile environment for radical Jewish socialism. Men like Cahan and Hillquit were very representative of the Jewish community that nurtured them. Both the socialist and socialistically inclined Jewish masses and their chieftains were responding to the same broad social and economic forces that drove Jews from militant socialism and then from socialism itself. These were the same forces that also drove their less radical coreligionists from the crowded ghettoes to the more spacious Bronx and eventually to the suburbs. America was freer than Russia. Jews were more likely to gain acceptance and face less anti-Semitism in the United States than in Eastern Europe. America did provide them with more economic opportunity than anywhere else in the world, especially the Pale. In these circumstances not many Jews, whether versed in Marxism or not, could be expected to follow the call of revolutionary socialists. (But those versed in Marxism could have been expected to question the underlying economic and historic reasons for America's benevolence rather than to attribute it to some inner goodness.) America had commenced the process of seduction for the socialist leaders and the socialist masses as soon as they stepped off the ships that delivered them from the misery of the Pale.

This process involves more than just being responsive to conservatizing forces. There were organizations and institutions that provided a context in which leaders and followers were made receptive to the lures of pragmatic socialism. It was these organizations that interpreted and mediated America for the immigrants so as to socially and psychologically prepare them for reform. The most important to those that stood at the vortex of the immigrant community were the needle trades unions. Rooted as they were in a highly insecure and competitive industry, these unions and their heads found cause to seek alliance with reformers, socialist, and others who could deliver practical benefits now and not at some future date. As their part of the bargain with these reformist allies, the unions delivered not only their organizations to the camp of reform but as much of the community as they could sway.

This emphasis on reform and practical benefits weakened the influence of socialism among the Jewish masses and eventually among the Socialist leaders who preached its virtues. Jewish Socialists, guided by their leaders and organizations, learned that socialism was honesty in government, municipal bath houses, the elimination of tenement workshops, the recognition of unions, and other such important things. When a nonradical party, such as the Democratic party, realized that such reforms did not conflict with capitalist principles, the Socialist party and socialism as New York Jews had learned to define it was doomed. Unlike the Socialist party, the Democratic party was more capable of delivering the goods. That was what the New York Jewish masses, educated on this by socialists as well as reformers, Republicans, and Tammany Democrats, had come to learn was the most important part of socialist politics.

A succession of reform Democratic governors in New York State (Al Smith, FDR, and Herbert Lehman) and the New Deal on the national level easily outdid the Socialists when it came to delivering practical benefits, especially as all were talking about roughly the same benefits. The politician who was the most adept at this maneuver of stealing the Socialist (or Communist) thunder was the Republican maverick Fiorello La Guardia, a long-time member of Congress and mayor of New York. His legislative program "duplicated the immediate demands of the Socialists, lacking only the ultimate objective of having the state own all productive property." La Guardia anticipated the direction in which his Socialist opponents would move when he told them that "the solution [to the labor problem] was not a radical third party but strong trade unions and a spokesman within a major party." In attacking them on the campaign trails, he warned Jewish and non-Jewish voters not to vote for Socialists as they would drain the votes away from reformers, such as himself, who were more capable in a capitalist political setting of improving conditions. He defined Marxism, with its grandiose verbiage and millennial visions, as "the opiate of the people."[78]

The Socialists were not the only leftists who facilitated the movement of Jews toward the Democratic party. The Communists, during their liberal phases, steered their Jewish (as well as non-Jewish) followers and supporters in the same direction. Many of these people were in occupational statuses that facilitated this type of political movement. Disproportionately, they were Jews in white-collar positions, often new to this status. The CP's positive emphasis on liberalism and democracy, as well as the New Deal, could not help but strike a responsive chord among such Jews. The reformism of the CP satisfied their yearning to be part of liberal America and still remain faithful to a radical heritage, while not endangering their material interests. Joseph Freeman voiced the feelings of many young middle-class Communists when he praised the bountiful rewards that flowed from the liberalism of the CP's United Front policies: "one could be simultaneously a Communist and a supporter of F.D.R. and jump on the sweetest bandwagon in all history." (A few years later, like so many of his literary peers, Freeman was off the bandwagon, or at least the Communist side of it.) [79]

LEFT PARTIES AND ETHNIC-JEWISH ISSUES

The Left's position on and handling of ethnicity was another major factor affecting its relationship with Jews and the Jewish community. The Jews' own feelings about themselves as immigrants, ethnics, and Americans caused them to attach importance to the way in which the radical parties dealt with the issues of immigration, ethnicity, and Americanism. The radical parties' treatment of these issues, particularly as they concerned Jews directly, became for many in the Jewish community a key to the way in which they related to those parties.

If we take the latter nineteenth century as our starting point, the realities of American life and the ethnic nature of the membership and supporters of the Left caused it problems. America in the late 1800s and in the first several decades of the 1900s was the refuge of millions of immigrants. The majority poured into the working class; for decades after the end of mass immigration in 1924, the American working class was heavily made up of the foreign-born. This was the class to which the Left primarily directed itself.

The heavily immigrant and ethnic composition of the working class in the latter nineteenth and early twentieth centuries evoked several types of responses from the radical parties. One of the more consistent responses was to pay ethnicity little heed and regard it as a problem to overcome. After all, Marxism, the informing ideology of the Left, emphasized societal universals; and ethnicity in this scheme of things was viewed as an ephemeral factor. Capitalism, industrialism, and urbanization would undoubtedly homogenize a nation's working class. To the extent that Marxists gave ethnicity consideration, it was to regard it as a troublesome factor. Ethnicity, or nationalist feelings, weakened the unity of the working class and destracted it from the task of achieving socialism. A united and unified working class was to be the principle agency of historical progress, the vehicle that would carry each nation to socialism.

This perspective on ethnicity was reinforced by other considerations. If the Left was to be receptive to national differences, it might find that it had attained a base in these ethnic groups. But that might put the Left in jeopardy of isolating itself from native Americans. Eventually time, schools, cities, and factories would combine to produce an American working class, if not among the immigrant fathers, then certainly among their American-born sons. If the Left were to have any hope of success in the United States, it would have to orient itself to America and to an American working class and not to immigrant or foreign-language groups within it. Stigmatization and isolation in a foreign community in the United States would be an onerous burden for the Left to bear.

There was another side to this problem. Despite Marxist ideology and abstractions about the American melting pot, the Left parties were confronted with the reality that most of their members and much of their support throughout most of the late nineteenth and early twentieth centuries came from ethnic and foreign-language groups. To ignore this reality or to force them to assimilate might jeopardize a base now for something intangible in the future. If the non-American base was alienated, there would not be much of an organization with which to reach out to the Americans in the future.

These problems were exacerbated because the fact that the members and supporters of the Left among the ethnic and foreign-language communities were not in agreement about the best way to deal with such issues. Some wanted to remain in their ethnic enclaves and have the Left parties succor them. Others desired to become Americans as soon as possible and to have the radical parties follow suit. The Jews were perhaps the group most troubled by disagreements on this issue.

The major Left parties in the United States were aware of the difficulties faced by a universalistic movement resting on a particularistic base. Unfortunately recognition of a problem does not guarantee that a solution will be forthcoming. And, unfortunately for the Left, it did not arrive at an adequate solution.

The Socialist Labor Party

This issue was first joined, as far as the Jews were concerned, within the context of the Socialist Labor Party (SLP). The Jews who entered this party were largely those who held little regard for a Jewish identity. They were largely the products of Russian schools and political movements where they had imbibed the spirit of Russian cosmopolitanism. They and their views were described by Meyer London's biographer, Harry Rogoff:

The intellectuals who preached socialism to the immigrant Jews in the 90's belonged to the "assimilative" school of Socialists. The problem of preserving Jewish nationalism never presented itself to them for they were not interested in it. They visualized the future socialist society as one in which race lines played no part. Questions such as the development of the Jewish language or the spreading of Jewish culture which were so vital to the Bundists in Russia were non-existent to the Jewish Socialists here.[80]

The SLP was an accommodating party as far as these and other Jews were concerned. Any language grouping, Jewish or not, that had a sufficient number of persons interested in joining the SLP could form their own language branch. Thus in the SLP there were German-, Hungarian-, French-, Russian-, Yiddish- and English-speaking language branches. In New York City at one time Jews, depending on their sense of identity, had the choice of at least three different language branches. For those who desired, or at least did not mind being identified as Jewish Socialists, there was the Yiddish-speaking branch, Branch 8. For those who remained caught up in their Russian identity, there was the Russian-speaking branch, Branch 17. And for those who wanted to relate to America as quickly as possible, there was an English-speaking section. However, the primary field of concentration for almost all Jewish SLP members, regardless of the branch they were in, was the Yiddish-speaking workers.[81]

Despite this flexibility, leading Jews within the SLP such as Hillquit and Cahan, were unhappy that its membership was so predominantly foreign and that it seemed to have little interest in reaching out to the American-born or the assimilated foreign-born. Cahan voiced the sentiments of many of his cosmopolitan Jewish peers when he wrote: "The German comrades understood that by themselves they could not achieve socialism in America. It was necessary to spread the doctrine and the party among the native Americans. They did much in this direction but one could not escape the impression that they were doing so only half-heartedly. Actually they looked condescendingly on the American masses and conducted their affairs as if the German-language socialist movement were the entire movement."[82] Cahan increasingly confined almost all his "activity to the English-speaking section of the movement," while keeping in steady contact with the Russian and Yiddish-speaking parts of the SLP.[83]

De Leon also believed that the SLP was not doing enough to reach the American workers. One of his major goals as leader of the party was to Americanize it. De Leon lashed out at the German-Americans for their failure to break out of their ethnic enclaves, in terms similar to those which Communist party leaders would use against non-English-speaking Communists decades in the future. In pitting himself against the *alte deutschen Genossen* (old German comrades) of the SLP, De Leon felt that he was opposing men who, having "evoked no response [from the American people,] shrank into social clubs—

singing and drinking and card-playing societies, with an occasional outing when a member dies, and periodical celebrations in which thrilling speeches were delivered by themselves to themselves. . . . A movement such as ours can be truly at the heart of those to whom, whether born here or not, America is their home. . . . To all others the movement can only be a sport or past-time."[84]

Despite their feelings, these non-Jewish Jews experienced difficulty acting upon them. The major obstacle in bringing their deeds in line with their words and thoughts was that the Yiddish-speaking workers, whose numbers were constantly growing, offered the best market for the socialist wares of these cosmopolitan Jewish ideologues. Other nationality groups were either less receptive to socialism or less receptive to its preaching among them. The Russian-speaking branch collapsed after an existence of only a few years because of these harsh realities. Men like Hillquit, who had belonged to Branch 17, and Cahan, who longed to work among the Americans, were forced by practical considerations to move into the Yiddish-speaking sphere. Even as they moved in this direction, they continued to harbor the hope of one day breaking out of this particularistic arena.[85]

The emergence of Debs and his Social Democracy organization in the latter 1890s, coinciding with the division of the SLP, encouraged the dissident Jewish SLP members to believe that there was now a genuine American Socialist movement in the United States that they could become part of. Despite De Leon's attempt to Americanize the SLP, it was still a predominantly non-American party in their minds. The membership was heavily foreign-born, as was its leader De Leon. It was not only the fact of his foreign birth that gave De Leon his non-American character; it was also his dictatorial style and uncompromising socialism that gave him and the organization he dominated a European tone.

The Socialist Party

Debs and Social Democracy appeared to be the antithesis of De Leon and the SLP. Debs, in addition to being a native-born midwesterner, was also a warm and humane person who believed in democratic leadership. This combination proved to be a magnetic attraction for the immigrant Jewish Socialists of New York. After meeting Debs for the first time, Cahan wrote: "Debs makes a deep impression on everyone with whom he comes in contact by his sincerity and genuine love for his fellow man, and we need a standard bearer of this kind."[86] When critics of Debs and his movement raised questions concerning the lack of a well-defined program and set of principles, his Jewish defenders replied by emphasizing the Americanness of Social Democracy and of Debs' personality. This would not be the last time that Jewish Socialists sought and found a standard bearer whose American background and personality overshadowed his political erudition or capabilities.

The Socialist party of America that the Jews helped to form was for them a truly American party. Not only did it have Debs at its head but it also had many other native-born Americans within its ranks. The Jewish Socialist immigrants were immensely gratified when they went to party conventions in the American heartland and discovered "old stock" American Socialists and a truly indigenous Socialist movement. These immigrants were socialist by upbringing; and they wanted to be Americanized. But sometimes socialism and being American seemed to them to be antithetical. The Western socialists, however, were living proof that it was possible to be American and still be socialist.[87] At last the assimilationist and cosmopolitan Jewish socialists seemed to have found an appropriate political home. Now they could be socialist in their politics without feeling un-American in their hearts.

The Socialist party soon came to function in a variety of ways as the vehicle for Jews to enter American politics and American society. It served this function for the sophisticated and semisophisticated Marxist, as well as for the average socialistically inclined Jew. This integrationist role became one reason why the immigrant Jews were so attracted to the SP. Paradoxically its very success as an agency of American socialization led the SP to function as a way station for immigrant Jews and their children en route to the mainstream of American politics and American society.

The SP's rise to prominence and influence in the United States coincided with the annual arrival of hundreds of thousands of Jewish immigrants. The SP that they found upon arriving was a different kind of socialist party then had ever existed before in the New World. Unlike its predecessors, it was largely an American organization and was not, like the SLP, located on the periphery of American politics and society. Respected American intellectuals, editors, lawyers, and ministers praised its works and, in some cases, even joined it. And it was a political organization of real significance. The party (in approximately 1910) appeared to be growing stronger and more capable of winning elections and influencing the direction of American politics.

The SP of America, whose fortunes intersected with that of the Jewish masses in the decade before World War I, had to be an attractive facet of the lives of those people as they acclimated themselves to the New World. It was the only major party to welcome Jews into its ranks and activities as equals. The leaders and spokesmen of the SP were men with personal qualities whom the Jewish immigrants could readily respect. They were men of integrity and erudition. Many were Jewish immigrants who by dint of education, sacrifice, and effort became not only leaders and influentials in the SP but respected professionals in the occupational sphere as well. They were also men whom Christian Americans respected, an important factor in the eyes of the

Yiddish-speaking Jews. At the head of the SP stood the East Side's beloved Debs. In addition the SP actually cared about the working and living conditions of Jews in the ghettoes and exerted itself to improve these conditions.[88] It was not difficult to understand why the Socialist party in New York was embraced by Jews. "Who was not a Socialist in our midst?" asked East Sider Harry Roskolenko.[89]

The SP was not the only party to vie for Jewish electoral support. The Republicans and Democrats also made their bids, as no party wished to forego votes. At the local level, particularly in New York City, the Democratic party was more successful among the Eastern European Jews than the Republican party or the SP. The Democratic organization's support of immigration and opposition to immigration restrictions won for it much support among the predominantly foreign born Jewish community. Despite occasional successful forays by progressive Republicans like Theodore Roosevelt into Jewish districts and despite the fact that Jews nationally favored Republican presidential candidates until 1928 (except for Wilson in 1916), the Democratic party in the first two decades of the twentieth century was the major rival of the Socialists for the Jewish immigrant vote in the cities.[90]

The Democratic party was somewhat handicapped in this contest. One of the important factors that caused many Jews to reject the Democrats was their ethnic character. When the Eastern European Jews arrived in New York and other major urban areas, the Democratic party was largely the creation of the Irish-Americans.[91] To the immigrant Jews the Irish Catholics appeared hostile and crude. The Irish and the Jews clashed in a variety of areas. Economic competition and Jewish encroachment upon the Irish residential turf led the Irish to exclude them from Irish-dominated jobs and unions. Jews were taunted and assaulted in the streets by hostile Irish groups. There was also mutual antipathy at the level of values and personal comportment. The Irish politicians of Tammany Hall openly smoked, gambled, drank, and caroused with women. Few among them spoke faultless English or went further in their education than grammar school. They were corrupt men who cheated their way to election victories.[92] The Socialists, by comparison, appeared saintly to the immigrant Jewish community. As one Lower East Side resident expressed it: "It seemed incomprehensible that a politician could also be a socialist. What had socialism to do with those one-flight-up political, unsavory clubs that inundated our streets?"[93]

The political treatment received by Jews from the Irish Democrats did not encourage Jews to flock to Tammany's banners. The Socialists treated the Jews as equals and with dignity, accepting them into the hierarchy of the party. Tammany leaders, on the other hand, did not endear themselves to "outsiders" when they boasted that "The Irish are natural leaders" and that other groups "want to be ruled by them."[94] The Irish did not conceal their hostility toward the Jewish newcomers until the size of the Jewish vote became appreciable. It was with reluctance that the Irish admitted them into the Democratic party organization. For as long as possible the Irish kept the Jews (as well as other ethnic groups) from positions of power and responsibility within the party. Most of those Jews who did manage to get inside did not get far beyond the status of meshores (messenger boy), even if they were a local judge or member of the United States Congress.[95] Scarcely any Tammany Jew ever reached the heights that Hillquit, Cahan, Vladeck and Waldman achieved within the Socialist party. By the same token, no Tammany Jew could compare in integrity and erudition to these men.

The election results testified to the fact that the immigrant Jews were capable of rising above petty ethnic prejudices and transcending differences in values on voting days. Even at the height of the Socialist party's prominence, Jewish voters, with some notable exceptions (Meyer London), usually cast more of their ballots for Democrats than Socialists. The Irish Democrats might not be as American or as honest or as nice to Jews as the Socialists, but they would do things for Jews that Socialists would not. The Democrats stopped police harassment of Jewish businessmen and performed other favors that the Socialists could or would not match. (If ever in power their ethics would have prevented them from effectively competing with Tammany at this level.)

However, the barriers and the hostility between the Tammany Irish and the immigrant Jews should not be considered politically insignificant. Even though Tammany succeeded in capturing the lion's share of Jewish votes, the differences with the Jews were sufficient to hinder some whose political self-interest should have directed them to the Democrats and to solidify for others their attachment to the non-Irish and American Socialists. And, though only a minority of Jews voted for the Socialist party in New York, their numbers (in terms of both Socialist voters and members) were sufficient to make it into a predominantly Jewish political party.

This development did not please the leaders of the Socialist party, especially the Jews among them. These Jewish leaders, as typified by Hillquit, did not want the Socialist party to become too closely identified with immigrant Jews. As Socialist politicians they realized that the ethnic divisions in American society and the existence of anti-Semitism made it perilous for a political party with state and national aspirations to rest on a narrow social base, particularly a Jewish social base. Such an identification might deter other ethnic groups from coming close to the Socialist party, especially native-born Americans.

Hillquit and the others wanted the Socialist party to be an American party. The American character of the early Socialist party had been one of its principal attractions. As the party's ethnic coloration began to change, they became even more concerned with maintaining and reinforcing the party's American character. Hillquit and the New York leaders were quite pleased at the time of World War I when they could draw such native Americans as Norman Thomas into their party. For Hillquit, Thomas was the prototype of the bright young American who would make the party more attractive to Americans. Hillquit and his fellow New York Jews worked to make Thomas' rise to power within the Socialist party as quick as possible.[96]

It was not only because these New York Jewish Socialist leaders were astute politicians that they wanted the Socialist party to broaden its base and avoid becoming a Jewish party. They were also motivated by their own Jewish identifications and by their conception of socialism. As Socialists they were universalistic and cosmopolitan; as Jews they were assimilationist or quasi-assimilationist. Loyalty to those ideals set these men on a collision course with Jewish Socialists who felt differently about their socialism and their Jewish identity and also proved costly in mobilizing Jewish support for the Socialist party and its candidates in elections.

The Socialist campaigns in the early 1900s in New York were curious affairs. Socialist campaigners preached the message of universalism to an ethnic community that constituted its major base of support. Historian Arthur Gorenstein stated: "Of all the parties in the ghetto the Socialist Party was least responsive to the ethnic interests of the residents of the ghetto. Cosmopolitan in outlook and faithful to its class allegiance, the Party was hostile to what it considered to be the conflicting loyalties invoked by 'nationality.' "[97] In this respect, these Jewish Socialist leaders were faithful to the socialism of pre-Bundist Russia.

It was only a matter of time before the sociological reality of the base came into conflict with the universalism of the ideology. Appropriately enough, Hillquit's electoral career became the principal sacrifice to this tension between base and ideology. Hillquit who had belonged to the Russian-speaking branch of the SLP, instead of joining a Jewish-speaking branch, continued his aloofness to Jewish parochial concerns while in the Socialist party. As a national leader of the party his cosmopolitan socialism was reinforced and stood him in good stead. Hillquit also had electoral ambitions, but here his universalistic socialism proved a major drawback. It was too difficult to run as a cosmopolitan socialist in a Jewish district and fight Tammany at the same time. Hillquit never won an election for public office. Ironically, his foreign birth prevented him from running for president on the SP ticket when presented with the opportunity in 1928. It was then that he advocated that the American Norman Thomas, a relative newcomer to the SP at the time, should be the party's national standard-bearer.[98]

Hillquit's 1908 bid for a seat in Congress from the East Side's Ninth CD provides a good illustration of the liabilities of being a cosmopolitan socialist in a Jewish district.[99] He launched his campaign at a time when the Jewish consciousness of the immigrant community was fed by the wave of recent pogroms in Russia and the flood of new arrivals fleeing this oppression. It was exacerbated by the fear emanating from public discussion and the filing of various immigration bills by restrictionist members of Congress that the United States might limit immigration, leaving the Jews in Russia in a hopeless situation. This consciousness was heightened even further by the charge of New York commissioner of police, General Theodore Bingham, that immigrant Jews were responsible for about half of the crimes in New York City.

Hillquit, throughout his campaign, paid little attention to these particular Jewish interests; instead, he stressed the theme of the universality of socialism. Speaking to his first campaign rally with Cahan at his side, he declared:

The issues thus defined by the Socialist Party in its National platform are also the issues in this Congressional District of New York. . . . The interests of the workingmen of the Ninth Congressional District are therefore entirely identical with those of the workingmen of the rest of the country, and if elected to Congress, I will not consider myself the special representative of the alleged special interests of this district, but the representative of the Socialist Party and the interests of the working class of the country so understood and interpreted by my party. . . .[100]

Hillquit's opposition responded by charging that he was indifferent to Jewish interests and a traitor to his people. The conservative Yiddish daily, the *Tageblatt*, declared: "Morris Hillquit belongs to those who hide their Jewish nationality . . . who crawls after Gentiles on all four." . . . Every right-thinking Jew will recognize that the Jews of New York should have as their representative in Congress a Jew who bears in mind Jewish interest. If Morris Hillquit were to be elected it would mean that New York Jewry would have no representative in the Congress of the United States."[101] The *Warheit*, another Yiddish-language daily supporting Daniel De Leon's candidacy for Congress also charged Hillquit with indifference to Jewish interests. It listed a series of crises affecting the immigrant community in which Hillquit had been noticeable by his absence. On the eve of the election, the editor of the *Warheit*, Louis Miller, wrote:

The American people have one position of high honor, the office of the President. . . . We Jews in this quarter possess only the office of Congressman. It is not much, perhaps, but it is all we have. To whom shall we give this office, to a person who has always been with us, or to a person who never cared to know us and has no desire to know us now, who when he comes among strangers denies that he is a Jew, who was, is and will always remain a renegade. Morris Hillquit's coming to us Jews when he wants our vote should by itself be sufficient reason for not voting for him.[102]

Of all the accusations, the most damaging to Hillquit was his stand on immigration. In 1904 and 1907 Hillquit, as a representative of the Socialist party in international Socialist congresses, had supported resolutions that called for the cessation of the immigration to developed countries of workers from "backward countries." He had tried to make it clear that this referred to Asians, "who are incapable of assimilation with the workingmen of the country of their adoption."[103] In the campaign Hillquit strove to reassure his Jewish electorate that the SP was not opposed to Jewish immigration. Even here he couched his reassurance in cosmopolitan socialist rhetoric and refrained from focusing directly on the special Jewish interest. According to Hillquit the SP was in favor of America opening its doors to certain kinds of immigrants "especially for the sufferers of economic exploitation, race and political attacks, refugees like the Russian Jews."[104] Hillquit also qualified his stance by pointing out that certain kinds of immigrants were not desirable—Asians and strikebreakers.

Hillquit's defense of his position on immigration did not quiet his opponents or allay the fears of his Jewish electorate. De Leon charged that the SP had violated basic socialist principles by dividing workers into "backward" and "progressive" races. There are no such types of races, De Leon exclaimed: "There is only a capitalist class and a workers' class. To divide the workers into races is the doing of capitalists. . . ."[105] De Leon went on to accuse Hillquit of being responsible for this SP position.

Probably the most serious aspect of Hillquit's position, as far as his Jewish electorate was concerned, was that he could not, without modification, support open immigration. A single desperate logic ruled the immigrant community: an open door for immigration. Restriction in any form would eventually affect Russian immigration. In such a situation, however Hillquit brilliantly couched his reservations, the Jewish quarter insisted on an unqualified stand for unrestricted immigration.[106]

Hillquit and his supporters did not completely ignore ethnic, specifically Jewish, themes in this election or others. It was usually made clear to the Jewish voters that Hillquit was a Jew. But, at the same time, Hillquit was not willing to stress this fact or publicly guarantee that he would push for Jewish interests.[107] Elections put Hillquit in a difficult position. On the one hand, there were personal and political considerations that inhibited his appealing to Jews qua Jews. First, he was an assimilationist Jew with little personal interest in Jewish questions. Second, he was a cosmopolitan socialist and a man who wished to be a national leader. On the other hand, he ran in areas where Jews constituted a major segment of the electorate. Unfortunately for Hillquit, there were not many assimilationists or cosmopolitan socialists among them.

Hillquit's universalistic creed and temerity in his approach to Jews were costly to him in election battles. It seemed clear that New York Jews, like any other ethnic group, did not want to endorse a candidate who was not willing to speak to their special interests. It was clear that if socialism wished to attract the masses of Jews and if Socialist candidates wanted to win in Jewish districts, then some compromise would have to be made. Socialism could not afford to remain too aloof from Jewish concerns. After all, the Jews of New York were among the party's strongest supporters and a major portion of the city's electorate.

The election campaigns and the triumphs of Meyer London indicate that the lesson of Hillquit's defeats did not go unheeded. London showed that Socialists could win elections if they were willing to subordinate their cosmopolitan socialism to a more Jewish brand of socialism. Unlike Hillquit, London had no qualms against running as a Jewish Socialist. London, unlike Hillquit, never left the East Side, remaining as a lawyer and a Socialist. Much of London's time, effort, and money were given to the cause of Jewish socialism; he was the friend, legal advisor, and political guide of the Jewish needle trades unions and the Workmen's Circle. When he chose to run for public office, these groups, plus the *Jewish Daily Forward*, constituted his campaign organization.

It was more than mere gratitude that earned London the support of the Jewish labor movement and the masses of East Side Jewry. He was not only favorable to Jewish interests, but he more than willingly championed them inside and outside of the SP. London was against any type of restriction on immigration.[108] He and his campaign leaders were not at all reluctant to stress his "Jewishness." As Louis Boudin, a Marxist theoretician, pointed out in the socialist daily, *New York Evening Call*: "In the London campaign, racial and subracial prejudices were appealed to. The Russian Jews were appealed to because Comrade London was also a Russian Jew."[109]

London's votes, especially his victories, legitimated particularistic socialism, Jewish socialism. The Hillquits and the Boudins could fume and fuss about the "pestilential atmosphere generated by the appeal to national or race feelings . . . [and] . . . unsocialistic practices. . . ."[110] But they and their principles did not win elections for Socialists in Jewish districts. London did bring election triumphs. As long as the number of votes and election victories were standards by which policies were evaluated, it was difficult for those who thought differently to seriously injure London with their criticisms. London's victories in the immigrant Jewish community (along with other factors) turned the tide with respect to the type of socialism that was preached among Jews. After 1910 the socialist deviant in the Jewish community would become the one that did not tailor his socialism to the specifications of his Jewish clients.

There is no doubt that London and his type of socialism furthered the cause of the SP among the immigrant Jews in the short run. He did, after all, win a seat in the United States Congress in three elections (1914, 1916, 1920) running as a Socialist—a feat rivaled by one other man in American political history, Victor Berger of Milwaukee. London's presence on a ticket did appear to boost the vote for other Socialists who were there with him. London probably also persuaded some Jews to move closer to socialism and may have reinforced the socialist ties of those who already believed in the principle and the party. London, after all, was a very popular figure on the East Side. As one ghetto youth said of him: "Meyer London was Samson, George Washington, Zane Grey—and the cop on the horse to me." [111]

It is, however, doubtful that London did much to further the cause of socialism and the SP beyond the short term. A good part of his vote was personal and not likely to carry over to other Socialist candidates. Even though he did seem to increase the vote of those other Socialists who ran with him, London's total was from two to four times greater than theirs. However, what was more important was the role he played in moving socialism and the Socialist party toward becoming Jewish communal phenomena. In his campaigns he appealed to a broad range of groups and classes on the East Side in which their Jewishness was emphasized. "The keynote of the [1910] campaign was 'split for London' and with this race prejudice was appealed to, and, in fact, everything except the class consciousness of these workers." [112] As the candidate himself told a victory rally before going to Congress for the first time in 1914: "When I take my seat in Congress I do not expect to accomplish wonders. What I expect to do is take to Washington the messages of the people. . . . I want to show them what the east side of New York is and what the east side Jew is." [113]

Socialism, as a Jewish communal phenomenon (as opposed to a working-class or even a Jewish working-class phenomenon), could not help but take a reformist character. To be successful at the ballot box it was necessary, as London had shown, to appeal to the broadest base of support as possible. To attract this broad base of support, purely working-class themes had to be muted. To maintain it the triumphant candidate could not afford to alienate this heterogeneous class base by advocating legislation of a militant working-class nature. London was quite aware of this. At a meeting for the unemployed in Union Square in 1915, when asked by an anarchist heckler what he (London) was going to do to bring about the "Social Revolution," London replied: "I am elected for only two years and that is too short a time in which to bring about the Social Revolution, so I am going to leave that job until later. *I am going to do hardly anything to bring it about. You see, I have to be re-elected in 1916 and I have to retain some votes in my district.*" [Emphasis added] [114]

True to his word, London did little to advance the cause of the Social Revolution. He did introduce and support socially worthwhile legislation, including measures endorsed by the Socialist party. Congressman London introduced bills against child labor, for a national system of unemployment insurance, and for a minimum wage law. [115] These measures, as capitalist politicians and parties soon found out, were compatible with capitalism. And, if they offended anybody in the Jewish community, it could only be the nastiest and most shortsighted among the employing class. This element would never have voted for London under any circumstances anyhow.

London effectively demonstrated that the road to Jewish socialism from cosmopolitanism ran in the same direction as the path from revolutionary to reform socialism. Cosmopolitan Jewish Socialists such as Hillquit had no difficulty finding their way to reform, although again by no means were all Jewish socialists reformists. Nevertheless, once socialism and the Socialist party moved closer to a Jewish base, the odds for it becoming reformist increased considerably.

Jewish Socialists Organize

The Socialist party's movement toward this ethnic base was hastened by its decision to recognize the Jewish Socialist Federation (JSF) as an official foreign-language affiliate in 1912. The JSF's formation and recognition by the SP represented a defeat for the cosmopolitan Jewish Socialists led by Hillquit.[116] The JSF was a concrete symbol that the ethnic factor in the Jewish community was a force that Socialists had to reckon with. It could not be wished away.

The cosmopolitans had long fought the establishment of a separate Jewish Socialist unit. But they, like the early Bundists, discovered that the Yiddish-speaking workers, whose numbers in America were constantly rising, required Yiddish-speaking Socialists to reach them. Again like the Bundists, they soon found that reaching and interacting with such a sizeable special constituency forced changes on organizational format which worked to alter their conceptions of socialism in a way that magnified the importance of the ethnic factor.

The initial wedge was the Jewish Agitation Bureau (JAB), which was organized in 1907. The Bureau's mandate was to propagandize and recruit Jewish workers into the ranks of the SP and the trade unions. This organization was hampered and restricted by Hillquit and the Old Guard cosmopolitans. They thought of the JAB as a possible vehicle for the expression of Jewish nationalistic tendencies.[117]

The Old Guard had long held a hostile attitude toward Jewish nationalism and toward Jewish nationalism within the ranks of the socialist movement. This concern and hostility had been exacerbated by the Kishinev pogrom in Russia in 1903 and the wave of pogroms that followed, which heightened Jewish nationalistic feelings among Russian Jews in Russia and the United States. Some Jewish socialists in the two communities, like Joseph Barondess, broke from socialism and moved to Zionism. In New York the executive committee of the SP cautioned Jewish Socialists to stand fast against the appeals of Jewish nationalism that were cascading around them.[118]

The Old Guard also went on the offensive against nationalistic incursions among Jewish Socialists. In 1903 the *Zukunft (Future)*, a Yiddish-language periodical controlled by the cosmopolitans, proclaimed:

The "Jewish Socialists" are quite a new species of humanity, which suddenly emerged after the Kishinev massacre. Most of them believe almost everything that the earlier ones do, except after the Kishinev murders, they began to evoke an undefined "Jewish feeling," began to praise Jewish characteristics as the best and the finest, and began proclaiming that Jewish Socialists must be first and foremost Jews.

Precisely what do they mean by this? What are we to do, and towards what are we to strive as Jews? This they have never specified. They are, therefore, not to be seriously reckoned with as a separate faction, since they have no positive program in their Jewishness. It is a temporary emotion. Such cheap phrase spouting also provides many with an opportunity to gain favor with the common Jewish masses.[119]

The *Zukunft* went on to caustically answer its own question. There was nothing special in the Jewish condition or tradition, it contended, that merited a Jewish nationalistic response, particularly by secular and socialist Jews:

What special demands can it [Jewry] present as a nation? What do Jews have in common besides a synagogue, a mikveh [ritual bath], a chazan [cantor], a shochet [ritual slaughterer], and a solemnizer of weddings? Give Jews civil rights, and what remains of the national demands? The language? The literature? Who is preventing the Jews from using their language and developing their literature, even today and even in Russia, where they have no rights at all? Who is preventing the Jews of New York from having six daily newspapers and four Jewish theatres . . . schools, Kosher meat and everything else? . . . And what more can they request as Jews? What traditions, what special culture, except the Talmudic culture? [120]

The opposition and the rational arguments of the cosmopolitans could not long stem the tide that merged Jewish nationalism with Jewish socialism. It was not only the pogroms that fueled this merger. The Bund and the Bundists also deeply influenced this development. The Bund's departure from the Russian Social Democratic Labor Party in 1903 and its embrace of a uniquely Jewish socialism made a significant impact on the Russian-Jewish immigrant community that closely paid attention to developments in Russia. Then came the arrival of thousands of Bundists and Bundist sympathizers. They brought with them rich experiences of the Bund. They also carried the message that Jewish socialism and Yiddish socialism were not only as legitimate as any other type of socialism but also a form of socialism that merited the enthusiastic support of proud Jews. In the face of these developments and such adversaries, the cosmopolitan socialist leaders were soon forced to retreat.

The defeat of the cosmopolitans was embodied in the JSF.[121] The JSF, established in 1912, stood for those principles that the cosmopolitans had most opposed since their arrival in America. It was Jewish socialism that committed the sin of dividing the Jewish from the non-Jewish socialists. But the cosmopolitans also had other reasons to oppose the JSF. The leaders and activists of this organization were drawn from their opponents among the former Bundists and their sympathizers. In fact the Bundists had been the principal force behind the establishment of the JSF. With the JSF these men had another means at their disposal to challenge the cosmopolitans for leadership of the Jewish Left community.

The Old Guard had another cause for opposing the ex-Bundists and the JSF. From their perspective these recent arrivals were too radical. The Bundists and the others who came after 1905 were individuals fresh from the oppression of the czar's government and fired with the rhetoric and experiences of militant socialism. This became more the case among those who immigrated at the time of the 1917 Russian revolution. The older cosmopolitans had become acclimated to America and more distant from the radicalizing experiences of their youth in Russia. Many had also entered the ranks of the middle class and had become less militant about their socialism. Eventually this would be the same route that the more recent, fiery Jewish immigrants would take as they became absorbed in America and its Jewish community.

The JSF symbolized particularistic Jewish socialism to assimilationist Jewish socialists. Even though a majority of Jews in the Socialist party never joined the JSF,[122] its mere existence brought home to the cosmopolitan Socialist Jews that the ethnic component, the Jewish component, of socialism had to be recognized if they were to maintain a base in the Jewish community.

There was also an ironical quality to their situation and that of other Jewish socialist leaders who came after them. In order to be a leader in the national SP, except for the few who had some overriding positive personal quality, such as Debs, it was necessary to have a base of power. For the Jewish Socialists the base was their ethnic constituency. If they became divorced from this constituency the likelihood was great that they would lose their positions of influence in the national party. They therefore had to follow their constituents in their move toward a heightened sense of Jewish consciousness and Jewish socialism. To stand on a national platform, they needed a Jewish step ladder.

The Old Guard begrudgingly accepted the triumph of Jewish socialism even though most remained in the English-language branches. There were some, like Hillquit and Cahan, who felt continually at odds with this development. They did not want to be identified as Jewish or regional barons in the national party. They wanted to feel free to walk unhindered on the national stage and feared that the rise of Jewish socialism would mean their separation from the mainstream of party life. In time this view was also shared by the former Bundists and Jewish-oriented Socialists who had initially opposed the Old Guard for its cosmopolitan views. As they became more Americanized, David Dubinsky, Sidney Hillman, and Charney Vladeck also

wished to gain access to the mainstream of party life and to the mainstream of American political life.[123]

In the second decade of the 1900s, when Jewish socialism became
more prominent a force, the ethnic divisions and barriers in the party
as a whole were also growing apace. This was the decade in which
Socialists in the foreign-language federations constituted less than a
third of the national SP at the beginning and more than half (53%) at
the end. The recency of the immigration of these diverse nationality
groups and the excitement about political events in their European
homelands, especially among the Russians and Eastern Europeans,
made for heightened ethnic consciousness. These new immigrants
who joined the SP or voted for its candidates were in reality joining or
supporting their own ethnic Socialist party. The insularity of these
foreign-language federations sorely troubled the SP leadership and
then (as we will see below) the Communists, when the situation was
replicated in the Communist party in the 1920s and 1930s.[124]

It was in this period that a boy on the Lower East Side remembered
asking his father: "Would you vote for a Socialist who was not Jewish?" He looked puzzled—then said "no."[125]

The end of mass immigration and the increasing Americanization of
the Jewish community did not eliminate the divisions between Jews
and non-Jews in the SP. These divisions held even as the importance
and usage of Yiddish declined. As the language issue lessened it became clear that there were other factors, primarily organizational and
financial, that sustained these Jewish and non-Jewish distinctions in
the party. The organizational and financial power of the party in the
post–World War I era largely rested on institutions dominated by the
New York Jews. The Jewish needle trades unions were the labor base
of the party. The *Jewish Daily Forward* and other Jewish organizations
such as the Workmen's Circle and the garment unions were its primary source of funds; and the New York Jewish community was its
leading source of votes.

These factors not only made up the SP's organizational and financial base, but, more directly, constituted the power base of the New
York Jewish leaders of the party. It was access to and control over
these Jewish unions, funds, and votes that gave them national prominence in the party. As a group they were not willing to dilute their
power base by sharing their resources without obtaining something in
return.

By the 1930s the distinctions within the New York Jewish Socialists
between the cosmopolitans and the noncosmopolitans had largely
faded away. Time, acculturation, and the existence of a shared power
base had done much to heal this particular division. Besides, each of
the two groups could now claim satisfaction. The former Jewish particularists had their Jewish enclave and Jewish power base. The
former cosmopolitans had their place on the national stage, even if it
was a stage "made in New York." In truth what had happened ran

contrary to the expectations of both the cosmopolitans and the particularists. Instead of being isolated in a Jewish Socialist party, as the cosmopolitans had feared, and instead of being submerged and losing their ethnic identity in an American party, as the noncosmopolitans had feared, the two groups had largely Judaicized the national party.

Norman Thomas and the Jewish Issues

The preeminence of Jews in the SP and the party's dependence on Jewish money and organizational strength could not help but become an issue and source of concern within the organization. The stance of the New York Jewish Socialists within the party in the 1920s and 1930s exacerbated the issue even more. Generally they aligned with the right wing of the Old Guard of the SP. Although the various factions in the SP in the 1930s had a considerable proportion of Jews within them and although the Old Guard consisted of more than New York Jews, the New York Jews and their power base were the principal force within and behind the Old Guard. The "Jewish issue" emerged at various times in the SP in the 1930s (and afterwards). Given the Jewish role and the influence of the party and that Jewish power was concentrated in one faction of a multifaction Socialist party, it was difficult for internal fighting not to take on some sort of Jewish coloration even when the major issues at the root of the squabbling had little to do with Jewish things as such.

As is the case in many political and ideological disputes, the issues became personalized. The major personalities involved in the battles over the Jewish issue were Norman Thomas, Morris Hillquit and Abraham Cahan. Ironically, Thomas had been attracted to the SP by Hillquit about the time of World War I and subsequently was boosted to a major role by Hillquit. By the latter 1920s and the early 1930s the two men had come to regard each other as rivals and threats to the future of the SP. It was in this period that Thomas assumed the position of opposition leader to the Old Guard.[126]

The dispute between these two men came to a head at the SP convention in May 1932. After Thomas was nominated to be the party's presidential standard-bearer, the convention turned its attention to the election of the national chairman, a largely honorific post. The incumbent was Hillquit, who had held this position since 1929 following the death of Victor Berger. Thomas and his allies, particularly the younger, American-born, and more militant Socialists, were opposed to the reelection of Hillquit. They believed that the time had come for a change and that the SP had to break from the restraints imposed upon it by the Old Guard, led by Hillquit. Thomas and the anti-Hillquit factions turned to Daniel Hoan, mayor of Milwaukee, to oppose Hillquit for the party chairmanship.

The struggle to replace Hillquit went beyond the issue of his political beliefs and those of his supporters. It became involved with the

questions of Hillquit's ethnicity and of the national image of the Socialist party. Thomas and other Hoan supporters believed that it was
time to Americanize the party. As one Milwaukee delegate expressed
it, "We want to attend to American problems. We want a national
officer who stays in America. [This is a reference to Hillquit's many
trips to Europe, a large portion of which were party-related.] . . . We
want an American Socialist Party." [127] And, according to a sympathetic biographer of Thomas, Murray Seidler: "The attempt to unseat
Hillquit was apparently part of Thomas' strategy to Americanize the
Socialist Party. . . . Undoubtedly Thomas believed that the
American-born Hoan, the mayor of a large American city, would be a
more appealing figure and a more suitable chairman than Hillquit . . ." [128]

This legitimate political position could, with little difficulty, be interpreted as having anti-Semitic overtones. Indeed, Hillquit and his
supporters made that interpretation and skillfully counterattacked.
Speaking to the issue of Americanization, the long-time leader of the
SP pointed out that he had "converted a good many 100% Americans
to Socialism. My distinguished friend, Mr. Thomas, is one of my converts." He also gave public recognition to the anti-Semitic allegations
in a convention speech prior to the election: "I 'apologize' for having
been born abroad, for being a Jew and for living in New York." [129]

By bringing the anti-Semitic allusion to the center of the convention
stage, Hillquit insured his reelection as party chairman. To vote
against him was to risk identifying the SP as an anti-Semitic organization. [130] As Thomas so aptly expressed it: "Once the anti-Semitic issue
was raised, even though unjustly, I was inclined to think it best that
Hillquit won." [131] It should also be noted that one day after Hillquit's
triumph, his fellow Old Guarders were ousted from their control of
the National Executive Committee by the same convention. [132]

This was not the first time that Hillquit had made allusions to
Thomas' prejudice against foreigners or Jews. In a letter to Algernon
Lee on June 24, 1931, Hillquit surveyed the reasons for his dislike of
Thomas: "It is obvious that Thomas wants to play the role of party
purist and of all men he is less entitled to assume this role than any
other. I cannot forget his several years of wooing 'liberals' and 'progressives,' his moralistic campaign against Tammany graft, *his statement in the press that his name is not 'Thomasky'.* . . ." [Emphasis
added.] [133]

Thomas also clashed with Cahan and the New York Jewish Socialist
establishment on other issues in the following years. Each time he did
so they became further alienated from him and moved closer to breaking with the SP. Thomas' confrontation with them over union democracy is particularly revealing. In his capacity as executive director of
the League for Industrial Democracy (LID) and as the symbol of the
SP, Thomas took open and critical stands against unions which violated the basic tenets of union democracy and socialist principles. For

example, in 1933, in a letter to the labor editor of the *Jewish Daily Forward* he denounced the leadership of the Boot and Shoe Workers Union (AFL) as a corrupt "strikebreaking bunch controlled by a bureaucracy which worked hand in glove with the bosses."[134] At the same time, Thomas praised the United Shoe and Leather Workers Union, a union independent of the AFL. The chairman of the labor committee of the SP of local New York, Louis Hendin, responded to Thomas' charges by asking him to desist from further attacks on the Boot and Shoe Workers Union because the *Forward* (which meant Cahan) was favorable to it.[135]

What really raised the ire of Cahan and the New York Jewish Old Guard was Thomas' intervention and action in a dispute between the left-wing and right-wing furriers' unions in New York City in 1933. In the course of his investigation, Thomas visited the headquarters of the left-wing furriers and then called the fur department of the Needle Trades Workers Industrial Union. Near the building he was recognized and surrounded by a crowd that asked him to speak out on his view of the internecine struggle. Thomas did so, attacking the right-wing International Furriers' Workers Union (IFWU) of the AFL for using injunctions and the police and for entering into an alliance with the Democratic mayor of New York in order to defeat its rivals. He told the crowd that "as a Socialist by no means could I support the attempt to organize labor through Mayor O'Brien, the Police Commissioner and injunctions."[136] That was not a statement delivered in the heat of the moment. In a private letter Thomas wrote about this incident, placing it in a larger context: "The Party in New York officially has shown by the action and lack of action of its Labor Committee and, more recently, by its actions in the Furriers' case, that it is willing to give blind support to AF of L leaders or groups no matter what tactics they use against, let us say, the Communists. I am as much opposed to Communist tactics as any man but we make our talk of class solidarity and of democratic methods plain hypocrisy."[137]

The negative reaction from Cahan's allies in the New York SP to Thomas' intervention in the furriers' dispute was overwhelming. He was accused of being ignorant of the fact that in the past the left wing had utilized police and gangsters against its socialist enemies. The real salvos were fired against the Socialist party leader for undermining the entire Jewish labor movement. Nathan Chanin, a leader of the Jewish Socialist Verband, the Yiddish-language branch of the SP, blasted Thomas on behalf of the right-wing Jewish labor movement:

As to your appearance on the platform of the left wing of the Union . . . it aroused protests among the right elements. After all you are a leading figure in the SP. . . . When I speak of the right elements in our movement, I mean not only the Furriers' right wing [IFWU], I also refer to the ILGWU, the Amalgamated, to the WC [Workmen's Circle], the 'Forward' and the Jewish Socialist Verband. Do you consider all those mentioned labor racketeers? I am certain that you do not. . . . Your appearance before the left wing of the

Furriers Union gave a new hold to such fellows as [Louis] Hyman and Ben Gold [left-wing furriers' leaders], as well as the Communist Party. You gave them new courage in the struggle being waged now, not only in the Furriers' Union but in the entire Jewish labor movement.[138]

By 1936 relations between Thomas and the New York Jewish Socialist establishment had reached a new low. The "Jewish interest," although not at the root of the deteriorated relationship, had by this time become interwoven with other issues. Thomas was increasingly attacked by Cahan's *Forward* and was at the same time, denied access to its pages in order to reply or to state the official position of the SP to the *Forward*'s Yiddish-language readers. Thomas was particularly embittered by this treatment as he ardently wished to use the *Forward* to respond to charges of anti-Semitism being circulated about him in the Jewish community.[139] When the Old Guard officially broke from the SP in 1936, it was the New York Jewish Socialist establishment led by Cahan and Waldman that led the right-wing dissidents out of the party.[140]

These years of hostility and acrimony between Hillquit, Cahan, and the New York Jewish Old Guard and Thomas and his supporters in the national SP took their toll on the historic relationship between Jews and the SP. This tie was further loosened when the Old Guard departed from the SP—further still when the American Labor Party was formed. Not all Jews drifted from socialism and the SP as a result of these factors (and others previously discussed). For many, the party and socialism were too important in their lives; they remained their commitments almost in deference to the legitimacy of their own biographies. However, a large number did leave, and noticeable among them were those who controlled the institutional infrastructure of Jewish socialism—the unions, press, and fraternal orders.

The departure of the Old Guard brought no respite for the Jews who remained in the SP and wished to harmonize their loyalty to the party with their Jewish consciousness. After 1936 the major issue in the party, Jewish community, and nation, became America's response to the forthcoming war. The policy of the SP, as enunciated in its 1940 national platform, was "Keep America Out of War!" Norman Thomas was the driving force behind this policy. For him World War II could only be a repeat of World War I, a struggle between rival imperialist powers. America's entry into the war would, in his view, bring with it "military dictatorship, the regimentation of labor and the ultimate economic collapse that must follow war." [141]

This noninterventionist stance became intolerable to many of the Jews who remained committed to the SP.[142] Each day these Jews and the Jewish community of which they were a part became progressively concerned with the Nazi menace to the Jews of Europe. Yet as this Jewish interest and the consciousness that went along with it became more extensive and intensive, Thomas persisted in his opposition to United States military intervention and to economic and military aid to the British and French. He did, however, valiantly and persistently call for the admission of thousands of refugees, Jewish and non-Jewish, to the United States as a way of saving them from the ravages of fascism. But this was not considered as significant as his opposition to military intervention. And what mattered even more, from the point of view of Jews inside the party and the Jewish supporters outside of its ranks, was that Thomas' position was shared by anti-Semitic isolationists. According to one biographer, Thomas was so consumed with the war issue that "at no time [was he] willing to divorce himself from any but the most extreme anti-Semites so long as they joined him in opposing the war." [143]

The reaction of many Jews and non-Jews to this situation was to sever their relationship with the Socialist party, a move that soon led to the severing of relationships with socialism as well. (It is difficult to remain committed to a principle without an organizational vehicle available to express that commitment.) In the face of Thomas' refusal to modify his antiwar position, the party's Jewish section, formed out of those from the Jewish Socialist Verband who remained loyal to the party after the Old Guard left, disbanded itself. Concerning them, Thomas wrote: "I'd rather have no section at all than one run in the spirit [of intervention]." It was not only the old Yiddish-speaking Socialists who broke from the party over the war issue but also the younger, American-born, and college-educated Jews who had sided with Thomas against the Old Guard in the mid-1930s. [144] Hitler had strengthened their Jewish identities while Thomas had weakened their Socialist commitment. One of their number told (in an interview with me) of how the Nazi invasion of Czechoslovakia in 1938 detonated his Jewish consciousness and led him away from the party:

I guess the turning point for me was Czechoslovakia. I was writing someplace, maybe in the *Socialist Call* . . . what should we do in Czechslovakia? "We, revolutionary socialists call upon the Czech workers to turn the war into a civil war. After you get rid of the lumpen bourgeoisie you can take up arms to fight Hitler." That was the formula. Then when I read it I said, oh no, I am out of my god damned head. This is the craziest advice you have ever given to anybody. You can't expect them to do anything like that. So I said to myself what would I do if I was there. *So I guess that is when I became Jewish.* I wouldn't care who gave me a gun. I wouldn't look at the label on the gun. I wouldn't care who my general would be. I'd just shoot Nazis, that is what I would do. If I was anyplace in the world I would shoot Nazis. . . . I was very sensitive on the issue because I was Jewish. [Emphasis added.]

This was the issue that caused him and others like him to break from the SP.

It was not only Jewish party members who broke with Thomas because of his stance on the war and their feelings about their Jewishness. The Jewish community also broke with the party for these reasons. The low vote that the partys 1940 presidential candidate obtained in Jewish districts is one indication of this. Another indicator was the refusal by the Workmen's Circle to endorse Thomas for president in 1940 or to even meet with SP leaders or discuss the party's position on the war. Poignantly the national executive committee of the WC wrote to Thomas: "We would have liked to cooperate with you now as we did in the past, but, regretfully, our views differ over an issue involving the life and death struggle between democracy and fascist totalitarians. . . . *As Socialists— and, to be frank, as Jews—* . . . it would be preposterous for us to help you spread your 'doctrine' that we consider dangerous and disastrous in the present catastrophe." [Emphasis added.] [145]

By the time that the war came, the SP as a political force was virtually dead. Although it was not only Jews who stopped supporting the SP, their break from the party hurt most as they had been its principal base. In 1939, for example, there were only about 150 dues-paying party members in New York City. In 1940 the presidential vote for the Socialists was 99,557, a significant decline from the 187,500 it received in 1936. In New York State it went from 86,897 to 18,950. In this latter election New York contributed the lowest percentage to the Socialist vote since the elections prior to World War I. In 1942 there were only about 1000 members in the entire SP.[146]

The virtual dissolution of the SP and the obvious cost of taking stands unpopular with the Jewish community did not deter Thomas from continuing to take such positions. His switch regarding the war after Pearl Habor to a policy of "critical support" of the United States did not earn him many plaudits from a nation that gave the president enthusiastic and noncritical support. Similarly, when the national and Jewish community's mood appeared to be highly in favor of punishing Germany severely, Thomas, in the midst of World War II, opposed the massive bombing of German cities and the policy of unconditional surrender. After World War II, Thomas continued to be out of step with Jewish opinion. When the Jewish community was overwhelmingly voicing its desire for a Jewish state in Palestine, the venerable Socialist leader urged the formation of a binational Jewish and Arab state. In 1956 he took a critical view of Israel's participation in the Suez War.[147] All these positions earned for Thomas the enmity of numerous Jews outside of the SP, particularly of former socialists like Cahan, and the displeasure of the few Jews who still claimed membership in the truncated party. Thomas was quite cognizant of this but did not let his Jewish colleagues and constituents deter him from taking the position dictated by his conscience. As he wrote with respect to the 1956 Suez War: "This Israeli business troubles me greatly. I would so like to go along with the great majority of my Jewish friends. Alas, as it seems to me, most of them have a blind spot on this subject." [148]

The Communists and the Jews

From its inception, the Communist party did not have clear and consistent positions on matters of Jewish concern and interest. The reactions of Communist and non-Communist Jews were not the major determinant of these policies. The CP rarely had the luxury of dealing with the Jewish question for extended periods in isolation from other pressing matters. Nevertheless, the policies it adopted and the actions it took that bore on matters of Jewish concern and interest significantly affected the level of Jewish participation in the party and the level of the party's support in the Jewish community.

Communist Party's Drive for Americanization

The CP's interests and Jewish concerns intersected in the course of the party's striving to Americanize itself and broaden the industrial base of its membership. The emphasis on Americanization stemmed from its having come into existence as a predominantly foreign-born organization. The early Communists came almost entirely from the foreign-language federations that had been expelled from the Socialist party in 1919. In the early 1920s about 90 percent of the Communists in the United States had been born abroad.[149]

The leaderships of both the American Communist party and the international Communist movement were very concerned about the predominance of the foreign-born within the American CP. They feared that unless this situation was remedied, the American CP could be stigmatized as a foreign group and isolated on the periphery of American society. The two leaderships realized that if the American CP were to have any hope of becoming a force in American political life, it must reach out and attract native-born Americans and English-speaking persons.

In the 1920s the international Communist movement continually prodded the American CP to become more of an American movement. In 1921 at the Third Congress of the Communist International, the American Communists were told to reach the American masses. Lenin himself advised them to launch an English-language newspaper.[150] In 1922 the Comintern instructed the American CP: "The most important task is to arouse the American-born workers out of their lethargy. The Party must systematically and willingly assist American-born workers . . . to play a leading part in the movement."[151] Five years later the Presidium of the Executive Committee of the Communist International chastized the American CP for its failure to attain adequate contact with the native-born American workers.[152] In 1929 the Comintern again leveled a similar criticism at the American CP.[153]

The Americanization of the CP and its acceptance by Americans as an American institution remained a concern of party leaders from the 1920s through the 1950s. During the 1930s, in the period of the Popular Front, this emphasis was at its height. In its 1936 platform the party declared: "Communism is twentieth-century Americanism. The Communist Party continues the traditions of 1776, of the birth of our country, of the revolutionary Lincoln, who led the historic struggle that preserved our nation."[154] It was in this period that the American flag replaced the red flag at party parades and the Star Spangled Banner was added to the International as the official hymns of party meetings.[155] At times this quest for an American identity and acceptance reached exaggerated proportions. In 1939 a writer in the *Young Communist League Bulletin* seriously declared:

Some people have the idea that a YCLer is politically minded, that nothing outside of politics means anything. Gosh no. They have a few simple problems. There is the problem of getting good men on the baseball team . . . of opposition from other ping pong teams, of dating girls, etc. We go to shows, parties, dances and all that. In short, the YCL and its members are no different from other people except that we believe in dialectical materialism as the solution to all problems.[156]

In 1956 American Communist leaders were still writing and talking about the need to Americanize the party.[157]

However, not all Communists in the United States believed in the necessity to Americanize their party. In the 1920s many of the foreign-born Communists had little regard for the political astuteness of the American masses. How could they make good Communists, the foreign-born contended, when the Americans were so divorced from the events and experiences of Russia? There were also other grounds for opposition to the mass entrance of Americans, as we shall presently see. The structural source of this opposition to Americanization was the foreign-language federations of the CP.[158]

It was therefore logical that one of the first concrete steps the party took in its effort to Americanize itself was the abolition of the foreign-language federations, which occurred in conjunction with the drive to "Bolshevize" the party in the mid-1920s. Bolshevization meant a variety of things. Overall it meant reorganizing the party so that it would be a more unified, centralized, and disciplined organization. With respect to ethnicity, "Bolshevization meant shifting the orientation of the average member from his ethnic group to his working group."[159]

From the point of view of Bolshevization, it was clear that the foreign-language federations would have to go. Their prominence and autonomy in the early 1920s made it difficult for the party to function as a unified organization. In addition, the federations isolated and insulated the members of each—not only from the English-speaking and American born, but also from fellow Communists who belonged to different federations. Federation members tended to be more concerned with events in their homeland or ethnic communities in the United States than with conditions in their shops and factories or with American political life.[160]

The Party was officially Bolshevized in 1925. The language federations were officially abolished and replaced with language fractions that consisted of "all members of the party speaking the same language within a subsection, section or city organization."[161] Unlike the federations, these language fractions were not centralized in the organizational structure of the party. The basic unit was now either a "shop nucleus," composed of members in the same place of employment, or a "street nucleus," also called an "international branch," composed of members in the same neighborhood who were not regularly employed or not employed in an enterprise where there were enough Communists to form a nucleus.[162] Despite their official abolition, however, foreign-language groups successfully resisted and remained alive in one unofficial form or another into the 1930s, much to the consternation of the party's officialdom.[163]

The Bolshevization policy proved nearly disastrous for the party. It caused the departure of too many members. For every seven members that went out, only two came in; to the dissatisfaction of the party, the new members were not very different socially from the old ones.[164] Foreign-language Communists, bereft of their federations, did not feel secure in interacting with Communists who could not speak their language, especially if the language they spoke was English. This reaction was informed by their experience with and location in separate ethnic ghettoes in America. Socially they were not accustomed to interacting with outsiders—nor did they wish to begin doing so even when ordered by the party. According to historian Theodore Draper, "The foreign language members, forced into shop and street nucleui either abandoned them or swamped them."[165]

Most members of the Yiddish-language Jewish Federation responded in a manner similar to other foreign-speaking Communists by abandoning the party. As one former member explained to me: "The autonomy of the Jewish Federation was dissolved, was abolished. And, of course, for the average Jewish worker he would feel himself at home in the Jewish branch where Yiddish was the language. He was not too comfortable in a branch where he couldn't express himself right, understand anything right. So this was one of the reasons you know that about three-quarters of the members left."

Many of those Yiddish-speaking Jews that did not quit the party over the language federation issue continued to behave as Yiddish-language Communists despite the party edicts and organizational forms. In 1928 a CP subsection organizer from New York City complained that "The greatest majority of our Party members are still filled with the Federation ideology and are supporters of their language paper [Freiheit] . . . in my sub-section . . . out of 150 members I found that 60 percent are still reading the Freiheit only, 10 percent reading the Freiheit and the Daily Worker, 25 percent the Daily Worker only, and 5 percent the New York Times and other capitalist papers only."[166]

Political security was another factor beside nostalgia and social security that informed the response of the Yiddish-speaking and other foreign-language speaking Communists to the abolition of the federations. By the mid-1920s the foreign-language Communists had already lived through several periods of police and governmental repression. Relating politically only to their fellow foreign-born ethnics in the language of the Old Country functioned as a means of protection. They assumed that police spies and government agents would not be able to speak their language with any degree of fluency. Conversely, a comrade that spoke English well was suspected as an undercover agent. For example, Max Shactman, who later became a prominent Trotskyist and Socialist, aroused a great deal of suspicion and hostility when he joined the party in 1920 because he spoke English too well.[167] Ten years later this fear of outsiders, particularly English-speaking ones, was still alive. In some areas it actually succeeded in paralyzing party activities. The situation in upstate New York in 1930 was described by a CP official: "Whenever an American joins the Party there is open suspicion that he is a spy. Five or six comrades suspended from the Party—American comrades, and everyone was suspected of being a spy and when I came there and started my work, they nearly accused me of being a spy because I took the part of these comrades."[168]

The CP's position on the abolition of the language federations was essentially correct but at the same time reflected ignorance about the ethnic nature of American society. A political party that had ambitions to play a major role in American politics could not rely on foreign-speaking members closeted in their ethnic organizations. It also, in practice, could not rely on these federations because of their inability or unwillingness to strive for political leadership within their respective foreign language communities. To become a significant political force, particularly after the cessation of mass immigration in 1924, the party had to do as much as possible to reach the English speaking and the American born. But, the problem here was that ethnic divisions and loyalties continued to obtain for decades and up through the present. The "American" ethnic identity and community, even for a second and third generation American, simply did not have the saliency of other ethnic identities and communities. To break party members or prospective members from their ethnic groups, particularly for those in the working class, in essence meant to cast them into some kind of ethnic limbo in which the party itself took on the attributes and functions of an ethnic group. Not very many Americans were willing to leave the security of their ethnic communities for some uncertain destination. This dilemma arising from the ethnic nature of American society was not fully appreciated by CP leaders or theorists.

The party's practical criticisms of foreign-language federations was also borne out in the 1930s with the opportunity stemming from the

Depression and the ferment among workers and unemployed for Communists to play significant political roles. But the foreign-language Communists who had resided in their ethnic enclaves typically did not rise to this occasion in the manner expected by the CP's officialdom. In essence, the foreign-language speaking Communists chose their ethnic comrades over their factory peers. Long years within the confines of a tightly knit language group had transformed many of them into cautious, conservative "social" Communists whose primary identity was derived from their fellow ethnics. One party official, writing in the internal CP publication, *Party Organizer*, provided a summary description:

. . . low level of political understanding, irregular attendance and participation in the so-called general Party work, a shirking from any activity that is not within the narrow shell of "society doings" . . . their activities in the main are in that of the old line federationalism. That is, limited to associating with their own friends, seeing the same faces year in and year out, having a dance here, a lecture there and of course giving financial support to their language press."[169]

This negative view of party officials toward the Communists involved in foreign-language organizations was not unique to them. Others noticed it also. One study of the United Automobile Workers (UAW) in the 1930s claimed that the foreign-born Communists in their foreign-language federations "remained insulated within their own language group and although their rhetoric was revolutionary, they almost never engaged in practical work in relation to other groups."[170]

Bolshevization of Communist Jews was not, however, limited to attacks on the foreign-language federations. Bolshevization also meant changing the occupational composition of the American CP. From the point of view of both the Comintern and the leadership of the American CP, the party had too many workers from the light industries and not enough from the heavy, basic ones. Or, looking at this problem in another way there were too many (Jewish) needle trades workers and not enough (Christian) coal miners and steel workers.[171] According to Benjamin Gitlow, the CP's vice-presidential candidate in 1924 and 1928: "The Comintern insisted that the working class base of the Communist Party must be radically changed from a preponderance of Jewish needle trade workers to non-Jewish workers employed in basic and mass production industries."[172]

Bolshevization and the emphasis on shop and factory nucleui was seen as a way of correcting this distortion. After Bolshevization the situation had not only failed to improve, it had worsened. The needle trades workers, comprising 9 percent of the party's members before the reorganization, constituted 21 percent after it. Conversely, the percentage of metal workers dropped from 15 to 11 between 1925 and 1928.[173] This unintended consequence arose because the party's primary source of strength in the basic mass industries, where Jews were few, was due to their foreign-language members. Since these same members contributed most to the exodus from the party after the reorganization of 1925, the party's existing strength in the basic industries immediately suffered a noticeable drop.[174] Thus industrially the party, due largely to its policy of Bolshevization, became more Jewish than it had been earlier in the twenties.

The CP in the interwar years was never able to establish the type of membership base envisaged by American and Comintern leaders in 1925. It was also unable to move into non-Jewish occupational arenas in a way that had a significant impact in reducing the proportion of Jews among its members. In fact, the percentage of Jews increased after 1925. In 1931, some six years after Bolshevization, only 16 percent of the CP's membership were factory workers; more than half of these were in factories with 100 or less workers. Needle trades workers in this year constituted the second largest occupational grouping in the party (618), the first being building workers (636). Five years later the situation had not changed appreciably.[175] The factories in which the majority still worked employed 100 or less workers. Those in light industries outnumbered Communists in basic industries by a margin of more than two to one (10,474 to 5000). There were even more professionals in the party (6221) than workers in basic industries.[176] In 1944 the party had approximately as many professionals in its rank (2,003) as steel workers (2,110). But the number of self-employed businessmen was even greater (2334) than the figure for steel workers.[177] Again, it is clear that the CP, despite its professed intentions in 1925, did not succeed in diminishing the proportion of Communists located in light industries and non-working-class occupations. Or, to express it in other terms, the party, despite its professed intentions and desires, almost reluctantly continued to be relatively successful in recruiting in occupational areas where Jews were disproportionately located.

The Jewish Search for Christians

The Communist party throughout most of the interwar years, especially prior to the latter 1930s, devoted relatively few resources to building its strength among Jews. The party appeared to act as if Jewish support could be taken almost for granted or the disproportionate number of Jews within it were an embarrassment.

One CP action that had the affect, whether intended or not, of blunting Jewish membership or support involved the geographical and ethnic placement of party organizers and cadres. The Communist leadership tended to remove Jewish cadres from "Jewish work" and from areas of Jewish population concentration. Instead of propagandizing and recruiting among Jews, these cadres went to such places as Ohio, New England, and Michigan to organize and propagandize among non-Jewish factory workers—not garment workers. A member of one such cadre sent to the party's New England district, an area containing only a handful of Jews, critically commented on this situation (many years later in an interview with me):

I knew nothing about New England. And here I was assigned to give guidance to textile and shoe workers. . . . Shoe workers are not Jewish and textile workers are certainly not Jewish and these were the two major industries at the time [early 1930s]. . . . I knew nothing about their industries and I learned as much as I could. But I grew up in the Bronx. I knew the Bronx and they knew me. *These were my roots and I could have been more effective among the people from which I came, who were very much like me.* [Emphasis added.]

This particular organizer was later dispatched to work among blacks in Harlem.

Knowledgeable informants have cited various reasons for dispatching Jewish cadres and functionaries to non-Jewish settings. Each sheds some light on the CP's attitude toward its Jewish members, or at least on the Jewish members' attitude toward and perception of the party's stance vis-à-vis Jews. According to the benign view, the distribution of Jewish cadres was almost solely determined numbers and available resources. In an interview with me, a member of such a Jewish cadre who had been dispatched to Ohio, expressed this viewpoint:

I would say that more Jews than any other nationality in the Communist Party [were removed from their ethnic communities for Party work]. In order to achieve a breakthrough in those areas where the Party was nonexistent or very weak, *you had to perforce send Jews because the Party didn't have anybody else. And if they were active in Jewish organizations, they would have to be taken out of Jewish organizations.* In order to make initial breakthroughs in areas where we were weak [which were non-Jewish areas for the most part], the Party had to use Jewish forces as it had no one else or it had very few others and in doing this its purpose was not to set out consciously to weaken its Jewish work. To the extent that it had to assign forces that were in Jewish work, to that extent, I suppose ipso facto you weaken your position [among Jews]. [Emphasis added.]

Others have confirmed this perspective by pointing out that it was not only a matter of quantity but also of quality. The best of the Jewish cadres were removed from Jewish work and Jewish population concentrations, thus weakening the party in those areas. The party itself openly admitted that it weakened itself among foreign-language Communists by taking the most able members from them.[178] The pressure from the party leadership to broaden its ethnic and industrial base—that is, to move out to non-Jewish groups and industries—led to a situation in which Jews became devalued relative to other ethnic groups. As one former Jewish functionary cynically expressed it: "If you were to put it in terms of values, one black recruit was worth ten Jewish recruits in the party at that time [1930's]. Consciously, one Italian was worth at least a half dozen Jews." This view-point was not unique to the CP. Other Left parties also shared this perspective on blacks, Italians and Jews, although the proportions may have varied.[179]

A more psychopolitical position was also put forth by the people I interviewed. They argued that the social-class backgrounds of the Jewish activists contributed to their being sent into non-Jewish arenas. These activists and the party were sensitive to the fact that they tended to come from petty bourgeois origins. As one interviewee expressed it: "We had to be apprehensive about that; concerned about it; we had to fight against and overcome the negative aspects of this kind of petty bourgeois Jewish background."[180] This member of a Jewish cadre in the 1930s and 1940s went on to amplify the position: " No one spoke specifically of Jewish petty bourgeois attitudes, but it was clearly implied. Jews were predominantly a merchant people, and when they joined the Party they had that past to overcome . . . there was no question about it that the attempt was being made to overcome one's background, the negative features of one's background, the trading origins of the Jew by involving the [Jewish] people who came into the Party in the general activities of the party [and in non-Jewish arenas]."

Work among non-Jewish proletarians in basic industry then became one way of repressing this Jewish background and establishing an identity more in line with the idealized notion of what a Communist should be. Whether this was a conscious or subconscious policy of the party is probably not as important as the feeling of the Jewish activists that it was the correct thing to do. When they went into the non-Jewish hinterland or into Harlem, they went with an obvious zest. In many ways they resembled their nineteenth century Jewish revolutionary counterparts in Russia who longed to radicalize, to go amongst and to be accepted by the non-Jewish Russian populace.

The Communist party of the United States, by sending Jews to politicize and live among non-Jews, was following the example of the Comintern, who, in dispatching its agents to a particular country never sent a national of that land to be its representative: "To send agents who were natives would, to be sure, have had the advantage of utilizing persons familiar with the local scene. But this advantage was consciously foregone in order to make sure that the agent was maximally protected from commitment to, or contamination by, local affiliations."[181] Thus, by separating its agents from their ethnic or national group and from their families, both the American CP and the Comintern could be more assured that their representatives would be dependent on the organization and therefore more likely to remain loyal to it.

In the case of the American Jewish activists in the CP, particularly the native-born and highly acculturated ones, this policy could also be interpreted as a way of de-Judaizing or deethnicizing them while contributing to the Americanization of the party. Sending these Jewish cadres to non-Jewish areas away from family, friends, and contacts with Jews was bound to weaken their Jewish ties and identities. After all, they would be spending years during which they would be relating almost only to the non-Jews whom they were politicizing and to their fellow party members. As previously indicated, the party contributed to making the national organization more balanced and more representative of America by transferring the cadres from Jewish arenas where the party was relatively strong to non-Jewish areas where it was weak.

But the locational consideration was only one aspect of the formal and informal process of de-Judaization. Another important facet of this process was the adoption of party names, which many members of the CP's cadres, both Jewish and non-Jewish did. This stemmed from both revolutionary tradition and reasons of personal security. The CP was not alone in this as Trotskyists (along with other radical organizations) also went in for the assumption of party names. The interesting thing here, though, is the character of the names that these Communists assumed. To my knowledge, none of the Jews in the party who changed their names chose ones that sounded Jewish. The transformation of Irwin Granich to Michael Gold is probably the most atypical. More typical were changes like Jacob Liebenstein to Jay Lovestone, Sol Regenstreif to John Gates, and James Wechsler to Arthur Lawson. (The same transformation occurred in the case of Jewish movie stars, e.g., Daniel Kaminsky to Danny Kaye and Bernie Schwartz to Tony Curtis.) In each case the new names were more Anglo-Saxon than the old. Party officials did not directly tell them that their new names had to be American sounding. There seemed to be an unspoken assumption by their party superiors as well as by the Jewish functionary or activist that the new name was to be more American than the old. (Non-Jewish functionaries also Americanized their names.)

These were various reasons for this type of name change. Political expediency was one reason advanced by several of the people I interviewed. An American or non-Jewish name, according to one former functionary who changed his own name, "avoid[ed] your being labeled or branded Jewish from the very beginning in a place where there was considerable anti-Semitism." (In the Soviet Union, Jews aspiring to high level party or governmental positions were advised to Russify their names.) [182] Such a name change can also be seen as a way of hastening assimilation and integration into America. There was little reason why devoted Communist Jews should want to reconstruct a new Jewish identity. The party, to whom these Jews were committed, made clear that it valued an American identity both for itself and its members. Conversely, it did not give things Jewish a very positive evaluation, at least before 1935 or so. Similarly, the institutions of American society stressed the virtues of assimilation and Americanization. "What is the point," said one Jewish ex-member of the Communist party I interviewed, "of creating a conspicuous Jewish name, a Jewish identity if it doesn't mean anything, either politically, socially, historically, or intellectually." Jewish self-hatred, either latent or manifest, may also have been involved, but it is difficult to estimate the weight of this factor.

In any event, the Americanization of names was undoubtedly viewed positively by the party. If the CP's appeal and recruitment procedures could not bring in as many non-Jews and native-born Americans as desired, then through name changing and other socialization procedures it could internally produce the image, if not the substance, of the type of ethnic organization desired. Again, the CP was not unique in this regard. An informant, a former Trotskyist, told of the reaction within his Trotskyist group to a recruit who did not adopt an "appropriate" party name. The name he originally chose was a Jewish sounding one (Rosen), and the leaders of his group strongly suggested that it would be better if he chose another, more suitable, name. He did. What makes this particular case so revealing is that the individual in question was an Italian-American. Perhaps for him, a Jewish name was a mechanism for assimilating into the dominant culture of his party group.

The Communist Party and Zigzagging on Jewish Issues

An overview of the Communist party's attitude toward things Jewish and the Jewish question indicates that the party did little or nothing to attract Jews to its banners prior to 1935. If they were attracted before, it almost had to be due to reasons that were not directly associated with their Jewishness. In fact, it might almost be said that throughout most of its first decade and a half of existence, the party (whether by design or accident) was relatively successful in reducing the size of its Jewish membership and constituency, which it had inherited from the Socialist party and from Russia through immigration. The treatment of the Jewish-language federation and the dispatch of Jewish activists to non-Jewish areas could be interpreted as part of an overall pattern of hostility toward Jewish interests and culture, although at no time in the party's existence could it be described as anti-Semitic. However, on occasions, it appeared to come very close.

The aforementioned elements were not the only ways in which the party revealed its negative attitude towards things Jewish. Attacks on rabbis and organized Judaism in the 1920s were another way. These attacks took the form of "widespread Communist anti-religious propaganda . . . conducted on the eve of the Jewish holidays, with mock Seders on Passover and anti-religious affairs and lectures on the Day of Atonement."[183] The *Daily Worker* and the *Freiheit* contributed to this campaign. The following item, which appeared on November 30, 1925, represents a sample of the *Daily Worker's* contribution: "The Talmud Torah is a free religious school where ancient rabbis are poisoning the minds of working class children, as most of them are, with religious ceremonies and superstitions and the dead Hebrew language. Knowing the value of such organizations for keeping workers mentally enslaved, the rich Jews are donating freely. They have plenty of cold cash exploited from their workers, either in factories or in their stores and pawn shops." Later, on September 28, 1927, on the occasion of Rosh Hashonah, one of the holiest days in Jewish religion, the *Daily Worker* announced: "A holiday is a holiday but why such a rebellious people as the Hebrews should tolerate the exorbitant admission fee of $10 to hear a cantor roar in a synagogue when they could hear as much noise for nothing in our print shop when the *Daily Worker* is being gotten ready for the press, is beyond my understanding." Judaism, it should be noted, was not the only religion to be attacked by the Communists in this decade. The assault on Judaism was only a part of the largest campaign that both the American and Soviet Communist parties waged against organized religion in general.[184]

The CP, because of its stance on religion, made it difficult for believers and near believers to belong to or support the party. In fact, during the 1920s some CP members were even expelled for attending religious services. Thus the party drew and constructed hard and fast barriers between those who chose to associate with religion and those who chose to associate with the party. Unlike the SP, the CP had no desire to tolerate within its ranks the Jew who went to both party branch meetings and the synagogue. Only the most secularized Jew could feel comfortable in the midst of a party with such a stance. This in turn meant that the CP, in effect, wrote off a large segment of the Jewish community who were in one way or another still positively tied to Judaism. Years later, it was to realize this error and change its ways.

Judaism was not the only aspect of Jewish life toward which the CP openly showed its disdain. In the course of the hard line Third Period, the party, intent on "proletarianizing" and Americanizing itself, demonstrated a negative attitude toward Jewish culture, history, and Yiddish. Jewish subjects and themes were deleted from the curriculum and books of the IWO *shules*. Jews eminent in the field of Yiddish culture and letters, if not Communists, were periodically singled out for attack by the *Freiheit*. On various occasions within this period, the usage of Yiddish at party functions was actively discouraged. (At the same time, however, the party allowed the Yiddish Workers University to function even though the curriculum was conducted in Yiddish and included Jewish history.) The Jewish Bureau of the National Committee, a linear descendant of the Jewish-language federation, was limited by party decree to work with only those Jews active in Yiddish work. Jews in the Jewish trade unions and other sectors were placed beyond its sphere.[185]

It is difficult to estimate the amount of support that the party lost in the Jewish community as a result of this Third Period attitude toward Yiddish and Jewish culture. Certainly it did not improve the position of the party among Jews, especially Yiddish-speaking ones, not already committed. In the 1930s the party, not unexpectedly, had great difficulty increasing its membership among Yiddish-speaking Jews.[186] Again, as with its stance toward Judaism, the CP further isolated itself from the Jewish community and provoked the hostility of this same community toward the party and toward Communism. And again, as with Judaism, it later changed its attitude toward Yiddish and Yiddish culture.

The party's attitude toward and position on the *yishuv* and Zionism in the 1920s and 1930s (prior to the Stalin-Hitler pact) was probably the most costly of all its actions bearing on Jewish interests and concerns. The CP, USA informed by Bundist and socialist traditions as well as by the policies of the Soviet leadership, was generally hostile to Zionism and, to a lesser extent, the yishuv as well. Zionism however did not occupy much of its attention throughout most of the 1920s. And the *yishuv,* when dealt with during this same period, was usually treated in a nonhostile fashion. However, in the latter 1920s, as the CP moved into its Third Period, Zionism and (to a lesser extent) the *yishuv* came in for more frequent and more hostile attention. The Arab uprising in Palestine in August 1929 and the assault on Jews gave the party a dramatic opportunity to demonstrate its hard line anti-Zionism. The *Daily Worker* took the lead in denouncing Jews in Palestine for their support of Zionism and British imperialism while the Arabs, who were killing and wounding Jews, were treated as heroes engaged in a struggle of national liberation. The *Freiheit,* which at first denounced the attacks against the *yishuv* as a pogrom and the work of hooligans, quickly fell into step with the *Daily Worker* and Communist policy. The *Freiheit* staff even conducted a mock public trial in September 1929 to convict the *Jewish Daily Forward* for betraying the Palestinian Arabs. For a time thereafter the Jewish Communists held meetings to rally support for the party's anti-Zionist position. At these gatherings there were banners that read "Zionists slaughter Arab men, women, and children!"[187] The reaction of the Jewish community to the Communist party's and the *Freiheit's* treatment of the Arab assaults on the Jews of the *yishuv* as noted earlier was overwhelmingly negative. The *Freiheit* was boycotted and lost much of its advertising. Its staff was expelled from the Yiddish Writers Union for anti-Jewish activities. In addition, Communists experienced difficulty in obtaining halls for meetings in the Jewish community. Those meetings that were held were either attacked or threatened with attack by enraged Jews.

This type of reaction was not limited only to Jews outside the party. Some Jews inside the CP and in its orbit disassociated themselves from Communism and the party. Leftist Jews in needle trade unions deserted the party. Several prominent contributors to the Freiheit severed their connection with the paper. All in all, the Communist treatment of the Arab uprising in 1929 proved a very costly venture in terms of the party's relationship with Jews.[188] Years later in 1957, the Freiheit editors and staffers admitted that the paper had made an error in its handling of this issue, and the 1929 Arab attack was once again labeled as a pogrom.[189]

The objectively anti-Jewish policy of the CP ended and was largely reversed as the party moved into the period of the Popular Front in the mid-1930s. This change was due in part to a sentiment within party ranks that it had gone too far in alienating the Jewish community. However, a more important cause of the change was the desire of the Soviet Union and the Comintern to forge a broad coalition of forces in order to combat the growing menace of fascism. Jews and the Jewish community were designated to be part of this grand Communist-inspired coalition. As John Arnold, editor of the newly formed New York CP publication, Jewish Life, candidly expressed it in 1937: "The Democratic Front in New York is not possible without the Jewish people."[190]

Guided by the spirit of the Popular Front, party leaders and spokesmen now sought ways to break out of the isolated position that their hard line policies had placed them in with respect to the Jewish Community and other ethnic groups as well. The Central Committee in June 1937 pointed to the new directions toward which the CP should move with respect to nationality groups: ". . . engage them in the American class struggle . . . it is necessary to smash through the sectarian isolation of our national bureaus and national press [for national read foreign language]; to throw them into the center of the community; to utilize its national traditions, issues, and peculiarities; to appeal to its national pride and culture, to find thus the road to Americanization, Americanization in our sense of the word."[191] He went on to say that the Jews were "among the largest and most important" national groups that the Party had to reach. In a resolution of the CP's Tenth Convention in 1938, the party officially went on record about the importance of recruiting and politicizing Jews and other nationality groups: "This convention raises before the entire Party the urgent necessity of speedily effecting a decisive turn in all phases of Party recruiting and mass work among the national groups and organizations, in the first place among the Italians, Poles, Jews, South Slavs and Spanish speaking peoples."[192]

The comrades concerned with Jewish work took the opportunity to chastize the party for its years of neglect and of hostility toward the Jewish community. As Moissaye J. Olgin, editor of the Freiheit said to the delegates of the Tenth State Convention of the New York State CP,

"Comrades, we . . . managed to alienate the Jewish masses. More than that, we managed to convey . . . that the Communists are hostile to Jewish national aspirations." [193] And, in a resolution adopted by the New York State Committee of the Communist Party entitled "Problems of New York Jewry and the Tasks of the CP," the party criticized itself for its failure "to appeal to the Jewish people in a given territory on the basis of the specific problems that agitate the Jews of the neighborhood or to properly combat anti-Semitism among non-Jews." [194]

Internally, long neglected political work in Jewish organizations and the Jewish community was resumed with vigor. The English-language *Jewish Life* was launched in order to reach the non-Yiddish reading Jews. And increasingly after 1935, the vanguard party of the working class directed appeals not specifically to the Jewish working class, but to the Jewish community. For the first time the Yiddish-language arm of the CP, the Jewish Bureau, according to Melech Epstein a former writer for the *Freiheit*, "was given the green light to approach the American born on *Jewish issues*." [Emphasis added.] [195] The CP in its time of need, in its quest for mass Jewish support, was now approvingly approaching Jews as Jews. This approach was exemplified by the position taken by the secretary of the New York State Jewish Bureau of the CP when he wrote (in 1937): "The Jewish people in the United States, regardless of their language and place of birth face common problems which are definitely noticeable in every locality with a Jewish population. Problems such as anti-Semitism, social discrimination, economic discrimination and the existence of forces that tend to stifle the creative expression of the Jews, tend to make of the Jews *an oppressed minority*." [Emphasis added.] [196]

The party's change in position and actions as related to Jews, Yiddish culture, and other Jewish matters in this Popular Front period (and afterward), as contrasted to what took place in the Third Period, bordered on the dramatic. Jewish culture and Yiddish in particular were extolled. Communist analysts and writers plumbed through the Old Testament to extract for public praise instances of the Hebrew people's courage, particularly when these could be portrayed as examples of a people's liberation movement. In this regard Passover, Channukah, and Purim were especially favored. The Communists moved so close to Judaism that at least one branch containing a large proportion of Jews cancelled its meetings if they conflicted with Jewish holidays. [197]

In line with the Popular Front ethos, it became necessary for the party to modify its position on the *yishuv* and Zionism. Too many Jews had too much of an emotional commitment from the party's point of view for it to remain adamant in its treatment of the *yishuv* and Zionism. But, despite the demands of practical politics, changes in the line toward Zionism were not quickly forthcoming. Jewish Communists, the older ones who carried with them Bundist and Bolshevik traditions of hostility toward Zionism, had a good deal of difficulty reversing a lifetime's stand because of immediate political necessity. However, even they were forced to bend to new political realities.

This new line became publicly evident in 1936. The party's spokesman on Jewish matters, J. Sultan, while continuing to voice opposition to Zionism, stressed the need for Communists to make quite evident that they, too, were concerned with the well-being of the Jews in Palestine. In an article in the journal *The Communist* Sultan wrote: "In the past, we have made the mistake that our struggles against Zionism took on a form which made the impression of a struggle against the Jews living in Palestine. This was not correct. We must make clear, even more than we have, that Communists are not against the Jewish masses living at the present time in Palestine; that the Communists are fighting for the lives and the interests of the toiling Jewish masses everywhere—in Palestine, as in other capitalist countries where they are being oppressed by imperialism, anti-Semitism, fascism, etc." At the end of his article Sultan made clear that the party was willing to change its attitude toward Zionism: "we are even ready to make united fronts with those Zionists that are willing to struggle for the interests of the Jewish masses in this country or abroad."[198]

In the several years following the publication of this new line, the party gradually moderated its position on Zionism. After the invasion of Russia by Germany in 1941, the CP became much friendlier, not only to Zionism, but also to the idea of a Jewish state. In 1944 Alexander Bittelman, the most prominent Jew in the CP, publicly praised the Zionists while condemning the *Forward* and the Bundist-oriented Jewish Labor Committee for propagating anti-Zionism. He even proudly claimed that there were Zionists in the *Morning Freiheit* Association, the association that formally owned the *Morning Freiheit*.[199] Then in July 1945 the convention of the Communist party of the United States solemnly revolved that it: "Support[s] the just demands of the Jewish people . . . for the rebuilding of a Jewish national homeland in a free and democratic Palestine in collaboration with the Arab people."[200] The party, indeed, had come a long way toward a rapprochement with Zionism.

However, if there was any one uniquely Jewish issue that stood out for special treatment and positive attention by the CP, that issue was anti-Semitism. The party had always been opposed to anti-Semitism, but after 1935 this position was advanced to the forefront and became the focus of a major multifaceted campaign. The Communist party emphasized the fact that the Soviet Union had eliminated anti-Semitism and made it illegal. In the United States the CP in 1936 was alone of any political party to publicly advocate that the propagation of anti-Semitism be barred by law.[201] Communists who ran for public office in Jewish districts in those heady days made anti-Semitism one of their major issues and points of identification with the Jewish community. In 1938 the *Freiheit*, in its coverage of Israel Amter's campaign for Congress declared: "Vote for Amter and Beat Anti-Semitism."[202]

It was not only domestic anti-Semitism that the Communists fought. The fight against Hitler and fascism was also carried out in this same context. In its opposition to the Nazis, the CP may have been the most militant public force in the Jewish community. The party led street demonstrations and marches when others focused on boycotts, petitions, or prayer days in synagogues.[203]

This pro-Jewish policy and the Communist party and the Soviet Union's militant attacks on anti-Semitism and fascism bore fruit among Jews in the 1930s and 1940s. One result was the virtual end to its isolation in the Jewish community. During the war, for example, the Jewish People's Fraternal Order of the IWO was admitted as an affiliate of the American Jewish Congress and the American Jewish Conference, an organization "set up by the major Jewish organizations to represent the point of view of American Jews in the postwar settlement."[204] Communist Jews also worked together with non-Communist Jews in the Jewish Council for Russian War Relief.[205]

This near end of the Communists' isolation among American Jews, together with the party's pro-Jewish policies, encouraged and facilitated the movement of Jews toward the CP. This is evidenced by voting and membership statistics (previously discussed). Jews in white-collar and professional positions whose careers were impeded by anti-Semitism were attracted in relatively large numbers to an organization that they believed was ardently fighting anti-Semitism. Numerous Jewish writers, artists, and intellectuals, like Daniel Boorstin, the historian, and Jerome Robbins, the choreographer, also came to the party because of its stands on anti-Semitism and fascism.[206] The literary historian Daniel Aaron wrote: "As the threat of Fascism mounted, lending support to ideological anti-Semitism in the United States, Jewish intellectuals [and not only they] naturally gravitated to a movement most vociferously committed to anti-Fascism and to the socialist state which alone seemed able and willing to check Nazi expansion."[207]

However, one major deviation from the Communist party's general support for Jewish issues and interests in this period, beginning in the mid-1930s, was caused by and coincided with the Nazi-Soviet nonaggression pact and lasted from its signing on August 24, 1939, to the time Hitler invaded Russia on June 21, 1941. The agreement between the hated Nazis and the Soviet Union shocked the Jewish community and almost wiped away the previous gains that the Communists had made among American Jews: "The reaction was volcanic . . . Jewish Communists were met by their shopmates with the Nazi salute and a 'Heil Hitler.' "[208] The scene in the *Freiheit* offices as word of the pact first became widespread has been described as follows: Sam Lipzin, a leader of a Communist faction in the Amalgamated Clothing Workers of America, rushed into the office to declare to the *Freiheit's* editor, Paul Novick, that ". . . the workers are making a revolution against us. They are driving us out of the market. What has Stalin done to us? Why did he sign the Pact? Everything we have built up in the last twenty years has been destroyed. I tell you, we are going to be stoned." Novick responded by throwing him out.[209]

The Communist party then proceeded to compound its difficulties in the Jewish community by pursuing a political strategy that dovetailed with the pact. It adopted a policy opposed to American intervention and of anti-British neutrality with respect to the belligerents. The party tried to sell this line to American Jewry. In May 1940, in a pamphlet entitled "The Jewish People and the War," Earl Browder declared: "This war is an imperialist war, and the Jewish people have nothing to gain from an Allied victory, just as they have nothing to gain from a victory by Hitler."[210] It was the Zionists in alliance with British imperialism who pushed for American involvement in the war contrary to the best interests of the Jewish masses, according to Novick.[211] The overwhelming Jewish vote (approximately 90 percent) for the "war monger" FDR in 1940 clearly demonstrated that the Jewish masses did not buy this Communist line.[212]

Relatively few Jews already strongly committed to the CP broke with it because of the pact; but some defections did occur, including writers, trade unionists, and members of the IWO.[213] One group of IWO dissidents formed the Committee of Action of the Members of the International Workers Order to protest the drastic change in policy of both the Communist party and the IWO—which followed suit. They felt strongly as Jews that Jewish interests had been sacrificed upon the altar of organization and political expediency: In their appeal to Jewish members of the IWO, they argued: "There is a loyalty which we must put above all things—a loyalty to the ideals of freedom and democracy and to the war against Nazism and its allies which are enemies of freedom and democracy, enemies of the Jewish people. To support the Stalin-Hitler agreement means the betrayal of the ideals of freedom of the working class and humanity; and it also means the betrayal of the ideas and interests of the Jewish masses."[214]

In most cases, again however, the Nazi-Soviet pact did not cause Jews loyal to the Communist party to sever their ties to it. Their faith in the Soviet Union was so prominent a feature in their lives that this one event was not sufficient in itself to make apostates out of them. A good deal of rationalization took place in their own minds to justify continuing allegiance to a movement that ostensibly aligned itself with the major enemy of the Jewish people. The position and feelings of these Jews with respect to the Stalin-Hitler pact was revealed to me by former high-level party officials (in the course of interviews). As one such person said: "I didn't like it. As a Jew my rationale was that Russia had a great many Jews and anything that would prevent a war against Russia that would endanger these Jews was good for them and therefore was something that I could support. . . . [Also] my thinking then was that it was good for socialism and, therefore, by extension to the Jews."

Another former high-level Jewish functionary writing in his memoirs about the period said: ". . . our faith held. The Soviet Union could not be wrong. It was still the socialist fatherland, the only force that could save the world from catastrophe. We managed to submerge our doubts. . . . The popularity we enjoyed in the days of national unity was important and immensely satisfying, but it had to yield to loyalty to the Communist line. It was a testing period in which we developed the ability to function as a militant, disciplined body, unmoved by mass hysteria."[215]

It is also interesting to note the views of a prominent party personage of Jewish ancestry—one who remained within the Communist party until his death. This individual [whom I interviewed in the national CP headquarters] was undoubtedly providing me with the official or at least quasi-official position of the party at this time (1975) to the Nazi-Soviet pact: "You see we accepted the non-agression pact as a necessary action by the Soviet Union to prevent this gang up on it [by the Allies and Hitler] and we considered this [the pact] to be as much in the interests of the Jewish people as anyone else."

There are indications that Communist party functionaires and activists harbored doubts and were uncomfortable about supporting the party's anti-Allied, anti-interventionist line. (Unfortunately this assertion is based on the retrospective statements and writings of informants.) It was not an easy matter to be abruptly transformed from a growing movement closely aligned to a popular national administration and, for the Jewish comrades in particular, a movement that was taking them toward the mainstream of the Jewish community to a party isolated from public support, especially in Jewish areas. These men may have been Communists but at the same time they were Jews. Their Jewish consciousness had been raised by party propaganda, their own activity in Jewish areas, and the Hitlerian menace to their fellow Jews abroad. In addition, many had families containing nonparty members with whom they maintained contact. One Jewish functionary described his feelings during the period of the pact: "Once I dared to speak on the Lower East Side, and the crowd was in an ugly mood. They listened in pain, however, as I retraced the appeasement history. No one would contradict me. Yet I could establish no bond with the people, for it was only part of the story, and I could feel the ache of uncertainty that continued for years to torment me and many of the comrades."[216] The argument that the Soviet partition of Poland (contained in the pact) was aimed at the protection of Polish Jews carried little weight among Jews, perhaps even among those very Communist Jews who advanced it.[217]

The Communist Party leadership did seem to be sensitive to the fact that its antiwar line was not being readily accepted by the Party faithful. "In this crisis, a tacit acceptance or even complete silence was sufficient for the party, as long as the individual did not come out publicly against the pact."[218] It also did not go out of its way to needlessly antagonize the membership by slavishily copying the Russians when they made drastic public relations mistakes. For example, on October 9, 1939, *Izvestia* printed an editorial on the war containing the statement: "One may respect or hate Hitlerism just as any other system of political views. This is a matter of taste." The *Morning Freiheit* and the *Daily Worker* both "tactfully deleted the phrase from their coverage of this editorial."[219]

Hitler's invasion of Russia on June 21, 1941, followed less than five months later by the Japanese attack on Pearl Harbor "liberated," to use the word of one Jewish CP interviewee, the American Communists. Once again they were reunited with the Roosevelt administration and in accord with the mainstream of Jewish public opinion. One Party leader described the situation:

With the invasion of the Soviet Union . . . everything changed. Overnight the "war" became a just war. . . . After Pearl Harbor, most Americans were disinclined to rake over the past; . . . the people gave warm support to the government program of all-out aid to the Soviet Union. In this atmosphere tensions dissolved rapidly and the overriding popular sentiment was for unity. We, too, felt the flush of patriotism and the resurgence of the anti-fascist feeling. It was a wonderful relief to share the people's enthusiasm for Churchill's Britain. . . . It was a wonderful feeling to walk the streets, to share the popular concern with the battle at Smolensk . . . and to hear Stalin referred to as "Uncle Joe." I will never forget the meeting at which Johnny Gates announced that he had volunteered for the Army and saluted the flag. [Both of Gates' actions were spontaneous. In addition he led the Communist meeting in the singing of the "Star Spangled Banner" while literally draping the American flag around his body.] It released a tremendous emotional feeling, as though by this exhibition we were atoning for the sins of the past.[220]

The CP recouped much but certainly not all of the losses it sustained during pact period by its vigorous support for the war effort and its drive for national unity behind Roosevelt. This was also true in the Jewish community. Once again the CP and the Soviet Union claimed to be in the vanguard of the struggle to save Jews. Soviet victories were portrayed as Jewish victories. Even the execution of two popular Bundist Polish leaders, Henryk Erlich and Victor Alter, by Stalin in December 1941 did little to detract Jewish support from the Soviet Union or the CP. At the war's end, despite the continued emnity of the American Jewish Committee, the Jewish Labor Committee, the Workmen's Circle, and the Jewish Daily Forward, there appeared to be no Jewish issue of major consequence capable of arousing the hostility of the Jewish masses to the CP.

The Communist Party and Jewish Issues After World War II

If there was any one party position that ensured Jewish good will after the war, it was the one dealing with Palestine. During World War II the CP had edged nearer to the endorsement of some kind of Jewish state in Palestine. In those years the party campaigned for Jewish support behind the slogan A Jewish National Homeland in Palestine. In 1946 in the wake of the reaction to Browderism and to the ideological "softness" of the former general secretary, the party, under William Z. Foster's leadership, drew back from its wartime position and took the opportunity to clarify its new Fosterian line on Palestine:

The Marxist position on the question of a Jewish National Homeland in Palestine is: (a) That only an independent Palestine will create the conditions for the free, national development of the Jewish Yishuv, which will thus realize its equal national rights side by side with the Arab people whose free national development in a united Palestine will be assured by the guarantee of the equality of national rights; (b) That this calls for Arab-Jewish struggle against all schemes for the partitioning of Palestine, since partition would make impossible any free national development of the Jews and Arabs in Palestine . . . ; (d) That the realization of the national rights of the Jewish Yishuv *will create a national homeland for the Jews in Palestine*. It will not be a homeland for the Jewish people of other countries.[221]

Even this Fosterian hard line stance on Palestine was light years away from the party's prewar position.

This 1946 definition of the CP's attitude toward a Jewish national homeland soon was modified due probably to pressure from the Soviet Union. On May 11, 1947, in an address before the General Assembly of the United Nations, Russian Foreign Minister Andrei Gromyko informed the world and the American Communist party of the thinking of his government on the issue of a Jewish national homeland: "The fact that not a single Western European state has been in a position to guarantee the defense of the elementary rights of the Jewish people or compensate them for the violence they have suffered at the hands of the Fascist hangmen explains the aspiration of the Jews for the creation of a state of their own. *It would be unjust not to take this into account and to deny the right of the Jewish people to the realization of such an aspiration* [emphasis added]." Gromyko went on to advocate the establishment of "one dual, democratic Arab-Jewish state." But, he said, "if Arab-Jewish relations are 'so bad' that this is impossible, that there be established an independent Arab state and an independent Jewish State."[222] By 1948 the United States CP, together with the Soviet Union, had become ardent public supporters for some form of a Jewish state in Palestine.

All of this was not just a public relations gambit, at least as far as the American Communists and especially the Jewish ones, were concerned. An important indication of the private nature of this commitment was the debate within the Morning Freiheit Association prior to the United Nations' vote on Israel. The debate concerned the future status of Jerusalem, but the discussion and its outcome reflected the feelings of those present on the larger question of Israel too. A majority of the Association who participated in the debate, according to Alexander Bittelman a participant, "wanted Jerusalem for the Jews, for Israel."[223]

After the establishment of Israel, Communists publicly pointed with pride to the role that the Communist movement had played in its creation. The shipment of Czechoslovakian arms to the Jewish forces, party spokesmen noted, had made a major contribution to the success of the Jews' armed struggle during a period in which the United States officially imposed an arms embargo to the area. In addition, the Soviet Union had been the first country to give *de jure* or legal recognition to the fledgling Jewish state. The attitude and position of the Communist party in 1948 to Israel was reflected to some extent in the platform of the Progressive Party in the course of the American presidential elections of that year. In its Israel plank, the Communist-endorsed Progressive Party called for:

. . . the immediate de jure recognition of the State of Israel . . . a Presidential proclamation lifting the arms embargo . . . [the United States to] safeguard the sovereignty, autonomy, political independence, and territorial integrity of the State of Israel . . . generous financial assistance without political conditions . . . [and] the United States Government to provide immediate shipping and other facilities for the transportation of Jewish displaced persons in Europe who desire to emigrate to Israel.[224]

This pro-Jewish and pro-Israel policy won considerable support for the CP in the Jewish community, as evidenced by the relative success of Communist-backed political candidates in Jewish areas from the mid-1940s through 1948 (see the earlier discussion in this chapter). The only time in these years that a Communist-endorsed candidate actually won in a Jewish congressional district occurred in 1948. This was the (aforementioned) by-election in the Bronx's Twenty-fourth CD. In the election the ALP's congressional nominee, Leo Isaacson, triumphed while running on a pro-Israel platform against a backdrop of the Soviet Union's advocacy of Jewish statehood.[225] No other party's platform even came close to matching the Progressive Party's pro-Israel stance.[226]

It was in the 1948 presidential election that the most (electoral) fruit was reaped for the Communist party's pro-Jewish and pro-Israel policies. Again, this was probably the high point of the Jewish support for Left- or CP-supported candidates. Communists directed appeals to Jews to vote for Henry Wallace because, as *Jewish Life* expressed it: "a repetition of the Hitlerite holocaust can be prevented only by a strong movement gathering about . . . Wallace."[227] Considerable attention was paid to Wallace and the Communist support of Israel, and much was made of the fact that the Truman Administration, in contrast, had done so little for the Jewish state, before or after its formulation.[228] One non-Communist political analyst, Samuel Lubell, later claimed that: "Truman's shilly-shallying on Palestine was the immediate cause of the large Jewish [Wallace] protest vote, [although] several additional factors are involved. . . ."[229] Again, one-third of the Wallace votes are estimated to have come from Jews.

The Jewish response to the Communists from the mid-1940s through the early 1950s can also be gauged by public opinion polls. The results from these indicate that the Jews as a group were always more favorable to the Communists or more supportive of their constitutional rights than either the Catholics or the Protestants. For example, in 1946, when given a choice of four statements dealing with United States-Soviet relations running the spectrum from very positive to very negative, 32 percent of the Jewish respondents chose the most favorable alternative: "It is very important to keep on friendly terms with Russia and we should make every effort to do so." Only 13 percent of the Christian respondents selected that alternative.[230]

Communist policies toward Jews and Israel not only made a positive impact among Jews outside of the Party, they also had a similar effect on Jews within its ranks, even those who long considered themselves cosmopolitans, internationalists, or Americans. One Communist who had been active primarily in non-Jewish work described the party's Jewish stand as producing within him a feeling of "coming home." Other Communist Jews also felt that party policies were facilitating their coming home to their Jewish people.

It was not only Communist policies as such that facilitated this "homecoming" for Communist Jews. The actual implementation of these policies and the social and historical context in which they occurred were also important factors. In the course of carrying out the Communist-inspired drive for Jewish unity, Jewish Communists were expected to and did interact with non-Communist Jews. This interaction amidst the backdrop of the Hitlerian threat, increased their Jewish consciousness. Bittelman told of what such contact did for him:

My Jewishness, I felt, was being deepened and enriched in a national sense. I was conscious of feelings of admiration for some of the nationalist-Zionist leaders of the [American Jewish] Conference. This was true especially of . . . Rabbi Stephen S. Wise. Many a time . . . I would find myself thinking such thoughts as these: if Jews like Rabbi Wise and his friends can work together for the good of our people with Salzman [head of the Jewish People's Fraternal Order], myself and our other friends, there must be something very deep and basic that is common to all of us. . . . The national content of our Jewishness, with all that it meant in the past, present and future, was assuming ever larger importance in my thoughts and feelings.[231]

Bittelman wrote those words almost two decades after the experience, so there is the possibility that time and his expulsion from the Communist party in 1960 may have colored his retrospective views. However, he was not the only one to report such experiences and feelings. The growth of this special Jewish feeling that stemmed from intensive interaction with fellow Jews was also facilitated by a set of special circumstances that obtained for only a few years, primarily the war years. For virtually the first time in their party lives, Communist Jews were expected and encouraged to be Jews, to relate to Jews, and to think of the Jewish people and the Jewish culture in a positive light. At the same time, non-Communist Jews, with some notable exceptions (e.g., those close to the Jewish Labor Committee, the Workmen's Circle, and the *Forward*), accepted their Jewish credentials and agreed to work with them in an all-Jewish context. Thus, for a brief but important period, Communist Jews found their identities as Jews and as Communists to be compatible, if not mutually supportive, and that these identities were acceptable to many of their ideological and ethnic kinsmen.

Finally, the role of the Holocaust proved significant in itself and in association with all of the above-mentioned developments. The destruction of European Jewry stimulated the Jewish consciousness of the Jews within the party just as it did for those outside of it. It made even the hardened assimilationist and cosmopolitan more receptive to a Jewish identity for himself, to the need to keep a collective Jewish identity alive, and to the need to support the creation and maintenance of a Jewish homeland. Again, during this period, the Communist party not only permitted Jewish Communists to express these feelings, but actually formulated policies in support of these uniquely Jewish interests.

The Postwar Cooling-Off Period

This homecoming period was short-lived. By the end of 1948 and the beginning of 1949, it once again became difficult for Communist Jews to be both Jews and Communists. Both the Jewish community and the Communist party, together with the Soviet Union, took actions and formulated positions that made the statuses of Jew and Communist virtually incompatible.

With onset of the Cold War, the Jewish community became, as did other segments of American society, caught up in the postwar anti-Communist fear. The institutions and organizations of American Jewry moved to isolate and purge actual and suspected Communist individuals and Communist groups from the Jewish community. In 1949 the Jewish People's Fraternal Order (JPFO) was expelled from the American Jewish Congress and later from the Jewish Community Councils around the nation. Communists and alleged Communists and their sympathizers in the employ of Jewish organizations were identified by zealous Jewish Communist hunters, and pressure was exerted (with some measure of success) to have them fired or politically sanitized. It did not seem to matter how active they were as Communists or how nonsensitive their jobs were. In the spirit of the times, various Jewish fraternal organizations also passed resolutions denouncing Communism.[232]

There were various Jewish and non-Jewish reasons why the Jewish community took these measures against real and imagined Communists in their midst. The leaders of the Jewish community and those that perpetrated and pushed for these measures were generally middle-class Americans who were as concerned as their non-Jewish counterparts with the Communist menace. But they also had Jewish reasons. One was the knowledge of the Soviet Union's destruction of Jewish leaders and cultural institutions. As knowledge of this spread and was publicized in the Jewish community, Jewish hatred of Russia and, by association, communism and Communists, mounted.[233] Another and probably more important reason was the fear of Jews and the Jewish community of being tarred with the brush of Communism, especially in the latter 1940s and early 1950s.

The fight against the stereotype of Communist-Jew became a virtual obsession with Jewish leaders and opinion-makers throughout America. Theirs was not a totally irrational paranoia. For example, in 1947, Representative John Rankin asserted in the House of Representatives:

I want to read you some of the names. . . . One of the names is June Havoc . . . her real name is June Hovick. Another one was Danny Kaye, and we find out that his real name was David Daniel Kaminsky. . . . Another one is Eddie Cantor, whose real name is Edward Iskowitz. . . . There are others too numerous to mention. They are attacking the Committee [House Committee on Unamerican Activities] for doing its duty to protect this country and save the American people from the horrible fate the Communists have meted out to the unfortunate *Christian* people of Europe. [Emphasis added.][234]

The arrest and trial of Julius and Ethel Rosenberg as atomic spies in the early 1950s further exacerbated the fears of Jewish establishment leaders. Their paranoia was heightened even further by the public campaign to save the Rosenbergs. It was a campaign in which the Rosenbergs' supporters drew much attention to their Jewishness imputing, if not charging, that the harsh treatment of the Rosenbergs was due to their being Jewish. The tendency of Jewish leftists to draw attention to their Jewish backgrounds when called before investigating committees did not do much to calm the anxieties of the Jewish communal leaders.

The mainstream Jewish leaders in the face of this felt compelled to alter what they felt to be the negative and near subversive image of Jews. Thus, in addition to purging Communists and fellow travelers from positions within the Jewish community, prominent Jewish defense organizations took steps to establish their own, as well as the Jewish community's, anti-Communist and American bona fides to the American public in general and to the official investigating committees in particular. In 1953 pursuant with these aims, the Anti-Defamation League of B'nai B'rith, the American Jewish Committee, and the Jewish War Veterans volunteered their cooperation and files to the House Committee on UnAmerican Activities (HUAC). When Julius and Ethel Rosenberg were convicted of conspiracy to commit espionage, Jewish organizations warned American Jewry to be on guard against what they considered to be a Communist-inspired campaign to save them. Indeed, spokesmen for the National Committee to Save the Rosenbergs were literally chased out of Jewish centers and synagogues and could find only a very few rabbis to assist in efforts to save the Rosenbergs. Even after they were executed, a leader in the struggle to save them was denied membership in a synagogue until he admitted that he had been wrong about the Rosenbergs.[235]

Commentary, a highly respected journal of ideas and opinions subsidized by the American Jewish Committee, was rigorously edited to ensure that nothing that appeared within it could be in any way construed as favorable to Communism. The editor, Elliot Cohen, also became more conscientious in selecting for publication extreme anti-Soviet and anti-Communist articles. This was, as his successor wrote, ". . . part of a secret program to demonstrate that not all Jews were Communists—even though, as all the world knew but as *Commentary* would have folded before admitting, Jews were disproportionately represented in the Communist Party."[236]

This concerted effort against Communism in the Jewish community did achieve a measure of success. Communist and alleged Communist groups were isolated, and Communists and fellow travelers had a great deal of difficulty finding employment in Jewish organizations and institutions. Communists and Communism were now definitely beyond the (Jewish) Pale. The campaign also achieved more than this. In that period of national and (Jewish) community trauma, the line could not be drawn against Communists and Communism alone. Soon individual Jews an Jewish organizations eschewed the public espousal of Left, Socialist, or controversial positions and issues lest this be construed as being Communist or pro-Communist actions. Jewish centers were advised by the National Jewish Welfare Board to bar not only Communists but controversial speakers as well. Even the League for Industrial Democracy, an organization closely associated with militant anti-Communist Socialist and ex-Socialist Jews took pains to point out that it was never a socialist organization, even during the period when its official name was the Intercollegiate Socialist Society. At the same time, few within the Jewish community publicly complained of the violations of individual civil liberties by the various governmental committees seeking out "subversives." There would be an occasional voice of protest or a gesture, such as when the Conference of American Rabbis, a Reform group, unanimously passed a resolution denouncing Senator Joseph McCarthy or when a Jewish Young Men's Hebrew Association would open its doors to the folk singer Pete Seeger.[237] But these were all too few.

During this same period, especially from the end of the 1940s through the middle of the 1950s, the Communists made it increasingly difficult for Communist Jews to remain loyal to the party. The most important impediment to the maintenance of this ideological commitment was the overt anti-Semitism of the Soviet Union and other Communist countries in Eastern Europe. From 1948 to 1956 the Soviet government was transformed in many Jewish Communist eyes from a stalwart defender of Jews to one of their major enemies. In 1952, 14 leading Czechoslovak Communists were placed on trial, charged with espionage and treason. Eleven of them were of Jewish origin, a fact that the prosecution did not hesitate to make reference to throughout the trial. Soon after there followed similar trials and purges of Jewish Communists in East Germany, Hungary, and Rumania. In 1953 in the Soviet Union, shortly before Stalin's death on March 5, a number of Jewish doctors were arrested and accused of plotting to murder the top Soviet leaders. The Russian authorities alleged that virtually every major Jewish organization in the world was implicated in the plot. Then in 1956 the full scope of the Soviet repression of the Jews was revealed in the Polish Yiddish-language Communist newspaper *Folkshtimme*. (This revelation came after several years during which Jewish Socialists and anti-Communists had made similar accusations.) The Communist government of the USSR, a country in which anti-Semitism was illegal, had, beginning in 1948, liquidated and imprisoned leaders, intellectuals, writers, artists, and actors of the Jewish community solely because they were Jewish. Jewish culture had been systematically all but eliminated with the forced closing of Jewish cultural institutions, theatres, and publications.[238]

Those revelations sent waves of shock and revulsion throughout American Jewry, eradicating for many any vestige of a positive association between communism and the Jews. Undoubtedly for many this feeling also extended by implication to socialism, even though Jewish Socialists and former Socialists had been among the most prominent opponents of the Communists in the nation at large as well as in the Jewish community.

The reaction of Jews in the Communist party was initially and unanimously one of horror and indignation. Afterwards the responses tended to vary along lines of age, class, and degree of assimilation and acculturation. The younger and more middle-class Jews, the American-born Jews, and the more highly acculturated Jewish Communists were more critical of the Soviet Union on the issue of anti-Semitism than were the older, working-class Communist Jews embedded in their Yiddish-Communist subculture. This was reflected in the differential treatment that this issue received in the *Daily Worker,* which was largely in the hands of the "Acculturationists" and the *Morning Freiheit,* the organ of the "Yiddishists". It was also reflected in the fact that more of the Acculturationists than the Yiddishists chose this issue as a reason to break with the party, both numerically and proportionately.[239]

The *Folkshtimme* revelations, against the backdrop of Nikita Khrushchev's speech denouncing Stalin and the Russian invasion of Hungary, commenced or hastened for many of the acculturationists and some Yiddishists a process that led them from Communism back to their Jewish roots. An acculturated American and a CP leader who had been jailed under the Smith Act in the early 1950s poignantly described the process—a description that applied to his peer group and generation:

How could we reconcile anti-Semitism with communism? How could we identify it with the party of Lenin, with the Soviet Union? Our whole world was falling apart. I had been a Communist for all these years [about two decades], and my proudest feeling was that the party encompassed all humanity, that only through communism could we abolish the hatreds and divisions among people. As an American and a Jew, I had become a Communist, and in time these parts of my social being had become fused. Now the unity had been shattered; as some of us sensed forever. . . . Now I would think of my Jewish origins, the emotions engendered by the plight of the Jews in Europe, the epic of the Warsaw Ghetto, and know with certainty that whatever my political beliefs now or in the future, *I was a Jew.* [Emphasis added.][240]

Another in the same group and also CP leader who had been imprisoned under the Smith Act asserted that the cumulative impact of the exposure of the doctors' plot as a fraud, the anti-Semitic revelations, and the Khrushchev speech produced in him a determination "to defend Jews, to defend Israel."

An example of the reaction of the more acculturated and English-speaking rank-and-file Jewish Communists and pro-Communists concerned with Jewish affairs is provided in the letters from the readers of *Jewish Life.* This periodical verified the *Folkshtimme* reports of the atrocities against Russian Jews and Jewish culture in the Soviet Union. The letter writers poured out their hurt, anger, and frustrations on the Soviet government, the United States Communist party, and the editors of *Jewish Life.* They voiced their feelings of betrayal, their intentions to cancel their subscriptions, and their plans to leave the Communist party.[241] One loyal Jewish Communist was driven to a nearly heretical position: "I understand for the first time, the Zionist sympathies of the mass of Jews: the belief that there can only be safety from persecution in a land of the Jews."[242] Another reiterated and elaborated on this theme: ". . . revelation of the impotence of the Soviet Communist Party in the face of a dotard and his criminal coterie make me wonder whether Zionism is not after all a safer theory, since,

no matter what other faults it may have, it cannot blunder into genoci-
dal anti-Semitism, a very important consideration for a Jew, for of
what value can a bright new tomorrow be to an annihilated Jewish
people." [243]

The older, foreign-born, Jewish Communists, although condemna-
tory of Soviet anti-Semitism, did not quickly follow the course of their
younger, more assimilated, ethnic counterparts. The older Yiddishists
also broke from the party, but their break was more gradual. Initially
they tried to construct arguments and rationalizations about how the
oppression of the Soviet Jews and their culture was an aberration from
the essence of the Soviet Union and of communism. Individuals like
Beria, chief of the Soviet secret police, and Stalin were blamed, and
their actions were interpreted as being deviations from the norms of
the Communist system. The *Morning Freiheit* even tried to demonstrate that the West was the real culprit. It was the West's support of
Hitler and other counterrevolutionaries and spies before and after him
that had made the Soviet authorities overly sensitive to real and
imagined internal adversaries. And the *Freiheit* pointed out that, although the destruction of Yiddish-culture institutions in the USSR
was wrong, it should be weighed against the positive things that the
Soviet Union had done on behalf of Jews. In an editorial on September
23, 1956, about five months after the *Folkshtimme* had published its
story on Soviet anti-Semitism, the *Freiheit* declared: "However important the preservation of facilities for the creative cultural expression
and development of the rich cultural heritage of the Jewish people is,
and its importance cannot and must not be underestimated, the physical preservation of the Jewish people is even of more decisive, indeed
ultimate, importance. As the Jewish addage goes, better a beardless
Jew than a beard without a Jew . . . [The] Soviet government . . .
saved millions of Soviet Jews and some 400,000 Polish Jews from ex-
termination by the Nazis."

Three months later the tone of the *Morning Freiheit* had altered.
The paper told its readers that, although Soviet officials had promised
to reestablish Yiddish-language and Yiddish-culture institutions,
months had passed without any action in that direction. And this failure opened up the possibility that anti-Semitism in the Soviet Union
was not just an aberration of a few individuals. However, the Yiddish-
language paper quickly assured its readers: "There cannot be any
question of political anti-Semitism in the Soviet Union, that is, of an
anti-Semitism encouraged or even tolerated by the State. The fact is
that Jews hold prominent positions in numerous fields beginning with
that of the government itself." [244]

It is interesting to observe that while the Yiddishist Jews around the
Freiheit were at the forefront of the attempt to mute criticism of the
Soviet Union and keep its Jewish readers loyal to the CP, the more
Americanized Jews who largely controlled and wrote for the *Daily
Worker* were at the center of the party's critics of the Soviet Union and

in the vanguard of its dissidents. It was the *Daily Worker* that printed the full text of the Khrushchev speech, thereby authenticating it beyond doubt, contrary to Soviet wishes. It was the *Daily Worker* that condemned the Soviet invasion of Hungary as an act against socialism and a betrayal of socialist principles. It was the *Daily Worker*, according to John Gates who was editor at the time, that immediately and directly "expressed its 'indignation, anger and grief' " concerning Soviet anti-Semitism after the *Folkshtimme* article was published and "its 'dissatisfaction' that the Soviet leaders had not offered any explanation of what took place." [245] Finally, it was, with some exceptions, the Jews centered around the *Daily Worker*, who openly broke, largely as a group, with the party.

Why the difference in reaction between the acculturated and Yiddishist Jews in the Communist party to the charges of Soviet anti-Semitism? There is, of course, no single reason. One of the most important is the role of subculture. The older Yiddish-speaking Communist Jews who were still in the party by the latter 1940s were a highly select group. Many had spent most of their adult lives within the confines of a working-class, Yiddish-speaking Communist subculture. They had existed for so long in this self-sustained and self-enclosed world that even evidence attested to by Communists of heinous crimes against Jews by Soviet authorities was insufficient to cause them to seriously question, much less attack and turn on, their lifelong commitment.

The consequences of breaking with their subculture over events that occurred so many thousands of miles from their everyday lives made such an act difficult to contemplate much less consummate. They knew, for example, that once they abandoned the party, the remaining comrades would shun them. For persons in their late-middle and old age, the thought of being ostracized by lifelong friends could not have been pleasant. And it was not only the social consequences with which they had to concern themselves. For many, their jobs, shops, and places of residence in some ways hinged on remaining within the Yiddish Communist subculture.

Another problem was the alternative. Where would they go and who would accept them after they broke with the party? The other Yiddish-speaking arenas in American society were controlled or dominated by their lifelong enemies, the social democrats around the *Jewish Daily Forward*, on the one hand, and Orthodox Jewry, on the other. To gain their acceptance would not only involve breaking with the Communist party but also denouncing a lifelong commitment to other principles, which they may not have been as ready to do. For these various reasons, then, the Yiddish-speaking old timers remained within their secure and comforting world throughout the mid-1950s.

The situation of the American-born and assimilated Jewish Communists was different. As a group they had spent less of their lives in the Communist party and were not as totally encapsulated in a Communist subculture as their elder, more Jewish counterparts. As American-born, college- or near college-educated, and occupants (or potential occupants) of middle-class positions, they had more meaningful contact with non-Communists and different points of view than did their elder coethnics. Many had also been separated from Communists and the world of communism by their army experience during the war or their prison experience after it. Thus through non-Communist books and personal relationships they became more cognizant of positions and attitudes other than the party's. Similarly, those who edited and wrote for the *Daily Worker,* by virtue of their position, were forced to come to grips with non-Communist ideas, interpretations, and personalities on a continuing basis. This tended to open them up to alternative perspectives that had intellectual credence.

Many from this heterogeneous acculturated group had also been initially and strongly attracted to the Communist party because of its role and the Soviet Union's in the struggle against anti-Semitism and the fight to save the Jews during the war. Thus, when the Soviet government was revealed to be guilty of anti-Semitism, they lost one of their major reasons for remaining in the party.

The experience of one American-born, college-educated Jewish Communist, related to me in an interview, gives insight into what was happening among his peers. He decided to join because of his wartime experiences, particularly his work with concentration camp inmates. He felt that the CP would be the political organization most effective in ensuring that the concentration camps and the Holocaust would never be repeated. After his military duty, he entered graduate school in a midwestern university, where he became active in the Labor Youth League (LYL). The Slansky [Czech] trials of 1952, however, set into motion a chain of developments that led to his eventual withdrawal from Communism:

I became aware of the Slansky trials and was really shocked. When I tried to raise questions about it with other LYL members, I found a lack of comprehension about what I was saying. They began to get uneasy about me and my questions; and I, with their reaction to me. I was fearful because almost all of my friends were in the LYL, and I had built my whole life around it. I knew what would happen if I continued to raise serious questions. And I didn't want to risk being ostracized until I knew that I was completely right. Then the doctors affair happened and I was convinced. I resigned and threw myself into my graduate studies.

Older people who more embedded in the Communist movement needed more evidence to make their move. One 1930s recruit from CCNY, who had so high a position in the party that the United States government imprisoned him as a leader, cited his reactions to those same events. This CP leader had a rich party life and more experience as a Communist to fall back upon than did the LYL member in interpreting the trials of the Eastern European leaders and the Soviet

Jewish doctors' plot. Regarding the trials, he told me in an interview: "It was shocking and difficult to believe but not impossible. In Spain [where he had fought in the Civil War] . . . Franco boasted about the fifth column operating within our ranks. . . . So that we were prepared to believe that the enemy had its agents working at all times within the ranks of the Communist Party. So while it was shocking . . . we were ready to believe it and above all if Stalin said it, it must be right." In prison when he learned about the charge that Jewish doctors had planned to murder Soviet leaders, he had no difficulty accepting it: "I had not even a single doubt in my mind. My first reaction was those son of a bitch Jews. [I had] the feeling of guilt, you know, look what they had done to us Jews. [I believed that] the whole bunch should be castrated and killed. It was almost like all Jews were a bunch of bastards." However, the exposure of the doctors' plot as a fraud followed by the *Folkshtimme* revelations and the Khrushchev speech proved too much even for this CP leader. His intellect, sense of justice, and his Jewish consciousness were subjected to too many violations, by the actions and words of his party, the Soviet government, and his hero Stalin. Then in 1958, after more than 25 years with the Communist party, this leader resigned and developed a strong Jewish identity which encompassed a fierce loyalty to Israel.

Again it should be stressed that the Jewish issues were not the only reason for the break of many Communist Jews from the party. The Jewish reasons cannot be totally isolated from everything else that was occurring or had occurred in the late 1940s and 1950s in and out of the party. Undoubtedly for many already discontented on other grounds, the Soviet Union gave them further incentive to leave as well as provided them with legitimation in their own eyes for the move. For other CP members, their Jewish identities strengthened by the Holocaust, the rise of Israel, and other considerations were too strong to allow them to remain within a party tainted with the sin of Soviet anti-Semitism.

The importance of the issue of Soviet anti-Semitism was heightened for Jews within the Communist movement by the actions of the Federal Bureau of Investigation. It was in this period that the FBI mailed anonymous letters to Jewish members of the party specifying the anti-Semitic practices of the Soviet Union.[246]

Jewish issues as factors inducing splits in the party did not end in the latter 1950s. The most important, after the issue of Soviet anti-Semitism, was Israel and Jewish nationalism. When the Soviet Union and the Communist party of the United States began to change their attitude toward Israel, they embarked on a course which led them into conflict with Jewish public opinion in general and Jewish Communist opinion in particular. The beginning of this development was most prominently expressed in the course of a meeting in May 1950 of members of the party's high-ranking National Committee, including General Secretary Eugene Dennis and Jewish Communist functionaries active in Jewish work. The Jewish Communists were severely taken to task for their shortcomings in a variety of areas but most specifically with respect to "bourgeois-nationalism."

> The National Committee is of the opinion that one of the most serious tasks confronting our Jewish comrades is to organize a more effective and consistent campaign against all expressions of bourgeois ideology that are penetrating the Jewish masses. . . . The main ideological danger among the Jewish people that must be exposed and fought against is the mounting influence of pernicious bourgeois nationalism. We cannot close our eyes to the fact that the cannibalistic fascist Hitler policy of the extermination of the Jewish people stimulated the growth of Jewish bourgeois-nationalist influences. These influences were further accentuated by the establishment of Israel as a state. . . . this bourgeois-nationalist influence on broad sections of the Jewish people penetrates into progressive and Left circles and brings its pressure to bear among some comrades in the Party. Today, many comrades in mass organizations, as well as some of the *Morning Freiheit* staff, tend to capitulate to this pressure of bourgeois-nationalism and do not fight it effectively. . . . the penetration of bourgeois-nationalism is seen in the J.P.F.O. children's schools. . . .[247]

It is important to note that this May 1950 attack on Jewish bourgeois-nationalism was aimed not only at the growth of Jewish and Communist Jewish support for Israel. It was also, in a less direct fashion, establishing the correct line with respect to the future of the Jewish community and Jewish people. Throughout the report on this meeting, it is clear that the party was stepping back from its 1946 position on the Jewish question. In 1946, in its "Program for Survival: The Communist Position on the Jewish Question," authored by Bittelman, the United States CP became the first party in the history of the international Communist movement to advocate the survival of the Jewish people as an ethnic entity. Implicit in this 1946 stance was the understanding that a Jewish community would and should persist within a socialist society.[248] Now, in 1950, the party leaders indicated that some form of assimilation, perhaps similar to the model of the Russian Jews, might be the most adequate solution to the Jewish question.

Tensions within the party between the leading Jewish activists and the leadership over the Israel and Jewish questions mounted after 1950. As Israel veered closer to the United States and the Soviet Union closer to the Arab countries, the Soviet government and the United States CP, while defending Israel's right to exist, grew increasingly critical of the Jewish state's domestic and foreign policies. And, in each of the Arab-Israeli wars from 1956 to 1973, both the United States CP and the USSR took positions hostile to Israel and in favor of the Arab combatants. Coincidental with this development, the party's stance on the future of Jewry hardened. According to one interviewee, "For a couple of years nobody used the word 'survival' in the Jewish Left [Communist Left]."

Those policies, coupled with the revelations of anti-Semitism in the Soviet Union, placed the CP on a collision course with many of its Jewish members, particularly those actively involved with Jewish work. After 1956 the *Morning Freiheit* cautiously and ambivalently increased its criticism of Soviet policies affecting Jews. In 1957, as mentioned above, policy-makers of the *Freiheit* openly began to question the stance that the paper had taken at the time of the Arab attacks on the *yishuv* (specifically Hebron) in 1929. There was an admission that it had been a mistake to portray these events "as an expression of the Arab national liberation struggle."[249] The collision between the Communist party and many of the remaining older and prominent Jewish Communists finally occurred in 1967 and 1968, prompted by the Six-Day War of June 1967, the third Arab-Israeli conflict since 1948.

Both the *Morning Freiheit* and the *Jewish Currents* (formerly *Jewish Life*), the two major expressions of the older, less acculturated and Yiddishist Communists and Communist-inclined Jews, openly contravened the party line on the Six-Day War. (By 1958 the Jewish Currents was independent of Communist Party Control, although some of its editors continued to remain in the party.) The CP defined it as a war of aggression. The Jewish Communist editors of the two publications defined it as a war of self-defense. In addition, the *Morning Freiheit* also aroused the hostility of the CP by opposing the organization's demands that Israel immediately return all captured Arab land. The Yiddishists of the *Morning Freiheit* and the English-speaking, Jews of the *Jewish Currents* had found and crossed their Rubicon.

But the Communist Jews around those two periodicals did not regard the differences as important enough for them to leave the party, and especially in an open and defiant manner. But this was not the viewpoint of the Communist party leaders, who felt that the *Morning Freiheit* and the *Jewish Currents* had gone too far, not only on the Israeli issue but on at least three others as well. Early in 1968 the party's leadership took the rare step of sending to the general membership a letter in which it attacked the *Freiheit* and *Jewish Currents* for significantly deviating from the line of the CP on four grounds.[250]

The first (not necessarily in order or in order of importance, as I have not seen the letter) concerned Israel. According to a major party figure whom I interviewed, the *Freiheit*, and by implication the *Jewish Currents*, has "more and more adopted the line of the Zionists and abandoned the line of the Communist Party." The second charge focused on the periodicals' position on the Jewish question in general and on the Soviet-Jewish situation in particular. The party accused them of being too critical of Russia's treatment of its Jews. One party official stated that Paul Novick (the *Freiheit* editor) was an antiassimilationist in general and had specifically accused the Soviet Union of engaging in the forced assimilation of Russian Jews. The third charge involved the New York City teachers' strike. The periodicals were accused of being more favorable to the largely Jewish teachers union than to the blacks who advocated community control of schools. The fourth charge dealt with the periodicals' position on the Soviet invasion of Czechoslovakia. Contrary to the United States CP line, the papers opposed it.

Shortly after the issuance of this letter, Morris Schappes (*Jewish Currents* editor) was separated from the party. Five years later, Novick was expelled at the age of 81, charged with "opportunistic capitulation to the pressures of Jewish nationalism and Zionism." The way in which these actions were handled, as well as the manner in which both sides dealt with the severance, gives some insight into the importance, even as late as 1973, of the Jews to the Communist party. In both cases, it was accomplished quietly. Schappes was severed from the party for failing to attend Communist meetings and for being lax in the payment of his dues. Novick was expelled, but neither the *Morning Freiheit* nor any party organ in the United States carried a word about it, although the fact was published by the Communist movement abroad. By handling the Schappes and Novick cases as it did, the United States CP did not run the risk of confronting and possibly alienating many of its relatively few remaining Jewish members. Although the *Freiheit's* circulation was under 6000 by 1973, these Jews whose reading of the paper implied either party membership or the holding of views favorable to communism, were too many for a small Communist party to needlessly antagonize by publicly condemning Novick. And Novick, in all probability, used the same sort of logic for not taking his case to the pages of the paper. Publication of the matter might have cost the *Freiheit* the support of those readers who were more loyal to the party than to the paper. For a newspaper with a readership of less than 6000, there seemed no need to take the risk of losing any readers. (It was not until 1977 that the United States CP openly denounced the *Morning Freiheit*.)

In 1971 the CP decided to publish a new periodical under its exclusive control in order to reach a Jewish audience. Called *Jewish Affairs*, it currently has a circulation of approximately 2000–2500. The editor of this publication, Hyman Lumer (a man long concerned with Jewish matters in the Communist party) explained, in an interview, the reason for its commencement and existence:

Why did we start it? Because we had no vehicle of expression. The *Morning Freiheit* was not a vehicle for the expression of the Party's views on this [Jewish] question. It was on the contrary carrying on an active campaign against them. The English language publication *Jewish Currents* was even more against us in this matter . . . but since there was no organ of expression of any kind, we received requests: "Why don't you publish some materials so that we know where you stand on this question and other questions [concerning Jewish or largely Jewish issues]?" So we started . . . in a city like New York, a large part of the Left movement is Jewish . . . so that there is a body of Jewish people in the city, but mostly older Jewish people who are not Communists but who do look to us for our position on some of these questions.

And it is to these and to our own Party members, Jewish and nonJewish, that it is addressed.

It should also be noted that *Jewish Affairs* is the only English-language publication of the Communist party published on a regular basis that is directed to or concerned with a specific ethnic or nationality group. Lumer, who recently died was the editor not only of *Jewish Affairs* but also of *Political Affairs*, the CP's leading theoretical journal. Lumer's successor as editor of *Jewish Affairs* was Herbert Aptheker, a major party theoretician. It does therefore seem that the Communist party still considers the Jews to be of some significance.

Nevertheless, the exit from the party of Schappes and the *Jewish Currents*, Novick and the *Morning Freiheit*, and Gates and other Jews around the *Daily Worker*, which began in the mid-1950s, testifies to the fact that the historic relationship between the Jews and the Communist party had, in effect, been severed as it had between the Jews and the Socialist party in the pre-World War II days.

This departure of Jewish activitists and cadres from the Communist party indeed marked the virtual end of the traditional association between Jews and the Old Left in the United States. (Some, like Schappes and Novick and the stalwarts clustered around the *Jewish Currents* and the *Freiheit*, continued to remain faithful to a Jewish left tradition, but their numbers are small, they are middle-aged, or older, and in general this surviving remnant has had little impact on the Jewish community or the current Left.) The assimilationist and anti-Israeli policies of the Soviet and United States Communist parties, against the backdrop of the Holocaust and a rising Jewish nationalism, placed many Jewish Communists in a conflict position. They were forced to choose between their ethnic identification and community and their universalistic political movement. This had also been the choice of their counterparts decades earlier in Russia and the United States. Now, however, the selection of ethnicity or socialism was different. How could a socialist movement—which in effect meant Communism—stained by anti-Semitic excesses and big power expediency make any claims to moral superiority over a movement associated with the near martyrdom of a people and a state—Israel—characterized by heroism and social democratic values, which was also the last refuge of the survivors of the Holocaust? Given such alternatives, it was no wonder that of those who made the choice between Jewishness and the Communist party, most chose their ethnic identity. The policies and actions of the Communist party in the United States and those of the Soviet leadership with respect to Israel and Jewish issues in particular succeeded in dealing a nearly mortal blow to Jewish ties with the Old Left.

THE LEFT AND THE PERSONAL JEWISH PROBLEM

There is one other aspect of the relationship between the Left parties and the Jews that bears special attention. From time to time we touched on the issue of the consequences for the Left of becoming too deeply imbedded in or identified with one ethnic group like the Jews. In order to thrive and to eventually succeed, the Left had to, and knew that it must, reach and attract far more than Jews to its banners. Even Jewish leftist leaders recognized this.

However, once the Jews became so important an element in the Left, a problem arose concerning its ability to reach non-Jews. There were various obstacles that inhibited close contact with and relationships between Jews and non-Jews in general—anti-Semitism, ethnic divisions, and different Jewish and non-Jewish life styles. Communist and Socialist party leaders rarely addressed this issue directly, in either their speeches or their writings. But at some level of consciousness they were aware of it, as were the rank-and-file members. In order to broaden its attraction, the Left had to overcome the obstacles that separated Jews from non-Jews. It had little or no success in eradicating these obstacles and this in turn played no small role in its failure (to date) to become a major political force in the United States.

A description and analysis of the various ways in which the Left and leftists handled or, more accurately, mishandled this Jewish issue, particularly at the level of interpersonal relations, will provide another perspective on the relationship between the Jews and the Left. As we shall see, the issue was a difficult one and produced many problems for the Left.

One of the major ways in which the Left dealt with its own internal Jewish question was to put on an American face (or at least as non-Jewish a public face as possible). Again, this may not have always been a conscious response to this issue, nor was such action taken only for "Jewish" reasons. Nevertheless, both the Socialist and Communist parties never advanced Jews as their presidential nominees. The closest that either of these parties came was in 1924 and 1928, when the Communist party nominated Benjamin Gitlow for vice-president. After 1928 the Communist party, despite its high proportion of Jews, particularly among its functionaries, never placed a Jew on its national ticket, reserving those spots for either Anglo-Saxons from the American heartland, like Earl Browder, or men of more acceptable immigrant stock, like the Irish-American William Z. Foster and the Finnish-American Gus Hall. Also, after Jay Lovestone's removal as party chairman by Stalin in 1929, no Jew ever again held the top post in the Communist party.

This tactic of presenting an American public face did not necessarily alienate Jews in the Left. As we have seen, Jews in the Socialist party were pleased to recruit Norman Thomas and elevate him quickly through the Socialist hierarchy. But this was not always the case, as evidenced by the bitter SP convention fight in 1932 over the election of Morris Hillquit to the position of national chairman. There was also an incident involving the Progressive Party in 1948 that alienated at least one Left Jew and, at the same time, indicated that the Progressive Party and the Communists associated with it were well aware of the need to project a non-Jewish (American) public image. This is best described in the words of a Jew and member of the Communist party:

The Progressive Party at Madison Square Garden, New York—that's the meeting . . . whole parade of speakers and I sat there . . . I had written speeches for Wallace and a lot of other people there. I was with them all the way, a hundred percent. I suddenly realized that in the city of New York, one-third of which was Jewish, the Progressive Party, about 75 percent supported [by Jews in New York City] . . . there was not a single Jewish speaker the entire evening, neither chairman, nor fund raiser, or anybody. I was so angry. I felt so violated by that that I became hostile to the Progressive Party. I mean I continued working for them but basically I had an underlying hostility which I tried to rationalize. I tried to rationalize the situation by saying "Well the guys who planned that meeting were pretty dumb." Yet I knew that these meetings were planned with a lot of people in a planning meeting. Everything is checked out with everybody else, everybody upstairs agreed, Wallace agreed, and the other guys agreed. That just got my goat.[251]

Paradoxically, at the same time that some Left Jews felt embittered about their exclusion from positions of public eminence and power, some non-Jews in and around the various Left parties felt resentful because they believed that the Jews had too much power and held too many important positions. The issue of Jewish power was closely interwoven with resentment toward the dominance of New York City in the affairs of the Left. New York City housed the headquarters of the Communist party after 1927 and of the Socialist party after 1938 and their major newspapers as well. New York was also the city with the largest Jewish population in the world and a cosmopolitan center whose culture was very much informed by that of the Jewish community. This Jewish-oriented culture also informed the attitudes and actions of the leftists that were politically active there—Jews and non-Jews alike. One leading Socialist, in an interview, admitted that "there was a latent kind of anti-Semitism feeling outside of New York. Part of it was directed at New York, which those in the Party outside of New York hated because it was the center." A prominent member of the Socialist Youth League (SYL) and the Young Socialist League (YSL) (post-World War II socialist youth organizations), in an interview, commented in the same vein: "We were very conscious of two things; one, we were the only group that we could think of where the leadership was not all Jewish and two, . . . we were centered in New York City." In order to counter this feeling, various Socialist organizations, according to informants, would bring Gentile members from outside of New York to headquarters positions in the city in order to dilute the image of control by New York Jews. One told of the joy of a party leader of Jewish background who uncovered a Protestant minister in the ranks on the West Coast who was willing to come to New York.

These concerns were also reflected, in an interview, by a non-Jewish female Communist from the Midwest. She voiced resentment (which she felt to be shared by her fellow cell members) toward New Yorkers, invariably Jews, who came to her city in order to transmit the party's orders. In many instances (too many as she and her midwestern comrades readily proclaimed), this "foreign" emissary would remain and instantly move into a local leadership position. For her, the issue of Jewish influence was an integral part of her party cell life: "I felt that the people whose words would be accepted as the last word in any discussions, educational or strategic or just general Party club meetings, were first men and second Jews . . . The pecking order in my group would start with Jewish men."

There were those non-Jews, however, who were not willing to participate in a movement that they believed to be dominated by Jews and either abandoned the Left entirely or searched for another radical movement where Jews were not so important a factor. One of the more bluntly outspoken opponents of the prominent role of Jews in the Left was Harold Cruse, a black intellectual and former Communist. He railed against the political and cultural dominance of the Jews within the Communist party, especially with respect to party policy toward blacks. Cruse believed that by the end of the 1920s there began

. . . the period of Jewish dominance in the Communist Party. It culminated in the emergence of Herbert Aptheker and other assimilated Jewish Communists, who assumed the mantle of spokesmanship on Negro affairs, thus burying the Negro radical potential deeper and deeper in the slough of white intellectual paternalism. The new inner group was composed of Old Guard, first-generation Communists from the Jewish Socialist Federation, plus a young wave that was to emerge as the Communists' intellectual and theoretical corps of the 1930's and 1940's. This younger group, who took command of the *Daily Worker*, *New Masses*, and *The Communist*, assumed various roles. Some remained Communist Jews, others became assimilated Jewish-American Communists, a few became triple threat experts on Jews, Negroes, and Gentile labor organizations, with foreign affairs thrown in for good measure.[252]

Cruse also contended that the Jewish experience in America had made them virtually incapable of Americanizing Marxism: "Certainly the Jews could not [Americanize Marxism] with their nationalistic aggressiveness, emerging out of East Side ghettoes to demonstrate through Marxism their intellectual superiority over the Anglo-Saxon *goyim*. The Jews failed to make Marxism applicable to anything in America but their own national-group social ambitions or individual self-elevation."[253] Cruse's views were no doubt also colored by the fact that Jews held most of the leadership positions in the Harlem branch of the

CP through the late 1930s, by which time the area was predominantly black.[254]

The Communist party and the (Trotskyist) Socialist Workers party did, however, take measures that resulted in Jews functioning in non-Jewish milieus, not only in leadership positions. This generally involved younger Americanized Jews with high school and college backgrounds who were sent into the Gentile hinterlands to recruit and organize for the Communist or Socialist Workers party. As discussed earlier, such dispersement of Jews apparently stemmed from their being a surplus talented commodity. As they were not needed or required for Jewish work, they could readily be spared for work among non-Jews. Also, this appears to have been done most in the Communist party—at least in the period in which it was most hostile to nationality formations, Jewish or non-Jewish.

Unfortunately for the Left, this dispersion tactic did not succeed in Americanizing the Communist party nor breaking down the ethnic barriers between Jewish Communists and non-Jews. The reason for the lack of success of these missionaries appears to hinge on the variables of time and mode of integration. These Jewish emissaries from New York usually did not spend much time in the Christian milieus. Rarely did anyone spend more than five continuous years in such places. John Gates, for example, was in Youngstown, Ohio, for about four years. Also, many of them did not actually work in the shops and factories alongside the Christian workers whom they were trying to recruit and organize. They usually spent most of their time interacting with other Communists and politicizing the workers from the vantage point of outsiders. Consequently, these Jewish Communists could not make a significant impact on the divisions between Jew and non-Jew. It was a question of overcoming not only the latent or manifest anti-Semitism of the Gentiles but also their own latent anti-Gentile feelings. One Jewish Communist I interviewed who had ventured into the Christian hinterlands admitted that his Jewishness and the Jewish image of the party inhibited non-Jews from coming to and staying in the CP: "Many times they didn't feel at home because many of the leaders were Jewish, and it was not what they were accustomed to. Many dropped out because they never felt at home in the Party [due to its Jewish atmosphere]."

Another insight into this problem of Jewish–non-Jewish interpersonal relations was given by a New York Jewish college graduate and intellectual who crossed the Passaic River to work alongside non-Jews in a steel plant in Harrison, New Jersey. In an interview his response to the question "Did you also have a social life with them [gentiles]?" was "A little bit, not much, their social life really appalled me. For the most part, social life consisted of playing cards and getting drunk or screwing prostitutes." In this regard, this young Jewish Trotskyist was very much in the tradition of the young radical Jewish intellectual of latter nineteenth-century Russia (cited earlier) who also could not abide the drinking of his Christian coworkers. Neither the Russian nor the American Jew experienced much success in spreading their brand of radicalism to their Christian colleagues. This ethnic-social class barrier was one of the root causes in both of their personal failures. The American Jewish Trotskyist, repelled by the crass behavior of his Gentile mates, would seize available opportunities to return to New York, a more familiar, more acceptable, more intellectual, and a more Jewish milieu.

But if the distance between New York and Harrison was great for the interviewee just discussed, it was even greater for the few non-Jewish workers he did manage to reach. In order to develop them beyond the one-to-one personal relationship and bring them into the SWP, he had to bring them with him to New York. He knew that he couldn't take them to the SWP's purely intellectual and political functions; but what else remained? The only possible social forum in which the potential Gentile working-class recruit could more or less interact with members of the SWP in any degree of comfort was a Saturday night party in which social life was combined with political life. But even this was unsatisfactory, as the Christian workers from New Jersey could not feel comfortable and relaxed among the Jewish intellectual types who dominated even the social functions of the SWP in New York City.

However, it was not only working-class Gentiles who experienced difficulties and discomfort in interacting with Jews and who, as a result, were inhibited in moving to the Left. Christian college students in a university context experienced similar problems. They felt out of place because of their Gentile and, in many cases, non–New York and noncosmopolitan backgrounds. One such person had in the 1950s been active on a Left fringe group on a campus where the number of Jews and Jewish culture was not significant. Later, upon moving to a school where he perceived Jews and Jewish culture to play a more marked role in Left groups, he ceased his active involvement. He did, however, continue to participate in Left-inspired activities, such as election campaigns and demonstrations in which comparatively large numbers of students and a broader cross-section of the student body were involved. In participating in these activities he was also removed from intimate contact with the core activists, who were primarily Jews. Of these core activists and their Left group, he commented in an interview: "I was uncomfortable there. They were almost all Jews and I got the feeling to belong one had to be Jewish."

Another interviewee, also a college educated non-Jew with Left sympathies, remarked about his personal difficulty in having intimate contact with liberal and Left Jews. An Ivy Leaguer, he had a somewhat different perspective on them than the Christian steel workers. To him the Jews on the Left were "scrufie, fuzzy types who didn't dress well. They were intense rather than cool. They lacked a command presence."

The ethnic barrier did not only affect Gentiles. It appeared also to make an impact upon Left Jews who, as a matter of life's (rather than party's) circumstances resided in non-Jewish areas. Thus in Rochester, New York, during the 1930s an observer noted that the foreign-born Jewish socialists, Yiddish-speaking garment workers who were members of the Workmen's Circle, would not join the local Socialist party unit. An explanation for this behavior was offered by a YPSL observer on the scene, himself an Americanized Jew from the Bronx. They didn't join, because the unit "was dominated by . . . 'American' types who had very little connection with the world of European socialism from which the Yiddish-speaking group derived." However, they did encourage their children to join the Rochester Young Peoples Socialists League (YPSL) in which Jews were a majority.[255]

It should also be noted that there were some non-Jews who were attracted to the Left because of the presence of Jews and of the cosmopolitan culture associated with them. Jews on the Left were regarded as being intellectuals, somewhat bohemian, and capable of letting loose and enjoying themselves. One interviewee, an ex-Communist and an ex-professor, asserted that he knew ". . . a dozen non-Jewish academics who were attracted to the CP because of its Jewish members intellectual intensity." One non-Jew in the late 1940s and early 1950s described his move toward the Left and simultaneously toward an intellectual life in terms of his attraction to Jews and their positive qualities (as he saw them). He remarked in an interview that the Jews in the Socialist party branch that he joined

. . . were very smart people. There would always be debates on a variety of topics including the Palestine issue. They would debate for the sake of debate. I learned a lot from them. The parties were always great too. Playing guitars, singing, and drinking wine; having lox and bagels until three or four in the morning. There was a swinging quality to the group. It was a little strange to me. At the same time I wasn't used to such sharp quick intellectualism. On occasion I would say the wrong thing and they would as a matter of course put me down because that's the way they were towards each other. I was a little offended but I felt that I was getting a lot out of the association.

There were other non-Jews, similar to the Young Intellectuals of pre–World War I years, who admired the Jews as an oppressed minority. During that era, in the wake of the Holocaust, the Jews through their suffering became defined as a morally worthy people. Intimate association with them, including marriage, became, according to sociologist Dennis Wrong, one way to demonstrate one's own liberalism or worthiness. For some, the struggle for the independence of Israel in which socialist *Kibbutzniks* and concentration camp survivors were depicted as battling for their lives against Arab reactionaries and British imperialists was especially attractive. In this period, to be pro-Jewish and pro-Israel placed one spiritually within the ranks of the Left. Michael Harrington, a prominent post–War Socialist leader and writer, in an interview described his movement to the Left around 1948 and pointed to this feeling as one of the factors:

I was . . . under the spell of the fight to create an independent Israel. I was Irish enough to accept without question the truth of Zionist attacks on British imperialism, and the Holocaust of the European Jews seemed to me the most monstrous evil since time began. I read with sympathy Arthur Koestler's apology for the terrorist wing of Zionism and I learned the melody of the "Hatikvah" from a record and the words from the Fireside Book of Folk Songs. To this day I am one of the few people I knew who can sing that Jewish anthem in English [emphasis added].

However, it is doubtful whether the factors engendering this "philo-Semitism" were salient enough for large numbers to overcome, especially in the area of personal relationships, the anti-Semitic feelings, attitudes, and opinions that Americans were exposed to in the 1920s, 1930s, and early 1940s. It would be expecting too much to think that prior to the latter 1950s or early 1960s the many Gentiles who had been exposed to the virus of anti-Semitism in their formative years could develop sufficient antibodies against it to intimately associate with persons who were both Jewish and radical, especially in the context of organizations where Jews were superordinates and much more experienced than they.

Also, Leftist Jews did not make it easy for non-Jews who wanted or might have wanted to cross the ethnic and political divide to join them on the Left. Jewish attitudes, styles, and modes of expression did not encourage Gentiles to interact and communicate with them, especially in the context of a tight-knit group that placed so high an evaluation on intellectual sharpness. There was a style of argument, debate, and writing within the Left that had a distinctive Jewish tone and style. It was aggressive, polemical, highly critical, and often personally derogative to even comradely opponents.[256] Non-Jews as well as noncosmopolitans experienced difficulty in relating to a milieu dominated by such Jewish values. There were some, like Michael Harrington and David McReynolds, who could throw themselves into this ambience with gusto. But undoubtedly there were many more who could not. Their own non-Jewish background and personal styles held them back.

The case of three Italian-American sisters is highly instructive in this regard and, at the same time, sheds considerable light on the problems inherent in a nonproletarian Jewish intellectual Communist party. The three sisters—Rosie, Anita, and Evelyn (fictitious names)—were New Yorkers and second-generation Americans of Italian descent. They all joined the CP in New York at approximately the same time during World War II. If their coming to the CP was noticed by the party leadership, it must have pleased them because the sisters were not only Italian, but also from working-class backgrounds. However, the sisters differed in their own lives with respect to what sociologists call socioeconomic level. Rosie's education did not extend beyond junior high school, Anita was a high school graduate, and Evelyn was a college graduate. Each had a job commensurate with their educational attainment. Evelyn was a teacher; Anita was a secretary; and Rosie was a genuine member of the working class, a garment worker.

The three also differed in terms of their commitment to and length of time spent in the CP. The one who spent the most time in the party and who also was the most committed to it was Evelyn. In fact, she was so loyal, the leadership selected her to be part of its underground apparatus in the early 1950s, where she remained until Khrushchev's denunciation of Stalin in 1956.

Rosie, the garment worker, had the shortest party career. The intellectual side of party life overwhelmed her. She, in the words of one of her family members, "felt stupid and out of it because of her lack of education." The Jewish and intellectual New York Communists, it would appear, had difficulty in integrating workers into the life of the party.

There was also another dimension to this Jewish style that inhibited close relationships between Jews and non-Jews in Leftist and liberal parties. Charles Liebman, a social scientist, commented on this:

. . . most "honorary" Jews learn that they really are not totally accepted into even the secularist humanist liberal company of their erstwhile Jewish friends. Jews continue to insist, in indirect and often inexplicable ways, on their own uniqueness. The promise of Jewish universalism in relations between Jews and non-Jews often has an empty ring. . . . We find Jewish political reformers breaking with their local parties which stress an ethnic style of politics and pressing ostensibly for universal political goals while organizing their own political clubs which are so Jewish in style and manner that non-Jews often feel unwelcome.[257]

There was also present among Jewish intellectuals and leftists a mixture of hostility and superiority toward Gentiles. This, in part, was a product of centuries of Christian anti-Semitism and Jewish defensive responses, including the emphasis on reliance on one's wits for survival. In the latter 1940s and early 1950s, the immediacy of the Holocaust and the insecurity of the Jewish position in America contributed to the maintenance of these attitudes.[258] They appeared to become almost part of the definition of what it meant to be a Jew: "Does there remain any way—any really important way in which the Jew can know and feel and do things that others cannot know and feel and do? The older answer was that fundamentally you have to be Jewish to be a good guy. We didn't parade that answer in public, but that's what most of us believed. Not, of course, that there weren't any decent non-Jews, but, if there were, they were decent by accident, we by design."[259]

The attitudes and values that Jews and non-Jews held about themselves and each other, on the whole, proved to be significant impediments to the development of a "successful" Left in the United States. Given the long-engrained tradition of ethnic antagonisms in a society where ethnic communities were and continue to be placed in the roles of rivals for scarce and desirable goods, services, and positions, no political movement in this country could be free from the debilitating tensions emanating from these ethnic rivalries. The problem of the Left was greatly exacerbated in this regard because of the highly prominent and visible role of the Jews within it. The vicious cycle of anti-Semitism and Jewish chauvinism and defensiveness, divisive elements emanating out of America's cultural and political history, proved to be especially onerous burdens for the Left in America.

These ethnic hostilities, particularly as they revolved around Jewish/non-Jewish attitudes and relationships, negatively affected the Left in at least two significant ways. First, these factors constituted barriers between the Left and those whose objective economic interests should have inclined them either toward membership or support of the movement. Second, many of those who did join or associate with the Left, both Jews and Gentiles, carried with them into the movement the divisive traditions and values of their prejudiced societies and ethnic communities. The intrusion of these tainted traditions and values into interpersonal relationships and the informal interaction of movement members and supporters made cooperation and mutual support and trust difficult to attain. These ethnically derived problems then constituted capitalism's highly effective "fifth column" within the socialist ranks. It would not be until the 1960s that the ethnic barriers would lower sufficiently, albeit briefly, to allow Jews and non-Jews in large numbers to join together in a Left-oriented movement—the New Left.

9 The New Left and Jewish New Left

INTRODUCTION

This chapter will be concerned with examining facets of the relationship that developed between Jews and the New Left in the United States from the mid-1950s through the 1970s. This relationship cannot and should not be considered as independent from that between the Jews and the Old Left. In many ways Jewish responses to the New Left were strongly influenced, if not conditioned, by the involvements, experiences, and reactions that individual Jews and sectors of the Jewish community had with and to the Old Left.

Links between Jews and the New Left that emanated from the Jewish association with the Old Left came largely from two sources—one familial and the other institutional. Many of the parents and close relatives of Jewish New Leftists had been part of the tens of thousands of Jews whose lives at one point or another had intersected with the Old Left and who had been able and willing to transmit to the younger generation a favorable view of Old Left ideals and politics. The other source was the institutional network that the immigrant generation had assembled to strengthen and perpetuate a commitment to the Left. Many of the New Leftists, particularly the early leaders and activists, had come into meaningful contact with this network as children and adolescents.

This chapter will also deal with the forces within the Jewish community that worked at severing the nexus between Jews and the New Left. In many respects these were the same that vitiated the ties between Jews and the Old Left. An ethnic community that was "making it" in American society and that was gripped by a powerful emotional commitment to a nation dependent on the United States for its survival was not going to support an antibourgeoise and antinationalist Old or New Left.

The actions and policies of the New Left as they bore on Jewish interests and concerns will also be considered. Again, as with the Old Left, the New Left made an impact upon Jewish political attitudes and behavior. The positions that the New Left took and the attitudes that it voiced on matters affecting Jews were at times decisive in determining levels of Jewish support and involvement.

Finally, we will look at the Jewish New Left, or Jewish Liberation Movement, that emerged as the New Left was fragmenting. This Jewish radical movement was similar in many ways to the Bund, and the likelihood is that it will suffer the same fate as that of the Bund. (In fact, it may already have done so.)

THE OLD LEFT'S FALL AND THE NEW LEFT'S RISE

Before discussing and analyzing the relationship between Jews and the New Left, it is first necessary to step back and deal with some of the more salient political circumstances that surrounded the origins and development of the New Left. Jews responded to the New Left not only as Jews but also as Americans and as members of various strata, occupational groupings, and classes. Therefore it is important to understand what was happening during the time which the New Left came into being and developed.

The New Left originated at a point in time at which the Old Left was at its nadir—the mid-1950s. These two developments were not coincidental. There was a real causal relationship between the rise of the New and the fall of the Old Left.

First, it is important to realize that the Communist party since the 1930s was the single most important component of the Old Left in the United States. It was the largest and best organized of all the organizations in the Left. Ideologically, the CP defined what were the Left positions in the 1930s and 1940s. Its impact was so great that the party literally controlled the terms of the discussion of all issues on the Left. The decline of the Old Left is well documented in other sources, but let us briefly review here the overall picture.[1]

The organizational, ideological, and moral hegemony of the party waned in the late 1940s and early 1950s. From 1950 to 1957, the party lost almost all of its membership, which declined from 55,000 to 3000. Its youth affiliate, the Labor Youth League (LYL), went from 6000 to 400 members during roughly the same period. And in 1957 the party dissolved the LYL.[2]

The party's ideological decline paralleled that of its organizational fall. It floundered from one position to another. It failed to adequately comprehend postwar social and economic developments. By 1953 liberal and reformist rationales similar to those of liberal Democrats increasingly substituted for theory.

The CP suffered the most telling blows to its claim to moral superiority in 1956, when Khrushchev, at the Twentieth Congress of the Russian Communist Party, denounced Stalin for crimes against socialism. The leader of world communism publicly admitted that many of the long-denied accusations that Trotskyists, Socialists, liberals, and conservatives had leveled against Stalin for years were true. As the full impact of this began to reverberate through the United States Communist party (and others as well), the moral armor of the Communist movement was further weakened by the revelations that the Soviet leadership had been guilty of anti-Semitism. It had destroyed Jewish cultural institutions as well as the lives of Jewish intellectual and political activists. The third blow in the same year was the Soviet repression of the Hungarian uprising. This made clear to many within the ranks and orbit of the Communist party that the USSR, even under non-Stalinist leadership, was more than willing to subordinate international socialist ideology to the cause of narrow great power and national interests. In the wake of these events, there were few who could still believe in 1956 that the Communist movement had much of a moral edge over its rivals in or out of the Old Left.[3]

The collapse of the Communist party in the 1950s was not due solely to factors internal to the Communist movement. The party, since the late 1940s, had been subject to a campaign of official and unofficial repression and harassment. Federal, state, and local authorities, trade unions, employer associations, veterans, and religious groups, as well as liberal organizations, all made their contributions to the creation of a political milieu that allowed and facilitated the harassment and repression of Communists in particular and radicals in general. Dozens of Communists and Communist sympathizers were jailed for their beliefs. Thousands of persons lost their jobs and were expelled from trade unions and professional associations for being a Communist, whether real or imagined. In the repressive climate of the 1950s, being a principled liberal was sufficient to place one's livelihood at risk.

The CP was, however, not the only Old Left party to erode the moral impact of socialism or blur the distinctions between socialism and other ideological forms. The Socialist party made its own independent contributions in this regard. By the 1950s it had become highly appreciative of the strengths of bourgeois American society and drew ever closer to the Democratic party. For example, in 1950 the SP endorsed the decision to send United States troops to fight in Korea. In 1952 Norman Thomas publicly declared that the Democratic party platform was one that social democrats could find congenial. The SP also engaged in red baiting in this decade. Most important, socialist perspectives and objectives faded from the Socialist party's consideration of issues. According to historian James P. O'Brien, "Its vision of socialism was growing ever closer to the reality of liberal capitalism . . . In effect the social democrats in the latter 1950s saw no basis for taking seriously their belief in either the need for socialism or the possibility of achieving it; they found America under a reformed capitalism to be a basically healthy society."[4]

The withdrawal of the Socialists from socialism and their increased commitment to America paralleled their decline as an organization. By the mid 1950s their organizational situation was almost as desperate as that of the Communists. In 1957 there were fewer than 3000 adult Socialists, and its youth wing, the Young People's Socialist League (YPSL) contained less than 150 individuals.[5]

The shambles and near demise of the Old Left proved fortuitous to the New Left in several respects. First, it meant that the field was clear for the New Left to grope toward an ideology and organizational identity of its own. In the latter 1950s it no longer had to fear ideological and organizational control by Old Leftists. Nor did the fledgling New Left have to waste many precious resources in combatting leftist competitors.

THE NEW LEFT EMERGES

The New Left that emerged in the latter 1950s and early 1960s was a conglomeration of ideas and organizations. There was little in the way of disciplined hierarchies or fully shaped ideologies. The New Left, especially in its earlier years, was a loose label that was applied to campus political parties and to various political organizations and protest groups on the liberal-to-left end of the political spectrum. Thus the New Left included campus parties such as Slate (at the University of California at Berkeley); peace groups such as the Student Peace Union; civil rights organizations such as the Congress of Racial Equality (CORE) and the Student Non-Violent Coordinating Committee (SNCC); and, most important, the Students for a Democratic Society (SDS). New Leftists came to mean those who belonged to those types of organizations and/or those who participated in activities sponsored by them.[6]

The ideology of the New Left in the late 1950s and early-to-mid 1960s was a mixture of ideals borrowed from a variety of sources. The more prominent of these were moral outrage, participatory democracy, decentralized power, humanistic socialism, and faith in the individual's capacity to resist evil and to express his humanity. In addition, New Left idealism was colored by a profound distrust of mainstream American liberalism and Old Left sectarianism and dogmatism.[7] These ideals were pulled together and beautifully expressed in the SDS' Port Huron Statement of 1962:

We regard men as infinitely precious and possessed of unfulfilled capacities for reason, freedom and love . . . We oppose the depersonalization that reduces human beings to the status of things . . . Men have unrealized potential for self-cultivation, self-direction, self-understanding and creativity. It is this potential that we regard as crucial and to which we appeal . . . The goal of men and society should be human independence . . . As a social *system* we seek the establishment of a democracy of individual participation, governed by two central aims: that the individual share in those social decisions determining the quality and direction of his life; that society be organized to encourage independence in men . . .[8]

It is important to stress here that the New Left did not represent an abrupt break with the past or with the Old Left. Many of its key people came from Old Left backgrounds. Many of its ideas came from radical pacifists, such as the Reverend A. J. Muste, and from socialists. The New Left, as did the Old Left, espoused a socialist future for

America. The primary difference was that the New Left's version of socialism was highly utopian and humanistic and paid scant attention to issues such as class conflict and the vanguard role of the proletariat.

The leaders and builders of the New Left came largely from the college-age sons and daughters of relatively affluent and well-educated parents. They tended to be drawn from the ranks of the more intellectually oriented, liberal arts students located at the more prestigious colleges and universities. And a strategic and sizeable minority of these New Left architects and cadres were not new to radical politics either having been involved in Old Left groups themselves or coming from Old Left families. Also, and particularly important for our purposes, a disproportionate number were Jews.

THE JEWISH ASPECT OF THE NEW LEFT

Earlier (in Chapter 2) the Jewish component in the New Left was described. It is appropriate at this time to briefly review the Jewish role in this movement before examining the social factors that underlie this presence. First, it should be pointed out that Jews, although important numerically and otherwise, did not constitute a majority of the New Left at any given time. Even though there was a larger proportion of Jews among the leadership than among the rank and file, Jews were rarely if ever a majority. As Norman Podhoretz, the anti–New Left editor of Commentary, pointed out with obvious relish: ". . . a great many of the more visible leaders of The Movement are not now and never have been Jews. David Dellinger is not Jewish; Tom Hayden is not Jewish; Staughton Lynd is not Jewish; Carl Oglesby is not Jewish; Timothy Leary is not Jewish and neither, it is somehow necessary to add, is Stokely Carmichael, nor Huey Newton, nor Angela Davis."[9]

It should also be noted that only a small minority of Jewish students were in the New Left. Simply stated, the number of New Leftists was considerably smaller than the number of Jews in colleges. During the 1960s, in any given year there were from 325,000 to 350,000 Jewish students. On the other hand, the very highest estimate of SDS membership was between 80,000 to 100,000 in the school year 1968–69. Thus, if all the SDS members had been Jews, which they were not, it would have meant that at most only about 30 percent of the Jewish students would have been members. The situation is similar to that of the Jews and the Old Left. In both cases, only a minority of Jews were radicals. But, when we shift our perspective to ask about the numbers and proportions of radicals who were Jews, instead of Jews who were radicals, the situation looks quite different. Seen from this point of view, the numbers and proportions of Jews are considerable. Of all ethnic and religious groups represented in the New Left, the Jews led the others in terms of the proportion of eligibles in an ethnic group participating in the movement.

Now, after making these qualifications, it is necessary to illustrate and document the role and influence that Jews did play in the New Left. As noted earlier, many of the important national officers in the SDS were of Jewish origin. These include the founder, Al Haber, Richard Flacks, Steve Max, Bob Ross, Mike Spiegel, Mike Klonsky, and Mark Rudd. Nearly half the delegates to the 1966 SDS convention were Jews. At one point in the latter 1960s, SDS presidents on the campuses of Columbia University, University of California at Berkeley, University of Wisconsin (Madison), Northwestern University, and Michigan University were Jews. In fact, the Jewish presence was so large that it concerned and, at times, even embarrassed the SDS leadership.[10]

An examination (done by the author) of the New Left's theoreticians and intellectual articulators again reveals a significant Jewish presence. From 30 to 50 percent of the founders and editorial boards of such New Left journals as *Studies on the Left, New University Thought,* and *Root and Branch* (later *Ramparts*), were of Jewish origin. They included such people as Norman Fruchter, Robert Scheer, Saul Landau, Martin Sklar, James Weinstein, David Horowitz, Otto Feinstein, Ronald Radosh, and Stanley Aronowitz. And, although they did turn to older Protestant intellectuals such as A. J. Muste, David Dellinger, and C. Wright Mills for guidance, these young New Left thinkers were also enlightened by and attracted to Jewish theorists and writers such as Paul Goodman, Herbert Marcuse, and Isaac Deustcher.

An overview of major New Left or Movement events in the 1960s again, reveals a major Jewish presence. Jews were approximately two-thirds of the Freedom Riders that went South in 1961. In 1964 they represented from one-half to two-thirds of the Mississippi Summer volunteers. At Berkeley in 1964, about one-third of the Free Speech Movement (FSM) demonstrators were Jews as were over half of the FSM leadership. In 1965 at the University of Chicago's Selective Service demonstration, 45 percent of the protestors were Jews. At Columbia University in 1968 one-third of the demonstrators were of Jewish origin; three of the four students killed at Kent State in 1970 were Jewish. All in all, if one uses a broad definition of the New Left, roughly one-third to one-half of those involved in this movement were Jewish.[11]

All those figures testify to the prominence of Jews in the New Left. But it is also necessary to stress that the issue is not solely that of numbers. In many instances Jews, even though a minority, were important for the tone that they set, the ambience that they established, and the patterns of debate and discourse that they shaped. These are the qualitative influences that are difficult to enumerate but essential to recognize in order to understand the scope of Jewish influence on and in the New Left.

It is interesting to observe, too, that the Jews who entered the movement were not a uniform group, the variations among them often correlating with their time of entry into the New Left. Although the data is scant, certain patterns are apparent: Typically, those Jews who came to the New Left in the late 1950s through the early-to-mid 1960s and who provided the bulk of the leadership were most likely to have Old Left backgrounds. They came from Communist and Socialist contexts as well as to a lesser extent from labor Zionist backgrounds. There was little that was overtly Jewish about this group, including those with labor Zionist experiences. They were also generally not religious or Zionist and usually ignorant of Yiddish. Typically, they were deracinated and acculturated third-generation Americans.

These members of Old Left Jewish familes could be described as non-Jewish Jews. It was perhaps in their politics as well as in their political style that they revealed their Jewish origins. They carried with them into the New Left a brand of politics that, by the latter 1950s, had become so highly identified and interwoven with things Jewish that it was difficult to differentiate the political from the ethnic in style and content.

The young Jews who came to the New Left after the mid 1960s are not as easy to identify and characterize as those who entered before them. The massive growth of the New Left in this period in terms of numbers participating in New Left activities and organizations meant that the Movement was attracting a broader and more politically heterogeneous base of support in the Jewish as well as non-Jewish student bodies. In general, though, those later Jewish New Leftists, compared to their peers of the earlier period, tended to be more liberal than Left in their politics and to have a stronger Jewish identity.

Our attention in the next section, unless otherwise indicated, focuses primarily on Jewish New Leftists from radical backgrounds and, to a lesser extent, on those from liberal contexts. The time span in the section will range from the late 1950s through the early-to-mid 1960s.

LINKS TO THE PAST

From an ahistorical perspective, the disproportionate presence of Jewish college students in the New Left can be considered a paradox. The Jewish community from which these students emanated was stable, relatively prosperous, and largely comprised of comfortable middle-class families. It was a highly organized community led by the wealthy, rabbis, and professional organizers. Levels of anti-Semitism, in the wake of the Holocaust, were at or near historical low points. Jews as Jews suffered few significant blockages to their mobility aspirations. The doors to the Ivy League schools and other prestigious private colleges and professional schools were no longer partially closed to Jews as students or as professors. Jewish intellectuals and writers were no longer locked in their ethnic enclaves and could move to the center of the national stage. Jewish writers moved to the top of the best seller lists, and Jewish social scientists and newspaper columnists became the accepted interpreters of the nation's norms and values.

In the post–World War II era there were no more Lower East Sides. No longer did there exist in the United States massive concentrations of Jewish immigrant workers plying the same trades and suffering the same abuses and exploitation. No longer were Jews separated into their own large enclaves by language, religion, custom, and anti-Semitism. There was also no sizeable radical Jewish intelligentsia, and the institution of Judaism was not in disarray.

Yet, out of this essentially stable bourgeois milieu, Jewish New Leftists were spawned. Various social theorists have sought to explain this phenomenon by invoking tradition as a causal variable.[12] Nathan Glazer, a sociologist and Jewish former (Old) Leftist, has argued that the primary cause was a radical secular Jewish tradition reinforced by a strong Jewish concern and involvement with matters intellectual: "Thus, the thrust of the Socialist background, instead of disappearing into suburban blandness, is maintained by the generally higher level of intellectual interest and strong emphasis on higher education."[13]

That argument, even accompanied by Glazer's modification, is, however, inadequate. It does not account for how the tradition is passed down nor for who does and does not choose to relay it through the generations. Furthermore, it neither explains nor predicts who of the young Jews will receive the tradition and act upon it and who will do neither. Glazer's notion of intellectuality reinforcing tradition is not without merit. But here, too, similar problems apply. Not all intellectuality is liberal or leftist oriented. Even in the humanities and social sciences, especially during the 1950s, there were moderate and conservative intellectuals as well as liberal and radical ones.

A political tradition that is capable of influencing behavior needs more than familial reminiscences and indirect reinforcement through correlative values. A tradition to have meaning in this sense needs *contemporary structural supports*. Jewish New Leftists had such supports available to them. (Non-Jewish New Leftists also had such supports. Indeed, there was some overlapping. But it was for Jews that they were most applicable.)

The organizations and institutions that reinforced the tradition of Jewish radicalism were largely those that the immigrant generation of Jewish Old Leftists had constructed—mainly the left wing schools, summer camps, and resorts. In these environments, young Jewish boys and girls were either politically socialized in conformity with the attitudes and values of their parents, or they were provided with exposure to a political perspective that reinforced that of their parents. It was in these places that they came to realize that the political views of their families had social legitimacy. It was in these settings, too, that these young Jews acquired cohorts and friends of their same general age who saw the world politically the same way as themselves. It was this overlay of political experience, political socialization, politically homogenous friendship and peer groups, and parental politics that proved so crucial in building receptivity in this generation to the New Left.

At this point, I wish to consider other issues in order to place the present argument in a broader and more meaningful context. First, it must be stressed that the focus here is on *Jewish* New Leftists. And we will therefore be primarily concerned with those factors most unique to Jews that influenced their political behavior. There are, of course, salient things that both Jews and non-Jews shared in common that drew both to the New Left. These should not and will not be ignored. But here we are concerned, not with New Leftists in general, but with Jewish New Leftists in particular.

Second, the thesis concerning structural supports that is being developed here applies largely to Jewish New Leftists who entered the movement in the latter 1950s and early-to-mid 1960s. After the New Left developed its own powerful internal dynamics, others—Jews and non-Jews—had less need of prior experiences because the movement now had considerable attractive powers of its own. It is easier to join an established social movement than it is to commit oneself to a small fledgling group.

Third, the experiences of a cohort or cohorts can have significance for others outside. It is not necessary to demonstrate that all Jews (or non-Jews) who came to the New Left in its early stages had some type of exposure to the Old Left structures. A cohort that is sufficiently large and, in social or intellectual ways, quite significant can be capable of drawing into its vortex individuals who have not shared the same childhood or adolescent experiences. The young people living in the neighborhood of the aforementioned Allerton Avenue "coops" in the Bronx would be an example of this.

Fourth, an emphasis on structural supports does not imply that what went on within families is incidental or superfluous. The political attitudes and values that parents pass on to their children are quite meaningful. However, a "deviant" political family *by itself* is in a very weak position to significantly influence the politics of their sons and daughters who are exposed everywhere else to conformist political norms and values. In the case of New Leftists who were exposed to Leftist institutions, it is difficult to parcel out parental from institutional political influences. The two mesh. For the most part, only leftist or leftist-inclined parents would send their children to such institutions to begin with.

Fifth, the emphasis on tradition, family, and Leftist social structures does not mean that there were not other factors at work motivating young Jews to come to the New Left. Earlier (in Chapter 7), the impact of parental occupations was noted. We will also consider others, including social location in college, New Left political orientation, and polical events that helped to bring into being a New Left with a disproportionate Jewish presence.

THE OLD NEW LEFT

Let us begin our analysis of the Jewish involvement with the New Left by first examining the historical continuity between the Old and the New Left and particularly the Jewish variants linking them. Once this is established, we can then detail the personal and structural underpinnings of the disproportionate Jewish presence in the New Left.

Various social analysts have called attention to the similarities and links between the New Left and the student movement of the 1930s. It has even been asserted that many New Leftists were the children of those 1930s activists.[14] What we do know for sure about the 1930s and 1960s student activists is that they were drawn from the same sociological pools, particularly the leaders and the activists—they were the brighter students, humanities and social science majors, and Jews.[15] And, as we saw in the case of the students of the Depression decade movement, the students in the New Left drew heavily on Old Leftists for leadership and cadres. At the vortex of both was the combination of Old Leftist Jews.

It is not necessary to go back to the 1930s to find links and similarities between the New Left and student radicalism of an earlier era. There were also student dissidents in the latter 1940s and 1950s, and the resemblance between them and the student radicals of the 1930s and 1960s is striking. It should be, because in all these cases the builders and early developers emerged out of the same or similar sociological constellations.

In the 1930s the colleges and universities emerged for the first time as important arenas for the Left. Previously, with some notable exceptions, the Left had generally disregarded them, choosing instead to focus its energies on workers or other disadvantaged groups. This was also true of the Jewish Left. But in the 1930s it was becoming clearer, especially with regard to Jews, that the nation's collegiate student body could not be ignored by the Left. More and more people were going on for higher education, and it made little political sense to write them off. What was true for the general population was even truer for Jews.

By the immediate post–World War II years, it was evident that the colleges and universities were for Jews the functional equivalent to the garment shops and factories of a bygone era. In 1950 there were more Jews in college in New York City than there were in all of the locals of the ILGWU combined. At that time there were 80,000 Jewish students in the greater New York area out of a Jewish college enrollment of 200,000 nationally.[16] Thus a handful of colleges in and out of

New York became points of concentration for young Jews, many of whom were liberal and a significant minority of whom were Left or sympathetic to the Left. The cadres of Left youth organizations realized that these disporportionately Jewish schools were more profitable arenas for recruitment and proselytization than were the factories. But it was not clear to them that a primary reason for this was the presence of large numbers of Jewish students.

These progeny of the immigrant Jews had politics that resembled that of their parents. That is, they were generally liberal with a significant minority being on the Left. The most comprehensive survey of student attitudes and opinions conducted in the 1950s—a survey of 11 colleges, What College Students Think—revealed that Jews were more likely than non-Jews to give liberal responses regardless of the area of the specific question, such as civil liberties, civil rights, attitudes toward labor unions, and so on. Interestingly, the Jewish students also differed from their Gentile peers when the responses were subdivided by socioeconomic class. There was a variation in the responses of the gentiles but much less so among Jews. That is, the pattern of responses of Jewish students from working-class families was very similar to those of their coreligionists from middle-class backgrounds. The data also indicated that Jewish students from conservative homes, as measured by Republican party affiliation, were more likely than non-Jewish students to shift to a liberal or Democratic party affiliation, suggesting the lack of depth of their ties to conservatism or their responsiveness to Jewish peer pressure. Altogether, then, the data from this survey, as well as those from other campuses such as Berkeley, confirm that the Jewish students were a liberal constituency.[17]

An interesting aspect of this relationship between liberalism and Jewish students was that it more or less held when Jewish students moved from the supportive environment of New York in the latter 1940s and 1950s. An increasing number and percentage of Jewish students attended schools outside of New York City, in part because of the movement of their parents and the establishment of Jewish population centers in other metropolitan areas, particularly Chicago and Los Angeles, and in part as a function of the movement of Jewish students from the New York City area. Some of the schools at which Jewish enrollments increased appreciably included the University of Chicago, the University of Wisconsin, the University of Minnesota, the University of California at Berkeley, the University of California at Los Angeles, Wayne State University, Antioch, Swarthmore, Oberlin, Harvard, Yale, and the University of Pennsylvania.[18]

Many of these colleges and those in New York City provided milieus in which students could feel comfortable in adopting nonconformist perspectives whether in politics or the arts. Some, such as Chicago, Wisconsin, Berkeley, Antioch, and Wayne State, had politically liberal traditions that encouraged the expression of political concerns outside the scope of the two major parties. The infusion of numerous Jews with liberal and Left backgrounds into these environments appeared to increase the political tempo on these campuses. Interviewees recalled the disproportionate presence of Jewish students in debating clubs, folk song societies, nonconventional political organizations, and avante garde circles. Michael Harrington, an Irish Catholic and principal Left youth activist of the 1950s attributed his conversion to socialism in large part to "nine months of ideological debates" with fellow Yale Law School students who were largely from such backgrounds.[19] Kenneth Kenniston, writing in 1962 about the political revival among American students, commented that a disproportionate number of the activists were from "recent European immigrant stock," an apparent euphemism for Jews, whose backgrounds gave them the capability of violating American norms and traditions that inhibited the participation of the more American types of students in politics.[20]

It was at the colleges with numerically or proportionately high Jewish enrollments that there existed in the 1950s the organization that constituted the Young (Old) Left. The Student League for Industrial Democracy (SLID), the Young People's Socialist League (YPSL), the Labor Youth League (LYL), the Socialist Youth League (SYL), and the Young Socialist League (YSL) had chapters or branches at such schools as Chicago, Wisconsin, Minnesota, CCNY, Berkeley, Brooklyn College, Antioch, and Wayne State. These were also sites of large pro-Wallace groups in 1948. Also found at these campuses were the largest and most active chapters of the Students for Democratic Action (SDA) and the NAACP, liberal groups that, in the context of those times, were often considered Left.[21] Very often their memberships, many times unbeknownst to them, significantly overlapped with those of the Left organizations.

The members and particularly the officers of the Left organizations were predominantly Jewish. Although no surveys were made of the religious and ethnic backgrounds of the membership of these groups, the small numbers involved—less than a thousand for most years in the 1950s—lends validity to the impressions of the leaders and activists who have commented on the matter. And the impression of virtually all who have stated an opinion on the matter is that the leftists were largely Jewish.[22] Andre Schiffrin, president of SLID in 1956–57 and himself of Jewish background, was very aware of the "foreign element" within the SLID: "For awhile, all our national officers, myself included were 'foreign born.'" He went on to comment that the militant rhetoric within the organization was ". . . usually voiced in a heavy Yiddish accent."[23] Others also noted the frequent usage of Yiddish expressions among the members. Another indication of the large Jewish component was the care that was taken to ensure that regional and national conventions of these Left nonsectarian groups would not coincide with important Jewish holidays. No such attention was paid to Christian holidays. On one occasion a Protestant minister was sharply critical of the SLID for scheduling a meeting on Good Friday.[24]

There tended to be an interdependency between the liberal climate, number and proportion of Jewish students, and the size and activity of the Left on a given campus. The liberal climate and tradition aided the legitimacy of the Left on the campus and gave some degree of encouragement to student leftists. The Jewish students served as a pool and a cushion for the Left. It was from among them that recruits and sympathizers were developed. They also provided some generalized support on which members of the Left could fall back in times of need. Also, their existence in sizeable numbers generally meant that a campus would not be polarized between a small, predominantly Jewish Left on the one hand and an overwhelming hostile or nonconcerned Christian student body on the other.

The situation at the University of Wisconsin at Madison in the 1950s provides a good case of the interaction between a liberal campus and a Jewish Left. Wisconsin had gained a reputation as one of the more liberal universities in the country. Its history was closely interwoven with that of the state's reforming progressives. Periodically it attracted national attention as a forthright defender of academic freedom. In the 1930s the university had been the setting for a vigorous student movement in which the Left played a prominent role.[25] Within the Left group at that time there was a large proportion of Jewish students from New York.[26] In 1948 the campus became a major center for the nationwide student-based Henry Wallace presidential campaign. The university was also a school with high academic standards, no out-of-state quotas, and a low tuition for out-of-state residents. These practical features, in addition to a liberal tradition, combined to make the school popular among liberals, leftists and out-of-state Jews, three categories that frequently overlapped.[27]

The Left found the Wisconsin campus to be a relatively hospitable arena compared to others around the nation during the 1950s. Although its strength and fortunes varied, the Left managed, together with liberal supporters, to make an impact there throughout most of the period. It spearheaded efforts to end discrimination in fraternities and sororities, to abolish compulsory ROTC participation, to curtail infringements on civil liberties, and to open up housing for minority groups. It participated in drives against Senator Joseph McCarthy, the junior senator from Wisconsin. The principal Left groups on the campus during the 1950s were the LYL, the Socialist Club, the SLID, and the editorial board of *Studies on the Left*. Ironically, the Communist LYL chapter at the university in Senator McCarthy's home state survived longer than any other chapter.[28]

The membership, and particularly the leadership, of these Left organizations and the SDA were primarily Jewish and generally from New York City. Many of these leftists thought of themselves, in the words of one of them, as the "Jewish intelligentsia." Once the Left was established at the Wisconsin Campus after the war, particularly the LYL, which functioned fairly openly, a pattern of self-recruitment began to develop. One Jewish leftist who had been a member of the LYL while in high school in New York City, when asked why he had chosen to go out to the University of Wisconsin for his undergraduate studies responded: "They had the only open chapter of the LYL in the McCarthy era. This led me to believe that it would be a relatively free campus politically in which I could function."

This predominance of New York Jews in the Left at Wisconsin lasted into the 1960s. Paradoxically in the early 1960s this caused difficulty for the SDS chapter at the university. As the SDS leadership saw it, part of the problem was that, unlike the old Left at other campuses, the Old Left had survived at the Wisconsin campus and was resistant to the overtures of what they considered to be a bunch of political novices. The SDS leaders were also aware of the sociological ground on which these leftists at the Madison campus stood. As Bob Ross, an SDS organizer, explained it in a letter to C. Clark Kissinger, an SDS officer, "my impression is that the Left at Madison is not a New Left, but a revival of the old . . . with all the problems that entails. I am struck by the lack of Wisconsin-born people [in the Left] and the massive preponderance of New York Jews. The situation at the University of Minnesota is similar." Kissinger responded to Ross, confirming his observations: Madison was "the home of the old left . . . As you perceived, the Madison left is built on New York Jews." [29]

It should be stressed at this point that the relationship with the past for the 1950s college generation Jewish Left was very much an organizational one. They did not found new organizations but instead joined those affiliated to Left parties and groups, whose leadership and traditions were rooted in the Jewish Left. Such was the case of the LYL and the Communist party, the YPSL and the Socialist party, the SYL and the Independent Socialist League (ISL), and the SLID and the League for Industrial Democracy (LID). There is some serious question about whether any of these youth groups could have survived as independent entities during the 1950s.

The 1950s Radicals and the New Left

The youthful Old Left of the 1950s—including those who were active and those who identified with Old Left politics of their parents—played an important role in the origin and development of the New Left. As individuals and organizations, they did much to build the foundation of this movement. And, again, when talking of the Old Left of the 1950s, we are talking about a primarily Jewish Old Left.

From 1956 to 1967, surveys of New Left activists—variously defined either in terms of participation in demonstrations or by self-designation—repeatedly arrived at the same finding with respect to their political backgrounds. They came primarily from parents who were liberal to left on the political spectrum and, as previously noted, disproportionately from Jewish parents who themselves were liberal to left. Richard Flacks, a social analyst of the New Left as well as a former officer of the SDS, an Old Leftist and son of a Jewish Old Leftist, after reviewing the various surveys estimated that "fifteen to twenty percent of the activists' parents are reported to be socialists or otherwise radical."[30] Samuel Lubell, on the basis of his own interviews and observations, identified the children of former Socialists, Communists, and other radicals as one of the three "key" streams feeding the New Left.[31]

Given the number of persons of parental age in the late 1950s and 1960s who had been involved in the Old Left, it is not surprising that so many of the *relatively few* New Leftists had this type of parentage. From the 1930s through the 1950s it is estimated that from one to two million persons passed through the Communist party alone. (The turnover rates were generally extremely high.) Also, the numbers go even higher when those involved in peripheral Left organizations are added.[32]

The same sort of findings pertain when the ideological roots of the earlier and more important leaders and cadres of the New Left are examined. James P. O'Brien, the historian who has done the most extensive study of the development of this movement, asserted that with respect to the sons and daughters of Communist parents alone, "at the most active schools probably between a fourth and a third of the core of the political activists come from this kind of a family background."[33] My own study of the political backgrounds of the members of the editorial boards of strategic New Left publications— *Studies on the Left, Root and Branch,* and *New University Thought*— revealed that in addition to being heavily Jewish, a proportion larger than a majority emerged from the Old Left. *Studies on the Left,* in particular, a University-of-Wisconsin-based journal, emerged almost wholly out of the Jewish Old Left organizations that had previously functioned on that campus.

Young Old Leftists and children of the Old Left figured quite prominently in the peace and civil rights groups and actions of the late 1950s and early 1960s. The Student Peace Union (SPU) founded in 1959, the most important of the peace groups, was organized by youth from Old Left and pacifist backgrounds. An early president of the SPU was a member of the YPSL, Philip Altbach. In fact, the leadership of the SPU became so predominantly YPSL in composition that the SPU soon lost its New Left aura. A similar phenomenon was at work in the northern civil rights arena. YPSL members were largely responsible for planning, organizing, and coordinating the major civil rights activities in this period, including the two marches on Washington in 1958 and 1959 on behalf of integrated schooling, the freedom rides of the early 1960s, and the northern picketing and demonstrations in support of black sit-ins in the South.[34] In both the peace and Northern civil rights activities of this period, New Left activities, a plurality if not a majority of the key leaders and participants were both Old Leftists and Jews.

This same phenomenon can also be seen in the case of the SDS, the vanguard organization of the New Left. Important leaders with Jewish and Old Left backgrounds included Al Haber, Richard Flacks, Steve Max, and Bob Ross. As with the ad hoc peace and civil rights groups, a significant number of the SDS members in the early-to-mid 1960s were from the YPSL, including its first president, Al Haber. Kirkpatrick Sale, an historian of the SDS, has described the early SDS members and the overlapping between politics and ethnicity that obtained among them: "They were overwhelmingly from the East and generally from the cities (although a sizeable number were from the midwest), and many (perhaps a third [a conservative estimate]) were Jewish, all of which went to produce a kind of sophistication, a cosmopolitanism, and a grounding in urban traditions. And they were often from families whose parents had had some contact with the Left, usually during the thirties.[35]

This blending of Old Left and Jewish backgrounds among the New Leftists of the late 1950s and early-to-mid 1960s was no accident of history. New social movements often draw upon individuals and groups who have had some sort of previous involvement in similar movements in the past. And if the Old Left was disproportionately Jewish, it would seem reasonable that the New Left would also have that distinguishing characteristic. But there still remains the issue of the manner in which this ethnic configuration was produced. In order to address this question, we now turn to the social mechanisms that were largely responsible.

THE IMPACT OF FAMILY AND ORGANIZED STRUCTURES

Family

The family's role in the political socialization of their children cannot be disregarded. This relationship also holds for the New Leftists. They were most likely to emerge from homes where parents were liberal to Left in their politics. These members of the New Left were not, for the most part, involved in a political conflict of generations.[36]

Let us begin our discussion and analysis of parental political impact by focusing on New Left activists from Jewish and Old Left backgrounds. The primary source of data here are my interviews with New Leftists of this type. I have also relied on interviews done by James P. O'Brien and various secondary sources. No claim is made to statistical representativeness for, among other reasons, there is no way of determining the composition of the universe to be sampled. At the same time, there is little reason to suspect that these interviewees were atypical.

Another methodological problem that merits attention is the nature of the samples used to draw inferences about parental influence. In almost all studies on New Leftists, including my own, the youthful activists are selected and then asked about the politics of their parents. This means that we do not really know much about liberal and Left parents who did not sire New Leftists. Perhaps, and this is not very likely, only a very small minority of these kinds of fathers and mothers produced such children. Unfortunately there is only one significant study that speaks directly to this methodological issue—"Family Congruence on Political Orientations of Politically Active Parents and Their Children" by Lamar Thomas. This study does reveal that parental politics is an important factor in the shaping of New Leftists.[37]

Before proceeding to the analysis, one final methodological issue should be addressed—the political heterogeneity of Old Left families. Parental ties with the Old Left mirrored the gamut. They varied from long-time, high level Communist party officials like Herbert Aptheker, CP theorist and editor, to a brief membership in a moderately leftist group. Also, in most cases among my own interviewees and others with whom I am familiar, their parents had ceased to be active in the Left by the time their activist children had reached middle and late adolescence. In some instances these young people did not find out about their parents' previous leftist past until after they themselves had become involved. It should also be recalled that the political atmosphere in the United States from the late 1940s throughout most of the 1950s was such that it not only discouraged formal membership in radical organizations but also inhibited open and frank discussions of radical views even within one's own home. This means that generalizations are being made about a fairly heterogenous political group.

In general, those whose parents had some form of association with the Old Left received little in the way of formal indoctrination. The politicizing effect was more indirect. Some sense of identification with the underdog, most notably the American black, informed their political development. As adolescents they also began to share their parents' concerns with the issues of peace and civil liberties, though these concerns and issues were rarely presented to them within a radical or Marxist perspective. At the same time, while they were growing up they felt themselves to be somewhat apart from their society, vaguely critical of the dominant institutions and values and, except in those instances when there were enough others similar to themselves to form some sort of quasi-dissident subculture, somewhat different from their school and neighborhood peers.

A good representation of the kind of person we interviewed can be obtained from J. Anthony Lukas' portrait of Dave, the Harvard SDS leader in his book *Don't Shoot—We Are Your Children*.[38] Dave was

Jewish and the son of former Communists, his father having been a leading member of the Progressive Party after 1948. The father, in a retrospective talk with Lukas, perceived the home while Dave was growing up to be a radical home, a dissenting one. The son concurred. "Dave agrees that he undoubtedly absorbed a great deal of political thinking at home. 'But, it came from the way my parents lived and dealt with the problems more than from any explicit political direction. Really, the only thematic statement we ever got was in the religious context. Above all, there was a pretty strong, firmly established atmosphere of love in the home. People were on the whole dealt with as human beings.' "[39]

Interestingly, these young Old Leftists we interviewed directed little hostility toward their parents for failing to live up to political ideals they held but did not practice. This differs from the findings of Richard Flacks and Kenneth Kenniston, who stressed the New Leftists' outrage at the political hypocrisy of their parents and the older generation in general.[40] Several factors appear to account for this discrepancy. First, at the time that James O'Brien and I interviewed the young Old Leftists they were older, especially my respondents, or they had spent more time in the movement than those who Flacks and Kenniston studied. Age and years of political experience temper moral outrage, a characteristic associated with youth and inexperience. Evidently age and experience afforded our respondents more of an opportunity to appreciate their parents' problems in actively adhering to their political principles. Second, our respondents, relative to those of Flacks and Kenniston, were more likely to have themselves experienced or emerged from a tradition that allowed them to appreciate the difficulties in sustaining left political activity in periods when such politics were the politics of a small, almost outcast minority.

However, returning to our original concern, several tentative conclusions can be drawn from this broad overview of the political impact of the Old Left parents on their children, at least the ones who were to become active participants in the New Left. First, these young persons from Old Left backgrounds appear to have been more ready to become part of a dissident subculture than their peers. Growing up in families that were considered nonconformist by neighbors and relatives because of the parents' unpopular political stands and ideas prepared their children when their time came to be part of an unpopular minority movement. Second, they were more exposed to and evidently more affected by the informal comments and conversations and feelings of their parents rather than by official doctrines. It was the moral and humanistic concerns espoused by their parents, rather than Marxist world view, that moved them toward a receptivity to the New Left.

At this point, the similarity between the liberal and Old Left families that spawned New Lefters should be noted. The social values of these two types of families did not appear to be very different. In liberal households, children were also exposed to feelings of concern for the underprivileged, particularly blacks. In all probability the intensity and frequency of these feelings of concern were greater in Old Left than in liberal families, plus the definition of the underdog was likely to be more extensive in the former than in the latter households. It should also be noted that in the 1950s even active Old Leftists, due to political circumstances, assumed the politics of concerned liberals. All in all, there did not seem to be too much difference between liberals and Old Leftists during this period, except, on the issue of anti-Communism.

There was also another similarity between liberal and Old Left families that contributed children to the New Left—the educational and occupational backgrounds of the parents. The findings about the social backgrounds of New Left activists in general seem, with some modification, particularly with respect to income, to hold for both Old Left and liberal scions. According to Richard Flacks (and other sociologists), "Activists" . . . are disproportionately . . . the sons and daughters of high income families in which both parents have at least four years of college and tend to be employed in occupations for which advanced educational attainment is a primary requisite."[41]

There is, in the abstract, nothing uniquely Jewish about the political, educational, and occupational backgrounds of the New Leftists' parents. The Jewish element enters in because of the disproportionate presence of Jews among Old Leftists, and of Jews with such politics among those who have at least four years of college and are in intellectually oriented positions. And (as noted in Chapter 7) the important thing is not the fact of being Jewish but the political baggage and tradition that Jews brought with them to these jobs. Once more, the political implications of these professional and intellectually oriented positions should be noted. These were types of occupations that tended either to facilitate a liberal perspective or at least not to challenge it. Therefore when a person with a liberal to Left background, like a Jew with an Old Left heritage, was in such an occupation, the combination was very likely to produce a person with liberal to Left politics.[42]

We have seen in this section that the families of New Leftists, particularly those from Jewish households, did seem to be highly influential in the shaping of their politics. This finding, however, should be placed in a proper context. Although politics were significant, it is necessary to consider other causative factors. There are at least two reasons for this. First, there is no one-to-one relationship between parents' and New Left children's politics. For example, the aforementioned study by Thomas found that although family politics was the single most important factor correlated with offspring's politics, it, by itself, was not sufficient to statistically explain the politics of a substantial proportion of the New Leftists in his study.[43] Second, and related to the first, the family is not the only agency of political socialization of young people. A politically deviant family in the midst of a hostile environment, as we noted earlier, would be hard pressed to successfully transmit its politics across generations if their offspring did not encounter some reinforcement outside of the family environment. This, indeed, was a major reason why Jewish Old Leftists constructed their institutional subculture. And we shall now see how politically prescient they were as we turn our attention to the role that those nonfamilial structures played in the generation and socialization of New Leftists.

Nonfamilial Structures

The organizations and structures constructed and maintained by the Jewish Old Left facilitated the development of the New Left by providing it with recruits favorably predisposed toward radicalism and socialism. This Jewish Left institutional subculture kept alive and legitimated Leftist values and traditions for significant numbers of young Jews (and non-Jews). In Cold War America it represented an organized oasis as the Left, together with its values and traditions, was driven from virtually every other arena of American life. It was in the context of this Jewish Left institutional network that leftist political socialization in various degrees took place. And it was in the context of these Left organizations and structures that proleftist networks and cohorts were produced—networks and cohorts that were to be important human foundation stones for the New Left.

The schools and summer camps of or associated with Jews of the Old Left carried a heavy political burden in the late 1940s and 1950s. The general absence of large and relatively politically Left Jewish neighborhoods in this period and the virulent antiradical atmosphere prevalent in America at the time meant that there were virtually no other places where young people, non-Jews as well as Jews, could find institutional and social support for the holding of even mildly leftist values and perspectives.

There were a variety of private schools that succored what were to be New Leftists. These schools varied in orientation. Approximately 100, with some 6000 students were institutions formerly affiliated with the Jewish People's Fraternal Order (JPFO). These schools gave considerable emphasis to the interrelationship between a Left perspective and progressive Jewish tradition. Another group were the Workmen's Circle schools where the Jewish or Yiddish culture was stressed and an appreciation of socialism and the working men's plight received some favorable mention. There were also private schools, some affiliated with liberal religious groups such as the Quakers and the Ethical Culture Society, with large enrollments of Jewish students from Left and liberal families. Many of the teachers in these schools had been fired or forced out of the public school system on political grounds, and a significant proportion were Jewish. The curriculum in these schools were generally humanistic, democratic, and prolabor.[44]

One of the more popular schools for Leftists of Jewish background was the Little Red School House elementary school and its associated Elizabeth Irwin High School in New York City. Although not formally part of the Jewish Old Left subculture, these schools were part of it. More than half of the student bodies were Jews and most students, Jews as well as non-Jews, came from Old Left backgrounds. It is difficult to estimate with any degree of certainty the number or proportion of the alumni of these schools that went on to the New Left, but interviewees and other sources indicate that they were substantial. Kathy Boudin, the scion of a prominent Jewish Old Left family, is perhaps the most famous New Left alumnus. Michael and Robert Meeropol, the sons of Julius and Ethel Rosenberg, and later active New Leftists also attended.

It is important here to stress that non-Jews from the Little Red School House and Elizabeth Irwin High School also went on to the New Left, although their numbers were fewer. Angela Davis, the black New Left and Communist party activist and theorist, is one famous example. The issue here is not one of counting Jewish and non-Jewish New Leftists from these schools. The point is that the number of Jews from leftist backgrounds at these progressive schools was sufficiently large to provide a student proleftist milieu that gripped Jews and non-Jews alike.

The manner in which schools like the Little Red School House and Elizabeth Irwin developed this proleftist milieu and affected the political development of future New Leftists was revealed by New Leftist member interviewees and other alumni that I interviewed. They spoke of the lasting political impact that the schools had made upon them. There they were exposed to courses on socialism, labor history, and minorities. They were taught and learned to think analytically and critically—skills that enabled them to penetrate and reject the accepted dogmas of American society. These New Left activists also cited the close interaction with fellow students and faculty who shared similarly liberal or Left political views as another factor in predisposing them toward an acceptance of a need for radical social change in America.

An examination of the curriculum and objectives of the Little Red School House and Elizabeth Irwin High School reveals what an oasis they must have been for the students in the 1950s. Students were guided in their study of the Civil War by the following generalizations: "The struggle between the North and South was partly a struggle between 'landlords and money lords' . . . At the same time it was also an upsurge of democratic tendencies, a movement for the liberation of the Negro people."[45] They also read about strikes, trade unions among garment and subway workers, and union leaders such as Eugene V. Debs and John L. Lewis. They were taught about prejudice and ". . . the drive for the emancipation of Negroes, of women, of labor."[46] One year for the school's Christmas program, the students danced and chanted a self-composed poem dealing with the Hebrews from the time of Abraham to the exodus from Egypt.[47]

Left summer camps were also instrumental in bringing Left young people together where their values and outlooks could be openly expressed and socially supported. These camps, particularly Camp Kinderland, reached out to many more persons than did the schools. Throughout the interviews with the activists of the late 1940s and 1950s, reference is continually made to their summer camp experiences. And these camps were primarily those of the Jewish Left, ranging from Communist to Labor Zionist. There is little question that the camps made a political impact that transcended the summer months and that actively predisposed many campers to involvement in the Left in later years. Again, it was in places like Camp Kinderland, which were similar to the progressive schools, that Left values were inculcated and supported. It was there that they learned and sang in public left wing folk songs. It was there, too, that young people learned about labor struggles, particularly those of the garment workers. In these camps they also met and listened to live radicals who talked not only of the Left's past but of its present and future as well. And, finally, it was in these progressive summer camps that long-term friendships were formed—friendships that proved important years later on college campuses in the formation of New Left groups and activities.

The progressive camps and schools were not the only features of the predominately Jewish Old Left institutional network that made a contribution to the New Left. There were others as well. It was the Old Left's organizational and financial support that was largely responsible for keeping campus liberal and Left groups alive in the late 1940s and in the 1950s and 1960s. Such groups as the YPSL, although not formally Jewish, were largely or disproportionately Jewish in composition.

The importance of Jewish Old Left and labor organizational and financial assistance to the New Left via the maintenance of these kinds of groups can be seen most clearly in the case of the SDS, the "flagship" of the New Left. The SDS had a long organizational involvement in and with the Jewish Old Left. Its direct and earliest ancestor was the Inter-collegiate Socialist Society (ISS), which was founded in 1905 on the Lower East Side with the assistance of socialists such as Morris Hillquit and Upton Sinclair.[48] The ISS later evolved into the LID, which in turn founded the SLID in 1932. The predominantly Jewish SLID led by Socialists played a significant role in the student movement of the 1930s. In 1936, the SLID broke from the LID to join the Communist-oriented National Student League (NSL) to form the American Student Union (ASU)—the organizational backbone of the Depression-decade student activism. In 1945 the LID revived its student affiliate, which was renamed the Students for a Democratic Society in 1960.

The LID and the SLID, as well as the SDS, were able for several years to maintain their existences and function because of the resources that flowed into them from the Jewish-led garment unions. The money from these unions purchased the printing of leaflets and brochures, paid for the salaries of officials, and provided the expenses necessary to hold symposia and conventions.

The garment unions, also, supplied the leadership and ideology for the LID, which in turn guided the SLID. The leaders were generally Jewish with Socialist backgrounds and had close ties to the primarily Jewish (and right wing) Social Democratic Federation. In 1944 Mark Starr of the ILGWU became president of the LID and in 1948 was succeeded by Nathaniel Minkoff, also of the ILGWU.

In the 1950s the SLID was not a large organization, or an active one, or very socialist in its politics. Its membership probably did not exceed 500 in any given year during the decade. But in this "silent" decade, the SLID was one of the more important of the groups associated with the Old Left that existed on American campuses. It conducted conferences and published pamphlets dealing with various aspects of economics and politics from a moderately socialist perspective. It was also one of the few organizations in the country to publicly challenge Senator Joseph McCarthy. The SLID, like other Old Left–oriented groups of the time, was predominantly Jewish and drawn largely from the student bodies of colleges with substantial Jewish enrollments, including CCNY, University of Chicago, Cornell, Wayne State, and University of Wisconsin.

The SLID had two major accomplishments relevant to the development of the New Left. First, it helped to keep alive within the student community an awareness of socialism and alternatives to capitalism. There were not many other organizations dealing with students (or adults) in the 1950s that performed this function. Second, it managed its own survival as an organization. This, of course, was important for leaders and members who, in the absence of the SLID, might not have joined any other like-minded group. Membership in an ongoing socialist-oriented organization provided a focus that was not as likely to have been attainable had it not existed. The SLID was also important for the continuity that it provided with a rich tradition and a potential vehicle for political action. It is easier (sometimes), as was the case with the SLID and SDS, to build upon an existing structure than to construct one from scratch.

The availability of the SLID for more vigorous political action was seen by Alan Haber, a member of the YPSL and the son of a man with close ties to the LID. Haber became vice-president of the SLID in 1959 and then later president and field secretary. Together with Tom Hayden and several other friends, Haber planned and worked to transform the SLID into a more activist and more radical organization. Their vision came to fruition in the SDS. It should also be noted that although the SDS and the LID soon clashed over various matters of policy, the SDS chose not to sever its financial and organizational ties with the LID. In 1965 the SDS, primarily at the LID's choosing, became an independent organization. From 1960 to 1965, despite the SDS's numerical growth and fame, the organization remained financially dependent upon the LID and the financial support associated with it.[49]

This connection with the LID and the Jewish-led garment unions was not the SDS's only association with the formal and informal Jewish Old Left. One of the SDS's first chapters in New York City was formed largely from young Jews with Old Left backgrounds who belonged previously to an organization called the FDR-Four Freedoms Club.[50] It is also interesting to observe that this club drew mainly upon Jews located in one of the last quasi-radical Jewish concentrations remaining in New York City—the upper West Side of Manhattan. Labor Zionist organizations also made their contributions to the New Left. In 1965, for example, the first two high school chapters of the SDS were formed by Jewish youth who had previously belonged to a labor Zionist movement *Habonim*. The SDS and the New Left in general also contained veterans of another labor Zionist movement, the *Hashomer Hatzair*.[51]

THE NEW LEFT AND JEWISH CONCERNS

The relationship between the New Left and Jews, similar to that between the Old Left and Jews, was a two-way street. The Jewish relationship to the New Left was very much affected by the policies and actions of the movement. The New Left did take positions that had direct and indirect impact on Jewish interests. (Direct interests are those that flow from the fact of being Jewish. Indirect ones emanate from social categories in which Jews are concentrated. Thus Israel's security would be an example of a direct Jewish interest, and job security for New York City school teachers would be an example of an indirect Jewish interest.) The New Left, like the Old Left before it, lost Jewish members, potential members, and supporters when it attacked Jewish interests or was perceived by Jews as being hostile to direct and indirect Jewish concerns. Conversely, the Movement attracted or did not inhibit the inflow of Jewish members and supporters when it was perceived by Jews as being positive or neutral to Jewish-related interests.

The New Left's relationship to Jews went through positive and then less positive phases. The former period lasted roughly from the latter 1950s through the early-to-mid 1960s, when the New Left did or said very little that could be interpreted as being negative to Jewish sensibilities. By the same token, the Movement did not endorse or promote direct Jewish interests in this period. Indirectly, however, it did facilitate the recruitment and support of Jews via formal and informal policies that were congenial to the interests of incumbents of social categories like students or professionals, in which Jews were disproportionately located.

Jewish issues in these years, despite or perhaps because of the large numbers of Jews in the movement, were publicly invisible. Scarcely anyone wrote or talked about such things in public. References to matters Jewish were generally found or alluded to in private conversations or correspondence, but even then they did not appear to be too plentiful.

The absence of public discourse on Jewish issues in the New Left from the late 1950s through the mid-1960s arises from a variety of sources. First, the New Left had little reason to address itself to matters pertaining to Jews. Jews did not constitute an oppressed and impoverished minority group. Anti-Semitism was at its lowest level and Jews were economically among the more prosperous groups in the country. If anything, the Jews' very success, particularly when reflected in ostentatious consumption patterns and in their "celebration of America," was embarrassing to idealistic New Leftist advocates of a more just and equitable society.

Similarly Israel, a focal concern of the American Jewish community, was not a major object of attention of the New Left in this period. The 1956 Sinai War had been fought prior to the New Left's birth and, unlike the 1967 Six-Day War, Israel and the Arabs did not create a long-term issue over the occupation of Arab territory. (Israel, under pressure from the United States and the USSR returned all captured territory in 1956.) From 1956 to 1967 Israel seemed securely established and was generally not considered much of a threat to the sovereignty and economies of the surrounding Arab countries. When the New Left did look beyond America's borders, there were more pressing matters than the Arab-Israeli situation to concern itself with—especially the Vietnam war. In addition, many Jewish New Leftists (and non-Jewish ones as well) had varying degrees of positive feelings about Israel, emanating in large part from their knowledge of and contact with the kibbutzim. More than a few of the Movement notables such as Jerry Rubin had spent some time on a kibbutz.[52]

A second major cause of the paucity of attention paid to Jewish issues emanated from the nature of Jewish identity and the social composition of the New Left. The New Left was the most "American" radical movement since the early Socialist party at around the turn of the century. The New Left was made up almost entirely of native-born Americans, who themselves were sired by native-born Americans. In this respect it embodied the dreams of Old Leftists who had long aspired to create such an entity. The movement was also more American than its predecessors in terms of ideology and dominant themes. Its appeals were rooted in American traditions. Marxism, to a certain degree a Jewish European import, although present, was not given the priority that it had had in Old Left parties. The issue that first gripped the New Left was also a very American one—the race issue.[53]

Public attention to and identification with Jewish concerns might have in some subtle ways undermined the American identity of the New Left. Jewish and non-Jewish New Leftists did not want to weaken this asset by bringing up Jewish matters. Also, some of those familiar with the Old Left through direct contact or indirectly were aware of problems emanating from its heavy Jewish identification. The New Left, although having a disproportionate number of Jews, did not have this kind of identification. And the movement obviously desired to keep it that way.

The Jewish identity and the attitude toward it on the part of many Jewish New Leftists also caused them to be very protective of the movement's American image. They had little reason to desire Judaicization of the New Left. Consciously a Jewish identity was not a salient factor. After all, many were third-generation Americans from families who did their best to assimilate into American society. This was true both for those from bourgeois families and from Old Leftist ones. Conversely their universalistic political identity did mean much to them. Similar to their cosmopolitan Jewish predecessors in the pre–World War I Socialist party and in the student movement of the 1930s, the Jewish New Leftists did not desire to be tied to particularistic primordial groups and identities. They wanted instead to be part of a universalistic movement devoted to breaking down artificial and irrational barriers. This may also have been a way, at some unconscious level, of assimilating into and being accepted by American society.

A third factor and related to the other two was that categories such as "ethnicity" and "religion" did not figure large in New Left thinking. Through the mid-1960s the New Left was primarily concerned with "the individual," "man," or "people." Class and occupational categories, although used, were not as significant. (This vagueness may have reflected the Movement's uncertainty as to who or what was its actual political constituency or constituencies.) Virtually the only ethnic division that the New Left was willing to give public attention to was that between whites and blacks. To this extent the educated and rational New Leftists were viewing the American social scene in ways not very different from their liberal or left parents and teachers.

A fourth factor inhibiting public discussion of Jewish and Jewish-related issues in the New Left that may have been working at different levels of New Leftists' consciousness was a fear of offending Jews. Jews were important to the New Left as members and potential members and as supporters, particularly financial supporters. To have publicly done anything else but praise things Jewish was to risk offending some Jewish groups. And since public praise of Jewish matters had other costs, it was perhaps better from the vantage point of the New Left's own self-interest to say nothing.

Indirectly the New Left appealed to Jews by emphasizing positions and themes that individuals from intellectually oriented professional and occupational backgrounds found congenial. These were the situations in which Jews were disproportionately located. Thus, as noted earlier, the Jewish scions of nonbureaucratic and nonmanagerial middle-class parents could more readily be drawn to a movement that emphasized morality and humanism as opposed to Marxism. They could more readily identify with the New Left's principal vehicle for social change—Man—than with the Old Left's working class. Finally, the issues that the New Left chose as the important ones—racism and war—and the lines that it drew between "good guys" and "bad guys" did little up to the mid-1960s to directly threaten the past or future status of middle-class Jews (or non-Jews, too, of course). The bad guys were not the bourgeoisie as much as they were racists, warmongers, and insensitive bureaucrats—statuses in which Jews were underrepresented. In many ways the New Left provided all the props necessary to act out a morality play. Young, highly educated Jews from intellectually oriented middle-class families were willing to serve as actors in this drama, especially when the roles that they played were such positive ones.

THE FALLING OUT

After 1967, the relationship between the New Left and Jews increasingly soured. The movement changed in ways that Jews inside and outside of it construed to be injurious to Jewish interests and sensibilities. It was in these years that the New Left or major segments thereof raised issues and supported causes that threatened Jews as Jews and as members of the middle class. The New Left's alienation of its white college-age middle-class constituency also alienated its Jewish constituency, given the relatively large numbers of Jews in this class.

The denouement between Jews and the New Left had three overlapping foci—Marxism, race relations, and Israel—a mix that affected Jews as Jews and as white middle-class Americans. The negative impact of the changes in New Left positions and on those issues was not felt immediately nor did it have the same behavioral result on all Jews. Responses varied according to experience, political background, and personality. But what is certain is that the level of actual and potential Jewish membership in and support for the New Left declined when it and its various elements took stands Jews perceived as hostile and insensitive to Jewish feelings and concerns.

MARXISM IN THE NEW LEFT

The humanist idealism that had facilitated the movement of middle-class Jews and non-Jews to the New Left in the late 1950s and early 1960s waned in the years that followed. As Marxism-Leninism (or variants thereof) began to supersede it, the middle-class youth withdrew its support from the movement. Since Jews aligned with the New Left were so largely middle- and upper-middle-class, the disaffection of these groups meant, ipso facto, the disaffection of much Jewish support.

The New Left had, of course, even in its earlier days, acknowledged its debt to Marxism. But at that time Marxism was only one of a variety of influences, and it was defined by the New Left leadership in broad, loose, and humanistic terms. This changed in the mid-1960s (due to a variety of factors that are not particularly germane to our purposes here), from which time Marxist themes moved to a more central position within the Movement. And the Marxism that the Movement incorporated was a harsh and dogmatic variant.[54]

One of the significant concomitant changes was the political role assigned to students. In the early days of the Movement, students had formally or informally occupied a vanguard position; as the 1960s unfolded, the New Left leadership assigned to them a minor supporting role. The students' vanguard role was allotted to the working class and to blacks, other oppressed minorities, and even to Third World peoples. White middle class Jewish and non-Jewish students were directed to go into their own communities and there to work for social change. For many this must have felt like being made to take a back seat to other groups whose life experience, skin color, and social class positions made them "real" forces for societal reconstruction.

The Movement's definition of the "enemy" of progress and social justice also underwent a change in line with the rise of Marxist influences. In the early years, that enemy was somewhat vague, like "the system" or "bureaucracy." However, that changed by the mid-to-latter 1960s, when the enemy was more clearly defined as liberals, liberalism, capitalism, and the supporters of capitalism, including well intentioned white-skinned liberal bourgeoisie.[55]

It is not easy for a strata—white middle-class college youth—to continually lend support to a political movement that (a) assigns it to a minor backseat role and (b) identifies it with the major enemy to be overthrown. The enemy in this case was the system that had offered up some of its riches to those college students and their parents and their class as a whole. In the face of this situation, rational self-interest demanded that they disengage from the New Left. Even though some students were able to transcend their class position and adopt new identities as revolutionaries, the bulk of middle-class youth could not and would not.[56] Consequently during the late 1960s and early 1970s, they withdrew from (or did not join) the Movement, leaving it more solidly in the hands of anti-middle-class, anti-liberal Marxist and Third World revolutionaries. (The process of withdrawal was not immediate or uniform. On given issues or events in the late 1960s or early 1970s such as the invasion of Cambodia in 1970, hundreds of thousands of white middle-class youths did become involved in the

Movement. But, typically, this involvement was increasingly short-lived.) Again, as Jews were so disproportionately concentrated in the affluent and liberal middle-class college strata, the withdrawal of this strata from the New Left also meant the withdrawal of a large number of Jews.

BLACKS VERSUS JEWS IN THE NEW LEFT

The metamorphosis from civil rights to black power in the 1960s strained relationships between blacks and whites in general and Jews and blacks in particular. White New Leftists who had worked with blacks on behalf of civil rights felt a sense of rejection when their allies demanded that the struggle for the realization of black interests be carried on in the context of separate all white and all black organizations. Jewish New Leftists were most likely to feel rejected because they were disproportionately in the forefront of the civil rights movement and had had the most direct contact with blacks. The strain for Jews was, however, not due to only the insistence that blacks have their own organizations. It also emanated from the attacks by blacks on Israel and Zionism, broadly defined, as well as on Jews as exploiters. The concomitance of all of these things, plus the New Left's tacit acceptance of black demands and charges, drove some Jews from the movement and weakened the commitment of many others.

The integration-oriented Northern civil rights movement of the late 1950s and early 1960s had an unreal quality. It was more like a morality play than a social movement. Altruistic whites, together with well-mannered, well-intentioned, and self-restrained blacks, were crusading together on behalf of the "Negro." White and black civil rights workers and the "Negro" had right and justice on their side, and their opponents were easily depicted as either amoral, immoral, or plain evil.

This was a scenario that had appeal to white middle-class college youth from liberal and Left families and particularly to the Jews among them. It gave them an opportunity to act out their liberal familial values without risking danger to their own socioeconomic status. It also gave some the opportunity to risk their lives on behalf of a worthy cause.

It was not Stokely Carmichael's advocacy of black power in 1966 that started this morality play on the road to oblivion. The social tensions of whites and blacks working together and the seeds of black power had been there before, but scarcely anyone in the civil rights movement of the New Left had been willing to call them to public attention. These tensions had been apparent and building within CORE, particularly since 1960. Whites tended to treat slights and accusations from blacks as personal problems and not as manifestations of social issues. Differences in social class and the life experiences of black and white civil rights activists, plus the guilt inspired by the privileges of white skin and economic affluence, generally blinded white movement people, preventing them from coming to grips with the actual inter-racial social dynamics involved in the struggle for civil rights.[57]

The sources of tension between blacks and whites in the civil rights movement and the genesis of black power were structured into the movement. Neither blacks nor whites, no matter how well meaning, could eradicate from their interactions those influences from the larger society in which both were located, that is, from the racism and social inequality that pervaded American society.[58]

The most pernicious of these influences could be seen in the racial distribution of leadership positions in the civil rights movement. Whites by virtue of their "superior" education and social class backgrounds assumed a disproportionate share of these positions. One white activist in a retrospective account acknowledged that "many of us had drifted into administrative roles . . . not because we wanted to be leaders, but because we were obviously better able to write press releases and answer the telephone than to approach frightened black people in remote rural communities. The objective result, however, was that we made more decisions than we should have made . . ."[59]

Blacks at the time, particularly the young college blacks, were well aware of what was happening and did not like it. For example, at the time that Freedom Summer (1964), a project to bring several thousand largely white college students to Mississippi, was proposed, black SNCC workers put forth a plan to counter the white domination that they expected. Their plan called for each Freedom Summer group to have a fixed racial ratio—ten blacks to each white. It was never carried out, largely because of the fear that if it were and it became public knowlege, white funds and support would be withdrawn. However, the black SNCCers fears were realized. The immediate consequence was the expression of hostility toward whites, which pained the white volunteers. Another consequence, though, was the heightened support that it engendered among blacks for black power and the control of their own organizations.[60] This, of course, this phenomenon was not limited to only SNCC. The same development occurred in other civil rights groups as well.[61]

Jews, because of their disproportionate presence in the civil rights movement and in leadership positions within it, bore a larger share of this black hostility. This anger, of course, could not help but disillusion many Jews and consequently lessen their active commitment to the civil rights cause—a primary arena of New Left activity. Kirkpatrick Sale, an historian of the SDS, described the sad reaction of white Jews and non-Jews SDS activists to SNCC's 1966 proclamation of black power and the exclusion of whites from the organizing of blacks: "It was the official pronouncement of the death of the dream, which of course was known to be dying, of multiracial organizing in multiracial communities for multiracial justice. And with it the generation of SDS leadership that had grown up inextricably entwined with

SNCC and the civil rights movement . . . the generation that had achieved its political consciousness through integration, found its past, like a rug in an old vaudeville routine, ripped from under its feet." [62]

The hostility and disillusion informing the relationship between blacks and Jews did not only feed off the relatively large number of Jews in the civil rights movement. The history and tradition of black-Jewish relationships in the larger society impinged upon the interactions of blacks and Jews in the movement. This became even more the case when the struggle of blacks shifted its focus from civil rights in the South to economic conditions in the cities of the North. Unfortunately for both blacks and Jews in the movement, the larger tradition of black-Jewish associations that informed theirs was one that contained a highly negative dimension.

Historically blacks and Jews, regardless of the content of their relationship, tended to enter into *unequal* patterned encounters—the black in the subordinate position and the Jew in the superordinate position. Often the context was an undesirable commercial one. Small or marginal Jewish storekeepers were pitted against low-income black customers; Jewish tenement owners confronted black tenants; and Jewish housewives (like Mrs. Portnoy) supervised black maids scrubbing Jewish floors on their knees. Even in the best of circumstances such contexts did little to promote racial and religious harmony and understanding. [63]

Unfortunately the form of the relationship was also present in what were seemingly more positive contexts. In the arena of public services, Jewish school teachers, Jewish social workers, and Jewish civil servants ministered to the needs of the less fortunate blacks. And when blacks were finally able to become school teachers, social workers, and civil servants, they had to deal with the fact of a Jewish supervisor. Such a pattern of unequal relationships, even outside of the marketplace, does little to inhibit the development of mutual suspicion and hostility between those in the subordinate and those in the superordinate locations.

This pattern permeated what were seemingly the most favorable contexts for black-Jewish interaction—older civil rights organizations like CORE and radical parties. But here too blacks could and did point to the preeminent role of Jews and the influence that they wielded over black strategy and tactics. Harold Cruise's (aforementioned) lament about the Jews' domination in areas affecting black interests in the Communist party is a famous case in point.

Thus, when young Jews of the New Left entered the civil rights movement and drifted toward positions of authority and influence, their actions could be interpreted as typical Jewish behavior. But the black political activists who, by the latter 1960s, were marching behind the banner of black power were in no mood to tolerate relationships in which blacks played subordinate roles. Unfortunately for

Jewish New Leftists and for black militants, the manner in which the black desire for autonomy was expressed felt much like rejection. And Jews, hurt by the bitter unwillingness of blacks to accept their hand of friendship, began to draw back and question their political commitments. (For at least one Jewish New Leftist this pain contributed to his suicide.)[64]

Black radicals also gave Jews other reasons to withdraw from the New Left, the major one being black attacks on Israel and Zionism. As one historian expressed it: "As a black sense of identification with Africa and the Third World began to grow, and especially after the cult of things Islamic began to flourish, militant blacks came to the defense of the Arab cause in the Mideast, much like other radicals."[65] After the Six-Day War of 1967, black militants condemned Israel in the strongest terms. Some even offered to take up arms in the Arab cause. Often the anti-Zionist expressions of blacks bordered on anti-Semitism.[66]

It was not only these black attacks in themselves that hastened the withdrawal of Jews from the New Left. The responses of the white New Left and of the organized Jewish community also played a role. First, scarcely anyone in the New Left challenged or was critical of black allegations against Jews or Israel. It was as if the white New Left gave tacit approval to these condemnations. On the other hand, the counterattack by Jewish groups and organizations was massive. Virtually the entire Jewish community defined the black militants as anti-Semites.[67] In this context, it was difficult for many Jewish New Leftists to resist accepting this definition as their own.

The rise of an anti-Semitic–tinged black power movement, against the backdrop of the exacerbated Arab-Israeli conflict and the heightened ethnic consciousness of the Jewish community, did more than just spur the withdrawal of Jewish support and membership from the New Left. These factors also stimulated another type of Jewish response on the part of some radical Jewish youth. Like their nineteenth-century predecessors who had directly encountered anti-Semitism from the Russian peasants and seeming indifference from their Christian comrades-in-arms, young radical and liberal Jews in the late 1960s and 1970s turned back toward their Jewish roots. The shift in this direction was also facilitated by the seeming legitimation that black separatism or nationalism obtained from radicals and nonradicals. Various young Jews, however, desired to hold onto their New Left principles at the same time as they moved closer to a Jewish identity. They were the ones that were crucial in the formation of the Jewish New Left, or Jewish liberation movement. (This will be discussed further below.)

ISRAEL AND THE NEW LEFT AFTER 1967

The most important of the confrontations between the New Left and its Jewish membership and constituency occurred over Israel. The Six-Day War and the Israeli occupation of Arab territories was largely responsible for placing Israel on the public agenda of the New Left. The attention given to Israel and the 1967 war made it exceedingly difficult for any organization concerned with politics and public affairs to avoid discussion of the Israeli situation. The New Left was expected to not only comment on the Arab-Israeli conflict but also take a public position on the issue.

A declaration of policy by the New Left with respect to the Arab-Israeli dispute could not be cost free for the movement. The strong emotions on the part of New Leftists and New Left supporters who held contrasting viewpoints on the issue left the movement no room for maneuvering. Whichever position it took was guaranteed to be costly.

The Six-Day War had heightened the already considerable commitment of American Jews to Israel. Though the Jewish state's victory had been swift and convincing, the war riveted in the minds of American Jews memories of the Holocaust and the potentially precarious position of Israel. Recall, too, that by this time organized Jewish life in the United States was completely dominated by an anti-radical Jewish bourgeoisie, virtually all of whom were enthusiastically dedicated to the cause of Israel. And this, in effect, meant Israeli dedication to government policy. These Jewish leaders, as well as the members of this Jewish community, were in no mood to consider even-handed lectures from radicals about Israel, much less critical comments and analyses. Thus the Jewish community and its leadership were highly primed to attack anyone that did not support Israel.

The other side of the coin was represented by an overlapping and heterogeneous group of black militants and ardent Marxists of various stripes. By 1967 the New Left was, as noted earlier, leaning in a more militant direction. More and more New Leftists, particularly blacks, strongly identified with the colored peoples of the Third World in their struggles against Western imperialism. The total endorsement of these struggles by the Communist nations also helped to give them a Marxist orientation. New Leftists came to vicariously participate in these battles, assuming the role of the underdog and interpreting the conflicts in Marxist and quasi-Marxist terms.

Thus, when the 1967 Arab-Israeli war occurred, New Leftists already had a framework available in which to place it. Militant blacks and dogmatic Marxists exerted a great deal of pressure on the New Left to treat the Arab-Israeli wars as one more example of underdeveloped peoples fighting for liberation against Western imperialists. Between these groups on the one side and the organized Jewish community on the other, the New Left, whatever position it took on Israel, was sure to alienate someone.

The difficulties for the Movement with respect to Jews was further complicated by the fact that the Movement was not centralized and hierarchical. The New Left was, as noted earlier, actually a loose coalition with the SDS being its most important and visible element. And the SDS was itself a loose and open organization containing a variety of factions. Therefore, when issues arose, the New Left's position was often enunciated by a variety of spokespeople representing different groupings whose views were not always similar. Thus, when virulently anti-Israel statements were made by specific factions and self-appointed spokespeople of the New Left, it was not always easy to discern how widespread and legitimate that particular position was. This also meant that those desiring to break the nexus between the Jews and the New Left could pick and choose the most appropriate movement pronouncements to suit their purposes.

In fact, the New Left did speak with a variety of voices on the Arab-Israeli conflict in 1967 and thereafter as the Middle East situation became a more important concern of the New Left. But many of those voices were harshly anti-Israel, reflecting the influence of Marxist and anti-imperialist ideologies. The National Interim Committee of the SDS, an important, official leadership body of that organization, published its position as a proposed resolution in the *New Left Notes,* an official SDS newspaper:

It is important that the American Left understand that Arab reaction is as valid as will be the reaction of blacks to whites in South Africa when that violence culminates against colonial settlers in that country. The importation of pro-Western settlers into the underdeveloped world to build a strong colonial base is hardly a new tactic of imperialism and is no more justifiable in Israel than in Kenya or Mozambique. The Israelis are no more at fault than white settlers anywhere else in the Third World, and no less; the Arabs are no more wrong than the Africans who will ultimately arise against those settlers.[68]

This position was quite similar to that taken by SNCC later in the same year. SNCC, too, lined up solidly with the Arab side and openly referred to Israel as an "illegal state."[69]

Probably the most even-handed New Left assessment of the Arab-Israel conflict came from the editors of *Ramparts.* This California-based magazine had been one of the earliest New Left publications (first as *Root and Branch*) and by 1967 had the largest circulation of any. Many of the people associated with it, including the lead writer of the major editorial defining its stance on Israel, came out of Jewish Old Left backgrounds. In an editorial entitles, "Arabs and Jews," *Ramparts* stated its position:

While there can be no doubt as to the basic legitimacy of the state of Israel, it is tragic that this small nation, which was to be a haven from war's violence, should now be forced to rely for its existence on preemptive military power. . . . It is unreasonable to deny the absolute right of the state of Israel to exist . . . it is equally unprincipled to maintain that Arab claims are irrational and that they have no legitimate grievances in the Holy Land. There is no question that the Arabs terrorized Israeli border communities, but it is also true that the Israelis discriminated against their native Arab population. It is also unfair to place the total responsibility for reconciliation upon the Jews.[70]

The editorial then went on to chastize American leftists who tried to simplify the conflict by making the Israelis into the "bad guys" of Western imperialism and the Arabs into the "good guys" of Third World socialism.[71]

The New Left position on Israel that received the most attention came from the National New Politics Convention (NNPC) held in Chicago on Labor Day weekend in 1967. (This convention was called in order to forge a unified political movement of all radical and liberal groups opposed to the war in Vietnam.)[72] In essence, however, it was a forum for New Left views as shaped by the black militants in attendance. The policy statement on the Middle East endorsed by the NNPC was in fact drafted by the Black Caucas. It put the NNPC on record as condemning "the imperialist Zionist war." In deference to Jewish sensibilities, the statement did add that "this condemnation does not imply anti-Semitism." An alternative resolution calling for Israel to withdraw to prewar borders and for Arab nations to respect these borders was rejected out of hand.[73]

The New Left positions on Israel, whether moderate or militant, unleashed a storm of protest in the Jewish community. Jewish spokesmen bitterly denounced the New Left, accusing it of being not only anti-Zionist but anti-Semitic as well. As Norman Podhoretz, the editor of *Commentary*, explained it: "Now it is perfectly true that anti-Zionism is not necessarily anti-Semitism. But it is also true, I fear, that the distinction between the two is often invisible to the naked Jewish eye, and that anti-Zionism has served to legitimate the open expression of a good deal of anti-Semitism which might otherwise have remained subject to the taboo against anti-Semitism that prevailed in American public life from the time of Hitler until, roughly the Six Day War."[74]

After 1967 it became quite difficult to be a Jew and a New Leftist. The attacks on Israel, which by this time was the focal point of Jewish concern and identity; the hostility of militant blacks toward Zionism, which bordered on anti-Semitism; and the turn toward militancy and dogmatic Marxism, on the one side, and the massive and concerted counterattack of nearly every segment of the organized Jewish community, on the other, subjected many Jews in the Movement to severe pressures and cross-pressures. These phenomena also had an impact on those younger Jews who might have joined.

This does not mean that Jews suddenly and totally abandoned the New Left in the months after the Six-Day War. It takes time for individuals to change their political course. It also takes time for policies enunciated in newspapers, in television interviews, and at conventions in foreign cities to drift down to and influence the attitudes and behavior of peers in local New Left groups. In addition, the Movement did not speak as one on the question of Israel (or most other questions of import). This provided those pro-Israeli Jews who wished to remain in the New Left with rationales for remaining.

There were also other considerations beyond the Movement that inhibited a swift exodus of Jews from New Left politics after 1967. The social forces and events that fed the Movement and assisted it in the politicizing, if not radicalizing, a generation of college students did not disappear in the late 1960s. The Vietnam War still raged, and the plight of the poor and blacks had not noticeably bettered. In fact events like the Cambodian invasion and the Kent State killings did more to radicalize the mass of students at the time (1970) than did any policies of the New Left or its contending factions. Indeed, those events moved students toward the left in spite of New Left politics— which were at that time characterized by internecine warfare, militancy, confusion, and withdrawal from the campuses.[75]

The sudden and massive exodus of Jews from the Movement was further restrained by the character of politics in the Jewish community. While the New Left became increasingly more radical and militant in the 1960s and early 1970s, American Jewry, especially as viewed through the eyes of idealistic and critical Jewish college students, appeared to be traveling in the opposite direction. Even though American Jews were still among the most Democratic and liberal of all ethnic and religious groups in the United States in this period, there was objective evidence to confirm their *relative* rightward drift. In the 1960s Democratic presidential candidates garnered between 80 to 90 percent of Jewish votes. In 1972, given a choice between a liberal Democrat candidate, George McGovern, and a conservative Republican, Richard M. Nixon, the Jewish Democratic vote declined to about 60 percent. Nixon and the Republicans did not accomplish this feat alone. They were assisted by Israeli leaders, Jewish intellectuals, Jewish communal leaders, and Jewish financial notables. Prime Minister Golda Meier and Israeli Ambassador Yitzhak Rabin made known their obvious preference for Nixon. Irving Kristol, the former CCNY radical, became Nixon's "house" philosopher. The Jewish community leaders who broke with the Democrats in this election included Herschel Schacter, former Chairman, Conference of Presidents of Major American Jewish Organizations and William Wexler, Chairman, World Conference of Jewish Organizations. The list of Jewish economic elites who openly supported Nixon or withheld support from McGovern included Stanley Goldblum, Chairman and President, Equity Funding Corp, E. V. Klein, Board Chairman, National General Corp, and Davis Factor, Board Chairman, Max Factor and Co.[76]

This defection from liberal politics was not limited to the 1972 presidential election. It occurred in other elections as well. In some local elections, such conservatives as Sam Yorty in Los Angeles, Frank Rizzo in Philadelphia, and Mario Procacchino in New York also appeared to have made some headway in chipping away at liberalism's strong hold on Jews, especially among the older and poorer Jews. Conversely, it also appeared that candidates, in gearing their appeals toward Jews, were adopting a more moderate, as opposed to a liberal, stance, reflecting what they believed to be a growing trend in the Jewish community.[77]

In New York City between 1966 and 1972 there were various issues and events that appeared to provide further evidence of a growing conservative trend within the Jewish community. In 1966 a referendum was held on the question of a civilian review board for the police—an institution fervently desired by liberals and radicals. Despite the pleas of Jewish favorites like Senators Jacob Javitz and Ted Kennedy, 55 percent of the Jewish votes were cast against this proposal.[78] Then in 1968 a highly publicized teachers' strike broke out, which focused on community control of the schools. The primary contestants were the disproportionately Jewish teachers' union on the one side and various black groups on the other. The media depicted the strike as a struggle between the Jewish teachers battling for their positions against a poor black community concerned with improving the quality of the education of black children.[79] Also in 1968 the Jewish Defense League was founded and it quickly attracted much attention as a militant Jewish foe of liberals and radicals.[80] Several years later Jews in the Forest Hills section of New York made headlines with their opposition to the establishment of low-income housing in their neighborhood.[81]

The conservative drift was also evidenced by the men that leading Jewish organizations chose to publicly honor. In the years 1966–1972 some of the nation's leading conservatives—Governor Ronald Reagan (California), Chief of Police Frank Rizzo (prior to his election as mayor of Philadelphia), San Francisco State President S. I. Hayakawa, Senator George Murphy (California), and Senator James Buckley (New York)[82]—were paid public tribute by such groups as the Jewish Anti-Defamation League.

Then there was also the Jewish intellectuals and public figures who appeared to both embody and legitimize the rightward movement of the Jewish community. Secretary of State Henry Kissinger and chairman of the Federal Reserve Board, Arthur Burns, were the most famous of the powerful conservative Jews. Norman Podhoretz and Commentary were perhaps the most visible examples as well as legitimators of Jewish caution and conservatism from the latter 1960s on. The once liberal-to-left Commentary now came out in opposition to almost all radical or quasi-radical tendencies in American life, from the student movement to women's liberation. Order, stability, caution, and measured change became the watchwords of Jewish former radicals and liberals centered around *Commentary* and the *Public Interest*, a neoconservative journal of opinion.[83]

The rightward shift of American Jewry should, however, be considered in a broader context. Jews may have become more conservative in the late 1960s and 1970s, but this was also true of many other segments of American society, most of which appeared to be moving in this direction at an even faster pace. Relative to almost any other ethnic and religious groups, Jews in this period still had the most liberal politics. Again, Jewish voters disproportionately cast their ballots for liberal and Democratic candidates. Relative to other groups, Jews still contributed more members and support to liberal and radical organizations. Jews as a group also were among the most liberal on virtually all social issues from Vietnam to social welfare.[84]

Jewish youth, either those still in the New Left or those who were liberal-to-Left inclined, tended not to place Jewish politics in a larger context or consider it in *relative* terms. For these young Jews the conservatizing trends within the American Jewish community were accentuated by the higher expectations they held concerning Jews. Robert Scheer, former editor of *Ramparts*, bluntly expressed this point of view at a symposium on Israel: "Yes, I ask more of the Jews."[85] This same perspective was also poignantly stated by another disillusioned Jewish youth, Danny Siegel:

Our synagogues are empty most of the year, and it is the adults who dismiss from their pulpits the few rabbis who have the courage to challenge the notion that Judaism must not become involved with the question of Vietnam, racism, and poverty. It is not only the young who are disgusted by the display of wealth so common in our celebrations of "religious" occasions . . . It is not only the young who understand that Jewish life is empty of real depth because it has accepted a life style which demands silence in the face of evil, submission to the authority of "experts," and surrender of moral accountability for the misfortune of others in exchange for the split-level homes, catered affairs, and pious (but very vague) resolutions calling for peace and brotherhood. We have indeed bought into the American economy, but we may have done so at the cost of our Jewish souls.[86]

Young Jews of college age in 1970, despite these pressures and cross-pressures, were still further to the left on the political spectrum than their non-Jewish peers. An extensive national survey of freshman in 1969 reported that of the male freshmen, 10 percent of the Jews identified their current political preference as "Left" compared to 3 percent of the non-Jews. Among those calling themselves "Liberal," Jews outnumbered others 47 to 30 percent.[87] In a 1971 survey of a random sample of Harvard Students, 65 percent of the radicals were identified as Jews in a total student population that was 29% Jewish.[88] Similar results were obtained from a survey of college students conducted in the wake of the Cambodian invasion and Kent State killings in 1970. This poll found that in colleges where demonstrations took place, 90 percent of the Jewish students participated, compared to 82 percent of the Catholics and 71 percent of the Protestants.[89]

The numbers of self-identified leftists, liberals, and demonstrators among Jews, although important, masked the changes that were taking place at the organization level. The pollsters and nose counters did not notice that, while larger numbers of Jews and non-Jews called themselves liberal and left and took to the streets to voice their anger against government policies and actions, the organizational core of the New Left was fragmenting and shrinking. And the Jewish presence in these groups was also declining. In 1970 only 2 of the top 11 SDS officers in the country were Jewish—the lowest proportion of Jews at this level since the founding of this organization.[90]

The pressures on Jews in the Movement, building since 1967, were increasingly exacting a toll. Anti-Israeli sentiments hardened and diffused throughout much of the ranks of the New Left as pro-Palestinian feelings grew stronger. At antiwar demonstrations Al Fatah or Palestinian guerrilla posters began to appear; New Lefters like Mark Rudd, a Jewish SDS leader, commenced the solicitation of funds for the Palestinian resistance. As one male interviewee said: "I was marching in a demonstration against the war and looked up to see an Al Fatah banner. I walked out of the parade and never participated in another New Left protest again." (He subsequently emigrated to Israel.) Other Jews departed out of disgust over the crudeness and insensitivity that pro-Palestinian and anti-Israeli New Lefters displayed to those unwilling to comply with this line. "Don't you know," said one Jewish radical on returning from talks with Palestinian guerrillas, "that Theodore Herzl had discussions with Hitler."[91] It soon became clear that one could not remain in New Left and radical organizations *and* be either pro-Israel or even neutral about Israel without the greatest difficulty. Many Jews in or around radical groups in the late 1960s and early 1970s simply could not tolerate such dissonance and resolved their problems by leaving the movement. One of those who quit the New Left because of its stance on Israel, David Balch, perhaps best expressed the feelings of his generation of Jewish radicals in an Op-Ed column in the (July 6, 1975) *New York Times* entitled: "The Jewish Radical: A Crisis of Conscience."

. . . The New Left caucus meeting in Chicago caused the first real crisis of conscience for the Jewish radicals in the Left establishment when it condemned Zionism and the basic validity of a Jewish homeland and nation. . . . The New Left today . . . now stands in direct and open opposition to the entity, safety, and aspirations of the Jewish people. In full combat, it has resorted to the most blatant anti-Semitism. It is now almost past time for Jews still associated with the reactionary left to open their eyes.

An important political and personal issue for these alienated New Leftists and radicals became the direction to pursue after their departure. Given that their Jewishness was involved in their decision to quit, it would seem logical that they might have sought a Jewish or Jewish-oriented alternative. But the middle-class life-style and the harsh antiradical orientation of the leadership of the Jewish community were, for many, roadblocks against moving in that direction. The dilemma of Jewish radicals (and liberals) who wanted to hold a radical or liberal commitment while continuing to maintain some aspect of Jewish identity was considerable. In many ways they were in the same position as their nineteenth-century predecessors in Russia. Sol Stern, an articulate Jewish New Leftist journalist, and primary author of the July 1967 *Ramparts* editorial, stated the case as follows:

> In the exertions of the Jewish Establishment, one sees the Left's arguments merely stood on their head. Where the Left has said to young Jews, "to be for the survival of Israel is to betray the world revolution," the Jewish Establishment seems to be saying, "if you are for the world revolution, you betray your people." All this makes for strange bedfellows, with the Left and the Jewish Establishment cooperating in the polarization of the Jewish community between pro-Israel cold warriors and simple minded, anti-Jewish revolutionaries.[92]

The contending and often emotional pressure upon Jews in the New Left and in radical groups of the late 1960s and 1970s forced them to consciously come to grips with their ethnic and political identity. There were scarcely any sanctuaries where such Jews could avoid going through this process. Their responses, as one might expect, were not uniform. (Unfortunately there is no study that measured how many of what kind of Jews went in which directions. I therefore had to rely upon my own impressions and that of key informants.)

Some Jewish radicals consciously chose to adopt a cosmopolitan position. For them, their political identities as radicals superseded their identities as Jews. However, even within this camp there were some variations, with some following Trotsky or Rosa Luxemburg and publicly declaring that they were revolutionaries or leftists and not Jews. Barry Sautman, a Columbia University SDS speaker, angrily replied to the hostile question " 'What the hell kind of Jew are you . . . ?' " by saying, " 'I don't consider myself a Jew . . . I'm an internationalist. I believe the only way to overcome the bosses of this world is for all the working people everywhere to rise up together.' "[93] Others like David Horowitz, a *Ramparts* editor, came to a similar position but tried to maintain continuity with secular Jewish traditions and the historical experience of the Jewish people. In this respect, Horowitz chose to model himself after the noted Jewish socialist and writer Isaac Deutscher, who stated:

> I am . . . a Jew by force of my unconditional solidarity with the persecuted and oppressed.

The Jewish *Ramparts* editor then went on to say:

The revolutionary belongs to a community of faith. It is a community that extends beyond the classes and the nations, and reaches across the boundaries that divide and oppress. Within every national group it forms the basis of a new human community and a new human identity. Today the revolutionary is isolated, obstructed by the divisions that form the cultural and political legacy of the past; the revolutionary is in nations but not of them . . . within each nation—Russia, America, Israel, Egypt—there are the aliens, the persecuted, the unassimilated, the "Jews" who know the heart of the stranger and who struggle for human freedom.

Horowitz ended the summation of his position by quoting from the Passover service:

This year we are slaves; next year we shall be free men and women. This year in the lands of our exile; next year in Jerusalem.[94]

Many Jewish youth in the face of the conflicts between the New Left and their Jewish identity chose to leave radical politics. It was simply too costly in emotional terms to be part of a political grouping subjected to such heavy attack from Jewish quarters and at the same time to have no support from within that movement for a Jewish identity. Some who were motivated by this dilemma and other considerations sought out movements of personal and spiritual growth in lieu of radical politics. Jerry Rubin of Yippie and Chicago Seven fame was perhaps the most famous example of those who went from politics to psychology.[95]

There was also a third response to the dilemma of being Jewish and radical in the late 1960s and 1970s, which involved the active blending of Jewishness or Zionism with radicalism. Collectively, the various Jewish radical groups and papers that came to this type of position was known as the Jewish New Left or Jewish liberation movement.

JEWISH NEW LEFT

In essence the Jewish liberation movement was born in the wake of the Six-Day War and had for its reluctant midwife the crude anti-Zionists of the New Left. In many cases it attracted individuals groping for an alternative structure that would allow them to comfortably be both Jewish or Zionist and radical. As one Jewish student expressed it: "How could I reconcile my leftist proclivities with my, now, admittedly Zionist ones? Did I have to choose between the Fatah supporting SDS and the ultra-middle class, lox and bagel breakfast club, "Hillel Society?' There could be no doubt but that the most interesting Jewish kids were on the left. The Jews of the anti-war movement were infinitely more intellectually exciting than the business majors of . . . Hillel. The choice was an impossible one. I felt that there had to be a third route." That third route was for him and many others, Zionist radicalism.[96]

The Jewish liberation movement was initially small, consisting of a few individuals, usually students, coming together in various localities to form a Jewish radical group or newspaper. But within a short period considerable growth occurred. In 1968 two radical Jewish newspapers commenced their publication, *The Jewish Radical* (Berkeley) and *The Jewish Liberation Journal* (New York). Within five years there were over 65 of this kind of paper. During the same period the number of Jewish radical groups grew from a handful to over 100. Increasingly they moved toward coordinating their strategies and approaches to common problems. In 1970 a number of radical Zionist groups banded together to form the Radical Zionist Alliance. By 1973 there were metropolitan unions of Jewish students in Philadelphia, Boston, Baltimore, Washington, Denver, Boulder, Los Angeles, and northern Ohio. Overall, the Jewish New Left was a loose confederation of many autonomous groups that more or less shared a variety of ideas and interests.[97]

The period in which the Jewish New Left was able to maintain some semblance of a balance between its Jewish and radical commitments proved to be relatively short, lasting from approximately 1968 to 1973 or 1974. In the Jewish New Left, as in the Jewish Old Left for many of the same sociological reasons, things Jewish came to take precedence over things radical. In the older movement the process had taken decades; in the younger it took a few short years. By the mid to latter 1970s, religion and Israel had become the focal concerns of the Jewish liberation movement, whereas radical concerns, by contrast, became markedly secondary and held by only a relative handful.

In order to understand how this metamorphosis came about, it is necessary to examine the backgrounds of Jewish New Leftists, their political strategies, and the historical context in which they were politicized. We turn our attention first to the Jewish community and the New Left in the years after 1967. The developments within these two political contexts, although they did not determine the political path of the Jewish New Left, most certainly strongly influenced the direction that this movement would take in the late 1960s and 1970s.

In the Jewish community after the 1967 Six Day War, the Jewish consciousness and the pro-Israel identification of American Jews rose significantly. The war in itself was a major factor underlying those changes. In addition, the actions taken by the leadership of organized Jewry also contributed to the resurgence of this consciousness and identification. Jewish schools, organizations, and fund raising drives took on a more decidedly pro-Israel orientation after 1967. In the same period, Zionist organizations developed the American Zionist Federation at the national level and Zionist federations at the local levels to more adeptly spread the Zionist message within the American Jewish community. Programs for sending various categories of Jews to Israel for either a few weeks, a year, or a lifetime were developed or expanded. They bore immediate fruit as the number of American Jews visiting, volunteering, or settling in Israel after 1967 increased dramatically and thereby increased the number of U.S. Jews with personal ties to the Jewish state.⁹⁸ The result of all of these developments was that young Jews who came to the American campuses after 1967, especially those who had some contact with the organs and institutions of Jewish life, were much more likely than their Jewish predecessors prior to 1967 to feel more positively toward Israel and to be more aware of their Jewish identities.

Once on campus, the New Left in its post-1967 phase was increasingly less able to gain the commitment of Jewish students in particular or of American students in general. Although specific events or causes such as the Cambodian invasion or "People's Park" in Berkeley continued to attract large numbers of Jewish and non-Jewish students to New Leftist-led demonstrations in the late 1960s and early 1970s, their involvement with the New Left was progressively more sporadic and short-lived.⁹⁹ Again, this was a period in which the New Left was fragmenting and moving toward a more sectarian and dogmatic Marxist line (or lines). It was a time when black power advocates at the forefront of the New Left espoused anti-Israel and at times anti-Jewish positions. And it was also the years in which the New Left became more anti-Israel and more pro-Palestinian. This Movement in this period of history then had little in its political arsenal capable of attracting Jewish college students either as liberals, scions of a bourgeoisie, or most especially as Jews.

These historical developments within the Jewish and New Left communities in themselves did not cause the Jewish New Left to evolve in less than a decade into a predominantly Jewish and non-Leftist movement. The experiences and outlooks that individual Jewish New Leftists brought with them to their movement, as well as the organizational strategies that they adopted, also made unique contributions to this metamorphosis. However, the real significance of these personal and organizational variables can only be understood by placing them within the larger historical context. This perhaps can be best demonstrated by focusing primarily on one Jewish New Left organization, the Radical Jewish Union (RJU).

The RJU, which is still in existence today, was one of the earliest and most important of the groups that came to be known as the Jewish New Left. It was founded in 1968 at the very heartland of the American student movement, the University of California at Berkeley. Its paper, The Jewish Radical, is and was perhaps the most thoughtful and best written of all Jewish liberation movement publications.¹⁰⁰

The RJU members and leaders brought to their organization a political heritage and orientation that combined liberal to Left politics with a Jewish and pro-Israel orientation. Both the leadership and membership were, in terms of contacts with Jewish organizations, institutions, and Israel prior to joining the RJU, markedly "Jewish." Two of the most important leaders of the group, David Biale and Shelly Schreter, had had meaningful Jewish experiences before coming to Berkeley. Biale came from a labor Zionist family and had been active as a camper and a counsellor in Jewish camping activities. Schreter had attended Jewish day schools and, as an undergraduate at McGill University, was president of the campus Hillel Foundation, an old traditional Jewish student organization associated with B'nai B'rith. Biale and Schreter were typical of the approximately 20 students who formed the core of the RJU. Virtually all of them had had some form of intimate involvement in Jewish day schools or youth movements, and just about every person in this group had spent time in Israel, typically as a volunteer on a kibbutz. As a group, according to David Biale, "RJU members were more Jewish than other [Jewish] students at Berkeley." These Jewish contacts and involvements meant or at least strongly implied that, as a group, those in the RJU were very conscious of their Jewish identities and had been exposed to the dominant currents circulating in the Jewish community after 1967.

The RJU leaders and members also brought to their organization a set of political attitudes and values. These attitudes, similar to those of non-Jewish students involved in the student movement, ranged from Marxist to liberal. But the most dominant orientation seemed to be labor Zionist. For example, David Biale came from this type of background. Many, if not a majority, of the members prior to their entrance into the RJU had had some form of involvement with a labor Zionist youth movement, either *Hashomer Hatzair* or *Habonim*. Thus, from the type of Jews that the RJU attracted, it is quite clear that the organization would be highly sensitive and responsive toward Jewish issues and interests.

This Jewish "tilt," however, did not prevent the RJU members either as a group or as individuals from becoming concerned about New Left-type issues or from getting involved in New Left-type activities. RJU members, as American college students and/or as an organization, took an active part in anti-war demonstrations, the strike of Third World students, and the People's Park campaign—issues and events that grabbed many if not most Berkeley students in this tumultuous period of time.[101]

In its earlier years, in particular, the RJU attempted to be simultaneously a Jewish and a New Left movement. This, in the context of the times, was a most difficult feat to accomplish. Jack Nusan Porter, a sociological analyst of the Jewish liberation movement (as well as a former member of Habonim and founder of the Jewish Student Movement at Northwestern University), described how Jewish New Leftists tried to maintain a balance between their two souls *circa* 1970:

. . . black and white radicals have taken anti-Israel and anti-Semitic stances. Jewish student movements have arisen to meet this challenge, to correct and refute these ideologies, and to seek a *rapprochement* with such revolutionaries . . . For the time being Jewish radicals will take what is *good* from blacks and SDSers but will reject what is *bad,* i.e. any invalid anti-Israel or anti-Jewish positions . . . radical Jews . . . will condemn Jewish slumlords, but will support Black Power demands of . . . more jobs, better housing, community control of schools . . . They will denounce the New Left's biased account of Zionism yet seek a homeland for the Arab Palestinians. They will denounce the Jewish establishment, yet will work within the Jewish structure to change it.[102]

The RJU, as with the Jewish New Left in general, however, was unable to maintain this balance. Increasingly the organization drew closer to its Jewish and pro-Israel pole and further from its New Left one. This shift was the result of an interplay of various factors.

First, there was the politics of the New Left. From the late 1960s through the 1970s, for reasons previously cited, the New Left lost its attraction for RJU members and Jewish New Leftists (as well as for American students at large). In the case of the RJU, a New Left identity was primarily maintained through ad hoc involvement in occasional "good" causes promoted by or associated with New Left elements, such as the aforementioned anti-war demonstrations or the People's Park campaign. This sporadic contact with the New Left reinforced the RJU's identification with this movement. But such reinforcement was minor compared to what was, from the perspective of RJU members, the New Left's repelling features: factionalism, dogmatic Marxism, and an anti-Israel stance.

Second, there was the previously cited developments within the American Jewish community after 1967. Jewish New Leftists like the RJU members, given their Jewish backgrounds and Jewish concerns, could not help but be influenced by the heightened Jewish consciousness and particularly the pro-Israel focus of the Jewish community in those years.

In fact, it is doubtful whether there would have been a Radical Jewish Union or a Jewish New Left without the heightened consciousness of that period. For approximately a decade before 1967, young Leftist-oriented Jews, including those with labor Zionist involvements and experiences in Israel, had made no serious attempt to form a Jewish Left movement on American campuses. Given the state of the New Left and the Jewish community, as well as the almost purposeful de-emphasis on ethnicity among intellectual opinion leaders in those years, the formation of a Jewish New Left movement prior to 1967 would have been a most formidable task, if not an almost unthinkable one, for young politically inclined Jews. The year 1967 marked the beginning of a new era and new generation of liberal to left Jews on American campuses. Their experiences and involvements in and with a changed New Left and Jewish community facilitated and encouraged them to think about and to form a Jewish New Left.

Third, the organizational character of the RJU and Jewish New Left and the primary constituency toward which they addressed themselves also played important roles in moving these Jewish New Leftists toward more purely Jewish concerns and a pro-Israel position. The RJU, like other Jewish New Left groups, organized as a Jewish body and focused on a Jewish constituency. Even on issues that had little intrinsic connection with purely Jewish matters, the Jewish liberation movement addressed itself primarily to Jews. Thus, at the time of the Cambodian invasion in 1970, the Radical Jewish Union sent its spokesmen into the synagogues to carry its case on the war as Jews to Jews.

The choice of such a constituency in this period seemed politically quite sensible. The New Left leaders, through their endorsement of members organizing in their own racial and ethnic communities, appeared to legitimize if not support the decision of Jewish New Leftists to direct themselves toward the Jewish community. (Jews as such, however, received little specific encouragement to take this action.) Jewish New Leftists, as Jewish Old Leftists before them, wanted to be politically significant and relevant. To accomplish these ends, it seemed necessary to have a special constitutency, American Jewry. Also, American Jews were politically an influential group in the larger society. It would have been the height of political folly for Jewish New Leftists to purposely cut themselves off from a community that needed to be informed and persuaded by political persons such as themselves, particularly when this was the community with which they had the most familiarity.

The selection of a Jewish constituency placed the RJU and the Jewish New Left in the same political position as the one that had confronted their Jewish Old Left predecessors in earlier decades. Both the Old and the New Jewish Left wished to push American Jewry further toward the liberal to Left end of the political spectrum and at the same time resist the pull to the center through such contact. In this quest the Jewish Old Left had a political arsenal that included a relatively well-honed ideology, experienced leaders, mass base, and solid organizational infrastructure. But in the end, despite these strengths, the pursuit of and involvement with this constituency proved to be primary factors in eroding the radical commitment of this movement. The New Left not only lacked the assets of its predecessors, but in addition faced considerably more formidable obstacles and opponents within American Jewry than had the Old Left. The contemporary Jewish community was largely middle class in composition, well organized, liberal to moderate in its politics, and led by a strata of respected rabbis, professionals, and men of wealth generally hostile to radicals and radicalism and not lacking in political acumen. It was also a community fervently united around and committed to the safeguarding of Israel. Under such circumstances, the chances for the

Jewish New Left avoiding the fate of the Jewish Old Left were nil. How could these young men and women gain any support from within such a community without compromising their New Leftist positions? And, without such compromise, they would have few if any constituents and thus no political relevance.

The major issues that the Jewish New Left chose to identify itself with also contributed to the weakening of its radical commitment. The most important issues or themes that Jewish New Leftists took with them to the Jewish community revolved around Israel, the campaign for Soviet Jewry and the Jewish power structure in America. This kind of agenda and the manner in which the Jewish New Left dealt with these items generated a dynamic that attenuated the movement's ties to the New Left while strengthening its Jewish or non-Leftist commitment.

This process can be viewed most clearly with respect to the Radical Jewish Union's and Jewish liberation movement's stance on Israel. Jewish New Leftists were genuine supporters of Israel's continued existence, even though they were critical of many of its governments' particular policies. The strongly held and often incompatible feelings about Israel held by the New Left and the Jewish community, however, gave the Jewish New Left precious little room to establish a position that would alienate neither New Leftists or American Jews. It was quite clear from the mood of American Jews and its leadership that if anything would ensure the enmity of this people, it would be criticism of Israel, no matter how tepid. Given their desire to do political work within the American Jewish community, as well as their own individual ties and contacts with this community prior to joining the Jewish New Left, the members of this movement were moved toward a more supportive position on Israel and into a relationship of conflict with the New Left.

The movement in this direction was also facilitated and encouraged by another level of association with Israel. These Jewish New Leftists chose to have an individual as well as a corporate Jewish and Left identity. Any identity needs validation and support from sources beyond the beliefs in the heads of the individual carrier or carriers. Jewish Old Leftists of an earlier day had the Yiddish language and culture associated with a vibrant and massive Jewish working class to validate both their Jewish and Left identities simultaneously. In contemporary United States neither this prop nor any other meaningful one was available to Jewish New Leftists. Thus, the only source of a Jewish and Left identity stemmed from Israel, particularly the Israeli *kibbutz*—a country and an institution about which almost every RJU member and probably most Jewish New Leftists were intimately and positively knowledgeable.

In Israel itself, it was also easier for Jews to maintain a combined Jewish and Leftist identity than was true in the United States. In America *circa* 1970, the Jewish and New Left communities' attitudes toward such an identity, and especially the New Left's hostility toward Israel, made it difficult, if not at times painful, for those who wished to hold a Jewish and New Left identity and be accepted by both the Jewish and New Left communities. In the Jewish state, Jewish radicals did not have their political legitimacy threatened and called into question by fellow radicals because of their Jewish identities or position on Israel. A considerable portion of Jewish New Leftists, including about 25% of the Jewish Radical Union, whether consciously or unconsciously influenced by this logic, eventually migrated to Israel.[103] And, for many of those who remained, the awareness of what a Jewish state could psychologically offer to Jewish radicals was probably one more reason to elevate a pro-Israel sentiment to the fore of their political concerns. But, whatever the direct or indirect cause, the rise in such a sentiment correlated with a waning commitment to the anti-Israel New Left.

One example of the manner in which the primacy of the Jewish New Left's commitment to Israel undercut its leftist leanings can be observed in the case of The Jewish Radical's treatment of Representative Ronald Dellums, a black liberal Democrat from Berkeley and Oakland. Dellums (is and) was one of the most progressive members of the House of Representatives. With respect to his legislative record, The Jewish Radical stated: "On Watergate, on spending for social programs, on civil rights, on many other issues, Dellums has always been on the side of the angels." The paper's only point of disagreement with Dellums was the fact that in 1969 he had voted against a $2.2 billion emergency arms appropriation for Israel. It admitted that, except for this, the liberal Congressman had an "excellent voting record." When it came to the point of endorsing Dellum's reelection bid, The Jewish Radical waffled: "Each voter will have to make up his own mind." Dellums' one vote against Israel was in the estimation of this Jewish newspaper sufficient in itself to outweigh or balance out his otherwise "excellent voting record." It became the single reason why The Jewish Radical denied him its endorsement.[104]

The escalation of Israel to the fore of the concerns of the Jewish New Left was a process that appears to have received encouragement from ostensible movement adversaries. The Youth and He-Chalutz Department of the Jewish Agency, an international organization close to the Israeli government that is primarily responsible for the disbursement of funds collected in the Diaspora on behalf of Israel, is alleged to have funneled funds through the American Zionist Youth Foundation to Jewish New Left groups for the purpose of underwriting their newspapers. Later, local federations like the Jewish Federation of Oakland provided funds for the same purposes. These monies, particularly those of the Jewish Agency, were crucial to the establishment and/or survival of papers such as The Jewish Radical. And, as such publications were usually at the heart of the activities and life of Jewish New Left groups, the Jewish Agency and the local federations then in effect played a highly significant role in the growth and development of the Jewish liberation movement itself.

The officials of the Jewish Agency, the American Zionist Youth Foundation, and the local Jewish federations, according to one highly informed recipient of this subsidy, tied no political conditions to their gifts. Indeed, during the period in which the subsidies were received, Jewish New Left newspapers did not cease their criticism of the American Jewish or Israeli establishments. The Jewish Radical, for example, despite its subsidization, did not cease its advocacy of a free and independent Palestinian state. What, then, did these alleged establishment donors receive in return for their apparent largesse?

It is clear that politics and not charity or good will was behind the distribution of such funds. The subsidization of these Jewish New Left papers and organizations was a subtle form of political manipulation. The officials of these Jewish establishment organizations in essence made a financial investment in the hope of reaping certain political returns. The return on this particular investment that they desired was a "Jewish" New Left student movement.

At the time in which these funds were originally given in the late 1960s, there was considerable political ferment on American campuses and among Jewish students. The political direction in which Jewish students would move was far from clear. The Jewish Agency money became one way of influencing the nature and direction of these particular students. What it did was to facilitate and encourage Jewish students to utilize uniquely Jewish channels as outlets for their politics. In the context of Jewish organizations, even if they were Jewish leftist organizations, those responsible for the subsidies apparently believed that eventually New Left attitudes and values would weaken while Jewish identities and commitments to Israel would grow stronger. In the pursuit of this goal these officials were willing to tolerate attacks on their political positions from those whom they subsidized. As the long-range results demonstrated, these political manipulators were correct.

The social class composition and the nature of the ideology of the Jewish New Left were also factors that inclined this movement away from a radical orientation. The Jewish New Left was (and is) made up almost entirely of college students and former college students from middle class families. This kind of base, as we saw earlier, does not facilitate the maintenance of a Marxist political commitment for any length of time.

The nature of the ideology of the Jewish New Left proved to be inadequate as a firm basis for the establishment and survival of a Left or Left-oriented movement. The ideology or perhaps ideologies of this heterogeneous and decentralized movement was only moderately socialist and paid little attention to class issues. The enemies were generally loosely defined as the Jewish establishment, large corporations, anti-Semites, the government, and American imperialism. One of the best statements of the ideals that informed the beliefs of Jewish New Leftists is that of the Jews for Urban Justice, one of the first radical Jewish groups to be formed in the 1960s. In language reminiscent of the SDS' Port Huron platform, the Jews For Urban Justice proclaimed:

As Jews we declare our intention to participate in the revolutionary process by synthesizing and following a new Halakhah. Our new way of life will consist of the same elements as the old: i.e., the love of life, respect for all of Nature, the encouragement of individual development within a communal context, an active passion for social justice and human equality, a recognition of human potentiality. However, it will also be framed in the context of the realities of our day: i.e., an expanding technology, imperialism, racism, sexism, ecological disaster. We recognize our obligation to denounce evil everywhere it appears and work in a united community to hasten its disappearance. We dedicate outselves to the creation of a decentralized socialist order, for that is the only way in which we can end our own oppression and that of all peoples.[105]

This statement, although a brief expression of one of many Jewish radical groups, does give us insight into the ideological shortcomings of the movement. There is no question that this formulation is both sensitive and moving. There is serious question, however, whether the ideology sketched out could be effective as a counterweight to and a rallying force against the prevailing capitalist ideology of the United States or the non-Left tendenceis within the Jewish community. Enemies are too vaguely defined. Courses of action are either too utopian or too susceptible to cooptation by the Jewish establishment and the non-Jewish establishment as well.

This statement, as a representative of the ideology of the Jewish New Left, also reflects a confusion and problem with the areas of class and constituency within American Jewry. Jews are appealed to as Jews as if they had no class interests and as if being Jewish was sufficient to elicit support for "just" causes. Essentially, the ideology espoused by the Jewish New Left was one of good and decent persons and congenial to the interests and outlook of Jewish New Leftists, who were themselves members of an educated, humanistic, and economically stable strata within middle class Jewry.

The problematic nature of the Jewish New Left's ideology, its political strategy, class composition, and the contrasting pressures exerted upon it by the New Left and the Jewish community, placed its radical commitment in a vulnerable position. Unfortunately, the movement did not have the political and organizational strength to protect its radical orientation from subversion by Jewish forces and currents. The Yom Kippur War of 1973 and the heightened Jewish consciousness and pro-Israel sentiment that followed in its wake gave greater strength and impetus to those internal and external forces working to transform the Jewish New Left into a more Jewish and a less left movement.[106]

The role that Israel and a Jewish consciousness played in the decline of the Jewish New Left's radicalism can perhaps best be seen in the two paths that many of the more idealistic Jewish New Leftists took in their departure from or in lieu of leftist-oriented politics in the United States. A significant proportion of those who were politically inclined emigrated to Israel and to kibbutzim where they hoped they could avail themselves of a milieu and subculture more supportive of a Jewish and/or radical Jewish identity. This drained the Jewish New Left in the United States of some of its more politically experienced and sophisticated leaders and activists, thus making the movement that much more vulnerable to forces pushing it from a radical to a more moderate political orientation. Another idealistic contingent traveled along a religious route in its quest for meaning and understanding. They either formed *havurahs*, religious communal groups with a focus on traditional Judaism, or chose to pursue rabbinical careers.[107]

The Jewish New Left as a radical movement is now (1978) a spent force. But this has not meant the extinction of a radical commitment among Jewish youth. Jewish leftists as individuals and in the context of organizations continue to exist, albeit in reduced numbers compared to those of 5 or 6 years earlier. Young Jewish socialists and those favorable to socialism can be found in organizations with strong ties to the Jewish Old Left: the Jewish Socialist Youth Bund, Habonim, and Hashomer Hatzair. There are also leftist and leftist-oriented Jews in a few remaining Jewish New Left organizations such as the Radical Jewish Union in Berkeley and the Jewish Socialist Community in New York City. Young (and not so young) Jewish radicals, many of whom are veterans of the Old and New Left, also constitute a significant part of the membership and leadership of non-Jewish radical organizations and publications such as the Social Democrats, the Democratic Socialist Organizing Committee, the New American Movement, and the Socialist newspaper, *In These Times* (which is edited by James Weinstein and Martin Sklar, two Jewish political activists of the Old and New Left).

The total number of Jews (and non-Jews) involved with these leftist organizations is not large. The combined membership of the Jewish Socialist Youth Bund, the Habonim, and the Hashomer Hatzair, for example, is approximately 3400. The readership of *In These Times*, a socialist newspaper read by Jews and non-Jews alike has, for example, not reached as high as 12,000.[108] But, the important point is that these Jewish leftists and Jewish left organizations exist. This fact suggests that perhaps when a new wave of radicalism sweeps the Jewish community in the near future there will be available an experienced and seasoned cadre ready to lead and fan the flames.

The question that of course remains is: How is any future Jewish radical movement or movement of radical Jews going to escape the pitfalls that befell the Jewish New Left and Jewish Old Left? Unfortunately, both of these movements found that they were unable to for any enduring length of time be simultaneously Jewish, radical, and relevant.

Summary and Conclusion

In a period no longer than the lifetime of one human being, the relationship between socialism and the Jewish community in America changed dramatically. Earlier in this century Jews were an important base for a significant socialist movement and provided a very large proportion of its leaders, activists, and spokesmen. In these same years men and women of the Left were held in respect by the masses of American Jewry, and some of them were also community leaders. Now the situation is different. Although Jews are still disproportionately present in radical organizations, their numbers as well as the total involved in such groups are small. In the Jewish community today, Leftists, if they are alive and politically active, generally command not respect but suspicion and animosity. If there are any Jewish radicals who might be called leaders within the Jewish community, they are typically leaders of only small handfuls of the faithful aged or the idealistic young.

The sociohistorical account and analysis of the fate and course of socialism in the Jewish community has already been provided in abundant detail. At this juncture a brief summary of the important themes and issues appears to be in order. This will enable us to take stock of the past relationship of the Jews and the Left and contribute to our understanding of what this association may be like in the future. In addition, the summary will provide a context and a forum for dealing with the interrelationship between class, ethnicity, and politics in a capitalist society.

The Rise of Socialism

The basic thesis of this monograph is that Jews as a people turned to socialism primarily as a consequence of their experience with capitalism, first in Russia and then in the United States. Russian and American capitalists proved to be unwitting marriage brokers, or *shadkhens*, between this religioethnic group and this ideology. Their most important contribution in this regard was to bring into being for the first time in Jewish history a large, concentrated, and embittered class of Jewish workers: a Jewish proletariat.

Capitalism not only brought forth this proletariat, it also worked to ensure that this working class would be imbued with class consciousness and be predisposed to socialism. This Jewish proletariat in both Russia and America was molded by its contacts and experiences with this politicoeconomic system in ways that made it resemble the ideal-typical model of a militantly class-conscious working class: a large group concentrated in the same or similar occupations and geographical areas, sharing common grievances at the hands of the same or similar exploiters. The characteristics that define this class facilitate intraclass communication, a feeling of solidarity, and a shared antagonism toward the oppressor class. Eventually, the interaction of all these factors ideally (in the Weberian sense of the term) leads this class toward an identification with socialism.

This particular proletariat was not an ideal-typical one, it was a Jewish proletariat. The "Jewish" component of its identity played a crucial role both in strengthening the ties between Jews and socialism and in weakening them. The ethnic factor as it mediated the relationship between Jews and the Left was very much a two-edged sword.

At the end of the nineteenth and the beginning of the twentieth century, the social physiognomy of the Jewish people with the proletariat at its core appeared to be most supportive of a socialist movement among Jews. This was a period in which Jews, especially in Russia, most resembled a nation-class or people-class—that is, a social collectivity within a multinational society in which all persons are simultaneously members of the same class and people or nation.[1]

In this period of time capitalists did much to ensure that nationality and class reinforced one another in the Jewish community. Their prime contribution in this regard was, of course, to bring into being a large Jewish proletariat. But capitalists did more than this. Capitalism also did yeoman work to undermine those elements within the Jewish community that functioned as its most valuable allies in resisting a Jewish turn toward radicalism. While building a Jewish proletariat, capitalism simultaneously weakened and diminished the influence and numbers of other classes and strata most antagonistic to a close relationship between the Jews and the Left. The rabbinate and the men of wealth, buttressed by religion and tradition, found their political leadership positions cut from under them by an economic system that had little respect for tradition and traditional relationships. Their role as agents of social control was also diminished by the fact that capitalism forced Jews from traditional locales and occupations into cities and occupational arenas and settings in which old mechanisms as well as old agents of social control were of little consequence.

Capitalism also made Jewishness into its enemy and impelled Jews as Jews toward radicalism at the same time that it was orienting Jews as workers in the same direction. The new, the modern, and the reputedly rational economic system that knocked aside tradition and inspired change and expectations for change proved to be remarkably respectful of the past when dealing with Jews. Rather than "liberating" Jews from the despised and marginal economic roles in which they had been confined by centuries of anti-Semitism, capitalists built upon and reinforced Jewish and non-Jewish divisions and distinctions. Jewish workers found that under capitalism as well as under feudalism their employment was to be in "Jewish" occupations and peripheral industries. Thus, there came into being a uniquely *Jewish proletariat*, one that was exploited and oppressed both as wage earners and as Jews.

This double yoke and concentration as Jews and as proletarians proved beneficial to the cause of socialism among Jews. It increased the bitterness and frustration of Jews while at the same time building a powerful sense of solidarity among them. Their relative isolation and insulation as Jews in similar occupations and industries as well as in ghettoes also gave new life and importance to the language and culture of the Jewish masses, Yiddish. Yiddish heightened Jewish workers' solidarity and their predisposition toward socialism by facilitating intraclass communication among the disadvantaged Jews and by cutting them off from contact with non-Jewish values and socializing agents supportive of the status quo.

Capitalism, it is important to point out, set the stage for Jews to move toward socialism, it did not determine this political direction for them. Jews chose to be socialists or prosocialists. This choice was, of course, very much influenced by the nature of their socioeconomic conditions, but it was still a choice. Not all Jews, not all Jewish workers, and not all impoverished Jewish laborers made this political choice. Some opted for nationalism or Zionism, while others remained largely politically apathetic. The selection of political radicalism as one alternative out of several was typically made by only a minority. But, it should also be noted, minorities are the ones who make history.

The level of activity, energy, and commitment of a small minority of Jews who gave themselves to socialism in Russia and the United States around the turn of the century was a very important factor in the movement of larger numbers of Jews on the path toward socialism. It was this dedicated and gifted minority that constructed a Jewish Left subculture and Jewish socialist organizations and parties. This subculture with its self-contained and self-sustaining values and institutions—parties, unions, newspapers, schools, fraternal orders, choral societies, and camps—reinforced the socialist commitment of Jews already committed to the cause and, at the same time, "tilted" Jewish individuals and organizations outside of its sphere toward a prosocialist orientation. The internal dynamism of this subculture and its leaders was such that for several decades (in the United States) it was able to function virtually independent of the concrete social and economic forces that supported and sustained it at the time of its creation. This self-sustaining character of the Jewish Left subculture proved to be vitally important for the maintenance and generation of radical or proradical Jews in later decades in America when the broader sociological and ecological bases underlying and supportive of the Jewish Left subculture and Jewish socialism were largely decimated in America by such processes as mass acculturation and mass upward socioeconomic mobility.

THE DOWNWARD SPIRAL

Just as the turn toward socialism by Jews was very much influenced by the nature of their contact with capitalism, so, too, was their turn from radicalism very much affected by their interaction with this socio-economic system. The different political responses flowed from the dissimilar types of capitalism that Jews experienced in Russia and then in America.

The socialist movement among Jews in the United States in the early decades of this century was very much indebted to the brutal confrontations that Jews had had with capitalism in Russia and to their experiences with unions and other radical organizations. Socialism in America benefited from the decision of radicals and proradicals to emigrate and from the decision of the committed Orthodox Jews and the rabbinate as well as men of wealth not to emigrate. The rise of a Jewish Left in the New World was not, however, simply a by-product of developments in Russia. The Jewish confrontation with capitalism in the United States, while generally not as bitter or as harsh as that with Russian capitalism, nevertheless did produce similar patterns and outcomes supportive of a Jewish bias in favor of socialism in the early years of this century.

American capitalists did not open wide the doors and routes of opportunity to Jews upon their arrival. Similar to Russian capitalists the Americans also "respected" and built upon existing ethnic and cultural divisions. American capitalists shunted Jews toward low-status and marginal occupations and industries, like the needle trades or peddling, while barring them from access to positions at the core of the economy. The result of this and of previous experiences in Europe was the concentration of a large number of immigrant Jews in the same or similar low-paying occupations and in overcrowded residential areas. In other words, capitalism in America, like capitalism in Russia, produced a Jewish working class with the classic ingredients necessary to move it in the direction of socialism.

There were differences though between the situation of the Jews in America and that of the Jews in Russia. These differences, as we have seen, were significant. American capitalists were not as efficient, thorough, and mean in their dealings with Jews as were their counterparts in Eastern Europe. Here, capitalism left more doors and mobility routes open than in Russia. Whatever the reasons for this, large numbers of Jews did tend to take advantage of these opportunities. Quickly after their arrival, many Jews did experience an income, occupational, and geographical mobility at a level and at a pace unheard of in Russia.

In the more dynamic soil of American capitalism even "Jewish occupations" which were dead ends in Russia became rungs on the ladder of mobility for many. Peddlers who in Russia remained peddlers scratching out a living for a lifetime became in America owners of stores and secure as well as insecure enjoyers of a middle-class lifestyle. As such they were weak rods to support a socialist movement.

Needle trades work, the "Jewish occupation" par excellence, also experienced a metamorphosis when located on American soil. In Russia, such employment ensured a lifetime of low wages, long hours, and dirty work. In America, an expansive garment industry offered a different set of rewards for its Jewish employees. Here many needle trades workers found that it was possible to improve their working conditions, incomes, and status in a relatively short span of time. The proportion that moved at least once from worker to boss within the garment industry was not inconsequential. In any event, those needle workers who experienced income or occupational mobility (or saw it occur between generations) and those whose dream of mobility was reinforced by such role models were not likely to retain, assuming they had one, an ardent commitment to socialism.

It should also be recalled that the garment industry was both a contributor as well as a deterrent to working-class consciousness. Typically the shops were independent, competitive, and small. Bosses used scarcity of work as a means to push "shop" loyalty over worker solidarity. Working-class consciousness was further diminished by the frequency of contact between employer and employee that characterized such small workplaces. The garment industry was not like the steel or coal industry where large numbers worked in impersonal settings, and the lines of demarcation between bosses and managers on the one hand and the workers on the other were hard and fast and quite difficult to cross.

The income, occupational, and geographical mobilities that Jews experienced in America in one or two generations were body blows to the maintenance of a sizable, concentrated, and economically homogenous Jewish working class. Although limitations on where Jews might work or live continued (and continue), the opportunities were such that Jews as a people rather quickly moved from the working class to the middle class in America. This socioeconomic metamorphosis could not but be damaging to the Jews' commitment to socialism.

A large and cohesive working class, though, was only one of the major bases underlying the Jews attachment to the Left. Their sense of peoplehood, or ethnicity, was the other major base. Both, of course, were intertwined and interdependent as well as quasi-autonomous of one another. The ethnic base of Jewish socialism was also undercut by American capitalism and the society that it shaped.

The Jewish sense of peoplehood that was supportive of a Jewish attachment to socialism was forged out of a common history of oppression—anti-Semitism— and a common language and culture that reflected this oppression—Yiddish. Both of these failed to receive much reinforcement in America and diminished in importance. The weaker they became, the less they could contribute to the maintenance and regeneration of a Jewish liaison with the Left.

Anti-Semitism, although never absent or at consistently low levels in the United States, was much less onerous here than in Russia. The contrast between anti-Semitism in the Old and New Worlds and the many examples of Jewish success in America reduced the magnitude and intensity of Jewish frustration and anger—a fuel that was very important to feeding the fires of socialism among Jews.

Yiddish virtually died of malnutrition in an inhospitable environment. America, a nation of immigrants, was determined not to be a nation of separate peoples speaking separate tongues. Jews, on their way to the middle class and desirous of acceptance, were generally willing to jettison their immigrant baggage in accord with their new homeland's dictates. Thus, when mass immigration ended in 1924, the fate of Yiddish as a viable language and culture was sealed. For the Jewish Left, it meant the loss of a political weapon and a shield that had insulated Jews from bourgeois, or American and antisocialist, norms, values, and ideals.

These cultural and socioeconomic changes that weakened Jewish ties to socialism also dovetailed with developments in the structure and identity of the American Jewish community that had the same type of political impact. The growing political power of the bourgeoisie among organized Jewry was very much related to the increase in numbers and wealth of this class and the backing it received from their Gentile counterparts in the non-Jewish world. The reinvigoration of a religious establishment and the development of a strong religious identity were encouraged and sustained by an acculturated and acculturating Jewish bourgeoisie complying with the desires, if not the dictates, of a white, Anglo-Saxon, Protestant ruling class. It was more than convenient to the interests of both these Jewish and Christian "gentlemen" that Jews in America be religious rather than atheistic, an American religious community rather than a "separate people," and have a strong and stable religious establishment rather than a weak and unstable one. The establishment of an American version of the rich and the rabbinate similar to the one that had ruled the Jews in Eastern Europe proved to be powerful competition for the Jewish Left and, with outside help, was successful in pushing it from the center of the Jewish political stage to the far wings.

It is important to stress that Jewish politics and political leadership was not a matter of disinterest to bourgeois and antisocialist forces in the United States. The economic and political powers and their allies viewed with disfavor the appearance of socialism in any quarter of the land, even a Jewish quarter. Their direct and indirect multifaceted campaign against socialism in the Jewish community and the society at large placed the Jewish (as well as non-Jewish) Left almost continually in a defensive and generally losing position.

Antisocialist political forces in American society were not the only elements to weaken the power and stature of the Left in the Jewish community. At various times American Left organizations and parties inadvertently accomplished the same end as their bourgeois rivals. Left sympathies and allegiances among Jews were periodically alienated by the crude and occasionally stupid manner in which parties like the Socialist and Communist, as well as movements like the New Left, dealt with matters of deep concern to the Jewish community. The Communist party's support of the Stalin-Hitler Pact is perhaps the most vivid example.

Yet, despite these inadvertent as well as intentional assaults on the position of the Jewish Left and the broader cultural and socioeconomic developments that eroded its base, there were Jews at different social or sociological locations who continued to retain a commitment to socialism. The transformation of Jews from an oppressed people and exploited working class to a quasi-legitimate middle-class religioethnic group did not bring in its wake the eradication of Jews with radical politics. Even though their numbers and influence declined with the passage of time, there continued to exist within American Jewry a prophetic minority who remained loyal to their secular faith.

There were various interrelated reasons for their continued existence. First, it takes time for the impact of centuries and generations of oppression and exploitation as a people and a class to become irrelevant to a people's political concerns and interests in the here and now, even in the best of countries.

Second, a Jewish working class did not disappear over night. As we pointed out earlier, a majority of Jews who entered the garment industry as workers ended their working lives with the same status. This dwindling class continued for many years to be a relatively strong base for Jewish socialism.

Third, anti-Semitism was never totally inconsequential in the United States. Subtle and crude forms of discrimination against Jews continued to keep the flame of Jewish socialism alive. The denial of employment in certain occupations and industries continued to generate embittered Jews who looked toward the Left for some relief of their predicament. It was also the heritage of European anti-Semitism as well as its continuing life in America that helped to direct Jews toward specific middle-class occupations like social work and teaching in which some form of radical commitment could be maintained.

Fourth, there was the aforementioned Jewish Left subculture. For decades and generations, this contraculture continued to attract and socialize and resocialize Jews for socialism. Jewish Left institutions were, in a society hostile to radicalism, enclaves in which similarly inclined Jews interacted, protected, and reinforced one another's political deviancy.

Fifth, the energy, dedication, courage, and intelligence of numerous socialist leaders and activists should not be overlooked. Their continuous political efforts and their keen articulation of a Leftist political perspective had to have some impact on the way Jews interpreted and responded to political issues.

ETHNICITY AND THE DECLINE OF JEWISH SOCIALISM

The continued existence of a small Jewish Left should not, however, detract our attention from the larger picture. The Jewish Left was a major political force in the Jewish community for a relatively short time. It remained a vital force in the American Left for a much longer period of years because the American radical parties and movements were typically small entities, and the contribution of other ethnic groups was, with the possible exception of the Finns, substantially less than that of the Jews.

American capitalism and the nature of the society, government, and politics that it inspired, we have already noted, played a major role in the decline and near demise of socialism in the Jewish community (and in the non-Jewish communities as well). But Jewish socialists and radicals also contributed to this fate. They and their political decisions were not irrelevant. Their choices were not determined by larger outside forces and the machinations of the capitalist system. Too many of the decisions that they made, unfortunately proved injurious to the socialist cause.

History presented Jewish socialists in Russia and in the United States with cruel and limited alternatives. As socialists they wished to revolutionize their societies. As Jew in ethnically segregated societies their political access was primarily limited to the Jewish community. Jewish radicals largely chose to remain within the ethnic community most hospitable to them and their cause. But, in the process of transforming a vice into a virtue, the chances for the success of their larger goal, namely a socialist America, were diminished. In theory and in the abstract it may be possible to achieve a socialist America by Jews and radicals in other ethnic groups restricting their political activities primarily to the confines of their respective ethnic communities. But in history and in practice in America, ethnic socialism as practiced by Jews was a contributor more to socialism's tragedy than to its triumph.

Psychologically, socially, and politically, it was quite difficult for individuals in the United States, particularly in those periods in which ethnic divisions and antagonisms were pronounced, to step beyond the boundaries of their ethnic or nationality group. For Jews, more than any other group—with the possible exception of blacks—it was a hard step to take.

Centuries of formal and informal discrimination and prejudice against Jews had fostered an intense solidarity and spirit of chauvinism among them. Similarly the same heritage of anti-Semitism coupled with a growth of narrow nationalism in the nineteenth and twentieth centuries made the Christian world, for the Jewish believer and apostate alike, an almost uniformly hostile, nearly impenetrable "enemy camp."

Socialists, like their non-socialist kinsmen, were also infected by the viruses of nationalism and ethnic chauvinism. A commitment to a rational, egalitarian, and internationalist creed proved no antidote to these diseases. Those comparatively few Jews whose unique life circumstances and strength of will enabled them to take leave of their own ethnic group found that the non-Jewish socialist movements were rife with ethnic divisions, chauvinism, and, not infrequently, traces of anti-Semitism. Such movements did not joyously throw open their arms to receive Jews, no matter how deracinated or assimilated they appeared.

It was not only formidable external obstacles and barriers that kept most Leftist Jews within the confines of their ethnic community, there were also positive attractions and benefits, especially in those years in which a large Jewish working class existed. A common heritage, culture, and background stemming from membership in the same ethnic group made it easier for Jewish radicals to politick among fellow Jews than among strange and often hostile Christians. The existence of Yiddish as a language and culture of the Jewish masses was recognized as a further boon to Jewish radicals (once they overcame their elitist snobbishness). In Yiddish they found a way of simultaneously insulating Jews from non-Jewish bourgeois norms and values and enhancing intraclass communication in a tongue and culture that they had skillfully succeeded in tilting toward the Left.

The comparative political returns from working and politicking among Jews as opposed to Gentiles was another factor that made it difficult for Jewish radicals to broaden their political horizons. Jews were simply more responsive to their efforts than non-Jews. The expenditure of the same amount of energy and resources produced greater positive results among Jews than among Christians. The Jewish radicals were seduced by their relative success. Work in the Jewish arena produced direct and immediate rewards. It made the Jewish Leftists feel relevant and effective. It gave them a sense of accomplishment. All of these rewards would certainly not have been so easily attainable if they had chosen to live, work, and politick among other ethnic groups. These benefits plus the many barriers that restricted them from leaving the Jewish community made remaining within its confines very enticing.

The most important problem of this political cost accounting was its historic specific, or limited, time frame. Immediate rewards were traded off, consciously or unconsciously, against long-term and crucial debits. At the time in which the Jews were most like an oppressed people and exploited working class, few Jewish radicals were willing to let abstract arguments about their particularistic politics influence their behavior. It seemed foolhardy not to devote as much time, energy, and resources as possible to politicking in so responsive a constituency as the Jewish working class. Conversely, it seemed equally foolhardy to devote much time, energy, and resources to politicking among non-Jewish peoples, who were generally nonresponsive to the message of socialism, especially when the messengers were Jews.

The decisions by Jewish Leftists to remain within the Jewish community, to build Jewish Left institutions, and to focus their attention largely upon an all Jewish constituency set into motion a tragic dynamic that eventually almost succeeded in sweeping away virtually all of their considerable accomplishments. Their choices led to the maintenance and strengthening of a Jewish identity among both themselves and their constituents. Simultaneously, the actions which flowed from these decisions of the Jewish Leftists detracted from the establishment and maintenance of a class loyalty that transcended ethnic boundaries. This does not mean that Jewish radicals did not make appeals to interethnic working-class solidarity and strive valiantly to bring this into being among Jews. But the fact that these appeals were delivered in Yiddish or in Yiddish accents or directed by Jews to largely all-Jewish groups tended to be more significant than the message itself. Again, it is important to realize that this did not seem that grave a problem when the term "Jew" was approximately synonomous with "oppressed" or "exploited."

This inadvertent strengthening of a sense of Jewish solidarity did become a grave problem and eventually a significant "enemy within the gates" as Jewish class structure became more differentiated and as Jewish nationalism or Zionism made greater inroads among Jews. These developments coincided with and spurred the rise of Jewish interest groups and classes whose politics were in conflict with or at least uncongenial to that of the socialists. These Jewish groups and classes, as they grew in size and influence, became increasingly effective in fighting with the Leftists for the allegiance of the Jewish masses.

As these events and developments unfolded on American soil, it became increasingly clear that the Jewish radicals had boxed themselves into an untenable tactical position. As Jewish leaders of Jewish organizations they could not allow their constituency to be won away from them by opposing forces in the Jewish community. The nonradicals' use of Jewish themes and issues to attract the allegiance of the Jewish masses forced the socialists into combat on a field in which their opposition had a decided advantage. Jewish radicals in the face of political competition from within their ethnic community chose to respond more as Jews than as radicals. The end result of this process was the further Judaization of both the socialists and their constituents and the simultaneous erosion of their radical faith.

Success and the way in which Jewish Leftists dealt with it led to the same outcomes. Success was the opiate of the leaders of Jewish radicalism, the heads of the organizations that comprised the Jewish Left subculture. In the process of building a meaningful and powerful set of institutions, these Jewish socialists made the choice not to risk their investments and attainments by directly challenging the structure of capitalism. Eventually, the goal of socialism in America was subordinated to the more immediate concern of protecting their organizational creations and their official positions within them.

Once this goal displacement began to take place, a conservative dynamic was set into motion. Many leaders soon realized that organizational effectiveness, in the context of a stable capitalist environment, required cooperation and some form of quid pro quo with bourgeois parties and groups. The price exacted for this assistance was the further reduction of an already attenuated socialist commitment.

Personal and organizational success and concern for the viability of their organizations also caused the leaders and officials of these bodies to draw closer to nonsocialist elements in the Jewish community. The diminution of their particular organizational and political base— the poor and working-class immigrant, Yiddish-speaking Jews— which the Jewish Left institutions' very effectiveness had helped to bring about, presented the officers of these groups with a dilemma.

The dilemma involved the direction in which to search for new and different bases and constituencies. Essentially two alternatives were available. One was to venture outside of the Jewish community and seek support from other socialist groups and the poor and working classes in other ethnic communities. The price for this would have involved the risk of becoming minor actors on someone else's stage— even if it was a socialist stage. The other was to develop ties and commitments to nonsocialist groups and classes in the Jewish community. The latter was the choice that was made. The price was a further attenuation of an already frayed socialist commitment.

The failure of Jewish (as well as non-Jewish) socialists to adequately deal with the issue of their own ethnicity crippled their struggle to bring socialism to this country. No socialist movement could have succeeded here that left in place and reinforced prevailing ethnic barriers and divisions. The ethnic communities from which Jewish and non-Jewish socialists derived were not merely separate cultural worlds embued with rich and distinctive heritages. In the context of capitalism they were also arenas and instruments that one peoples used to gain competitive advantage over other peoples. Workers and radicals who remained within the boundaries of these parochial and competitive social and cultural worlds could not erect and sustain the inter-ethnic class consciousness and political unity necessary to defeat capitalism.

Jewish socialists in America have been actors in an historic tragedy. They entered a multi-ethnic society in which their greatest political resource proved to be their own ethnicity and ethnic group. But, it was the reliance on this very source of strength that also proved to be a fatal weakness. Jewishness was a two-edged political sword that Jewish socialists grasped in the absence of any other significant weapon. This sword allowed them to engage in a mighty but ultimately to date at least a futile battle.

In conclusion, the options and the opportunity of Jewish socialism, past, present and future have best been stated by Rabbi Hillel:

"If I am not for myself, who will be for me? And if I am only for myself, what am I? And if not now, when?"

Epilogue: A Prediction

THE REEMERGENCE OF SOCIALISM AMONG JEWS

At this point I would like to offer a prediction about the future of socialism among Jews in America. Socialism, I contend, contrary to popular impressions, will be on the future agenda of the American-Jewish community. The conditions, the situations, and the circumstances that led many Jews, particularly the best and the brightest, to socialism in the past will in various forms reemerge to play a similar role for Jews in the future. I believe that, in America in the forthcoming decades, the Jewish community's harsh confrontation with capitalism will result in a renewed Jewish commitment to socialism.

Yet if one were to take a snapshot of the present-day Jewish and American communities, a superficial reading of the film would not indicate the imminent presence of a revivified socialist movement, particularly with respect to the Jews. For the society as a whole, despite several years of high unemployment and a decline in real income, there are not many indicators to suggest a rise in the level of working-class, much less socialist, militancy. The poor, the colored minorities, and the working class—those who primarily bear the brunt of the twin scourges of joblessness and inflation—occasionally do strike out in ways that can be interpreted as quasi-socialist forms. But more typically they either stoically accept their fate, turn to religion, or seek out other nonpolitical outlets for the expression of their plight and frustration.

In the political realm, conservatives and conservatism are on the ascendancy. The 1976 presidential election, the defeat of Democratic congressional candidates in Democratic strongholds in Washington and Minnesota in 1977, and Daniel P. Moynihan's defeat of Bella Abzug in the New York senatorial primaries attest to this rightward drift in the nation. The national debate on the issue of the Panama Canal treaties and the lack of such a debate on even a watered down version of the Humphrey-Hawkins full-employment bill are other indications of the growing strength of the Right and the weakness of the Left as well as the vacuity of American politics.

A glance at the political spectrum to the left of the Democratic Party reveals some wide, nearly empty spaces. The student movement is dead. The women liberationists are on the defensive. Pockets of Leftists and New Leftists exist in and around the Democratic Party, some unions, universities, poverty programs, and small publications, but there is no Left or New Left party or organization of any consequence that still functions.

Socialism's fate in the Jewish community seems even more dire. The economic and occupational bases that once sustained a meaningful Jewish Left are now largely a thing of the past. In terms of income and occupations Jews appear to be among the most favored of the nation's ethnic and religious groups. The organs and organizations that are dominant in the Jewish community reflect the predominance of its bourgeois base. Power and influence among American Jews are concentrated in its wealthier strata and in the rabbis, administrators, and bureaucrats of community organizations, and the intelligentsia allied with and attuned to it.

Jewish radicals, whether of the Old Left, New Left, or Jewish New Left varieties, are few in number. The organizations that constituted the sinews of the Jewish Left subculture, if in existence, either serve only a handful or are now politically blander and more moderate than was true in past decades. Jewish radical newspapers and periodicals tend to be in financial difficulty and on the verge of extinction or bankruptcy. Their readership can be counted in the hundreds or low thousands, while their more conservative ideological competitors are read by the tens of thousands.

The status of Jewish radicals in the Jewish community today is a far cry from what it was prior to World War I. Now they have little influence in community affairs. Now, as opposed to the earlier period, they are viewed by a large segment of American Jewry with suspicion, even with hostility. Leftists, whether Jewish or non-Jewish, Old or New, are regarded by many Jews as being opposed to basic Jewish economic and political interests, that is, Israel's security, a militarily strong United States, and a seemingly bountiful capitalist system. The only socialist honored by this community are those who have been embalmed in nostalgia.

The prospects for a revival of socialism in the American Jewish community, however, is not as bleak as these facts may at first appear to suggest. There are two factors that will promote this revival. The first is the existence of organized Jewish radicalism. The second is the peculiar location of the Jews in a maturing monopolistic capitalist society.

Jewish radical organizations, although few in number and in potency at this time, can serve important political functions with respect to any future resurgence of leftism among Jews. The Jewish Socialist Youth Bund, Habonim, Hashomer Hatzair, the Jewish Socialist Community, the Radical Jewish Union, the *Jewish Currents*, the *Morgen Freiheit*, the Bund, and Camp Kinderland all help to keep alive the historical tradition and legitimacy of Jewish socialism. The importance of the availability of radical traditions to groups or nations concerned with dramatic social change should not be underestimated. Such a tradition reduces the time and energy spent in groping for meaningful political alternatives and also serves as a rallying force for those concerned with the radical transformation of their societies. Indeed, this was a fact of which the early fathers of the Zionist movement were well aware.

This is not the only real or potential contribution that such Jewish radical organizations have to make to a future revival of Jewish socialism. In addition to tradition, they keep radical political people alive. In these explicitly leftist Jewish contexts (as well as in leftist contexts in which Jews do not participate specifically as Jews, such as *In These Times*), a small but not insignificant number are being politically educated. Also, a small but not insignificant number are gaining experience in radical politics. Thus, when a thrust for meaningful change arises among Jews in the future there will be, directly or indirectly available to those generations, men and women who can provide a socialist direction. Sociologists and historians of social movements have often noted that key persons and groups in the rise of new social movements many times are those with experience in and involvement with old ones. And, a handful of astute and experienced individuals can make a difference. Indeed, was it not a handful who made an important difference in the initial successes of the Bund and the Bolsheviks?

A few individuals and organizations by themselves, however, cannot produce a radical movement. Their potency is circumscribed by larger structural considerations. It is to these structural considerations, namely the occupational and economic structure of American Jewry within this monopolistic capitalist society, to which we now turn our attention.

Jewish Occupations and Industries

Jews, though largely middle class, are not dispersed at random throughout the labor force. Values, traditions, historical experiences, previous successes, and anti-Semitism have all come together to produce a Jewish occupational structure today that is unique. I contend that this special pattern of Jewish location in the occupational and industrial world will play a major part in placing Jews once again in that vanguard of a socialist movement.

To understand this point, it is necessary to look beyond income levels and the glitter of the gilded ghettoes. Once this is done it becomes clearer that the occupational roles that Jews currently occupy do not give them access to the levers of societal power. Basically Jews are located in peripheral and dependent positions and stand outside of the politico-economic core where real power is vested. It is this concentration of Jews in these types of economic arenas and the consequential political and economic vulnerability that will revive socialism in the American Jewish community.

Let us commence this brief analysis by sketching a map of the occupational and industrial locations of Jews in the United States today. Industrially, as social analyst Allon Gal has noted, ". . . the center of gravity of American Jewry's economic life is the *field of trade and finance*," a field in which nearly half of all economically active Jews are employed.[1] This proportion is approximately two times larger than that for non-Jews in the same field. In manufacturing, Jews are disproportionately located in light manufacturing or the consumer-goods industries. Jews in business also differ from their Christian counterparts in terms of the type of enterprise with which they are associated. Jews are more likely to be found in proprietorships and partnerships, while Christians are more likely to be located in corporations.[2]

Occupationally Jews are distinct from the rest of the population. Whereas approximately one-tenth of the national labor force is self-employed, the percentage for Jews is about 50 percent, or nearly five times greater. A similar but not as sharp a disparity also obtains with respect to representation in specific occupational categories. Seventy percent of Jews in the labor force are either professionals (29%) or managers and administrators (41%). The comparable percentage for non-Jews in both these categories is close to 30 percent, or proportionately less than half of that of Jews.[3]

These current occupational and industrial concentrations of Jews are a product of a combination of various historic and contemporary factors. The positions of Jews today in the economy are in many cases extensions of the types of field and activities that they entered and in which they were successful in earlier decades. These contemporary concentrations also reflect the considerable educational and economic mobility of the Jews as a group. But, most important for our present concern, the nonrandom location of Jews in the economy also indicates the existence of a pattern of exclusion from the central position of economic power.

Jews are virtually absent from the executive suites of the large corporations situated at the core of politico-economic power in this society. (Irving Shapiro, Board Chairman of DuPont, is a singularly notable exception.) As William Domhoff, a sociological student of the power elite, described the wealthy Jews (and their Cowboy or Southwestern allies): "The Jewish-Cowboy group is the major fringe group in an overwhelmingly Anglo-Saxon power elite rooted in commercial banking, insurance, public utilities, railroads and [heavy] manufacturing—precisely the areas from which people of Jewish background are almost completely excluded. Even where the Jews and the Cowboys are highly visible as in investment banking, oil and real estate, they are decidely minor leaguers compared to the even wealthier gentiles."[4] The statistics of Jewish exclusion from the corporate power elite are quite jarring. In the field of commercial banking the percentage of Jews in executive positions at the larger banks is approximately 1 percent. In 1973 the American Jewish Committee found that of the

176 senior executives in the 15 largest commercial banks not one was Jewish. The pattern is almost identical in the auto industry. Not one of the top officers of General Motors, Chrysler, and Ford is Jewish. Those Jews who are highly paid in the auto industry are primarily technicians, engineers, and scientists; and even they are relatively few in number. Again, the same pattern is found in the oil industry, where Jews constitute from about 1 to 4 percent of all high-level officials. In public utilities, the percentage is less than 1 percent. In the insurance industry, the picture for Jews is only slightly better.[5]

The fact of Jewish exclusion from positions of corporate power is more salient than the reasons behind it. But some brief attention should also be paid to the underlying reasons. Jews in the past (as noted earlier in the volume) were excluded from these industries and consequently sought out other economic arenas more hospitable to them and their talents. After a while a pattern tends to be established, and it is possible that Jews may overlook new opportunities within sectors that were previously regarded as hostile to them. However, the major difficulty with this line of reasoning is that many if not most of the doors closed to Jews in the past remain firmly closed in the present owing to the current locks installed by the contemporary gate keepers. These major corporations apparently do not actively recruit on campuses with large proportions of Jews. For example, one recent study found that the number of visits to campuses by bank recruiters searching out future executives varies inversely with the percentage of Jews in the student body. Even when the Jewish students, such as those graduating from the Harvard Business School, appear to be eminently qualified for the trek to the high-level executive suites, they tend not to be chosen. The objectively anti-Semitic policies of the corporate power elite are also reflected in the social clubs that they dominate. More than half of these clubs—in which many of the big business decisions are made—actively discriminate against Jews.[6]

The exclusion of Jews from the corporate power structure means that Jews are in a vulnerable position. Decisions that non-Jews make about the economy and decisions in which Jews do not participate determine in essence the Jewish economic fate. The expansive nature of the American economy in the several decades following World War II up until approximately 1970 and the need then for talents in fields where Jews did have access masked the impact of this power distortion. Income and status success in a variety of economic arenas made the exclusion from a few easier to bear. The anti-Semitic policies and practices of the economic power elite was treated by Jewish defense organizations as more a status irritant than as a major blockage to Jewish economic mobility or a significant threat to the fundamental position of Jews in the economy or society.

These *judenrein* corporations, particularly the oligopolies, constitute an actual threat in the present and an even greater one in the future to the economic and social attainments and security of American

Jewry. The simultaneous growth of monopoly capitalism and the contraction of the economy that we are currently experiencing underscore
the gravity of the situation for American Jewry. The economic giants
will block Jewish mobility and invade traditional Jewish economic
arenas, while the competition from other sectors and strata in the society for the relatively few economic plums that exist beyond the sphere
or concern of the corporate magnates becomes more intense. This is
the scenario for the economic, political, and status decline of Jews in
America of the future. It is also the scenario that will lead American
Jewry back to a renewed and vigorous commitment to socialism.

THE ECONOMIC THREAT

Let us now examine the various ways in which the predominantly
Jewish economic and occupational arenas and mobility channels are
being and will continue to be eroded. First, we will turn our attention
to small business—the traditional Jewish economic metier. The economic data clearly reveal that small businesses in America in the last
several decades have declined, using virtually any indicator of economic performance. At the same time, the wealth and influence of the
large corporations, the conglomerates, and the oligopolies have grown
considerably. Between 1950 and 1962, for example, the 20 largest corporations' share of all corporate assets increased from 21 to 25 percent. By 1962 the net profits of the five largest manufacturing corporations were approximately 200 percent greater than those of the
178,000 smallest manufacturing corporations.[7] Or, to use another example, ". . . The 100 largest firms in 1968 held a larger share of manufacturing assets than the 200 largest in 1950; the 200 largest in 1968
controlled as large a share as the 1000 largest in 1941."[8] By 1966 the
concentration of economic power had grown to the point where the
top four firms in aerospace, motor vehicles, computers, tires, ciga-
rettes, soap detergent, and photographic equipment accounted for approximately two-thirds or more of the total output in each of these industrial groupings. This phenomenon was not only restricted to
manufacturing. The same pattern also applied in the banking and insurance worlds as well. Small businesses' share of assets, output, and
profits could not keep up with that of the giants.[9]

It was not only the sheer growth of large businesses that proved injurious to the interests of small firms. It was also the nature of that
growth. Prior to the 1960s corporations had tended to expand within
narrow limits, generally within the boundaries of their industries or
in related sectors. But in the 1960s and 1970s, aggressive corporations
moved up and out in various directions ingesting firms in diverse industries.[10] And again where large corporations ruled the roost, Jews
were generally not welcome.

It should also be noted that despite the flurry of corporate growth and mergers there was a considerable degree of stability among the owners and influentials who controlled big business. The same or similar family groupings such as the Rockefellers, the Mellons, the Fords, and the Hannas that controlled much of the banking and industrial worlds 50 years ago generally still control them now.[11] Jews are generally not to be found in these kinds of family circles. Thus, not even via marriage can Jews get into the charmed circle of the corporate elite.

The decline of small businesses in the 1960s and 1970s proved especially injurious to the interests of Jews. It was the trade and light manufacturing sectors of the small business world—areas in which Jews were heavily concentrated—that suffered the most economic misfortune.[12] The growing power of the large corporations on the one hand and the increased competition from abroad placed the type of enterprises and occupations in which Jews were disproportionately concentrated in the grips of an ever tightening vise.

A cruel paradox in this situation was that success or relative success provided not guarantees that the interests of the Jewish community would be protected. If small or medium-size Jewish businesses were too profitable, they ran the risk of being bought or taken over by a large and avaricious non-Jewish corporation. Even the growth of a Jewish firm that was not absorbed by outsiders did not necessarily insure its remaining within a Jewish sphere. Both Sears Roebuck and the Radio Corporation of America, for example, commenced life and flourished for many years under the aegis of Jews. As large concerns, however, they have followed, according to sociologist E. Digby Baltzell, the pattern of Jewish exclusion common to large industries in America.[13] There is also a similar sort of dynamic at work at the pinnacle of the Jewish business world, the prestigious investment houses. Here Jewish houses will for purposes of business, hire or appoint Christian partners, but Christian investment firms do not tend to acquire Jewish partners.[14] And there is also the problem of the highly successful Jew who, in the process of achieving upward mobility and interacting with Christian peers, either converts or intermarries, or has children who do. A significant percentage of the progeny and spouses of upper-status Jewish families considered by Stephen Birmingham in his book *Our Crowd*, for example, are not part of "their crowd."[15]

The general point here, however, is that small and medium-size businesses are increasingly less able to perform the positive economic functions for Jews that they did in the past. This sector of the economy, which was once a major route of upward mobility and a source of a relatively comfortable middle-class existence for this ethnic group, is suffering in absolute and relative terms. These types of enterprises are evolving, for the most part, into dead-end propositions or fragile economic bases that cannot or will not be able to sustain bourgeois life-styles. As such economic realities intrude into the consciousness of Jews, they will begin to realize that their interests and those of the capitalist system are no longer parallel.

These doubts and feelings of discontent will not be limited to Jewish businessmen. The expansion of large corporations carrying their policies of Jewish exclusion with them into increasingly larger areas of business life and the decline of small businesses within the context of a contracting economy will produce a negative "multiplier affect" upon middle-class Jews who are not the owners and managers of the small and medium-size firms under attack. The Jewish economy is a highly integrated one, as is the national economy, and both are very much interrelated at this time. It is therefore not possible for one important sector of the Jewish economy to experience assaults without having other parts of it suffer as well.

One of the other Jewish economic arenas that is feeling and will continue to feel the impact of the blows raining down upon small businesses is the professions—an important basis of Jewish middle-class existence. Consider, for example, the case of Jewish lawyers. At the present time, with some exceptions, Jews are generally not found in the higher echelons of major corporate law firms, especially at the level of senior partners. This stems from a variety of sources. Historically, lawyers associated with such prestigious firms have had a long and not very noble history of animosity toward Jews and other minority groups in the profession.[16] More important for our present concerns, however, is the structural source. The personnel of the large corporate law firms usually are mirror images of their clientele, and the clientele for these law corporations are typically the white Anglo-Saxon Protestants from the world of corporate business. Conversely, Jewish firms, again with some notable exceptions, especially when government contacts and specific expertise are needed, do the legal work of small to medium-size businesses. (The non-Jews that Jewish lawyers are most likely to serve are those in need of nonmainstream legal services such as those relating to criminal, matrimonial, or personal injury. These Christian clients, needless to say, are not likely to be in the upper or upper-middle classes.) It follows, then, that the fewer the number of profitable Jewish businesses in existence, the fewer the number of clients Jewish law firms will have.[17] This will eventually mean a decline in the number of Jewish lawyers or a decline in the income of Jewish attorneys. There is no reason to believe that the same process will not affect Jews in other middle-class service occupations.

The Jewish professional bastion has also come under attack from another quarter. The growth of big business, the decline of small firms, and the general contraction of the economy have increased the competition among the professions. Blacks, Puerto Ricans, non-Jewish women, and Catholics have become increasingly less willing to concede these positions to Jews either for merit or other reasons. An important focal point in the struggle for these positions has been at the level of admissions to the professional schools. Jewish defense organizations have actively fought against quota systems and other devices designed to increase the enrollments of underrepresented minorities in the professions. Their struggle is informed by a history of anti-Semitic quota systems. But it is also informed by the present-day fact that the more seats in professional schools that go to non-Jews, the fewer there will be available for Jewish students. The briefs submitted by Jewish organizations on behalf of the law school applicant De Funis and the medical school applicant Bakke—alleged victims of reverse discrimination—represent concrete attempts by the Jewish community to protect and preserve admission by merit so that the enclaves that Jews have fought long and hard to establish will not be diminished.

The struggle for professional and middle-class positions between Jews and non-Jews has not been limited to professional school admissions. In New York City, Jews and blacks continue to fight each other for jobs in the school system. Similarly, Jews are waging struggles to preserve their faculty positions in the nation's colleges and universities, which are being threatened by minority groups backed by affirmative action guidelines and policies.

This competition in the educational sector between Jews and non-Jews is occurring during a period in which the number of teachers at all levels has either reached a plateau or is beginning to decline. For Jews, who are so concentrated in the teaching profession—about 50 percent of New York City's school teachers and approximately 9 percent of the nation's professors [18]—this contraction by itself has to be a troublesome development. But the contraction, together with the vigorous competition endorsed and supported by government, means that in the future Jews will lack this important institutional bulwark to their middle-class status that was there in the past.

This same pattern of present and future erosion of the overall position of Jews in American society is apparent in the sphere of politics as well. Jewish political power is overrated. The prominence and visiability of Israel as the premier Jewish interest in the last three decades has distorted the reality of Jewish capabilities. Support for Israel by American politicians, until very recently, has been, in domestic political terms, a relatively cost-free endeavor. Presidents and Congressmen have much to gain in terms of votes and campaign contributions by providing aid to Israel and little to lose except from fringe groups. Political and economic assistance to Israel, furthermore, does not in any way challenge or disturb the socioeconomic status quo on the homefront.

The vaunted political clout of the Jewish community seems to have produced relatively little payoff in Jewish interest areas other than Israel. For example, Jewish political muscle was unable to stem the decline of the domestic garment industry, particularly in geographical locations like New York in which Jews were the strongest.[19] Jewish political strength was also unable to prevent the implementation of affirmative action policies in disproportionately Jewish occupational and institutional arenas. Even in New York City and even during the administration of the first Jewish mayor in that city's history, Jews were unable to prevent blacks and other groups from encroaching on Jewish enclaves in the civil service and educational bureaucracies.[20]

Politically, organized Jewry has not had much success in its dealings with the corporate elite. Jewish organizations have made no effort to stem the encroachment of big business upon the disproportionately Jewish small-business sector. It is almost as if Jewish political leaders regard this evelopment as an "act of nature" that man cannot stop. Jewish political efforts vis-a-vis the Gentile giants have focused largely upon forcing them to open their executive suites to Jews. This campaign has generally not reaped huge dividends as our previous accounting of Jews in top-level positions in the banking, oil, and automobile industries has made clear. Irving R. Shapiro may have recently become chairman of the board of DuPont, but it is extremely doubtful whether he represents a wave of the future.

Ironically, if Jewish political power has made any significant impact upon the corporate elite, it has been to bolster rather than weaken corporate economic power. This irony stems from the effectiveness of the Jewish lobbying on behalf of Israel. The concern for Israel's security has inclined Jews and Jewish organizations toward a more favorable stance on an ever-increasing United States defense budget. The logic is straightforward. If the American military is to be the ultimate defender of Israel, then the United States armed forces have to be strong. Such strength requires a huge expenditure of funds. Therefore, it follows that Jews should push for bigger defense budgets. *And they are.*[21]

Defense spending may or may not help Israel in the long run, but it most certainly is injurious to Jewish domestic interests in the short, or long, run. This is because these military dollars go largely to a few corporate giants with interests in economic sectors beyond military hardware. In 1968, for example, about 60 percent of these dollars went to 50 such firms.[22] This defense money significantly strengthens the overall economic position of those businesses most dangerous to Jewish economic concerns. The Jewish clout exercised on behalf of Israel turns out to be deleterious to other important Jewish interests and to the economic base upon which the clout rests.

Thus, when the major economic and political tendencies pertaining to American Jewry are assessed, the picture for the Jewish middle class in the future is bleak. After several generations and decades of upward socioeconomic mobility, the mobility that will occur among Jews in the decades to come will be downward. The continued multifaceted growth of judenrein corporate giants into the "Jewish" sectors of the business world will have a substantial negative impact upon the economic fate of Jewish businessmen and upon the Jewish professionals who service them. The economic decline of American Jewry cannot but be paralleled by a decline in its political power as well. And as the political clout of American Jewry is diminished so is its ability to protect its economic and occupational interests. What we have then is an intertwined downward spiral.

This bleak future will not be averted by the logic and values that now guide the political strategy of Jewish leaders and defense agencies. In the face of a powerful threat to Jewish interest by the Gentile corporate magnates, the heavy Jewish artillery has been trained against blacks and other minority groups, politically and economically weak strata that are not very capable of severely injuring basic Jewish interests. Jewish spokesmen will loudly and vociferously protest the morality and legality of affirmative action programs in universities and government designed to redress in some small degree of shameful heritage of racial and sexist discrimination. But there is not equivalent campaign conducted against the major financial, legal, and manufacturing corporations that are serious threats to Jewish interests.[23] The Gentile corporate and financial elite are subjected to quiet studies and gentle entreaties to open their doors while the blacks and other minority groups sniping at the heels of the bourgeois Jewish community are subjected to massive and bitter public relations and legal salvos. In a recent study of anti-Semitism done by two eminent and long-time leaders of the Anti-Defamation League, one of the most effective Jewish defense agencies in the country, the authors barely mention corporate anti-Semitism. Instead, the dominant focus is placed almost totally on weak political groups such as blacks, the radical Left, and the extremist right with some nod also given to the Arabs.[24]

The problem, however, is more significant than a poor choice of targets and the differential level and intensity of campaigns. When banks, corporations, law firms, public utilities, and insurance companies are targeted by Jewish defense agencies, the nature of their attacks is woefully lacking. The entire emphasis is usually placed upon employment practices and scarcely any attention is paid to the business and economic policies of these shapers of the American economy.

It will do the American Jewish community and the non-Jewish poor, working and middle classes little good if Jewish hands at the helm of the nation's economy lead in the same disastrous direction as elite Gentile hands. The admission of a small number of bourgeois Jews into the nation's economic elite will not stem the downslide in the more Jewish areas of the economy. It may have been prestigious for American Jewry to have Arthur Burns serve as Chairman of the Federal Reserve Board but the conservative fiscal policies pursued by him have not helped Jewish economic interests. Jews, like other people, cannot eat prestige. The entrance of a Jewish bourgeoisie into the ruling economic class will not change the basic policies that have led to high rates of unemployment, inflation, and small-business failures. A Judeo-Christian corporate elite, should one come into existence, will be no more capable than a WASP elite in dealing with the basic contradictions and internal weaknesses of capitalism.

The drive for acceptance into the Gentile corporation suites and clubs is shortsighted in another manner as well. It is based on the premise that the exclusion of Jews stems from personal or individual predilections. If these could be overcome, according to this perspective, then Jews could demonstrate how well they perform as executives and senior partners and thus lower the barriers for other Jews to enter the corporate sanctuaries. But the barring of Jews is not due to individual or personal tastes or prejudices. It is due to economic and institutional considerations. Corporate anti-Semitism protects the vested interests of the strata that occupy the seat of economic power in American society. There is no rational reason why they would have any self-interest in sharing their lucrative and powerful positions with any group of outsiders, except perhaps for a token few, no matter how talented they are. Ethnic and religious distinctions between the corporate elite and potential challengers provide the former with a convenient and popular rationale for protecting the socioeconomic status quo.

The shortsighted and narrow politicoeconomic policies of the American Jewish leadership stem from their bourgeois socioeconomic status and political socialization. It is these leaders' identification of their community's interest with that of the status quo and capitalism that makes them so ineffective in stemming the economic and political decline of American Jewry that is currently under way. This identification and their socialization experiences in America also blind them to the real nature and function of corporate anti-Semitism.

THE REVIVAL OF SOCIALISM

This ongoing deterioration of the economic and political position of the American Jewish community in the context of a society rent by ethnic and class divisions will eventually cause socialism to rise once again as a force in the Jewish community. As in czarist Russia, the Jews' harsh confrontation with the realities of capitalism linked with anti-Semitism will again turn them toward socialism.

There are differences, to be sure, between nineteenth and early twentieth century czarist Russia and contemporary America as there are between the position of the Jewish communities within each. But these differences as they apply to the relationship between Jews and socialism do not overshadow the similarities. In czarist Russia and in contemporary and future America, capitalism confronted, confronts, and will confront Jews in vulnerable economic positions outside the core of the economy. In Russia, the government and the businessmen combined to block the access of Jews to legitimate channels of upward mobility. In America, the powerful corporate and financial elite, as their power increases, will be more effective in denying Jews entree into a declining number of meaningful routes of upward mobility. In Russia, developing capitalism forced Jews from their middle-class or middle-strata positions of artisans and small shopkeepers downward into the ranks of the proletariat or nearly impoverished petty bourgeoisie. In America, maturing monopoly capitalism will force Jews from their small and medium-size businesses while at the same time creating the conditions for a "squeezing" of the Jewish professional strata. The end results will be, as in Russia, downward mobility, frustrated aspirations, and a turn to socialism.

The contours and social physiognomy of the American Jewish community will come to resemble in some that of the Russian Jewish community in late nineteenth and early twentieth century czarist Russia. Jews in their downward drift will find themselves concentrated in positions as objectively or relatively low-paid wage workers and petty merchants scratching out a living. In their ranks there will be large numbers of frustrated intellectuals and professionals. Thus, once again Jews will be amassed in large numbers, sharing the same or similar occupational plight and economic misfortune, and containing among themselves many intellectuals ready to lead and articulate the demands and aspirations of the masses. These facts plus their common ethnic origins and experiences will facilitate intraclass communication, the development of class solidarity, as well as hostility toward their common exploiters and oppressors. Finally, this will culminate, I contend, in a revivification of socialism among Jews.

Such a development will not be rapid or smooth. Some Jews will try to seek out alliances with their oppressors. But the institutional and objective anti-Semitism present among the corporate elite and its satellites will frustrate such endeavors. If they barred Jews from their doors when Jews were relatively prosperous and politically influential, why would the corporate magnates be willing to change their policy when Jews were in so weak a position? After much floundering and resisting, increasing numbers of Jews will come to see that their interests as Jews, as downwardly mobile persons, as members of an exploited working class, and as an impoverished, or nearly impoverished, strata of petty traders and merchants are antithetical to the powerful American bourgeoisie. The American Jews of the future will also be confronted by a situation that their kinsmen in czarist Russia did not have to face—the absence of a sanctuary. The world capitalist economy of the future will ensure that American Jews have no supportive and economically expansive capitalist enclave—including Israel—in which to seek refuge.

Thus, at some time in the not too distant future, the elements necessary to produce a new and reinvigorated Jewish commitment to socialism will fall into place. A relative or objective decline in socioeconomic circumstances and the narrowing if not closing of channels of mobility in combination with a living radical tradition and cadre will constitute those necessary elements.

The Jewish socialist movement of the future will hopefully not be an isolated phenomenon. Ideally it will be a center piece of an ethnically heterogeneous socialist movement capable of converting the United States into a humane, democratic socialist society.

Notes

CHAPTER 1

1. Max Weber, "Ethnic Groups," in *Theories of Society*, Talcott Parsons et al., Eds. (New York: Free Press, 1961), p. 306.
2. Benjamin Disraeli, *Lord George Betinck: A Political Biography* (New York: E. P. Dutton, 1905), pp. 323–324 (originally published in England, 1852); Vladimir Lenin, "Critical Remarks on the National Question," in *Lenin On the Jewish Question*, Hyman Lumer, (New York: International Publishers, 1974), p. 107 (originally published in 1913); and Robert Michels, *Political Parties: As Sociological Study of the Oligarchical Tendencies of Modern Democracy* (New York: Free Press, 1962), pp. 244–248 (originally published in 1915).
3. These include Wesley and Beverly Allinsmith, "Religious Affiliation and Politico-Economic Attitude: A Study of Eight Major U.S. Religious Groups," *Public Opinion Quarterly*, 12:3 (Fall 1948), 124–130; Werner Cohn, "The Politics of American Jews," in *The Jews: Social Patterns of an American Group*, Marshall Sklare, Ed. (Glencoe, Ill.: Free Press, 1960), pp. 614–626; Lawrence Fuchs, *The Political Behavior of American Jews* (Glencoe, Ill.: Free Press, 1956), pp. 124–130; Seymour Martin Lipset, *Revolution and Counter-Revolution: Change and Persistence in Social Structure*, rev. ed. (Garden City: Anchor Books, 1970), pp. 152–153, 383; Jack N. Porter, "Jewish Student Activism," *Jewish Currents* 24:5 (May 1970), 28–34; and Louis Ruchames, "Jewish Radicalism in the United States," in *The Ghetto and Beyond: Essays on Jewish Life in America*, Peter I. Rose, Ed. (New York: Random House, 1969), pp. 228–252.
4. Moses Rischin, *The Promised City: New York's Jews, 1870–1914* (New York: Harper Torchbooks, 1970), p. 166.
5. Nicolas Berdyaev, *The Russian Revolution* (Ann Arbor, Mich.: University of Michigan Press, 1961), pp. 69–70.
6. Cited in Louis Harap, *The Image of the Jew in American Literature: From Early Republic to Mass Immigration* (Philadelphia: Jewish Publication Society, 1974), pp. 292–293.
7. Lawrence Fuchs, "Sources of Jewish Internationalism and Liberalism," in *The Jews*, Marshall Sklare, Ed., pp. 598–611. Twenty years after first advancing this position, Fuchs continues to subscribe to it, albeit in a more modified form. See L. Fuchs, "Introduction," *American Jewish Historical Quarterly*, 66:2 (December 1976), pp. 182, 606, 611.
8. Salo W. Baron, *The Russian Jews Under Tsars and Soviets* (New York: Macmillan, 1964), pp. 70–71; Leonard Schapiro, "The Role of the Jews in the Russian Revolutionary Movement," *The Slavonic and East European Review*, 40:4 (December 1961), 163; and Ezra Mendelsohn, "The Dilemma of Jewish Politics in Poland: Four Responses," in Bela Vago and George L. Mosse, eds., *Jews and Non-Jews in Eastern Europe 1918–1945* (New York: Wiley, 1974), pp. 206–213.
9. L. Fuchs, *Political Behavior of American Jews*, p. 50.
10. Alan Fisher, "Continuity and Erosion of Jewish Liberalism," *American Jewish Historical Quarterly*, 66:2 (December 1976), 328–329.
11. Solomon F. Bloom, "Karl Marx and the Jews," *Jewish Social Studies*, 4:1 (January 1942), 3–16.
12. Robert S. Wistrich, *Revolutionary Jews from Marx to Trotsky* (New York: Harper & Row, 1976), pp. 3–5.

13. Isaac Deutscher, "The Non-Jewish Jew," in *The Non-Jewish Jew and Other Essays*, Tamara Deutscher, Ed. (New York: Hill and Wang, 1968), pp. 25–41.
14. Ezra Mendelsohn, *Class Struggle in the Pale: The Formative Years of the Jewish Workers' Movement in Tsarist Russia* (New York: Cambridge University Press, 1970), pp. 104–108.
15. Charles S. Liebman, *The Ambivalent American Jew: Politics, Religion and Family in American Jewish Life* (Philadelphia: Jewish Publication Society, 1973), pp. 142–144; and Joseph Zietlin, *Disciples of the Wise: The Religious and Social Opinions of American Rabbis* (Freeport, N.Y.: Books for Libraries Press, 1970), pp. 113–130, 139–158.
16. Nathan Glazer, *American Judaism*, 2nd ed., rev. (Chicago: University of Chicago Press, 1972), pp. 138–141; and Zeitlin, *Disciples of the Wise*, pp. 177–185.
17. The relatively few Jews in the United States generally means that studies not purposely generating a sizeable Jewish sample wind up with a very small absolute number of Jews. The size factor, then, precludes virtually any form of multivariate analysis or the introduction of sociological "controls."
18. Seymour M. Lipset and E. C. Ladd, Jr., "Jewish Academics in the United States: Their Achievements, Culture and Politics," in the *American Jewish Yearbook, 1971* (Philadelphia: American Jewish Committee and Jewish Publication Society, 1972), p. 121.
19. C. S. Liebman, *Ambivalent American Jew*, pp. 143–144.
20. David Badain, "Uniformity nd Diversity in Jewish Voting Patterns: New York's 13th Congressional District, A Case Study," unpublished class paper, State University of New York at Binghamton, 1976, pp. 16–46.
21. Richard Reeves, "Splitting the Jewish Vote," *New York*, 6:25 (June 18, 1973), 57–63.
22. Mordecai Soltes, The Yiddish Press: An Americanizing Agency (New York: Teachers College, Columbia University, 1950), pp. 15, 22, 23.
23. Meir Kahane, *The Story of the Jewish Defense League* (Radnor, Penn.: Chilton Book Co., 1975), pp. 72, 179–185; and E. Mendelsohn, "The Dilemma of Jewish Politics in Poland," pp. 211–213.
24. B. Disraeli, *Lord George Betinck*, 322–324.
25. C. S. Liebman, *Ambivalent American Jew*, p. 140.
26. Ibid., pp. 140, 141; Lewis S. Feuer, *The Scientific Intellectual* (New York: Basic Books, 1963), p. 303; and Miriam K. Slater, "My Son the Doctor: Aspects of Mobility 'Among American Jews,' " *American Sociological Review*, 34:3 (June 1969), 372.
27. Jerold S. Auerbach, "From Rags to Robes: The Legal Profession, Social Mobility and the American Jewish Experience," *American Jewish Historical Quarterly*, 56:2 (December 1976), 281–284; Michael Wyschograd, "Discussion," *Judaism*, 13:2 (Spring 1964), 145; and Mark Zborowski and Elizabeth Herzog, *Life Is With People: The Culture of the Shtetl* (New York: Schocken Books, 1965), pp. 105–123, 214–238.
28. M. Wyschograd, "Discussion," p. 145.
29. Irving Howe, *World of Our Fathers* (New York: Harcourt Brace Jovanovich, 1976), p. 623.
30. Lionel Kochan, "Moved to Revolution," *Times Literary Supplement*, 20 August, 1976.
31. Marvin Olsen and Judy C. Tully, "Socioeconomic-Ethnic Status Inconsistency and Preference for Political Change," *American Sociological Review*, 37:5 (October 1972), 562.
32. R. Michels, *Political Parties*, 247–248.
33. Ibid., 247.
34. See Chapter 6 in this volume.
35. William Schneider, Michael D. Berman, and Mark Schultz, "Bloc Voting Reconsidered: 'Is There A Jewish Vote?' " *Ethnicity*, 1:1 (December 1974), 179.

36. Edgar Litt, "Ethnic Status and Political Perspectives," *Midwest Journal of Political Science*, 5:3 (August 1961), 280.
37. Janet L. Dolgin, *Jewish Identity and the JDL* (Princeton, N.J.: Princeton University Press, 1977), p. 12; and Kahane, *Story of the Jewish Defense League*, pp. 58–96, 219–220.
38. Edmund Silberner, "Was Marx an Anti-Semite?" *Historia Judaica*, 11:1 (April 1949), 13, 17, 18.
39. The most recent example of this can be found in Wistrich, *Revolutionary Jews*.
40. Edward O. Laumann and David R. Segal, "Status Inconsistency and Ethnoreligious Group Membership as Determinants of Social Participation and Political Attitudes," *American Journal of Sociology*, 77:1 (July 1971), 36–61; and Olsen and Tully, "Status Inconsistency and Political Change," pp. 560–574.
41. These are the subjects studied by Wistrich, *Revolutionary Jews*. . . .
42. This point was well articulated by Michels, *Political Parties*, pp. 238–253.
43. William O. McCagg, "Jews in Revolutions: The Hungarian Experience," *Journal of Social History*, 6:1 (Fall 1972), 78–105.
44. See Chapter 2 in this volume.
45. Stephen Birmingham, *Our Crowd: The Great Jewish Families of New York* (New York: Harper & Row, 1967), p. 399; and L. Fuchs, *Political Behavior of American Jews*, pp. 41–50.
46. See Chapter 6 of this volume.
47. See Chapter 3 of this Volume.
48. Mark R. Levy and Michael S. Kramer, *The Ethnic Factor: How America's Minorities Decide Elections* (New York: Simon and Schuster, 1973), pp. 104–109; Lipset, *Revolution and Counter-Revolution*, pp. 342–343; W. Schneider, M. D. Berman, and M. Schultz, "Bloc Voting Reconsidered," pp. 359, 369.
49. E. O. Laumann and D. R. Segal, "Status Inconsistency and Ethnoreligious Group Membership," pp. 36–61.
50. David R. Segal, "Status Inconsistency, Cross Pressures, and American Political Behavior," *American Sociological Review*, 34:3 (June 1969), 357.
51. M. Olsen and J. C. Tully, "Status Inconsistency and Political Change," pp. 571–573.
52. E. O. Laumann and D. R. Segal, "Status Inconsistency and Ethnoreligious Group Membership," p. 55.
53. Ibid., pp. 46, 49, 54; and Lipset, *Revolution and Counter-Revolution*, pp. 342–343.
54. This position has been advanced by Werner Cohn, "Sources of American Jewish Liberalism—A Study of the Political Alignments of American Jews," unpublished doctoral dissertation, New School for Social Research, 1956; and Lucy S. Dawidowicz and Leon J. Goldstein, *Politics in a Pluralist Society* (New York: Institute of Human Relations Press, 1963), pp. 70–80. See also J. L. Talmon, *Israel Among the Nations* (London: Leidenfeld and Nicolson, 1970), pp. 1, 9–13; and Albert Memmi, *The Liberation of the Jew* (New York: Viking, 1966), pp. 228–229.
55. W. Cohn, "Politics of American Jews," p. 615.
56. See note 54 and Michels, *Political Parties*, pp. 245–247.
57. C. S. Liebman, *Ambivalent American Jews*, pp. 147–148.
58. Ibid.; and Walter Laqueur, *A History of Zionism* (New York: Schocken Books, 1976), pp. 270–285.
59. Walter Laqueur, "Zionism, the Marxist Critique and the Left," *Dissent* 18:4 (December 1971), 560–574; and Robert S. Wistrich, "Socialism and Antisemitism in Austria before 1914," *Jewish Social Studies*, 37:3–4 (Summer–Fall 1975), 323–332. For an extended discussion of this point, see Bela Vago, "The Attitude Toward the Jews As A Criterion of the Left-Right Concept," in Vago and Mosse, *Jews and Non-Jews in Eastern Europe*, pp. 21–50.
60. Milton M. Gordon, *Assimilation in American Life: The Role of Race, Religion,*

and National Origins (New York: Oxford University Press, 1964), pp. 38–39.
61. This concept was coined by J. Milton Yinger. As it is used here, contraculture is very similar to Yinger's. The major difference is that I include institutions and structures as part of a counterculture. See J. Milton Yinger, "Contraculture and Subculture," *American Sociological Review*, 25:5 (October 1960), 625–635.
62. Karl Marx did not set down in one place his analysis of the formation of class consciousness. Parts of it can be found in his various works including: Karl Marx and Friedrich Engels, *Manifesto of the Communist Party* (New York: International Publishers, 1932); Karl Marx, *The German Ideology* (New York: International Publishers, 1939); Karl Marx, *Capital* (New York: International Publishers, 1967); Karl Marx, *The Eighteenth Brumaire of Louis Bonaparte* (New York: International Publishers, 1963). Max Weber's analysis can be found in his classic article, "Class, Status and Party," in *From Max Weber: Essays in Sociology*, H. H. Gerth and C. Wright Mills, Eds. (New York: Oxford University Press, 1958), pp. 180–195. Contemporary social scientists who have fruitfully drawn upon this model in their work include Al Gedicks, "Ethnicity, Class Solidarity and Labor Radicalism Among Finnish Immigrants in Michigan Copper Country," unpublished paper presented at the American Sociological Association, New York, September 1976; James A. Geschwender, *Class, Race and Worker Insurgency: The League of Revolutionary Black Workers* (New York: Cambridge University Press, 1977); Seymour Martin Lipset, *Agrarian Socialism: The Cooperative Commonwealth Federation in Saskatchewan, A Study in Political Sociology* (Garden City, N.Y.: Anchor Books, 1968); Seymour Martin Lipset, *Political Man: The Social Basis of Politics* (Garden City, N.Y.: Doubleday, 1960); Clark Kerr and Abraham Siegel, "The Interindustry Propensity to Strike—An International Comparison," in *Industrial Conflict*, Arthur Kornhauser, Robert Dubin, and Arthur Ross, Eds. (New York: McGraw-Hill, 1954), pp. 189–212; and James Petras and Maurice Zeitlin, "Miners and Agrarian Radicalism," *American Sociological Review*, 32:4 (August 1967), 578–585.
63. Marxists have not been able to adequately incorporate ethnicity into their schema. See Tom Nairn, "The Modern Janus," *New Left Review*, 94 (November–December 1975), 3–29.

CHAPTER 2

1. For a description of many of these parties and the splits and feuds within the Left from the latter nineteenth century through World War II, see Robert J. Alexander, "Splinter Groups in American Radical Politics," *Social Research*, 20:3 (Autumn 1953), 282–320.
2. The principal method used here in the studies dealing with Jewish voting behavior relies on data gathered from the official election results in "predominantly" Jewish neighborhoods, districts, or wards. This means that we do not know if the vote for a particular candidate was derived from purely Jews or some mixture. But given high Jewish registration and voting rates, a consistent pattern over time in different cities and states, and a knowledge of the political background of Jews, we can be secure in using the results from elections.
3. Much of the material on the early years is derived from Melech Epstein, *Jewish Labor in the USA: An Industrial, Political and Cultural History of the Jewish Labor Movement, I* (New York: Ktav Publishing House, 1969), pp. 108–272; Irving Howe, *World of Our Fathers* (New York: Harcourt Brace Jovanovich, 1976), pp. 101–118; and Ezra Mendelsohn, "The Russian Roots of the American Jewish Labor Movement," *YIVO Annual of Jewish Social Science*, 26 (1976), pp. 150–177.
4. M. Epstein, *Jewish Labor*, p. 143.
5. Morris Hillquit, *Loose Leaves From a Busy Life* (New York: Macmillan, 1934), p. 41.

6. Nathan Fine, *Labor and Farmer Parties in the United States: 1828–1928* (New York: Russell and Russell, 1961), p. 115.

7. Ibid., p. 116.

8. Abraham Cahan, *The Education of Abraham Cahan*, translated by Leon Stein, Abraham P. Conan, and Lynn Davison from the Yiddish Autobiography *Bleter Fun Mein Leben* by Abraham Cahan, Vols. I and II (Philadelphia: Jewish Publication Society of America, 1969), pp. 347, 410.

9. Friedrich Engels, "The Labor Movement in the United States," in *Marx and Engels: Basic Writings on Politics and Philosophy*, Lewis S. Feuer, Ed. (Garden City, N.Y.: Anchor Books, 1959), pp. 495–496. For further discussion of the "German" problem in 19th century American socialism, see Philip S. Foner and Brewster Chamberlin, eds., *Friedrich A. Sorge's Labor Movement in the United States* (Westport, Conn.: Greenwood Press, 1977), pp. 15–17, 37, 198–204, 240–246.

10. M. Epstein, *Jewish Labor*, pp. 149–150.

11. Ibid., p. 152; and I. Howe, *World of Our Fathers*, p. 366.

12. Moses Rischin, *The Promised City: New York's Jews, 1870–1914* (New York: Harper Torchbooks, 1970), p. 273. Not all of the 8th Assembly District voters were, of course, Jews. In the absence of valid opinion surveys, we will throughout most of this study draw most of our inferences about Jewish voting behavior from the distribution of votes cast in what reliable authorities consider to be areas disproportionately inhabited by Jews. This method undoubtedly has its flaws; but in the absence of any better alternative, it is the best we have available.

13. Ibid., pp. 272–273; and William Leiserson, "The Jewish Labor Movement in New York," unpublished paper, University of Wisconsin, 1908, p. 45.

14. Samuel T. McSeveney, *The Politics of Depression: Political Behavior in the Northeast, 1893–1896* (New York: Oxford University Press, 1972), pp. 60, 61, 118, 119, 160, 161, 296.

15. Morris Hillquit, *History of Socialism in the United States* (New York: Funk and Wagnalls, 1903), pp. 258–259; M. Hillquit, *Loose Leaves*, p. 18; and Morris U. Schappes, "The Political Origins of the United Hebrew Trades," *Journal of Ethnic Studies*, 5:1 (Spring 1977), 14.

16. N. Fine, *Labor and Farmer Parties*, p. 180.

17. M. Rischin, p. 227; and Carl Shorske, *German Social Democracy 1905–1917* (New York: Harper Torchbooks, 1972), p. 4. The year 1892 was the last in which more than 100,000 German immigrants arrived in America. From 1893 to 1914 they averaged about 30,000 per year. U.S. Bureau of the Census, *Historical Statistics of the United States, Colonial Times to 1957* (Washington, D.C.: U.S. Government Printing Office, 1960), p. 56.

18. David A. Shannon, *The Socialist Party of America* (Chicago: Quadrangle Books, 1967), pp. 1–42; and M. Hillquit, *Loose Leaves*, p. 290. See also James Weinstein, *The Decline of Socialism in America, 1912–1925* (New York: Vintage Books), pp. 1–62.

19. N. Fine, *Labor and Farmer Parties*, p. 234.

20. D. A. Shannon, *Socialist Party*, pp. 12–13.

21. J. Weinstein, *Decline of Socialism*, pp. 23–24.

22. Ibid., p. 26; and William Z. Foster, *History of the Communist Party of the United States* (New York: International Publishers, 1952), p. 95.

23. D. A. Shannon, *Socialist Party*, pp. 43–44.

24. Daniel Bell, *Marxian Socialism in the United States* (Princeton, N.J.: Princeton University Press, 1967), p. 79; M. Epstein, *Jewish Labor*, pp. 338–340; and M. Hillquit, *Loose Leaves*, p. 290.

25. N. Fine, *Labor and Farmer Parties*, p. 232; and J. Weinstein, *Decline of Socialism*, pp. 94–102.

26. D. Bell, *Marxian Socialism*, pp. 79–80; D. A. Shannon, *Socialist Party*, pp. 62–80, 104; and J. Weinstein, *Decline of Socialism*, pp. 158–159, 172.

27. Arthur Gorenstein, "A Portrait of Ethnic Politics: The Socialists and the 1908 and 1910 Congressional Elections on the East Side," *American Jewish Historical Quarterly, 50*:3 (March 1961), 202, 221, 226; and J. Weinstein, *Decline of Socialism*, p. 107.

28. Melvyn Dubofsky, "Success and Failure of Socialism in New York City, 1900–1918: A Case Study," *Labor History, 9*:3 (Fall 1968), 370–371; Zosa Szajkowski, *Jews, Wars, and Communism, I: The Attitude of American Jews to World War I, the Russian Revolutions of 1917, and Communism (1914–1945)* (New York: Ktav Publishing House, 1972), pp. 153–154; and J. Weinstein, *Decline of Socialism*, pp. 118, 169.

29. *American Labor Yearbook, X, 1929* (New York: Rand School of Social Science), pp. 143–144; D. A. Shannon, *Socialist Party*, p. 247; and D. Bell, *Marxian Socialism*, p. 97.

30. N. Fine, *Labor and Farmer Parties*, p. 230.

31. *American Labor Yearbook, 1916* (New York: Rand School of Social Science), pp. 97–98; and *American Labor Yearbook, X, 1929*, p. 144.

32. D. A. Shannon, *Socialist Party*, pp. 198, 247, 255.

33. I. Howe, *World of Our Fathers*, p. 311.

34. Charles Leinenweber, "Socialists in the Streets: The New York City Socialist Party in Working Class Neighborhoods, 1908–1918" (unpublished paper: Dept. of Sociology, State University College at New Paltz, n.d.), p. 25. An abbreviated version of this paper with the same title appeared in *Science and Society, 41*:2 (Summer 1977), pp. 152–171.

35. Harry Rogoff, *An East Side Epic: The Life and Work of Meyer London* (New York: Vanguard Press, 1930), pp. 15–16.

36. A. Gorenstein, "Portrait of Ethnic Politics," p. 220.

37. See I. Howe, *World of Our Fathers*, pp. 360–374; and Harry Roskolenko, *The Time That Was Then: The Lower East Side, 1900–1914: An Intimate Chronicle* (New York: Dial Press, 1971), pp. 196–199.

38. C. Leinenweber, "Socialists in the Streets," pp. 3–5.

39. I. Howe, *World of Our Fathers*, p. 312.

40. A. Gorenstein, "Portrait of Ethnic Politics," p. 220.

41. E. P. Hutchinson, *Immigrants and Their Children, 1850–1950* (New York: John Wiley and Sons, 1956), pp. 262–264.

42. C. Leinenweber, "Socialists in the Streets," p. 4.

43. I. Howe, *World of Our Fathers*, pp. 360–374. See also Samuel Ornitz, *Haunch Paunch and Jowl* (Garden City, N.Y.: Garden City Publishing Co., 1923) for a good literary treatment of this kind of social welfare—business corruption.

44. *American Labor Yearbook, 1917–1918* (New York: Rand School of Social Science), p. 340; Melech Epstein, *The Jew and Communism: The Story of Early Communist Victories and Ultimate Defeats in the Jewish Community, U.S.A.: 1919–1941* (New York: Trade Union Sponsoring Committee, 1959), p. 102; and Franklin Jonas "The Early Life and Career of B. Charney Vladeck, 1886–1921: The Emergence of an Immigrant Spokesman," unpublished doctoral dissertation, New York University, 1972, p. 102.

45. Alexander Bittelman, "Things I Have Learned: An Autobiography," unpublished manuscript on file in Tamiment Library, New York University, 1962, p. 271.

46. Nathan Glazer, *The Social Basis of American Communism* (New York: Harcourt Brace and World, 1961), p. 24.

47. Benjamin Gitlow, *I Confess: The Truth About American Communism* (New York: E. P. Dutton, 1940), p. 21.

48. Letter from Melech Epstein to Werner Cohn contained in Werner Cohn, "Sources of American Jewish Liberalism—A Study of the Political Alignments of American Jews," unpublished doctoral dissertation, New School for Social Research, 1956, pp. 134–135.

49. M. Dubofsky, "Success and Failure," p. 362.

50. D. Bell, *Marxian Socialism*, pp. 168–177; and D. A. Shannon, *Socialist Party*, p. 250.
51. Patti M. Peterson, "The Young Socialist Movement in America from 1905 to 1940: A Study of the Young People's Socilist League," unpublished doctoral dissertation, University of Wisconsin, 1974, pp. 36, 90–96, 135; *American Labor Yearbook*, XII, *1931*, pp. 153–154, *American Labor Yearbook*, *1932*, pp. 96–97, and *American Labor Yearbook*, *1915*, p. 154 (New York: Rand School of Social Science).
52. P. M. Peterson, "Young Socialist Movement," p. 36.
53. W. Z. Foster, *History of Communist Party*, p. 113; D. A. Shannon, *Socialist Party*, p. 246; John H. M. Laslett, *Labor and the Left: A Study of Socialist and Radical Influences 1881–1924* (New York: Basic Books, 1970), pp. 98, 131–134; and C. Leinenweber, "Socialists in the Street," p. 40.
54. Louis Waldman, *Labor Lawyer* (New York: E. P. Dutton, 1944), pp. 270–273.
55. Bernard K. Johnpoll, *Pacifist's Progress: Norman Thomas and the Decline of Socialism* (Chicago: Quadrangle Books, 1970), pp. 27, 54, 55.
56. Norman Thomas Papers, New York Public Library.
57. Much of the historical background on the Communist Party is derived directly or indirectly from the two works of Theodore Draper, *American Communism and Soviet Russia: The Formative Period* (New York: Compass Books, 1963), and *The Roots of American Communism* (New York: Viking Press, 1957).
58. T. Draper, *Roots of American Communism*, p. 206.
59. Ibid., pp. 190, 206, 207.
60. N. Glazer, *Social Basis*, pp. 39, 58.
61. Ibid., pp. 99–100; and *American Labor Yearbook*, VII, *1926* (New York: Rand School of Social Science), p. 247.
62. Glazer, *Social Basis*, p. 130; and Epstein to Cohn in W. Cohn, "Sources of American Jewish Liberalism," pp. 134–135.
63. Kenneth Newton, *The Sociology of British Communism* (London: Penguin Press, 1969), pp. 78–79; Richard V. Burks, *The Dynamics of Communism in Eastern Europe* (Princeton, N.J.: Princeton University Press, 1961), pp. 158, 161–169; and Albert Memmi, *Portrait of a Jew* (New York: Viking Press, 1962), p. 277.
64. N. Glazer, *Social Basis*, p. 131.
65. M. Epstein, *Jew and Communism*, pp. 29–30.
66. Epstein to Cohn in W. Cohn, "Sources of American Jewish Liberalism," p. 134.
67. Ibid.; and N. Glazer, *Social Basis*, p. 136.
68. *American Labor Yearbook*, VII, *1926* (New York: Rand School of Social Science), p. 247; and T. Draper, *American Communism and Soviet Russia*, p. 191.
69. M. Epstein, *Jew and Communism*, p. 202.
70. T. Draper, *American Communism and Soviet Russia*, p. 191.
71. Ibid., pp. 187–188; and *American Labor Yearbook*, VII, *1926*, p. 247.
72. N. Glazer, *Social Basis*, p. 130.
73. Epstein to Cohn in W. Cohn, "Sources of American Jewish Liberalism," p. 134. In testimony before the Dies Committee of the House of Representatives in 1939, Earl Browder, then leader of the American Communist Party, claimed that the Jewish Communist Party members numbered 2500, or 2½ percent [Samuel Halperin, *The Political World of American Zionism* (Detroit: Wayne State University Press, 1961), p. 371]. That figure is so far out of line with those of other sources, those cited as well as Communist and former Communist Party members, that one can only conclude that Browder was being less than frank with the committee.
74. N. Glazer, *Social Basis*, pp. 220–221.
75. George Charney, *A Long Journey* (Chicago: Quadrangle Books, 1968), pp. 57, 73.
76. N. Glazer, *Social Basis*, p. 220.
77. Z. Szajkowski, *Jews, Wars, and Communism*, p. 416.
78. Ibid., p. 415.
79. Epstein to Cohn in W. Cohn, "Sources of American Jewish Liberalism," p. 135.

80. John Gates, *The Story of An American Communist* (New York: Thomas Nelson & Sons, 1958), pp. 110–111.

81. Cited in Gabriel Almond, *The Appeals of Communism* (Princeton, N.J.: Princeton University Press, 1954), p. 202.

82. N. Glazer, *Social Basis*, p. 71.

83. T. Draper, *American Communism and Soviet Russia*, p. 189.

84. Joseph Starobin, *American Communism in Crisis, 1943–1957* (Cambridge, Mass.: Harvard University Press, 1972), pp. 112–113.

85. *American Labor Yearbook, X, 1929* (New York: Rand School of Social Science), p. 154.

86. There is a dispute as to the veracity of the *Freiheit*'s circulation figures. *Freiheit* intimates who later became anti-Communists have challenged the figures reported in *Ayer's Directory of Newspapers and Periodicals* and those given to the United States Post Office. They claim that at no point in its history did this paper have a circulation in excess of 20,000. Even if this is true, we do not know whether the same charge of "inflated" figures could not also be leveled against all the other Communist papers. Even if more weight is given to the challengers' numbers than to those provided by the *Freiheit*, its *relative* position among the Communist periodicals would not be seriously challenged. See M. Epstein, *Jew and Communism*, p. 138; W. Z. Foster, *History of Communist Party*, p. 262; and N. Glazer, *Social Basis*, p. 206.

87. N. Glazer, *Social Basis*, pp. 71–73, 77–79.

88. Benjamin Gitlow, *The Whole of Their Lives: Communism in America—A Personal History and Intimate Portrayal of Its Leaders* (New York: Charles Scribner's Sons, 1948), p. 130.

89. W. Z. Foster, *History of Communist Party*, pp. 298–305; and Irving Howe and Lewis Coser, *The American Communist Party: A Critical History* (New York: Frederick A. Praeger, 1962), p. 256.

90. N. Glazer, *Social Basis*, p. 115.

91. Ibid., pp. 217–218. William Z. Foster in his discussion of these union tactics complained bitterly that the Communist Party did not get much of a direct return for the considerable investment of resources that it put into union activities. The Communists, he claimed devoted "themselves wholeheartedly to the building of the [United Steel Workers Union]." With reference to the automobile industry, but applicable to other industries as well, Foster wrote: "The main weakness of the Communists and the real progressives . . . was that they did not develop a sufficiently independent line" (W. Z. Foster, *History of Communist Party*, pp. 348–353). Although Foster may not have been the most objective observer in these matters because the union policies of the 1930s were those of his arch rival, Earl Browder, other sources with smaller or different axes to grind have also corroborated his general position.

92. N. Glazer, *Social Basis*, pp. 138–147; and G. Charney, *Long Journey*, p. 170.

93. See the history of the furriers by Philip S. Foner, *The Fur and Leather Workers Union: A Story of Dramatic Struggles and Achievements* (Newark, N.J.: Nordan Press, 1950). Regarding these 11 unions, see F. S. O'Brien, "The 'Communist Dominated' Unions in the United States Since 1950," *Labor History*, 9:2 (Spring 1968), 184–209.

94. F. S. O'Brien, "The 'Communist Dominated' Unions," p. 189.

95. *American Labor Yearbook, VI, 1926*, p. 261, and *American Labor Yearbook, X, 1929*, p. 155 (New York: Rand School of Social Science).

96. Lawrence H. Fuchs, *The Political Behavior of American Jews* (Glencoe, Ill.: Free Press, 1956), pp. 154, 166–168.

97. William Spinrad, "New York's Third Party Voters," *Public Opinion Quarterly*, 21:4 (Winter 1957), 550.

98. Lillian Gates, "New York's 1949 Elections," *Political Affairs*, 28:12 (December 1949), 48.

99. Benjamin J. Davis, *Communist Councilman from Harlem: Autobiographical*

Notes Written in a Federal Penitentiary (New York: International Publishers), pp. 106, 107, 112.

100. G. Charney, *Long Journey*, pp. 176–177; David A. Shannon, *The Decline of American Communism: A History of the Party Since 1945* (New York: Harcourt, Brace, 1959), pp. 99–101; and David J. Saposs, *Communism in American Politics* (Washington: Public Affairs Press, 1960), pp. 80, 81, 83.

101. L. H. Fuchs, *Political Behavior of American Jews*, pp. 80, 108, 154, 155; Curtis D. MacDougall, *Gideon's Army*, III (New York: Marzani and Munsell, 1965), pp. 645–646; and Philip G. Altbach, *Student Politics in America: An Historical Analysis* (New York: McGraw-Hill, 1974), pp. 141–163.

102. D. J. Saposs, *Communism in American Politics*, pp. 93, 94, 105.

103. L. H. Fuchs, *Political Behavior of American Jews*, pp. 76–107; and Stephen D. Isaacs, *Jews and American Politics* (Garden City, N.Y.: Doubleday, 1974), pp. 151–152.

104. For an overview of the ideology and programs of the New Left during the early to mid-1960s, see Paul Jacobs and Saul Landau, *The New Radicals* (New York: Vintage Books, 1966), pp. 3–8, 42–58, 74–81; Mitchell Cohen and Dennis Hale, Eds., *The New Student Left* (Boston: Beacon Press, 1967); and Martin J. Sklar and James Weinstein, "Socialism and the New Left," *Studies on the Left*, 6:2 (March–April 1966), 62–70.

105. Nathan Glazer, "The Jewish Role in Student Activism," *Fortune*, 79 (January 1969), 112; and Kirkpatrick Sale, *SDS* (New York: Random House, 1973), pp. 89, 203–658, 663–664.

106. Richard G. Braungart, "Family Status, Socialization and Student Politics: A Multivariate Analysis," unpublished doctoral dissertation, Pennsylvania State University, 1969, p. 142; Jack Nusan Porter, "Jewish Student Activism," *Jewish Currents*, 24:5 (May 1970), 4; and Sale, *SDS*, pp. 663–664.

107. "Jewish Young Freedom Fighters and the Role of the Jewish Community: An Evaluation," *Jewish Currents*, 19:9 (July–August 1965), 6, 14, 18; Stanky Rothman et al., "Ethnic Variations in Student Radicalism: Some New Perspectives," in Sweryn Bialer (ed.), *Radicalism in the Contemporary Age: Sources of Contemporary Radicalism*, 1 (Boulder, Colorado: Westview Press, 1977), p. 155.

108. Personal knowledge, and Lewis S. Feuer, *The Conflict of Generations: The Character and Significance of Student Movements* (New York: Basic Books, 1969), p. 423; and Robert H. Somers, "The Mainsprings of the Rebellion: A Survey of Berkeley Students in November 1964," in *The Berkeley Student Revolt: Facts and Interpretations*, Seymour M. Lipset and Sheldon S. Wolin, Eds. (Garden City, N.Y.: Doubleday Books, 1965), p. 548.

109. Richard W. Flacks, "The Liberated Generation: An Exploration of the Roots of Student Protest," *Journal of Social Issues*, 23:3 (July 1967), p. 65.

110.. *Time*, 20 September 1968, p. 42.

111. Seymour M. Lipset, *Rebellion in the University* (Boston: Little, Brown, 1972), p. 93; Alexander W. Astin, "Personal and Environmental Determinants of Student Activism," *Measurement and Evaluation in Gudiance*, 1:3 (Fall 1968), p. 153.

112. N. Glazer, "Jewish Role in Student Activism," p. 112.

113. For this poll, see S. M. Lipset, *Rebellion in the University*, p. 86. This same source also provides a summary of the major survey results, pp. 8–123. See also David E. Drew, *A Profile of the Jewish Freshman*, American Council on Education Research Report (Washington, D.C.: 1970), pp. 25, 26.

CHAPTER 3

1. See S. M. Dubnov, *History of the Jews in Russia and Poland*, 3 Vols. (Philadelphia: Jewish Publication Society, 1916–1920), for a good historical overview.

2. Arthur Ruppin, *The Jew in the Modern World* (London: Macmillan, 1934), p. 113.

3. Ibid., pp. 113–115; Moses Rischin, *The Promised City: New York's Jews*,

1870–1914 (New York: Harper Torchbooks, 1970), pp. 19–31; and Ezra Mendelsohn, *Class Struggle in the Pale: The Formative Years of the Jewish Workers' Movement in Tsarist Russia* (Cambridge: Cambridge University Press, 1970), pp. 1–26.

4. Jonathan Frankel, "Socialism and Jewish Nationalism in Russia, 1892–1907," unpublished doctoral dissertation, Cambridge University, 1961, p. 60.

5. William J. Fishman, *Jewish Radicals: From Czarist Stetl to London Ghetto* (New York: Random House, 1974), p. 30.

6. A. Ruppin, *Jew in the Modern World*, p. 44; J. Frankel, "Socialism and Jewish Nationalism," pp. 59–61; and Lucy S. Dawidowicz, *The Golden Tradition: Jewish Life and Thought in Eastern Europe* (Boston: Beacon Press, 1967), pp. 47–48.

7. L. S. Dawidowicz, *Golden Tradition*, pp. 46–47; and J. Frankel, "Socialism and Jewish Nationalism," pp. 59–61.

8. W. J. Fishman, *Jewish Radicals*, pp. 29–30.

9. J. Frankel, "Socialism and Jewish Nationalism," pp. 22–28.

10. Samuel Joseph, *Jewish Immigration to the United States: From 1881 to 1910* (New York: Arno Press, 1969), p. 68.

11. W. J. Fishman, *Jewish Radicals*, p. 28.

12. S. Joseph, *Jewish Immigration*, pp. 68–69.

13. There are no precise figures for converts. See the discussion on subject in Salo W. Baron, *The Russian Jew Under Tsars and Soviets* (New York: Macmillan, 1964), pp. 159–167.

14. Simon Kuznets, "Immigration of Russian Jews to the United States: Background and Structure," in *Perspectives in American History*, Donald Fleming and Bernard Bailyn, Eds. (Cambridge, Mass.: Charles Warren Center for Studies in American History, Harvard University, 1975), pp. 48–49.

15. S. Joseph, *Jewish Immigration*, pp. 98–104.

16. S. M. Dubnov, *History of the Jews*, Vol. III: pp. 66–75, 85.

17. S. Joseph, *Jewish Immigration*, pp. 100–101; A. Ruppin, *Jew in the Modern World*, pp. 45, 47; and Mark Wischnitzer, *To Dwell in Safety: The Story of Jewish Migration Since 1800* (Philadelphia: Jewish Publication Society of America, 1948), p. 105.

18. S. Joseph, *Jewish Immigration*, pp. 69–80, 105–116; and M. Rischin, *Promised City*, pp. 31–33.

19. A. Ruppin, *Jew in the Modern World*, p. 45; and M. Rischin, *Promised City*, p. 33.

20. S. Kuznets, "Immigration of Russian Jews," pp. 44, 51.

21. S. Joseph, *Jewish Immigration*, p. 139.

22. Ibid., pp. 183–184.

23. A. Ruppin, *Jew in the Modern World*, pp. 51–52.

24. S. Joseph, *Jewish Immigration*, p. 46; and E. Mendelsohn, *Class Struggle in the Pale*, pp. 4–5.

25. A. Ruppin, *Jew in the Modern World*, p. 113 and E. Mendelsohn, *Class Struggle in the Pale*, pp. 4–5.

26. Tamara Deutscher, Ed., *The Non-Jewish Jew and Other Essays* (New York: Hill and Wang, 1968), p. 27.

27. Henry J. Tobias, *The Jewish Bund in Russia: From Its Origin to 1905* (Stanford, Calif.: Stanford University Press, 1972), p. 8; A. Ruppin, *Jew in the Modern World*, pp. 40–41; and Israel Cohen, *Vilna* (Philadelphia: Jewish Publication Society, 1943), pp. 304–357.

28. W. J. Fishman, *Jewish Radicals*, p. 22; and M. Rischin, *Promised City*, p. 31.

29. M. Rischin, *Promised City*, p. 30.

30. Ibid., pp. 20–31; and E. Mendelsohn, *Class Struggle in the Pale*, pp. 1–26.

31. These statistics are not highly reliable. They come from government and Jewish agencies that did not gather the most complete data available. However, if anything, they overstate the size of Jewish factories as the smaller ones were pre-

cisely those most likely to avoid being sampled or inspected. I. M. Rubinow, "Economic Conditions of the Jews in Russia," *Bulletin of the Bureau of Labor, No. 7* (Washington, D.C.: U.S. Government Printing Office, 1907), pp. 536–548; Leon Trotsky, *1905* (New York: Vintage Books, 1972), pp. 20–22 (first published in 1909).

32. E. Mendelsohn, *Class Struggle in the Pale*, pp. 8–26; and Rubinow, "Economic Condition of the Jews," pp. 545–546.
33. L. S. Dawidowicz, *Golden Tradition*, p. 58; S. Joseph, *Jewish Immigration*, pp. 44–45; and I. M. Rubinow, "Economic Conditions of the Jews," pp. 519–523.
34. Ber Borochov, *Nationalism and the Class Struggle: A Marxian Approach to the Class Struggle* (New York: Young Pole Zion Alliance of America, 1937), pp. 65–69; and I. M. Rubinow, "Economic Conditions of the Jews," pp. 498–499, 520, 524.
35. E. Mendelsohn, *Class Struggle in the Pale*, p. 6.
36. M. Rischin, *The Promised City*, pp. 22–31; E. Mendelsohn, *Class Struggle in the Pale*, pp. 14–15; and A. L. Patkin, *Origins of the Russian Jewish Labour Movement* (London: F. W. Chesire Pty., 1947), pp. 36–39.
37. B. Borochov, *Nationalism and the Class Struggle*, pp. 61–63, 187–189; and E. Mendelsohn, "Economic Condition of the Jews," p. 9–10.
38. E. Mendelsohn, *Class Struggle in the Pale*, pp. 6–10.
39. B. Borochov, *Nationalism and the Class Struggle*, pp. 186–187.
40. One of the better sociological discussions of the impact of size on workers' political and class attitudes occurs in Seymour M. Lipset, Martin Trow, and James Coleman, *Union Democracy: The Internal Politics of the International Typographical Union* (Glencoe, Ill.: The Free Press, 1956).
41. For an insightful discussion of the value system of the Jews in Eastern Europe in the nineteenth century, see Mark Zborowski and Elizabeth Herzog, *Life Is With People: The Culture of the Shtetl* (New York: Schocken Press, 1962).
42. A. Ruppin, *Jew in the Modern World*, p. 113.
43. B. Borochov, *Nationalism and the Class Struggle*, p. 62.
44. Ibid., p. 188.
45. E. Mendelsohn, *Class Struggle in the Pale*, pp. 9–13.
46. Ibid. and A. L. Patkin, *Russian Jewish Labour Movement*, p. 39.
47. B. Borochov, *Nationalism and the Class Struggle*, p. 78.
48. E. Mendelsohn, *Class Struggle in the Pale*, p. 10.
49. Ibid., pp. 28–29; A. L. Patkin, *Russian Jewish Labour Movement*, p. 44; and H. J. Tobias, *Jewish Bund*, pp. 1–37.
50. Erich Goldenhagen, "The Ethnic Consciousness of Early Russian Jewish Socialists," *Judaism*, 23:4 (Fall 1974), 483 and Robert J. Brym, *The Jewish Intelligentsia and Russian Marxism: A Sociological Study of Intellectual Radicalism and Ideological Diversity* (London: Macmillan Press, 1978), pp. 53–58.
51. L. S. Dawidowicz, *Golden Tradition*, p. 37; and M. Rischin, *Promised City*, p. 39.
52. L. S. Dawidowicz, *Golden Tradition*, pp. 14–33, 81–82; and J. Frankel, "Socialism and Jewish Nationalism," pp. 16–19, 46.
53. L. S. Dawidowicz, *Golden Tradition*, p. 82.
54. Ibid., p. 48.
55. E. Goldenhagen, "Ethnic Consciousness," p. 483.
56. Brym, *Jewish Intelligentsia*, pp. 53–58.
57. L. S. Dawidowicz, *Golden Tradition*, pp. 42–46; and J. Frankel, "Socialism and Jewish Nationalism," pp. 42–49.
58. L. S. Dawidowicz, pp. 47–48; and J. Frankel, pp. 59–60.
59. J. Frankel, "Socialism and Jewish Nationalism," pp. 69–71; and E. Goldenhagen, "Ethnic Consciousness," pp. 492–494.
60. E. Goldenhagen, "Ethnic Consciousness," p. 493.
61. Ibid., p. 492.
62. E. Goldenhagen, "Ethnic Consciousness," p. 491.

63. Norm Levin, *While Messiah Tarried: Jewish Socialist Movements, 1871–1917* (New York: Schocken Books, 1977), pp. 54–55.
64. Melech Epstein, *Jewish Labor in the U.S.A.: An Industrial, Political and Cultural History of the Jewish Labor Movement, 1882–1914* (New York: Ktav Publishing House, 1969), pp. 19–22 and Abraham Menes, "The *Am Oylom* Movement," *YIVO Annual of Jewish Social Science*, IV (1949), pp. 9–33.
65. M. Epstein, *Jewish Labor*, pp. 22–23.
66. Ibid., pp. 30–32; and Elias Tcherikower, *The Early Jewish Labor Movement in the U.S.*, translated by Aaron Antoovsky (New York: YIVO Institute for Jewish Research, 1961), pp. 44, 50.
67. William M. Leiserson, "The Jewish Labor Movement," unpublsihed paper, University of Wisconsin, 1908, p. 10.
68. A. Menes, "The *Am Oylom* Movement," p. 33.
69. Walter Laqueur, *A History of Zionism* (London: Weidenfeld and Nicolson, 1972), pp. 75–76.
70. J. Frankel, "Socialism and Jewish Nationalism," pp. 75–84.
71. M. Epstein, *Jewish Labor in the U.S.A.*, p. 17.
72. E. Mendelsohn, *Class Struggle in the Pale*, pp. 33–35; and H. J. Tobias, *Jewish Bund*, pp. 16–18.
73. J. Frankel, "Socialism and Jewish Nationalism," pp. 77–86.
74. H. J. Tobias, *Jewish Bund*, p. 18.
75. J. Frankel, "Socialism and Jewish Nationalism," pp. 2–3; E. Mendelsohn, *Class Struggle in the Pale*, pp. 29–44; and H. J. Tobias, *Jewish Bund*, pp. 28–32.
76. Quoted in J. Frankel, "Socialism and Jewish Nationalism," p. 89.
77. E. Mendelsohn, *Class Struggle in the Pale*, pp. 56–61.
78. This general line of argument was used by Ber Borochov, prominent labor Zionist theoretician, in his attack on the Bund [B. Borochov, *Nationalism and the Class Struggle,*
79. See "Engels to Marx in London" (Manchester, October 7, 1858) and "Engels to H. Schluter in New York" (London, March 30, 1892) in *Karl Marx and Frederick Engels: Selected Correspondence* (Moscow: Progress Publishers, 1965), pp. 110, 444; V. I. Lenin, *Imperialism, The Highest Stage of Capitalism* (Moscow: Foreign Languages Publishing Houses, n.d.), pp. 16–17 (originally published in 1917); and an incisive discussion of this issue in Bryan D. Palmer, "Most Uncommon Men: Craft, Culture and Conflict in a Canadian Community, 1860–1914," unpublished doctoral dissertation, Binghamton: State University of New York at Binghamton, 1977, pp. 18–22.
80. B. D. Palmer, "Most Uncommon Men," pp. 11–27; Peter N. Stearns, *Revolutionary Syndicalism and French Labor: A Cause Without Rebels* (New Brunswick, N.J.: Rutgers University Press, 1971), pp. 32, 33, 96; E. P. Thompson, *The Making of the English Working Class* (New York: Vintage Books, 1963), pp. 234–268.
81. I. M. Rubinow, "Economic Conditions of the Jews," pp. 522–532.
82. Epstein, *op. cit.*, pp. 119, 131–146 and Emanuel Hertz, "Politics: New York," in Charles S. Bernheimer (ed.), *The Russian Jew in the United States* (Philadelphia: John C. Winston, 1905), p. 61.
83. J. Frankel, "Socialism and Jewish Nationalism," pp. 33–35; and Mendelsohn, *Class Struggle in the Pale*, pp. 32–33.
84. Quoted in Mendelsohn, *Class Struggle in the Pale*, p. 33.
85. L. S. Dawidowicz, *Golden Tradition*, p. 70; J. Frankel, "Socialism and Jewish Nationalism," pp. 33–35; and H. J. Tobias, *Jewish Bund*, pp. 50–53.
86. J. Frankel, "Socialism and Jewish Nationalism," pp. 195–197.
87. L. S. Dawidowicz, *Golden Tradition*, p. 64.
88. Quoted in J. Frankel, "Socialism and Jewish Nationalism," p. 57.
89. Ibid., pp. 94–103; and H. J. Tobias, *Jewish Bund*, pp. 32–35.
90. Quoted in Ibid., p. 103.
91. I. L. Peretz, "What Our Literature Needs," in *Voices From the Yiddish: Essays,*

Memoirs, Diaries, Irving Howe and Eliezer Greenberg, Eds. (Ann Arbor, Mich.: University of Michigan Press, 1972), p. 30.

92. L. S. Dawidowicz, *Golden Tradition,* pp. 22, 64–69; I. Howe and E. Greenberg, "Introduction," in *Voices From the Yiddish,* pp. 1–10; J. Frankel, "Socialism and Jewish Nationalism," pp. 94–103; E. Mendelsohn, *Class Struggle in the Pale,* pp. 116–125; Abraham Leissen, "When Yiddish Literature Became Socialist," in Dawidowicz, pp. 422–525; Peretz, "What Our Literature Needs," pp. 22–31; H. J. Tobias, *Jewish Bund,* pp. 32–46; and Hayim Zhitlowsky, "The Jewish Factor in My Socialism," in Howe and Greenberg, pp. 126–134.

93. E. Tcherikower, *Early Jewish Labor Movement,* p. 44.

94. Quoted in J. Frankel, "Socialism and Jewish Nationalism," p. 286.

95. M. Rischin, *Promised City,* p. 45.

96. J. Frankel, "Socialism and Jewish Nationalism," pp. 132–136; and H. J. Tobias, *Jewish Bund,* pp. 67–77.

97. Frankel, pp. 110–132; and Tobias, pp. 22–28.

98. Quoted in A. L. Patkin, *Russian Jewish Labour Movement,* p. 132.

99. Quoted in Koppel S. Pinson, "Arkady Kremer, Vladimir Medem, and the Ideology of the Jewish 'Bund,' " *Jewish Social Studies,* 7:3 (July 1945), 245.

100. Quoted in J. Frankel, "Socialism and Jewish Nationalism," p. 134.

101. Ibid., pp. 134–135.

102. Ibid.

103. Ibid., pp. 177–184; and H. J. Tobias, *Jewish Bund,* pp. 86–88.

104. Quoted in J. Frankel, "Socialism and Jewish Nationalism," p. 178.

105. Ibid., pp. 169–173.

106. Quoted in K. S. Pinson, "Ideology of the Jewish 'Bund,' " p. 248.

107. J. Frankel, "Socialism and Jewish Nationalism," pp. 239–242.

108. Ibid.

109. Ibid.

110. Quoted in H. J. Tobias, *Jewish Bund,* p. 165.

111. Vladimir I. Lenin, "The Position of the Bund in the Party," in *Lenin on the Jewish Question,* Hyman Lumer, Ed. (New York: International Publishers, 1974), p. 48.

112. Quoted in V. I. Lenin, "Position of the Bund," p. 49.

113. Ibid.

114. V. I. Lenin, " 'National Culture'," in H. Lumer, *Lenin on the Jewish Question,* p. 107.

115. Ibid.

116. V. I. Lenin, "Does the Jewish Proletariat Need an 'Independent Political Party'," in H. Lumer, *Lenin on the Jewish Question,* pp. 20–21.

117. J. Frankel, "Socialism and Jewish Nationalism," p. 208.

118. Quoted in Joseph Nedava, *Trotsky and the Jews* (Philadelphia: Jewish Publication Society of America, 1972), p. 91.

119. Isaac Deutscher, *The Prophet Armed, Trotsky: 1879–1921* (New York: Oxford University Press, 1970), pp. 72–73.

120. Ibid.

121. Quoted in J. Nedava, *Trotsky and the Jews,* p. 91.

122. Quoted in Patkin, *Russian Jewish Labour Movement,* pp. 185–186.

123. Quoted in ibid., p. 186.

124. Quoted in ibid., p. 188.

125. I. Deutscher, *Prophet Armed,* p. 74.

126. Quoted in J. Nevada, *Trotsky and the Jews,* p. 94.

127. Quoted in J. Nedava, *Trotsky and the Jews,* p. 94.

128. Quoted in ibid., pp. 95–96.

129. Quoted in ibid., p. 91.

130. Brym, *Jewish Intelligentsia,* pp. 37–46, 61–85.

131. Quoted in Deutscher, *Prophet Armed,* p. 75.

132. J. Frankel, "Socialism and Jewish Nationalism," p. 212.

133. A. L. Patkin, *Russian Jewish Labour Movement*, pp. 145–146; K. S. Pinson, "Ideology of the Jewish 'Bund,' " pp. 260–261; and W. Lacqueur, *History of Zionism*, pp. 273–274.
134. Quoted in W. Lacqueur, *History of Zionism*, p. 274.
135. Quoted in A. L. Patkin, *Russian Jewish Labour Movement*, p. 146.
136. H. J. Tobias, *Jewish Bund*, p. 342.
137. The Bund's membership statistics do not clearly differentiate members from organized supporters. However, for our purposes, this is not a crucial distinction (J. Frankel, "Socialism and Jewish Nationalism," p. 237).
138. H. J. Tobias, *Jewish Bund*, pp. 238–239.
139. M. Rischin, *Promised City*, pp. 44–45.
140. B. Borochov, *Nationalism and the Class Struggle*, p. 78.
141. quoted in H. J. Tobias, *Jewish Bund*, p. 224.
142. Ibid., pp. 224–225.
143. Ibid., pp. 236–237.
144. Ibid., p. 306.
145. Quoted in ibid., pp. 299–300.
146. Quoted in ibid., p. 309.
147. J. Frankel, "Socialism and Jewish Nationalism," pp. 227–228.
148. Quoted in E. Mendelsohn, *Class Struggle in the Pale*, p. 106.
149. H. J. Tobias, *Jewish Bund*, p. 229.
150. Quoted in ibid., p. 229.
151. Quoted in E. Mendelsohn, *Class Struggle in the Pale*, p. 105.
152. H. J. Tobias, *Jewish Bund*, pp. 256–257, 405.
153. Charles E. Woodhouse and Henry J. Tobias, "Primordial Ties and Political Process in Pre-Revolutionary Russia: The Case of the Jewish Bund," *Comparative Studies in Society and History*, 8:3 (April 1966), 349–357.
154. J. Frankel, "Socialism and Jewish Nationalism," p. 240.
155. C. E. Woodhouse and H. J. Tobias, "Primordial Ties," pp. 353–355.
156. Quoted in L. S. Dawidowicz, *Golden Tradition*, pp. 66–67.
157. B. Borochov, *Nationalism and the Class Struggle*, pp. 61–62; and J. Nedava, *Trotsky and the Jews*, p. 154.
158. Quoted in E. Mendelsohn, *Class Struggle in the Pale*, p. 153.
159. Quoted in ibid., p. 154.
160. Ibid., pp.153–155; and H. J. Tobias, *Jewish Bund*, pp. 340–343.
161. J. Frankel, "Socialism and Jewish Nationalism," p. 237.
162. Melech Epstein, *The Jew and Communism: The Story of Early Communist Victories and Ultimate Defeats in the Jewish Community, U.S.A., 1919–1941* (New York: Trade Union Sponsoring Committee, 1959), pp. 5–7; and H. J. Tobias, *Jewish Bund*, p. 241.

CHAPTER 4

1. Samuel Joseph, *Jewish Immigration to the United States: From 1881 to 1910* (New York: Arno Press, 1969), pp. 162–164; Mark Wischnitzer, *To Dwell in Safety: The Story of Jewish Migration Since 1800* (Philadelphia: Jewish Publication Society of America, 1948), p. 289; and Kuznets, "Immigration of Russian Jews," p. 39.
2. I. M. Rubinow, "Economic Conditions of the Jews in Russia," p. 502.
3. Joseph, *Jewish Immigration*, p. 195.
4. Morris U. Schappes, "Jewish Mass Immigration from Europe, 1881–1914," *Jewish Life*, 8:10 (Nov. 1954), 20–21.
5. Moses Rischin, *The Promised City: New York's Jews, 1870–1914* (New York: Harper & Row, 1970), pp. 93–94; and Thomas Kessner, *The Golden Door: Italian and Jewish Immigrant Mobility in New York City, 1880–1915* (New York: Oxford University Press, 1977), pp. 132–134.
6. T. Kessner, *Golden Door*, p. 148.

7. M. Rischin, *Promised City*, pp. 93–94.

8. Milton Doroshkin, *Yiddish in America: Social and Cultural Foundations* (Rutherford, N.J.: Farleigh Dickinson University Press), p. 191.

9. Seymour Martin Lipset, *Political Man: The Social Bases of Politics* (Garden City, N.Y.: Anchor Books, Doubleday, 1963), pp. 263–267.

10. United States Industrial Commission, *Reports of the Industrial Commission on Immigration and Education*, Vol. XV (Washington, D.C.: U.S. Government Printing Office, 1901), p. 486.

11. Quoted in ibid., pp. 476–477.

12. Melech Epstein, *Jewish Labor in the U.S.A.: An Industrial, Political, and Cultural History of the Jewish Labor Movement, 1882–1914*, Vol. I (New York: Ktav Publishing House, 1969), p. 102; M. Rischin, *Promised City*, p. 88.

13. Maurice Fishberg, "Health and Sanitation: New York," in *The Russian Jew in the United States*, Charles S. Bernheimer, Ed. (Philadelphia: John C. Winston, 1905), pp. 294–295.

14. M. Rischin, *Promised City*, pp. 90–91.

15. Samuel Ornitz, "Hirsch and Freund," [from *Haunch, Paunch, and Jowl: An Anonymous Autobiography* (1923)] in *On Being Jewish: American Jewish Writers from Cahan to Bellow* Daniel Walden, Ed. (Greenwich, Conn.: Fawcett Publications, 1974), pp. 164–165.

16. Irving Howe, *World of Our Fathers* (New York: Harcourt Brace Jovanovich, 1976), pp. 67–118.

17. Irving Howe and Eliezer Greenberg, Eds., *Voices From the Yiddish: Essays, Memoirs and Diaries* (Ann Arbor, Mich.: University of Michigan Press, 1972), p. 2.

18. Nathan Glazer, *American Judaism*, 2nd ed. (Chicago: University of Chicago Press, 1972), pp. 39–66; Rischin, *Promised City*, pp. 95–111.

19. Lloyd Gartner, "Immigration and the Formation of American Jewry, 1840–1925," in *Jewish Society Through the Ages*, H. H. Ben-Sasson and S. Ettinger, Eds. (New York: Schocken Books, 1973), p. 306.

20. Data of this nature cannot be considered highly accurate, but it is very suggestive. Uriah Z. Engelman, "Jewish Statistics in the U.S. Census of Religious Bodies (1850–1936)," *Jewish Social Studies*, 9:1 (January 1947), 136–138.

21. M. Doroshkin, *Yiddish in America*, p. 29.

22. M. Rischin, *Promised City*, p. 105.

23. Arthur Goren, *New York Jews and the Quest for Community: The Kehillah Experiment, 1908–1922* (New York: Columbia University Press, 1970), p. 20.

24. Louis Wirth, *The Ghetto* (Chicago: University of Chicago Press, 1928 and 1956), pp. 222–223.

25. Quoted in M. Doroshkin, *Yiddish in America*, p. 137.

26. Elias Tcherikower, *The Early Jewish Labor Movement in the U.S.*, trans. Aaron Antonovsky (New York: YIVO Institute for Jewish Research, 1961), pp. 132–134.

27. M. Epstein, *Jewish Labor*, pp. 273–297.

28. Mordecai Soltes, *The Yiddish Press: An Americanizing Agency* (New York: Teachers College, Columbia University Press, 1950), pp. 14–29; M. Epstein, *Jewish Labor*, pp. 318–334.

29. Samuel Niger, "Yiddish Culture," in *Jewish People: Past and Present*, Vol. IV, A. Menes, Ed. (New York: Jewish Encyclopedic Handbooks, 1955), p. 289.

30. S. L. Blumenson, "Culture on Rutgers Square: The Fervent Days of East Broadway," *Commentary*, 10:1 (July 1950), 69; and M. Soltes, *Yiddish Press*, pp. 23–24.

31. John Higham, "Social Discrimination Against Jews in America, 1830–1930," *Publication of the American Jewish Historical Society*, 47:1 (September 1957), 8.

32. Lloyd P. Gartner, "Immigration and the Formation of American Jewry, 1840–1925," in H. H. Ben-Sasson and S. Ettinger, Eds., *Jewish Society Through the Ages*, pp. 302–308; Irving A. Mandel, "Attitudes of the American Jewish Community Toward East European Immigration," *American Jewish Archives*,

3:1 (June 1950), 30–35; M. Rischin, *Promised City*, pp. 95–106; and Zosa Szajkowski, "Paul Nathan, Lucien Wolf, Jacob H. Schiff and the Jewish Revolutionary Movements in Eastern Europe, 1903–1917," *Jewish Social Studies*, 29:1 (January 1967), 21–26.

33. Quoted in M. Wischnitzer, *Jewish Migration Since 1800*, p. 126.
34. Stephen Birmingham, *Our Crowd: The Great Jewish Families of New York* (New York: Harper & Row, 1967), p. 291.
35. L. Gartner, "Formation of American Jewry," pp. 307–308.
36. S. Birmingham, *Our Crowd*, p. 291.
37. Mordecai M. Kaplan, *Judaism as a Civilization: Toward A Reconstruction of American-Jewish Life* (New York: Schocken Books, 1972), pp. 93–94.
38. Bernard D. Weinryb, "Jewish Immigration and Accommodation to America," in *The Jews: Social Patterns of an American Group*, Marshall Sklare, Ed. (Glencoe, Ill.: Free Press, 1960), p. 628.
39. Bernard H. Bloom, "Yiddish-Speaking Socialists in America: 1892–1905," in *Critical Studies in American Jewish History: Selected Articles from American Jewish Archives*, Vol. III (New York: Ktav Publishing House, 1971), p. 30.
40. E. Tcherikower, *Early Jewish Labor Movement*, p. 218.
41. L. Gartner, "Formation of American Jewry," p. 306.
42. Stuart E. Rosenberg, "Some Attitudes of Nineteenth Century Reform Laymen," in *Essays on Jewish Life and Thought: Presented in Honor of Salo W. Baron*, Joseph L. Blau et al., Eds. (New York: Columbia University Press, 1959), pp. 414–415.
43. Quoted in Rischin, *Promised City*, p. 104.
44. Harry L. Lurie, *A Heritage Affirmed: The Jewish Federation Movement in America* (Philadelphia: Jewish Publication Society, 1961), pp. 49–50.
45. Ibid., pp. 52–53; B. D. Weinryb, "Jewish Immigration, p. 19.
46. Zosa Szajkowski, *Jews, Wars, and Communism, II: The Impact of the Red Scare on American Jewish Life* (New York: Ktav Publishing House, 1974), p. 122.
47. Ibid., p. 119.
48. B. H. Bloom, "Yiddish Speaking Socialists," pp. 31–32.
49. H. L. Lurie, *Jewish Federation Movement*, pp. 78–79.
50. The political weakness and the defensiveness of this strata is insightfully portrayed in Abraham Cahan, *The Rise of David Levinsky* (New York: Harper Torchbooks, 1960), a novel about an immigrant Russian Jewish garment manufacturer first published in 1917. A. Goren, *New York Jews*, pp. 18–19.
51. See Kurt Lewin's "Self-Hatred Among Jews" for the social-psychological dynamics underlying this process: in *Resolving Social Conflicts: Selected Papers on Group Dynamics* (New York: Harper & Row, 1948), pp. 186–200. See also E. Digby Baltzell, "The Development of a Jewish Upper Class in Philadelphia: 1782–1940," for a historical-sociological analysis of this process, in M. Sklare, Ed., *The Jews*, pp. 271–287.
52. T. Kessner, *Golden Door*, pp. 33–34.
53. Charles S. Liebman, *The Ambivalent American Jews: Politics, Religion and Family in American Jewish Life* (Philadelphia: Jewish Publication Society, 1973), p. 53.
54. Lucy S. Dawidowicz, "From Past to Past: Jewish East Europe to Jewish East Side," *Conservative Judaism*, 22:2 (Winter 1968), 25.
55. Interview with man who immigrated to the United States from Russia in 1913.
56. M. Rischin, *Promised City*, pp. 146–147.
57. A. Goren, *New York Jews*, p. 88.
58. L. Wirth, *The Ghetto*, p. 178.
59. N. Glazer, *American Judaism*, p. 73; H. L. Lurie, *Jewish Federation Movements*, p. 422.
60. U. Z. Engelman, "Jewish Statistics," p. 149; and A. Goren, *New York Jews*, pp. 20–21.

61. A. Goren, p. 20; I. Howe, *World of Our Fathers*, pp. 190–197; and C. S. Liebman, *Ambivalent American Jews*, pp. 56–57.
62. Liebman, p. 53.
63. A. Goren, *New York Jews*, pp. 76–77.
64. Ibid.
65. Abraham J. Karp, "New York Chooses a Chief Rabbi," *Publications of the American Jewish Historical Society*, 44 (March 1955), pp. 129–198.
66. A. Goren, *New York Jews*, pp. 76–77; and N. Glazer, *American Judaism*, p. 78.
67. Milton Konvitz, "Change and Tradition in Modern Judaism: A Letter to David Daiches," in *Tradition and Contemporary Experience: Essays in Jewish Thought and Life*, Alfred Jospe, Ed. (New York: Schocken Books, 1970), pp. 28–29.
68. E. Tcherikower, *Early Jewish Labor Movement*, p. 137.
69. Ibid., pp. 138–139; M. Rischin, *Promised City*, pp. 148–149.
70. Morris U. Schappes, *The Jews in the United States: A Pictorial History: 1654 to the Present* (New York: Citadel Press, 1955), p. 153; and Philip S. Foner, History of the Labor Movement in the United States, Vol. III (New York: International Publishers, 1964), p. 134.
71. The most thorough discussion of Jewish radicalism in England from the 1880s until World War I is by William J. Fishman, *Jewish Radicals: From Czarist Stetl to London Ghetto* (New York: Pantheon Book, 1974).
72. Ibid., pp. 156–157, 164–165, 206–207, 211–215, 306; Lloyd P. Gartner, *The Jewish Immigrant in England, 1870–1914* (London: George Allen and Unwin, 1960), pp. 140–142.
73. L. P. Gartner, *Jewish Immigrant in England*, p. 113.
74. B. H. Bloom, "Yiddish Speaking Socialists," pp. 25–26; N. Glazer, *American Judaism*, p. 67; M. Rischin, *Promised City*, p. 164.
75. Quoted in W. J. Fishman, *Jewish Radicals*, pp. 211–212.
76. Melvin Urofsky, "The Emergence of Brandeis As A Zionist," *Midstream*, 21:1 (January 1975), 49–53; Walter Lacqueur, *A History of Zionism* (London: Weidenfeld and Nicolson, 1972), pp. 158–159.
77. Joseph, *Jewish Immigration*, p. 187. It should be noted that the "No Occupation" category was large for Jews, nearly half. This is because women and children were lumped together with men when the data were collected, and these groups constituted a large proportion of the Jewish immigrants.
78. Rubinow, "Economic Conditions," p. 502.
79. Joseph, *Jewish Immigration*, p. 190.
80. Rudolph J. Vecoli, "Contadini in Chicago: A Critique of the Uprooted," in *The Aliens*, Leonard Dinnerstein and Frederic C. Jaher, Eds. (New York: Meredith Corp., 1970), pp. 224–225.
81. M. Rischin, *Promised City*, p. 59.
82. M. Epstein, *Jewish Labor*, pp. 78–80; and M. Rischin, *Promised City*, pp. 59–60.
83. Alice Kessler Harris, "The Lower Class As a Factor in Reform: New York, the Jews and the 1890's" (Ph.D. diss., Rutgers University, 1968), p. 179; M. Rischin, *Promised City*, pp. 59–61; and Joel Seidman, *The Needle Trades* (New York: Farrer & Rinehart, 1942), pp. 43–49.
84. A. Ross Eckler and Jack Zlotnick, "Immigration and the Labor Force," *Annals of the American Academy of Political and Social Sciences*, 262 (March 1949), 100.
85. A. Goren, *New York Jews*, p. 18; Judith Greenfield, "The Role of the Jews in the Development of the Clothing Industry in the U.S.," *YIVO Annual of Jewish Social Science*, II–III (1947–1948), 203; and J. Seidman, *Needle Trades*, pp. 7, 43.
86. E. Tcherikower, *Early Jewish Labor Movement*, p. 99.
87. A. Cahan, *Rise of David Levinsky*, pp. 270–271.
88. M. Rischin, *Promised City*, p. 61.
89. Alice Kessler Harris, "Organizing the Unorganizable: Jewish Women and Their Unions," Working Paper, Center for the Historical Study of Societies, State University of New York at Binghamton, 1975, p. 22.

90. Louis Levine, *The Women Garment Workers: A History of the International Ladies Garment Workers' Union* (New York: B. W. Heubsch, 1924), pp. 1–13; J. Seidman, *Needle Trades*, pp. 14–17.
91. J. Seidman, pp. 335–345.
92. M. Rischin, *Promised City*, pp. 66–67.
93. M. Epstein, *Jewish Labor*, pp. 96–97; M. Rischin, p. 183; Industrial Commission, *Reports*, pp. 324–327.
94. Quoted in M. Epstein, pp. 92–93.
95. Melvyn Dubofsky, *When Workers Organize: New York City in the Progressive Era* (Amherst: University of Massachusetts Press, 1968), pp. 7–13.
96. Philip S. Foner, *The Fur and Leather Workers' Union: A Story of Dramatic Struggles and Achievements* (Newark: Nordan Press, 1950), pp. 31–32.
97. M. Dubofsky, *When Workers Organize*, p. 12.
98. Kessler Harris, "The Lower Class," p. 179.
99. M. Dubofsky, *When Workers Organize*, p. 8; M. Epstein, *Jewish Labor*, pp. 93–95.
100. Jacob Riis, *How the Other Half Lives* (New York: Charles Scribner's Sons, 1900), p. 108.
101. Quoted in M. Epstein, *Jewish Labor*, p. 99.
102. Industrial Commission, *Reports*, p. 345.
103. Ibid., p. 318.
104. Katherine Stone, "The Origin of Job Structures in the Steel Industry," in *Root and Branch: The Rise of the Workers Movement*, Jeremy Brecher et al., Eds. (Greenwich, Conn.: Fawcett Publications, 1975), p. 154.
105. Quoted in M. Epstein, *Jewish Labor*, p. 97.
106. Quoted in K. Stone, "Origin of Job Structure," p. 135.
107. J. Seidman, *Needle Trades*, pp. 82–84, 100–101.
108. William M. Leiserson, "The Jewish Labor Movement in New York," (B.A. thesis, University of Wisconsin, 1908), pp. 17–18; and Ezra Mendelsohn, "The Russian Roots of the American Jewish Labor Movement," *YIVO Annual of Jewish Social Science*, XVI (1976), 166–167.
109. W. M. Leiserson, pp. 7–10; and Mendelsohn, pp. 154–155. See discussion in Chapter 3.
110. Alexander Bittelman, "Things I Have Learned: An Autobiography" (manuscript at Tamiment Library, New York University, 1962), p. 249.
111. This impression is based on interviews with older Jewish radicals and ex-radicals. See also, Melech Epstein, *The Jew and Communism: The Story of Early Communist Victories and Ultimate Defeats in the Jewish Community, U.S.A., 1919–1941* (New York: Trade Union Sponsoring Committee, 1959), pp. 23–24.
112. E. Tcherikower, *Early Jewish Labor Movement*, p. 50.
113. Alexander Berkman, *Prison Memoirs of an Anarchist* (New York: Mother Earth Publishing Association, 1912), p. 5.
114. Ibid., pp. 9–10.
115. E. Tcherikower, *Early Jewish Labor Movement*, pp. 203–209.
116. Quoted in M. Epstein, *Jewish Labor*, pp. 139–140.
117. B. H. Bloom, "Yiddish Speaking Socialists, p. 20; M. Epstein, *The Jew and Communism*, pp. 3–8; W. J. Fishman, *Jewish Radicals*, pp. 260–265; and Louis J. Swichkow and Lloyd P. Gartner, *A History of the Jews of Milwaukee* (Philadelphia: Jewish Publication Society, 1963), p. 245.
118. M. Epstein, *Jewish Labor*, p. 350.
119. W. J. Fishman, *Jewish Radicals*, p. 207.
120. Robert E. Park, *The Immigrant Press and Its Control* (New York: Harper, 1922), p. 93.
121. L. Levine, *Women Garment Workers*, pp. 142–143.
122. M. Rischin, *Promised City*, 162–164; Henry Shukman, "The Relations Between the Jewish Bund and the RSDRP, 1897–1903," (Ph.D. diss. Oxford University, 1961), pp. 39–41; and Henry Tobias, *The Jewish Bund in Russia: From Its Origins to 1905* (Stanford, Calif.: Stanford University Press, 1972), pp. 92–93, 241.

123. Quoted in Charles E. Zaretz, *The Amalgamated Clothing Workers of America: A Study in Progressive Trades-Unionism* (New York: Avon Publishing Co., 1934), p. 94.
124. W. J. Fishman, *Jewish Radicals*, p. 207.
125. L. P. Gartner, *Jewish Immigrant in England*, p. 141.
126. James Weinstein, *The Decline of Socialism in America, 1912–1925* (New York: Vintage Books, 1969), p. 27.
127. Allen F. Davis, *Spearheads for Reform: The Social Settlements and Progressive Movement, 1890–1914* (New York: Oxford University Press, 1967), pp. 3–25, 8–122; M. Dubofsky, *When Workers Organize*, pp. 21–27; Richard Hofstadter, *The Age of Reform* (New York: Vintage Books, 1955), pp. 131–371; Seymour Martin Lipset, *Rebellion in the University* (Boston: Little, Brown, 1972), pp. 152–154.
128. Irwin Yellowitz, *Labor and the Progressive Movement in New York State, 1897–1916* (Ithaca, N.Y.: Cornell University Press, 1965), pp. 71–127.
129. M. Dubofsky, *When Workers Organize*, p. 26.
130. Henry May, *The End of American Innocence: A Study of the First Years of Our Own Times: 1912–1917* (Chicago: Quadrangle Books, 1964), pp. 282–283.
131. Ibid., p. 283.
132. M. Dubofsky, *When Workers Organize*, pp. 21–27, 47, 50–51.
133. Ibid., pp. 21–23; Bureau of the Census, *Historical Statistics of the United States: Colonial Times to 1957* (Washington, D.C.: U.S. Government Printing Office, 1960), pp. 682–683; I. Howe, *World of Our Fathers*, pp. 360–385; Samuel T. McSeveney, *The Politics of Depression: Political Behavior in the Northeast, 1893–1896* (New York: Oxford University Press, 1972), pp. 103–104; and J. Weinstein, *Decline of Socialism*, pp. 27, 28, 93, 100.
134. John Higham, "Social Discrimination Against Jews in America, 1830–1930" *Publication of the American Jewish Historical Society*, 47:1 (September 1957), 16, quoted in Stephen Steinberg, *The Academic Melting Pot: Catholics and Jews in American Higher Education* (New York: McGraw-Hill, 1974), pp. 9–10; and E. Tcherikower, *Early Jewish Labor Movement*, p. 140; T. Kessner, *Golden Door*, p. 98.
135. S. Birmingham, *Our Crowd*, p. 147; J. Higham, "Social Discrimination," pp. 16–17.
136. The most famous one occurred in 1914. Leo Frank, the manager of a pencil factory in Atlanta, was lynched by a mob after being found guilty of murdering one of his female employees, whom, it was rumored, he had sexually molested. The mob lynched Frank after the governor's commutation of the death sentence. John Higham, *Strangers in the Land: Patterns of American Nativism: 1860–1925* (New York: Atheneum, 1963), p. 111. The other killing took place in 1868 when the Ku Klux Klan lynched S. A. Bierfield in Franklin, Tenn. The Klan was incensed over his publicly expressed views on behalf of Negro equality. Schappes, *Pictorial History of Jews*, p. 100.
137. J. Higham, "Social Discrimination," p. 13.
138. S. Birmingham, *Our Crowd*, p. 253.
139. McSeveney, *Politics of Depression*, pp. 186–187.
140. S. L. Blumenson, "Rutgers Square," p. 67.
141. Richard Drinnon, *Rebel in Paradise: A Biography of Emma Goldman* (New York: Bantam Books, 1973), pp. 81–114; J. Higham, *Strangers in the Land*, pp. 52–111.
142. Quoted in M. Dubofsky, *When Workers Organize*, p. 14.
143. See studies dealing primarily with non-Jewish Eastern and Southern Europeans in the steel mills and coal mines for their attitudes and political and economic responses to their situation in America. David Brody, *Steel Workers in America: The Non-Union Era* (New York: Harper Torchbooks, 1969); Victor R. Greene, *The Slavic Community on Strike: Immigrant Labor in Pennsylvania Anthracite* (Notre Dame: University of Notre Dame Press, 1968); and Michael Nash, "Conflict and Accommodation: A Study of the Political Behavior of America's Coal

Miners and Steel Workers, 1890–1920," (Ph.D. diss., State University of New York at Binghamton, 1975). See also broader statements in support of this assertion by Stephan Thernstrom, "Urbanization, Migration, and Social Mobility in Late Nineteenth Century America," in *Towards a New Past: Dissenting Essays in American History*, Barton J. Bernstein, Ed. (New York: Vintage Books, 1969), pp. 161–163.

144. Ephraim E. Listzky, "In the Grip of Cross Currents," in *Jewish-American Literature: An Anthology*, Abraham Chapman, Ed. (New York: New American Library, 1974), p. 220.

145. See studies cited in note 142.

146. M. Rischin, *Promised City*, pp. 92–94.

147. Ibid., p. 93.

148. Industrial Commission, *Reports*, p. 477.

149. Nathan Glazer, "Social Characteristics of American Jews, 1654–1954," *American Jewish Yearbook*, 56 (Philadelphia: American Jewish Committee and Jewish Publication Society, 1955), pp. 8–11; M. Rischin, *Promised City*, pp. 92–93.

150. T. Kessner, *Golden Door*, pp. 114, 170. In Boston the Jews rate of mobility from blue- to white-collar was double that for Catholics and Protestants. Stephan Thernstrom, *The Other Bostonians: Poverty and Progress in the American Metropolis, 1880–1970* (Cambridge, Mass.: Harvard University Press, 1973), pp. 149–151.

151. Industrial Commission, *Reports*, p. 477.

152. Ibid., p. 319.

153. E. Tcherikower, *Early Jewish Labor Movement*, p. 339.

154. W. L. Leiserson, "Jewish Labor Movement," p. 50.

155. S. Thernstrom, "Urbanization, Migration, and Mobility," p. 168.

156. M. Rischin, *Promised City*, p. 187.

157. M. Epstein, *Jewish Labor*, pp. 257–258.

158. S. Thernstrom, "Urbanization, Migration and Mobility," p. 160.

159. L. Levine, *Women Garment Workers*, pp. 380, 405–406.

160. J. Seidman, *Needle Trades*, pp. 9–10.

161. For a good description of the role of the contractor in the garment industry, see Industrial Commission, *Reports*, pp. 345–369; and as quoted in J. Seidman, p. 18.

162. L. Levine, *Women Garment Workers*, p. 521; M. Rischin, *Promised City*, p. 66.

163. Seymour Martin Lipset, Martin Trow, and James Coleman, *Union Democracy: The Inside Politics of the International Typographical Union* (Glencoe, Ill.: Free Press, 1956), p. 152.

164. A. Cahan, *Rise of David Levinsky*, p. 378.

165. Industrial Commission, *Reports*, p. 346.

CHAPTER 5

1. Melech Epstein, *Jewish Labor in the U.S.A.: An Industrial, Political and Cultural History of the Jewish Labor Movement, 1882–1914*, Vol. I (New York: Ktav Publishing House, 1969), pp. 108–191; Louis Levine, *The Women Garment Workers: A History of the International Ladies Garment Workers' Union* (New York: B. W. Huebsch, 1924), pp. 40–43; Joel Seidman, *The Needle Trades* (Farrar and Rinehart, 1942), pp. 79–94; Elias Tcherikower, *The Early Jewish Labor Movement in the U.S.*, translated by Aaron Antonovsky (New York: YIVO Institute for Jewish Research, 1961), pp. 273, 290–296, 316; and Isaac A. Hourwich, *Immigration and Labor: The Economic Aspects of European Immigration to the United States* (New York: Arno Press, 1969), p. 373 (originally published in 1912).

2. Samuel Gompers, *Seventy Years of Life and Labor: An Autobiography* (New York: E. P. Dutton, 1925), p. 153.

3. United States Industrial Commission, *Reports of the Industrial Commission on*

Immigration and Education, XV (Washington, D.C.: U.S. Government Printing Office, 1901), p. 327.

4. Alice Kessler Harris, "The Lower Class as a Factor in Reform: New York, the Jews and the 1890's" (Ph.D. dissertation, Rutgers University, 1968), pp. 157–158.

5. Industrial Commission, *Reports*, p. 313; see also Victor R. Greene, *The Slavic Community on Strike: Immigrant Labor in Pennsylvania Anthracite* (Notre Dame: University of Notre Dame Press, 1968), pp. 13–32; and Rudolph J. Vecoli, "Contadini in Chicago: A Critique of the Uprooted," *Journal of American History*, 51 (December 1964), 404–417.

6. M. Epstein *Jewish Labor*, pp. 125–127; S. Gompers, *Seventy Years*, pp. 152–154; A. Rosenberg, "How Our Unions Were Built," *American Federationist*, XXXVI (December 1929), 1454–1455; and Joel Seidman, *The Needle Trades* (New York: Farrar & Rinehart, 1942), pp. 870–891.

7. Abraham Cahan, *The Education of Abraham Cahan*, translated by Leon Stein, Abraham P. Conan, and Lynn Davison from the Yiddish autobiography, *Bleter Fun Mein Leben*, Vols. I & II (Philadelphia: Jewish Publication Society, 1969), p. 300.

8. M. Epstein, *Jewish Labor*, pp. 387–420 and Melvyn Dubofsky, *When Workers Organize: New York City in the Progressive Era* (Amherst: University of Massachusetts Press, 1968), pp. 40–85.

9. The fullest discussion in English on the origin of the UHT can be found in Morris U. Schappes, "The Political Origins of the United Hebrew Trades, 1888," *Journal of Ethnic Studies*, 5:1 (Spring 1977), 13–44. For views of participants see Cahan, *Education of Abraham Cahan*, p. 237 and Morris Hillquit, *Loose Leaves From a Busy Life* (New York: Macmillan, 1934), pp. 16–17.

10. M. Hillquit, pp. 20–21.

11. M. U. Schappes, "United Hebrew Trades," p. 24.

12. Joseph Brandes, "From Sweatshop to Stability: Jewish Labor Between Two World Wars," *YIVO Annual of Jewish Social Science*, 16 (New York: YIVO Institute for Jewish Research, 1976), pp. 132–134; and Leo Wolman, *The Growth of American Trade Unions: 1880–1923* (New York: National Bureau of Economic Research, 1924), pp. 137–157.

13. L. Wolman, pp. 137–157.

14. Fred Beal, *Word from Nowhere: The Story of a Fugitive from Two Worlds* (London: Robert Hale, 1937), pp. 24, 36, 37, 39; Len De Caux, *Labor Radical, From the Wobblies to the CIO: A Personal History* (Boston: Beacon Press, 1970), pp. 284–288; and A. Ross Eckler and Jack Zltonick, "Immigration and the Labor Force," *Annals of the American Academy of Political and Social Science*, 262 (March 1949), 100.

15. J. B. S. Hardmann, "The Needle Trade Unions: A Labor Movement at Fifty," *Social Research*, 27:3 (Autumn 1960), 341; John H. M. Laslett, *Labor and the Left: A Study of Socialist and Radical Influences in the American Labor Movement, 1881–1924* (New York: Basic Books, 1970), pp. 117–119; L. Levine, *Women Garment Workers*, pp. 109–115; and James Oneal, *History of the Amalgamated Ladies Garment Cutters' Union Local 10 (ILGWU)* (New York: Local 10, 1927), pp. 217–220.

16. Melvyn Dubofsky, "Success and Failure of Socialism in New York City, 1900–1918: A Case Study," *Labor History*, IX:3 (Fall 1968), 362–366; John M. Laslett, *Labor and the Left*, pp. 118–120; and "Proceedings of the Third Biennial Convention of the Amalgamated Clothing Workers Association," Baltimore, May 13–18, 1918, p. 52.

17. J. H. M. Laslett, *Labor and the Left*, p. 110.

18. M. Dubofsky, "Success and Failure of Socialism," p. 363.

19. David A. Shannon, *The Socialist Party of America: A History* (Chicago: Quadrangle Books, 1967), p. 246.

20. Daniel Bell, *Marxian Socialism in the United States* (Princeton, N.J.: Princeton University Press, 1967), pp. 97, 98, 168; Murray Seidler, "The Socialist Party and American Unionism," *Midwest Journal of Political Science*, 5:3 (August 1961), 214–219.
21. J. H. M. Laslett, *Labor and the Left*, pp. 118–123.
22. Ibid., p. 121.
23. Ibid., p. 123; and J. Seidman, *Needle Trades*, p. 216.
24. L. Levine, *Women Garment Workers*, pp. 352–353.
25. Nathan Glazer, "Social Characteristics of American Jews, 1654–1954," in *American Jewish Yearbook*, 56 (Philadelphia: Jewish Publication Society, 1955), p. 17.
26. Charles E. Zaretz, *The Amalgamated Clothing Workers of America: A Study in Progressive Trade Unionism* (New York: Ancon Publishing, 1934), pp. 280–282; and J. Seidman, *Needle Trades*, p. 294.
27. M. Epstein, *Jewish Labor*, p. 350; J. H. M. Laslett, *Labor and the Left*, pp. 99–101; and Murray Seidler, "The Socialist Party and American Unionism," *Midwest Journal of Political Science*, 5:3 (August 1961), 214–216.
28. M. Seidler, p. 215.
29. Edwin Fenton, *Immigrants and Unions, A Case Study: Italians and American Labor, 1870–1920* (New York: Arno Press, 1970), p. 495.
30. Paul Jacobs, *Is Curly Jewish?* (New York: Vintage Books, 1965), p. 113.
31. Irving Howe, "The Significance of the Jewish Labor Movement," in *The Jewish Labor Movement in America*, Israel Knox and Irving Howe (New York: Jewish Labor Committee, 1958), p. 27.
32. J. B. S. Hardmann, "Needle Trades Unions," p. 331; J. H. M. Laslett, *Labor and the Left*, pp. 117–118; L. Levine, *Women Garment Workers*, pp. 142–143, J. Oneal, *Ladies Garment Cutters' Union*, pp. 150–152; Selig Berlman, "Jewish American Unionism, Its Birth Pangs and Contribution to the General American Labor Movement," *American Jewish Historical Quarterly*, 41:4 (June 1952), 305–306.
33. Moses Rischin, "The Jewish Labor Movement in America: A Social Interpretation," *Labor History*, 4:3 (Fall 1963), 237–238.
34. Cited in ibid., p. 238.
35. Raymond Munts and Mary L. Munts, "Welfare History of the I.L.G.W.U.," *Labor History*, 9 (Spring 1968), 82–97.
36. M. Seidler, "Socialist Party," pp. 214–215, 225–226.
37. Benjamin Gitlow, *I Confess: The Truth About American Communism* (New York: E. P. Dutton, 1940), p. 337.
38. J. H. M. Laslett, *Labor and the Left*, pp. 105–107; and L. Levine, *Women Garment Workers*, pp. 122–142.
39. Philip Foner, *The Fur and Leather Workers Union* (Newark, N.J.: Nordan Press, 1950), pp. 233–524; B. Gitlow, *I Confess*, p. 357; J. Oneal, *Ladies Garment Cutters' Union*, p. 357; and J. H. M. Laslett, *Labor and the Left*, pp. 105–107.
40. E. Fenton, *Immigrants and Unions*, pp. 38, 52, 60, 64, 69.
41. Cited in Moses Rischin, *The Promised City: New York's Jews, 1870–1914* (New York: Harper Torchbooks, 1970), p. 251.
42. Matthews Josephson, *Sidney Hillman: Statesman of American Labor* (Garden City, New York: Doubleday, 1952), pp. 109, 231, 400.
43. Ibid., 439.
44. Ronald Radosh, "The Development of the Corporate Ideology of American Labor Leaders," (Ph.D. diss., University of Wisconsin, 1967), p. 356.
45. M. Epstein, *Jewish Labor*, II, pp. 228–229; M. Seidler, "The Socialist Party," p. 219; D. A. Shannon, *Socialist Party of America*, pp. 245–247; and W. A. Swanberg, *Norman Thomas: The Last Idealist* (New York: Charles Scribner's Sons, 1976), pp. 199–201.
46. The discussion of the Protocol and the circumstances surrounding it is based on the facts, but not the interpretations, located in the single best study of it,

Hyman Berman, "Era of the Protocol: A Chapter in the History of the International Ladies Garment Workers' Union, 1910–1916," (Ph.D. diss., Columbia University, 1956).

47. Cited in J. H. M. Laslett, *Labor and the Left*, p. 113.
48. H. Berman, "Era of the Protocol," p. 348.
49. Cited in J. Seidman, *Needle Trades*, p. 276.
50. C. E. Zaretz, *Amalgamated Clothing Workers*, pp. 177–194.
51. M. Epstein, *Jewish Labor*, II, p. 160.
52. Ibid., p. 414.
53. Ibid.
54. J. Brandes, "Sweatshop to Stability," pp. 35–36.
55. R. Radosh, "Development of the Corporate Ideology," p. 327.
56. Epstein, *Jewish Labor*, II, pp. 168, 191; and Irving Howe, *World of Our Fathers* (New York: Harcourt Brace Jovanovich, 1976), p. 337.
57. J. B. S. Hardmann, "The Situation in 1926," J. B. S. Hardmann Papers, Tamiment Library, New York University, New York.
58. Norman Thomas to Morris Hillquit, December 21, 1926, Norman Thomas Papers, New York Public Library, New York.
59. B. C. Vladeck to David Dubinsky, July 18, 1929, B. C. Vladeck Papers, Tamiment Library, New York University, New York.
60. Charles Zimmerman, a retired Vice President of the ILGWU claimed that the vice president who headed the Out of Town Dept. of the ILGWU in the 1920s could single handedly influence the course of conventions through his control of the ballots of the small locals outside of the major metropolitan areas. See Zimmerman's comments in David Dublinsky and A. H. Raskin, *David Dubinsky: A Life With Labor* (New York: Simon and Schuster, 1977), pp. 88–89.
61. The information for this section is derived primarily from David Gurowsky, "Factional Disputes Within the I.L.G.W.U., 1919–1928," (Ph.D. diss., State University of New York at Binghamton).
62. P. Foner, *Fur and Leather Workers Union*, pp. 93–116.
63. See Dubinsky's account of his eight hour taxi ride with the president of the manufacturers' association, during which they both plotted strategy for the rebuilding of the ILGWU under Dubinsky's leadership. Dubinsky and Raskin, *Dubinsky*, pp. 76–78. See also Julia S. Brown, "Factors Affecting Union Strength: A Case Study of the ILGWU, 1900–1940," (Ph.D. diss., Yale University, 1942), p. 214.
64. M. Epstein, *Jewish Labor*, II, pp. 184–197; J. Seidman, *Needle Trades*, pp. 187–208; Zaretz, *Amalgamated Clothing Workers*, pp. 28–30, 297.
65. U.S. Bureau of the Census, *Historical Statistics of the United States: Colonial Times to 1957* (Washington, D.C.: U.S. Government Printing Office, 1960), pp. 91–99.
66. This policy of uniform wage rates did have certain limitations. The Amalgamated did not, for example, believe it necessary that its officials share the uniform wage of their members. Thus in 1920, when J. B. S. Hardmann was hired as the Amalgamated's first head of the newly formed educational department, his request that his wages be commensurate with that of a worker was denied. His union employers told him that it was necessary for him to take a higher salary than that of a worker in order to show the membership that he was not a "piker." Workers, he was informed, would have more respect for him if he earned more money. Remember this transpired in one of the more radical of the unions in America at the time. J. B. S. Hardmann interview, Irving Howe Collection, YIVO Institute of Jewish Research.
67. M. Epstein, *Jewish Labor*, II, pp. 163, 186–192; and Zaretz, *Amalgamated Clothing Workers*, pp. 28–30, 177–194.
68. Dubinsky and Raskin, *Dubinsky*, p. 130.
69. Herbert Hill, "The Racial Practices of Organized Labor: The Contemporary

Record," in Julius Jacobson, Ed., *The Negro and the American Labor Movement* (Garden City, New York: Anchor Books, 1968), p. 333.

70. North American Congress on Latin America (NACLA), *Latin America and Empire Report*, 11:3 (March 1977), 25–26.

71. H. Hill, "Racial Practices of Organized Labor," p. 333.

72. Ibid., p. 328.

73. L. Levine, *Women Garment Workers*, p. 101.

74. J. Seidman, *Needle Trades*, p. 69.

75. Roy B. Helfgott, "Trade Unionism Among the Jewish Garment workers of Britain and the United States," *Labor History*, II:2 (Spring 1961), 208.

76. M. Epstein, *Jewish Labor*, II, pp. 159–160, 198–205; H. Hill, "Racial Practices of Organized Labor," p. 325; and NACLA, *Report*, p. 26.

77. Ibid., p. 17.

78. Ibid., p. 18.

79. J. Oneal, *Ladies Garment Cutters' Union*, pp. 151–152.

80. J. Seidman, *Needle Trades*, pp. 138–139.

81. M. Epstein, *Jewish Labor*, II, pp. 53–54; and Leo Wolman, *The Growth of American Trade Unions 1880–1923* (New York: National Bureau of Economic Research, 1924), pp. 118–119.

82. Milton Cantor, "The Radical Confrontation with Foreign Policy: War and Revolution, 1914–1920," in *Dissent: Explorations in the History of American Radicalism*, Alfred F. Young, Ed. (DeKalb, Ill.: Southern Illinois University Press, 1968), p. 246.

83. Cited in Zosa Szajkowski, *Jews, Wars and Communism: The Attitude of American Jews to World War I, the Russian Revolutions of 1917, and Communism (1915–1945*, vol. I (New York: Ktav Publishing House, 1972), p. 531.

84. "Proceedings of the Third Biennial Convention."

85. Ibid., p. 321.

86. M. Epstein, *Jewish Labor*, II, pp. 155–156.

87. Ibid., p. 202; and Brandes, "From Sweatshop to Stability," pp. 70–71.

88. J. Seidman, *Needle Trades*, p. 198.

89. D. A. Shannon, *Socialist Party of America*, pp. 245–246; and W. A. Swanberg, *Norman Thomas*, pp. 199–201.

90. Will Herberg, "Jewish Labor Movement in the United States: World War I to the Present," *Industrial and Labor Relations Review*, 6:1 (October 1962), 54.

91. M. Josephson, *Sidney Hillman*, pp. 397–398.

92. M. Seidler, "Socialist Party," p. 225.

93. Dubinsky and Raskin, *Dubinsky*, p. 264.

94. Ibid.

95. M. Epstein, *Jewish Labor*, II, pp. 228–229; M. Seidler, p. 219; and D. A. Shannon, *Socialist Party of America*, pp. 245–247.

96. Mark R. Levy and Michael S. Kramer, *The Ethnic Factor: How America's Minorities Decide Elections* (New York: Simon & Schuster, 1973), pp. 104, 121, and M. Seidler, "Socialist Party," pp. 225–229.

97. The unions' continued reliance in 1963 on a policy of uniform wage rates to protect the market position of New York City, still a major garment manufacturing center at the time, can be ascertained from the stand of the ILGWU on a city minimum-wage bill. From 1959 to 1963 there was agitation in New York for the establishment of minimum wage legislation. In 1963 the City Council voted for and the mayor signed a bill setting the minimum wage in the city at $1.50 per hour. This was 25 cents higher than the federal minimum wage. The ILGWU and its political representatives in the Liberal party, at best, did virtually nothing to support its enactment and, at worst, opposed it. In a critical vote on the matter in the Citizen's Commission on the City Economy, the ILGWU's representative, Howard Molisani, Manager-Secretary of the ILGWU, abstained. This prompted Murray Kempton, a liberal New York newspaper columnist, to write:

"How marvelous is the ILGWU. It has a position on Vietnam and Algeria; but it has no position on wages in its hometown."

98. Cited in the *American Labor Yearbook 1923–1924*, V (New York: Rand School of Social Science, 1924), p. 132.
99. Cited in J. A. M. Laslett, *Labor and the Left*, p. 133.
100. Correspondence to and from Norman Thomas from June to November, 1933, Norman Thomas Papers (New York Public Library, New York.)
101. Contained in the William Edlin Papers, YIVO Institute of Jewish Research, New York.
102. M. Epstein, *Jewish Labor*, II, p. 85; and *American Labor Yearbook*, V, p. 137.
103. Cited in M. Seidler, "Socialist Party," p. 227.
104. Cahan, *Education of Abraham Cahan*, p. 237.
105. M. Epstein, *Jewish Labor*, pp. 132–146, 168–191; Philip S. Foner, *History of the American Labor Movement in the United States*, II (New York: International Publishers, 1955), pp. 34–38; William M. Leiserson, "The Jewish Labor Movement in New York," (B.A. thesis, University of Wisconsin, 1908), pp. 51–59; A. Rosenberg, "How Our Unions Were Built," pp. 1454–1457; and M. U. Schappes, "United Hebrew Trades," pp. 13–33.
106. J. Brandes, "Sweatshop to Stability," pp. 10–16; M. Hillquit, *Loose Leaves*, pp. 28–30; and M. U. Schappes, "United Hebrew Trades," pp. 32–33.
107. S. Gompers, *Seventy Years*, p. 153. According to M. U. Schappes, "United Hebrew Trades," pp. 32–33, Gompers was quite hostile to the UHT in its early years and became more supportive of it when the UHT became less socialistic in its orientation.
108. Cited in M. Epstein, *Jewish Labor*, pp. 182–183.
109. W. M. Leiserson, "Jewish Labor Movement," pp. 56–57.
110. J. B. S. Hardmann, "Needle Trade Unions," pp. 305–308, 331–332.
111. Cited in M. Rischin, *Promised City*, p. 179.
112. Ibid., pp. 178–180.
113. J. B. S. Hardmann, "The Jewish Labor Movement in the United States: Jewish and Non-Jewish Influences," *American Jewish Historical Quarterly*, III:2 (December 1962), 117.
114. M. Dubofsky, *When Workers Organize*, pp. 43–66; M. Rischin, *Promised City*, pp. 243–250; and Hyman Berman, "The Cloakmakers' Strike of 1910," in *Essays on Jewish Life and Thought Presented in Honor of Salo W. Baron*, Joseph L. Blan et al., Eds. (New York: Columbia University Press, 1959), pp. 63–94.
115. M. Epstein, *Jewish Labor*, p. 402.
116. B. C. Vladeck to Herbert H. Lehman, February 26, 1930, in Baruch C. Charney Vladeck Papers, Tamiment Institute Library, New York University, New York.
117. M. Epstein, *Jewish Labor*, II, p. 155.
118. Samuel Halperin, *The Political World of American Zionism* (Detroit: Wayne State University Press, 1961), pp. 158–162; and Jonathan Shapiro, *Leadership of the American Zionist Organization* (Urbana, Ill.: University of Illinois Press, 1971), pp. 17, 160–162, 195–297.
119. Philip Friedman, "Political and Social Movements and Organizations," in *The Jewish People: Past and Present*, Vol. IV, Abraham Menes et al., Eds. (New York: Jewish Encyclopedic Handbooks, 1955), pp. 168–169.
120. M. Epstein, *Jewish Labor*, II, p. 66; and Franktin Jones, "The Early Life and Career of B. Charney Vladeck, 1886–1921: The Emergence of an Immigrant Spokesman," (Ph.D. diss., New York University, 1972), p. 175.
121. J. H. M. Laslett, *Labor and the Left*, p. 121.
122. S. Halperin, *American Zionism*, pp. 160–162; and J. Shapiro, *American Zionist Organization*, pp. 252–262.
123. J. Brandes, "Sweatshop to Stability," pp. 120–121.
124. Raskin, "Dubinsky," *op. cit.*, p. 17.
125. J. Brandes, "Sweatshop to Stability," pp. 121–122.

126. W. Herberg, "Jewish Labor Movement," pp. 57–59.
127. Ibid., p. 105; and Jacob Loft, "Jewish Workers in the New York City Men's Clothing Industry," *Jewish Social Studies*, 2:1 (January 1940), 63.
128. Paul Jacob, *Is Curly Jewish?: A Political Self Portrait Illuminating Three Turbulent Decades of Social Revolt 1935–1965* (New York: Vintage Books, 1965), p. 125.
129. William M. Leiserson, *Adjusting Immigrant and Industry* (New York: Harper and Bros., 1924), p. 203; and J. Seidman, *Needle Trades*, pp. 86–89, 100.
130. C. E. Zaretz, *Amalgamated Clothing Workers*, pp. 97–98.
131. Ibid.
132. David J. Saposs, *Left Wing Unionism: A Study of Radical Policies and Tactics* (New York: Russell and Russell, 1926), pp. 112–113.
133. Much of the information on the Italians in the ILGWU from 1900 to 1920 is derived from E. Fenton, *Immigrants and Unions*, pp. 458–558.
134. I. Hourwich, *Immigration and Labor*, pp. 326–328.
135. Ibid.
136. Most of the Italian radicals in America appeared to be from northern Italy. For the role of northern Italians in unions and radical unions in Argentina and France at approximately the same period, see Samuel L. Baily, "The Italians and Organized Labor in the United States and Argentina: 1880–1910," *International Migration Review*, 1:3 (Summer 1967), 56–66; and R. P. Serge Bonnet, "Political Alignments and Religious Attitudes Within the Italian Immigration to the Metallurgical Districts of Lorraine," *Journal of Social History*, 2:2 (Winter 1968), 123–155.
137. E. Fenton, *Immigrants and Unions*, p. 485.
138. Ibid., p. 483.
139. M. Epstein, *Jewish Labor*, II, pp. 420–422; and H. Hill, "Racial Practices of Organized Labor," pp. 344–345.
140. We have already discussed the disproportional representation system at the international level. At the level of joint board, the process is similar: all locals within the domain of a joint board are entitled to the same number of board members. Thus a local with 200 persons has the same number of representatives as a local with 2000. See L. Levine, *Women Garment Workers*, pp. 454–455; and J. Oneal, *Ladies Garment Cutters' Union*, p. 350.
141. J. B. S. Hardmann, "Needle Trade Unions," pp. 336–337.
142. H. Hill, "Racial Practices of Organized Labor," pp. 323–324; and Vivian Gornick, "Union Blues: The Failure of the ILGWU," *Village Voice*, October 17, 1974.
143. Joyce Purnick, "New Head of the ILGWU," *New York Post*, June 7, 1975.
144. The restrictions pertain to convention delegate status and longevity in the Union. H. Hill, "Racial Practices of Organized Labor," p. 323.
145. P. Jacob, *Is Curly Jewish?* pp. 113–114; and J. Purnick, "New Head of the ILGWU."
146. M. Epstein, *Jewish Labor*, II, p. 344.
147. Ibid.
148. Ibid., pp. 244–245.
149. Mike Royko, *Boss: Richard J. Daley of Chicago* (New York: New American Library, 1971), pp. 61, 62, 132.
150. H. Hill, "Racial Practices of Organized Labor," p. 333; and Paul Jacob, *The State of the Unions* (New York: Antheneum, 1963), p. 126.

CHAPTER 6

1. Milton Doroshkin, *Yiddish in America: Social and Cultural Foundations* (Madison, N.J.: Farleigh Dickinson University Press, 1969), pp. 136–169, 228–242; and I. E. Rontch, "The Present State of the Landsmanchaften," *Jewish Social Service Quarterly*, 15:4 (June 1939), 360–378.

2. M. Doroshkin, *Yiddish in America*, pp. 157–162; and Melech Epstein, *Jewish Labor in U.S.A.*, Vol. I (New York: Ktav Publishing House, 1969), pp. 298–307.
3. M. Doroshkin, pp. 162–163.
4. Isaiah Trunk, "The Cultural Dimension of the American Jewish Labor Movement," *YIVO Annual of Jewish Social Science*, XVI (New York: YIVO Institute for Jewish Social Research, 1976), p. 364.
5. Bernard D. Weinryb, "The Adaptation of Jewish Labor Groups to American Life," *Jewish Social Studies*, 8:4 (October 1946), 230.
6. M. Epstein, *Jewish Labor*, II, p. 309.
7. Melech Epstein, *The Jew and Communism: The Story of Early Communist Victories and Ultimate Defeats in the Jewish Community, U.S.A., 1919–1941* (New York: Trade Union Sponsoring Committee, 1959), p. 8; and B. D. Weinryb, "Jewish Labor Groups," p. 230.
8. Official Minutes of the Forty-Sixth Convention of the Workmen's Circle, Detroit, Michigan, May 5–11, 1946, YIVO Institute of Jewish Research, New York.
9. Judah J. Shapiro, *The Friendly Society: A History of the Workmen's Circle* (New York: Media Judaica, 1970), pp. 210–213.
10. The following section is informed by the Minutes of the National Executive Committee of the Workmen's Circle from 1924 through 1940, YIVO Institute of Jewish Research, New York.
11. Secretary's Report, National Executive Committee of WC, September 1, 1931, YIVO Institute of Jewish Research.
12. M. Epstein, *Jewish Labor*, I, p. 311.
13. M. Epstein, *Jew and Communism*, p. 145.
14. Samuel Niger, "Yiddish Culture in the United States," in *Jewish People: Past and Present*, Vol. IV, Abraham Menes et al., Eds. (New York: Jewish Encyclopedic Handbooks, 1955), p. 302; and I. Trunk, "Cultural Dimension," pp. 360–361.
15. I. Trunk, pp. 362–363.
16. B. D. Weinryb, "Jewish Labor Groups," pp. 232.
17. I. Trunk, "Cultural Dimension," p. 372.
18. M. Epstein, *Jewish Labor*, II, pp. 275–279.
19. Max Rosenfeld, "Zhitlovsky: Philosopher of Jewish Secularism," in *Jewish Current Reader* (New York: Jewish Currents, 1966), p. 87.
20. Cited in I. Trunk, "Cultural Dimension," p. 361.
21. Cited in M. Epstein, *Jewish Labor*, II, p. 276.
22. B. D. Weinryb, "Jewish Labor Groups," p. 233.
23. Cited in J. J. Shapiro, *Friendly Society*, p. 191.
24. I. Trunk, "Cultural Dimension," p. 372.
25. M. Epstein, *Jewish Labor*, II, p. 289.
26. Workmen's Circle Papers.
27. Cited in Irving Howe, *World of Our Fathers* (New York: Harcourt Brace Jovanovitch, 1976), p. 387.
28. Workmen's Circle Papers, YIVO Institute of Jewish Research, New York.
29. I. Trunk, "Cultural Dimension," pp. 365–367.
30. William E. Mitchell, "Descent Groups Among New York City Jews," *Jewish Journal of Sociology*, 3:1 (June 1961), 125; and Nathan Peskin, "The Other Side of the Mountain," *The Call*, 45:3 (May 1976), 9.
31. Open Letter, April 14, 1946, in the Workmen's Circle Papers.
32. M. Epstein, *The Jew and Communism*, pp. 211–213, 281–283; and Richard A. Reuss, "American Folklore and Left Wing Politics" (Ph.D. dissertation, Indiana University, 1971), pp. 52–53.
33. The information used in the following section on the Coops was derived largely from three sources: (1) four interviews with former residents and persons highly knowledgeable about this cooperative housing project; (2) *The United Workers Cooperative Colony, 50th Anniversary, 1927–1977* (New York: Semi-Centennial Coop Reunion, 1977); and (3) M. Epstein, *Jew and Communism*, pp. 215–218.

34. Whitman Bassow, "Growing Up in the Coops," in *United Workers Cooperative Colony*, p. 27.
35. *United Workers Cooperative Colony*, p. 27.
36. Ibid., p. 36.
37. Ibid., p. 40.
38. Calvin Trillin, "U.S. Journal: The Bronx," *New Yorker*, August 1, 1977.
39. The information used in the following section on the International Workers Order and the Communist-oriented Jewish subculture was derived largely from (1) two interviews with former members and (2) *The International Workers Order Papers*, (Ithaca, N.Y.: Labor Management Documentation Center, Cornell University), hereafter referred to as *IWO Papers*.
40. Draft memorandum, "Guiding Policy for the Communists in Their Leadership and Work in the International Workers Order," *IWO Papers*, pp. 2–3. (Although undated, the references within this document indicate that it was written prior to the passage of Social Security legislation in the latter 1930s.)
41. *IWO Bulletin*, May 1951.
42. Cedric Belfrage, *The American Inquisition, 1945–1960* (Indianapolis, Ind.: Bobbs-Merrill Co., 1973), p. 181; M. Epstein, *The Jew and Communism*, pp. 151–155; "Defend Progressive Jewish Education," *Jewish Life*, 8:3 (January 1954), 4–5; *Brief for Respondent in the Matter of the Application of the People of the State of New York by Alfred J. Bohlinger, Superintendnent of Insurance of the State of New York, Petitioner-Appellant-Respondent For an Order Directing Him to Take Possession of the Property and to Liquidate the Business, and Dissolve the Corporate Existence of the International Workers Order, Inc.*, Supreme Court, Appellate Division, First Department, May 12, 1952. Hereafter referred to as *Brief for Respondent*.
43. "Guiding Policy for Communists," p. 2.
44. Benjamin Gitlow, *I Confess: The Truth About American Communism* (New York: E. P. Dutton, 1940), pp. 288–291; David A. Shannon, *The Decline of American Communism: A History of the Communist Party Since 1945* (New York: Harcourt, Brace, 1959), p. 107; Nathan Glazer, *The Social Base of American Communism* (New York: Harcourt, Brace & World, 1961), pp. 163–164; Betty Yorburg, *Utopia and Reality: A Collective Portrait of American Socialists* (New York: Columbia University Press, 1969), p. 92; and Max Vorspan and Lloyd P. Gartner, *History of the Jews of Los Angeles* (San Marinoc, Calif.: Huntington Library, 1970), p. 202.
45. *Brief for Respondent*, pp. 61–68.
46. Cited in *Communist Indoctrination and Training of Children in Summer Camps*, Report of the Joint Legislative Committee on Charitable and Philanthropic Agencies and Organizations, New York Legislative Document No. 62 (1956), p. 18.
47. "Defend Progressive Jewish Education," pp. 4–5; and Sam Pevzner, "A Progressive Jewish School," *Jewish Life*, 7:5 (March 1953), 28. "Memorandum on the Schools of the Jewish Peoples' Fraternal Order," *IWO Papers*, p. 1.
48. Alfred Henley, "Bringing Up Our Children for Jewish Survival," *Jewish Currents*, 13:4 (April 1959), 29.
49. Cited in Sid Resnick, "Recalling My Shule Days," *Jewish Currents*, 29:1 (January 1975), 12–13.
50. S. Yefroikin, "Yiddish Secular Schools in the United States," in *Jewish People: Past and Present*, Vol. II, Abraham Menes et al., Eds. (New York: Jewish Encyclopedic Handbooks, 1948), p. 146.
51. Kalmon Marmor, "Rosh Hashanah: Day of Judgment," *Jewish Life* 8 (October 1954), 17.
52. "Defend Progressive Jewish Education," p. 5.
53. A. Henley, "Bringing Up Our Children," pp. 29–33.
54. M. Epstein, *Jew and Communism*, pp. 219–220.
55. Elsie Suller, "A Secular Camp," *Jewish Currents*, 15:6 (June 1961), 25–26.
56. Ibid.

57. Remarks by Elsie Suller from the audience, as recorded in "Jewish Young Freedom Fighters and the Role of the Jewish Community: An Evaluation," *Jewish Currents*, 19 (July–August 1965), 32.
58. *Communist Indoctrination*, pp. 30–33.
59. J. C. Rich, "60 Years of the *Jewish Daily Forward*," *New Leader*, 40:22, Section II (June 3, 1957), pp. 15–20; Mordecai Soltes, *The Yiddish Press: An Americanizing Agency* (New York: Teachers College Press, Columbia University, 1950), p. 24; M. Epstein, *Jewish Labor*, II, pp. 318–325; and James Weinstein, *The Decline of Socialism in America: 1912–1925* (New York: Vintage Books, 1967), pp. 94–102.
60. S. Niger, "Yiddish Culture," p. 272.
61. Ibid., p. 273.
62. Ibid., p. 274.
63. M. Doroshkin, *Yiddish in America*, pp. 217–218.
64. Abraham Cahan, *The Education of Abraham Cahan* (translated by Leon Stein, Abraham P. Conan, and Lynn Davison from the Yiddish autobiography *Bleter Fun Mein Leben* by Abraham Cahan, Vols. I & II [Philadelphia: Jewish Publication Society, 1969], pp. 223–225); and S. Niger, "Yiddish Culture," pp. 288–99.
65. S. Niger, p. 289.
66. M. Epstein, I, *Jewish Labor*, pp. 319–24; S. Niger, pp. 297–98; and J. C. Rich, "60 Years of the *Foward*," pp. 10–22.
67. Cited in M. Doroshkin, *Yiddish in America*, p. 116.
68. M. Soltes, *Yiddish Press*, p. 24.
69. Ronald Sanders, *The Downtown Jews* (New York: New American Library, 1969), pp. 217–218.
70. I. Howe, *World of Our Fathers*, pp. 537–538.
71. J. C. Rich, "60 Years of the *Forward*," pp. 22–23; and R. Sanders, *Downtown Jews*, pp. 210–226.
72. J. C. Rich, p. 25.
73. Cited in Zosa Szajkowski, *Jews, Wars, and Communism, I: The Attitude of American Jews to World War I, the Russian Revolutions of 1917, and Communism (1914–1945)* (New York: Ktav Publishing House, 1972), p. 535.
74. Ibid., p. 181; and Moses Rischin, *The Promised City: New York's Jews 1870–1914* (New York: Harper Torchbooks, 1970), p. 235.
75. J. C. Rich, "60 Years of the *Forward*," pp. 26–28.
76. Norman Thomas to Clarence Senior and Others, Norman Thomas Papers, New York Public Library, New York.
77. J. C. Rich, "60 Years of the *Forward*," pp. 29–34.
78. Cited in M. Doroshkin, *Yiddish in America*, p. 115.
79. Cited in R. Sanders, *Downtown Jews*, p. 212.
80. J. C. Rich, "60 Years of the *Forward*," pp. 20–21.
81. Isaac Metzker, ed. and comp., *A Bintel Brief: Sixty Years of Letters from the Lower East Side to the Jewish Daily Forward* (New York: Ballantine Books, 1972), pp. 98–99.
82. Cited in M. Rischin, *Promised City*, pp. 160, 182.
83. Ibid., p. 167.
84. Daniel Bell, *Marxian Socialism in the United States* (Princeton, N.J.: Princton University Press, 1967), p. 98.
85. M. Epstein, *Jewish Labor*, II, pp. 324–328.
86. M. Doroshkin, *Yiddish in America*, pp. 202–203.
87. I. Metzker, *Bintel Brief*, p. 48.
88. I. Howe, *World of Our Fathers*, p. 529; Louis Harap, *The Image of the Jew in American Literature: From Early Republic to Mass Immigration* (Philadelphia: Jewish Publication Society, 1974), pp. 488–489. One example of a Cahan sentence cited in Harap: "Ich vel scrobben dem floor, klinen die vindes, un polishem dem stove" (p. 488).
89. L. Harap, p. 489.

90. S. Niger, "Yiddish Culture," p. 205; and J. C. Rich, *"60 Years of the Forward,"* p. 25.
91. Cited in M. Rischin, *Promised City*, pp. 160–161.
92. Cited in S. Niger, "Yiddish Culture," p. 307.
93. Ibid., p. 295.
94. Arthur Gorenstein, "A Portrait of Ethnic Politics: The Socialists and the 1908 and 1910 Congressional Elections on the East Side," *American Jewish Historical Quarterly*, 50:3 (March 1961), 209–15 and S. Niger, p. 297.
95. Shortly after the *Forverts* was launched, Cahan quit to work as a journalist on the *New York Commercial Advertiser*. Also, in 1935, echoing a theme that he had initially stated upon arriving in America, Cahan attacked the Yiddish-language schools of the Workmen's Circle on the grounds that "Yiddish culture is alien to the American conditions in which we live." Cited in Z. Szajkowski, *Jews, Wars, and Communism*, p. 125.
96. One of the reasons that Cahan returned to the *Forverts* in 1902 was that his English-language articles did not sell well. John Higham, *Send These to Me: Jews and Other Immigrants in the United States* (New York: Atheneum, 1975), pp. 96–97.
97. A. Gorenstein, "Ethnic Politics," p. 211.
98. Ibid., p. 224.
99. Louis Marshall to Postmaster General A. S. Burleson January 5, 1918, in *Louis Marshall: Champion of Liberty*, Charles Rezbikoff, Ed. (Philadelphia: Jewish Publication Society, 1957), p. 975.
100. Lucy S. Dawidowicz, "Louis Marshall and the Jewish Daily Forward: An Episode in Wartime Censorship, 1917–1918," *For Max Weinreich on His Seventieth Birthday* (The Hague, 1964), p. 43.
101. M. Epstein, *Jew and Communism*, pp. 67–141.
102. Ibid., p. 95
103. M. Epstein, *Jewish Labor*, II, p. 127.
104. Correspondence to and from Norman Thomas, from June 1, 1933, to March 2, 1936, Norman Thomas Papers, New York Public Library, New York.
105. Norman Thomas to B. Charney Vladeck, August 3, 1934, Baruch C. Charney Vladeck Papers, Tamiment Library, New York University, New York.
106. J. C. Rich, "60 Years of the *Forward*," pp. 31–33.
107. Ibid., pp. 31–38; and M. Epstein, *Jewish Labor*, II, p. xlii.
108. Paul Jacob, *Is Curly Jewish: A Political Self Portrait Illuminating Three Turbulent Decades of Social Revolt—1935–1965* (New York: Vintage Books, 1973), p. 312.
109. M. Epstein, *Jewish Labor*, II, p. xlii.
110. Z. Szajkowski, *Jews, Wars, and Communism*, p. 183.
111. Much of the following information is derived from an interview with Paul Novick, editor of the *Freiheit*, December 18, 1974.
112. M. Epstein, *Jew and Communism*, pp. 223–233.
113. Cited in ibid., p. 224.
114. Ibid., pp. 224–225.
115. Ibid., p. 226.
116. Ibid.
117. Ibid., pp. 302–303.
118. Samuel Halperin, *The Political World of American Zionism* (Detroit: Wayne State University Press, 1961), p. 38.

CHAPTER 7

Mark Wischnitzer, *To Dwell in Safety: The Story of Jewish Migration Since 1800* (Philadelphia: Jewish Publication Society, 1948), p. 289; and "Jewish Immigration," *American Jewish Yearbook*, Vol. 51 (Philadelphia: Jewish Publication Society, 1950), p. 75.

2. U.S. Bureau of the Census, *Historical Statistics of the United States, Colonial Times to 1957* (Washington, D.C.: U.S. Government Printing Office, 1960), p. 56.
3. John Higham, *Strangers in the Land: Patterns of American Nativism 1860–1925* (New York: Atheneum, 1963), pp. 308–324.
4. E. P. Hutchinson, *Immigrants and Their Children 1850–1950* (New York: John Wiley, 1956), p. 5.
5. James Weinstein, *The Decline of Socialism in America, 1912–1925* (New York: Vintage Books, 1969), pp. 181–209; Theodore Draper, *The Roots of American Communism* (New York: The Viking Press, 1957), p. 190; Nathan Glazer, *The Social Basis of American Communism* (New York: Harcourt, Brace, & World, 1961), p. 100; and *Historical Statistics of the U.S.*, p. 65.
6. William J. Fishman, *Jewish Radicals: From Czarist Stetl to London Ghetto* (New York: Random House, 1974), pp. 254–275, 279, 300–309; and Roy B. Helfgott, "Trade Unionism Among the Jewish Garment Workers of Britain and the United States," *Labor History* II, 2 (Spring 1961), 211–213.
7. Nathan Goldberg, *Occupational Patterns of American Jewry* (New York: Jewish Teachers Seminary, 1947), pp. 40–41.
8. Sidney Goldstein and Calvin Goldscheider, *Jewish Americans: Three Generations in a Jewish Community* (Englewood Cliffs, N.J.: Prentice-Hall, 1968), p. 74; Nathan Glazer, "The Social Characteristics of American Jews, 1654–1964," *American Jewish Yearbook*, 56 (Philadelphia: Jewish Publication Society, 1955), pp. 26–27; and Will Maslow, *The Structure and Functioning of the American Jewish Community* (New York: American Jewish Congress and the American Section of the World Jewish Congress, 1975), p. 8.
9. N. Glazer, *op. cit.*, pp. 25–27; and W. Maslow, *American Jewish Community*, p. 8.
10. Jacob Lestschinsky, "The Economic Development of the Jewish People in the U.S.," in *Jewish People: Past and Present*, Vol. I, Abraham Menes et al., Eds. (New York: Jewish Encyclopedia Handbooks, 1946), pp. 398–399; Ben Seligman, "The Jewish Population of New York City: 1952," in *The Jews: Social Patterns of an American Group*, Marshall Sklare, Ed. (Glencoe, Ill.: Free Press, 1958), p. 105; and Marshall Sklare, *America's Jews* (New York: Random House, 1971), p. 62.
11. N. Glazer, *op. cit.*, pp. 16, 20, 21.
12. B. Seligman, "Jewish Population of New York," p. 105.
13. E. P. Hutchinson, *Immigrants and Their Children*, pp. 335–349.
14. Melech Epstein, *Jewish Labor in the U.S.A.: An Industrial, Political and Cultural History of the Jewish Labor Movement*, 2 Vols. (New York: Ktav Publishing House, 1969), p. xiv.
15. Harry Roskolenko, *The Time That Was Then: The Lower East Side, 1900–1914, An Intimate Chronicle* (New York: Dial Press, 1971), p. 33.
16. Julia S. Brown, "Factors Affecting Union Strength: A Case Study of the ILGWU: 1900–1940," (Ph.D. diss., Yale University, 1942), p. 311; and Joseph Brandes, "From Sweatshop to Stability: Jewish Labor Between Two World Wars," *YIVO Annual of Jewish Social Science*, 26 (New York: YIVO Institute for Jewish Research, 1976), p. 105.
17. *Historical Statistics of the U.S.* p. 74.
18. N. Glazer, p. 16.
19. Stephen Thernstrom, *The Other Bostonians: Poverty and Progress in the American Metropolis, 1880–1970* (Cambridge, Mass.: Harvard University Press, 1973), p. 136.
20. Nathan Glazer and Daniel P. Moynihan, *Beyond the Melting Pot: The Negroes, Puerto Ricans, Jews, Italians and Irish of New York City*, 2nd ed. (Cambridge, Mass.: The M.I.T. Press, 1970), p. 323; and E. P. Hutchinson, *Immigrants and Their Children*, pp. 335–349.
21. James Oneal, *A History of the Amalgamated Ladies' Garment Cutters' Union Local 10* (New York: Local 10, ILGWU, 1927), p. 342.

22. Melech Epstein, *Jewish, Labor,* II, p. 422; and N. Glazer and D. P. Moynihan, *Beyond the Melting Pot,* pp. 144–145.

23. M. Epstein, *Jewish Labor,* II, p. 140; and Herbert Hill, "The Racial Practices of Organized Labor: The Contemporary Record," in *The Negro and the American Labor Movement,* Julius Jacobson, Ed. (New York: Anchor Books, 1968), pp. 343–348.

24. Alfred Jospe, "Jews in American Universities Since the End of the 19th Century," mimeographed, 1970, p. 1.

25. John Higham, "Social Discrimination Against Jews in America, 1830–1930," *Publication of the American Jewish Historical Society,* XLVII: i (September 1957), 21.

26. Stephen Steinberg, *The Academic Melting Pot: Catholics and Jews in American Higher Education* (New York: McGraw-Hill, 1974), pp. 16–30.

27. "Jewish College Students in the United States," *American Jewish Yearbook: 1965* (Philadelphia: Jewish Publication Society, 1964), p. 133.

28. National Commission, B'Nai B'Rith Vocational Service, *Jewish Youth in College* (Washington, D.C., 1967).

29. M. Sklare, *America's Jews,* p. 55.

30. Philip G. Altbach, *Student Politics in America: A Historical Analysis* (New York: McGraw-Hill, 1974), pp. 42–45, 72–83.

31. S. Willis Rudy, *The College of the City of New York: A History, 1847–1947* (New York: City College Press, 1949), p. 247.

32. Seymour Martin Lipset, *Rebellion in the University* (Boston: Little, Brown, 1972), pp. 178–180; and P. G. Altbach, *Student Politics,* pp. 72–84.

33. S. M. Lipset, pp. 179–180.

34. P. G. Altbach, *Student Politics,* pp. 76–84.

35. This phenomenon is true for not only American college students but others as well. See Arthur Liebman and James Petras, "Class and Student Politics in Chile," *Politics and Society,* 3:3 (Spring 1973), 329–345.

36. Joseph Freeman, *An American Testament: A Narrative of Rebels and Romantics* (New York: Farrar and Rinehart, 1936), pp. 120–121.

37. P. G. Altbach, *Student Politics,* pp. 45, 72–85; Robert W. Iversen, *The Communists and the Schools* (New York: Harcourt, Brace, 1959), p. 123; and S. M. Lipset, *Rebellion in the University,* pp. 182, 190.

38. Melech Epstein, *The Jew and Communism: The Story of Early Communist Victories and Ultimate Defeats in the Jewish Community, U.S.A., 1919–1941* (New York: Trade Union Sponsoring Committee, 1959), p. 202.

39. Interview with Morris U. Schappes, May 22, 1975.

40. M. Epstein, *Jew and Communism,* p. 202.

41. P. G. Altbach, *Student Politics,* pp. 72–84; R. W. Iversen, *Communists and the Schools,* pp. 123–139; and James Wechsler, *Revolt on Campus* (New York: Covici-Friede Publishers, 1935), pp. 94–99, 359.

42. J. Wechsler, p. 359.

43. Lewis S. Feuer, *The Conflict of Generations: The Character and Significance of Student Movements* (New York: Basic Books, 1969), p. 371.

44. John Gates, The Story of an American Communist (New York: Thomas Nelson & Sons, 1958), pp. 16–23; N. Glazer, *Social Basis of American Communism,* p. 137; R. W. Iversen, *Communists and the Schools,* p. 125; and S. M. Lipset, *Rebellion in the University,* p. 181.

45. R. W. Iversen, pp. 146–147.

46. Cited in S. M. Lipset, *Rebellion in the University,* p. 181.

47. James Wechsler, *The Age of Suspicion* (London: Andre Deutsch, 1954), pp. 129–130.

48. J. Higham, *Strangers in the Land,* p. 278; and S. W. Rudy, *College of the City of New York,* p. 399.

49. Cited in R. W. Iversen, *Communists and the Schools,* p. 125.

50. J. Wechsler, *Revolt on Campus, op. cit.,* p. 359.

51. S. W. Rudy, *College of the City of New York*, p. 398.
52. J. Wechsler, *Revolt on Campus*, p. 359.
53. Interview with Morris U. Schappes, May 22, 1975.
54. A. Jospe, "Jews in American Universities," p. 2.
55. J. Gates, *An American Communist*, p. 16.
56. L. Feuer, *Conflict of Generations*, p. 361.
57. J. Gates, *An American Communist*, pp. 18–19.
58. Ibid., p. 17.
59. L. Feuer, *Conflict of Generations*, p. 371.
60. A. Jospe, "Jews in American Universities," p. 2.
61. See Jerold S. Auerbach, "From Rags to Robes: The Legal Profession, Social Mobility and the American Jewish Experience," *American Jewish Historical Quarterly*, 56:2 (December 1976), 265–279; Irving Howe, "The New York Intellectuals," *Commentary*, 46:4 (October 1968), 29–51; Norman Podhoretz, *Making It* (New York: Bantam Books, 1967); and Daniel Aaron, "Some Reflections on Communism and the Jewish Writer," in *The Ghetto and Beyond: Essays on Jewish Life in America*, Peter I. Rose, Ed. (New York: Random House, 1969), pp. 253–269.
62. See relevant polls in Charles H. Stember et al., *Jews in the Mind of America* (New York: Basic Books, 1966), pp. 219–229; and Gertrude J. Selznick and Stephen Steinberg, *The Tenacity of Prejudice* (New York: Harper & Row, 1969), pp. 69–169.
63. This is the perspective that pervades the autobiography of Norman Podhoretz, *Making It*. It is not by any means unique to him.
64. *Partisan Review*, 19:3 (May–June 1952), 284.
65. Norman Podhoretz, "The Young Generation of U.S. Intellectuals," *The New Leader*, 40:10 (March 11, 1957), 9.
66. Leo Grebler, *Housing Market Behavior in a Declining Area: Long Term Changes in Inventory and Utilization of Housing on New York's Lower East Side* (New York: Columbia University Press, 1952), p. 254.
67. Ibid., pp. 114–115.
68. Ibid., p. 116.
69. Ibid., pp. 114–115, 236.
70. N. Glazer and D. P. Moynihan, *Beyond the Melting Pot*, pp. 160–161; Sidney Goldstein, "American Jewry, 1970: A Demographic Profile," *American Jewish Yearbook*, 72 (Philadelphia: Jewish Publication Society, 1971), pp. 39–41; Mark R. Levy and Michael S. Kramer, *The Ethnic Factor: How America's Minorities Decide Elections* (New York: Simon & Schuster, 1973), p. 98; and *Jewish Currents*, 30:2 (February 1976), 46.
71. Louis Wirth, *The Ghetto* (Chicago: University of Chicago Press, 1928 and 1956), p. 243; S. Goldstein and C. Goldscheider, *Jewish Americans*, pp. 46–61; and J. Higham, "Social Discrimination Against Jews," pp. 18–19.
72. L. Grebler, *Housing Market Behavior*, p. 141; and J. Higham, "Social Discrimination Against Jews," p. 19.
73. N. Glazer and D. P. Moynihan, *Beyond the Melting Pot*, pp. 160–161; J. Higham, "Social Discrimination Against the Jews," p. 20; and Stanley Lieberson, *Ethnic Patterns on American Cities* (New York: Free Press of Glencoe, 1963), pp. 127–131.
74. J. Higham, "Social Discrimination Against the Jews," p. 20.
75. In commenting on the election results in New York City in 1949, a Communist party writer commented approvingly on the fact that the Jews on the East Side had maintained their commitment to the Communist-influenced American Labor Party. Lillian Gates, "New York's 1949 Election," *Political Affairs*, 28:12 (December 1949), 52. Benjamin J. Davis, a Communist, in describing his successful 1943 election to a seat on the New York City Council, mentions the importance of the Lower East Side Jewish vote: "The tremendous vote I received from the Jewish community was one of the highlights of the election." Benjamin J.

Davis, *Communist Councilman From Harlem* (New York: International Publishers, 1969), p. 107.

76. See Chapter 8 for further discussion of this particular point.

77. Cited in Arthur Gorenstein, "A Portrait of Ethnic Politics: The Socialists and the 1908 and 1910 Congressional Elections on the East Side," *American Jewish Historical Quarterly, 50*:3 (March 1961), 207–208.

78. L. Grebler, *Housing Market Behavior*, p. 123; and S. Goldstein and C. Goldscheider, *Jewish Americans*, pp. 49–52.

79. Senate Committee on the Judiciary, *The Communist Party of the United States of America* (Washington, D.C.: U.S. Government Printing Office, 1955), p. 54.

80. N. Glazer, "Social Characteristics of American Jews," p. 17.

81. L. Grebler, *Housing Market Behavior*, p. 236.

82. Joshua A. Fishman, *Yiddish in America: Socio-Linguistic Description and Analysis* (Bloomington, Ind.: University of Indiana Press, 1965), p. 55; Samuel Halperin, The Political World of American Zionism (Detroit: Wayne State University Press, 1961), p. 56; and Ira Rosenwaike, "The Utilization of Census Mother Tongue Data in American Jewish Population Analysis," *Jewish Social Studies, 33*:2–3 (April–July 1971), 143.

83. Circulation figures for the various years can be found in the annual *Ayer Directory of Newspaper, Magazine and Trade Publications*. Also see Joshua A. Fishman, et al., *Language Loyalty in the United States* (The Hague: Mouton, 1966), p. 53; S. Halperin, "American Zionism," p. 56; and Mordecai Soltes, *The Yiddish Press: An Americanizing Agency* (New York: Teachers College, Columbia University Press, 1950), p. 24.

84. J. A. Fishman, *Language Loyalty in the U.S.*, p. 66.

85. Interview with Morris U. Schappes, August 2, 1975.

86. Nathan Goldberg, "The Jewish Population in the United States," in *Jewish People: Past and Present*, Vol. II, Abraham Menes et al., eds. (New York: Jewish Encyclopedic Handbooks, 1948), pp. 30–31; and S. Goldstein and C. Goldscheider, *Jewish Americans*, pp. 225–227.

87. The major work on this subject is by Arthur Goren, *New York Jews and the Quest for Community: The Kehillah Experiment, 1908–1922* (New York: Columbia University Press, 1970).

88. Ibid., p. 45.

89. Cited in Moses Rischin, *The Promised City: New York's Jews, 1870–1914* (New York: Harper Torchbooks, 1970), p. 243.

90. A. Goren, *New York Jews*, p. 35.

91. Cited in ibid., p. 196.

92. Naomi W. Cohen, *Not Free to Desist: The American Jewish Committee, 1906–1966* (Philadelphia: Jewish Publication Society, 1972), pp. 8–21; and Naomi W. Cohen, "An Uneasy Alliance: The First Days of the Jewish Agency" in *A Bicentennial Festschrift for Jacob Rader Marcus*, B. W. Korn, Ed. (New York: Ktav Publishing House, 1976), p. 110.

93. Harry C. Lurie, *A Heritage Affirmed: The Jewish Federation Movement in America* (Philadelphia: Jewish Publication Society, 1961), pp. 39–55.

94. Zosa Szajkowski, "Concern and Discord in American Jewish Overseas Relief, 1914–1924," *YIVO Annual of Jewish Social Science*, 14 (New York: YIVO Institute of Jewish Social Science, 1969), pp. 99–158; and A. Goren, *New York Jews*, pp. 215–217.

95. M. Epstein, *Jewish Labor*, II, pp. 57–62; and Louis J. Swichkow and Lloyd P. Gartner, *A History of the Jews of Milwaukee* (Philadelphia: Jewish Publication Society, 1963), p. 269.

96. Philip Friedman, "Political and Social Movements and Organizations," in *The Jewish People: Past and Present*, Vol. IV, Abraham Menes et al., Eds. (New York: Jewish Encyclopedic Handbooks, 1955), p. 168.

97. Cited in H. C. Lurie, *Heritage Affirmed*, p. 78.

98. Cited in Mordecai M. Kaplan, *Judaism as a Civilization: Toward A Reconstruction of American-Jewish Life* (New York: Schocken Books, 1972), p. 60.
99. Ibid., p. 48.
100. S. Halperin, "American Zionism," pp. 157–175.
101. H. C. Lurie, *Heritage Affirmed*, pp. 78–79.
102. W. Maslow, *American Jewish Community*, pp. 20–22.
103. Daniel J. Elazar, "Decision Making in the American Jewish Community," in *The Jewish Community in America*, Marshall Sklare, Ed. (New York: Behrman House, 1974), pp. 96–97; Salo W. Baron, "American Jewish History: Problems and Methods," *Publications of the American Jewish Historical Society*, 39: Part 3 (March 1950), 252; and Ira Silverman, "How Much Democracy And for Whom?" *Present Tense*, 4:2 (Winter 1977), 59–63.
104. Harry S. Linfield, *The Communal Organization of Jews in the United States* (New York: American Jewish Committee, 1927), pp. 20, 33.
105. S. Halperin, "American Zionism," p. 144.
106. *Reform Judaism in the Large Cities: A Survey* (Cincinnati: Union of American Hebrew Congregations, 1931), p. 10.
107. I. E. Rontch, "The Present State of the Landsmanschaften," *Jewish Social Service Quarterly*, 15:4 (June 1939), 370.
108. M. M. Kaplan, *Judaism as a Civilization*, p. 48; and H. S. Linfield, *Communal Organization of Jews*, p. 20.
109. S. Halperin, "American Zionism," p. 377.
110. Nathan Glazer, *American Judaism*, 2nd ed. (Chicago: University of Chicago Press, 1972), p. 108; H. S. Linfield, *Communal Organization of Jews*, p. 33; *American Jewish Yearbook*, 45–46 (Philadelphia: Jewish Publication Society, 1945), p. 644; and W. Maslow, *American Jewish Community*, p. 24.
111. *American Jewish Yearbook*, 45–46, p. 20.
112. N. Glazer, *American Judaism*, pp. 108–109; and Will Herberg, *Protestant-Catholic-Jew: An Essay in American Religious Sociology* (Garden City: Anchor Books, 1960), p. 190.
113. H. S. Linfield, *Communal Organization of Jews*, p. 21.
114. M. Sklare, *America's Jews*, p. 122.
115. Charles S. Liebman, *The Ambivalent American Jews: Politics, Religion and Family in American Jewish Life* (Philadelphia: Jewish Publication Society, 1973), p. 72.
116. Ibid., p. 72.
117. H. S. Linfield, *Communal Organization of Jews*, p. 69.
118. James E. Carlin and Saul H. Mendlovitz, "The American Rabbi: A Religious Specialist Responds to Loss of Authority," in *The Jews*, M. Sklar, Ed., pp. 378–414.
119. Much of the following discussion is indebted to Marshall Sklare's *Conservative Judaism: An American Religious Movement* (Glencoe, Ill.: Free Press, 1955).
120. Ibid., pp. 161–165.
121. W. Maslow, *American Jewish Community*, p. 25.
122. M. Sklare, *Conservative Judaism*, pp. 245–247.
123. Ibid., pp. 219–220.
124. In 1934 the periodical *The World Tomorrow* asked over 17,000 clergymen the following question: "Which economic system appears to you to be less antagonistic and more consistent with the ideals and methods of Jesus and the noblest of the Hebrew prophets?" Forty-nine percent of the rabbis who responded chose Socialism or Communism, compared to 1 percent of all the clergymen. No clergy from any of the 13 other denominations listed approached the Jewish figure. Cited in Ralph L. Roy, *Communism and the Churches* (New York: Harcourt, Brace, 1960), p. 142.
125. N. Glazer, *American Judaism*, pp. 138–140.
126. S. Halperin, "American Zionism," pp. 110–111.
127. C. S. Liebman, *Ambivalent American Jews*, pp. 143–144; and Seymour M. Lipset

and Everett C. Ladd, "Jewish Academics in the United States: Their Achievements, Culture and Politics," *American Jewish Yearbook*, 72 (Philadelphia: Jewish Publication Society, 1971), pp. 121–123.

128. Isaac Deutscher, "The Non-Jewish Jew," in *The Non-Jewish Jew and Other Essays*, Tamara Deutscher, Ed. (New York: Hill and Wang, 1968), pp. 32–41.

129. S. Halperin, "American Zionism," p. 329; Isaac M. Fein, *The Making of an American Jewish Community* (Philadelphia: Jewish Publication Society, 1971), pp. 195–200 (Baltimore); L. J. Swichkow and L. P. Gartner, *Jews of Milwaukee*, pp. 255–256, 350–352 (Milwaukee); and W. Lloyd Warner and Leo Srole, *The Social Systems of American Ethnic Groups* (New Haven: Yale University Press, 1945), p. 286 (Newburyport).

130. S. Halperin, "American Zionism," p. 313; and Jonathan Shapiro, *Leadership of the American Zionist Organization, 1897–1930* (Urbana, Ill.: University of Illinois Press, 1971), pp. 53–54, 129.

131. S. Halperin, "American Zionism," pp. 10–11.

132. Ibid., p. 327.

133. J. Shapiro, *American Zionist Organization*, pp. 102–105, 119, 166, 184–194.

134. S. Halperin, "American Zionism," pp. 211–214, 215.

135. Ibid., pp. 313–314.

136. Ibid., pp. 325–326.

137. Ibid., p. 327.

138. See discussion in Chapter 8.

139. S. Halperin, "American Zionism," p. 38.

140. Ibid., pp. 37–39.

141. Marshall Sklare and Benjamin B. Ringer, "A Study of Jewish Attitudes Toward the State of Israel," in *The Jews*, M. Sklare, Ed., pp. 440–441.

142. M. M. Kaplan, *Judaism as a Civilization*, p. 66.

143. S. Halperin, "American Zionism," pp. 13, 331.

144. Ibid., p. 25.

145. Hannah Arendt, "Zionism Reconsidered" (1945) in *Zionism Reconsidered: The Rejection of Jewish Normalcy*, Michael Selzer, Ed. (New York: Macmillan, 1970), p. 243.

146. S. Halperin, "American Zionism," pp. 306–307.

147. Ibid., pp. 157–169.

148. J. Sultan, "On the Communist Approach to Zionism: A Reply to a Memorandum," *The Communist*, 15:7 (July 1936), 670.

149. S. Halperin, "American Zionism," pp. 170–173.

150. Cited in ibid., p. 171.

151. Cited in Irving Howe and Lewis Coser, *The American Communist Party: A Critical History* (New York: Praeger, 1962), p. 343.

152. Cited in S. Halperin, "American Zionism," p. 172.

153. Alex Bittelman, *The Jewish People Will Live On* (New York: Morning Freiheit Association, 1944), pp. 36–47.

154. Interview with a former Communist. See also N. Glazer, *Social Basis*, p. 156.

155. Joseph Neveda, *Trotsky and the Jews* (Philadelphia: Jewish Publication Society, 1972), pp. 223, 226, 231.

156. Isaac Deutscher, "Israel's Spiritual Climate," in *Non-Jewish Jew*, T. Deutscher, Ed., pp. 111–112.

157. Alexander Bittelman, "Things I Have Learned: An Autobiography," manuscript, Tamiment Library, New York University, 1962, pp. 612, 683.

158. On the importance of Israel to Jews in America, especially on the organizational aspect of this propensity, see Daniel J. Elazar, *Community and Polity: The Organizational Dynamics of American Jewry* (Philadelphia: Jewish Publication Society, 1976), pp. 341–377; and C. S. Liebman, *Ambivalent American Jew*, pp. 88–108.

159. See Irving Louis Horowitz and Maurice Zeitlin, "Israeli Imperatives and Jewish Agonies," in *Israeli Ecstacies/Jewish Agonies*, Irving Louis Horowitz, Ed. (New

York: Oxford University Press, 1974), pp. 3–36; Sol Stern, "My Jewish Problem—And Ours: Israel, the Left, and the Jewish Establishment," in *Jewish Radicalism: A Selected Anthology*, Jack Nusan Porter and Peter Dreier, Eds. (New York: Grove Press, 1973), pp. 351–375; and Seymour Martin Lipset, *Revolution and Counter-Revolution: Change and Persistence in Social Structures*, Rev. ed. (Garden City, N.Y.: Anchor Books, 1970), pp. 375–400, or Chapter 10, "The Left, the Jews and Israel."

160. See, for example, Walter Lacqueur, "New York and Jerusalem," *Commentary*, 51:2 (February 1971), 38–46; and Nathan Glazer, "Jewish Interests and the New Left," in *The New Left and the Jews*, Mordecai S. Chertoff, Ed. (New York: Pitman Publishing, 1971), pp. 152–165, for a strong expression of this point of view. *Commentary* is published by the American Jewish Committee.

161. I. Howe, *World of Our Fathers*, p. 628; and Judah J. Shapiro, "The Philistine Philanthropists: The Power and Shame of Jewish Federations," in *Jewish Radicalism*, J. N. Porter and Peter Dreier, Eds., *op. cit.*, pp. 202, 208.

162. I. Howe, *World of Our Fathers*, p. 628.

163. J. Higham, *Strangers in the Land*, pp. 194–282.

164. The best account of this campaign and the source that has most informed this discussion of it is Zosa Szajkowski, *Jews, Wars and Communism, I: The Attitude of American Jews to World War I, the Russian Revolutions of 1917, and Communism (1914–1915)*, (New York: Ktav Publishing House, 1972), pp. 141–161, Chapter 11, "Jews and the New York City Mayoralty Election of 1917."

165. Zosa Szajkowski, *Jews, Wars, and Communism, II: The Impact of the 1919–20 Red Scare on American Jewish Life* (New York: Ktav Publishing House, 1974), pp. 8–9, 122–124.

166. See Z. Szajkowski, *Jews, Wars, and Communism, II*, for the most detailed account of the relationship between what has been called the Red Scare and anti-Semitism.

167. See J. Higham, *Strangers in the Land*, pp. 277–286; and Seymour Martin Lipset and Earl Raab, *The Politics of Unreason: Right Wing Extremism in America, 1790–1970* (New York: Harper & Row, 1970), pp. 110–145.

168. S. M. Lipset and E. Raab, p. 142.

169. Ibid., p. 143.

170. Emory S. Bogardus, *Immigration and Race Attitudes* (Boston: D.C. Heath, 1928), pp. 24–25.

171. J. Higham, *Strangers in the Land*, p. 309.

172. Ibid., pp. 300–330.

173. J. Higham, "Social Discrimination Against Jews," pp. 21–23; and S. Steinberg, *Academic Melting Pot*, p. 19–31.

174. J. Higham, *Strangers in the Land*, p. 278.

175. J. Higham, "Social Discrimination Against Jews," pp. 20–21.

176. Frederick Lewis Allen, *Only Yesterday: An Informal History of the 1920's* (New York: Perennial Library, Harper & Row, 1964), pp. 53–54.

177. For a general account of this period and an analytic description of anti-Semitism in the 1930s, see S. M. Lipset and E. Raab, *Politics of Unreason*, pp. 150–202.

178. Charles H. Stember, "The Recent History of Public Attitudes," in *Jews in the Mind of America*, George Salomon, Ed. (New York: Basic Books, 1966), pp. 54, 65, 69, 126.

179. Ibid., p. 55.

180. John Higham, *Send These to Me: Jews and Other Immigrants in Urban America* (New York: Atheneum, 1975), p. 190.

181. Heywood Broun and George Britt, *Christians Only* (New York: Vanguard Press, 1931), p. 105.

182. For analytic discussion of the role of relative deprivation in social movements, see James A. Geschwender, "Explorations in the Theory of Social Movements," in *The Black Revolt: The Civil Rights Movement, Ghetto Uprisings, and Separatism*, James A. Geschwender (Englewood Cliffs, N.J.: Prentice-Hall, 1971), pp.

6–17; and Ted R. Gurr, *Why Men Rebell* (Princeton, N.J.: Princeton University Press, 1970), pp. 22–154. Also see James C. Davies, "Toward a Theory of Revolution," *American Sociological Review*, 6:1 (February 1962), 5–19; and James C. Davies, Ed. *When Men Revolt and Why: A Reader in Political Violence and Revolution* (New York: Free Press, 1971), which contains selections from de Tocqueville, Marx, and others on the role of relative deprivation in social movements, especially the section entitled "Some General Theory."

183.   See, for example, the character of Dr. Irwin Metger, a Jewish dentist who was unable to get into medical school, in the novel by Harvey Swados, *Standing Fast* (New York: Ballantine Books, 1970). Nathan Glazer makes the following observation on this subject, "It is generally believed by the knowledgeable that Communist dentists were more common than lawyers or doctors," in *Social Basis of American Communism*, p. 147.

184.   S. M. Lipset and E. Raab, *Politics of Unreason*, pp. 160–184.

185.   See discussion in Chapter 8.

186.   Ibid.

187.   S. M. Lipset and E. Raab, *Politics of Unreason*, p. 111.

188.   Seymour Martin Lipset, *Political Man: The Social Bases of Politics* (New York: Anchor Books, 1963), pp. 346–347.

189.   Abbott L. Ferriss, *Indicators of Trends in American Education* (New York: Russell Sage Foundation, 1969), pp. 383, 387, 393; and *Historical Statistics of the U.S.*, pp. 34, 74, 75, 208, 210, 211.

190.   *Historical Statistics of the U.S.*, p. 97.

191.   N. Glazer, "Social Characteristics of American Jews," p. 24.

192.   Ibid.

193.   N. Glazer, *Social Basis*, p. 146.

194.   In his analysis of national survey data, Richard F. Hamilton has found that lower-middle-class persons who are the offspring of working-class, Democratic fathers have a high propensity to adopt their fathers' politics. Richard F. Hamilton, *Class and Politics in the United States* (New York: John Wiley, 1972), p. 343.

195.   R. W. Iversen, *Communists and the Schools*, pp. 32, 53, 103; and Celia L. Zitron, *The New York City Teachers Union, 1916–1964: A Story of Educational and Social Commitment* (New York: Humanities Press, 1968), pp. 9–28.

196.   C. L. Zitron, pp. 30–45, 183–184, 228–240, and Cyril Graze, "Repression in New York Schools," *Jewish Life*, 6:6 (April 1952), 20–22.

197.   N. Glazer, *Social Basis*, pp. 139–140.

198.   Ibid., p. 143; and John E. Hayes, "The 'Rank and File Movement' in Private Social Work," *Labor History*, 16:1 (Winter 1975), 78–98.

199.   R. W. Iversen, *Communists and the Schools*, p. 151. A fraction, to use Iversen's definition, is: "The Communist device for working within a nonparty organization . . . [it] is established whenever there are two or more party members in that organization. 'The fraction is the instrument of the Party in carrying out its policy.'"

200.   Ibid., p. 152.

201.   Interview with Morris U. Schappes, Spring 1975. Much of this section is indebted to the information supplied by Mr. Schappes.

202.   See Richard Flacks, "The Liberated Generation: An Exploration of the Roots of Student Protest," *The Journal of Social Issues*, 23:3 (July 1967), 65–66; Nathan Glazer, *Remembering the Answers: Essays on the American Student Revolt* (New York: Basic Books, 1970), pp. 223–224; Richard G. Braungart, "Family Status, Socialization and Student Poitics: A Multivariate Analysis," (Ph.D. diss., Pennsylvania State University, 1969), pp. 142, 153; and S. M. Lipset, *Rebellion in the University*, pp. 80–94.

203.   See note 202 and Seymour Martin Lipset and E. C. Ladd, Jr., "Jewish Academics in the United States: Their Achievements, Culture and Politics, in *American*

Jewish Yearbook, 72 (Philadelphia: Jewish Publication Society, 1971), pp. 110–125.

204. S. M. Lipset and E. C. Ladd, pp. 112–113.
205. Ernest Greenwood, "The Attributes of a Profession," in *Man, Work, and Society,* Sigmund Nosow and William H. Form, Eds. (New York: Basic Books, 1962), pp. 212–214.
206. For a discussion of the ideology of the New Left that obtained throughout most of the 1960s, see G. David Garson, "The Ideology of the New Student Left," in *Protest: Student Activism in America,* Juliam Foster and Durward Long, Eds. (New York: William Morrow, 1970), pp. 184–201; Jack Newfield, *A Prophetic Minority* (New York: New American Library, 1966), pp. 27–33; and Paul Jacobs and Saul Landau, *The New Radicals* (New York: Vintage Books, 1966), pp. 3–7.
207. E. Digby Baltzell, *The Protestant Establishment: Aristocracy and Caste in America* (New York: Random House, 1964), pp. 329–334.

CHAPTER 8

1. This debate over the political merits and consequences of reformism in the socialist movement have engaged the attention of numerous sociaist theorists, including: Eduard Bernstein, *Evolutionary Socialism* (New York: Schocken Books, 1961; first published in German in 1899); Morris Hillquit, *Socialism Summed Up* (New York: H. K. Fly Co., 1912); V. I. Lenin, *What Is To Be Done* (Moscow: Foreign Languages Publishing House, n.d.; first published in Russia in 1902); V. I. Lenin, 'Left-Wing' Communism, An Infantile Disorder (New York: International Publishers, 1969; first published in Russian in 1920); Rosa Luxemburg, "Social Reform or Revolution," in *Selected Political Writings of Rosa Luxemburg,* Dick Howard, Ed. (New York: Monthly Review Press, 1971), pp. 52–134 (first published in German in 1899). This debate is still continuing among socialists. See Max Gordon, "The Communist Party of the Nineteen Thirites and the New Left," *Socialist Revolution,* 6:1 (Jan.–March 1976), 11–47, the "Response" by James Weinstein in the same issue, pp. 48–58, and the "Reply" by Max Gordon in the same issue, pp. 59–66. See also Andre Gorz, *Socialism and Revolution* (Garden City, N.Y.: Anchor Books, 1973); originally published in French in 1967).
2. Quoted in A. Gorz, *Socialism and Revolution,* p. 141.
3. Samuel Gompers, *Seventy Years of Life and Labor: An American Autobiography* (New York: E. P. Dutton, 1925), pp. 313, 325.
4. Abraham Cahan, *The Education of Abraham Cahan* (translated by Leon Stein, Abraham P. Conan, and Lynn Davison from the Yiddish Autobiography *Bleter Fun Mein Leben* by Abraham Cahan, Volumes I and II) (Philadelphia: Jewish Publication Society, 1969), pp. 347, 410.
5. Melech Epstein, *Jewish Labor in the U.S.A.: An Industrial, Political and Cultural History of the Jewish Labor Movement,* 2 vols. (New York: Ktav Publishing House, 1969), p. 150.
6. David Herreshoff, *American Disciples of Marx: From the Age of Jackson to the Progressive Era* (Detroit: Wayne State University Press, 1967), pp. 110–112.
7. A. Cahan, *Education of Abraham Cahan,* p. 331.
8. M. Epstein, *Jewish Labor,* I, p. 248; and Moses Rischin, *The Promised City: New York's Jews, 1870–1914* (New York: Harper Torchbooks, 1970), pp. 224–235, 272–274.
9. Quoted in M. Epstein, *Jewish Labor,* I, p. 248.
10. Ira Kipnis, *The American Socialist Movement 1897–1912* (New York: Columbia University Press, 1952), p. 16.
11. Ibid., p. 17.
12. M. Hillquit, *Socialism Summed Up,* p. 303.
13. M. Epstein, *Jewish Labor,* I, p. 255.

14. Morris Hillquit, *Loose Leaves From A Busy Life* (New York: Macmillan, 1934), pp. 46–47; Morris Hillquit, *The History of Socialism in the United States* (New York: Funk and Wagnalls, 1903), pp. 323–325; and David A. Shannon, *The Socialist Party of America* (Chicago: Quadrangle Books, 1955), pp. 10–11. Hillquit's position in opposition to dual unionism was similar to that of Lenin's as put forth in '*Left-Wing' Communism*, pp. 30–39.

15. S. Gompers, *Seventy Years*, pp. 87–91.

16. M. Epstein, *Jewish Labor*, I, pp. 220–272; D. Herreshoff, *American Disciples of Marx*, pp. 113–130; Howard H. Quint, *The Forging of American Socialism: Origins of the Modern Movement* (Indianapolis, Ind.: The Bobbs Merrill Co., 1953), pp. 300–301; M. Rischin, *Promised City*, pp. 225–227.

17. H. H. Quint, *Forging of American Socialism*, p. 300.

18. Melvin Dubofsky, "Success and Failure of Socialism in New York City, 1900–1918: A Case Study," *Labor History*, 9:3 (Fall 1968), 369; Charles Leinenweber, "Socialists in the Streets: The New York City Socialist Party in Working Class Neighborhoods, 1908–1918," unpublished paper, Dept. of Sociology, New Paltz, pp. 39–41; and D. A. Shannon, *Socialist Party*, p. 13.

19. C. Leinenweber, "Socialists in the Streets," p. 40.

20. M. Dubofsky, "Socialism in New York City," p. 369.

21. Lawrence H. Fuchs, *The Political Behavior of American Jews* (Glencoe, Ill.: Free Press, 1956), pp. 124–125.

22. M. Rischin, *Promised City*, pp. 124–125, 166–167, 234–235; and Abraham Menes, "The East Side Matrix of the Jewish Labor Movement," *Judaism*, 3:4 (Fall 1974), 376.

23. M. Rischin, *Promised City*, p. 151.

24. Irving Howe in his discussion of the Jewish Left rarely deals with the strength that the radical or left-wing socialists, at various times, enjoyed in the Jewish community. He very much is in agreement with Hillquit's and London's socialist perspectives and values. In the 1920s, when discussing the rise of Communist support among Jewish needle trades workers, Howe cannot bring himself to admit the possibility that the Communists must have done something positive to attract this support. Instead, he sees this Jewish pro-Communist attitude among garment workers as a reaction to the corruption and loss of elan of the right-wing socialists. See Irving Howe, *World of Our Fathers* (New York: Harcourt Brace Jovanovich, 1976), pp. 321–324.

25. Harry Roskolenko, *The Time That Was Then: The Lower East 1900–1914: An Intimate Chronicle* (New York: Dial Press, 1971), p. 29.

26. *New York Call*, November 19, 1914.

27. I. Kipnis, *American Socialist Movement*, p. 171. See also Richard W. Fox, "The Paradox of Progressive Socialism: The Case of Morris Hillquit, 1901–1914," *American Quarterly*, 26:1 (March 1974), 127–140, for an analysis of Hillquit's conservative socialism.

28. M. Dubofsky, "Socialism in New York City," p. 366.

29. M. Rischin, *Promised City*, p. 235.

30. M. Epstein, *Jewish Labor*, II, p. 78.

31. Ibid., p. 145.

32. James Weinstein, *The Decline of Socialism in America 1912–1925* (New York: Vintage Books).

33. Quoted in H. Roskolenko, *Time That Was Then*, p. 31.

34. Gorenstein, "A Portrait of Ethnic Politics: The Socialists and the 1908 and 1910 Congressional Elections on the East Side," *American Jewish Historical Quarterly*, 50:3 (March 1961), 225.

35. Quoted in Ibid.

36. Ray Ginger, *Eugene V. Debs: A Biography* (New York: Collier Books, 1962), p. 325.

37. Ibid., pp. 279, 280, 326; and D. A. Shannon, *Socialist Party*, pp. 8–10. Weinstein argues that fragmentary evidence indicates that the lawyers, ministers, and edi-

tors generally were more prominent among the elected leadership in the larger, as opposed to the smaller, towns and cities. J. Weinstein, *Decline of Socialism*, pp. 42–43.

38. Daniel Bell, *Marxian Socialism in the United States* (Princeton, N.J.: Princeton University Press, 1967), pp. 55–90; D. A. Shannon, *Socialist Party*, pp. 62–80, 126–149; and J. Weinstein, *Decline of Socialism*, pp. 117–233.

39. Charles Leinenweber, "The World of Our Fathers as Socialist History," unpublished paper, pp. 4–5.

40. Quoted in Melech Epstein, *The Jew and Communism: The Story of Early Communist Victories and Ultimate Defeats in the Jewish Community, U.S.A., 1919–1941* (New York: Trade Union Sponsoring Committee, 1959), p. 57.

41. D. Bell, *Marxian Socialism*, p. 169.

42. For discussions of the Third Period see Theodore Draper, *American Communism and Soviet Russia: The Formative Period* (New York: Viking Press, 1963), pp. 302–314; William Z. Foster, *History of the Communist Party of the United States* (New York: International Publishers, 1952), pp. 265–279; and James Weinstein, *Ambiguous Legacy: The Left in American Politics* (New York: New Viewpoints, 1975), pp. 43–56.

43. T. Draper, *American Communism and Soviet Russia*, p. 189; W. Z. Foster, *History of the Communist Party*, pp. 261, 307; and Nathan Glazer, *The Social Basis of American Communism* (New York: Harcourt Brace and World, 1961), pp. 92–93.

44. See Georgi Dimitrov, *For the Unity of the Working Class Against Fascism: Report to the 7th Congress of the Communist International, 1935* (London: Scientific Booksellers, n.d.); and Earl Browder, *The People's Front* (New York: International Publishers, 1938).

45. These figures are gleaned from a variety of sources, including various issues of the *Party Organizer*, an internal CP publication; M. Epstein, *Communism and the Jew*, p. 277; and M. Gordon, "Communist Party of the Nineteen-Thirties," pp. 18–22. Theodore Draper contends that in the 1920s, about 100,000 passed through the ranks of the CP (*American Communism and Soviet Russia*, p. 189).

46. M. Gordon, "Communist Party of the Nineteen-Thirties," p. 25.

47. There is some debate about the extent to which socialism was subordinated. See the exchange between Max Gordon and James in *Socialist Revolution*, 6:1 (January–March 1976), 11–66.

48. E. Browder, *People's Front*, pp. 146–149.

49. Irving Howe and Lewis Coser, *The American Communist Party: A Critical History* (New York: Praeger, 1962), p. 425.

50. Ibid., p. 427.

51. See Joseph R. Starobin, *American Communism in Crisis, 1943–1957* (Berkeley: University of California Press, 1975), pp. 20–106; and I. Howe and L. Coser, *The American Communist Party*, pp. 319–436.

52. See Peter Friedlander, *The Emergence of a UAW Local, 1936–1939* (Pittsburgh: University of Pittsburgh Press, 1975), pp. 122–125, for a discussion of this in Detroit.

53. Max Steinberg, "Problems of Industrial Units in New York City," *Party Organizer*, 10:6 (June 1937), 12.

54. George Charney, *A Long Journey* (Chicago: Quadrangle Books, 1968), p. 75.

55. Again, see exchange between Max Gordon and James Weinstein, *Socialist Revolution*, pp. 11–66.

56. G. Charney, *Long Journey*, p. 101.

57. Ibid., p. 94.

58. Ibid., p. 77.

59. David A. Shannon, *The Decline of American Communism: A History of the Communist Party Since 1945* (New York: Harcourt, Brace, 1959), pp. 256–257.

60. N. Glazer, *Social Basis*, p. 149.

61. I. Howe and L. Coser, *American Communist Party*, p. 337.
62. G. Charney, *Long Journey*, p. 73.
63. N. Glazer, *Social Basis*, pp. 114–117, 130; and J. R. Starobin, *American Communism in Crisis*, p. 100.
64. G. Charney, *Long Journey*, pp. 156–157.
65. N. Glazer, *Social Basis*, pp. 78, 116–118.
66. Daniel Aaron, "Some Reflections on Communism and the Jewish Writer," in *The Ghetto and Beyond: Essays on Jewish Life in America*, Peter I. Rose, Ed. (New York: Random House, 1969), p. 253.
67. Joseph Nedava, *Trotsky and the Jews* (Philadelphia: Jewish Publication Society, 1972), p. 123.
68. Ezra Mendelsohn, "The Russian Roots of the American Jewish Labor Movement," *YIVO Annual of Jewish Social Science*, 16 (New York: YIVO Institute for Jewish Research, 1976), p. 156.
69. M. Hillquit, *Loose Leaves*, pp. 8–9.
70. A. Cahan, *Education of Abraham Cahan*, p. 228.
71. Franklin Jonas, "The Early Life and Career of B. Charney Vladeck, 1886–1921: The Emergence of an Immigrant Spokesman," (Ph.D. diss., New York University, 1972), pp. 104, 117.
72. Quoted in M. Epstein, *Jew and Communism*, p. 63.
73. D. Herreshoff, *American Disciples of Marx*, p. 133.
74. R. Ginger, *Eugene V. Debs*, pp. 279–280, 325–326; W. Z. Foster, *History of the Communist Party*, pp. 102–120; and J. Nedava, *Trotsky and the Jews*, pp. 111, 131–136.
75. J. Nedava, p. 131.
76. Ibid., p. 132.
77. The source for this was Joseph Freeman in a private communication to Daniel Aaron, June 8, 1958 [Daniel Aaron, *Writers on the Left* (New York: Avon Books, 1965), p. 150.]
78. Arthur Mann, *LaGuardia: A Fighter Against His Times, 1882–1933* (Chicago: Chicago University Press, 1969), pp. 60, 99, 152.
79. D. Aaron, *Writers on the Left*, p. 287.
80. Harry Rogoff, *An East Side Epic: The Life and Work of Meyer London* (New York: Vanguard Press, 1930), p. 115.
81. M. Epstein, *Jewish Labor*, I. p. 248.
82. A. Cahan, *The Education of Abraham Cahan*, p. 347.
83. Ibid., p. 412.
84. D. Herreshoff, *American Disciples of Marx*, pp. 132–133.
85. Elias Tcherikower, *The Early Jewish Labor Movement in the U.S.*, Aaron Antonovsky, trans. (New York: YIVO Institute for Jewish Research, 1961), pp. 227–245.
86. M. Epstein, *Jewish Labor*, I, p. 335.
87. D. A. Shannon, *Socialist Party*, p. 12.
88. M. Rischin, *Promised City*, p. 234; and D. A. Shannon, pp. 12–13.
89. H. Roskolenko, *Time That Was Then*, p. 28.
90. Melvyn Dubofsky, *When Workers Organize: New York City in the Progressive Era* (Amherst, Mass.: University of Massachusetts Press, 1968), pp. 22–23; and L. H. Fuchs, *Political Behavior of American Jews*, pp. 50–74.
91. William V. Shannon, *The American Irish: A Political and Social Portrait* (New York: Collier Books, 1966), pp. 137–140.
92. I. Howe, *World of Our Fathers*, pp. 369–377.
93. H. Roskolenko, *Time That Was Then*, p. 196.
94. Arthur Mann, *LaGuardia Comes to Power, 1933* (New York: J. P. Lippincott, 1965), p. 92.
95. I. Howe, *World of Our Fathers*, pp. 365–377.
96. Bernard K. Johnpoll, *Pacifist's Progress: Norman Thomas and the Decline of American Socialism* (Chicago: Quadrangel Books, 1970), pp. 27, 54, 55.

97. Gorenstein, "A Portrait of Ethnic Politics," p. 203.
98. B. K. Johnpoll, *Pacifist's Progress*, pp. 54–55.
99. This account of the Hillquit campaigns is drawn primarily from A. Gorenstein, "A Portrait of Ethnic Politics," pp. 202–240.
100. Ibid., p. 211.
101. Ibid., p. 214.
102. Ibid., p. 212.
103. Ibid., p. 217.
104. Ibid., p. 218.
105. Ibid., p. 217.
106. Ibid., p. 218.
107. Irwin Yellowitz, "Morris Hillquit," unpublished paper, 1976, pp. 8–10.
108. A. Gorenstein, "A Portrait of Ethnic Politics," p. 223.
109. Ibid., p. 224.
110. Ibid., p. 225.
111. H. Roskolenko, *Time That Was Then*, p. 197.
112. A. Gorenstein, "A Portrait of Ethnic Politics," p. 225.
113. Ibid., p. 226.
114. D. A. Shannon, *Socialist Party*, pp. 11–12.
115. Melech Epstein, *Profiles of Eleven* (Detroit: Wayne State University Press, 1965), pp. 174–175.
116. A. Gorenstein, "A Portrait of Ethnic Politics," p. 222.
117. Ibid., and M. Epstein, *Jewish Labor*, I, p. 350.
118. Gorenstein, "A Portrait of Ethnic Politics," p. 214; and Yonathan Shapiro, *Leadership of the American Zionist Organization 1897–1930* (Urbana, Ill.: University of Illinois Press, 1971), p. 43.
119. Cited in Bernard H. Bloom, "Yiddish Speaking Socialists in America, 1892–1905," in *Critical Studies in American Jewish History: Selected Articles from American Jewish Archives*, III (New York: Ktav Publishing House, 1971), p. 24.
120. Ibid., pp. 26, 27.
121. M. Epstein, *Jewish Labor*, I, pp. 350–351; and F. Jonas, "Life and Career of B. C. Vladeck," p. 102.
122. C. Leinenweber, "The World of Our Fathers as Socialist History," p. 7.
123. M. Epstein, *Jewish Labor*, II, p. 247.
124. See Benjamin Gitlow, *I Confess: The Truth About American Communism* (Freeport, N.Y.: Books for Libraries Press, 1972), pp. 21–25 (originally published in New York in 1939).
125. H. Roskolenko, *Time That Was Then*, p. 29.
126. B. K. Johnpoll, *Pacifist's Progress*, pp. 77–101.
127. *Milwaukee Journal*, May 24, 1932.
128. Murray B. Seidler, *Norman Thomas: Respectable Rebel* (Syracuse: Syracuse University Press, 1961), p. 110.
129. M. Seidler, *Norman Thomas*, p. 110.
130. Ibid.
131. W. A. Swanberg, *Norman Thomas: The Last Idealist* (New York: Charles Scribner's Sons, 1976), p. 133.
132. B. K. Johnpoll, *Pacifist's Progress*, p. 93.
133. Norman Thomas Papers, New York Public Library, N.Y.
134. Norman Thomas to Louis Shafer, December 27, 1933, in Norman Thomas Papers, New York Library.
135. Louis Hendin to Norman Thomas, January 13, 1934, in Norman Thomas Papers, New York Library.
136. Norman Thomas to Louis Shafer, June 5, 1933, in Norman Thomas Papers, New York Library.
137. Norman Thomas to George Steinhardt, July 21, 1933, in Norman Thomas Papers, New York Public Library.

138. Nathan Chanin to Norman Thomas, June 8, 1933, in Norman Thomas Papers New York Public Library.
139. Norman Thomas to A. B. Lewis, March 2, 1936, in Norman Thomas Papers, New York Public Library.
140. Louis Waldman, *Labor Lawyer* (New York: E. P. Dutton, 1944), pp. 192–225.
141. "Socialist Platform of 1940," in Kirk H. Porter and Donald Bruce Johnson, comps, *National Party Platforms: 1840–1964* (Urbana, Ill.: University of Illinois Press, 1966), pp. 398, 399.
142. B. K. Johnpoll, *Pacifist's Progress*, p. 222.
143. Ibid., pp. 212–213.
144. Ibid., pp. 221–223.
145. M. Epstein, *Jewish Labor*, II, p. 248.
146. B. K. Johnpoll, *Pacifist's Progress*, p. 234; and D. A. Shannon, *Socialist Party*, p. 250.
147. W. A. Swanberg, *Norman Thomas*, pp. 248–305, 392.
148. Ibid., p. 392.
149. N. Glazer, *Social Basis*, pp. 38, 44; and T. Draper, *Roots of American Communism*, pp. 159, 190, 206, 207.
150. T. Draper, *Roots of American Communism*, p. 279.
151. N. Glazer, *Social Basis*, p. 44.
152. *American Labor Yearbook*, X (New York: Rand School, 1929), p..166.
153. N. Glazer, *Social Basis*, op. cit., p. 59.
154. "Communist Party Platform of 1936," in K. H. Porter and B. Johnson, *National Party Platforms*, p. 360.
155. I. Howe and L. Coser, *American Communist Party*, p. 339.
156. Cited in Hal Draper, "The Student Movement of the 30's: A Political History," in *As We Saw the Thirties*, Rita James Simon, Ed. (Urbana, Ill.: University of Illinois Press, 1967), p. 181.
157. John Gates, *The Story of an American Communist* (New York: Thomas Nelson, 1958), p. 173.
158. Alexander Bittelman, "Things I Have Learned: An Autobiography," manuscript, Tamiment Library, New York University, New York, 1962, pp. 315–319; and B. Gitlow, *I Confess*, pp. 37–39.
159. N. Glazer, *Social Basis*, op. cit., p. 47.
160. See discussion of this subject by P. Friedlander, *Emergence of a UAW Local*, pp. 123–144.
161. T. Draper, *American Communism and Soviet Russia*, p. 161.
162. N. Glazer, *Social Basis*, p. 50.
163. Ellis Paterson, "Are There Language Fractions or Sections in our Party," *The Party Organizer*, 2:5–6 (May–June 1928), 22–24; "Shortcomings of Party Fractions in Language Work," *The Party Organizer*, 3:4 (June–July 1930), 17–18; and John Roman, "Language Work in Youngstown Section," *Party Organizer*, 7:4 (April 1934), 15–19.
164. T. Draper, *American Communism and Soviet Russia*, p. 188.
165. Ibid., p. 191.
166. J. L. Cooper, "More Party Readers for the Daily Worker," *Party Organizer*, 2:3–4 (March–April 1928), 22–23.
167. Betty Yorburg's interview with Max Schactman, May 15, 1965, in Columbia Oral History Project, Columbia University Library, New York.
168. N. Glazer, *Social Basis*, pp. 62–63.
169. J. Roman, "Language Work in the Youngstown Section," p. 17.
170. P. Friedlander, *Emergence of a UAW Local*, p. 123.
171. T. Draper, *American Communism and Soviet Russia*, p. 192.
172. Benjamin Gitlow, *The Whole of Their Lives* (New York: Charles Scribners, 1948), p. 130.
173. T. Draper, *American Communism and Soviet Russia*, p. 192.
174. Ibid.

175. J. B. S. Hardman, "The Radical Labor Movement," manuscript, Tamiment Library, New York University, New York, 1932, pp. 32–33.
176. F. Brown, "New Forms of Party Organization Help Us to Win the Masses," *Party Organizer*, 9:7–8 (July–August 1936), 8–10.
177. "Communist Party Registration, 1944" in Earl Browder Papers, Syracuse University, Syracuse, N.Y.
178. N. Glazer, *Social Basis*, p. 70.
179. See a literary treatment of this attitude as it pertained to members of a Trotskyist group in Buffalo in Harvey Swados, *Standing Fast* (New York: Ballantine Books, 1971).
180. In 1923 Trotsky had expressed similar feelings: "Part of us, fighters of the Communist Party, originate from a bourgeois and petty-bourgeois environment. I was not fortunate, as some others were, to be born into a workers' family" (J. Nedava, *Trotsky and the Jews*, p. 123).
181. Lewis Coser, *Greedy Institutions* (New York: Free Press, 1974), p. 132.
182. *New York Times*, November 26, 1977, p. 7.
183. M. Epstein, *Jew and Communism*, p. 255.
184. Ralph Lord Roy, *Communism and the Churches* (New York: Harcourt, Brace, 1960), pp. 33, 38, 58, 59.
185. M. Epstein, *Jew and Communism*, pp. 252–261.
186. Ibid., pp. 278–279.
187. Ibid., pp. 223–233; and Stuart E. Knee, "Jewish Socialists in America: The Debate on Zionism," *The Wiener Library Bulletin*, 33, 34 (1975), pp. 19–21.
188. Ibid.
189. *Morning Freiheit*, October 24, 1976.
190. M. Epstein, *Jew and Communism*, p. 320.
191. N. Glazer, *Social Basis*, p. 159.
192. Ibid.
193. M. Epstein, *Jew and Communism*, p. 302.
194. "Problems of New York Jewry and the Tasks of the CP," *Jewish Life*, 2:4 (April 1938), 6.
195. M. Epstein, *Jew and Communism*, p. 319.
196. H. I. Costrell, "Perspectives," *Jewish Life*, 1:1 (August 1937), 16.
197. M. Epstein, *Jew and Communism*, p. 323; and N. Glazer, *Social Basis*, p. 161.
198. J. B. Sultan, "On the Communist Approach to Zionism," *The Communist*, 15:7 (July, 1936), 669, 670.
199. Alexander Bittelman, *The Jewish People Will Live On* (New York: Morning Freiheit Association, 1944), pp. 36–47.
200. Samuel Halperin, *Political World of American Zionism*, (Detroit: Wayne State University Press, 1961), p. 173.
201. "The Election Platform of the Communist Party [1936]," in K. H. Porter and B. Johnson, *National Party Platforms*, p. 359.
202. M. Epstein, *Jew and Communism*, p. 319.
203. Ibid., p. 294.
204. N. Glazer, *Social Basis*, p. 155.
205. Z. Szajkowski, *Jews, Wars, and Communism*, I, p. 460.
206. For some impression of the role of the CP's battle against anti-Semitism in the movement of Jewish artists and intellectuals to the party, see the testimony of Elia Kazan, Jerome Robbins, and Daniel Boorstin, among others, before the House Committee on Un-American Activities contained in Eric Bentley, Ed., *Thirty Years of Treason: Excerpts from Hearings Before the House Committee on Un-American Activities 1938–1968* (New York: Viking Press, 1971).
207. D. Aaron, "Communism and the Jewish Writer," p. 264.
208. M. Epstein, *Jew and Communism*, p. 351.
209. B. Gitlow, *Whole of Their Lives*, p. 313.
210. Philip Jaffe, *The Rise and Fall of American Communism* (New York: Horizon Press, 1975), p. 48.

211. Paul Novick, "Zionism and the Imperialist War," *The Communist*, 19:5 (May 1940) 475–479.
212. L. H. Fuchs, *Political Behavior of American Jews*, pp. 73–74; and Isaacs, *Jews and American Politics, op. cit.*, p. 152.
213. M. Epstein, *Jew and Communism*, pp. 364–370.
214. Committee of Action of the Members of the International Workers Order, "The Stalin-Hitler Pact and the International Workers Order," Tamiment Library, New York University, New York, October–November 1939.
215. G. Charney, *Long Journey*, p. 125.
216. Ibid.
217. Ibid., p. 277.
218. M. Epstein, *Jew and Communism*, p. 369.
219. Ibid., p. 355.
220. Ibid., p. 126.
221. "Communist Work Among the American Jewish Masses: Resolution of the National Groups Commission of the C.P. U.S.A., October, 1946," *Political Affairs*, 25:11 (November 1946), 1037.
222. Morris U. Schappes, "The Jewish Question and the Left—Old and New: A Challenge to the New Left," *Jewish Currents*, Reprint No. 7, 1970, pp. 14–15.
223. A. Bittelman, *Things I Have Learned*, p. 710.
224. "Progressive Party Platform, 1948," Porter and Johnson, *National Party Platforms*, p. 440.
225. Charney, *Long Journey, op. cit.*, p. 177.
226. "Campaign of 1948," Porter and Johnson, *National Party Platforms, op. cit.*, pp. 419–468.
227. "Wallace for President," *Jewish Life*, 2:4 (February 1948), 4.
228. Ibid., pp. 3–4.
229. Samuel Lubell, *The Future of American Politics* (Garden City, New York: Doubleday, 1956), p. 207.
230. Cohn, "Sources of American Jewish Liberalism," pp. 119–122.
231. Bittelman, "Things I Have Learned," p. 689.
232. Cedric Belfrage, *The American Inquisition, 1945–1960* (Indianapolis, Ind.: Bobbs-Merrill, 1973), p. 179; Naomi W. Cohen, *Not Free to Desist: The American Jewish Committee, 1906–1966* (Philadelphia: Jewish Publication Society of America, 1972), pp. 347–354; Louis Harap, " 'Commiphobia' and the American Jewish Committee," *Jewish Life*, 5 (December 1950), pp. 6–7; Paul Jacobs, *Is Curly Jewish?* (New York: Vintage Books, 1965), pp. 149–154, 165–174; "Memorandum of the ADL," *Jewish Life*, 7 (September 1953), pp. 7–8; and Ruth Simon, "Fifth Column in the Jewish Community," *Jewish Life*, 2:5 (March 1948), pp. 10–14.
233. See Lucy S. Dawidowicz, "American Reaction to Soviet Anti-Semitism," *American Jewish Yearbook*, 55 (Philadelphia: Jewish Publication Society of America, 1954), pp. 146–155.
234. Stephan Kafner, *A Journal of the Plague Years* (New York: Atheneum, 1973), p. 73.
235. See note 232.
236. Norman Podhoretz, *Making It* (New York: Bantam Books, 1969), p. 101.
237. L. H. Fuchs, *Political Behavior of American Jews*, p. 176; N. Cohen, *Not Free to Desist*, pp. 351–354; and letter from Harry W. Laidler, executive director of the League for Industrial Democracy, to James Loeb, executive secretary of the Americans for Democratic Action, April 10, 1947 in the LID Papers, Tamiment Library, New York University Library, New York.
238. L. S. Dawidowicz, "American Reaction to Soviet Anti-Semitism," pp. 146–155.
239. My own interviews with former Communists. See also, N. Glazer, *Social Basis*, pp. 164–165; and D. A. Shannon, *Decline of American Communism*, p. 320.
240. G. Charney, *Long Journey*, p. 277.
241. See *Jewish Life* from May to July 1956. *Jewish Life* was originally published and

subsidized by the Morning Freiheit Association. In 1953 this relationship was severed, more for reasons of political security than for reasons of politics. The report of the Soviet atrocities were first carried by the *Folks-Shtimme (People's Voice)* on April 4, 1956. They were then published in the *Morning Freiheit* on April 11, 1956, and in the May 1956 issue of *Jewish Life.*

242. Letter to the Editor, *Jewish Life*, 10:8 (June 1956), 37–38.
243. Letter to the Editor, *Jewish Life*, 10:9 (July 1956), 42.
244. *Morning Freiheit*, September 16, 1956.
245. J. Gates, *The Story of An American Communist*, (New York: Thomas Nelson, 1958), p. 163.
246. UPI dispatch in Binghamton Press, August 16, 1975.
247. John Williamson, "For a United-Front Policy Among the Jewish People—Sharpen the Struggle Against Bourgeois Nationalism," *Political Affairs*, 29:6 (July 1950), 61.
248. M. U. Schappes, "Jewish Question and the Left," pp. 14–15.
249. *Morning Freiheit*, Oct. 24, 1976.
250. Interview with former Communist active in Jewish affairs while in the party.
251. Most of this section is based on my interviews with current and former Jewish Communists, Socialists, and Trotskyists.
252. Harold Cruse, *The Crisis of the Negro Intellectual* (New York: William Morrow, 1971), p. 147.
253. Ibid.
254. Ibid., p. 163; and G. Charney, *Long Journey*, p. 87.
255. P. Jacobs, *Is Curly Jewish?*, p. 69.
256. For a general discussion of this New York–Jewish intellectual style, see Irving Howe, "The New York Intellectuals: A Chronical and A Critique," *Commentary*, 46 (October 1968), pp. 29–51.
257. Charles S. Liebman, "Toward a Theory of Jewish Liberalism," in *The Religious Situation, 1969*, Donald R. Cutler, Ed. (Boston: Beacon Press, 1969), pp. 1056–1057.
258. For some idea of the feelings of envy, hostility, and superiority that were held by a young second-generation Jew and intellectual in the late 1940s and 1950s, see N. Podheretz, *Making It.* For a survey on Jewish attitudes toward non-Jews in 1952, see Andrew Greeley, *Why Can't They Be Like Us?* (New York: Institute of Human Relations Press, 1969), pp. 195–200.
259. Leonard Fein, "The Dilemma of Jewish Identity on the College Campus," *Judaism*, 17 (Winter 1968), p. 16.

CHAPTER 9

1. Two of the best accounts of the Left's decline are David A. Shannon, *The Decline of American Communism: A History of the Communist Party Since 1945* (New York: Harcourt, Brace, 1959); and Joseph R. Starobin, *American Communism in Crisis, 1943–1957* (Berkeley: University of California Press, 1975).
2. W. R. McIntyre, "Student Movements," *Editorial Research Reports* II, 1957, pp. 926–927.
3. See John Gates, *The Story of an American Communist* (New York: Thomas Nelson, 1958), pp. 157–194, for an account by the former editor of the *Daily Worker* of the impact that these events had on him and other CP members, particularly Jewish ones.
4. James P. O'Brien, "The Development of a New Left in the United States," (Ph.D. diss., University of Wisconsin, 1971), p. 7.
5. Philip G. Altbach, *Student Politics in America: A Historical Analysis* (New York: McGraw Hill, 1974), p. 157; and D. A. Shannon, *Decline of American Communism*, p. 362.
6. The single best study of the origins of the New Left is J. P. O'Brien, "Development of a New Left."

7. The most extensive collection of original documents and portions thereof dealing with the ideology of the New Left from the late 1950s to the early-to-mid-1960s is contained in Massimo Teodori, Ed., *The New Left: A Documentary History* (Indianapolis, Ind.: Bobbs Merrill, 1969).

8. Students for a Democratic Society, "The Port Huron Statement," (mimeographed, 1962), pp. 4–6.

9. Norman Podhoretz, "Issues: The Tribe of the Wicked Son," *Commentary*, 51:2 (February 1971), 6.

10. See Chapter 2 in this volume. For documentation on this embarrassment, see Irwin Unger, *The Movement: A History of the American New Left 1959–1972* (New York: Harper & Row, 1974), p. 129.

11. See Chapter 2 in this volume; Jack N. Porter and Peter Dreier, "Introduction: The Roots of Jewish Radicalism," in *Jewish Radicalism: A Selected Anthology*, Jack N. Porter and Peter Dreier, Eds. (New York: Grove Press, 1973), p. xxi; and Stanley Rothman et al., "Ethnic Variations in Student Radicalism: Some New Perspectives," in S. Bialex, Ed., *Radicalism in the Contemporary Age* (Boulder, Col.: Westview Press, 1977), p. 155.

12. Richard Flacks, "Who Protests: The Social Bases of the Student Movement," in *Protest: Student Activism in America*, Julian Foster and Durward Long, Eds. (New York: William Morrow, 1970), p. 138; and Nathan Glazer, *Remembering the Answers: Essays on the American Student Movement* (New York: Basic Books, 1970), pp. 222–249.

13. N. Glazer, *Remembering the Answers*, p. 237.

14. Norman Birnbaum and Marjorie Childers, "The American Movement," in *Student Power* Julian Nagel, Ed. (London: Merlin, 1969), p. 133.

15. See Chapter 7 and Seymour Martin Lipset, *Rebellion in the University* (Boston: Little Brown, 1971), pp. 80–123, 178–184.

16. Herberg, "Jewish Labor Movement in the U.S.: WWI to the Present," p. 59; National Commission, B'nai Brith Vocational Service, *Jewish Youth in College* (Washington, D.C.: B'nai Brith Vocational Service, 1957), p. 4.

17. Rose K. Goldsen et al., *What College Students Think* (Princeton, N.J.: D. Van Nostrand, 1960), p. 102–103. The same data was more intensively analyzed by Norman Miller, "Social Class and Value Differences Among American Colleges," Ph.D. diss., Columbia University, 1958), pp. 53–56, 104, 159–165, 203. For data on Jewish students at Berkeley in the 1950s, see Seymour Martin Lipset, "Opinion Formation in a Crisis," *Public Opinion Quarterly*, 17 (Spring 1953), pp. 26–27; and Hanan C. Selvin and Warren O. Hagstron, "Determinants of Support for Civil Liberties," *British Journal of Sociology*, 11 (March 1960), pp. 63–64.

18. B'nai Brith, *Jewish Youth in College*, pp. 3–9; S. Norman Feingold et al., "An Analysis of Major Trends in Jewish College Enrollment," mimeographed, Washington, D.C., B'Nai B'Rith Vocational Service, n.d., pp. 1–10; Alfred Jospe, "Jewish College Students in the United States," *American Jewish Yearbook*, 65, 1964, (Philadelphia: Jewish Publication Society, 1964), pp. 131–134.

19. Michael Harrington, *Fragments of the Century* (New York: Saturday Review Press, 1973), p. 64.

20. Kenneth Kenniston, "American Students and the 'Political Revival'," *The American Scholar*, 32 (Winter 1962–1963), p. 53.

21. P. G. Altbach, *Student Politics in America*, pp. 141–163.

22. Andre Schiffrin, "The Student Movement in the '50's: A Reminiscence," *Radical America* 3 (May–June, 1968), pp. 2–4; J. P. O'Brien, "Development of a New Left," pp. 62, 229; and virtually all our interviewees.

23. A. Schiffrin, "Student Movement in the '50's," pp. 2–3.

24. Letter from Reverend J. Henry Carpenter to Harry Laidler, March 17, 1950, in Student League for Industrial Democracy Papers, Tammiment Library, New York University, New York.

25. Richard Hofstadter, *The Development of Higher Education in the United States*

(New York: Columbia University Press, 1952), pp. 45–46; Dario Enrico Longhi, "Higher Education and Student Politics: The Wisconsin Experience (M.A. thesis, University of Wisconsin, Madison, Wisconsin, 1969), pp. 8–38; Shlomo Swirski, "Changes in the Structure of Relations Between Groups and the Emergence of Political Movements: The Student Movement at Harvard and Wisconsin, 1930–1969," (Ph.D. diss., Michigan State University, East Lansing, Michigan, 1971), pp. 165–169.

26. Zosa Szajkowski, *Jews, Wars and Communism* (New York: Ktav Publishing House, 1972), pp. 418–419.
27. By the latter 1950s, the Jewish enrollment in the University of Wisconsin approached 2000. The vast majority of these students were from out of state, most probably from the New York and Chicago areas. We unfortunately lack survey data on their political attitudes and positions. Two of our interviewees who attended the University at different times in the 1950s believed that most of the Left students, and many of the liberal students, were Jews. In a 1967 survey by Dario Enrico Longi, the data revealed that the Jewish out-of-state students were disproportionately liberal and Democratic in their politics. There is no reason to believe that similar findings would not have been obtained ten years earlier. It is interesting to note that in 1971 the University of Wisconsin Board of Regents imposed a quota on the number of out-of-state students to be admitted. The Jewish students interpreted this as a device to limit the number of Jews at the university, particularly Jewish radicals, a group that had played a prominent role in the student demonstrations of the 1960s [Longi, "Higher Education and Student Politics," pp. 36–37; and *Attah* (Jewish student newspaper at the University), May 1972, p. 1].
28. C. M. McIntyre, "The Influence and Influence Strategies of the Wisconsin Student Association on University Policy Making, 1938–1970," (Ph.D. diss., University of Wisconsin, Madison, Wisconsin, 1972), pp. 144–193.
29. From Bob Ross to C. Clark Kissinger, November 17, 1964, Students for a Democratic Society papers, Wisconsin Historical Society Archives, Madison, Wisconsin.
30. R. Flacks, "Who Protests," p. 139.
31. Samuel Lubell, "The Generation Gap: Where the New Left Dissidents Come From," *Boston Globe*, October 10, 1968.
32. Kirkpatrick Sale, *SDS* (New York: Random House, 1973), p. 89; and J. R. Starobin, *American Communism in Crisis*, p. 230.
33. J. P. O'Brien, "Development of a New Left," p. 230.
34. Donald McKelvey, "SPU and SDS: Continuity and Change," mimeographed, n.d., P. G. Altbach, *Student Politics in America*, pp. 275–277; Lawrence S. Wittner, *Rebels Against the War: The American Peace Movement* (New York: Columbia University Press, 1969), p. 270; YPSL *Challenge*, I: 1 (November 1958); Martin Oppenheimer, "The Genesis of the Southern Negro Student Movement: A Study in Contemporary Negro Protest," (Ph.D. diss., University of Pennsylvania, 1963), pp. 118–120; Maurice Pinard, Jerome Kirk and Donald Von Eschen, "Processes of Recruitment in the Sit-In Movement," *Public Opinion Quarterly*, 33 (1969), p. 356–369; and interviews with four YPSL activists of the period.
35. K. Sale, *SDS*, p. 89.
36. The best study to address the political connections between parents and children in the New Left era is Lamar E. Thomas, "Family Congruence on Political Orientations of Politically Active Parents and Their College Age Children," (Ph.D. diss., University of Chicago, 1968).
37. Ibid.
38. J. Anthony Lukas. *Don't Shoot—We Are Your Children!* (New York: Dell Publishing, 1971), pp. 7–57.
39. Ibid., 22.
40. Richard Flacks, "The Liberated Generation: An Exploration of the Roots of Student Protest," in *The Seeds of Politics*, Anthony M. Orum, Ed. (Englewood

Cliffs, N.J.: Prentice-Hall, 1972), pp. 358–361; and Kenneth Kenniston, *Young Radicals* (New York: Harcourt, Brace, 1968), pp. 30–31, 84–85.

41. R. Flacks, "Who Protests," p. 137.
42. See Chapter 7 in this volume.
43. L. E. Thomas, "Family Congruence," pp. 76–77.
44. Interviews with former students of these schools and an educator intimately involved with them.
45. Agnes De Lima and the Staff of the Little Red School House, *The Little Red School House* (New York: Macmillan, 1948), p. 276.
46. Ibid., 239, 279.
47. Ibid., 86–87.
48. This account of SLID is based on LID and SLID papers and Harry Laidler papers in the Tamiment Library, New York University, and on K. Sale, *SDS*, pp. 673–693.
49. K. Sale, pp. 237–240.
50. Data from an informant who was one of the key persons in the FDR–Four Freedoms Club.
51. J. N. Porter and P. Dreier, *Jewish Radicalism*, p. xxii.
52. See Rick Margolies, "On Community Building," in *The New Left: A Collection of Essays*, Priscilla Long, Ed. (Boston: Porter Sargent, 1969), pp. 359–360, for positive comments from a New Leftist on the kibbutz.
53. See Arthur Liebman, "Students and Politics in the 1950s and 1960s," Paper Delivered at the American Sociological Association Meetings, 1971, pp. 10–13.
54. This shift to dogmatic Marxism in these years can be clearly seen in K. Sale *SDS*, pp. 317–650.
55. I. Unger, *The Movement*, pp. 149–208; and K. Sale, pp. 455–650.
56. This is not unique to New Leftists in America. The same disaffiliation of the middle class occurred in movements of dissent elsewhere, when their focus changed from moral, or nonclass issues, to class ones. For England, see Frank Parkin, *Middle Class Radicalism: The Social Bases of The British Campaign for Nuclear Disarmament* (Manchester, England: Manchester University Press, 1968); for Latin America, see Arthur Liebman and James Petras, "Class and Student Politics in Chile," *Politics and Society*, 3:3 (Spring 1973), 329–345.
57. For varying accounts of this interpersonal and interracial social tension operating inside the civil rights movement, see Paul Cowan, *The Making of An Un-American* (New York: Viking, 1970), pp. 28–49; Inge Powell Bell, *CORE and the Strategy of Non-Violence* (New York: Random House, 1968), pp. 147–168; N. J. Demareth III et al., *Dynamics of Idealism: White Activists in a Black Movement* (San Francisco: Jossey Bass, 1971), pp. 68–135; Linda R. Forcey, "Personality in Politics: The Political Commitment of a Suicide," unpublished doctoral dissertation, State University of New York at Binghamton, 1978; and August Meier and Elliot Rudwick, *CORE: A Study in the Civil Rights Movement* (New York: Oxford University Press, 1973), pp. 194–210.
58. For an insightful analysis of structural sources of strain within egalitarian-oriented interracial movements, see Gary T. Marx and Michael Useem, "Majority Involvement in Minority Movements: Civil Rights, Abolition, Untouchability," *Journal of Social Issues*, 27:1 (1971), 81–104.
59. Staughton Lynd, "The Movement: A New Beginning," *Liberation*, May 14, 1969, p. 14.
60. P. Cowan, *Making of an Un-American*, pp. 39–49.
61. I. P. Bell, *CORE*, pp. 147–190.
62. K. Sale, *SDS*, p. 276.
63. For a sociohistorical overview of these kinds of unequal patterned encounters between blacks and Jews, see Robert G. Weisbord and Arthur Stein, *Bitter-Sweet Encounter: The Afro-American and the American Jew* (New York: Schocken Books, 1972).

64. This was James Robert Starobin. See L. R. Forcey, "Personality in Politics," for Starobin's political biography.
65. I. Unger, *The Movement*, p. 130.
66. See *SNCC Newsletter*, June–July 1967; and R. G. Weisbord and A. Stein, *Bitter-Sweet Encounter*, pp. 100–110.
67. R. G. Weisbord and A. Stein, pp. 101–104.
68. *New Left Notes*, June 19, 1967.
69. *New York Times*, August 15, 1967.
70. "Arabs and Jews: An Editorial," *Ramparts*, July 1967, pp. 2–3.
71. Ibid., p. 3.
72. For two accounts of this "sorry" convention, see Renata Adler, *Toward a Radical Middle: Fourteen Pieces of Reporting and Criticism* (New York: Random House, 1969), pp. 239–259 (originally published in the *New Yorker*, September 23, 1967, under the title "Radicalism in Debacle: The Palmer House"); and Walter Goodman, "When Black Power Runs the New Left," *New York Times Magazine*, September 24, 1967, pp. 28, 124–127.
73. W. Goodman, p. 124; and *New York Times*, September 3, 1967.
74. Norman Podhoretz, "A Certain Anxiety," *Commentary*, 52:2 (August 1971), 6.
75. K. Sale, *SDS*, pp. 557–657. I witnessed the same process while at Harvard University between 1969 and 1971. There the SDS literally turned its back on a student constituency while attempting to develop one among blue-collar workers. Thus, when the Cambodian invasion and the Kent State killings occurred, mobilizing students in so massive a fashion, the New Left cadres and organization were not present in any meaningful fashion.
76. Irving Louis Horowitz, *Israeli Ecstasies/Jewish Agonies* (New York: Oxford University Press, 1974), pp. 102–103; and Melvin I. Urofsky, *We Are One!: American Jewry and Israel* (Garden City, N.Y.: Anchor Press, 1978), pp. 387–390.
77. For descriptions and analyses of these elections, see Alan Fisher, "Continuity and Erosion of Jewish Liberalism," *American Jewish Historical Quarterly*, 56:2 (December 1976), 322–348; Stephen D. Isaacs, *Jews and American Politics* (Garden City, N.Y.: Doubleday, 1974), pp. 140–197; Henry Cohen and Gary Sandrow, "Philadelphia Chooses a Mayor, 1971: Jewish Voting Patterns," mimeographed, American Jewish Committee, New York, 1972); American Jewish Committee, "Jewish Voting in Recent Elections," (mimeographed, New York, 1969); Milton Himmelfarb, "Jewish Class Conflict?" *Commentary*, 49:1 (January 1970), 37–42; Nathan Glazer and Milton Himmelfarb, "McGovern and the Jews: A Debate," *Commentary*, 54:3 (September 1972), 43–51; Norman Podhoretz, "Between Nixon and the New Politics," *Commentary*, 54:3 (September 1972), 4–8; Richard Reeves, "Splitting the Jewish Vote," *New York Magazine*, 6:25 (June 18, 1973), 57–63; William Schneider, Michael D. Berman, and Mark Schultz, "Bloc Voting Reconsidered: 'Is There a Jewish Vote?' " *Ethnicity*, 1:1 (December 1974), 345–392; *Time*, November 15, 1976, pp. 19–20.
78. See David W. Abbott, Louis H. Gold, and Edward T. Rogwosky, *Police, Politics and Race: The New York City Referendum on Civilian Review* (New York and Cambridge: American Jewish Committee and Joint Center for Urban Studies, Harvard-MIT, 1969) for a description and analysis of this referendum.
79. "The Burden of Blame: Report on Ocean Hill-Brownsville," *Civil Liberties in New York*, 16:9 (November 1968), 1–8; and Diane Ravitch, *The Great School Wars: New York City, 1805–1973* (New York: Basic Books, 1974), pp. 312–398.
80. Janet L. Dolgin, *Jewish Identity and the JDL* (Princeton, N.J.: Princeton University Press, 1977), pp. 12–30.
81. Mario Cuomo, *Forest Hills Diary: The Crisis of Low Income Housing* (New York: Vintage, 1974).
82. J. N. Porter and P. Dreier, *Roots of Jewish Radicalism*, pp. xxxvi–xxxix; Paul Jacobs, "Understanding the New Left," *Congress Bi-Weekly*, 40:7 (April 13, 1973), 13–14.

83. N. Glazer, *Remembering the Answers*, pp. 3–32; and Isidore Silver, "What Flows From Neo-Conservatism," *Nation*, July 9, 1977, pp. 44–51.

84. Andrew M. Greeley, *Ethnicity in the United States: A Preliminary Reconsideration* (New York: John Wiley, 1974), pp. 187–209; and Norman H. Nie, Sidney Verba, and John R. Petrocik, *The Changing American Voter* (Cambridge, Mass.: Harvard University Press, 1976), pp. 263–269.

85. Quoted in *Morning Freiheit*, December 17, 1967.

86. Danney Siegel, "The Essence of My Commitment," *Midstream*, 16:3 (March 1970), 39.

87. David E. Drew, "A Profile of the Jewish Freshman," American Council on Education *Research Report*, 5:4 (1970), 25.

88. S. Rothman et al., "Ethnic variations . . .", 55.

89. Seymour M. Lipset, *Rebellion in the University* (Boston: Little Brown, 1972), p. 93.

90. K. Sale, *SDS*, 517.

91. Sol Stern, "My Jewish Problem—and Ours: Israel, the Left and the Jewish Establishment," *Ramparts*, 10:2 (August 1971), 30.

92. Ibid., p. 38.

93. Alan Adelson, *SDS: A Profile* (New York: Charles Scribner's, 1972), p. 199.

94. David Horowitz, "The Passion of the Jews," *Ramparts*, 13:3 (October 1974), 60.

95. For an insight into one Jewish New Left activist's conversion from politics to psychology, see Jerry Rubin, *Growing Up at 37* (New York: Warner Books, 1976).

96. M. J. Rosenberg, "My Evolution as a Jew," *Midstream*, 16:7 (August–September, 1970), 52.

97. J. N. Porter and P. Dreier, "The Roots of Jewish Radicalism," pp. xxx–xxxii and Aron Manheimer, "Radical Zionism Reconsidered," *New Outlook* 16:5 (June 1973), pp. 33–35.

98. For a description of these developments, see Daniel J. Elazar, *Community and Polity: The Organizational Dynamics of American Jewry* (Philadelphia: Jewish Publication Society, 1976), pp. 74–77, 79–86, 198–200, 222–227, 263–264, 288, 332, and 341–377.

99. The People's Park issue involved a struggle between Berkeley students and "street people" on the one hand and university authorities and the police on the other over control of an empty lot near the Berkeley campus. At the height of the confrontation between these two forces in May 1969, over 3000 students battled about 600 policemen.

100. My information about the Radical Jewish Union comes from reading *The Jewish Radical* in the years from 1968 to 1978 and from interviewing David Biale, one of its most important leaders.

101. The Third World strike occurred at Berkeley in 1969. It initially involved Third World or minority students who wished to have their own autonomous academic and cultural programs. Other students were drawn into the struggle because of alleged police brutality and administrative overreaction in the treatment of the initial strikers.

102. Jack N. Porter, "Jewish Student Activism," *Jewish Currents*, **24**, 5 (May 1970), p. 32.

103. The emigration estimates come from my own personal knowledge, David Biale, and J. N. Porter and P. Dreier, "The Roots of Jewish Radicalism," p. xxxix.

104. *The Jewish Radical*, **6**, 3–4 (Winter–Spring, 1974), p. 5.

105. Jews For Urban Justice, "The Oppression and Liberation of the Jewish People in America," in J. N. Porter and P. Dreier, *Jewish Radicalism*, p. 345.

106. For the impact of the Yom Kippur War on American Jews, see section entitled "United States of America: Overview and Perspectives," by Daniel J. Elazar et al. in Moshe Davis, Ed., *The Yom Kippur War: Israel and the Jewish People* (New York: Arno Press, 1974), pp. 1–94.

107. This observation stems from my own personal knowledge; information derived

from knowledgeable informants such as David Biale, Director of Judaic Studies, the State University of New York at Binghamton and Arieh Leibowitz, a participant and observer of the Jewish New Left; and Manheimer, "Radical Zionism Reconsidered," p. 36.

108. These figures are based on information provided to me by the offices of these organizations on October 17 and 18, 1978.

SUMMARY AND CONCLUSION

1. This formulation is very much indebted to the work of my distinguished colleague, James A. Geschwender. See his recent books, *Class, Race, and Worker Insurgency: The League of Revolutionary Black Workers* (New York: Cambridge University Press, 1977) and *Racial Stratification in America* (Dubuque, Iowa: William C. Brown, 1977) for further exposition of this concept.

EPILOGUE

1. Allon Gal, *Socialist-Zionism: Theory and Issues in Contemporary Jewish Nationalism* (Cambridge, Mass.: Schenkman Publishing Co., 1973), p. 22.
2. Ibid., pp. 22, 23, 63, 64.
3. Ibid., p. 29; and Will Maslow, *The Structure and Functioning of the American Jewish Community* (New York: American Jewish Congress, 1974), p. 8.
4. G. William Domhoff, *Fat Cats and Democrats: The Role of the Big Rich in the Party of the Common Man* (Englewood Cliffs, N.J.: Prentice-Hall, 1972), p. 54.
5. Stephen L. Slavin and Mary A. Pradt, "Corporate Anti-Semitism," *Jewish Currents, 32:* 2 (February 1978), 29–32.
6. Ibid., pp. 29–30 and Irving Howe, *The World of Our Fathers* (New York: Harcourt Brace Jovanovich, 1976), pp. 611–612.
7. U.S. Department of Commerce, *Statistical Abstract of the United States, 1976* (Washington, D.C.: U.S. Government Printing Office, 1976), pp. 507–526; and Willard F. Mueller, "The Measurement of Industrial Concentration," in *Superconcentration/Supercorporation*, Ralph L. Andreano, Ed. (Andover, Mass.: Warner Modular Publications, 1973), reprint 324, pp. 1–19.
8. Edward S. Greenberg, *Serving the Few: Corporate Capitalism and the Bias of Government Policy* (New York: John Wiley, 1974), pp. 38–39.
9. Ibid., p. 39.
10. W. F. Mueller, "Measurement of Industrial Concentration," pp. 13–19; and John M. Blair, *Economic Concentration: Structure, Behavior, and Public Policy* (New York: Harcourt Brace Jovanovich, 1972), pp. 41–81.
11. Ibid., pp. 18–19; and Maurice Zeitlin, "Corporate Ownership and Control: The Large Corporation and the Capitalist Class," in *American Society, Inc.*, Maurice Zeitlin, Ed. (Chicago: Rand McNally, 1977), pp. 246–249, 256–265.
12. See *Statistical Abstract, 1976*, p. 526, for listings of commercial and industrial failures by industry and occupation of debtor.
13. E. Digby Baltzell, *The Protestant Establishment: Aristocracy and Caste in America* (New York: Vintage Books, 1964), p. 321.
14. G. W. Domhoff, *Fat Cats and Democrats*, p. 48.
15. Stephen Birmingham, *Our Crowd: The Great Jewish Families of New York* (New York: Dell Books, 1967).
16. See Jerold S. Auerbach, *Unequal Justice: Lawyers and Social Change in Modern America* (New York: Oxford University Press, 1976), especially pp. 102–130.
17. Jerome E. Carlin, *Lawyers' Ethics: A Survey of the New York City Bar* (New York: Russell Sage Foundation, 1966), pp. 27–40, 125–129.
18. Nathan Glazer and Daniel P. Moynihan, *Beyond the Melting Pot: The Negroes, Puerto Ricans, Jews, Italians and Irish of New York City* 2nd ed. (Cambridge, Mass.: MIT Press, 1970), p. 146; and Seymour Martin Lipset and E. C. Ladd, Jr.,

"Jewish Academics In the United States: Their Achievements, Culture and Politics," *American Jewish Yearbook 1971*, 72 (New York and Philadelphia: American Jewish Committee and Jewish Publication Society, 1971), p. 92.

19. "Capital's Flight: The Apparel Industry Moves South," *NACLA's Latin America and Empire Report*, XI: 3 (March 1977), 5–12.

20. *New York Times*, January 9, 1978.

21. *New York Times*, January 11, 1977. Saul Bellow, Norman Podhoretz, and Eugene V. Rostow joined together with such military luminaries as Admiral Zumwalt and General Maxwell Taylor to push for increased defense spending to meet the Soviet menace.

22. Michael Reich and David Finkelhor, "Capitalism and the Military Industrial Complex," in *The Capital System*, Richard C. Edwards, Michael Reich, and Thomas Weisskopf, Eds. (Englewood Cliffs, N.J.: Prentice-Hall, 1972), pp. 392–401.

23. For example, the American Jewish Committee chose not to publicize the fact that the major public utilities between 1963 and 1971 had not changed their exclusionary policies toward Jews. S. L. Slavin and M. A. Pradt, "Corporate Anti-Semitism," p. 32.

24. Arnold Foster and Benjamin R. Epstein, *The New Anti-Semitism* (New York: McGraw-Hill, 1974).

Index